Drive-In Dream Girls

ALSO BY TOM LISANTI AND FROM McFARLAND

*Fantasy Femmes of Sixties Cinema: Interviews with
20 Actresses from Biker, Beach, and Elvis Movies*
(2001; paperback 2010)

*Hollywood Surf and Beach Movies:
The First Wave, 1959–1969* (2005; paperback 2012)

Glamour Girls of Sixties Hollywood: Seventy-Five Profiles (2008)

WITH LOUIS PAUL

*Film Fatales: Women in Espionage Films
and Television, 1962–1973* (2002)

BY GAIL GERBER WITH TOM LISANTI

*Trippin' with Terry Southern:
What I Think I Remember* (2009)

Drive-In Dream Girls

A Galaxy of B-Movie Starlets of the Sixties

TOM LISANTI

Foreword by Carole Wells

McFarland & Company, Inc., Publishers
Jefferson, North Carolina, and London

The present work is a reprint of the illustrated case bound edition of Drive-in Dream Girls: A Galaxy of B-Movie Starlets of the Sixties, *first published in 2003 by McFarland.*

LIBRARY OF CONGRESS CATALOGUING-IN-PUBLICATION DATA

Lisanti, Tom 1961–
Drive-in dream girls : a galaxy of B-movie starlets of the sixties / Tom Lisanti ; foreword by Carole Wells.
p.   cm.
Includes bibliographical references and index

ISBN 978-0-7864-7165-2
softcover : acid free paper ∞

1. Motion picture actors and actresses—United States—Biography.
2. Actresses—United States—Biography.   3. B films—United States.
I. Title
PN1998.2.L566   2012   791.43'028'092273   [B]   2003001323

BRITISH LIBRARY CATALOGUING DATA ARE AVAILABLE

© 2003 Tom Lisanti. All rights reserved

No part of this book may be reproduced or transmitted in any form or by any means, electronic or mechanical, including photocopying or recording, or by any information storage and retrieval system, without permission in writing from the publisher.

On the cover: Sue Ane Langdon

Manufactured in the United States of America

*McFarland & Company, Inc., Publishers
Box 611, Jefferson, North Carolina 28640
www.mcfarlandpub.com*

To ALL my friends
but especially Ernie, Teresa, John, Mark,
Alan, Matt, Pete, Scott, Phil, and Shawn.
Thanks for your continued support.

Acknowledgments

First and foremost, my sincerest thanks to the following lovely ladies for allowing me to interview them: Sue Casey, Jackie DeShannon, Andrea Dromm, Gail Gerber (a.k.a. Gail Gilmore), Laurel Goodwin, Sharyn Hillyer, Suzie Kaye, Sue Ane Langdon, Donna Loren, Vitina Marcus, Arlene Martel, Marlyn Mason, Luree Nicholson (a.k.a. Luree Holmes), Quinn O'Hara, Melody Patterson, Cynthia Pepper, Hilarie Thompson, Darlene Tompkins, Beverly Washburn, Carole Wells, and Lori Williams. A special thanks to Carole Wells who found time to write the foreword while on vacation touring Africa and to Sue Casey, Sue Ane Langdon, Quinn O'Hara, Hilarie Thompson, Darlene Tompkins, Beverly Washburn, Carole Wells, and Lori Williams for graciously providing photographs from their collections for use in this book.

A lot of people helped me locate these actresses. I would like to thank actress Barbara Luna in leading me to Suzie Kaye, manager Rick Saphire for contacting his clients Cynthia Pepper, Darlene Tompkins, and Beverly Washburn on my behalf, and Nile Southern for leading me to his father Terry Southern's longtime companion, Gail Gerber. Finally a huge thank you to actor Aron Kincaid, a great guy, who not only got me in contact with Luree Holmes and Quinn O'Hara but offered comments and supplied a number of photographs from his vast collection.

I would like to express my gratitude to the staff at The New York Public Library where I work. Thanks to photographer Maria Alos for her expert scanning capabilities. Also my gratitude goes to the staff at the Billy Rose Theatre Collection of The New York Public Library for the Performing Arts for putting up with me every Saturday with a special nod to Jeremy Megraw, Karen Nickeson, and Dan Patri.

I would like to thank my family and friends for all their continued support of my bringing long overdue recognition to '60s actresses. Special thanks, as always, to Ernie DeLia for his encouragement and patience. My family: Joan Lisanti, Rose DeFeo, Joe and Beth Lisanti, Lorraine and Richie Nicolo, Donna and Mike Cates, Joe Casamento and Barbara Klein, Al and Barbara Reisinger, Paul Reisinger and Marta Skorynkiewicz, and Lori Ann Reisinger. My nephew Vincent Nicolo and nieces: Emily Lisanti, Kelly Cates, McKayla Cates, and Christina Nicolo. My friends: Keith Aden, Rob Andrews, Diane Bonfanti, Jim Campbell, Shaun Chang, Kenn Connors, John Covelli, Jim Cullen, Teresa DeTurris, Matt Fletcher, David Gabriel, Diane Goldstein, Scott Hannibal, Pete Kaiser, Tom Kazar, Judy and Rick Keifer, John Kelly, Jeannie and Tony Koproski, Phil Lindow, Jim McGann, Jim Napoleon, Alan Pally, Louis Paul, John Rowell, Mark Tolleson, and Kevin Winkler. And a special nod to all my friends on the *Ryan's Hope* message board on Soapnet.

Table of Contents

Acknowledgments
vii

Foreword by Carole Wells
xi

Preface
1

The Interviewees

Sue Casey	3	Arlene Martel	105
Andrea Dromm	14	Marlyn Mason	117
Gail Gilmore	21	Quinn O'Hara	129
Laurel Goodwin	33	Melody Patterson	140
Sharyn Hillyer	44	Cynthia Pepper	151
Luree Holmes	54	Hilarie Thompson	160
Suzie Kaye	64	Darlene Tompkins	172
Sue Ane Langdon	75	Beverly Washburn	180
Donna Loren	89	Carole Wells	193
Vitina Marcus	97	Lori Williams	205

More Drive-In Dream Girls

Brenda Benet	217	Patti Chandler	232
Diane Bond	221	Nancy Czar	236
Cindy Carol	223	Jackie DeShannon	239
Regina Carrol	228	Jill Donohue	244

Table of Contents

Joan Freeman	246	Laurie Mock	292
Susan Hart	252	Valora Noland	296
Anne Helm	258	Angelique Pettyjohn	299
Mary Hughes	264	Pat Priest	303
Mikki Jamison	266	Juliet Prowse	307
Candy Johnson	268	Bobbi Shaw	313
Marta Kristen	270	Ulla Stromstedt	316
Meredith MacRae	275	Wende Wagner	318
Dodie Marshall	281	Debbie Watson	322
Claudia Martin	283	Venita Wolf	326
Jenny Maxwell	286		
Mary Mitchel	289		

Web Sites
329

Bibliography
331

Index
339

Foreword
by Carole Wells

Seeing your name lit up on theatre marquees across the country, seeing your face on the covers of popular magazines, and being chauffeured in long limousines to glamorous parties given for the stars is intoxicating and addictive. Everyone believes this is show business, but there are sacrifices, conditions, and responsibilities that cause great concern and tension for actresses, which no one else understands.

Working in television and motion pictures since the age of twelve has been a wonderful and rewarding experience for me. Performing was my way of life for twenty-five years. I knew I would be an actress since the age of three. Television was new and most of the shows were taped live with an audience, so one had to be a stage performer accomplishing a perfect job. There were no re-takes. The later television series were filmed. Making a motion picture was easier. There was more time for preparation, bigger budgets and the filming was more relaxed.

The actresses of the late fifties and sixties were a small and elite group who became friends easily. We visited with each other several times a month in the casting rooms at the studios while waiting to be interviewed for roles. We were happy when others were working as well as ourselves and praised each other for jobs well done. I never felt jealous when another actress landed a part. It felt natural to compete for roles. I knew one person wasn't right for every part but I was lucky, as I worked frequently.

Time was precious and always spent productively. We spent our hours filming and then studying for school. While our classmates were going to football games and parties, being cheerleaders, and surfing at the beach, we were taking lessons perfecting our art—tap dancing, ballet, singing, piano, acrobatics, and even horseback riding—all in preparation for another role. There wasn't time for socializing. We spent hours in isolation memorizing lines. Because we were alone so much of the time, when we did have a chance to be together there was a true camaraderie among us. We knew we were different from others. We stood out wherever we went. The press always reported where we were going, whom we were dating and what we were wearing. Our lives were constantly scrutinized. It was like living in a fish bowl. Our schoolmates had no understanding of our sacrifices and commitment to our work. Sometimes they were cruel or jealous of our high profiles. It wasn't easy acting like just one of the

Carole Wells

girls when everyone already knew who you were and had formed an opinion of you even before meeting you. We actresses welcomed the opportunity to share our fears, disappointments, and joys with fellow actors—we understood each other.

The girls of the sixties also contributed their spare time generously to charities and fundraisers. Later, the Vietnam War brought us together to entertain the troops and injured boys at the veterans' hospitals.

Some actresses that started working early in show business chose to have more complete lives—getting married and having children or returning to school to pursue other careers. They had the full run of the glamorous life and I marvel how well these actresses re-entered "normal life." As I matured and grew farther away from the glitter of the entertainment world, I realized how special we were—how we tried to be examples to other young girls growing up. Our lives were so remarkable and so unique to be a few selected as the most talented and the most beautiful in the world. Having our images blown up larger than life on the big screens across the nation was a tremendous responsibility. Any physical flaw was exaggerated so we constantly worked toward perfection—dieting all the time, getting enough sleep, keeping our skin out of the sun—all the things that other teenagers never had to think about. We worked with the best crews and were trained by professionals at the top of their careers and we were expected to act just as professionally. It was extraordinary to be surrounded by that quality of greatness all the time.

The most difficult part of living life in the "real world" is dealing with mediocrity. There is still a constant striving for perfection in every walk of life—how we look, how we uphold ourselves, how we conduct our lives, how we raise our children, even how we decorate our homes. It must drive our husbands and families crazy. But this exposure at such an impressionable young age gave us an awareness of excellence and the necessity of giving back by helping others not as fortunate as we. Striving to live at the highest level of integrity haunts us, but we continue to stand out as beacons of light encouraging others to greatness.

PREFACE

Drive-in Dream Girls: A Galaxy of B-Movie Starlets of the Sixties is a companion piece to my first book *Fantasy Femmes of Sixties Cinema: Interviews with 20 Actresses from Biker, Beach, and Elvis Movies*.* The focus is on actresses who worked in B-movies aimed at the teenage drive-in movie audience. Some of the actresses were leading ladies while others toiled in the background. Some appeared in nothing but teenage movies while others had careers outside this genre or on television. What they all have in common is that each one was a beauty who for a brief period in movie history enthralled the audiences that frequented the drive-ins across the country.

While deciding what actresses to include, I tried to select a cross section of women from various popular teenage movie genres. The Elvis Presley musical was a staple of drive-ins across the country. Some of his leading ladies included here such as Sue Ane Langdon, Marlyn Mason, and Juliet Prowse are remembered for other more important films while co-starring with Elvis was the high point for Laurel Goodwin, Darlene Tompkins, Anne Helm, Joan Freeman, Dodie Marshall, and Jenny Maxwell. Presley's leading ladies were also plucked from the small screen as former series stars Cynthia Pepper of *Margie* and Pat Priest of *The Munsters* had the pleasure of being romanced by the King.

The beach movie genre was another big moneymaker for drive-in theater owners during the sixties. *Beach Party* (1963) from American International Pictures was the official kick-off of the genre and it was quickly followed by *Muscle Beach Party* (1964), *Pajama Party* (1964), *Beach Blanket Bingo* (1965), etc. Fans know that these films starred Annette Funicello but included herein are the beach girls that supported her including Luree Holmes, Donna Loren, Meredith MacRae, Susan Hart, and Bobbi Shaw.

The major studios also began releasing beach movies to compete with AIP. Soon flooding the drive-ins across the country were *Ride the Wild Surf* (1964), *The Girls on the Beach* (1965), *A Swingin' Summer* (1965), *Beach Ball* (1965), and *It's a Bikini World* (1967), among others. From these films

*Includes interviews with Jean Hale, Joy Harmon, Linda Harrison, Jill Haworth, Karen Jensen, Deanna Lund, Diane McBain, Chris Noel, Joan O'Brien, Eileen O'Neill, Judy Pace, Julie Parrish, Salli Sachse, Joan Staley, Tisha Sterling, Pamela Tiffin, Irene Tsu, Lana Wood, Celeste Yarnall, and Francine York. Brief profiles on Pamela Austin, Joan Blackman, Yvonne Craig, Shelley Fabares, Mimsy Farmer, Annette Funicello, Dolores Hart, Jocelyn Lane, Patty McCormack, Mary Ann Mobley, Nancy Sinatra, and Deborah Walley are also contained.

profiled in this book are such bikini girls as Gail Gilmore, Suzie Kaye, Quinn O'Hara, Brenda Benet, Mikki Jamison, Claudia Martin, Mary Mitchel, and Wende Wagner, among others. Vocalist Jackie DeShannon also made the requisite beach movie appearance in *Surf Party* (1964). And though technically not a beach movie, *Gidget Goes to Rome* (1963) sent everybody's favorite surfing sweetie (now played by Cindy Carol) on an Italian holiday.

By 1966, the popularity of the beach movies and Elvis musicals was waning at the box office. Drive-in movie theater owners needed fresh product. In 1966, AIP released *The Wild Angels* and Russ Meyer gave the world his violent cult classic *Faster, Pussycat! Kill! Kill!* starring Tura Satana, Haji, and Lori Williams as three go-go dancing hellcats out for kicks. The biker and hot rod genre became extremely popular and needed young actresses to play various types of roles ranging from the innocent victims terrorized by biker gangs to tough talking hog-riding motorcycle mamas exemplified by Regina Carrol and Angelique Pettyjohn. It is interesting to see who was recruited for these films. Having hung up her cowgirl outfit as Wrangler Jane on the TV sitcom *F Troop*, Melody Patterson co-starred in *The Angry Breed* (1968) with former beach bunny Suzie Kaye and *The Cycle Savages* (1969). Perennial TV starlet Arlene Martel made her lone excursion onto drive-in movie screens across the country in *Angels from Hell* (1968). Fifties child star Beverly Washburn matured into a lovely woman during the sixties and played a sluttish racecar driver groupie in *Pit Stop* (1969).

AIP also began producing its alienated youth movies about teenagers fighting the establishment, doing drugs, and practicing free love. Hilarie Thompson made a career of playing hippies in exploitation fare such as *Maryjane* (1968) and *Getting Straight* (1970). Laurie Mock's brief career including starring roles in *Hot Rods to Hell* (1967) as a good girl and *Riot on Sunset Strip* (1967) as a pot-smoking bad girl.

Lastly, there is included in this book a few actresses who became more known for their TV work than their movies. Model Andrea Dromm parlayed her TV commercial success as the spokesperson for National Airlines and Clairol Summer Blonde into a brief movie career. Carole Wells, Marta Kristen, Vitina Marcus, Sharyn Hillyer, and Debbie Watson were more popular from television but they too made an occasional teenage drive-in movie appearance.

I've tried to be as thorough and accurate in my research using the vast resources of the Billy Rose Theatre Collection of The New York Public Library of the Performing Arts and the Margaret Herrick Library of the Academy for Motion Pictures Arts and Sciences. For biographical information on some of the actresses I had to rely on not the most trusted sources. These include press releases, which sometimes were padded by over zealous press agents, and fan magazines such as *Photoplay* and *Modern Screen*. In all cases, I tried to do my best in double checking the facts.

The film appearances of each actress are listed in release order. For television appearances, I have tried to embody every type of program the actresses appeared on. I have scoured back issues of *TV Guide* and have used numerous reference guides and Internet sources to verify episode titles and air dates where possible. Some of the actresses' roles were so minor that this information can't be obtained. A few of the actresses (Sue Ane Langdon, Meredith MacRae, and Juliet Prowse) had so many game and talk show credits that I separated them from their appearances on comedy, drama, and variety series. I've also tried to include any awards or nominations that the actresses received for their work.

THE INTERVIEWEES

☆ SUE CASEY ☆

Though actress Sue Casey was older than the other starlets in this book during the Swinging '60s, she was still too young-looking to be playing the mother of teenage children. It was this offbeat casting that brought instant camp value to her three drive-in movie classics. A former Goldwyn Girl, the statuesque Casey was similar to another voluptuous brunette, Francine York, who also played lead roles in B-movies in between small roles in major productions during the '60s. Casey had numerous credits before landing the part of a seductive, booze-swilling stepmother in the camp classic *The Beach Girls and the Monster* (1965). Garnering the only good reviews that film received at the time, Casey was cast in similar roles playing a barefootin' hillbilly ma in *Swamp Country* (1966) and a forger in the beach film *Catalina Caper* (1967).

Sue Casey was born in Los Angeles. Her father was a builder, and the family lived in Beverly Hills until the stock market crash of 1929, which sent them packing to live on the other side of town. When she was ten years old, the Casey family moved again, this time to West Hollywood. As a child Sue had no particular interest in acting. While in high school she worked at a high-end clothing store called Desmond's. A talent agent noticed her and took her around on interviews to the various studios. *Holiday in Mexico* (1945) was the teenager's first film, followed by *Words and Music* (1948), before she landed a bit as Danny Kaye's boss's secretary in *The Secret Life of Walter Mitty* (1947) at Goldwyn Studios. This led to an audition for Sam Goldwyn, who wanted to send her to South America with some of the other Goldwyn Girls, but Casey declined because she was married with a very small child. She did a bit in one of his movies instead. Sue soon learned that the Goldwyn Girl title was more for publicity purposes, as the studio would send her and the others out on radio and TV shows, charity events, parades, and the like. Still, Casey found work consistently through the late forties until the mid-fifties. "I was cast as showgirls, models, and in bit parts in literally dozens of films," remarks Casey. "It was fabulous. Back then you would be on a movie for three months at a time. I worked with Esther Williams in

Sue Casey in promotional photo for *Who's Got the Action?* (Paramount, 1962).

five movies. In most of her films I am swimming right next to her and some people can't tell us apart. I tell everyone that she's the one with the better costume."

During this time Casey had to keep working to support her child, as her husband was overseas in the navy. Fortunately, her mother was alive and would care for Casey's daughter during the day while she played showgirl after showgirl in movie after movie. Her films during this period included the Academy Award-winning musicals *Annie Get Your Gun* ("Judy Garland was originally cast as Annie, but they fired her and replaced her with Betty Hutton. At the time none of us liked Betty because we all missed Judy. But Betty does a wonderful job and was just fabulous") and *An American in Paris* ("Gene Kelly taught me how to come down the stairs in an enormous headdress without looking into the risers"). Casey could also be seen in *Road to Bali* ("Bing Crosby was just so smart and sweet") and *Three Ring Circus* ("Zsa Zsa Gabor was very kind to me on this movie and offered to help me get an agent"). In 1953 director Raoul Walsh named Sue Casey as "the most beautiful extra in pictures today."

Sue Casey also became a sought after model during this period, posing for artists and photographers. Her first modeling assignment was for Gantner's swim suits. She posed for the artist Henry Clive, who sketched movie personalities dressed up as famous people from history for the cover of the entertainment section of the *L.A. Sunday Examiner*. She also worked for Tom Kelly, who photographed the infamous shot of a nude Marilyn Monroe. "One time I was doing a Pabst Blue Ribbon Beer shot for one of his calendars," recalls Sue. "At that time he and his wife were still working together, but I understood that they were separated. They had studio space on Seward St. in Hollywood. She took me to the bedroom and pointed out one of those nude paintings on velvet hanging over the bed. They wanted to do a photo like that and asked me if I would do it. I said no because I was a mother. In retrospect, that was the first of three offers I had to take off my clothes. Marilyn Monroe said yes, and as they say, the rest is history. For a time, Marilyn and I worked for the same modeling agency called the Snively Agency."

Back on the big screen, one of Casey's greatest experiences was working for esteemed director Alfred Hitchcock on *Rear Window* (1954). "I can't find myself in it," laughs Casey. "But my kids say they see me. I was hired to play one of the two girls who are supposedly sunbathing on their rooftop. We were on this film for weeks sitting around and having such fun. It was great because we got to watch everything and we didn't have to work. Alfred Hitchcock had such a sense a humor. He was so droll and would say things like , 'I think the costumer today will be Mr. Ward Robe.' I got to know Grace Kelly too, and one day while we were having our hair done she said to me, 'What does your husband *do*?' I told her that he was a film editor. A week later she got engaged to the Prince!"

Casey took a hiatus from her career in the mid-fifties to have three more children. In 1959, she began doing television commercials, which were convenient to a working mother, because they were usually shot in one day and paid very well. She would go on to appear in over 200 commercials for such products as Chrysler, Wesson Oil, Maxwell House Coffee, Del Monte, and Kelloggs, among many others.

As Casey began to get her feet wet again in the acting business, her husband was working at the studio where *The Lucy-Desi Comedy Hour* was filmed. "Jerry Thorpe was directing one episode," says Sue. "For one of the guest roles he called around and said, 'I want a Sue Casey type.' Someone said, 'How about *Sue Casey*?'" On this episode Casey played one of the girls competing with Lucy Ricardo to be Paul Douglas' co-host of an early morning TV program. "Lucille Ball was a very bright woman. She was very serious and not a lot of fun to work with. A few years later I worked with her again on *The Lucy Show*. The funny thing about that one was that I ran into Edith Head, who was looking for someone to model this dress on the show. She didn't think I had the right figure for it but I told her I'd get into it. The dress was a beautiful midnight blue color and it looked gorgeous. I wanted the job just to wear Edith's creation, even though all I had to do on the show was bump into Lucy."

Casey began the '60's playing a party guest in the musical *Bells Are Ringing* (1960), starring Judy Holiday and Dean Martin. ("In the musical number 'Drop That Name,' Judy's character looks in this window and we are all standing around wearing these gorgeous sleek gowns. The dresses were so tight that we couldn't sit down in them so they had to provide leaning chairs for us.") In 1961, Casey did a bit role in *The Errand Boy*, her fifth time working with Jerry Lewis. "He is a fascinating guy and way ahead of the times," comments Casey. "He was the first director to use a monitor while filming to help him know immediately if he wanted to save the shot. He was always very nice to me. I had been working with a children's charity called The Footlighters for years and he was always very generous towards us."

During the '60s, Casey continued playing uncredited or small roles in such major MGM and Paramount productions as *Two Weeks in Another Town* (1962), *Who's Got the Action?* (1962) as Eddie Albert's girlfriend, *A New Kind of Love* (1963), *Where Love Has Gone* (1964), and *The Carpetbaggers* (1964), the last two directed by Edward Dmytryk. ("Eddie was the cutest thing. Back then I had a little voice that wasn't as deep as it is now. I came to the set one day with a cold. Eddie said, 'Well, you finally sound like you look.' I thought, 'Okay, got to get my voice down.' With singing lessons, I did.") Sue finally copped a leading role, albeit in the cult B-movie *The Beach Girls and the Monster* (1965). "There is a interesting story of how I got this," says Sue. "I was doing a TV commercial when I ran into a gal [Joan Janis] that I went to high school with. She told me that her husband [Edward Janis] was producing this movie and asked if I'd come over and read for the lead. I went to her house and of course there was Jon Hall. I still haven't been able

The Beach Girls and the Monster (AIP, 1965) starred Sue Casey as the slinky stepmother of a teenage surfer boy.

to figure it out, but it seemed to me that Jon Hall by that time owned a lot of stock footage like the scene of the Mercedes crashing used at the end of the movie. They must have offered him a package deal to direct and star in exchange for loaning the stock footage."

The Beach Girls and the Monster was filmed on location in Los Angeles on an extremely low budget. ("There was no money in this film to do anything," exclaims Sue, laughing. "I did my own hair, my own make-up and supplied all the clothes I wore.") Jon Hall starred as Otto Lindsay, an oceanographer with a zesty young wife named Vicky (Casey) and teenage son Richard (Arnold Lessing), who would rather surf and hang out at the beach with his girlfriend Janie (Elaine DuPont) than follow in his father's footsteps as a researcher. The movie opens with the murder of a teenage girl (Gloria Neil) by a hideous monster on the beach. Richard, whose life is complicated enough trying to fight off his stepmother's enticing advances and his father's controlling manner, discovers the girl's body. Later, Richard and Janie head to a beach party where one of the surfers turns up dead. All evidence points to Richard's crippled friend Mark (Walter Edmiston), who is a sculptor. Meanwhile, the monster watches Vicky when she goes alone for a swim and later, after taunting her husband with her amorous plans with Mark, she is murdered by the creature. ("I had this beautiful scar that ran across my face down to my chest.") The monster also attacks Mark, and during a struggle he stabs the creature and pulls off the mask, revealing Otto. The injured scientist makes it to his car and drives off. However, weakened from his injuries, he loses control of his vehicle and plunges over a cliff.

Casey enjoyed working with the younger cast members but not with Jon Hall. "I tried to not have a lot of interaction with him because he was not kind," comments Sue. "We'd do a take and he would never get it right. He'd finally get it by say the eighth take, but I'd do something wrong and he would save that one. He would also shoot the back of my head a lot. It was not much fun working with him. I think that also may have been him in the monster suit but I never watched him actually put on the costume.

"The scenes where I leave my house at night to go out with my boyfriend were shot at Hall's ex-wife's house," continues Casey. "It was one of those Hawaiian-motif homes, architecturally speaking. I don't recall if this was that house but there were shots of me going up the walk to the beach. The funny part was that Walter Edmiston, who played the crippled sculptor, created the monster because he worked on a popular child's TV show back then called *Beany and Cecil*, so he knew how to make monster get-ups. But with that pathetic face which was so sweet, it was hardly monstrous."

Suffice it to say *The Beach Girls and the Monster* was not a critical success nor a box office hit, even among the drive-in crowd. However, Casey is a hoot playing a vixen and her sexy patter with her disgusted teenage stepson is the film's highlight. The critic in *Variety* noted that Casey "deserves a better break; she does all right with a one dimensional role." In the late sixties, the rights were sold to television and the film was re-titled *Monster from the Surf* for no apparent reason. The producers were able to recoup some of their losses, which helped the actors because "we never got paid for it. When the producers sold it to TV they came to us with these contracts to approve and paid us a little bit of what they owed us, but we had to sign our lives away so that it could play on TV forever without the actors getting any more money." The movie became a staple of the late-late show and early Saturday morning movie airings. "That's where my kids' friends saw the film. They loved it and thought it was a hoot. We lived on the beach and in the movie you see the guys and girls dancing around on the shore with this flat surf. Then the guys decide to go surfing and all of a sudden there are these huge swells. This movie has always been a

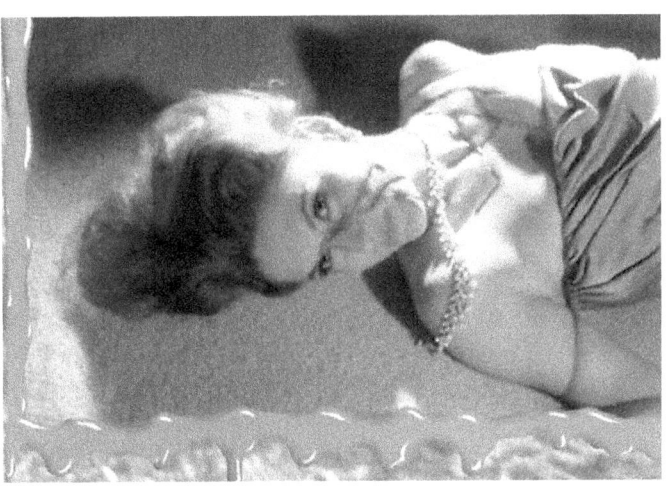

Sue Casey's bad girl meets a bad end in *The Beach Girls and the Monster* (AIP, 1965).

joke in my family because it was just so silly."

Silly or not, *The Beach Girls and the Monster* has developed quite a large cult following and lots of recommendations from various web sites as a true gem worth renting. "I am very surprised that this film has such a following because it is just awful," laughs Sue. "I remember being interviewed by somebody a few years ago who was writing a book on the one hundred worst movies ever made. I can say that certifiably that it *is* one of the worst movies ever made. It was so comical. I did it because I thought, 'What the heck. Maybe somebody will see it.' Actually, I got a couple of jobs out of it. I couldn't believe it. The roles were all in these crummy movies but it was work."

One of these crummy movies was the low-budget *Swamp Country* (1966), filmed on location in the Okefenokee Swamp of Georgia. Casey played the hillbilly mother of a teenage girl (Carole Gilbert) who aids a fugitive (David DaLie) on the run after being falsely accused of killing a gangster's moll (Kiva Lawrence). The town's sheriff (Rex Allen) and his deputy (Lyle Waggoner) pursue them through the swamps.

"My daughter was pregnant and living in Boston with her husband," explains Casey. "I wanted to go see her and the producers offered to pay the airfare to Boston and then Georgia for my three kids and me if I agreed to take the part. The character was similar to the part Patricia Neal played in *Hud* except mine was barefoot. I thought, 'This isn't so bad.' Well, was I wrong! The original director was a Russian guy and one of the actors had a fight with him and punched him out. The producer Robert Patrick had to take over as director. I remember doing make-up one morning with Rex Allen using pancake and coffee. It was such an up-in-the-air shoot. I don't know what happened to this film. I remember going to a screening and when I saw on screen somebody get killed with oozing bluish red blood, I thought, 'Well, that's the end of that.'"

Casey's last drive-in movie from the '60s was the beach movie *Catalina Caper* (1967), which was originally titled *Never Steal Anything Wet*, starring Walt Disney cast-off Tommy Kirk as Don, *Flipper* refugee Ulla Stromstedt as Katrina, and the "Miss Clairol" spokeswoman Venita Wolf as Tina. Lyle Waggoner (of *Swamp Country*) is also in this film playing a thug who is the jealous boyfriend of Stromstedt's Katrina. ("Lyle was so nice to work with and my children really liked him. But I don't remember a thing about the young kids in this.") Casey was cast as Anne Duval, a conniving mother, who along with her husband (Del Moore) is involved with a museum scam. In their possession is a stolen priceless Chinese scroll which they plan to duplicate, since Anne is an artist, and sell to a Greek billionaire while returning the original back to the museum. Trouble occurs when the scroll is knocked overboard from their yacht docked in Catalina Island. The Duvals' teenage son Tad (Peter Duryea) becomes friendly with Don, Tina, and her brother Charlie (Brian Cutler), who are expert scuba divers. The Duvals then decide to use the kids to retrieve the scroll, but the mistrusting Tad and the gang figure out what is going on first.

After appearing in three low-budget drive-in movies, Casey found herself in the big budgeted musical, *Camelot* (1967), starring Richard Harris as King Arthur, Vanessa Redgrave as Guenevere, and Franco Nero as Sir Lancelot. "One of the guys I worked with during by MGM days, Joel Freeman, was the associate producer on this. A lot of my friends were working on the film as dancers and in the background. Joel called me in to interview because they needed someone to play Vanessa's best friend. Of course, I'm tall and she's tall. The costume designer [John Truscott] who went on to win an Academy Award really liked me, so I got the part."

Casey was cast as Lady Sybil, the confidante to Redgrave's Guenevere. Though Casey received prominent billing, she hasn't much screen time, as one of her major scenes was cut. However, she is featured noticeably in the lively number "It's May" with Vanessa Redgrave (whom Casey never got to know very well because she, "spent all her [free] time with Franco Nero"). Guennevere and the young members of her court celebrate the season of spring as they frolic and sing in a grassy knoll. "During the audition Joshua Logan said I would have to run during one of the musical numbers," recalls Sue. "I lived in the bluffs above Beverly Hills and since I was no spring chicken anymore I began running up and down the hills. It was a good thing I did because that number was very strenuous. Also it was supposed to be springtime but we shot this in January. Even though we were in Southern California, it is cold in the mornings. What I did was every morning I would take a cold shower and drive to work with the windows opened. I did this because I knew they would attack me with the cold body make-up, because we wore this light spring dresses with no stockings and shoes. We had to run barefoot through the woods. You just had to grit your teeth and bare with it."

After landing a lead guest role on the sitcom *Family Affair* as a paramour of Brian Keith's character Uncle Bill who keeps standing her up to spend time with his niece Buffy (Anissa Jones) while on holiday in Puerto Rico, Casey decided it was time she got herself an agent. Unbelievably, she was able to land work throughout the decade without one. She

Sue Casey as mother and art forger in *Catalina Caper* (Crown-International, 1967).

played a gym instructor in *The Happy Ending* (1969), starring Jean Simmons and directed by Richard Brooks. ("I was wearing a pink sweat suit and I was running and talking to these ladies in the scene. But you never knew what you were doing with Richard Brooks because he never gave the dialog out until that day. He was one of those secretive directors.") Casey also got herself cast without the help of her agent in the overblown musical *Paint Your Wagon* (1969), starring Lee Marvin, Clint Eastwood, and Jean Seberg. "There is a funny story how I got this role," says Sue. "I knew the casting people from my days working at Paramount with Jerry Lewis and I knew the director, Joshua Logan, from *Camelot*. I called Hoyt Bowers at casting and he said, 'I'm sorry darling, all we need are gals to play prostitutes who speak fluent French.' I spoke French but not fluently. Then about a week later he called and told me that Josh Logan wanted to meet with me. John Truscott, the costume designer from *Camelot,* was also working on this and he recommended me for this part because he liked the way I looked in his clothes."

Paint Your Wagon was based on the hit Broadway musical about a gold mining town in 1840s California, featuring a score by Alan Jay Lerner and Fredrick Loewe. In the movie, Sue Casey was cast as Sarah Woodling, one of the two wives of Mormon Jacob Woodling (John Mitchum, Robert Mitchum's brother). The trio stumbles upon a gold mining camp while traveling to Utah. Since she had just given birth to a son, mean-spirited Sarah encourages her husband to sell the other wife Elizabeth (Jean Seberg) to the highest bidder amongst the gold miners, since they need the money to care for their child. After drunken Ben Rumson (Lee Marvin) wins the fair-haired lady, the Woodlings depart the camp, leaving Elizabeth with her new spouse.

"Boy was this a hard job," exclaims Casey. "We filmed it in Oregon during the middle of the summer. They built a whole town right on location. They tried to be authentic as possible, so I was wearing a corset, a wool dress, a shawl, and a bonnet outside in the hot sun. Before I was hired, nobody ever asked me if I could ride a horse. On location they gave me a mule to ride on down this river that was full of rocks. And then they gave me a real baby to hold. Being a mother, it was amazing to me that anyone would come out and offer up their children without knowing if I could ride. I am not really a rider but I did have the smarts before they gave me the baby to ask for another mule because the first one was not minding. This should have been only a two-day shoot for me, but there was so much infighting. Lee Marvin wouldn't work with Josh Logan. I would see Alan Jay Lerner [one of the producers] and plead, 'I want to go home!' But he said no because the studio was deciding if they were going to fire Josh. I was hot and miserable the whole time I was there." Incredibly, Casey readily agreed when Logan invited her to stick around to play a second small role of a dance hall hostess.

In *Paint Your Wagon*, Casey once again had another leading lady who was preoccupied with her male co-star. "Jean and I would go into wardrobe and make-up together, but she would always run off. She was very pretty and a hard worker, but we had no interplay. Lee Marvin was not a nice man. He was just gross. I hate talking ill of the dead, but he was as crude as could be."

During the seventies, Casey worked intermittently. She did a bit as a human who orders her ape slave to light her cigarette in *Conquest of the Planet of the Apes* (1973). Another job that came her way was a bigger part in *The Main Event* (1979), starring Barbra Streisand and Ryan O'Neal.

"This was a wonderful experience," says Sue. "Barbra was just so kind. She produced the movie with Jon Peters. I was supposed to do this little scene where I am coming on to Ryan O'Neal. We filmed this at a house in Malibu. As we were doing a run through, Ryan just went off on the director [Howard Zieff] about the changes in the scene. I thought, 'What am I supposed to do?' I just patted his arm and sat down. Ryan demanded to see Barbra. She came in and said, 'Let's just try a rehearsal.' She went behind the camera and rolled. It was perfect on one take. I had always heard that Ryan had a temper. It is always very difficult for the little guy in that type of situation. But it turned out okay and I looked *great*. The funny part was that the cinematographer [Mario Tosi] was the same guy who had filmed *Swamp Country*! It was just so incredible and lovely to see him have that success."

Today, Sue Casey is still going strong. When not busy with her successful real estate career, she could be seen playing feisty older ladies on TV (i.e. a mature Rita Hayworth on *Mysteries and Scandals*, an aging movie star in a rest home on the Olsen Twins' sitcom *So Little Time*, etc.) and the occasional film. She had the pleasure of playing a sophisticated woman looking to buy a house in the Academy Award–winning *American Beauty* (1999). "When I went on the audition I thought I didn't get it," admits Sue. "So when I got a call back I thought it was for another role where I was to play a grandmother so I dressed in plaid pants with a sweater. I was so embarrassed

The musical *Paint Your Wagon* (Paramount, 1969) featured John Mitchum as a Mormon with two wives, Jean Seberg (*bottom left*) and Sue Casey (*center*).

when I got there and realized what I had done. The casting director took me in to meet Sam Mendes and the writer. When I read the script I thought, 'My God! This reads like a porno film!' But it was hilarious especially my scenes where Annette Bening is determined to sell me this house that is in a shambles." Alas, except for a brief shot of Sue walking into the house, the scene with Bening landed on the cutting room floor. "*Nobody told me,*" exclaims Sue incredulously. "I brought my son to the premiere and felt so foolish when I realized they excised our scene." But being the veteran that she is, Sue Casey shrugs her shoulders and says, "that's show business," as she just takes it in stride and awaits her next acting gig.

Film Appearances

1945   **Holiday in Mexico** (MGM) d. George Sidney

1947   **The Secret Life of Walter Mitty** (RKO Radio Pictures) d. Norman Z. McLeod

1948   **Words and Music** (MGM) d. Norman Taurog

1949   **Neptune's Daughter** (MGM) d. Edward Buzzell
The Great Sinner (MGM) d. Robert Siodmak
It's a Great Feeling (Warner Bros.) d. David Butler
Madame Bovary (MGM) d. Vincente Minnelli

1950   **The Yellow Cab Man** (MGM) d. Jack Donohue
Wabash Avenue (20th Century–Fox) d. Henry Koster
Annie Get Your Gun (MGM) d. George Sidney
The Toast of New Orleans (MGM) d. Norman Taurog
Mrs. O'Malley and Mr. Malone (MGM) d. Norman Taurog
For Heaven's Sake (20th Century–Fox) d. George Seaton

1951   **The Scarf** (United Artists) d. Ewald Andre Dupont
Show Boat (MGM) d. George Sidney
Secrets of Monte Carlo (Republic) d. George Blair
An American in Paris (MGM) d. Vincente Minnelli

1952   **The Las Vegas Story** (RKO Radio Pictures) d. Robert Stevenson
Something to Live For (Paramount) d. Dwight Taylor
The Big Trees (Warner Bros.) d. Felix E. Feist
Sound Off (Columbia) d. Richard Quine
She's Working Her Way Through College (Warner Bros.) d. H. Bruce Humberstone
We're Not Married (20th Century–Fox) d. Edmund Goulding
The Merry Widow(MGM) d. Curtis Bernhardt
Son of Paleface (Paramount) d. Frank Tashlin
Million Dollar Mermaid (MGM) d. Mervyn LeRoy
Road to Bali (Paramount) d. Hal Walker
The Bad and the Beautiful (MGM) d. Vincente Minnelli

1953   **Abbott and Costello Go to Mars** (Universal) d. Charles Lamont

1954   **The French Line** (RKO Radio Pictures) d. Lloyd Bacon
Rear Window (Paramount) d. Alfred Hitchcock
A Star Is Born (Warner Bros.) d. George Cukor
Three Ring Circus (Paramount) d. Joseph Pevney
There's No Business Like Show Business (20th Century–Fox) d. Walter Lang

	The Other Woman (20th Century–Fox) d. Hugo Haas
1955	Son of Sinbad (RKO Radio Pictures) d. Ted Tetzlaff
1960	Bells Are Ringing (MGM) d. Vincente Minnelli
1961	The Errand Boy (Paramount) d. Jerry Lewis
1962	Two Weeks in Another Town (MGM) d. Vincente Minnelli Who's Got the Action? (Paramount) d. Daniel Mann Billy Rose's Jumbo (MGM) d. Charles Walters
1963	A New Kind of Love (Paramount) d. Melville Shavelson
1964	The Carpetbaggers (Paramount) d. Edward Dmytryk Where Love Has Gone (Paramount) d. Edward Dmytryk
1965	The Family Jewels (Paramount) d. Jerry Lewis The Beach Girls and the Monster (AIP) d. Jon Hall
1966	Swamp Country d. Robert Patrick
1967	Catalina Caper (Crown International) d. Lee Sholem Camelot (Warner Bros.) d. Joshua Logan
1969	Paint Your Wagon (Paramount) d. Joshua Logan The Happy Ending (United Artists) d. Richard Brooks
1971	The Marriage of a Young Stockbroker (20th Century–Fox) d. Lawrence Turman
1972	Skyjacked (MGM) d. John Guillerman
1973	Conquest of the Planet of the Apes (20th Century–Fox) d. J. Lee Thompson
1975	Lucky Lady (20th Century–Fox) d. Stanley Donen
1979	The Main Event (Warner Bros.) d. Howard Zieff
1981	Evilspeak (Moreno Co.) d. Eric Weston
1983	Hysterical (Direct-to-Cable) d. Chris Bearde
1994	Till the End of the Night (Motion Picture Corp. of America) d. Larry Brand
1996	A Very Brady Sequel (Paramount) d. Arlene Sanford Full Circle (TV-movie) d. Bethany Rooney What Love Sees (TV-movie) d. Michael Switzer
1999	American Beauty (DreamWorks)* d. Sam Mendes

*Scenes deleted.

Television Appearances

Lux Video Theatre "The Wayward Saint" 8/30/1956 NBC
The Lucy-Desi Comedy Hour "Lucy Wants a Career" 4/13/1959 CBS
77 Sunset Strip "The Kookie Caper" 10/9/1959 ABC
The Ann Sothern Show "Doubting Devery" 3/24/1960 CBS
Gunsmoke "The Hunger" 11/17/1962 CBS
Gunsmoke "The Bad One" 1/26/1963 CBS
The Dick Van Dyke Show "Big Max Calvada" 11/20/1963 CBS
The Lucy Show "Lucy Meets Danny Kaye" 12/28/1964 CBS
The Bailey's of Balboa "Sam's Dream" 1/14/1965 CBS
The Farmer's Daughter "A Plague on Both Their Houses" 1/29/1965 CBS
The Beverly Hillbillies "The Big Bank Battle" 5/5/1965 CBS
Family Affair "To Love with Buffy" 1/6/1969 CBS
Emergency! "The Lighter-Than-Air-Man" 11/1/1975 NBC
The White Shadow "One of the Boys" 1/27/1979 CBS
Delta House "Parents Day" 3/3/1979 ABC
Divorce Court (episode—title unknown) 1985 SYN

Hotel "Restless Nights" 12/10/1986 ABC
Dallas "Daddy's Little Darlin'" 12/18/1987 CBS
Family Medical Center (episode—title unknown) 1988 SYN
Dallas "Wedding Bell Blues" 2/24/1989 CBS
The Trials of Rosie O'Neill "The Gang's All Here" 11/26/1990 CBS
Hunter "The Reporter" 1/30/1991 NBC
Bodies of Evidence "Whispers of the Dead" 3/30/1993 CBS
Red Shoe Diaries "Juarez" 1995 SHO
The Faculty "Parents' Night" 6/5/1996 ABC
Boy Meets World "Last Tango in Philly" 12/5/1997 ABC
Mysteries and Scandals "Rita Hayworth" 1998 E!
Diagnosis: Murder "Seven Deadly Sins" 11/18/1999 CBS
So Little Time "The Volunteer" 3/2/2002 Fox Family Channel

Also

The Colgate Comedy Hour, All Star Revue, The Ray Bolger Show, The June Havoc Show, The Red Skelton Show, The Bob Hope Show, The Carol Burnett Show (2), *Arnie, Marcus Welby, MD, Hart to Hart, Unsolved Mysteries* (2) and *Haggerty*

☆ ANDREA DROMM ☆

Andrea Dromm, a willowy, blue-eyed sun-drenched blonde, is more famous as a model than actress. Cast as a flight attendant in a commercial for National Airlines in 1963, Dromm's career took off with the words, "Is this any way to run an airline? You bet it is!" Hollywood beckoned, and Andrea was cast as the teenage babysitter in *The Russians Are Coming, the Russians Are Coming* (1966) and a bikini-clad secret agent working undercover in the Bahamas in *Come Spy with Me* (1967). However, disillusioned with Hollywood, Dromm returned to modeling and was known throughout the late sixties for her Clairol Summer Blonde commercials. Her popular California-girl image led the native New Yorker to host a TV special on surfing in 1967.

Andrea Dromm was born on February 18. She was raised in the affluent community of Manhasset on the north shore of Long Island. At the age of six, Dromm began modeling. "According to my mom, my uncle took pictures of me, and he said I looked good so he thought I should do it," says Andrea. "I enjoyed it for awhile. Conover signed me and I had to go into the city a lot. I was dragged all over the place and had to take buses and trains. I was pulled out of school frequently. I stopped modeling as a child because I decided I would rather stay in school. It was interfering too much with my studies."

Dromm let the modeling drift during high school and purportedly worked as a hatcheck girl at Jones Beach, among other jobs. After graduation she entered the University of Connecticut, where she studied drama. Among her stage credits are productions of *The Diary of Anne Frank, The Crucible* and *Romeo and Juliet*. She quit school during her senior year and went to San Francisco where she worked at Saks. After a year or so, she returned to the East Coast to complete her degree. She also returned to the world of fashion as a runway model for various houses in New York City's garment center. "When I got out of college I realized I really wasn't suited to do very much," admits

Dromm. "A publishing house hired me to do secretarial work, but my typing wasn't that good, so I decided I might as well try modeling again. I had nothing to lose. I wasn't as tall or thin as they wanted me to be but I was determined to model and I did it. I pounded the pavement and posed for a lot of pictures. Eileen Ford didn't want me in the beginning, so I went with another agency. When I had a good portfolio put together I went back to her and she signed me. I took acting classes too, which led to commercials."

The commercial that made her an overnight TV star was for National Airlines. Recalling her big break, where she was the last of hundreds of actresses to audition, Dromm says jokingly, "Maybe they were tired of looking at people and just gave up. I don't know but it worked out very well for me."

For a short time, the National Airlines catchphrase became entrenched with the masses. Most actresses did not get to Hollywood on the strength of a TV commercial, but according to Andrea Dromm, "People remembered me from the commercial so it wasn't a hindrance at all. It was great and an asset, as a matter of fact." At first though, Dromm was reluctant to leave her steady modeling gigs for the bright lights of Hollywood. "During the sixties, when a model became an actress, they didn't want you to model any more," explains Dromm. "I had reservations about going to California because I still wanted to be in New York part of the time and model. It was a difficult decision."

Dromm finally made the big move to the Coast to pursue acting in 1965. Her first acting job was playing Yeoman Smith in the second *Star Trek* pilot produced by Gene Roddenberry, entitled "Where No Man Has Gone Before." It introduced regulars William Shatner as Captain Kirk, James Doohan as Scotty and George Takei as Mr. Sulu. Leonard Nimoy as Mr.

Is this any way for Andrea Dromm to look? You bet it is!

Spock was the only actor from the first pilot kept aboard. Continuing Roddenberry's vision of the Captain's yeoman (played by Laurel Goodwin in the first pilot), Yeoman Smith was still young and cute but with a less obvious crush on her captain as compared to the previous Yeoman Colt's more overt feelings. This may not have been intentional, but this episode gave Dromm absolutely nothing to do but to stand stoically alongside Kirk when he was on the bridge. ("Gene Roddenberry liked me a lot and I think he just wrote the part in for me. There wasn't much dialog.") Instead, the pilot focused on Sally Kellerman as a sympathetic doctor and Gary Lockwood as a crewmember and old friend of Kirk's who develop super human powers after being hit with an electric beam. When Lockwood becomes a threat to the Enterprise, Kirk has to make the decision to destroy him.

Regarding Dromm and Roddenberry,

Herb Solow wrote in his book *Inside Star Trek: The Real Story*, "Model Andrea Dromm ... came aboard for the second pilot as Yeoman Smith. Actually, it was a non-part. But during the casting process, director Jimmy Goldstone overheard Gene say, 'I'm hiring her because I want to score with her.' It was not only a non-part, I'm sure it was a non-score as well...." He was right, but this surprises Dromm, who says of Rodddenberry, "I had no problems with Gene at all. I thought he was a very nice man."

Recalling her experience working with the *Star Trek* cast, Dromm says, "William Shatner was very pleasant and professional. Gary Lockwood and Sally Kellerman were guest stars in the pilot. Gary was especially friendly and helpful because there were a lot of things I had to react to without dialog like the ship rocking, and I did not know what to do. This was my first real acting job and this was all new to me. I was a little nervous and not quite sure of myself and did not know how to approach those scenes. The director wasn't telling me very much, but Gary helped me out and I just did my best."

The character of Yeoman Smith was to become a regular on the series, but Dromm passed on it. Explaining her decision, Andrea Dromm says matter-of-factly, "I was offered a role in *The Russians Are Coming, the Russians Are Coming*. They told me that you either do the film or the series. I chose the film but if I had known that *Star Trek* would become such a phenomenon, I probably would have opted for the series. But this episode was still only a pilot. Not only did nobody know if it was going to be picked up as a series but nobody had a clue that it was going to turn out as big as it did. In fact, William Shatner told me that if the show didn't hit he didn't know what he was going to do. Since *Star Trek* was only a pilot they could keep you under option for six months and change your character or even worse drop you from the show. [A fate that had befallen Laurel Goodwin.] You had no guarantees that they would sign you for the series. I thought doing the movie would be more exciting and a great thing to do. That was a choice I had to make and you can't look back."

No doubt acting talent is required to make it in Hollywood, but luck also plays a factor, as Andrea Dromm found out. One night, she was eating with her agent and some friends at an Italian restaurant. Sitting at the table next to hers was director Norman Jewison. "My agent introduced us and Norman Jewison asked me if I'd be interested in auditioning for a role in his new movie, *The Russians Are Coming, the Russians Are Coming*. I said yes and that is how I got the part."

The Russians Are Coming, the Russians Are Coming (1966) was a hilarious cold-war comedy about a Russian submarine that comes aground on a sandbar off the coast of Maine. Alan Arkin, in his film debut, played the sub's second-in-command, Lt. Rozanov, who comes ashore with eight of his men to find a boat to free them. The Russians land at the summer home of Walt Whittaker (Carl Reiner), his wife (Eva Marie Saint), two children and one fetching babysitter named Alison (Dromm). Rozanov persuades Whittaker to sneak them into town, leaving young Kolchin (John Phillip Law) to guard Whittaker's family. The Russians steal a car from the town's postmistress and when she is untied she reports what happened to the switchboard operator (Tessie O'Shea). Soon, wild rumors are circulating that the Russians have invaded, as Sheriff Mattocks (Brian Keith) and his inept assistant Norman Jonas (Jonathan Winters) try to calm the townspeople and investigate what actually happened. As all this craziness is taking place, Kolchin has fallen in love with Alison. While some critics felt

In *The Russians Are Coming, the Russians Are Coming* (United Artists, 1966) Carl Reiner tries to protect his wife Eva Marie Saint, children Sheldon Collins and Cindy Putnam, and neighborhood teenager Andrea Dromm from the "invading" Russian Navy.

the young love story was slow and hampered the pace, Jewison filmed most of these scenes on the wind-swept beach, as the striking-looking Law and Dromm made a wonderful counterpoint to all the character actors in the film. The reviewer for *Variety* remarked, "Miss Dromm ... is good in a role which must convey suspicion, then compassion, then romance. The pair's [Law and Dromm] interactions are fine...."

Andea credits her good performance to director Norman Jewison, whom she describes as being "a lovely and terrific director. He used to be an actor so he is very giving. He worked with us a lot, especially when we had our close ups and things like that. Most directors leave you on your own. They really don't direct you. You have to improvise and hope you do an okay job. It was not like that at all with Norman Jewison.

"Coincidentally, I just ran into Norman Jewison on the beach in South Hampton," continues Dromm. "He was walking and I said, 'Gee, I think I know that guy.' I started to sort of stalk him. He was with Greg Kinnear and Peggy Siegel. I wanted to get close enough to hear him speak clearly because he has a very distinctive voice. I finally said, 'Pardon me, are you Norman Jewison?' He turned around and said, 'Yes.' 'Well, I'm Andrea Dromm.' He gasped, 'Oh, good grief! I haven't seen you in years.' We talked for awhile and he called me 'America's sweetheart,' which I thought was very endearing. It was very nice seeing him again."

As for the cast, Dromm has nothing but the highest praise for them. "It was a great bunch of people," remarks Dromm. "For me it was a honor to work with them because they were all so professional." As for John Phillip Law, Dromm found him to be "friendly and a very conscientious actor." What stands out most for Dromm is the film's climax. As the Russian commander takes his submarine into the town's harbor and threatens to blow it up, a small boy slips from his perch on the roof of a church and hangs from the gutter. The Russians help the townsmen form a human pyramid to rescue him. According to Dromm, "There was almost one accident in this scene. When John Phillip Law took the boy, Johnny Whittaker, off whatever he was suppose to be caught on, he almost dropped him. That was really kind of scary. For some of those shots they really were high up. For the close ups they weren't."

When *The Russians Are Coming, the Russians Are Coming* opened on May 25, 1966, it received critical raves and went on to become the year's fifth highest grossing film. The movie won the Golden Globe for 'Best Motion Picture–Comedy/Musical,' the Photoplay Gold Medal award for 'Most Popular Film' and went on to receive four Academy Award nominations including 'Best Motion Picture.' ("I thought *The Russians Are Coming* was a good film with a lot of wonderful actors but I was surprised with all the recognition it received," admits Dromm.) Even so, she was able to ride the crest of the film's success to a starring role in her next movie.

20th Century–Fox tapped the winsome blonde to star opposite Troy Donahue ("He was a very nice man") in her next and final film *Come Spy with Me* (1967). "I knew the director, Marshall Stone, who I had worked previously with in commercials," divulges Dromm. "This was the only film he ever directed. I don't know what happened to him after that." Dromm played secret agent Jill Parsons, who is sent on assignment to Jamaica. Her mission—to solve the murders of two Americans killed just before a big meeting of the world's leaders aboard an aircraft carrier in the island's waters. Villainous financier Walter Ludecker (Albert Dekker) has been laying bombs throughout the ocean floor to destroy the cruiser and to create an international incident. Parsons masquerades as a skin diver contestant in a competition hosted by swinging ex-surfer Pete Barker (Donahue) on his boat. She goes diving, does the new dance craze "the Shark" at a local discotheque and lounges by the pool. Oh and she also finds time to locate Barker's kidnapped friend Samantha (Valerie Allen), uncover Ludecker's plot and defuse the bombs.

Regarding the on location work in *Come Spy with Me*, Andrea Dromm recalls, " I had to learn how to ride a motorcycle, dive into the water and scuba dive for this. The thing is I thought the scuba diving was very dangerous. I didn't take an official course and they had us go down in really quite bad weather as practice. They wound up using a double for me because I was really nervous doing it and I just didn't want to take my life in my hands. When they shot the scene I think the regulators weren't checked properly and one of the actors—it may have been Troy Donahue—got into some trouble under the water. One of the other actors, Martin Hewitt, who had taken a scuba diving course, had to save him."

Come Spy with Me was a confusing secret agent film that was overshadowed later that same year by Fox's other female secret agent film, *Fathom*, starring Raquel Welch. Though both films were greatly

Lobby card for *Come Spy with Me* (20th Century–Fox, 1967) starring Troy Donahue and Andrea Dromm.

helped by their on-location filming—*Come Spy with Me* in the Caribbean and *Fathom* in Spain—Fox devoted more of a budget and effort to the other film and sometimes the cinematography in *Come Spy with Me* seems "of uncertain focus." Hence, Dromm's movie opened at the bottom of a double bill with *One Million Years B. C.* starring, coincidentally, La Welch. This didn't surprise Andrea, who found the film to be "kind of rough around the edges. I don't know if it had a professional script. It definitely wasn't up to the caliber of *The Russians Are Coming, the Russians Are Coming*." The critics couldn't have agreed more and seem to try to outdo each other with quips on the title or Dromm's TV commercial past. Robert Salmaggi, writing in the *NY Herald Tribune*, remarked, "The film belongs on top of the sky-high pile of crummy I spy losers" and ended his review with "Come die with me." The reviewer in *Variety* wrote, "It this any way to make a motion picture? You bet it isn't.'" The reviewer also went on to speculate that the film may have been originally shot in 16m and later blown up to the 4:3 aspect ratio.

Between movies, Andrea Dromm stayed active by appearing in commercials. Beginning in 1966, she was once again the toast of the small screen as the cute sun-drenched beach bunny in Clairol's Summer Blonde campaign. The ads proved so popular that Dromm was tapped to host the special *Hit the Surf*, which was "An on-the-scene, behind-the-scene, make-the-scene look at the surfing boom!" Cameras followed Andrea from California to Hawaii in search of the perfect wave. In Huntington Beach, Dromm learned how and why people surf from surfers Roy Krump and Kemp Aaberg, who give Dromm a lesson in catching a wave. Next, Dromm took viewers to a surfboard factory and then to some of the world's most dangerous surfing areas in Hawaii's Banzai Pipeline. Dromm doesn't remember too much about this show except that, "They tried to teach me how to surf a little bit. I always wanted to surf and tried it but I wasn't good at it. It takes awhile to get the hang of it and I didn't have the patience for it."

After the special Dromm returned to New York. She continued modeling and making commercials until the early seventies and then completely quit. Regarding her decision to stop acting, she told *Look Magazine* in 1967, "[Hollywood] is no place to learn acting. In the movies, you don't have to be a great actress: you're just a type. They expect you to do sexy things, like seduce people with your eyes. I felt susceptible and trapped." Looking back today, Dromm sighs, "I don't know what happened that made me stop acting. Hollywood is very competitive. I guess you really had to want it very badly and there was an awful lot of competition. I wasn't aggressive. It goes against my nature. It is also a hard life because you are not always working. You have to be prepared for that. I wasn't. While I was working in New York, I was working all the time. In Hollywood, lots of times you had to

Tonight!
July 20, 9:30-10:00
in color on ABC!

"HIT THE SURF"

An on-the-scene, behind-the-scene, "make-the-scene" look at the surfing boom! See what (and who) makes surfing a multimillion-dollar tidal wave, coast to coast!

STARRING
ANDREA DROMM
and featuring some of the nation's top surfers.

SPECIAL!
Brought to you by Clairol, creators of the exciting natural look in beauty.

© Clairol Inc. 1966

Promotional ad for the TV special *Hit the Surf* (1967) hosted by Andrea Domm. *Billy Rose Theatre Collection, The New York Public Library for the Performing Arts, Astor, Lenox and Tilden Foundations.*

sit around and wait for a long time. When you are used to being busy and then you are sitting around waiting for something to happen, you can get lonely and discouraged. I also met a guy at the time. Hollywood was also very wild in the late sixties. I eventually left and moved back East."

People Magazine tracked Dromm down in 1988 for its "Where Are They Now" issue. Despite dividing her time between her homes in Florida and Long Island (reportedly Dromm made some very successful investments in California real estate), she professed a return to acting in movies, theater or commercials. Unfortunately, it never came to be. "I still have a desire to return to acting but it is a hard business to get back into," says Dromm. "I would love to give it a try but it is still so competitive. You have to be very lucky." Today it is still an endless summer for Clairol's former Summer Blonde as Andrea Dromm continues wintering in balmy Palm Beach and summering in the Hamptons.

Film Appearances:

1966 **The Russian Are Coming, the Russians Are Coming** (United Artists) d. Norman Jewison
1967 **Come Spy with Me** (20th Century–Fox) d. Marshall Stone

Television Appearances

Star Trek "Where No Man Has Gone Before" 9/22/1966 ABC
The Mike Douglas Show 2/13/1967 SYN
Hit the Surf (special) [hostess] 7/20/1967 ABC

☆ GAIL GILMORE ☆

A cute blonde with an unconventional personality, hence the name changes, Gail Gilmore (a.k.a. Gail Gerber, a.k.a. Gail Gibson) came to Hollywood in 1963 and appeared in six movies in 1965. In that short period of time, she left an indelible impression on fans of '60s teenage drive-in movies. Gilmore appeared in two Elvis Presley musicals, playing a vacationing coed in *Girl Happy* and a dancing gypsy in *Harum Scarum*. She then frolicked on the seashores of sunny Southern California in *The Girls on the Beach* and *Beach Ball*, before growing to gigantic proportions along with five other delinquent teenagers who terrorize a town in *Village of the Giants*. Gilmore met writer Terry Southern on the set of *The Loved One* (1965) and abandoned Hollywood in 1966 to live with him in New York and then Connecticut, where she remained his constant companion until his death thirty years later.

Gilmore was born Gail Gerber in Edmonton, Alberta, Canada, on October 4, 1937. ("I was older by five to ten years than all the other actors I worked with in my movies.") When she reached her twelfth birthday Gail became an equity performer. Also being a very talented dancer, she became a member at the age of fifteen of Les Grands Ballets Canadiens in Montreal. "I was the youngest dancer in the company. We all lived in a big house and we would all go to gay bars together. I had a wonderful childhood and youth. It was just grand."

Gail left her dance troupe and moved

Gail Gilmore or Gail Gerber? It really doesn't matter to drive-in movie fans since Gail looks fantastic.

to Toronto, where she was hired as one of the regular dancers for the series *Music '60 Presents The Hit Parade*. Using her birth name, she began acting and landed 'the girl' roles in a number of live *Playhouse 90*-type TV series. ("This was exciting work. It was just like being on stage.") Gail was also one of the last people to work with Smith and Dale of The Sunshine Boys fame. "They were headliners in burlesque," says Gilmore. "They hadn't spoke to each other or worked in a long time. Wayne and Schuster brought them up twice to Canada to appear on their show. They sat on opposite sides of the stage during rehearsal and never spoke a word to each other. I got to work with them in some of their classic sketches. We all then went on *The Ed Sullivan Show*—following a dog act!" Critics began taking note of the promising young actress, and in 1962, the Canadian magazine *Top Hit Club News* picked Gail as the performer "On the Way Up" and described the TV actress as "being more attractive in person with the added dimension of color and a sparkling personality."

By 1963, Gilmore had relocated to Hollywood. "I had to get out of Toronto," reveals Gail. "I was afraid to come to New York because I felt I was okay enough for comedy but not a good enough actress to cut it there. I found out many years later that I was right when studying in New York with Lee Strasberg and Stella Adler. But I knew I could succeed in Los Angeles." Never having been to California, the brash newcomer checked into the Beverly Hills Hotel and headed straight to her favorite network—NBC. After talking her way through the gate, she was directed by the guard to the building where casting was located. The casting agent was impressed with Gilmore's list of credits but advised her to get a talent agent and randomly recommended the Armstrong–Deuser Agency.

"Sam Armstrong was just wonderful," remarks Gilmore fondly. "He was a classy older gentleman who always wore three piece suits and smoked those long cigarettes with the ash that doesn't fall off. We'd make the casting rounds with Sam introducing me as his latest discovery. Sam would drive me in his big car and we'd drift from lane to lane as he would fill my head with stories about the old days of Hollywood and how much more exciting it was and how this was now the doldrums with the studios collapsing. He told me about one of his clients, Louise Rainer, who won two Academy Awards and then ran off with a writer and was never heard from again. It was a cautionary tale. I didn't know it at the time."

Gail's first job in Hollywood was the lead role on stage in *Under the Yum Yum Tree* at the Ivar Theatre. ("I became friends with the black stage manager who told me that I would never make it in Hollywood because 'My brains weren't tied to my ass,'" says Gails, chuckling.) After doing a couple of guest shots on TV, the petite, brown-eyed blonde appeared in six movies in 1965—five of which were geared to the teenage audience. She made her film debut, billed as Gale Gerber, delivering a perky performance as Georgia, a man-hungry, wisecracking coed in *The Girls on the Beach*, which featured a catchy title tune sung by the Beach Boys who also appear in the film. In this pleasant teenage beach romp, a gaggle of sorority sisters (Noreen Corcoran, Linda Marshall, Lana Wood and Gerber) have just learned from their housemother that the mortgage is due. When she explains to them about a "ten thousand dollar balloon payment" Gerber's ditzy Georgia asks, "Who bought a ten thousand dollar balloon?" When they suggest that they use their "nest egg," she confesses she has squandered it helping other less fortunate friends. With foreclosure imminent, the girls enter their other sorority sisters (including Mary Mitchel, Lori Saunders and Anna Capri) into various contests to win prize money. Meanwhile, a trio of surfer boys (Martin West, Aron Kincaid and Steve Rogers) is trying to think of a way to impress the girls. Thinking they are starstruck, the guys boast that they know The Beatles. The girls disbelieve the guys until they receive a phone call from 'Ringo,' which changes their minds. But it is actually West on the phone out in the parking lot crinkling newspaper to make it sound like static. When all the sorority girls come up losers in the contests, they decide to take the guys' offer and mount a fundraiser with the Beatles as headliners. When the girls learn that the guys have duped them, they don some Beatles' wigs and impersonate the Fab Four. Gilmore is seen on the

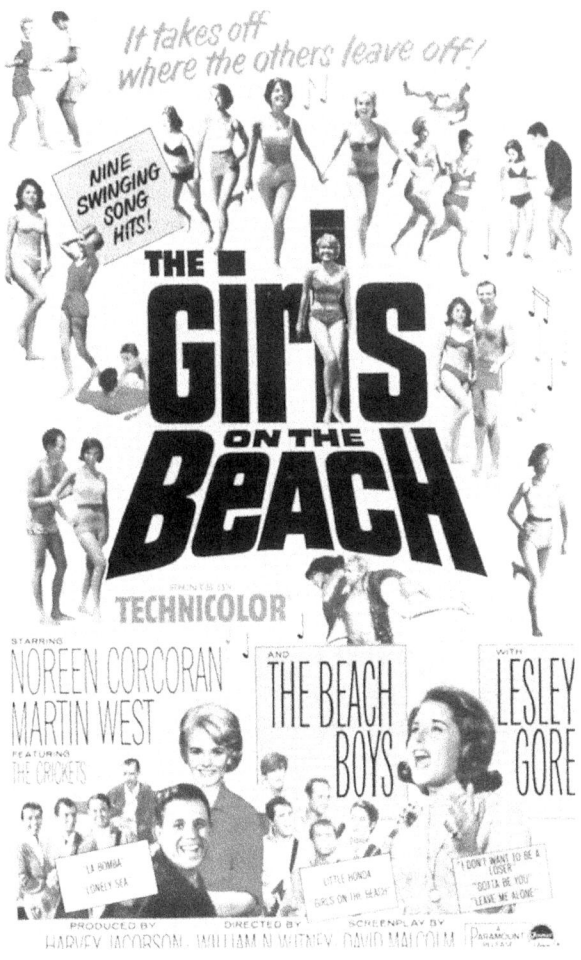

Poster art for *The Girls on the Beach* **(Paramount, 1965).**

drums pretending to be Ringo Starr. The audience goes wild and the show is a big success even after the girls' ruse is exposed. Sans wigs, they sing "I Wanna Marry a Beatle" and raise enough money to save the sorority house. When the film was released most reviews were in line with *Variety*'s, which called the movie a "pleasant teenage entry" and noted that Gail Gerber "offers fresh support."

"Lana Wood and I sort of didn't fit in with the rest of the girls in this," reveals Gail. "I was a little older than the others. As for Lana, they weren't sisters of stars and they may have held that against her. Lana did advise me about make-up during this. She told me that her sister Natalie suggested that after you come out of make-up you go and put more on. I told the make-up guy this and he said, 'You know what's going to happen Gail? You are going to wind up with two black holes around the face.' He was right. If you look at pictures of us there is light around Noreen Corcoran's and my eyes but not Lana's. The make-up guys know their work but they made us all come out looking alike. When I happen upon this movie on TV, sometimes I can't tell which one is me." This is true, as brunette Noreen Corcoran's hair was dyed blonde and styled into a bouffant which matched Gilmore and Linda Marshall's.

The Girls on the Beach was directed by William Witney (whom Gail describes as being "a great old guy") and produced by Gene Corman. The film was shot on a strict budget in two weeks with no time to goof off. Co-star Aron Kincaid recalls, "Gail was this tough little blonde. We just completed a number of takes on a scene, and the director only allowed us a ten-minute break. Gail sat down, lit a cigarette and said very loudly, 'Who do you have to fuck to get *off* this picture.'" Smiling, Gail admits, "That is a true story. It is an old line from the thirties and forties. Someone like Ida Lupino said it first. I just used it for the occasion."

Gilmore and the other girls on the beach dance up a storm in this beach bon bon. But according to Gail, she took it upon herself to turn down the gyrations for one number because "the director asked me to dance around this young girl [Lesley Gore] who was performing this song ["It's Gotta Be You"]. I thought, 'if I danced—like the way Joy Harmon can dance—I would just wipe out this girl during the intro to her song. I downplayed it and did a little vamp. Later on I had to dance in front of the Beach Boys [while performing "Little Honda"]. I'm dancing around and I am thinking, 'if they don't yell cut pretty soon there is nothing more in my repertoire that I can do. *This music is so boring—I can't stand it. If they play that riff one more time I'm going to kill somebody!*' They just kept banging away. Thirty years later I am reading about the leader of the Beach Boys [Brian Wilson] describing this scene in his early youth, which he said was his lowest moment because there was this girl gyrating out in front during his very important song. I am sorry I caused him so much grief. If only we were able to read each other's mind."

After completing *The Girls on the Beach*, Gail changed her last name on advice from her agent. "Sam Armstrong acted so cosmopolitan but he didn't have a passport and had never been out of Los Angeles," says Gail laughing. "He said to me, '*Gerber is a German name. This is a Jewish town.*' I tried Gail Gilmore first because in Canada I had a friend and dance partner named Glen Gilmore. His sister, who was also a ballet dancer, was named Gail so I just sort of stole her name." It is as Gail Gilmore that drive-in movie fans know Gail best.

As just one of thousands of young Hollywood hopefuls, Armstrong advised Gail that she needed publicity to get noticed. She attended an opening of a Mexican restaurant in Hollywood for a photo shoot arranged by one of the teen movie rags of the time, but her date was noted writer Henry Miller. ("I forgot to tell Terry that he stole me from Miller. He would have loved that so much.") Miller may have thrilled the owner but no doubt young readers of the publication were hoping for Troy Donahue or Jimmy Darren. More outrageously, Gilmore got talked into a rather bizarre publicity stunt worthy of Jayne Mansfield. Under advisement from "a demimonde guy from Montreal," she borrowed a small dog and walked to the mailbox in front of Schwab's Drugstore to send a package. She not only slipped the parcel into the mailbox but the dog as well. She then began screaming. The police and fire crews were called to rescue the pooch that was unharmed. Also as planned, reporters showed up and Gail got her face splashed across the newspaper. Gilmore says laughing, "It was after this that I started to get letters from Toronto saying 'Congratulations on how well you're doing in your career in Hollywood.' I thought, 'Oh, irony!' I told Terry this story and he thought it was the funniest thing."

After learning that she got a small role in an Elvis Presley musical, Gilmore decided to do her homework and see a Presley movie. She hopped into her '52 Dodge and drove down from her home in Laurel Canyon to see *Viva Las Vegas*. "I needed to see what I was getting into. As

The Girls on the Beach (Paramount, 1965) featured (left to right) Lana Wood, Aron Kincaid, Gail Gerber, Martin West, and Noreen Corcoran as beach-loving college students. *Courtesy of Aron Kincaid.*

I was limping back up the hill in my '52 Dodge, I am thinking, 'This is crazy. The whole story was about young men and women diving into back seats of cars just to get laid!" In *Girl Happy* (1965), Gilmore played Nancy, a pretty blonde who is romanced by Gary Crosby ("a really talented guy"), who played one of Elvis' combo members on spring break in Fort Lauderdale. Their idyll is constantly interrupted by the antics of a mobster's daughter (Shelley Fabares) they are hired to secretly chaperone. Gilmore recalls that "Elvis's guys kept inviting me to his house and I kept declining. I must confess that I was a terrible snob. I wasn't familiar with Elvis Presley's music because I came from the world of classical and jazz music. I had been married to a piano player in Montreal. I wasn't aware of Elvis' importance until I met Terry Southern."

Gilmore joined practically every starlet in Hollywood at the time to appear, albeit briefly and uncredited, in *The Loved One* (1965), which was adapted from the Evelyn Waugh novel that satirized the Southern California funeral industry and Hollywood's British 'colony' of actors. The screenplay was co-written by Christopher Isherwood and Terry Southern, the literary hipster as he was referred to, who was the author of numerous short stories and the novels *The Magic Christian* and *Candy*, among others. Director Stanley Kubrick hired Southern to (according to his son Nile Southern) "employ a satirical touch" to the movie *Dr. Strangelove*, which began his short stay in Hollywood as a screenwriter. "Terry Southern was one of the first writers or maybe *the* first writer to always be on the set," says Gilmore. "In those days, you handed in your script and you went home. Terry was on the set writing all these wonderful vignettes for all these incredible people. He loved to tailor his work to a specific person or write with a specific person in mind. The actors loved his work and dialog so much [the director] couldn't get them to stop."

According to Gail, director Tony Richardson was signed to direct the black comedy before he won his Best Director Academy Award for *Tom Jones*. When he tried to renegotiate his deal with MGM, they refused and held him to his contract. "He then tried to undermine the whole production," reveals Gilmore. "He cast an American [Robert Morse] in the lead role of the British young man who comes to Los Angeles and hired Anjanette Comer for the female lead [Amiee Thanatogenos]. Tony barred the producer Martin Ransohoff from the set and would have elaborately catered screenings of yesterday's dailies every morning. He purposely went over budget and extended the shooting schedule by weeks."

Gilmore does not have much to do in *The Loved One* and you will be hard pressed to find her. However, costumed identically to Comer's character, a cosmetologist at a funeral home called Whispering Glades, Gilmore does have a brief close up during Comer's first scene with Rod Steiger as embalmer Mr. Joyboy. "I was sitting around earning more money than I would tell any ballet dancer ever," says Gilmore. "There was a whole bunch of us making all this money doing nothing. We were all dressed like Anjanette Comer but we were never really used. One day I was thinking that I was going to die there. I was working twelve hours a day and having absolutely nothing to do. I saw a chair unobtrusively in the corner and I thought, 'Maybe I can make it to that chair and disappear, then the day will pass.' I moved to the chair—I guess Terry was standing a ways away—when one of the crew guys said, 'That one is a dancer.' His friend said, 'How can you tell?' He replied, 'I can tell by the way she sits down.' Terry looked at who they were talking about and came over to me." After

Brenda Benet (left) and Gail Gilmore (right) as gypsies shake that tambourine as Elvis Presley croons another song in *Harum Scarum* (MGM, 1965). *Billy Rose Theatre Collection, New York Public Library for the Performing Arts, Astor, Lenox and Tilden Foundations*

introducing himself to her, Terry asked Gail if she would be interested in coming to his office for a drink. "I replied, 'Certainly!'"

"We went upstairs and Terry poured a drink," continues Gail. "He then said, 'I also have a bestseller out—the novel *Candy*.' I said, 'I don't read bestsellers.' I guess you don't tell a writer that because I wasn't able to get rid of him for thirty-one years!"

After informing Terry that she had worked with Elvis Presley in *Girl Happy*, she was surprised to learn that he was a big fan of the King's. "Terry told me that Elvis was very influential in the crossover of what was called race music. He also told me that when he was living in Geneva, Switzerland, he'd play all these Elvis Presley records and that his jazz friends and literary friends would have rather run out into a blizzard than listen to Elvis. When the second film [with Elvis] came along, Terry wanted to meet Elvis Presley."

That second film was *Harum Scarum* (1965), which took great advantage of Gilmore's dancing prowess and gave her more to do than in her two last films, though she is almost unrecognizable wearing a long, dark wig. "When I first came to Hollywood my agent told me not to tell anyone that I could dance because I would be typed," discloses Gilmore. "I really wanted to dance with Elvis so I revealed to them my background as a dancer." David Winters was the film's choreographer and his second in command was Wilda Taylor, who joined Gilmore and Brenda Benet as a trio of dancing gypsies.

In *Harum Scarum*, Gilmore played Sapphire, a Middle Eastern dancer and member of a band of thieves who help Elvis, as kidnapped singing star Johnny Tyrone, thwart a plot to assassinate the King of Lunacan by a band of rebels led by Fran Jeffries and Theo Marcuse. Along with Benet (as Amethyst) and Taylor (as Emerald), Gilmore does an exotic dance in the town square while Elvis croons "Shake That Tambourine" and later they do another dance as entertainment for the king. The finale finds Gilmore, Benet and Taylor in Vegas as part of Johnny's revue as Elvis sings "Harem Holiday," the original title of *Harum Scarum*.

Recalling her experience working with Elvis on *Harum Scarum*, Gilmore recounts, "Elvis had a bunch of guys around him and they'd play touch football between takes. He sent one of them—a guy with red hair who I think was nicknamed 'Red'—to my trailer and he said to me something like, 'Well, I see you're back again. Maybe you'll be coming to some of the parties this time?' When I told him that I now had a boyfriend, he told me to bring him to the set. Terry was a genuine person and extremely shy. He met Elvis outside my trailer. Presley said to him, 'We watched *Dr. Strangelove* sixteen times.' Terry said, 'You went to the theatre *sixteen times* to see it?' But in those days, Elvis was such a big star he was able to get films and show them at his house. The two of them had a nice mutual respect for one another.

"I had so much fun working with Elvis on this movie," continues Gail warmly. "I got to dance with him and play tambourine. I even showed Elvis how to do Chaînès Finger Turns for the film's last number. I had a picture of us going off stage. He was not planted right but we did it and nobody broke their neck. Outside of his trailer he had soda pop bottles that stood in the water like they have in the south. I was very impressed by that. He also used to practice his Karate moves and try to break bricks with his hands. Elvis was intelligent, quiet and very sweet. But at that time he seemed like a young man in turmoil—sort of like a *'who do I have to fuck to get off this picture'* kind of thing. Elvis was a tortured guy who obviously hoped for something better [than *Harum Scarum*]."

In Gilmore's fourth film, *Beach Ball*, she played Deborah and co-starred with Chris Noel ("She was darling and such a pretty girl"), Mikki Jamison and Brenda Benet as four staid coeds. As members of their college's finance committee, the girls decide to give a loan to poor music student Edd Byrnes, who needs the cash to pay for his band's instruments. When the gals decide to deliver the check in person, they discover a wild party going on at Byrnes' Malibu beach house. Realizing that they have been tricked and that Byrnes and his buddies (Robert Logan, Aron Kincaid and Don Edmonds) are dropouts and beach bums, they rip up the check and flee the boys' swinging Malibu shindig. Back in their dorm, the coeds come up with a plan to get the guys to go back to school. To reach that end, the girls take off their glasses, tease up their hair and trek to the beach. One especially amusing scene is when the girls are pressured to don bikinis and slink out of the beach house. Gilmore's character is especially reluctant to bare any skin and crawls out of the cabana in embarrassment wearing a skimpy yellow bikini. Deborah is then paired with Bango (Logan), the Wigglers' drummer, as the girls convince the guys that if they win a Battle of the Bands contest they would return to school.

As with *The Girls on the Beach*, *Beach Ball* too received mostly positive notices or as good a review a beach movie can get.

The critic in *Variety* commented, "A bouillabaisse of all the tried and true surfing ingredients, this loud, lively pic should prove a winner with the adolescent set" and that the "pic is well-acted, which is to say that everyone is likable...."

Gail Gilmore's last film was the teenage exploitation classic *Village of the Giants,* loosely based on the H.G. Wells' story "Food of the Gods." The movie was produced and directed by Bert I. Gordon who previously gave the world *The Amazing Colossal Man* and *Attack of the Puppet People*. The film opens excitedly as a group of delinquents (including Gilmore, Beau Bridges, Joy Harmon, Tim Rooney, Tisha Sterling and Bob Random) pile out of their wrecked auto after crashing on a mountain road during a rainstorm. They then begin dancing in the mud to composer Jack Nitzsche's awesome rhythms heard throughout the movie. Meanwhile, boy genius Ronny Howard develops a mysterious substance called "goo," which is eaten by a cat and two ducks that grow giant-size. When the pack of troublemaking mud-clad teenagers come to the small town, they take refuge in an abandoned theatre. After cleaning up they decide to go to the local discotheque. Gilmore as Elsa is applying make-up when she hears the groovy sounds of the Beau Brummels emanating from the dance club. She then utters the classic line,

Village of the Giants (Embassy, 1965) starred Joy Harmon, Tisha Sterling, Tim Rooney, Bob Random, and Gail Gilmore as juvenile delinquents who grow to giant proportions and terrorize a town. *Billy Rose Theatre Collection, New York Public Library for the Performing Arts, Astor, Lenox and Tilden Foundations.*

"Dig that nitty gritty!" (*"Did I actually say that?"* asks Gail incredulously.) There the pack of teens hear about this secret "goo" and steal it, thanks to Elsa's tricking Genius into revealing its whereabouts. They then sprout to mammoth proportions and terrorize the small town in the process. The local teens (led by Tommy Kirk and Johnny Crawford) join forces with the police to thwart the marauding giants who have an axe to grind with the adult establishment. When the good teens fail in stopping the overgrown delinquents, Howard develops a smoke gas that counteracts the growth formula. The "giant" teens shrink to normal size and are then run out of town.

Regarding *Village of the Giants*, Gail remarks, "This has not been in my mind for forty years. It was a sweet, sweet moment in my life but it was only a moment. I remember every note of *Brandenberg Concerto No. 2* but I don't remember wallowing in that mud! Joy Harmon is a lovely and sweet girl. But she was so formidable and so big in so many ways I was a bit put off by her. Terry, though, loved Joy. Tisha Sterling was the prettiest thing I ever saw. Beau Bridges was just charming. He was just a kid then. If I ever meet him again, I would hate to say—because he has done some wonderful, fine work—that we worked together on *Village of the Giants*. He'd probably take out a gun and shoot me!"

A number of sixties actresses felt that they were exploited by frolicking in beach movies wearing nothing but a skimpy bikini or by posing scantily clad for cheesecake photographs but Gail did not. "Oh, no, I did not feel exploited in the least," exclaims Gail. "I knew where I was and what I was doing. I didn't do it for very long because I was more horrified by what I saw as the celebrity life. God forbid you should become famous—you lose everything in terms of your privacy."

Before leaving the acting world, Gail appeared in a few segments of the religious TV anthology series *This Is the Life* (including one episode as the grasping daughter who pressures her father to accept a high-paying job in a big city). She also did a guest stint in an episode of the steamy Southern primetime soap opera, *The Long Hot Summer*. "Terry taught me how to do a Southern accent for this," reveals Gail. "I went through all my lines learning this great accent. We get on the set and it doesn't work on that level. As long as I was in the scene with the guy who was the star of the show [Roy Thinnes] his accent was fine. But when I wasn't in a scene with him he lost his accent."

In 1967, Gilmore moved to New York with Terry Southern and gave up her career in Hollywood. Encouraged to keep acting by Southern, she studied with Stella Adler and was accepted by the Actor's Studio as a professional observer due to Geraldine Page and Rip Torn. "I then decided *I didn't want to be an actor*," says Gail with a laugh. "I don't have that instrument so I went into teaching and taught ballet for twenty-five years."

Gilmore was also privy to the making of the hip counterculture film, *Easy Rider* (1969), directed by Dennis Hopper. The screenplay was written by Terry Southern but credited to Southern, Hopper and Peter Fonda. Years later, however, Hopper falsely claimed sole authorship. Gail explains, "Dennis and Peter Fonda were living in our house on East 36th Street [in New York City] when Terry wrote *Easy Rider*. He called the Screenwriters Guild—which has a rigid rule that you have to contribute more than 51 percent to get a screenwriting credit—to get a credit for 'the lads.' That is what he called Dennis and Peter. The Guild said no, but Terry said he felt that they contributed 51 percent. Then Dennis and Peter completely screwed Terry out of the millions of dollars they made off this film. They are assholes with bad karma and it will follow them through many lives. Actually Dennis was mad and insane from the very beginning when I knew him. Terry was attracted to and loved outrageous people. That is why he just thought Joy Harmon was the best thing in the whole world. She was just so *wonderfully* outrageous. Dennis was too. We'd go over to his house and he'd rant and rave all night. Terry couldn't have been happier with someone like that."

Before filming began on *Easy Rider*, Dennis Hopper's volatile side surfaced in public. Arriving late for dinner at an Upper East Side restaurant, Hopper joined Southern, Gilmore, Fonda, John Carpenter and Rip Torn, for whom Southern had written the role of the Southern attorney. According to Gail, "Dennis came in very hostile and said—I'm paraphrasing—'You guys are here in New York and I've been scouting locations. I just came from Texas and I was lucky I wasn't killed with my long hair. You're from Texas, aren't you, Rip? What a bunch of assholes.' Rip replied, 'Yes, I'm from Texas but don't judge all assholes by me.' This went on a bit longer until Dennis who was still standing picked up a knife and began jabbing it at Rip Torn. Rip is a virile guy from the military. He didn't get up but just grabbed Dennis' arm and the knife dropped to the table. Rip has a very short fuse but he very gentlemanly got up from the table and left. Den-

In *Village of the Giants* (Embassy, 1965) bad girl Gail Gilmore tries to attract the attention of an uninterested Tim Rooney.

nis sat down and we ordered our food. Rip was waiting outside when we got back [to their apartment] to either give his apologies or fight it out [with Dennis]." Wisely, Torn withdrew himself from the movie and was replaced by Jack Nicholson.

Gilmore accompanied Terry Southern down to New Orleans where *Easy Rider* was being shot. Since this was a low budget production, Gilmore was put to work holding a sun gun while Peter did his mother monologue in the mud. "We all stayed in a motel near the airport," recalls Gail. "It was so weird with Dennis screaming and hollering that after a couple of days I just got on a plane and went back to New York. Terry came back a few days later. They had Terry's script so they went on to finish the movie. Terry said that Dennis never knew what the movie was about. They kept most of Terry's scenes intact but he was most proud of the ending. Whoever edited the film did a wonderful job. Dennis was holed up with the film for over a year and wouldn't give it up. Finally, they had to send someone over to wrest the film from Dennis."

In 1970, Gilmore resurfaced on screen in the rarely seen movie entitled *End of the Road*, directed by Aram Avakian and featuring a screenplay by Terry Southern adapted from the novel by John Barth. Originally rated X, it was the story of an unstable college professor, recently released from an asylum called "the Farm," who becomes involved with his colleague's wife. Starring in the film are Stacy Keach, Harris Yulin, Dorothy Tristan and James Earl Jones. Gail played Miss Gibson, one of Stacy Keach's students. "The only reason I am in this is because they were shooting in Great Barrington [part of the Berkshires] and the local high school students were supposed to play Keach's students," says Gilmore. "Someone thought we were shooting a dirty movie and they wouldn't let the kids participate. They then had to round up anyone who looked young, like the script girl, the gofer, some typists and me. It was a funny scene."

Unfortunately, many of Gilmore's fans may have missed her in *End of the Road* because she is billed as "Gail Gibson." The name change was due to esteemed French director Roger Vadim, who found it difficult to pronounce Gilmore. "I thought it is not very good if Vadim can't say it. One day, I was reading in the paper about the latest fashions and the Gibson Girl. I thought, 'Maybe Vadim can say Gibson.' By this point I really wasn't into my career. As Terry used to say a lot, 'you can call me anything you like—just don't call me late for lunch.'"

As for the *Easy Rider* incident, it lay dormant for thirty years except within the industry as Dennis Hopper told everyone that Rip Torn pulled a knife on him. Torn ignored Hopper's fabrication until Dennis went too far and told this lie on a major talk show in 1992. "Rip was just beside himself," recalls Gail. "He asked Terry and I if we would give depositions." Torn sued Dennis Hopper, and Gilmore flew to Los Angeles to testify. By the time the case reached the courts, Southern had sadly passed away. Even still, with only Gail's testimony Torn won the case. ("I think he is getting his money in installments—one hundred dollars here, fifty dollars there.") Southern too was vindicated, as Gilmore went with the original *Easy Rider* script by Terry, which clearly proved he wrote it and not Dennis Hopper.

Gail Gilmore, now once again Gail Gerber, taught ballet for twenty-five years after she gave up acting. Terry Southern died from respiratory failure in October 1995 and his only child, Nile Southern, is trying to extend his father's legacy. As for Gail, after a brief stay in New York City, she is living and working in Chicago." She is also writing her memoirs on her exciting unorthodox life with Terry Southern.

Film Appearances

1965 **Girl Happy** (MGM) d. Boris Sagal
The Girls on the Beach (Paramount) d. William Witney
Beach Ball (Paramount) d. Lennie Weinrib
Village of the Giants (Embassy) d. Bert I. Gordon
The Loved One (MGM) d. Tony Richardson
Harum Scarum (MGM) d. Gene Nelson

1970 **End of the Road** (Allied Artists) d. Aram Avakian

Television Appearances

Music '60 Presents The Hit Parade [dancer] 10/12/1959 to 7/11/1960 CBC

The Ed Sullivan Show 4/9/1961 CBS
Mr. Novak "The Exile" 1/14/1964 NBC
My Three Sons "The Chaperone" 1/30/1964 ABC
Perry Mason "The Case of the Careless Kidnapper" 4/30/1964 CBS
Wagon Train "Those Who Stay Behind" 11/8/1964 ABC
The Littlest Hobo (episode—title unknown) 3/24/1965 SYN
The Long, Hot Summer "Track the Man Down" 12/30/1965 ABC
This Is the Life (episode—title unknown) 11/6/1966 SYN

Also

The Wayne and Shuster Show, *The Joan Fairfax Show* and *The Teenager*

☆ LAUREL GOODWIN ☆

A former model, Laurel Goodwin's only acting experience was doing summer stock until producer Hal B. Wallis saw her photograph in the Paramount studio publicity department and tapped her to play a lead role opposite Elvis Presley in *Girls! Girls! Girls!* (1962). Goodwin was cast as rich girl Laurel Dodge who vies with a sultry torch singer for the charms of fisherman Elvis Presley amid the lush scenery of Hawaii. With her fresh-faced, adorable look, strawberry blonde hair and charming screen persona, Goodwin was a hit in her film debut and won over the critics and fans alike. However, Hollywood typecast her in prim and proper-type roles. After playing Jackie Gleason's daughter in the comedy *Papa's Delicate Condition* (1963), she did two B-oaters before getting a good part in the Sam Peckinpah scripted-western *The Glory Guys* (1965), her last movie. Goodwin's most famous role though was not in film but on TV. She played Ensign Colt opposite Jeffrey Hunter as Captain Pike in the original pilot for *Star Trek* called "The Cage." When *Star Trek* finally became a series, William Shatner, Leonard Nimoy and the other cast regulars traveled the galaxies while Goodwin pounded the pavement in Hollywood for a few more years before calling it quits in 1971.

Laurel Goodwin was born on August 11, 1942, in Wichita, Kansas. When she was a few weeks old her family relocated to San Francisco. As a child, Goodwin describes herself as "always a bit of a ham at home." She began working from about the age of seven as a child model. Her mother was in the garment business and

Laurel Goodwin and Elvis Presley tango the night away in *Girls! Girls! Girls!* (Paramount, 1962).

which kind of bothered the hell out of me," says Laurel with a laugh. "We were of a slightly similar type and age group. Carol was in every magazine and on every cover. I was in *Seventeen Magazine* also but not on the cover."

Modeling gave Goodwin the courage to appear in a few school plays. However, at that time she had no desire to pursue it as a career. After graduating Lowell High School (which was a college prep school and the oldest high school west of the Mississippi) she entered San Francisco State University majoring in science and math with a minor in drama. An invitation from her drama instructor to be a part of his summer stock troupe would change her life forever, as she became friendly with the still photographer Kurt Gunther, who was working on the film *Hell Is for Heroes*. To thank her for babysitting his children, he took a number of photos of her. When Gunther returned to Paramount Studios, he included her photos in with the still photographs he took for the film. There were no women in *Hell Is for Heroes*, so when the press department saw the pictures of Laurel Goodwin they wanted to know who she was. "Paramount called me to hear the tone of my voice because they thought I was fourteen," recalls Goodwin. "When I proved I wasn't fourteen and was legal tender, they invited me down to meet them. They put my mother and me up in the Roosevelt Hotel. I had a meeting with all the top Paramount executives and they offered me a seven-year option contract, which the other studios were not doing anymore. I was probably the last studio contract player under the

had gotten her younger sister modeling at eighteen months old. Goodwin began when "they needed an older girl to show off this line of clothes called 'The Little Dress That Grows.' It was very special party dresses. The House of Charm, one of the major modeling agencies in San Francisco at that time, represented us. My sister and I did quite a bit of modeling. The difference was that she was two and thought it was a great lark and I was seven and was terrified."

Goodwin eventually got over her fears and continued modeling through her teens. She became one of the most successful teen models in the Bay Area. However, the most famous teenage model at that time was Carol Lynley. "I constantly had to live with 'the Carol Lynley image,' old system. Universal was putting actors under contract, but that was with doing optional TV shows. Mine was a complete 'grooming me to be a star' contract. I got in during the very last remnants of the old studio system, which believe me, lasted about six to eight months. I did a lot of press when Paramount signed me."

Producer Hal Wallis spotted her picture hanging in the photo studio at Paramount. When he found out who she was, he set up an appointment to meet her. At the time, Wallis was looking for a leading lady to star opposite Elvis Presley in his next film. He originally wanted Dolores Hart but she just had stunned Hollywood with her decision to enter a convent to become a nun. Pamela Tiffin was also being considered (and may have turned the film down). "I do not know for sure who was the second choice," says Goodwin. "But I remember the choreographer on the film said, 'Oh how boring! Why don't we go with this girl [Laurel] instead.' And that is apparently what happened. I was going through make-up tests, wardrobe tests, all kinds of things, and what I was getting from Mr. Wallis and everybody else was, '*If* Laurel should do this picture maybe she should wear this.' This went on for weeks. I then did a screen test. I had a bit of a chipped tooth—this was never a problem in still photography but film-wise it looked like a real big point. They said, '*If* Laurel does this picture she'll need that tooth capped.' About three weeks before filming began I was notified that I got the part and that I had a dental appointment the next day."

Though Goodwin was thrilled to be making her film debut opposite Elvis Presley, she was a bit apprehensive about working with Hal Wallis, who had a reputation in Hollywood for being "an old letch," as Julie Parrish described him in *Fantasy Femmes of Sixties Cinema*. "Hal Wallis made me a little nervous," comments Goodwin. "But by the time that we were in a position where there might have been a problem for me, he had a personal crisis. Wallis then had to leave the shoot in Hawaii and return to the mainland. I took a sigh of relief and really didn't have to face that issue but I saw it coming around the corner, so to speak. He was always a gentleman with me but I knew what was lurking."

Goodwin also did not know what to expect of Elvis Presley. She had never met him and none of her screen tests were with him. Before she left for Hawaii, she had talked to an actress who had worked with the King. She learned that Elvis would not be a problem but his entourage could be. The guys who shadowed him were known for being very possessive, jealous and overly protective. "I made a very big effort not to be threatening to his entourage who had IQs of about eighty," quips Laurel chuckling. "I kept my English simple and I didn't challenge anyone about anything. I did not have any problems with them. After about four or five days, the entourage was doing for me what they were doing for Elvis—bringing me a chair, lighting my cigarettes, inviting me to play football with them, etc. I was one of the gang."

As with a number of actresses who worked with Presley, Goodwin did not meet him until the first day of shooting in Hawaii. She had a chance to the prior evening when she received a call about ten o'clock at night from Joe Esposito, inviting her to meet Elvis in his suite. "I had to be up at five A.M. so it wasn't convenient for me. I told Joe to thank Elvis for the invite and to send him my regrets but I'd see him in make-up in the morning. And that's where we first met—in make-up. I was a big fan of Elvis' music but meeting *Elvis Presley* did not knock me out. He was charming and sweet. He apologized for calling me in the middle of the

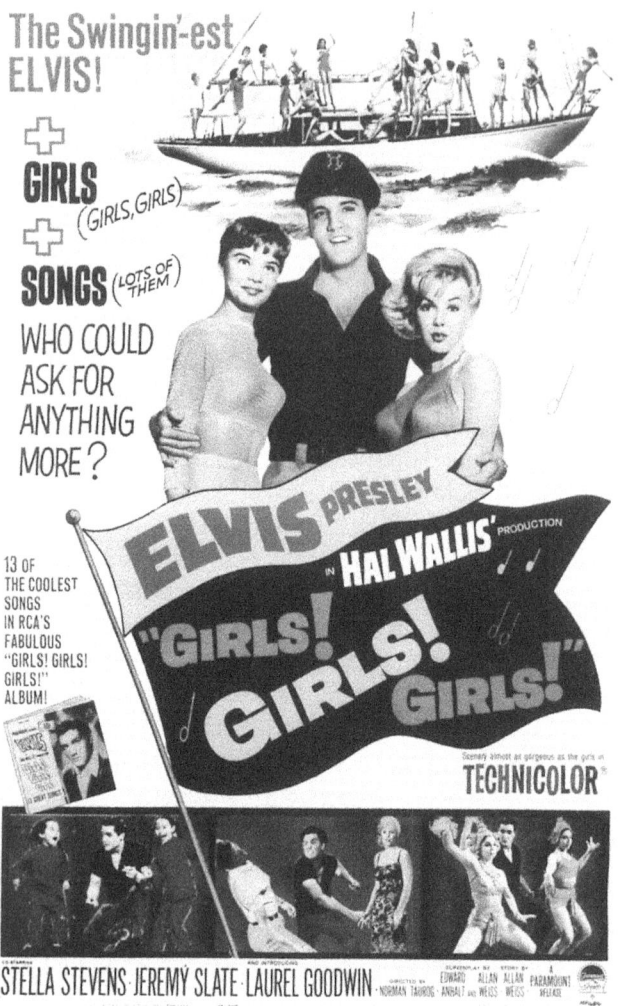

Poster art for *Girls! Girls! Girls!* (Paramount, 1962).

night. I told me I was sorry that I was too tired to come down. We got along famously and had no problems whatsoever.

"Elvis did not like *Girls! Girls! Girls!*. He didn't like it at all. He was very uncomfortable with performing. He also felt very unsure of himself as far as acting went. He deferred to me continually because he felt I knew more about *acting*, whatever the hell that is. He was not comfortable with making movies, but it was a living and he was indulged. He made quite a bit of money and he supported a lot of people. Hal Wallis had him on a bare-bones contract because Elvis signed a multiple picture deal with Wallis very early on. Once Elvis commented to me, 'One thing about working with Wallis is that he spends a lot of money on the production, the accommodations and the catering because he has me so cheap. With the money he makes on my movies, he then can afford to go off and do [a film like] *Beckett*.'"

Though Goodwin and Elvis hit it off beautifully, their idyll was interrupted by co-star Stella Stevens, who was cast in the role of the torch singer who vies with Laurel's character for the charms of Presley. For years, Stevens has made it known in interviews that doing *Girls! Girls! Girls!* was one of the worst experiences of her life. Stevens commented in 1999 to Linnea Quigley, writing in *Femme Fatales*, "I felt I was so mistreated by the producer [Hal Wallis] and the director [Norman Taurog] that I would never see the film, and I never have. I wish I had never met Elvis and worked with him.... Sometimes you meet people you think could be your idol and then, after you meet them, you're so disappointed that you don't even like them anymore." Regarding Stevens, Goodwin opines, "I think what you've been hearing from Stella is sour grapes. The scuttlebutt on Stella was that she wanted my role. Hal Wallis told her no and that she was going to play the other role because she was under contract. She then told Wallis that she would do it if she could sing, because she fancied herself a singer. He told her, 'You *won't* sing and you *will* do the role.'

"I had not met Stella Stevens prior to this, even though we were on the [Paramount] lot together," continues Goodwin. "I had seen photos of her and was familiar with her work. I kind of was looking forward to meeting and working with her. From my point of view in that time of my life, she was the image of a 'Hollywood glamour girl.' She was a very pretty, buxom blonde. Knockers were in then *and she certainly had a set of those!*"

Goodwin first met Stevens in the limousine that came to the hotel to take them to the location site on a gorgeous Hawaiian morning. Goodwin remembers, "The chauffeur opened the door, I got in, and I said, 'Good morning, Miss Stevens. Welcome to Hawaii. I'm Laurel.' She said, 'Hello, I'm Stella.' I then said, 'It's a pleasure to meet you. How do you feel about being in Hawaii? It's just beautiful, isn't it?' She replied, 'Oh, God. This is just not my kind of place. I'm like a mushroom. I like dark, dank places.' I thought, 'Oh, what a pain in the ass!' I really wanted to like her and have admiration for her, but Stella was over there under duress by Hal Wallis, so she decided that she didn't like anything about it. She was very aloof to everybody, even to Elvis. They didn't have very much to say to each other. It wasn't even what I would call a professional relationship. Stella did not make any effort whatsoever to be pleasant or friendly to anyone and she was not well liked by any of the crew. I heard gossip and stories about her from wardrobe to make-up to hairdressing. They called her *Madame Stella*—she thought she was some great stellar star. And she wasn't really much of anything at that time."

Despite the presence of Stevens, Goodwin enjoyed making *Girls! Girls!*

Laurel Goodwin and Elvis Presley make nice with hated co-star Stella Stevens during publicity shoot for *Girls! Girls! Girls!* **(Paramount, 1962).**

Girls! with Elvis, whom she describes as being "a sweetheart and a Southern gentleman with glorious manners." They spent a lot of time together and shared a number of private moments. "I became his sort of confidante," reveals Goodwin. "He was uncomfortable with the fact that his father had a girlfriend. He was still in a great deal of pain over the loss of his mother. We became very close on this level of conversation. I told Elvis that just because his father has a new woman in his life, that did not have anything to do with how he felt about his mother. His father was only about fifty years old and I said to Elvis, 'Your father is young. Do you want him to be alone for the rest of his life? You should be delighted that he has found some pleasure.' Elvis and I were very companionable and very good friends."

Being with Elvis also showed Goodwin the trappings of fame. "I remember when we were filming in Hilo I came onto the set and Elvis asked me what I did last night. I said, 'I walked into the village and I went to this great place. I had a wonderful dinner and had a lot of fun.' He said, 'Oh, boy. I'd really like to do that.' I said, 'You can come with me anytime you want to. However, you can't wear your sunglasses and your hat and make a big scene. And you especially can't bring your fourteen guys. If you want to go with me, I guarantee you that you will not be bothered.' That evening, he and I walked over into town and went to that wonderful little place. Even though everybody knew it was Elvis nobody hassled him. We danced, we ate, and we drank and had a marvelous time. We did that about three times while we were in that area. I think it was one of the few times in his life after he became popular that he really had a fun, laid back evening."

After filming wrapped in Hawaii, the cast returned to Hollywood to shoot the film's interiors. Most of these scenes took place in the nightclub where Presley and Stevens' characters performed. After working six days a week in Hawaii, Goodwin was relieved to be back home, as her working days were supposed to decrease to five. However, that did not happen. Scheduled to be off her first day in weeks, Goodwin was surprised to see her name on the call sheet, though she was not in any scenes. She recalls, "I went to the assistant director and said, 'Why do I have a ten o'clock call?' He said, 'Elvis would like you to be here. You don't need to do makeup or anything like that. Elvis doesn't feel comfortable filming these nightclub scenes and he'd like you to be behind camera.' I said, 'Okay, no problem.' Previously, I had taught Elvis how to do the Twist. He didn't know how to do it and he needed to for the nightclub scenes. Anyway, I showed up at ten o'clock and watched Elvis while he was lip-synching the songs and dancing. He was singing and dancing to me and I was behind the camera going crazy encouraging him to do things. He was not that comfortable with public performance. That's why I worked that day. This happened a number of times."

Though they were terribly fond of each other, a romance never took place. "Elvis was quite a bit older than I was but I felt like he was my kid brother. Here was the world's most popular singer, who most women would kill to just touch his shoes, and I felt like his sister! After filming *Girls! Girls! Girls!* we only got together one more time. Elvis knew I was involved with somebody else. I also really wasn't interested in any kind of long-term relationship with him. The guy had too many problems and he was very nervous about getting into the Las Vegas scene. He really didn't want to do that."

When *Girls! Girls! Girls!*, directed by Norman Taurog, was released, it became one of Presley's biggest hits, grossing $2.7 million, and contains one of his most popular songs, "Return to Sender." In his eleventh film, Elvis played Ross Carpenter, a down-and-out tuna fisherman who is trying to buy back the boat his father built called the *West Wind* from kindly Alexander Stavros (Frank Puglia). Ross also moonlights singing at a nightclub, where his former lover Robin (Stella Stevens), who still carries a torch for him, also performs. Enter one night, Laurel Dodge (Goodwin), a nice wholesome rich girl on a blind date with a heckler. When Ross saves her from the cad, she agrees to have dinner with him. Ross' rival Wesley Johnson (Jeremy Slate) buys the *West Wind* from a desperate Stavros to keep

Ross from owning it and immediately puts it up for sale to the highest bidder. Keeping her wealth hidden, Laurel secretly buys the boat for Ross and when he finds out his male pride gets the worst of him. As with all of Elvis' films it all ends on a happy note.

Girls! Girls! Girls! was Wallis attempt to recapture the glory of *Blue Hawaii* (1961) and he succeeded. The film was pleasant and tuneful, featuring pretty girls and lush scenery. It took the Laurel Award for Best Musical, placing third in the poll. Elvis looks great, acts with ease and sings well. Goodwin received excellent notices for her performance. *Variety*, in particular, raved, "The most striking thing about the picture is the introduction of Laurel Goodwin." She received a 1962 *Photoplay* Gold Medal Award nomination for "Most Promising New Star (Female)" but lost out to Suzanne Pleshette. "I look back at my performance now and think, 'Hot damn! For a kid who had never done a motion picture before I was pretty good,'" boasts Laurel laughing. "Also realize that what ended up in the film was not necessarily the best take of my performance. A lot of those scenes took thirteen to twenty-two takes. My biggest challenge was to try on each take to keep my performance at the level that was acceptable, because the one that Elvis or Stella did best would be chosen as the print."

After receiving her kudos (including being voted a Hollywood Deb Star), Goodwin found herself typecast as "Beth the preacher's daughter, Beth the preacher's daughter, and Beth the preacher's daughter. There aren't a whole lot of those roles but I got to do *all* the preachers' daughters." One role that got away was Gidget in *Gidget Goes to Rome* (1963). Laurel was hired for the role, only to be fired and replaced by Cindy Carol. Goodwin explains, "They thought I was a great Gidget and then they asked, 'By the way, how tall are you?' I lied and said 5'5". But I am really 5'7". James Darren [who played Moondoggie] wasn't very tall and Gidget was a girl midget." Another role that Laurel lost out on was the part of Susan Hayward's troubled daughter in *Where Love Has Gone* (1964). Reportedly, Goodwin, Deborah Walley, Patty Duke, and Lana Wood auditioned vigorously for the role, which ultimately went to Joey Heatherton.

Goodwin did get to play Jackie Gleason's daughter in *Papa's Delicate Condition* (1963), directed by George Marshall and featuring the Academy Award–winning song, "Call Me Irresponsible." This turn-of-the-century comedy was based on the memoirs of Corinne Griffith, focusing on the relationship between her (Linda Bruhl in the movie) and her father, a tipsy railroad inspector (Gleason). Goodwin played the older daughter who, along with her mother (Glynis Johns), is embarrassed by his shenanigans, including buying a carnival so Corinne could have a pony. Her father's quirkiness costs Goodwin her rich boyfriend, whose family forbids him from seeing her.

"Over the years, people not in the business have asked me about Jackie Gleason," says Laurel. "I used to be real down and dirty truthful. I'm not that way anymore. Fans don't want to hear that Jackie wasn't wonderful and that he was a pain. They think of him as Ralph Kramden from *The Honeymooners*. And there was a lot of *Honeymooner* in him. *There was also a lot of other stuff!* He was another gruff person to work with. I took one look at him and decided that I was going to hide behind my role. So I completely stayed in character when I was around Jackie. He was always very nice to me but he treated me like I was a child, which was swell with me. But with Glynis Johns, who played my mother and who was *fabulous*, I was my adult, sophisticated self. We had a lot of laughs together. But whenever Jackie was around I would be the prim and proper daughter. Also our director was a pit of a chaser and a letch. I decided it was a wiser way to just stay in character, which would eliminate any problems with him also."

Goodwin next appeared in two B-oaters for A. C. Lyles, who produced a number of cheap westerns during the mid-sixties featuring veteran casts. *Stage to Thunder Rock* (1964), directed by William F. Claxton, starred Barry Sullivan as a sheriff transporting an outlaw to jail. Much of the action takes place in the station owned by Lon Chaney, Jr. (whom Goodwin describes as being "a sweet, wonderful man who brought all kinds of pathos and intensity to his role") as they await the stagecoach to Thunder Rock. Goodwin was cast as Chaney's daughter, who is desperate to leave town. Goodwin also had a small role in Lyle's *Law of the Lawless* (1964), starring Dale Robertson and Yvonne De Carlo, but her name does not appear in the credits and her scenes may have been cut from the final print.

Between movie roles, Goodwin also did a few TV guest shots, including a role in the pilot for a little series called *Star Trek*. She met with producer Gene Roddenberry to interview for the role of Ensign Colt. All she knew of the character was that she had to have long legs, so she brought a portfolio of publicity stills including a shot showing off her gams. "I had good legs—still do," exclaims Laurel with a laugh. "Gene looked at the photo

Papa's Delicate Condition (Paramount, 1963) starred Jackie Gleason as a tipsy schemer with Laurel Goodwin (left) and Linda Bruhl (right) as his loving daughters.

and said, 'Yes, I guess those qualify. Can I see the real thing?' I said, 'Sure!' So I stood back away from the desk a little bit and I hiked up my skirt. He said, 'They're real—that's for sure. Great.' Then he asked me what I felt about the concept for *Star Trek*. I replied, 'I think it sounds like wonderful fun! I love the idea. Personally, I think the timing is about right for something along these science fiction lines with a little intelligence. I think it would be a great project.' I got called in again and then I was hired." As Ensign Holt, the most the script gave Goodwin to do was to moon over her captain.

Recalling her first day on the set of "The Cage," Goodwin says, "I went to make-up not knowing who was going to be there, and who walks in but my dear pal and ex-drama coach Leonard Nimoy. I hadn't seen him in a couple of years so we had a great reunion." Meeting co-star Majel Barrett was less enchanting, however. "At that time, Majel lived in Gene Roddenberry's guesthouse on his estate and babysat his children. I met her on the set and I was *not* the least bit impressed with her. I thought, 'My god! Why did they cast her in this? There are so many more handsome, talented, intelligent actresses out there.' Majel had her nose in Roddenberry's ear and her hand on his butt all the time we were there. She had no time for the rest of us and obviously had a great deal to say. We all sort of assumed and figured there was more going on than met the eye—she was *not* just the babysitter. She wasn't much fun to work with either. She was civil to all of us, but there was no real communication except between she and Gene Roddenberry. If you ask any of the original cast members, I think they would verify that fact."

Goodwin had better luck working with Jeffrey Hunter (whom she says, "was one of the prettiest men in the world with the most magnificent powder blue eyes. We got along wonderfully"). Susan Oliver also impressed Goodwin. "She was a lovely spirited human being," remarks Laurel. "Susan was just marvelous to work with. She didn't want to do that scene where she transforms from her pretty self to the old woman. Susan told Gene, 'I know how this stuff works. It's going to take three days to shoot.' Gene said, 'No, no, no, Susan. We'll do it in two hours.' Well, it took a full day. But she was such a good sport about it. I'd usually go to lunch with some of the crew and most of the cast—right down to the extras. And Susan would always join us. She was just so kind and friendly."

After the pilot was complete, it was shown to all three networks, who passed on it. NBC, though, thought it had potential, but they felt it was too surreal and that the audience would not accept a woman as second in command. NBC commissioned a second pilot. All the actors were dropped except for Leonard Nimoy and Goodwin. Two weeks before filming began, Goodwin learned that she too was being let go. "I was not replaced—the role was just dropped. I was mad because I missed out on other work during the pilot season from the previous year. Except for the experience of doing the pilot itself and helping develop all of that and seeing it become such a grand success, the rest of it is a bummer. It upset me terribly that I didn't continue with it." Goodwin never knew why she was fired and never asked. She was happy (though she didn't get much remuneration wise) that two years later fans got to see her work in the pilot when it was edited into the two-part episode entitled, "The Menagerie."

Goodwin made her next film appearance in the rousing medium-budgeted western, *The Glory Guys* (1965), directed by Arnold Laven from a script by Sam Peckinpah. The film starred hot newcomers at the time Tom Tryon, Harve Presnell and Senta Berger, but it was back to playing the "preacher's daughter" for Goodwin. Tryon and Presnell portrayed a cavalry captain and his scout, respectively, involved with making the territories safe for settlers by driving off the Sioux to reservations. However, their commander (Andrew Duggan) wants to annihilate them instead. When they are not busy chasing Indians, both men vie for the charms of a busty widow (Senta Berger). James Caan also co-stars as an Irishman with Michael Anderson Jr. as Goodwin's love interest, a young enlistee who she helps nurse back to health after a barroom brawl. The film ends with an exhilarating climactic battle with the Indians surprisingly coming out on top.

Recalling her experience working on *The Glory Guys*, Goodwin remarks, "I adored Tom Tryon dearly. I worked with a lot of good-looking men and Tom was one of the handsomest. He is six foot, three inches, slim, and fun to work with. Tom was a very generous human being, while Harve Presnell was self-absorbed. Harve—who has a hell of a singing voice and was brilliant years later on Broadway in *Annie*—was a bit pompous and a total pain in the neck. He was obsessed about his wardrobe. There is one scene where he is wearing this pink paisley silk scarf. We're talking about a western and I thought, '*What is this!?!*' It was shortly thereafter when I found out that he was totally bald. All those blond curls were from a wig! Senta Berger was a beautiful woman. Unlike most actresses, she was very sweet, generous, and helpful. My philosophy was the play is the thing. Unfortunately at that particular time, most actors felt that *it's my role and my vision of what I'm doing* rather than the play be the thing. Senta shared my attitude.

"James Caan was absolutely darling in this movie," continues Goodwin. "We became good pals. I used to run into him quite frequently at auditions. I was really amazed that his career at that time [mid-sixties] didn't do more. In the late seventies I ran into him at the Cannes Film Festival—I was there with my husband who was running the film office for New York City—and Jimmy was still as charming as ever. Michael Anderson Jr. became a good friend as well."

The Glory Guys was Goodwin's last film appearance, but it wasn't by design. Though she hadn't gotten the notices she did in her first film, *Girls! Girls! Girls!*, she gave more than competent performances in her subsequent films and proved that she had screen presence. With her blonde good looks and low-key charm, she would have been perfect for the beach movies that were so prevalent during the mid-sixties. However, Goodwin had bigger aspirations. Reflecting on what happened to her film career in the mid-sixties, Goodwin opines, "A lot of what happened had to do with the business itself. Prior to that each studio put out sixty films per year. In the late sixties and early seventies *the entire industry* put out roughly sixty films per year. How many roles are there for someone in my age group? And how many people were there? We had Carol Lynley, Tuesday Weld, Stefanie Powers, Hayley Mills and Sandra Dee, who in particular got a couple of roles I was up for. There was also an entity called Ann-Margret and a little gal named Jane Fonda. There was very little work and an *awful* lot of competition."

In 1974, Godwin moved to New York with her husband, renowned film producer Walter Wood, whose movie *The Hoodlum Priest* won an award at the Cannes Film Festival in 1961. Wood was the first person hired to run the mayor's office for motion pictures and television. In his position, he also became one of the founders of the Astoria Studios. During his tenure he assisted the producers of such blockbusters as *Superman* and *King Kong* to get these films done in New York with as little stress as possible. As for Goodwin, she didn't quit acting entirely, as she continued doing commercial work. "My husband's position required a lot of socializing, so I had to be available for that," says Laurel. "Doing commercials was something that was controllable. I didn't want to get involved in location work—not that they were going to be beating down my door necessarily—but I didn't pursue that. I purposely decided that what was convenient and what would work in terms of what was going on in my life was commercial work and I was fairly successful at it."

In the eighties, the Woods returned to the private sector. They jointly produced *Stroker Ace* with Burt Reynolds and Loni Anderson. Recalling the infamous couple, Goodwin states, "This is when Burt and Loni first met. Burt was pleasant to work with, but Loni acted like a Queen Bee. She was a bit self-impressed."

Today Laurel Goowin and her husband reside in Palm Springs. Walter Wood is semi-retired and Laurel is a certified nursing attendant assistant. "I get a great deal of satisfaction out of that—I've always been the nurturing type," says Goodwin. "I enjoy it and am very good at it. Where I am today in my life, I think I'm now an old collector's item—I worked with Elvis Presley, Jackie Gleason, and I did the initial pilot for *Star Trek*. When I'm ninety there'll probably give me a lifetime achievement award!"

Publicity shot of Majel Barrett, Jeffrey Hunter and Laurel Goodwin (left to right) as Enterprise crew members in the first pilot for *Star Trek* (Paramount Television, 1964).

Film Appearances

1962   **Girls! Girls! Girls!** (Paramount) d. Norman Taurog

1963   **Papa's Delicate Condition** (Paramount) d. George Marshall

1964   **Law of the Lawless** (Paramount)* d. William F. Claxton
       Stage to Thunder Rock (Paramount) d. William F. Claxton

1965 The Glory Guys (United Artists) d. Arnold Laven

*Scenes deleted.

Television Appearances

The Bob Hope Show (special) [Hollywood Deb Star] 3/13/1963 NBC
The Virginian "A Gallows for Sam Horn" 12/2/1964 NBC
Star Trek (unaired pilot episode: "The Cage") 1964 NBC
Run, Buddy, Run "Steam Bath and Chicken Little" 9/12/1966 CBS
Get Smart "Anatomy of a Lover" 9/17/1966 NBC
Hero "The Matchbreaker" 10/20/1966 NBC
Star Trek "The Menagerie" [edited version of "The Cage"] 11/17 & 11/24/1966 NBC
The Beverly Hillbillies "Robin Hood of Griffith Park" 9/27/1967 CBS
The Beverly Hillbillies "Robin Hood and the Sheriff" 10/4/1967 CBS
Call to Danger (pilot) 7/1/1968 CBS
Mannix "A Question of Midnight" 10/25/1969 CBS
Partners "Our Butler Didn't Do It" 12/4/1971 NBC

☆ SHARYN HILLYER ☆

The sultry Sharyn Hillyer was one of a number of sexy starlets who graced drive-in movies and the television landscape during the '60s. With honey brown hair and *Vogue*-like looks, Hillyer was immediately discovered by Ozzie Nelson after she graduated high school. She played numerous bit roles on his family sitcom *The Adventures of Ozzie and Harriet* beginning in 1960, before progressing to the recurring role of coed Sally Taft. After leaving the comedy series, Hillyer went on to play a variety of small decorative parts on TV. But drive-in fans will remember her most as the seductive U.N.C.L.E. agent Wanda, who was forever half-heartedly fighting off the advances of the virile Robert Vaughn as agent Napoleon Solo in the big screen capers *The Spy in the Green Hat* (1966) and *The Karate Killers* (1967).

Sharyn Hillyer (born in 1943 in Downey, California) was the daughter of a businessman and his wife. Hillyer's early life, growing up in sunny Southern California, would make any teenager freezing up north envious. The popular coed was a bouncy song leader for the Warren High School Bears and she went on to be crowned Miss Downey in 1959. This led to the Miss California contest in 1960 where Ozzie Nelson and singer Tony Martin spotted her. "Both of them contacted the contest officials to meet me," recalls Hillyer. "I spent the summer traveling with Tony and dancing in his act [though she never had a lesson]. I came back and started working on the Ozzie and Harriet show.

"Working on *The Adventures of Ozzie and Harriet* was wonderful," continues Hillyer. "Coming right out of high school, I felt I was back at school. It was a lot like it seemed on the show. Some of the actors brought in were people the Nelson boys would meet and liked. They started to invite them on the show and a lot of them had never acted before. When I first met with Ozzie, I knew nothing about show business and had never taken an acting class. He suggested that I also work as an extra to learn more. A lot of the people on the show did both. We'd swing back and forth between roles and doing extra work. They liked people to just hang around and be part of the show."

Hillyer progressed from doing background work on the sitcom to small parts during her first two years on the show. ("Ozzie said that I played everyone's girlfriend at one time but his. He used to kid and say that he was going to write a show for me to play his girlfriend.") During the 1962–63 season, Hillyer finally got to play a character on a steady basis. She was cast as Sally Taft, the girlfriend of Ricky Nelson's college buddy Wally (Skip Young). One episode in particular, "Any Date in a Storm," gave Hillyer a chance to shine as she and Charlene Salerno as Ginger are trapped in a resort while their beaus Wally and Rick decide to ask out two other girls (Pamela Austin and Mikki Jamison).

During this season Ricky was supposed to be a student away at college but the producers still gave him every opportunity to sing. Sharyn says, "I remember a lot of the musical numbers from this show. We'd all stand there and try to look at Ricky all dreamy. But when the camera was on Ricky alone while he was singing, we'd try to make him laugh. We'd cross our eyes and make faces at him, but he sang with his eyes closed most of the time so we could rarely get even a chuckle out of him."

Recalling her experiences with the Nelson family, Hillyer remarks, "From what I saw, Ozzie seemed to get along very well with his wife and sons and everyone

Sharyn Hillyer swoons in the arms of virile agent David McCallum as Illya Kuryakin in still promoting the new spy series *The Man from U.N.C.L.E.* **(MGM-TV, 1964).** *Inset:* **Sharyn Hillyer strikes a sultry pose.** *Billy Rose Theatre Collection, The New York Public Library for the Performing Arts, Astor, Lenox and Tilden Foundations.*

was very respectful of him. He had a very special directing style. Harriet blew me away when I would see her smoking or cussing. I'd think, 'Mrs. Nelson!' I dated Ricky for a little while and he was such a down-to-earth guy—David too. Like I said, they'd just meet someone that they liked and invite them to come be on the show. We'd all play Frisbee between the set ups and go to lunch together. After shooting, we'd all go to parties. At one time, Rick and David were roommates and a small group of us used to go to their house every week to watch the show together. It was a lot of fun and I felt very protected and very safe, like with a family."

After the 1962–63 season, Hillyer left *The Adventures of Ozzie and Harriet*. She made her film debut in 1963 in the Academy Award–winning film *Hud*, starring Paul Newman and Patricia Neal. Though she didn't have many lines ("I say one word!"), she was the catalyst for a big fight scene in a Texas diner. Dressed in a very form-fitting, flower-patterned dress ("It was so tight I needed help getting in and out of it"), Hillyer's Myra slinks into the diner trailed by her slovenly jerk of a boyfriend. Layabout Hud (Newman) and his shy nephew Bud (De Wilde) immediately notice her. Hud prods Bud to talk to the girl. He strolls up to her and begins flirting. This justifiably angers the boyfriend and the punches begin to fly. "I was initially very intimidated working with Paul Newman," admits Hillyer. "But he was so easygoing and playful! My one line was 'no' and he spent all day long telling me different ways that I should do it—to milk that 'no' for more. He'd kept feeding me the line and I'd reply, 'Um, nooo!' He was wonderful and so was Brandon DeWilde."

At this point in Hillyer's career, film roles were scarce, but she was becoming a fixture on the small screen. She played a high school student in an episode of *Mr. Novak*, starring James Franciscus as the fresh-faced novice English teacher at Jefferson High. She also popped up three times on *Burke's Law* playing, among other roles, a debutante and a chorus girl. Hillyer was such a standout for the producers that they chose her (along with series co-star Eileen O'Neill and frequent guest star Joan Staley) to appear on the cover of *TV Guide* with series lead Gene Barry. "*Burke's Law* was a lot of fun to do," comments Hillyer. "I liked working with Gene Barry very much. It was always a nice and easy-going set. Harlan Ellison wrote several of the shows that I was in. I enjoyed him a lot because he just had this wonderful quirky mind." Though she took pleasure in the camaraderie on the *Burke's Law* set, things were different on *The Man from U.N.C.L.E.* soundstages. Hillyer played a stewardess in the pilot episode and was invited back to discuss becoming a regular. However, the hit spy show's original producer propositioned her and when she turned down his advances, she unjustly lost the role.

By this time in Sharyn Hillyer's career, her name was becoming somewhat familiar to television fans. *TV Guide* even did a feature story on her in May 1965 entitled "The World's Most Low-Pressure Actress." Married at the time to Bill Doherty, who owned PJs, a hip Hollywood nightclub, Hillyer admitted then and now that she wasn't very ambitious when it came to her career. "That's why my roles were small. I had so many opportunities and I was discovered so many times but I never really followed through. I didn't have real high self-esteem or a lot of confidence. I just went along with things. If someone called and offered me a part, I took it. But I wasn't pushy or assertive in those days. A few people approached me at different times from different studios but nothing ever came of it. I had no real training and was sort of flying by the seat of my pants. I didn't have the confidence to really put myself out there and go after roles and follow through with the contacts."

In 1966, Hillyer must have been surprised when the new producer from *The Man from U.N.C.L.E.* came calling. With Norman Felton, the original producer of the pilot, and Sam Rolfe, the producer of the first season's crop of episodes, both gone, replacement Boris Ingster offered Hillyer the role of helpful U.N.C.L.E. agent Wanda in two episodes during the second season. This role was previously played by a number of different actresses. When the third season began, Hillyer was Ingster's choice to essay the role of Wanda on a recurring basis. If she was not available (her son was born around this time), another actress would be brought in and the name changed to something different. For an actress, the role of Wanda was not an acting challenge in the least. The helpful agent was usually seen scurrying around the New York headquarters bringing U.N.C.L.E. chief Mr. Waverly (Leo G. Carroll) news of the whereabouts of agents Napoleon Solo (Robert Vaughn) or Illya Kuryakin (David McCallum) or producing dossiers on THRUSH agents. When Wanda did appear in scenes with Solo, there was usually a playful flirtation between them, as the suave agent was always trying to get a date with the coy Wanda.

Surprisingly, it was *The Man from U.N.C.L.E.* that introduced Hillyer to the legions of drive-in moviegoers during the '60s. Since the series became so popular and the James Bond craze was just taking off, the producers began re-editing and adding new scenes to most of the two-part episodes. Hillyer was first seen on the big screen in *The Spy in the Green Hat* (1966), which was the film version of "The Concrete Overcoat Affair." In the film, Robert Vaughn's Solo gets entangled in Italy with a pretty girl (Leticia Roman) and her retired gangster uncles as he investigates THRUSH's plot to divert the Gulf Stream with heavy water. Jack Palance and Janet Leigh are the film's chief villains, but Hillyer's scenes were only with the U.N.C.L.E. agents back at headquarters. The two-part episode, "The Five Daughters Affair," was edited into the feature *The Karate Killers* (1967). This film's plot had U.N.C.L.E. agents Solo and Kuryakin (David McCallum) traveling around Europe with a dead scientist's daughter (Kim Darby) in tow. Their assignment is to locate her three half-sisters to retrieve from them pieces of her father's formula for extracting gold from sea water before THRUSH can get their hands on it. Again, Hillyer is only seen in scenes back at U.N.C.L.E. headquarters.

As for working with the stars of *The Man from U.N.C.L.E.*, Hillyer comments, "Robert Vaughn was friendly enough but he kept to himself and wasn't much fun. David McCallum was playful and would have lunch with me. Leo G. Carroll was very nice and always courteous." For unknown reasons, the new producer, Anthony Spinner, dropped Sharyn Hillyer as Wanda during the show's fourth season. However, *The Man from U.N.C.L.E.* was not around much longer, as it was cancelled in January 1968.

In between her appearances on *The Man from U.N.C.L.E.*, Hillyer could be seen playing a nurse on the sitcom *Please Don't Eat the Daisies* and joining Joy Harmon portraying guests at a women's health spa run by Zsa Zsa Gabor in the comedic TV western *The Rounders*. Back on the big screen, Hillyer was in a hilarious vignette in the hit sex comedy *A Guide for the Married Man* (1967), starring Walter Matthau, Inger Stevens and Robert Morse. As Morse's libidinous character instructs Matthau's happily married husband in the ABC's of adultery, famous guest stars are featured as "technical advisors" in the vignettes. Hillyer plays the mistress of Joey Bishop's philandering husband whose screeching wife (Alice Pearce) catches them together. This vignette was to teach Matthau that if caught—deny *everything*. Even though the wife walks in on Bishop and Hillyer in bed together, the cheating husband disputes everything the wife accuses him of (including that there is a girl there). The cheating duo nonchalantly get out of bed, get dressed, make the bed and leave the room, leaving the wife standing

Sharyn Hillyer as U.N.C.L.E. agent Wanda flirts with Robert Vaughn as Napoleon Solo while David McCallum (Illya Kuryakin) looks on in *The Spy in the Green Hat* (MGM, 1966).

there open-mouthed in disbelief. Kathleen Carroll, writing in the *NY Daily News*, praised all the vignettes enthusiastically but singled out this one in particular and described Hillyer as being "luscious."

Sharyn Hillyer knew going into *A Guide for the Married Man* that her part required nudity. "I was a nervous wreck," reveals Hillyer. "I had never done anything like that before. I took the first tranquilizer that I ever took in my life in order to do this. They put pasties on me because I was nude from the waste up. Joey Bishop knew my husband at the time and he *still* came on to me. I was so angry at that *asshole*. I just felt he was an absolute creep, especially since he was friendly with my husband. That made it very uncomfortable doing this scene over and over with him all day. Then I'd look up and see all the crew and it made it even more difficult for me. But it was a great scene. The timing had to be precise as we got out of bed, fixed it up, got dressed and left the bedroom. Gene Kelly [the director], though, was very sweet and respectful of me. He would make sure there was someone there all the time with a robe for me right away."

Back on television, Hillyer played small roles on *Mannix*, starring Mike Connors ("He was very friendly and gracious"), and as a thirties era gun moll on *Star Trek*, starring William Shatner ("He would show up on the set and that was it"). She had another smallish part playing a sexy blonde mini-skirted airline passenger who becomes just another victim of agent Maxwell Smart's clumsiness on *Get Smart*. On an airplane bound for Iowa, Max (Don Adams) tries to be a Good Samaritan when his seatmate (Hillyer) can't raise the window shade. Reaching over her with a drink in one hand, he yanks the shade while spilling his martini down her cleavage. When he glances at his empty glass, he at first doesn't think he spilled it on her until she thrusts his olive at him. As Hillyer passes him to go dry off Max gets hit with the tray table when she leaves and returns. "Don Adams had me laughing the whole time," remembers Sharyn. "I was always cracking up around him. He knew my then-husband and he was constantly cracking jokes."

In 1968, Hillyer got another chance to show her comedic talents in a guest lead role on *The Monkees*. She was reunited with actress Joy Harmon, who had previously worked with Hillyer in episodes of *Burke's Law* and the western comedy *The Rounders*, starring Ron Hayes and Patrick Wayne. "I hated working with Joy, which I told her one time," says Sharyn Hillyer with a laugh. "She was an absolute delight and so adorable. But she was an effervescent bubbly blonde and I felt like a mud hen around her. Every time we'd be cast in the same show I'd think, 'Oh no, not again!' Joy was a sweetheart, but I just felt so dull next to her."

Married Joey Bishop is caught in bed with sexy Sharyn Hillyer by his wife Alice Pearce in one of the amusing vignettes in *A Guide for the Married Man* **(20th Century–Fox, 1967).** *Billy Rose Theatre Collection, The New York Public Library for the Performing Arts, Astor, Lenox and Tilden Foundations.*

In Hillyer's episode entitled "The Monkees on the Wheel," Mickey Dolenz and his showgirl girlfriend Zelda (Joy Harmon) accidentally win big money at a roulette table in Las Vegas, unaware that the wheel was fixed to make a gangster, Biggy (Pepper Davis), win. When The Boss (David Astor) finds out, he orders Hillyer as Della the Decoy to swipe the money back. She masquerades as a seductive maid and diverts the boys' attention while Biggy tries to locate the cash, but the plan doesn't work, which leads to a series of misadventures in the casino. Although the episode is considered one of the series zaniest, Hillyer did not enjoy doing the show at all.

"Working on *The Monkees* was one of the worst experiences of my career," exclaims Hillyer. "Those guys were out of control! The director had a hell of a time trying to keep them in line. I never hung out with them. I really tried to stay away from all of them. They were just kind of bouncing off the walls. [They were probably stoned, since it has been reported that the guys like to smoke pot in the Black Box, a private room the studio built for them.] I was really naïve at that point. The little one [Davy Jones] was just so odd. You know how there are some men who are always sniffing around women all of the time. He was sort of like that. Every time I turned around he was next to me."

Hillyer's last big screen appearance was a small role in the Sandra Dee-George Hamilton comedy, *Doctor, You've Got to Be Kidding!* (1968). Dee played an aspiring singer who winds up pregnant by her boss (Hamilton). The film opens with her being rushed into the delivery room trailed by her three friends who propose marriage to her (Bill Bixby, Dwayne Hickman and Dick Kallman). The movie then uses flashbacks to show how Dee got herself into that predicament. Hillyer played one of the many paramours of Bixby as Dee's swinging bachelor neighbor. ("Bill was a very open and pleasant to work with. He was also flirty but in a playful way just to make me more comfortable.")

In 1969, Hillyer's agents asked if she would be interested in going to Vietnam on a USO tour. She had a few meetings with the USO and reconnected with her costar from *The Adventures of Ozzie and Harriet*, Skip Young, who was also asked to participate. Despite the protestations of her husband ("My marriage was just about over anyway") and the concerns of her family that she would be in danger, Sharyn agreed to go and left in April on a twenty-two day handshaking tour of South Vietnam. Unlike Bob Hope's tours at the time, Hillyer was not part of a big troupe with musicians and costumes. It was just three women and Young. "We visited all the big bases but we also went to small bases and even some outposts with only two men stationed there," recalls Sharyn. "Before we left for Vietnam, we heard a lot of stories about the group that went before us. They had quite an attitude and were difficult to be with. The four of us decided that we were going to be a 'yes' group and that we were just going to say yes to everything and be really positive. That's what we did and because of that we saw things and did things that most USO people didn't do. We'd go to bed at night with rockets firing in the distance. They'd ask us if we'd mind adding an hour or two to our schedule to visit some guys who never got a chance to see anybody. We'd always say sure. Everywhere we went the guys did everything they could to make us feel welcome and give us the best of whatever they had. Sometimes that was just a roll of Lifesavers or a clean washcloth. It was an incredible experience.

"Our first day in Vietnam we went to one of the big bases," continues Hillyer. "We met with the officers who told us that there was a big troop coming in from the field. They took us out to the edge of the camp so we would be the first people they would see when they returned. When they saw us, hundreds of guys came charging towards us. They surrounded us, and it was a little scary at first but it turned out to be fun. Later on that night we had dinner with the officers who took us to their R&R club. We were up on the stage dancing and we would let a couple of the guys come up and dance with us. Then another couple of guys would take their place. The energy was just building and building and building. Someone came along behind us and said that they were going to give us a signal to run to the left as fast as we can because they knew it was about to get out of hand. It was getting harder and harder to handle the guys and keep them off the stage. Finally, someone gave us the signal and we ran off and headed to our little van. In moments, we were surrounded and the guys were shaking it. The MPs showed up and got us out of there. It was just like that scene in *Apocalypse Now*."

Returning home, Hillyer found her feelings regarding the US presence in Vietnam had changed dramatically. She also suffered from a case of depression, which affected many returning servicemen, entertainers, and volunteers who journeyed to Vietnam. "Before I went to Vietnam I had been sort of apolitical," admits Sharyn. "I hadn't paid much attention to the war. I was involved with my family and my acting career and always had faith in our military authority figures. I came back very depressed, which lasted

Doctor, You've Got to Be Kidding! (MGM, 1968) featured Sandra Dee (left) as a pregnant singer, Bill Bixby as her playboy neighbor, and Sharyn Hillyer as one of Bixby's many paramours.

about a month. It was really hard being home. I would read the paper about who was wounded or killed and wonder if I had sat and had lunch with them or if they have my picture in their pocket. I felt so badly about all the men over there and the hideous things they went through. I became a flaming liberal after that and very much anti-war. I attended many protest rallies."

In 1969, Hillyer divorced her husband and returned to work. Hillyer was the top choice for the female lead in *The Seven Minutes* (1971), directed by Russ Meyer, known for his sex-filled romps of the mid-sixties, such as *Vixen* and *Faster, Pussycat! Kill! Kill!*. ("I was a little concerned at first that the director was Russ Meyer. But my agent assured me that it was going to be an upscale film.") Her years toiling in small parts were finally going to pay off with a starring role in a major motion picture from 20th Century–Fox. Based on a novel by Irving Wallace, *The Seven Minutes* was a straightforward court room drama tackling the subject of pornography vs. free speech when a teenager purchases an erotic novel and is later arrested for rape. Hillyer was up for the role of Maggie, the girlfriend of the attorney (Wayne Maunder) who defends the banned book and preaches about the evils of censorship. Hillyer was one of the final candidates for the part but her new relationship got in the way. "I met with Meyer and the producer a couple of times," says Hillyer. "I had the script and was supposed to go back for the final reading on a Monday morning. My boyfriend was just so sure that I was going to get the part that all of a sudden he proposed marriage over the weekend because he couldn't conceive being wed to an actress. I called my agent and told them I was quitting. I then called the producers and told them I was not going to come in for the third reading. I quit acting just because he waved marriage in front of me. I was a stupid female at the time." Regrets aside, *The Seven Minutes* was panned by the critics and was a box office flop. It also did nothing for the acting career of Marianne McAndrew, who was cast as Maggie, as her next film was the dreary horror opus *The Bat People*.

After her remarriage, Hillyer concentrated on raising her child and did volunteer work. In the mid-seventies, she and her husband took a visualization class related to his work, and out of the blue Hillyer had a thought that she was going to be a psychologist. "I had never been to therapy at that point," marvels Hillyer. "No one in my family ever had. It was so alien to me. I had never gone to a day of college because I had started acting right out of high school. But the thought was so compelling that within weeks I had enrolled in school and started from scratch. I got a Bachelor's Degree and then a Master's Degree. I eventually got my license to be a marriage family therapist and I love the work.

"After that I never had the desire to return to acting but I role play with some clients," continues Hillyer. "I act out their mothers or their husbands. For awhile I was doing a public access TV show and I have appeared on a number of talk shows as an expert guest. I kept my hand in a little bit but I don't miss it. Acting was something that I was never quite that comfortable with. I never studied or really knew what I was doing. But I get a kick looking back on these shows because it was so long ago and my life is so different now. The roles I played were very minor. Coming from Downey though, they were a big deal, but in reality they weren't. It was a fun time, especially since I was right out of high school when I began acting. It was sort of the ideal American dream."

The closest Sharyn Hillyer came to a

return to acting was when she appeared on two episodes of the acclaimed TV drama series *China Beach*, starring Dana Delaney as a nurse stationed in Vietnam during the war. "They did a lot of interviewing of people before they ever started *China Beach*. I had been interviewed and gave them lots of my stories. I shared my various experiences there and things that happened.

"I think a lot of the audience didn't get the first episode that I did [the Emmy award–winning "Vets"]," opines Sharyn. "They were interspersing real people who had gone to Vietnam with scenes of the characters in the show. What they were trying to convey was that this series was based in truth. I don't know if the audience quite understood what they were trying to do with these episodes."

Today, Sharyn Hillyer is a renowned psychotherapist and relationship and life coach. She is quoted in many magazine articles about marriage and commitment problems. And if you are lucky enough, you may see her as the in house expert on any of the daytime talk shows. Coincidentally, one of Hillyer's last acting roles was in an episode of *Love, American Style* called "Love and the Marriage Counselor." Prophetic, wasn't it?

Film Appearances

1963   Hud (Paramount) d. Martin Ritt

1966   The Spy in the Green Hat (MGM) d. Joseph Sargent

1967   A Guide for the Married Man (20th Century–Fox) d. Gene Kelly

       The Karate Killers (MGM) d. Barry Shear

1968   Doctor, You've Got to Be Kidding! (MGM) d. Peter Tewksbury

Television Appearances

The Adventures of Ozzie & Harriet "A Sweater for Rick" 11/9/1960 ABC

The Adventures of Ozzie & Harriet "The Girl Who Loses Things" 1/4/1961 ABC

77 Sunset Strip "The Space Caper" 3/10/1961 ABC

The Adventures of Ozzie & Harriet "A Question of Suits and Ties" 4/5/1961 ABC

The Adventures of Ozzie & Harriet [recurring as Sally Taft] 9/27/1962–9/5/1963 ABC

Channing "Collision Course" 1/6/1963 ABC

Burke's Law "Who Killed Alex Debs?" 10/25/1963 ABC

Burke's Law "Who Killed the Kind Doctor?" 11/29/1963 ABC

Mr. Novak "To Break a Camel's Back" 5/26/1964

The Man from U.N.C.L.E. "The Vulcan Affair" 9/22/64 NBC

Burke's Law "Who Killed the Strangler?" 1/6/1965 ABC

The Man from U.N.C.L.E. "The Project Deephole Affair" 3/18/1966 NBC

The Man from U.N.C.L.E. "The Indian Affairs Affair" 4/15/1966 NBC

The Man from U.N.C.L.E. "The Sort of Do-It-Yourself Dreadful Affair" 9/23/1966 NBC

The Rounders "The Scavenger Hunt" 10/11/1966 ABC

The Man from U.N.C.L.E. "The Pop Art Affair" 10/21/1966 NBC

The Man from U.N.C.L.E. "The Off-Broadway Affair" 11/18/1966 NBC

The Man from U.N.C.L.E. "The Concrete Overcoat Affair" 11/25 & 12/2/1966 NBC

The Man from U.N.C.L.E. "The My Friend the Gorilla Affair" 12/16/1966 NBC

The Man from U.N.C.L.E. "The Pieces of Fate Affair" 2/24/1967 NBC

The Man from U.N.C.L.E. "The When in Roma Affair" 3/17/1967 NBC

Please Don't Eat the Daisies "When I Was a Young Man" 3/25/1967 NBC

The Man from U.N.C.L.E. "The Five Daughters Affair" Pt. II 4/17/1967 NBC

Mannix "Turn Every Stone" 12/9/1967 CBS

The Monkees "Monkees on the Wheel" 12/11/1967 NBC

Star Trek "A Piece of the Action" 1/12/1968 NBC

Get Smart "Snoopy Smart vs. the Red Baron" 9/28/1968 NBC

Gomer Pyle, USMC "All You Need Is One Good Break" 11/8/1968 CBS

Love, American Style "Love and the Marriage Counselor" 2/27/1970 ABC

China Beach "Vets" [as herself] 3/15/1989 ABC

China Beach "Souvenirs" [as herself] 1/17/1990 ABC

☆ LUREE HOLMES ☆

The daughter of the founder of American International Pictures, statuesque Luree Nicholson Holmes began as an extra in a few of that studio's juvenile delinquent movies of the fifties. As a young adult she graduated to playing a beach girl in *Beach Party* (1963) and went on to appear in every film of the series. As one of the suntanned lovelies (along with actresses Salli Sachse, Mary Hughes and Patti Chandler) that surrounded Frankie Avalon and Annette Funicello, Luree was usually relegated to the background. However, she was given more screen time in *Pajama Party* (1964), *Ski Party* (1965) and *The Ghost in the Invisible Bikini* (1966), her last film appearance.

Luree Holmes was born Luree Nicholson on April 24, 1942, in Los Angeles. Her father was renowned film producer James H. Nicholson, who founded American International Pictures in 1955. According to Luree, "Originally my mother and father started the company in 1954 as American Releasing Corp. Sam Arkoff was the attorney and he had 25 percent interest in it in return for doing all of the legal work. The $3,000 that they talk about the company being started with came from a friend of the family who was the grandfather of Nathan Moriety, who recently produced *The Fast and the Furious* [2001]. The idea for the company began when my father saw Roger Corman's movie [*The Fast and the Furious*] that was turned down by Realart [in 1954].

He went to Roger and made the proposal to distribute the film. They didn't have the money yet so my father went out to raise the money from distributors. Sam didn't go with my father on those trips. He made it sound like he did but he really didn't. My father owned theaters before he produced movies. He knew all of the distributors and the exhibitors. He knew what they wanted. He knew what they could and were willing to do. He knew how they bought their films and he knew that they needed product. He plan was to fill that market and need, because as an independent theater owner he couldn't get any films either [from the major studios].

"When Sam Arkoff saw the company starting to take off, he talked to my father about becoming partners" continue Holmes. "My father was the senior partner. That is why his name is always listed first. Even then Sam only handled the legal and financial aspects of the company. My father totally stayed out of that part of the business. He didn't want anything to do with it. I would love in retrospect to ask my dad how he felt Sam handled that, because I don't think Sam was completely fair. Sam may have been legally correct but I don't think he was always ethical. One of the stories Sam told in his book is that my father insisted that the exhibitors have more time to pay fees and be charged lower percentages. Every time Sam would want to raise the fees, my father would say no. It was the only battle with Sam over fees that he won. But in the choice of what films to produce my father always had the final say."

Running a company and traveling across the country, you would expect Nicholson to be more of an absentee father and not be able to spend much time with his daughters, Loretta, Luree and Laura, but not so says Luree. "My father did a lot of work at home. My sisters and I were with him on the set and we often traveled with him when he did promotion for the films. My mother didn't believe in babysitters, so we were never left with anybody. He never raised his voice and he never spanked us. He was very philosophical, quoting Shakespeare, Plato, etc., and into spiritual beliefs like mind over matter and the continuation of the soul after death." Nicholson also solicited his teenage daughters' opinions regarding their likes and dislikes about movies. He had a projection room built at the Nicholson home in 1956 so they could watch movies as a family. "One of the things we kids always complained about was that in every movie—other than my father's—the teenagers were always old. The actors looked thirty-five. Kids didn't like that. It made the film so fake and so phony. My father remembered this when casting the beach movies, so taking kids literally off of the beaches of southern California became an important part of the films.

"My father also asked us what we thought of the actors in his films. The one guy my sisters and I loved was John Ashley. He was gorgeous. We got to know John very well because he came up to our house many times. My father always thought John Ashley would become a big star. [This may explain why Ashley is the only actor from the AIP juvenile delinquent films to appear in the beach movies.] John was such a nice guy."

Though Luree never had a desire to act, she began doing background work in the early black and white AIP exploitation films including *I Was a Teenage Werewolf*. "My sisters and I were always invited to be in everything, but it was left up to us if we wanted to or not," says Luree. "We got paid for it, so that was another benefit." Luree received her first on screen credit as "Luree Nicholson" in *Diary of a High School Bride* (1959) playing a friend of Anita Sands, a teenager trying to hold on to her marriage to an older medical

Publicity pose of Luree Holmes and Aron Kincaid in *Ski Party* (AIP, 1965). *Courtesy of Aron Kincaid.*

student while dealing with a psychotic ex-boyfriend. In *The Comedy of Terrors* (1963) Luree played the servant of wealthy Basil Rathbone, who won't stay dead, in this comedy about undertaker Vincent Price, who with his assistant Peter Lorre, murders rich old men to collect hefty commissions when their families enlist their services. "Basil Rathbone became a good friend of the family," recalls Luree. "He was basically quiet but interesting. He and my father got along very well. The older actors who appeared in AIP movies usually became friendly with my dad. Vincent Price, in particular, was at our house often."

In 1963, Luree was cast as a beach girl in AIP's *Beach Party* (1963). Though she rarely has any lines in the core films, Holmes is known to fans by her trademark long, waist-length brown hair that is worn in a variety of wild hairstyles. ("They were always putting my hair up in these funny hairdos so they would match from scene to scene for the beach shots.") In *Beach Party*, singing sensation Frankie Avalon and Mouseketeer cast-off Annette Funicello play college sweethearts, Frankie and Dolores, who head for the beach to spend an idyllic two weeks alone. But unbeknownst to Frankie, Dolores has invited all their surfer friends and their girls (including John Ashley, Jody McCrea, Valora Noland, Delores Wells, Mike Nader, Luree, etc.) to come along for a beach party. Amid the sun worshipping, surfing and dancing, comes a staid college professor (Robert Cummings) and his girlfriend (Dorothy Malone) bent on secretly observing the vacationing young people to catalogue their morals and sex habits for a book. Throw in fumbling motorcycle leader Eric Von Zipper (Harvey Lembeck) and his gang of Rats and Mice, plus a Hungarian vamp (Eva Six) with the hots for Frankie and AIP had an instant hit.

Luree reveals, however, that, "Sam Arkoff didn't want *Beach Party* to be made. He thought that it would be a complete loser. Of course that is not the story he told afterwards. Sam's brother-in-law, Lou Rusoff, wrote *Beach Party*. My father had the idea to make a movie about teenagers on the beach and he asked Lou to write the script. Lou had teenage sons, so he just started watching and analyzing them—sort of like what Robert Cummings did in the film. That's how the basics of the movie came about. The kids were initially to be all-American kids. There was to be no smoking, no drinking and no swearing—not like you could do that on screen anyway in those days."

The combination of the chemistry between Frankie and Annette, the beach, the surfing footage, a zany supporting cast and authentic surf rhythms provided by Dick Dale & His Del-Tones made *Beach Party* a must see for the Clearasil set. The adult guests, including Cummings, Malone, and Morey Amsterdam, made it appealing to older audiences as well. But *Beach Party* was aimed more at the teenage psyche. It combined their hormonal thirst for titillation (e.g. scantily clad boys and girls twitching and singing about love and heartache on the shores of Southern California) without straying from the moral attitudes of the time. *Beach Party* was an enormous hit by AIP standards and received pretty good reviews. It won a 1964 Laurel Award for the year's Best Sleeper.

AIP knew they started a successful formula in *Beach Party* and in quick succession released *Muscle Beach Party* (1964) and *Bikini Beach* (1964). These popular follow up films starring Frankie and Annette mixed stars from *Beach Party* with newer faces and different plots. What was key to the remaining films were the pretty beach girls who surrounded Frankie and Annette. Luree Holmes was part of a company that went on to include Mary Hughes, Salli Sachse, Patti Chandler,

In *Muscle Beach Party* (AIP, 1964) beach girls Valora Noland (third from right) and Luree Holmes (second from right) look down admiringly as Annette Funicello tends to Frankie Avalon.

Laura Nicholson, Linda Opie, Sue Hamilton, and Jo Collins, who decorated the remaining *Beach Party* movies. Richard Warren Lewis, writing about the beach girls in the *Saturday Evening Post* remarked, "Their sole specialty is the manner in which they fill a bikini. In every beach film, for little more money than minimum union scale, they twist their torsos to unknown music while alert cameramen focus on their spectacular anatomy."

In *Muscle Beach Party*, the surfer gang tangles with a bunch of bodybuilders and fitness nuts (including Peter Lupus and Amedee Chabot) led by comedian Don Rickles. *Bikini Beach* saw the return of Erich Von Zipper and his motorcycle gang as the beach crowd mingles with snooty builder Keenan Wynn and a hot rod racing British pop star the Potato Bug (also played by Avalon). "What my father did was choose veteran actors who were his favorites to be in these movies as well as current television personalities and young kids," remarks Luree. "This helped make the beach movies appeal to a wide audience."

In both films, Luree was once again relegated to the background. Though these two films didn't give her much to do, she became very friendly with series star, Annette Funicello. Both young women

In *Ski Party* (AIP, 1965) Frankie Avalon is surrounded by lots of pretty girls including Luree Holmes (center) and Salli Sachse (right) as he croons the song "Lots Lots More." *Billy Rose Theatre Collection, The New York Public Library for the Performing Arts, Astor, Lenox and Tilden Foundations.*

were very quiet and introverted compared to the other more outgoing and playful young actors who came from the beaches of Southern California. Luree was a bridesmaid at Annette's wedding and later, Annette and her husband Jack Gilardi named their daughter Gina Luree.

The main reason for Holmes' lack of screen time was director William Asher. Luree was the first to admit that she was not an actress but was offered work on the beach movies by Nicholson. "I did hear that some people were saying that I was only in the films because of my father and that I was taking jobs from actors who really wanted to act," reveals Luree. "Those comments didn't bother me and I ignored them, because I could see why people would perceive it that way. It was true that I wouldn't have been in the movies if it weren't for my father. I had no desire to pursue an acting career—I was interested in psychology. But I had a lot of fun and enjoyed working in the beach movies."

But Holmes' enjoyment was not enough to satisfy her director. "William Asher handpicked a lot of the girls to be in the beach movies," divulges Holmes. "He favored girls like Salli Sachse and Linda Opie because they had the best figures. I definitely understood that. Since

I was tall—5'7"—he was always telling me to stand in the back. In a lot of the scenes you had to be really upbeat, and because I wasn't very outgoing it was difficult for me. The only time he ever complimented me was when we did the scene in *How to Stuff a Wild Bikini* where the girls were on top of the guys' shoulders and we had to knock each other off. I really had a great time doing that. I was part of the last two couples standing. Asher said to me, 'Well, that was great! You finally came alive.' It was a backhanded compliment. Except for that scene, I was never able to put on the show he wanted.

"Annette also had problems working with William Asher," continues Luree. "She voiced her displeasure to me about him, and I remember telling my father that she didn't like Asher very much. But that was about it. Asher may have given Annette a hard time because he didn't want her for the films. I think he and Sam Arkoff wanted Sandra Dee or someone of her ilk. When my father hired Annette, Asher was not so supportive. Though Annette didn't like him, being a professional, she never said she wouldn't work with him or request another director. She is not that kind of person."

AIP's last beach movie for 1964 was *Pajama Party*, an off-shoot from the series starring Tommy Kirk as a Martian who crashes the beach party and falls for Annette Funicello as Dee Dee, despite the presence of her boyfriend Big Lunk (Jody McCrea). The film's director, Don Weis, picked Luree Holmes to work with Buster Keaton in a standout comedic scene. When Keaton as Chief Rotten Eagle accompanies Bobbi Shaw to a dress shop, he browses in front of perfume girl Holmes' counter. In a hilarious silent bit, she lightly sprays him with a little perfume. He then squirts her back right in the face and the perfume battle begins. After both are drenched with different exotic fragrances, it ends with Luree dumping a whole bottle of cologne over Keaton's head. "Buster Keaton was wonderful in terms of acting and doing the scene," exclaims Luree. "But he was very quiet otherwise. He sort of kept to himself. We really didn't do too much rehearsing for this. We ran through it once and then just shot it." This was not the end, as the duo meet up again during the film's finale at the poolside pajama party, with Holmes dumping her soft drink over Keaton's head. These scenes are arguably Keaton's funniest bits from all the beach movies he appeared in.

Pajama Party also featured Luree's three-year-old daughter as a model for the topless bathing suit during the dress shop scenes. At this time, Luree was the only one of the younger actresses doing beach movies who was married with children, which stood her apart. "We shot the films in about two to three weeks, so it wasn't like it was a lot of work and I was leaving my kids for any long period of time," says Luree. "Sometimes I would even bring them to the set. My husband was very possessive and he didn't like me to do things that I enjoyed without him. I was going to school for awhile and he made it so unpleasant for me that I quit. By the time the movies came along I had smartened up and told him that I didn't like doing them. He said, 'You have to. We need the money.' He encouraged me to do it as long as I was not having fun. But I was having a *great time* and loved the people—Annette in particular."

Though Holmes performed well in *Pajama Party* it was a return to the background for her in the William Asher directed features *Beach Blanket Bingo* (1965) and *How to Stuff a Wild Bikini* (1965). *Ski Party* (1965) gave her much more screen time due to a different director, Alan Rafkin. "On the beach movies, the director would decide who is going to be in the scenes," explains Luree. "On the set one day, Alan Rafkin said something negative about my father and Susan Hart [his girlfriend] to a group of us. He didn't know who I was. Somebody then told him and he came to me and apologized profusely. I think that is why he used me a lot."

Breezy and entertaining, *Ski Party* (which surprisingly received a 1966 Laurel Award for Best Musical, placing fifth in the poll) was another offshoot from the core *Beach Party* movies as the beach gang trades in their surfboards for skis. When college kids Frankie Avalon, Dwayne Hickman, Deborah Walley, Yvonne Craig and the rest of the crew hits Sun Valley for a ski vacation, all the girls go gaga over suave ski champion Freddie Carter (Aron Kincaid). Trying to determine what Freddie has that they lack and what girls want in a guy, Avalon and Hickman masquerade as two English lasses. Needless to say, complications ensue, especially when the pompous Freddie falls for Hickman's 'Nora.' "*Ski Party* was one of the most fun movies that we made," says Holmes fondly. "I think part of it was because we shot almost the whole movie on location in Sun Valley. One of the cameramen on this picture was the first to mount a camera on a helmet and he skied down the mountain to get all those ski shots. Some days it was freezing and we had outdoor scenes where we had to wear bathing suits.

Salli Sachse (extreme left) and Luree Holmes (extreme right) as just two of the many female robots created by Vincent Price (center) as a mad scientist and Jack Mullaney as his assistant in *Dr. Goldfoot and the Bikini Machine* **(AIP, 1965).**

To keep warm, we wore skin color tights that made it look like that we had nothing on but we did." In this film, Avalon serenades Holmes and the other beach girls by poolside as he sings the catchy song, "Lots, Lots More." Luree then joins Salli Sachse and Patti Chandler for a pajama party with Walley, Craig and Avalon and Hickman, disguised as their female alter egos, that ends in a frantic pillow fight after the gals spend the time bashing their boyfriends.

As with all the beach movies, there was a dynamic regarding the entire cast that was broken down into the leading players, the supporting contract players and the first timers or guest stars. Luree explains, "It was very clear on all of the movies that there were levels of how well known you were. Frankie, Annette, Dwayne Hickman, Deborah Walley, Yvonne Craig, etc. were a group. Harvey Lembeck and the actors who played his motorcycle gang members stayed together. The beach boys and girls [Luree, Salli Sachse, Mike Nader, Patti Chandler, Mary Hughes, Ed Garner, etc.] who were contract players were another group. Finally, there were the one-time only actors who were not part of the AIP stable.

"This really shook out during *Ski Party*," continues Luree. "The four leads pretty much stuck to themselves. Frankie Avalon was very friendly if you approached him but he was not very outgoing. Even with me, I would have to go up to him to start a conversation. Poor Aron Kincaid was a newcomer to AIP when he did this movie and he didn't know where he fit in. For publicity purposes they would pair up the actors by height. Since we are both tall and I had a bigger than usual role in this film, Aron and I were partnered together. I became friendly with Aron and that automatically made him part of our group. I think the contract players realized that our jobs were safe and that there were other actors who would come and go. If we got to know them in any way they would hang out with us. Aron was very nice and I think everybody liked him a lot. Doing *Ski Party* without Annette or my other good friend, Donna Loren, I began branching out and getting to know some of the other people more. I eventually became friendly with the other beach girls, particularly Salli Sachse. She was married, so we had something in common. We spent a lot of time together and got to know each other quite well. Her husband was killed in a plane crash two years later."

During 1965, things began getting chaotic at American International Pictures when Luree's father Jim Nicholson left his wife for actress Susan Hart. ("I always thought my mother was very harsh and cold so I was not surprised when my father left her. I told him at that time, 'I don't blame you for divorcing her. I just don't like the way you did it.'") Luree claims the rift widened between Sam Arkoff and her father when Nicholson lost controlling interest in the company to Sam after divorcing Luree's mother. Arkoff now owned fifty percent of AIP, with Nicholson and his ex-wife each owning twenty-five percent. "I think that all along Sam Arkoff craved to be in charge of AIP," comments Holmes. "I never liked Sam very much and didn't feel comfortable around him. Until his death, Sam had been re-writing history for years. He wrote a book about AIP that was released in 1991 when he got his star on the Hollywood Walk of Fame. He sent copies to my sisters and I. After reading it I became so livid and so angry that I wanted to picket his getting that star. He rewrote history and took credit for almost everything my father created. When he was confronted, his response was that 'He's dead. I'm alive.' We are working on a book about AIP that will tell the truth."

Luree Holmes did two more movies

for AIP before calling it quits. She played a bikini-clad robot in the spy spoof *Dr. Goldfoot and the Bikini Machine* (1965) starring Vincent Price, Frankie Avalon and Susan Hart. In *The Ghost in the Invisible Bikini* (1966) starring Tommy Kirk, Deborah Walley and Aron Kincaid, Holmes, looking fantastic with frosted hair cut shoulder-length, was given more to do as Karen, a friend of Nancy Sinatra's. After she stopped working, Luree had three more children. She also became interested in the field of anger management and ending violence and child abuse. She worked as a family counselor and educator who trained with Dr. George R. Bach, the psychologist and author of the best-selling *Creative Aggression* and *The Intimate Enemy*. In 1980, Luree went on to co-author with Laura Torbet the book called *How to Fight Fair with Your Kids and Win*.

More recently, Luree Nicholson, which is the name she now uses, was also instrumental in getting the documentary entitled *It Conquered Hollywood! The Story of American International Pictures* produced for American Movie Classics. "Initially, they couldn't get anybody to come in to be interviewed," discloses Luree. "They had sent letters to people like Roger Corman asking them to talk about the wonderful, fabulous Sam Arkoff. When they contacted my sister Laura and I, we asked how they were portraying my father and what is the documentary really going to be

Aron Kincaid and Mary Hughes, Janice Levinson, Salli Sachse, Luree Holmes, and Patti Chandler (left to right) relax between takes while filming *The Ghost in the Invisible Bikini* (AIP, 1966). *Courtesy of Aron Kincaid.*

about. The producer and director told us they had heard so many discrepancies in the AIP story that they wanted to present an accurate picture. I said, 'If you are going to present the truth I will call these people you want to interview and let them know that is what you are doing. The letter you sent is not going to get you anybody.'

"It took them two and a half years to edit the film," continues Luree. "At first, they were thinking of showing version one, Sam Arkoff's side of the story, and version two, everybody else's view. They did a nine-hour interview with Sam, and I think they found the only couple of times Sam said, 'Jim and I' that gave any credit to my father. Everybody else who spoke said, 'Jim and Sam.' When the narrator spoke, he said 'Sam and Jim.' Though they erred in a couple of places—Blaxpoitation films were my father's idea—I think they did an excellent job. Susan [Hart] was very upset about the documentary and strongly felt the narrator should have said 'Jim and Sam' throughout. She sued to stop the film from airing. Susan is very protective of my father's place in AIP but she goes about it in strange ways." Though she and her sister were interviewed on film for the documentary, they were not used in it. Luree feels that is because they were able to get bigger names to participate and that they revealed too much information contradicting Sam Arkoff.

Today, Luree is writing another book now tentatively called *Anger and the Spirit*, which is about how to transform anger into compassionate action. She is also a grandmother with a granddaughter that just loves the beach movies. "She wants to watch them over and over," says Luree with a laugh. "That is a bit too much for me. But I think it is great that there is an audience for these films that were good clean fun."

Film Appearances

1959 **Diary of a High School Bride** (AIP) d. Burt Topper

1963 **Beach Party** (AIP) d. William Asher
      The Comedy of Terrors (AIP) d. Jacques Tourneur

1964 **Muscle Beach Party** (AIP) d. William Asher
      Bikini Beach (AIP) d. William Asher
      Pajama Party (AIP) d. Don Weis

1965 **Beach Blanket Bingo** (AIP) d. William Asher
      Ski Party (AIP) d. Alan Rafkin
      How to Stuff a Wild Bikini (AIP) d. William Asher
      Sergeant Deadhead (AIP) d. Norman Taurog
      Dr. Goldfoot and the Bikini Machine (AIP) d. Norman Taurog

1966 **The Ghost in the Invisible Bikini** (AIP) d. Don Weis

Television Appearances

The Wild Weird World of Dr. Goldfoot (special) 11/18/1965 ABC

☆ SUZIE KAYE ☆

Either as a sultry brunette or dippy blonde, Suzie Kaye was a talented actress who made her mark in '60s drive-in movies. The petite Kaye made her film debut as a Shark girl in the Academy Award–winning *West Side Story* (1961). She went on to play small roles in a few more films, including *Wild Wild Winter* (1966), with her natural dark hair. Feeling her career needed a boost, Kaye went blonde, which seemed to suit her perky personality better. As with Gail Gilmore, who she resembled, Suzie Kaye too went on to work in beach movies and with Elvis Presley. The vivacious beauty could be seen singing and dancing in the Elvis film *Clambake* (1967), *It's a Bikini World* (1967) with Tommy Kirk, and *C'mon, Let's Live a Little* (1967) with Bobby Vee. After playing James MacArthur's biker babe in *The Angry Breed* (1968), Kaye was cast as one of the early seventies' most memorable daytime vixens on *Love Is a Many Splendored Thing*.

Suzie Kaye was born Susan Helene Klein in New York City to a show business family. Her mother was a singer named Ethel Bennett and performed at the Old Romanian on Allen Street. Her father was a drummer. Living on Ocean Parkway in Brooklyn, the Kleins immediately enrolled their musically inclined daughter to take classical piano lessons from her uncle, who was professor at Juilliard. When she was six years old the determined girl made her parents take her over the river into Manhattan. "We went to see *The Red Shoes* and later *South Pacific*," recalls Suzie. "To perform on stage became my dream but my parents wanted me to wait until I was at least ten years old. Years later I was on the same stage [as *South Pacific*] in *The Music Man*, playing one of the River City kids. I'd set goals and think, 'I'll be in this theater' and surprisingly (like the maniac that I was) most of those things came true."

As a child Suzie began taking tap and ballet lessons in the neighborhood, despite her pleas to study in Manhattan. Though hoping their daughter would not remember the pact they made with her, on Suzie's tenth birthday she reminded them of it. "We went into Manhattan for my first audition," recalls Suzie. "I got a show at the Charlie Lowe's School of Dance called *Bonnie Maid*. A lot of kids my age went here and some later became stars, like Elliot Gould. A week later I got cast along with Connie Francis, Bobby Darin, Patti Austin, and Lenny Dale in a TV revue show called *Star Time Kids*. We ran a new show every week for six years. I literally grew up on this from ten to sixteen years old with Johnny Olson. I got a lot of experience. It was like a juvenile version of *Caesar's Hour*."

During the summer breaks of her TV show, Suzie performed on stage at resorts in the Poconos. One year she even did a show in Los Angeles at the La Ciniega Theater called *Crawling Arnold* with Katheleen Freeman, Rue McClanahan, Yvonne Wilder, and Bert Convy. "I was the kind of girl who would walk into an audition with five hundred other girls when they needed only one," says Kaye. "I pushed myself into the front because I was so scared and knew I had to do that, because I believed in the adage, 'Try three times harder and maybe you'll make it.' It worked for me and I got *The Music Man*. I sang in the "76 Trombones" number. I did the show with the original lead Robert Preston, then Eddie Albert and Bert Parks."

Suzie Kaye and Don Edmonds frolic in the snow in *Wild Wild Winter* (Universal, 1966). *Billy Rose Theatre Collection, The New York Public Library for the Performing Arts, Astor, Lenox and Tilden Foundations.*

Though just cast in a big Broadway musical, everybody looked at Kaye, bewildered, when the following week she auditioned for the movie version of *West Side Story*. Recalling the casting process, Kaye says, "It was like you see in *A Chorus Line* and *All That Jazz*. There were about three hundred people auditioning at first and then you get whittled down. I was not auditioning for one particular role. We did Jets and Sharks combinations. I was called back to screen test for Anita. Then I tippy-toed in *The Music Man* for another six months when I received a phone call one night [from the casting director of *West Side Story*]—'Can you be here?' I said, 'You bet!' I was brought out to L.A. to play one of the featured roles of Rosalia. That started a new life for me on the West Coast." However, since she was not yet eighteen, Kaye had to go to court along with fellow cast members Eliot Feld and Eddie Verso to get permission to do the movie. She turned eighteen during filming.

In an ironic note of casting, the Jewish girl from Brooklyn was cast as Rosalia, a Puerto Rican gang member. Though she auditioned for the bigger role of Anita, which went to Rita Moreno, Kaye was not the least disappointed and was thrilled to be in the movie. "I think Jerome Robbins always had Rita Moreno in mind," states Suzie. "He had worked with her in *The King and I*. But quite a few ladies tried out. I know BarBara Luna was one of them and she was wonderful. Later I played Anita on stage at the Seattle Opera House and the Vancouver Queen Elizabeth. I went in for Luna as Anita in San Diego on two hours notice, because she had hurt her eye on opening night. I hadn't done the show in over a year and I was in the bathtub with my hair in rollers when I got the call. At first I said, 'No, I won't do it!' But I did."

As most filmgoers know, 1961's Academy Award–winning Best Motion Picture *West Side Story* was a masterful reworking of Shakespeare's tragic love story *Romeo and Juliet,* featuring a wonderful score by Leonard Bernstein and Stephen Sondheim and energetic dance numbers choreographed by Jerome Robbins. The Bard's feuding Montague and Capulet families of 18th century Verona were transformed into the feuding white and Puerto Rican street gangs, the Jets and the Sharks, of New York City's Upper West Side. Romeo and Juliet became Polish-American Tony (Richard Beymer) and Maria (Natalie Wood), newly immigrated from Puerto Rico. Maria's brother Bernardo (George Chakiris) was the leader of the Sharks while Tony's best friend Riff (Russ Tamblyn) led the Jets. Tensions between the gangs come to a head when the young lovers are drawn to each other at a school gym and dance together, infuriating Bernardo. The Jets and Sharks set a time and place to rumble, but Maria begs Tony to stop it. He tries, but during the course of the fight Bernardo stabs Riff fatally. In retaliation, an enraged Tony kills Bernardo. Despite his actions, Maria forgives Tony and they make love. Bernardo's girlfriend Anita (Rita Moreno) is infuriated with her friend until Maria convinces her of her love for Tony. When Anita agrees to help Maria run away with Tony by delivering a message to him at Doc's Drugstore, the Jets rough her up ("Bernardo's girl wants to help? She only wants to help get Tony!"). Enraged, Anita spits out that Shark member Chino shot Maria dead. This lie brings Tony out from hiding. In a school playground, he rushes towards Maria just as a bullet is fired from Chino's gun. Sadly, he dies in his lover's arms.

West Side Story was brilliantly co-directed by Robert Wise and Jerome Robbins, who shared the Academy Award for Best Director. ("Robert Wise was going to do the dramatic scenes and Jerry was going to direct the musical and dance numbers.") Kaye's character of Rosalia was one of Maria's friends who work with her at a dress shop. She is featured in two of the film's biggest production numbers—the "Dance at the Gym" where the Jets and Sharks try to out Mambo each other and "America" where the Shark girls sing about the good things in America while their boyfriends refute them. She and the other Shark girls also accompany Maria on the song "I Feel Pretty." They think she is excited about Chino, but it is Tony she is happy about. Robbins directed all these numbers. "I was so in love with Jerome Robbins' aura—it was like he was God," exclaims Kaye. "I was just so awe stricken that he had the ability to make you do things that you could never imagine you could do. I was so scared that I dared *not* do what he wanted because I thought I would have been invited back to New York and dumped in the East River! We killed ourselves working on that movie. Saul Chaplin was the musical director and he would rehearse with us. He was a darling man."

The one number that Suzie found to be most difficult was "America." She explains, "I had this ego problem where I liked my feet to look small, so I bought a pair of Papagalo Shoes to wear during this number. I got a pair that was half a size too small, which was the worst thing I could have done. I would go home at night and my feet would be bleeding and blistering. We were putting chamois on each other to bring our temperatures down so as not to pass out. It was a painful situation, but at that age pain is a pleasure. It all depends on what you are doing it for."

Though Kaye and the cast may have been in awe of Jerome Robbins, the film's producers and the studio became fed up with his budget overruns. They parted ways halfway through the filming. Kaye remembers, "We were filming 'I Feel Pretty' and were going over and over budget because Jerry Robbins was a perfectionist. One day we came in and Jerry had left. It was like, 'what?' Bob Wise took over and we just moved on—that's show business, as they say. But we missed Jerry a lot."

Recalling the cast, Kaye says, "Natalie Wood was fine to work with but a little distant. I think she was fearful and a bit uncomfortable being around all these New York dancers. I never had any run-ins with her." As for the dancers, "Off the set we were gangs through and through. We even played cards separately. We didn't mix because a lot of us were Method Actors—I know I was. We just stayed in character most of the time because it made it easier."

While many of her *West Side Story* cast mates disappeared or got work behind the camera, Suzie Kaye was determined to be an actress. ("It was my goal to have an acting career. I went on to do many acting roles in B-movies—*but I also did good theater*.") On TV, she was one of the

Lobby card for *Wild Wild Winter* (Universal, 1966) starring Chris Noel, Suzie Kaye, and Vicky Albright as snow bunnies.

"discoveries" on *Talent Scouts* and played a high school flapper on the sitcom *Margie*, starring Cynthia Pepper. Back on the big screen she had a one-line role as a friend of Sandra Dee's in *Tammy and the Doctor* (1963).

In 1966, Suzie Kaye was cast in the low-budget grade-Z movie *Women from the Prehistoric Planet* (1966). "This was a *raging* success," jokes Kaye. "I wound up doing a Mambo with flaming red hair on a rocket ship." Suzie portrayed a space explorer who is part of Admiral Wendell Corey's crew (which also included John Agar, Merry Anders, and Stuart Margolin) from the planet Centaurus who receive a distress signal from another ship that has crashed on an uninhabited planet full of prehistoric animals and wild natives. "The sets were so cheap that they needed to be propped up, because they thought it was going to fall over. Melissa Gilbert's father, Paul Gilbert, played my boyfriend."

That same year, Kaye appeared in *Wild Wild Winter*, her first of five drive-in movies aimed at the teenage audience. This beach movie set in the snow was the second musical about the college crowd from producer Bart Patton and director Lennie Weinrib. As with the duo's *Beach Ball* (1965), the enjoyable and colorful *Wild Wild Winter* (billed as a "Surfin' Snow Ball") is packed with rock acts including Jay and the Americans, The Beau Brummels, The Astronauts, and the sweet duo of Jackie and Gayle. Kaye gives a sprightly performance (*Variety* called her "a cutie") as Sandy, a coed and member of a sorority headed by the prim Susan (Chris Noel), who instructs her Zeta-Theta sisters to distrust men because all they want is a "hi and a goodbye." Long-in-the-tooth Gary Clarke ("He looked like our father," laughs Suzie) was cast as Lonnie, a surfer bum and ladies man who is coaxed to leave the shores of Malibu to attend Alpine University by his friends Burt (Don Edmonds) and Perry (Steve Rogers). The plan is for Lonnie to romance and distract Susan so they could move in on her friends, Sandy and Dot (Vicky Albright). Of course, Susan eventually uncovers Lonnie's ruse and he is forced to participate in a championship ski contest against her snobbish boyfriend John (Steve Franken). Lonnie wins the competition by a fluke and gains the love of Susan.

In 1966, Kay was unhappy with the path her career was going. She was liked by a lot of people in the business but was not getting the roles in films or television that she craved. The stage was the only medium to take advantage of her talent. "I had a lot of people who really enjoyed to come see me perform, like Carl Reiner, Garry Marshall, and Goldie Hawn, who married Gus Trikonis, the actor who played my boyfriend in *West Side Story*," says Kaye. "Goldie came back stage one night while I was playing Dulcie in *The Boy Friend* and she said to me, 'I am going to an audition tomorrow.' There was something I did in the show that she wanted to use at her reading. I said, 'Sure!' It turned out that the audition was for *Rowan and Martin's Laugh-In*! She got the role and has had a brilliant career ever since. Garry Marshall used to always say to me, 'Suzie, do you think it will *ever* happen? Just don't quit.'

"I think one of my problems was that I did a few TV pilots [including one called *Easy Aces*] that would tie me up for a whole year sometimes," continues Kaye. "I couldn't do much of anything else until the networks decided to pick it up as a series or not. One of them, *Run, Buddy, Run*, was picked up *but not with me!*"

Also around this time Suzie Kaye was distracted from her career when her boyfriend, Laurence Stone, came out to California from New York to work as an agent at APA. "He wasn't *my* agent—I wanted him to be," admits Kaye. "You know that adage that when you are standing across the room and your eyes meet. It was like the song "Some Enchanted Evening." I saw him when we were in high school in a friend's basement. He was standing with another guy and they were both handsome. I was thinking, 'Mmm, which one?' In the Performing Arts High School there was about twenty girls to one guy, if not more. I chose Laurence because his hair was a little darker. As I did with films and theater (and Las Vegas I might add), I just went for it and picked him. We were married for twenty-five years. We're still together as friends now. The other guy standing next to him was Al Pacino. So there you have it—the luck of the draw."

Kaye's career went into high gear when she simply went from a brunette to a blonde. "I think I got typecast with the dark hair because of *West Side Story*," opines Suzie. "I thought I'd get more roles as a blonde, which I did, but I was always cast as a bit of a dopey blonde." Back on the big screen, the newly flaxen-haired Suzie Kaye played a supporting role in *Clambake* (1967) starring Elvis Presley as Scott Heyward, the son of an oil baron who switches identities with Will Hutchins as Tom Wilson, a ski instructor. Scott takes Tom's job working at the Shores Hotel in Miami Beach, while Tom masquerades as the super rich Scott. Kaye played a kooky blonde named Sally on vacation in Florida with Shelley Fabares as Dianne and Angelique Pettyjohn as Gloria who are out to snare rich husbands. All

Publicity photo of Elvis Presley surrounded by Suzie Kaye (left) and Angelique Pettyjohn (right) in *Clambake* **(United Artists, 1967).**

of them are attracted to suave playboy James Jamison III (Bill Bixby). Sally however falls for Tom (when he asks her to go on a treasure hunt for a sunken pirate ship loaded with bullion the dippy blonde squeals, "Oh! *Soup?*"). Scott is attracted to Dianne, a self-confessed golddigger who fights her feelings for the poor ski instructor and focuses her attention on Jamison. The two rivals duke it out in a speed boat race competition. Scott wins both the race and Dianne, who faints when Scott reveals his true identity.

Clambake didn't give Kaye much to do, however, she is a standout in her silver lamé bikini singing and dancing with Elvis during the rousing production number "Clambake" set on the beach. She also contributes nicely to the mod dance number "Hey Hey Hey," belted out by Elvis while pretty girls dance around his garaged speedboat. As for working with the King, Kaye gushes, "Elvis Presley was divine—what a dream! This was before his come down so he was so handsome. Both men and women loved him. He was so sweet and a total gentleman. He also paid attention to you if you had a problem, like I did. While we'd be waiting for a shot to be set up, we'd talk in a corner and he'd listen. He wasn't just fluff.

"Shelley Fabares was so nice too," continues Kaye. "Angelique was a lovely girl and we used to hang out together for awhile. I knew she had cancer and thought she was going to beat it—that's wishful thinking. Bill Bixby was handsome and sexy. I was a close friend with Brenda

Lobby card for *It's a Bikini World* **(Trans-American, 1966) featuring a fetching blonde Suzie Kaye.**

Benet [Bixby's wife]. I couldn't believe what happened to her. It [her suicide] was such a tragedy."

Bikini roles continued for Suzie Kaye, as her next film was the aptly titled *It's a Bikini World* (1967), directed by a Stephanie Rothman. "It was nice being directed by a woman," admits Suzie. "I felt more comfortable. I was awestruck, because to me it was magical to have a female director. The film was still exploitation but Rothman did it in a more wholesome form—I didn't do anything embarrassing. She would let the scene play." The film was an independent production from Trans American Arts but distributed by American International Pictures and is most notable for an outstanding lineup of rock acts including the Animals, the Gentrys, and the garage band the Castaways, performing their hit, "Liar, Liar."

In the last of the beach movies (whose tag line proclaimed, "The Bikini-Bunnies are Bustin' Out All Over"), Kaye is wasted playing Pebbles, the best friend of the athletic and spirited Delilah (Deborah Walley), who keeps spurning the advances of cocky athlete Mike Samson (Tommy Kirk). To win over the beautiful redhead, Mike masquerades as his nerdy and shy brother Herbert. However, complications ensue when Delilah challenges Mike to compete in a series of beach sporting events including skateboard, swimming, and speedboat races. Delilah is helped by Pebbles, whose boyfriend is Sampson's best friend Woody (played by Bob Pickett of "The Monster Mash" fame). Mike wins all the heats except the last one where he allows Delilah to beat him. When his ruse is uncovered, Delilah is furious for being deceived, but when she finds out that he let her win one race she declares that there is hope for him and they resume their romance. Though *It's a Bikini World* had a feminist slant to it with the competition between "Samson" and "Delilah," by 1967 it was out of date compared to the new crop of exploitation movies featuring biker gangs, hippies, and reckless youth being produced for the teenage drive-in audience.

Kaye's last film, released in 1967, was the college musical *C'mon, Let's Live a Little,* starring pop stars Bobby Vee and Jackie DeShannon. "They were cool," remarks Kaye. "I didn't get to know Jackie that well because I rehearsed my musical numbers separately. We did have a couple of scenes together but we didn't get that tight. She was working quite a bit then writing and singing. She was wonderful." Tackling the issue of free speech, this picture was a mild entry in the series of campus unrest movies released in the late sixties and early seventies. Kaye played Bee Bee Vendemeer—college coed by day and go-go dancer by night. Her best friend is Judy Grant (DeShannon) a student at Waymount College and also the daughter of the dean (Russ Conway). She tries to help Arkansas country boy Jesse Crawford (Vee) get into school after he saves her from a car wreck. After passing his entrance exams, Jesse enrolls, where his singing talent comes to light. Ambitious senior Rego (John Ireland, Jr.) decides to use Jesse as a draw to get students to attend his political rally to rile up the students against the dean and the college.

Kaye's Bee Bee has little to do with the plot in *C'mon, Let's Live a Little,* but she sings and dances up a storm. She even performs the film's rousing title song, which was a bit of a surprise considering that female lead Jackie DeShannon had a number of hit records. "I had the star production number in this—Suzie and her boys," remarks Kaye. "I danced with about eight guys who threw me around and up in the air—all that joyful fun. This was a blast." The critics agreed. The reviewer in *Variety* raved that this production number is "chirped by Suzie Kaye, standout in the

Suzie Kaye and Bob Pickett in *It's a Bikini World* (Trans-American, 1966)

picture..." and "Suzie Kaye is cute and saucy," while Howard Thompson of the *New York Times* commented, "And a twittery blonde eel named Suzie Kaye raises the roof of the off-campus twist hangout...."

Due to her outstanding output of work in 1967, Suzie was voted a Hollywood Deb Star in 1968. Her sponsors were Danny Thomas and Ronnie Jacobs. "There was one person who shall remain nameless on the voting team who didn't like me," says Suzie. "He or she brought my scores down because I was close to winning. If I had won, I was supposed to do *The Mod Squad*. Since I lost, Aaron Spelling dumped me and the part went to Peggy Lipton!"

Despite the setback, TV producers finally began to take notice of Kaye's singing talent. She was booked on a number of variety and talk shows, including *Shindig*, *The Tonight Show Starring Johnny Carson*, and *The Milton Berle Show*. Kaye also appeared on *The Merv Griffin Show* with almost disastrous results. "I was very nervous about performing my number," reveals Kaye. "During the dress rehearsal I was *so* incredibly wonderful! Then comes the taping. Before the show I said to Stoney [Laurence Stone], 'Please get me a martini so I could calm my nerves.' Of course, he forgot. I went on and had a panic attack. Luckily, the tape broke so you couldn't tell that I was dancing like a crazy person—all you heard was heavy breathing. I have never forgiven Stoney for it! He is *so* on my list."

By the late sixties musicals were a dying breed. Elvis was now playing a ghetto doctor in *Change of Habit* and a gunslinger in the western *Charro!* The beach party was long over, and the youth-oriented musicals trickled down to one or two a year, if that. Kaye traded in her bikini and surfboard for a mini-skirt and motorcycle for her next film, *The Angry Breed* (1968). She played Ginny, a fierce biker chick and girlfriend of crazed gang leader Deek Stacey (James MacArthur). Reduced to the fourth female lead, this film showcased Suzie's physical attributes rather than her acting prowess. ("What I remember most is that we wore tight fitting mini-dresses and had to get on a back of a motorcycle in them. It was tough.") Her last film appearance was a cameo role in *The Comic* (1969), directed by Carl Reiner and starring Dick Van Dyke as a silent film star with a destructive ego. The movie featured many reenactments of classic silent movie bits with famous guest stars. "Carl Reiner, who I adored (he used to call me his little Nanette), offered me a nice size part in *The Comic*, but I couldn't play it due to another commitment. So I did a smaller role that we shot in a few days where I was tied to a stake ready to be shot. Mickey Rooney saves me."

As with most '60s actresses who hadn't hit the big time by the late sixties, film roles began to dry up for Suzie Kaye. But the ambitious blonde kept persevering. "I did a nightclub act in Las Vegas and I played at the Tropicana in the Blue Room," boasts Kaye. "If it wasn't happening in L.A. I had to cover all bases. I'd go to Vegas and if nothing was happening there I'd go to New York." It was in the Big Apple where Kaye's next success occurred. While visiting her parents, she had dinner with her friend, actress Donna Mills, who was starring on the soap opera *Love Is a Many Splendored Thing*. Mills informed Kaye that there were two roles coming up on the soap, one of which was a rival of Mills' character. "Since Donna was blonde they wanted a brunette for that role," says Suzie. "Of course, I was blonde too. Anyway, Donna set up an interview for me with Jon Conboy, the producer. I went down to make-up and then they screen tested me. I was very good. They ordered a couple of dark wigs for me for a second screen test. I said, 'Thank you very much,' and then started to get ready to go back to California. Stone and I were driving back at the time. Two days after I arrived back in L.A., they called and said, 'Can you come back to New York? We'd like you to sign a five year contract.' I said, 'I'll be there!'"

Debuting in 1969, Kaye was a sensation as the vile Angel Allison Chernak, who at first tried to steal Mark Elliot (played by David Birney that year) away from his wife, ex-nun Laura Donnelly (Donna Mills, who vacated the role in 1970 and was replaced by Veleka Gray). Angel then gave up on Mark and married Dr. Peter Chernak. "Angel Chernak was an absolute villainess until she got cancer and then atoned," laughs Suzie. "I played opposite three actors as Peter Chernak. The first guy was Paul Michael Glaser [1969–70], then Michael Zaslow [1970], and lastly Vincent Bagetta [1970–73]. It takes a few weeks to get used to playing opposite someone new, but when you are an actor

1968 Deb Stars (in foreground) Suzie Kaye and Monica Peterson played rich girls who ask Ron Ely as Tarzan to help find Peterson's missing uncle on an episode of *Tarzan* (NBC-TV, 1968)

you are an actor. The first three years of the show were done live. I was used to changing my clothes underneath cameras and dodging cable because I grew up on live TV in the fifties. We were cancelled in March of 1973."

After the soap ended, Suzie Kaye was burned out and took a year off, because "it got to be a point where it was really work. I labored hard to get where I was with my acting career but I started to look around and only saw cement walls and no windows. I didn't like it anymore. After time off, I got involved in another whole life where I became addicted to alcohol and drugs for the next ten years.

"I have been clean and sober for twenty-one years," continues Kaye proudly. "I went through recovery, and rather than go back to the mish-mosh of acting I decided to move on. Today I own with Stone a computer supply company. It's nice because I have a good head for business. I am sober and grateful for things that I didn't have time to be grateful for before. When they say, 'too much, too soon,' they're right. I have a wonderful life right now. I look pretty good and people have asked me if I wanted to try acting again. I did do a 'making of' *West Side Story* documentary a while back, but that is about it for me. I was supposed to do another one but I didn't get to New York after 9/11. We had a party out here in L.A. Rita Moreno came and we hugged each other and had a blast. We watched a film that my friend Bob Banas took on the set while we were shooting the movie. We might do something with that. But I am really not interested in acting. My ego does not need that anymore."

Film Appearances

1961 **West Side Story** (United Artists) d. Robert Wise & Jerome Robbins

1963 **Tammy and the Doctor** (Universal) d. Harry Keller

1966 **Women of the Prehistoric Planet** (Realart) d. Arthur C. Pierce
Wild Wild Winter (Universal) d. Lennie Weinrib

1967 **Clambake** (United Artists) d. Arthur Nadel
It's a Bikini World (Trans American) d. Stephanie Rothman
C'mon, Let's Live a Little (Paramount) d. David Butler

1969 **The Angry Breed** (Commonwealth United) d. David Commons
The Comic (Columbia) [cameo] d. Carl Reiner

Television Appearances

Star Time Kids (series regular) 9/1951 to 6/9/1957 WABC-TV
Margie "The Shimmy Dress" 12/21/1961 ABC
The Many Loves of Dobie Gillis "Sweet Smell of Success" 4/24/1962 CBS
Talent Scouts 8/20/1963 CBS
Arrest and Trial "Some Weeks Are All Mondays" 12/15/1963 ABC
Shindig [singing "Jerk and Twine"] 3/3/1965 ABC
Bob Hope Presents the Chrysler Theater "Mr. Governess" 11/10/1965 NBC
The Smothers Brothers Show "Heaven Help the Drop-Out" 2/25/1966 CBS
Run, Buddy, Run "Steam Bath and Chicken Little" 9/12/1966 CBS
The Jones Boys (pilot) 8/21/1967 CBS
The F.B.I. "By Force and Violence" 10/22/1967 ABC
Tarzan "Trina" 4/5/1968 NBC
Love Is a Many Splendored Thing (series regular as Angel Allison Chernak) 1969 to 3/23/1973 CBS

Also

Hey Landlord, The Merv Griffin Show, The Milton Berle Show, and *The Tonight Show Starring Johnny Carson*

☆ Sue Ane Langdon ☆

With her curvaceous figure and perky personality, blue-eyed blonde Sue Ane Langdon played a variety of kooks, goofy dames and sexy showgirls throughout the sixties. As with Stella Stevens and Jill St. John, Langdon had a flair for light comedy and was at her best playing the naïve sexy dingaling in such films as *The Rounders* (1965), *Frankie and Johnny* (1966) with Elvis Presley and *A Fine Madness* (1966). However, in her teenage drive-in films Langdon expertly essayed the role of the temptress, giving her unsympathetic characters a comedic edge—a fortuneteller lusting after Elvis in *Roustabout* (1964), a golddigging chorus girl in *When the Boys Meet the Girls* (1965) and a vain starlet in *Hold On!* (1966). In 1966, Langdon received lots of press regarding her semi-nude spread touting her new film *A Fine Madness*, starring Sean Connery, in the pages of *Playboy* magazine. The following year she played the sexy housewife who tempts Walter Matthau to cheat in *A Guide for the Married Man* (1967). As the sixties came to an end, the voluptuous sexpot surprisingly morphed into a dutiful housewife (and won a Golden Globe Award in the process) on the amusing sitcom *Arnie*.

Sue Ane Langdon was born on March 8, 1936, in New Jersey. Her father died when she was two years old, leaving her opera singer mother, whose professional name was Grace Wallis Huddle, to make ends meet to support them. While earning her master's degree at the University of Michigan, Grace became a college voice instructor. It was while she was mounting a production of the operetta *The Bartered Bride* at Coe College in Cedar Rapids, Iowa that Langdon got the acting bug. Grace, not wanting to hire a babysitter, took Sue to rehearsals and decided to incorporate her into the production. As a four-year-old, little Sue Ane stole the show! "Since I felt perfectly at ease on stage and enjoyed myself, my mother cast me in many productions at the colleges where she taught around the country," says Sue Ane. "I continued performing as I grew up and went to elementary school, high school, and on to college in Texas and Idaho." Then mother and daughter relocated to New York because "it was the Mecca of theatre show business."

Langdon began singing in the chorus at Radio City Music Hall. ("Coincidentally, this was the first job my mother had had in New York City many years prior.") She then understudied Jane Kean in the flop Broadway musical *Ankles Aweigh*. Undeterred, the determined newcomer landed a role in a destined for Broadway show called *Copper and Brass* starring Nancy Walker. However, Langdon was let go from the show because "Walker did not like pretty ladies." The musical never reached Broadway. ("Hah! Hah! Nancy Walker," jokes Sue Ane.) Langdon had better luck on TV, appearing on *The Ray Bolger Show*, *The Perry Como Show*, *The Steve Allen Tonight Show*, and *The Phil Silvers Show*. In 1957, she hosted, along with Richard Hayes, *Get Set, Go*, a variety program produced by the U.S. Army. Between television appearances, Sue Ane also appeared in summer stock productions of *Guys and Dolls*, *Brigadoon*, and *The Most Happy Fella*.

In 1958, Sue Ane landed a gig at the Riviera Hotel in *The Ziegfeld Follies* starring Jane Morgan. Langdon sang in the show and worked with comedian Dickie Henderson. It was after the show one night that she met her future husband Jack Emrek, who was an actor/director at the time. Their first date was horseback riding during the early morning hours. According to Sue Ane, "Somewhere during the ride he said, 'Come to Hollywood. I'll make you a star!'" After her show closed, Langdon took Emrek up on his offer. However, she couldn't find work (it was Christmastime) and returned to New York. But the persistent Emrek would not give up. "Jack had his agent call me to tell me that he had a job for me and to fly right out to L.A.," remembers Langdon with a laugh. "The lying agent hung up the phone and said to Jack, 'She's coming. Now *I* gotta get her a job!'" He did get her an interview, and with her beauty and talent, Langdon snagged a leading role opposite John Cassavetes on the TV anthology series *Lux Playhouse* in 1959. That same year she also became Mrs. Jack Emrek and landed a semi-regular role playing sexy but scatterbrained Kitty Marsh, the secretary to John Forsythe's *Bachelor Father*.

In 1960, Langdon made her film debut playing one of Ernie Kovacs' girlfriends in *Strangers When We Meet*, about suburban infidelity. In *The Great Imposter*, starring Tony Curtis as Ferdinand de Mera, she played a prison warden's daughter. Langdon was off the big screen for four years but she was very active on TV, playing a variety of characters. Among her comedic roles were a dumb burlesque queen on *Thriller*, the girlfriend of Sheriff Andy Taylor on *The Andy Griffith Show* and a ditzy exotic dancer on trial for diamond smuggling on *The Dick Van Dyke Show*. She also began making her mark in the western genre with appearances on *Gunsmoke*, *Bonanza*, and *Tales of Wells Fargo*. Langdon's versatility seemed to have gotten her noticed when The Great One, Jackie Gleason, picked her to play Alice Kramden and other roles on his new variety series entitled *Jackie Gleason and the American Scene Magazine* in 1962. "Jackie Gleason was not easy to work with," states Langdon, matter-of-factly. "He was the kind of person who would do *everything* if he could—from playing his part to playing your part to re-writing the script. I think he would have sold tickets in the lobby if he had the time to. He never came in to rehearse. I would run the lines and do the blocking with his stand-in. When it came time to do the live performance, Jackie would read his part off the teleprompter and he would change everything. I would have liked to have winged it too because I don't like to rehearse either. But when the scene has been rehearsed and blocked it made it difficult when Jackie came in and changed everything. Even so I was thrilled to have played Alice even for a short time with Jackie and Art Carney. Art was adorable! He got very sick and couldn't work, so *The Honeymooners* skit was dropped from the show. There was less and less for me to do on the program so I left."

Langdon returned to the big screen playing a small role as a drug addict forced to go "cold turkey" in *The New Interns* (1964) and got her first taste of drive-in movie fame playing opposite Elvis Presley in *Roustabout* (1964). "I almost didn't do *Roustabout*, because doing an Elvis Presley movie at the time was not really much of a steppingstone," admits Langdon. "Now I'm glad I did the two films with Elvis because they're the main things I'm remembered for today." In *Roustabout*, Langdon, wearing a dark wig, played Estelle, a.k.a. Madame Mijanou, a sexy palm reader working at a carnival owned by Maggie Morgan (Barbara Stanwyck) and run by embittered Joe Lean (Leif Erickson). Elvis Presley played rebellious Charlie Rogers, who has just been hired as a roustabout after being accidentally run off the road by Lean. Estelle meets Elvis when he comes to her tent to help her set up for the carnival's opening. After some witty innuendo, Estelle puts the moves on

Elvis who happily obliges, and they kiss. But when he finds out that her boyfriend is a knife thrower with the carnival he leaves. This doesn't stop Estelle from trying to seduce Charlie every chance she gets, causing trouble when Charlie's true love Cathy (Joan Freeman), Joe's daughter, catches them in a clinch. Later Estelle, wearing a very tight fitting dress, corners Charlie late at night. Tired of her come-ons, Charlie calls her bluff. An enraged Estelle then tells a smug Charlie to beat it. Later she encourages Cathy to try to get Charlie to come back to the carnie after he deserts it for a more lucrative gig. As with all Elvis Presley movies, it closes with a happy ending as Charlie returns, gets the girl, Joan Freeman, and saves the carnival from going bust.

"I thought Elvis Presley was very nice and very, very polite," comments Sue Ane. "It was 'Yes, Sir, Yes, Ma'am.' To me it was 'Yes, Madam,' because I played Madame Mijanou. He'd say it with that little giggle of his. Elvis also liked to tease me and thought I'd be a good 'business woman' in some 'house' somewhere. Despite that little joke he was a very shy, Southern gentleman. I enjoyed working with him and can't say one bad thing about him. Ladies thinks it was so amazing that I was lucky enough to have kissed him. All I can say is that his lips were very soft."

As for working with the esteemed Barbara Stanwyck, Langdon comments, "I was quite thrilled to meet and work with her, as she was an actress that I had admired. She was from a time in Hollywood when 'stars were *stars*,' and I felt quite

The flexible Sue Ane Langdon.

privileged to ride out to location in her private car with her everyday. She was quite pleasant and while I was on the set everybody seemed to get along. But I think Stanwyck was a bit too strong of a lady for Elvis. He was quite sensitive and she didn't pull any punches. I also don't think she was too thrilled to be in an 'Elvis' movie."

Though *Roustabout* did not receive as much praise as Presley's previous musical, *Viva Las Vegas*, the critics were kind, even the staid *New York Times*, whose critic Howard Thompson described *Roustabout* as being "tuneful and colorful." Coming from the *Times*, that was a rave in itself. The film made money too, grossing $3 million at the box office.

Roustabout (Paramount, 1964) featured Sue Ane Langdon as a carnival psychic who wants to read more than the mind of roustabout Elvis Presley.

Langdon continued her vixenish ways playing a scheming chorus girl (*Variety* remarked, "Miss Langdon remains the most impressive of the principals: she makes a first rate shrew") in the mundane teenage musical *When the Boys Meet the Girls* (1965), starring Connie Francis and Harve Presnell. As the trade ads proclaimed, "The Boys ... The Girls ... and that wild, way-out, wicked, wonderful beat!" Basically, this was a remake of *Girl Crazy*, complete with George and Ira Gershwin's tunes plus a dollop of 1965 rock and roll from Herman's Hermits ("Listen People") and Sam the Sham and the Pharoahs ("Monkey See"). Langdon played Tess, who leads a bunch of chorus girls singing "Treat Me Rough" in a variety show at her suitor Danny's (Presnell) all-male college. After getting caught with Tess in his dorm, Danny breaks up with her. The showgirl then shows her true colors as a blackmailing barracuda and slaps a breach-of-promise suit against him. To escape from her threats, Danny transfers from his high brow university to his father's alma mater in a remote section of Nevada to pursue his master's degree in engineering. There he literally runs into Ginger (Francis), as the daughter of the local mailman Phin (Frank Faylen) whose gambling debts have forced him to put his ranch up for sale. As love blooms between the two after a rocky start, they decide to save Ginger's homestead by turning it into a dude ranch for divorcees. Tess shows up and joins in cahoots with local gamblers out to stop Danny, but their scheme is foiled and true love conquers all.

That same year, Langdon made headlines when she and Hope Holiday bared their backsides in the hit western comedy *The Rounders* (1965), directed by Burt Kennedy. Glenn Ford and Henry Fonda starred as two aging cowpokes who make their living breaking in wild broncos used to round up stray cattle out west. However, their dream of retiring to an island paradise is always hampered by their love of booze and gals. Langdon and Holiday played two fun-loving exotic dancers who hook up with the two rascals. They both briefly revealed their shapely derrieres during the film's most hilarious scene after they've skinny-dipped with the two broncbusters, who attempt to cover those derrieres with cowboy hats. "I really did bare my behind in *The Rounders*," admits Langdon. "It was just so fast as you see it in the movie. It was terribly easy to do. I agreed to do it because I thought it was funny. Whenever I agreed to do anything like that it was usually done for a laugh." However, Langdon was not that happy that it had to appear that she was topless for part of that same skinny dipping scene. "Hope Holiday and I were a tad modest and prudish appearing like that on the set. We were allowed to wear bikini bottoms because that part of our body was immersed in the water but it had to look like we were bare on top. We conceived of the idea to paste falsies over the boobs. So we were able to get onto the set and into the water but we forgot that the water would loosen the glue. Our pasties came floating to the top and ruined the shot but it was good for a laugh on the set. We were well covered by the water and when it came time to get out they covered us with towels.

"Burt Kennedy directed *The Rounders* and he was just so enjoyable to work with," continues Langdon. "I also loved working with Henry Fonda and Glenn Ford. Hank was dating Shirlee, his to-soon-to-be wife at that time, so we didn't see too much of him because he was always running back to the trailer to be with her. I worked with him again on *The Cheyenne Social Club*. Hank was a very fine actor and a very fine person but he was very quiet. I spent more time with Glenn Ford, who was very nice to me. I really liked him."

Langdon was reunited with the British rock group Herman's Hermits in her

Sue Ane Langdon (center) as a greedy showgirl in *When the Boys Meet the Girls* **(MGM, 1965).**

next drive-in film, *Hold On!* (1966), co-starring Shelley Fabares. As the tagline asked, "Looking for a show to blow your cool? Well, swing loose, bust out, and HOLD ON ... you've never heard faster beats or seen wilder fun!" Produced by Sam Katzman, the movie was shot quickly and rushed into theatres to capitalize on the group's popularity. In the film, with her hair dyed a Lucille Ball orange, Langdon breezily played Cecilie Bannister, an ambitious, publicity-hungry starlet out to land a movie contract. To reach her goal, she hires two inept PR men (Mickey Deems and Phil Arnold) to get pictures of her with Herman's Hermits for publicity purposes. Pretending to be "an old friend of the group's" Cecilie meets up with NASA scientist Edward Lindquist (Herbert Anderson), who is also trying to get near the Hermits to investigate if they are worthy of having an American space capsule named for them. Cecilie and Harry cozy up to each other thinking that the other one will get them closer to the group. When that fails, Cecilie decides to crash a charity event where the Hermits are going to perform, because "The Hermits are news and if I'm going to be news I have to be where it is." Disguised as a nurse, she enters in an ambulance and causes a riot when the Hermits' fans storm the stage in pursuit of the "sickly" Herman.

Hold On! turned out to be a surprise box office hit. Lead singer Peter Noone, who had a very sweet aura about him, charmed the teenage audience and the critics alike. However, acting kudos went to Langdon, who received excellent notices. For example, the *NY Daily News*' critic remarked that Langdon "shows a flair for comedy," while the reviewer in *Variety* raved, "Sue Ane Langdon registers quite strongly as the brassy babe who cons her way into the headlines."

Langdon next had another opportunity to work with Elvis Presley and this time she didn't hesitate, accepting a role in the musical *Frankie and Johnny* (1966). A bit different than the typical Elvis Presley film, *Frankie and Johnny* was based loosely on the classic folk song. Set on a Mississippi gambling-showboat circa 1865, it featured Elvis as Johnny, a singer and gambler who loves Frankie (Donna Douglas), but she refuses to marry him until he gives up gambling. Together they perform on a showboat owned by Clint Braden (Anthony Eisley). Johnny tries to give up gambling, but a fortune teller reveals that a beautiful redhead will soon enter his life and change his luck. Things get complicated when the redhead turns out to be Nellie Bly (Nancy Kovack), the former lover of Braden. Frankie becomes jealous of Nellie, who is only using Johnny to get Braden to marry her, and Braden becomes jealous of Johnny. Amidst this complicated quadrangle, Langdon livens up the proceedings as Mitzi, Frankie's ditzy lovelorn showgirl friend. David Fader, writing in *Films and Filming*, thought Langdon brought "considerable personality" to her role. The critic in *Variety* remarked that "Langdon gets a chance at a number of cute situations," and Ann Guarino in the *NY Daily News* wrote, "[Langdon] makes the most of her comic lines." She even received a 1966 *Photoplay* Gold Medal Award nomination for Favorite Comedy Star.

"I truly enjoyed my part of Mitzi in *Frankie and Johnny*," says Langdon. "I had a great time with that role. I didn't notice any change with Elvis. He seemed pretty much the same—still a very nice guy. Donna Douglas was of interest to him at that time, and he was spending a lot of time with her. I just hung out with the guys on the set like I did on *Roustabout*. Whenever you were with Elvis for the most part you were with his entourage. Those guys were always around but they

Poster art for *Hold On!* (MGM, 1966).

were all very nice. I really had a great time working with Elvis but I don't think he was that comfortable appearing in movies. He was much more relaxed as a singer on stage. Sometime after doing these movies I saw him in concert at the International in Las Vegas. I thought he was *fantastic*! He was so sexy, dynamic, and strong vocally. That's when I became a true fan. I went backstage afterward and thought I was going to faint when he kissed me hello. I wish we could have shot those movies scenes again because I would have insisted on lots of rehearsal!"

Today, Elvis fans are split about *Frankie and Johnny*, but back in 1966 the critics seemed to like it, as it offered something different from the typical Presley fare. The movie grossed more than some of Elvis' previous movies and it received a 1966 Laurel Award for Best Musical, placing fourth in the poll.

Langdon's next film, *A Fine Madness* (1966), was a more adult film that led to her notorious layout in *Playboy* magazine. Trying to break free of the James Bond mold he felt typecast in, Sean Connery played Samson Shillitoe, a married poet who has a way with women. They just melt in his presence and he keeps getting distracted by them from completing his latest poem. Not many people know this movie because the public totally rejected Connery in this type of role and the film was a box office dud. Langdon played the small role of brassy receptionist Miss Walnicki, who encounters Connery's Samson at her office, which he is hired to clean. However, the prim Walnicki too wilts under his charms and soon the two are rolling around on her boss' couch as his Samson's carpet cleaner is running and making foam, which seeps under the door. All of the office staff see the foam and rush in on them. "I call this nookie with Nicki," jokes Langdon with a laugh. "It was so much fun working with Sean. I adored and admired him. He was so cool and a really relaxed person! Kissing him was quite an experience! We really had some fun on the couch. He was like a big bear but totally charming. I was married and he knew my husband, so he respected that. Sean was very confident and comfortable with his persona, unlike Elvis who was not all that confident except when he was performing on stage."

During the making of the film, Langdon was asked if she would recreate the scene with Connery for a photographer from *Playboy*. Since it was promotion for the film she agreed as they were also shooting Jean Seberg. Recalling the layout, Langdon says, "For the most part, I was pretty well covered. I don't know how that side shot of me got in. Even so, I'm not too exposed, especially compared to what they show today. I think the side shot must have been taken after I sat up. Those photographers get in there and you forget sometimes that they're clicking away. I was wearing panties and Sean covered the top part of me as we were lying on the couch. I remember grabbing my 'Teddy' when I got up and I was pretty well covered with it. Sean was very nice about doing this. Everybody handled it just beautifully. I wasn't that embarrassed."

Langdon's last official '60s drive-in movie was the low-budget spy adventure *A Man Called Dagger* (1967), directed by Richard Rush and featuring music by Steve Allen. "I thought Steve was one of the sharpest, cleverest people I ever knew," exclaims Sue Ane. "He and Johnny Carson were by far the best *Tonight Show* hosts. We saw Steve at a party shortly before he passed away. He was the guest of honor and his acceptance speech was amazing! He was just so talented. Steve's score for *A Man Called Dagger* was a take off on some of the James Bond music and he was able to weave it in pretty well."

Sue Ane Langdon, Elvis Presley, and Donna Douglas (left to right) in *Frankie and Johnny* **(United Artists, 1966).** *Courtesy of Sue Ane Langdon.*

In this James Bond knock-off, Langdon makes a sexy and duplicitous femme fatale who tangles with virile secret agent Dirk Dagger (Paul Mantee) and his partner Harper Davis (Terry Moore). Asked how she landed the role of Ingrid, the owner of a health spa and paramour of the film's villain, Nazi Rudolph Koffman (Jan Murray), Langdon replies frankly, "I knew Terry Moore. She called and asked me if I would do this part. That's really all that I remember. But I'm sure I had to meet Dick Rush. I don't recall how we arrived on the accents for the movie. I think I was trying for a German or Swedish accent and I thought Maureen Arthur, who played one of my attendants [and who also sang the theme song by Allen], was trying for a Carol Channing sound. I guess it was an effort on Dick's part to make this film as goofy as he could. My character had different colored hair, which matched my dog. Even so, I don't think we were much competition for James Bond.

"Paul Mantee was a very nice guy but not quite a Sean Connery," continues Langdon. "I recently saw him at a collector's show in North Hollywood. I hadn't seen him since we did the movie. Jan Murray was great fun. If you goofed up a line he'd say, 'Wrong' all the time, just like he did when playing his character, Rudolph. I've seen him a number of times since then. Here was the consummate

Jewish comedian playing a German Nazi and driving around in a Mercedes-Benz. He makes a joke that he forgave the Germans all in one year. He was supposed to attend my ceremony when they gave me my Star in Palm Springs. But he does his comedy act on cruise ships and he couldn't make it. He is still a character."

Langdon took a respite from movie making when she replaced Barbara Harris in the hit Broadway musical *The Apple Tree* in 1967. She wowed the reviewers, even getting a rave from the *New York Times* critic Clive Barnes, no fan of Hollywood actors on Broadway, who described her as being "charmingly dreamy."

As the swinging '60s came to a close, Langdon could be seen playing an adulterous suburbanite in the hilarious comedy *A Guide for the Married Man* (1967) and a "happy whorelet" named Opal Ann in *The Cheyenne Social Club* (1970). In the former, Walter Matthau starred as a married man who is getting the itch to cheat on his beautiful attentive wife, Inger Stevens. His best friend, played by Robert Morse, is a big time philander and instructs his friend on the art of infidelity. Langdon deliciously played Matthau's curvy neighbor from next door who is always coming on to him. In the film's finale, Matthau backs out on his rendezvous with the elegant Claire Kelly because he realizes he really does love his wife. Morse, the seasoned cheater, gets caught in bed with Langdon! In the light-hearted western *The Cheyenne Social Club*, Langdon has less to do as one of a number of prostitutes living in a beautiful brothel inherited by disapproving cowboy James Stewart. While he thinks of ways to close the place down and turn it into a boardinghouse despite the protestations of the ladies of the social club and the townsmen, his laconic friend (Henry Fonda) samples the "fine ladies," including his barber—Opal Ann.

"*A Guide for the Married Man* is one of my most favorite films, because I think it was one of the funniest movies ever made," exclaims Langdon. "Walter Matthau is so adorable as the husband and Robert Morse is also very good. And all the famous actors who played the technical advisors were hilarious. Gene Kelly brilliantly directed *Guide*. I worked with him again on *The Cheyenne Social Club*. I had a great time working on this film too. It featured an amazing cast. I liked the character I played in this film as well. She was goofy and happy doing her job! I liked playing those roles. I was really in heaven working on this film. Jimmy Stewart was just wonderful to work with. We did a publicity tour for the film. Jimmy, Gene Kelly and I promoted the film in the western states. It was just so delightful to be around them. I miss them both."

Though she was appearing on drive-ins across America from 1964 to 1967, Langdon still found time to play a number of TV roles. She played a Russian naval officer assigned to PT 109 on *McHale's Navy*, a klutzy wife whose husband is kidnapped by a modern day pirate on *The Man from U.N.C.L.E.* and a Hollywood actress staring in a military training film on *No Time for Sergeants*. On *The Wild Wild West* Langdon's fans probably did a double take, as she first appeared as a prim young scholar. However, the episode's villain hypnotizes her character to only want to have fun and she morphs into a saloon girl (a role her fans expected) where she dances, drinks, and whoops it up with the town's cowboys. By the episode's end she returns to her dull self.

In 1970, Langdon was cast as Lillian Nuvo, the wife of Greek blue-collar foreman Arnie Nuvo (Herschel Bernardi) who is promoted to management in the sitcom *Arnie*. "I was shocked when they cast me as a housewife in *Arnie*," comments Sue Ane. "During my acceptance speech at the Golden Globe Awards I said, 'I never knew I would make it as a mother.' I had known Grant Tinker for years and adored him and his wife, Mary Tyler Moore. One day he called me to come up to his office and talk with him about this role in a pilot he was producing. To this day, I have no idea what possessed him to think of me to play a housewife."

Langdon reveals that the pilot for *Arnie* was very different from the series. In the pilot, Bernardi's Greek ethnicity was played up, as were the characters on the loading dock. The series focused on Arnie's relationship with his persnickety polo-playing boss (Roger Bowen) and his home life with his wife, children and crazy neighbor (Charles Nelson Reilly), the star of a TV cooking show. *Arnie* was predicted to be the big hit of the upcoming television season. "I did a lot of promotion for it," remembers Langdon. "Everybody felt our show was going to be the hottest thing on the air. CBS had so much confidence in us that they scheduled *Arnie* as the lead-in to *The Mary Tyler Moore Show* to help bring in a big audience for Mary. As it all turned out later, Mary surely didn't need us! When we came back to begin shooting the series, the creator of the show David Swift—rightly named—was gone. Grant Tinker wasn't involved anymore either. They brought in a whole new creative team who downplayed Arnie's Greek ethnicity and wrote off some characters. It became a completely different show and we were constantly trying to find the magic that we had in the pilot. They shifted the focus from the loading dock to the office. Roger Bowen played the boss and he was very funny. But we had an overall humorous situation with the pilot which wasn't there with the new writers. We struggled and struggled. Even with all that, the public liked us—we had a 36 share, which most shows would die to have. But we were not the mega hit that we were supposed to be. CBS had thought they were going to have another *All in the Family*." After its second season, the network cancelled the show.

Though disappointed with the creative team, Langdon won accolades for playing against type as Arnie's wife. She received back to back Golden Globe nominations, winning for the second season. Surprisingly, both years she was snubbed by the Emmys and failed to get even a nomination. "My producers told me that they had submitted my name for Emmy

Sue Ane Langdon celebrates St. Patrick's Day, Hollywood starlet-style.

consideration, but they hadn't," reveals Langdon. "I was very disappointed. To this day I don't understand it. It was one of those things that happen in your career that you can never figure out."

The '70s found Sue Ane Langdon concentrating on television over film. After *Arnie* was cancelled in 1972, Langdon did a number of TV guest stints. She was a regular on the short-lived dramatic series *Grandpa Goes to Washington* during the 1978–79 season, playing the daughter-in-law of Jack Albertson as a liberal political science professor elected senator who clashes with the ideals of his son (Larry Linville), a general in the Pentagon. ("*Grandpa* was short-lived because Jack Albertson became ill during the filming and passed on shortly after the conclusion.") Another short-lived series for Langdon was the situation comedy *When the Whistle Blows* in 1980, which centered around the blue-collar crew of an L.A. construction company. Langdon owned a Western bar with a "bucking bull" where the crew hung out after work.

The talented actress returned to feature films in 1979 playing supporting roles in two low budget horror films. *The Evictors* (1979) with Vic Morrow was about a couple who move into a haunted house in Louisiana, and *Without Warning* (1980), with Jack Palance and Martin Landau revolved around an alien who hunts humans with flesh-eating parasites. More lighthearted were her roles in the *Carrie* spoof *Zapped* (1982) with Scott Baio, its sequel *Zapped Again* (1990), and in the "totally awesome" comedy *The Vals* (1982). She also appeared with Peter Fonda and Jack Elam in the western, *Hawken's Breed* (1987).

Sue Ane Langdon's last film appearance was playing Weird Al Yankovic's aunt in the comedy *UHF* (1989). When asked why she hasn't worked since, Langdon reflects, "The parts I played in the '60s and '70s were fun and there is just not that kind of humor around anymore. The innocence is gone from films and all entertainment today. There is no gentle humor, it's all harsh, brash, and fast with absolutely no set up and no timing, and it's not funny! Everything is so 'real.' Seems like we've totally forgotten the goofy, zany, happy side of life. Even if the ladies I played were 'worldly' they still had an innocence and warmth about them—a reflection of the times, I guess. These parts and these people don't seem to exist anymore.

"I don't miss acting and I think it's probably not much fun being an actress today," continues Sue Ane Langdon. "Only occasionally do I see a part I wish I could have played. I've done films, TV, theatre, and starred on Broadway. I guess I got most of it out of my system." Instead, Langdon concentrates on meeting her fans at conventions and film festivals around the country. She has even emceed a number of them. "I get a kick out of goofing around with the audience and the people I introduce. It's fun seeing how much 'humanness' and laughter you can reach in a two or three minute conversation!"

Film Appearances

1960 **Strangers When We Meet** (Columbia) d. Richard Quine
The Great Imposter (Universal) d. Robert Mulligan

1964 **The New Interns** (Columbia) d. John Rich
Roustabout (Paramount) d. John Rich

1965 **The Rounders** (MGM) d. Burt Kennedy
When the Boys Meet the Girls (MGM) d. Alvin Ganzer

1966 **Hold On!** (MGM) d. Arthur Lubin

Frankie and Johnny (United Artists) d. Frederick De Cordova

A Fine Madness (Warner Bros.) d. Irvin Kershner

1967 **A Guide for the Married Man** (20th Century–Fox) d. Gene Kelly

A Man Called Dagger (MGM) d. Richard Rush

1970 **The Cheyenne Social Club** (National General) d. Gene Kelly

1972 **The Victim** (TV-movie) d. Herschel Daugherty

1979 **The Evictors** (AIP) d. Charles P. Pierce

1980 **Without Warning** (Filmways) d. Greydon Clark

1982 **Zapped!** (Embassy) d. Robert J. Rosenthal

The Vals (Jensen Farley Pictures) d. James Polakof

1987 **Hawken's Breed** (New World Pictures) d. Charles P. Pierce

1989 **UHF** (Orion) d. Jay Levey

1990 **Zapped Again!** (Direct-to-video) d. Douglas Campbell

Television Appearances: Drama, Comedy, & Variety Series

Get Set, Go! (co-host 6/9 to 9/22/1957) SYN
The Steve Allen Show 4/27/1958 NBC
Lux Playhouse "The Dreamer" 4/3/1959 CBS
Bachelor Father (recurring role as Kitty Marsh) 12/3/1959 to 9/1961 NBC
Bourbon Street Beat "The Light Touch of Terror" 12/7/1959 ABC
Alcoa Goodyear Theatre "All in the Family" a.k.a. "Togetherness" 3/28/1960
Shotgun Slade "Crossed Guns" 9/19/1960 SYN
Dan Raven "The High Cost of Fame" 9/23/1960 NBC
Coronado 9 "Blonde Herring" 9/28/1960 SYN
Surfside 6 "Local Girl" 10/31/1960 ABC
Three to Get Ready (unaired pilot) 1961 ABC
The Outlaws "Culley" 2/16/1961 NBC
Tales of Wells Fargo "Fraud" 3/13/1961 NBC
Surfside 6 "The Bhoyo and the Blonde" 5/15/1961 ABC
77 Sunset Strip "Mr. Goldilocks" 6/30/1961 ABC
Harrigan and Son "On Broadway" 9/22/1961 ABC
Perry Mason "The Case of the Crying Comedians" 10/14/1961 CBS
The Joey Bishop Show "The Bachelor" 10/25/1961 NBC
The Detectives "A Barrel Full of Monkeys" 10/27/1961 ABC
Bonanza "The Many Faces of Gideon Finch" 11/5/1961 NBC
Gunsmoke "Catawomper" 2/10/1962 CBS
Room for One More "The Girl from Sweden" 2/17/1962 ABC
Thriller "Cousin Tundifer" 2/19/1962 NBC
Margie "The Dangerous Age" 2/22/1962 ABC
The Dick Van Dyke Show "One Angry Man" 3/7/1962 CBS
Follow the Sun "The Inhuman Equation" 3/11/1962 ABC
The Andy Griffith Show "Three's a Crowd" 4/9/1962 CBS
Jackie Gleason and His American Scene Magazine (series regular) 9/29 to 11/18/1962 CBS
The Bill Dana Show "Jose the Playboy" 10/6/1963 NBC
77 Sunset Strip "The Fumble" 12/13/1963 ABC
Bob Hope Presents the Chrysler Theatre "The Square Peg" 3/6/1964 NBC
McHale's Navy "Comrades of PT 73" 3/17/1964 ABC
Summer Playhouse: The Apartment House (pilot) 9/5/1964 CBS
The Man from U.N.C.L.E. "The Shark Affair" 10/13/1964 NBC
Perry Mason "The Case of the Scandalous Sculptor" 10/18/1964 CBS
Bonanza "Hound Dog" 3/21/1965 NBC
No Time for Sergeants "The Velvet Wiggle" 5/3/1965 ABC
The Wild Wild West "The Night of the Steel Assassin" 1/7/1966 CBS

Perry Mason "The Case of the Avenging Angel" 3/13/1966 CBS
Summer Fun: Little Leatherneck (pilot) 7/29/1966 ABC
Ironside "The Challenge" 2/8/1968 NBC
Mannix "Merry-Go-Round for Murder" 4/5/1969 CBS
The Name of the Game "Give Till It Hurts" 10/31/1969 NBC
Arnie (series regular as Lillian Nuvo) 9/19/1970 to 9/9/1972 CBS
Love, American Style "Love and the Happy Couple" 12/11/1970 ABC
Love, American Style "Love and the House Bachelor" 12/17/1971 ABC
Rowan and Martin's Laugh-In [cameo] 1/24/1972 NBC
Super Comedy Bowl 2 (special) 1/12/1972 CBS
Rowan and Martin's Laugh-In [cameo] 2/28/1972 NBC
Rowan and Martin's Laugh-In [cameo] 11/13/1972 NBC
Police Surgeon (episode—title unknown) 1/23/1973 SYN
Honeymoon Suite (pilot) 3/12/1973 ABC
Here We Go Again (episode—title unknown) 3/17/1973 ABC
ABC Wide World of Mystery "Nightmare Step" 3/27/1973 ABC
Wrinkles, Birthdays and Other Fables (special) 10/29/1973 PBS
Police Story "Collision Course" 11/20/1973 NBC
Banacek "The Vanishing Chalice" 1/15/1974 NBC
Good Heavens "Coffee, Tea or Gloria" 6/26/1976 ABC
Grandpa Goes to Washington (series regular as Rosie Kelley) 9/7/1978 to 1/16/1979 NBC
When the Whistle Blows (series regular as Darlene Ridgeway) 3/14/1980 to 7/27/1980 ABC
Jackie Gleason: The Great One (special) 9/17/1980 CBS
The Love Boat "The Captain's Triangle/ Boomerang/ Out of This World" 12/13/1980 ABC
Three's Company "Urban Plowboy" 2/9/1982 ABC
Happy Days "All I Want for Christmas" 12/14/1982 ABC
Hart to Hart "Bahama Bound Harts" 2/22/1983 ABC
General Hospital [short-term role as Marge Pulaski] 1991 ABC

Television Appearances: Game & Talk Shows

Snap Judgement 6/26 to 6/30/1967 NBC
The Hollywood Squares 6/26 to 6/30/1967 NBC
The Hollywood Squares 8/14 to 8/18/1967 NBC
Pat Boone in Hollywood 9/18/1967 SYN
Pat Boone in Hollywood 2/6/1968 SYN
PDQ 2/19 to 2/23/1968 NBC
Pat Boone in Hollywood 3/13/1968 SYN
The Donald O'Connor Show 1/23/1969 SYN
The David Frost Show 7/14/1970 SYN
The Real Tom Kennedy Show 8/15/1970 SYN
The Hollywood Squares 10/12 to 10/16/1970 NBC
The Merv Griffin Show 10/20/1970 CBS
The Virginia Graham Show 3/18/1971 SYN
The Virginia Graham Show 4/29/1971 SYN
The Virginia Graham Show 6/1/1971 SYN
The Virginia Graham Show 7/12/1971 SYN
The Mike Douglas Show 7/19/1971 SYN
The Mike Douglas Show 8/28/1971 SYN
This Is Your Life "Hershel Bernardi" 10/21/1971 SYN
The Movie Game 10/15 to 10/29/1971 SYN
The Virginia Graham Show 11/5/1971 SYN
The Hollywood Squares 3/27 to 3/31/1972 NBC
The Virginia Graham Show 4/20/1972 SYN
The Virginia Graham Show 5/24/1972 SYN
The Hollywood Squares 5/92 to 6/2/1972 NBC
Jerry Visits 8/26/1972 SYN
It's Your Bet 12/11 to 12/15/1972 NBC
Celebrity Sweepstakes 9/2 to 9/6/1974 NBC
Cross-Wits 2/26 to 3/2/1979 SYN
All-Star Beat the Clock 1/21 to 1/25/1980 CBS

Also

The Ray Bolger Show, The Perry Como Show, The Phil Silvers Show, and *Kid Talk*

☆ Donna Loren ☆

The All-American girl, Donna Loren was a talented singer and one of the most popular teenage performers during the mid-sixties. In 1963, she became the "Dr. Pepper Girl" and the pretty vocalist propelled herself into a record contract and then drive-in movie nirvana. Her duet with Dick Dale in *Muscle Beach Party* (1963) so impressed the founders of AIP that she was signed to a multi-picture deal and quickly followed this up with demurely clad roles in *Bikini Beach* (1964) and *Pajama Party* (1964). Loren had a banner 1965, as she could be seen on the small screen as the in-house female vocalist on *Shindig*, while she flickered on the big screen in *Beach Blanket Bingo* and *Sergeant Deadhead*. But by the time free love and LSD were the rage, the newly married Loren quietly faded from the spotlight to raise a family.

The 5'3½" beauty was born Donna Zukor in Boston, Massachusetts, on March 7, 1947. Her adopted father, Morris Zukor, was an artist-animator who relocated his family to Los Angeles when Donna was an infant. She made her public singing debut at the age of five in a local amateur show. ("I was very shy but I loved to sing, so my parents convinced me to perform because I was 'making people happy.'") This led her to a small role on *Playhouse 90*, then to a regular gig on the live radio program *Sqeakin' Deacon* with James Burton. Her first TV commercial was singing the jingle for Meadowgold Ice Cream.

Though she did not become a Mouseketeer, Walt Disney was impressed enough to feature her in the segment "Talent Round-Up" on *The Mickey Mouse Club* in 1957. ("I met Annette Funicello when I appeared on *The Mickey Mouse Club*. She was fourteen. I never developed a relationship with either one," jokes Loren.) Donna's singing caught the attention of a record promoter and she recorded for various labels but did not score a hit record. She did get a name change. "Jimmy Bowen produced my record 'Hands Off' and paired my first name with Loren from a L.A. phonebook. It is my legal name."

In late 1963, Loren beat out hundreds of young females to become the "Dr. Pepper Girl." As spokesperson for the soft drink, she appeared in TV and radio spots, on billboards, in magazines and made personal appearances across the country to promote Dr. Pepper to a younger market. Her contract with the soda company got her frequent exposure on *American Bandstand* ("Dick Clark was always supportive of me") and then a chance to sing on the big screen in *Muscle Beach Party* (1964). Loren was teamed with Dick Dale and sang the song "Muscle Bustle" written by Gary Usher, Roger Christian, and Brian Wilson of the Beach Boys. Unlike the scantily glad beach boys and girls around her, Loren remained prim and properly clad. In her later appearances she wore only one-piece or occasional modest two-piece bathing suits. Her contract with Dr. Pepper and the image she wished to project to the teenagers of America forbade her from shaking her body in a bikini. She commented to writer Christopher Gardner of *Parade* magazine in 1965, "You have to leave something to the imagination. Just because a girl's navel is showing doesn't make her more interesting. Besides, my first allegiance is to the soda firm I represent and I can't destroy my demure young lady image, now can I?" On the same subject, Loren was more candid with the *Saturday Evening Post* and remarked, "I don't believe in going up there and sticking a bikini on and shaking around."

Donna Loren, the "Dr. Pepper Girl," singer, and actress.

However, in 1965 Loren's morals may have loosened up a bit as she was photographed frolicking in the surf with boyfriend Paul Petersen for a photo layout for *Modern Screen*.

Loren was such a hit in *Muscle Beach Party* that American International Pictures signed her for four more films. In *Bikini Beach* (1964) Loren had no lines but was given a solo number to perform. Clad in a two-piece bathing suit with the bottom a pleated skirt, she rocked on the song "Love's a Secret Weapon" by Jerry Styner and Guy Hemric, while Candy Johnson and the surfer crowd danced a wild Watusi around her. When asked what stands out for her most from her first two beach movies, Loren responds, "I was most impressed with the make-up men completely 'tanning' all the body builders [in *Muscle Beach Party*]." Loren never mingled with the actors playing the surfer boys and beach girls because she was well chaperoned by her adopted father. Frequent beach girl Salli Sachse commented in *Fantasy Femmes of the Sixties*, "I remember Donna Loren's father was always on the set. He was very overprotective of her and would even follow her to the bathroom! He was just so afraid that some guy was going to hit on her or something." It must be remembered that Donna was only sixteen to eighteen years old when she appeared in these movies, while the other actors were in their early twenties. Loren commented to the *Saturday Evening Post*, "On one of these sets you can learn about life in three weeks. Thank God, I have parents who are guiding me and helping me."

In the fall of 1964, Donna Loren became a semi-regular on the new music TV series *Shindig*, created and produced by Jack Good who had previously produced teen music shows in Great Britain. This was the first rock music show to feature live (not lip-synched) performances by some of the decade's biggest superstars. L.A. disc jockey Jimmy O'Neill hosted the program, which also featured an array of semi-regular performers including Loren, Bobby Sherman ("He was definitely a teen idol"), Darlene Love and the Blossoms, and the Wellingtons. During the course of its one and a half seasons on the air, a number of top rock acts made appearances including the Rolling Stones, Aretha Franklin, the Beach Boys, James Brown, the Supremes, Tina Turner, Sonny and Cher, the Dave Clark Five, Marvin Gaye, Herman's Hermits, and Lesley Gore. Loren recalls, "When the Turtles were on I offered to give one of them a hair cut (a hobby of mine usually reserved for that special someone in my life). So the dress rehearsal was the long version and the show was the short cut. Another time, the Kinks mooned me from their dressing room. Another fond memory is when Bill Medley [of the Righteous

Brothers] sang 'Georgia on My Mind' to Ray Charles with Billy Preston on organ. Ray loved it. It was never televised." During its first season *Shindig* aired for an hour. With the start of the second season it was shown twice a week in half-hour installments. Loren appeared much less frequently during this season. Her last episode was in November of 1965, and *Shindig* was cancelled soon after in January 1966 to make room on the ABC schedule for *Batman*.

Back on the big screen, Loren not only sang but also had a speaking role in her third AIP movie *Pajama Party* (1964). She played Vicki, the ex-girlfriend of Big Lunk (Jody McCrea) who is now dating Dee Dee (Annette Funicello). Vicki tries to give Dee Dee advice when the under appreciated girl complains of Big Lunk's lack of attention. Though not a typical *Beach Party* movie—Frankie Avalon cameos as a Martian while leading man chores are taken over by Tommy Kirk—the movie nevertheless has one of the better soundtracks, featuring tunes by Jerry Styner and Guy Hemric. Though Annette sings most of them, the songwriters handed Loren arguably the film's best song called "Among the Young." Loren warbles the tune on a bandstand at the beach (backed by the rock group the Pyramids) while perennial go-go girl Candy Johnson sets the stage afire with her wild dance gyrations.

In early 1965, Loren still was focusing her attention on her singing career. The previous year, Voyle Gilmore signed

Muscle Beach Party (AIP, 1964) featured Donna Loren in her screen debut singing a duet with Dick Dale.

her to a record deal with Capitol Records. He was the man who was partly responsible for bringing the Beach Boys to the same label. He first saw Loren perform at the Aragon Ballroom where she opened for Dick Dale. Gilmore remarked to Mark Heater, writing in the November 1979 issue of *California Music* magazine, that "I was sitting in the audience when Donna came on to sing. In thirty years in watching performers I have never seen one to match her in stage presence and ability to capture attention. The amazing thing is that this same rapport is evident on her records."

Donna released two singles with Capitol in 1964 but neither one charted. Even though Loren had a national venue

No bikinis allowed for good girls Annette Funicello (left) and Donna Loren (right) seen here in *Pajama Party* (AIP, 1964). *Billy Rose Theatre Collection, The New York Public Library for the Performing Arts, Astor, Lenox and Tilden Foundations.*

to perform some of them on *Shindig,* none caught on with the teenage public. This may have been due to the advent of the British invasion. Performers from across the ocean such as The Beatles, the Rolling Stones, Herman's Hermits, the Dave Clark Five, Petula Clark, etc. knocked most of the American acts off the charts. Especially hurt during this was the Girl Group sound, which Loren fell into. Though she was extremely popular on TV and in movies, it didn't translate to record sales, probably due to the times, as Loren was a talented vocalist along the lines of Lesley Gore. She even sang one of Gore's hit records, "Sunshine, Lollipops, and Rainbows" on *Shindig.* As proof of Donna's singing ability, her performance in her next beach movie is truly a standout. Loren turns up early in *Beach Blanket Bingo* (1965) to sing the heart wrenching song (and her personal favorite), "It Only Hurts When I Cry," by Guy Hemric and Jerry Styner. As she sings, Jody McCrea as Lunkhead is seen with tears streaming down his cheeks. By the end of the song it is revealed that he has been peeling onions.

The movie was another big hit for AIP, and in an unusual move, Capitol Records issued the soundtrack album entitled *Beach Blanket Bingo* with all the songs re-recorded by Donna Loren. The tie-in LP was produced by David Axelrod and arranged and conducted by H. B. Barnum. Loren cut all the tracks in fourteen hours for her one and only album. Axelrod and songwriter Guy Hemric thought "Cycle Set" (originally sung by The Hondells in the film) was the album's best record and tried pushing it as a single. Loren sang it on *Shindig* and other televised teenage music shows, but the song never charted. She followed this up with the single "New Love," but that too failed. As for the album, though Loren's voice is in top form, the LP sold a disappointing 20,000 copies despite Capitol's big push. Loren released one more single for Capitol, a silly dance craze song entitled "So, Do the Zonk" before her contract with the record label came to an end in 1966.

In 1965, Loren began concentrating more on acting. Because of her dark hair and features, Loren was suitable for various ethnic roles on TV. Between *Shindig* appearances, she played her first dramatic role, that of Italian-American Anna Perrona, a high school dropout who is waiting anxiously to see if she will be chosen to receive a kidney transplant in a multipart story arc on *Dr. Kildare*. Loren's hard work paid off and the charming beauty was chosen a Hollywood Deb Star for 1965.

After being notably absent in AIP's *Ski Party* (1965) and *How to Stuff a Wild Bikini* (1965), it was back to the big screen for Loren, who scored her biggest acting role in *Sergeant Deadhead* (1965), her last drive-in movie for the studio. She played the naïve Susan, a WAF and best friend to the befuddled Col. Lucy Turner (Deborah Walley) whose wedding day to Sgt. O. K. Deadhead (Frankie Avalon) is approaching. However, Deadhead was accidentally trapped in a rocket and launched into space. Though rescued, the ride into space has altered his personality, turning the mild-mannered serviceman into a crazed girl-chaser. The Air Force imprisons Deadhead on his wedding day and sends his look-alike Sgt. Donovan (Avalon) to take his place. Deadhead escapes and is able to take his rightful place on the honeymoon as his original personality emerges. Loren, along with Bobbi Shaw and some of the other girls, helps out Deborah Walley on the song "How Can You Tell," performed in the barracks and later she sings solo "Two-Timin' Angel," during the couple's wedding reception. Guy Hemric and Jerry Styner wrote both songs. Loren impressed the editors of *Photoplay* enough, who nominated her for the magazine's Gold Medal Award in 1965 for Most Promising New Star (Female) [Pat Morrow of TV's *Peyton Place* won].

Loren's last appearance on *Shindig* was on Nov. 20, 1965, singing "Take Me in Your Arms." The series was cancelled shortly after that in January of 1966. Loren continued making the TV music show rounds, as she was pushing her newest Capitol single "If You Really Loved Me" on *Where the Action Is* and *American Bandstand*. Loren then turned up on a two-part *Batman* episode playing Susie, a misguided, greedy high school cheerleader ("The reason I've taken up crime is so I could get a taste of the finer things in life"). The nefarious Joker (Cesare Romero) recruits the teenager to join his gang called the Bad Pennies. "I remember that this show was the fourth one being filmed," says Donna. "While driving onto the [studio] lot, fans were literally climbing on the chain-link fence. I must admit Adam West had very soft lips the one and only time he kissed me—strictly platonic."

In the fall of 1966, Loren was signed to appear in four episodes of Milton Berle's new variety series that was entitled (what else?) *The Milton Berle Show*. Loren and singer Bobby Rydell were added to the series in hopes of attracting a younger audience. They didn't, as this misfire (a

WAFs Donna Loren (center) and Deborah Walley (right) panic when their base is put on red alert in *Sergeant Deadhead* (AIP, 1965).

throwback to Berle's earlier *Texaco Star Theater*) was cancelled after only thirteen episodes, despite the appearances of some top-flight guest stars including Lucille Ball, Joey Bishop, David Janssen, and Adam West. "Milton Berle was tough," remembers Loren. "One of the character actresses showed up on crutches for rehearsal and specifically asked him to take it easy on her. He deliberately treated her very rough and showed no sympathy for her broken leg."

Donna Loren remained busy in 1967 and 1968. She left Capitol Records and signed with Warner Bros./ Reprise. However, continuing with her unlucky streak the two singles she cut for her new record label went nowhere. Despite this, Donna Loren was as popular as ever. The "Dr Pepper Girl" began writing two monthly columns for *Movie Life Magazine* called "Let's Talk It Over" and "Donna Loren's Young Hollywood." She was in demand on television, appearing on the game show and talk show circuit while still accepting acting offers. On *The Monkees*, she played an Arabian princess named Colette whose father, King Yahuin of Naduhi, decides it is time for her to marry. She rejects his choice of the sinister Prime Minister and chooses Davy Jones from a magazine instead. All sorts of trouble follows when The Monkees are whisked off to Naduhi and the fellows try to keep a smitten Davy from saying, "I do." ("I was a very happy princess on *The Monkees*," reveals Donna. "Of course, Casanova Davy Jones won my heart for a long moment.") In the TV pilot *Two for Penny*, Loren was cast in the title role of a young put-upon Greek-American whose two older well-meaning brothers (Michael Constantine and Lou Antonio) not only run a delicatessen but Penny's life as well. Lastly in 1968, ala *Romeo and Juliet*, Loren convincingly played a Hungarian-American girl who gets Gomer (Jim Nabors) to intervene when her old-fashioned parents won't let her marry the son from a feuding family on *Gomer Pyle, USMC*.

By mid–1968, Loren shocked Hollywood and her young fans when she completely walked away from her singing and acting career at the height of her popularity. On her twenty-first birthday, she had her contract with Dr. Pepper terminated and shortly thereafter married Lenny Waronker, president of Warner Bros. Records. She then devoted her time to her marriage and children.

Today, Donna Loren resides in Hawaii and is a fashion designer. Loren always had a desire to create her own line of clothing. She began sewing her own clothes when she was a teenager and when she was seventeen years old she became the spokesperson for Simplicity Jiffy patterns. Loren and her current husband Jered Cargman head the ADASA Hawaii fashion design house featuring clothes by Loren, who has begun developing a reputation as a world-class couture designer with her own line of hand-made French silk fashions. Each of these exquisite creations is made by Loren's own hand with the aid of various seamstresses in a studio above her shop. "When I moved to Hawaii, I had enough time for myself and I developed a more serious interest in promoting my designs," says Loren. "It is incredibly inspirational watching Hawaiian sunsets, so I started producing hand-painted French silk jersey sunset T-shirts, which sold out. Then I moved into growing roses and having them painted, as well as other flowers, by professional silk painters on my rare French silk. One of these dresses was chosen to be on the cover of *Honolulu Magazine*. Since then I've been encouraged to make my work more visible." In 1998, Donna Loren was chosen by *Honolulu Magazine* as one of Hawaii's best new designers.

Though Loren has a new life miles away from the Hollywood scene, she has not totally abandoned her past. In 2001, her *Beach Blanket Bingo* LP was reissued

Donna Loren, the girl-next-door.

on CD as *The Very Best of Donna Loren* from Collectible Records with nine bonus tracks including "So, Do the Zonk" and Loren's haunting version of "Call Me." It can be purchased, along with Donna's creations, from her web site.

In conclusion, Donna Loren says emphatically, "I enjoy rekindling my interests and sharing them with the public, so that's what I'll do until I roll over for the last time. Life has been good to me within the roller coaster rides, so onward and upward!"

Filmography

1964 **Muscle Beach Party** (AIP) d. William Asher
   Bikini Beach (AIP) d. William Asher
   Pajama Party (AIP) d. Don Weis
1965 **Beach Blanket Bingo** (AIP) d. William Asher
   Sergeant Deadhead (AIP) d. Norman Taurog

Television Appearances

The Mickey Mouse Club "Talent Round-Up" 3/7/1957 ABC
American Bandstand 11/23/1963 ABC
Shindig [singing "Wishin' and Hopin'"] 9/16/1964 ABC
Shindig [singing "It's All Right"] 9/30/1964 ABC
Shindig [singing "Down the Line" & "That's What Love Is Made Of"] 10/21/1964 ABC
Shindig [singing "African Waltz"] 11/18/1964 ABC
Shindig [singing "Too Many Fish in the Sea"] 11/25/1964 ABC
Shindig [singing "Rock Me in the Cradle of Love" & with Bobby Sherman, "Casting My Spell Over You"] 12/2/1964 ABC
Shindig [singing "Santa Claus Is Coming to Town" & with Bobby Sherman, "Keep on Searching"] 12/23/1964 ABC
Shindig [singing "Ten Good Reasons"] 12/30/1964 ABC
The Hollywood Deb Stars of 1965 (special) [Deb Star] 1/2/1965 ABC
Shindig [singing "90 Day Guarantee"] 1/6/1965 ABC
Shindig [singing "Rock 'n' Roll Music," "Ten Good Reasons" & "Boys"] 1/20/1965 ABC
American Bandstand 1/30/1965 ABC
Shindig [singing "Personality" & "Ave Maria"] 2/3/1965 ABC
American Bandstand 2/6/1965 ABC
Shindig [singing "The Boy from New York City"] 2/10/1965 ABC
Shindig [singing "Blue Suede Shoes" & "With the Wind and the Rain in Your Hair"] 2/24/1965 ABC
Shindig [singing "I'm Ready" & with Bobby Sherman, "Just One Look"] 3/10/1965 ABC
Shindig [singing "Goldfinger"] 3/24/1965 ABC
Shindig [singing "Got to Get You Off of My Mind"] 4/7/1965 ABC
Shindig [singing "Talk About Love" & "Finger Poppin'"] 4/14/1965 ABC
Shindig [singing "I Know a Place" & with Bobby Sherman, "Heebie Jeebies"] 4/28/1965 ABC
Shindig [singing "Cycle Set" & "Into My Heart"] 5/19/1965 ABC
Go! Go! 5/24/1965 SYN
Celebrity Game 6/17/1965 CBS
What's This Song? 6/21 to 6/25/1965 NBC
Shindig [singing "Rock Me in the Cradle of Love," "My Boyfriend's Back" & with Bobby Sherman, "Casting My Spell on You"] 6/30/1965 ABC
Shindig [singing "Shakin' All Over" & "Bad Boy"] 7/7/1965 ABC
Shindig [singing "Long Live Love," "To Know Him Is to Love Him" & "Reelin' and Rockin'"] 7/28/1965 ABC
You Don't Say! 8/2 to 8/6/1965 NBC
Shindig [singing "Sunshine, Lollipops and Rainbows" & "All My Loving"] 8/11/1965 ABC
Shindig [singing "You've Got Your Troubles"] 9/28/1965 ABC
Shindig [singing "The Way of Love"] 10/14/1965 ABC
Dr. Kildare "The Life Machine" 10/26/1965 NBC

Dr. Kildare "Toast the Golden Couple" 11/1/1965 NBC
Dr. Kildare "Wives and Losers" 11/2/1965 NBC
Dr. Kildare "Welcome Home, Dear Anna" 11/8/1965 NBC
Dr. Kildare "A Little Child Shall Lead Them" 11/9/1965 NBC
Shindig [singing "Where Have All the Flowers Gone?"] 11/13/1965 ABC
Dr. Kildare "Hour of Decision" 11/15/1965 NBC
Dr. Kildare "Aftermath" 11/16/1965 NBC
Shindig [singing "Take Me in Your Arms"] 11/20/1965 ABC
Hollywood a Go-Go 1/14/1966 SYN
Where the Action Is [singing "If You Really Love Me"] 2/3/1966 ABC
The Red Skelton Show [singing "Johnny One-Note" & "The Way of Love"] 2/15/1966 CBS
American Bandstand [singing "If You Really Love Me"] 2/26/1966 ABC
Batman "The Joker Goes to School" 3/2/1966 ABC
Batman "He Meets His Match, The Grisly Ghoul" 3/3/1966 ABC
You Don't Say 4/11 to 4/15/1966 NBC
American Bandstand [singing "I Believe"] 7/23/1966 ABC
The Milton Berle Show [series regular] 9/16 to 10/21/1966 NBC
The Hollywood Squares 11/28 to 12/2/1966 NBC
The Hollywood Squares 1/30 to 2/3/1967 NBC
American Bandstand [singing "Let's Pretend"] 7/8/1967 ABC
The Monkees "Everywhere a Sheik, Sheik" 9/25/1967 NBC
The Pat Boone Show 1/29/1968 NBC
The Woody Woodbury Show 2/2/1968 SYN
The Mothers-in-Law "Herb's Little Helpers" 2/11/1968 NBC
The Danny Thomas Hour: Two for Penny (pilot) 3/11/1968 NBC
Gomer Pyle, USMC "Love and Goulash" 3/29/1968 CBS
Hollywood Rocks the Movies: The Early Years (1955–1970) (special) 7/2/2000 AMC

Also

Playhouse 90

☆ VITINA MARCUS ☆

Vitina Marcus (now known as simply Vitina) was an exotic beauty who was typecast as jungle women, Indian maidens, and space girls in films and television throughout the '60s. A student of Lee Strasberg, Vitina was probably the most well trained starlet to ever don a loincloth on screen. Drive-in fans remember her best as the helpful native girl in *The Lost World* (1960) while to TV viewers she will always be Athena, the Green Girl from *Lost in Space*.

Dolores Vitina Marcus was born in Brooklyn, New York. Her parents were Rose and Frank Marcus, though Vitina confessed she felt closer to her Sicilian grandmother who also named Vitina. As a young girl in Bensonhurst she studied ballet and took violin lessons. She blossomed into a striking beauty and when a teenager she was voted Miss Bensonhurst before moving into Manhattan to pursue a career in dance. Vitina modeled for the Huntington Hartford Agency and began studying acting at the prestigious Lee Strasberg's Actor's Workshop. "I was about seventeen years old when I started," recalls Vitina. "I had to choose my first scene for Lee Strasberg's class playing a prostitute—he required this for all new actresses. I was very innocent at that time—perhaps most of us were all innocent in those days—so I

Exotic and wild, Vitina Marcus as the Native Girl in *The Lost World* (20th Century-Fox, 1960) had every teenage boy's heart racing.

The newcomer studied at the Actor's Workshop during the time Marilyn Monroe was there. "I was very impressed with her extreme sensitivity and sweetness," says Vitina fondly. "We talked and we did some Improv. She told me that she thought it was so great that I was in the class learning so much. It was a very good experience for me." Vitina's next teacher in New York was Frank Corsaro, who had done the Broadway show *A Hatful of Rain*. He cast her in the part of Putski in an Off-Broadway version of it. "Putski was a highly sex-charged woman who is naked under a raincoat. It was my first taste of playing to a large audience and I loved the energy. It just turned me on. I think that's what's part of the addiction of being an actor—the exchange of energy along with everything else."

During this time, Vitina was also working as a showgirl on *The Jackie Gleason Show*. Recalling The Great One, she says, "Jackie Gleason was very gallant. After each show, he'd send every girl a dozen roses in a box. I was chauffeured around in limousines to make personal appearances for the show. It was very exciting for me since I was only seventeen at the time."

In 1958, Vitina landed her first film role in *Never Love a Stranger*, based on the novel by Harold Robbins. ("I was having something to eat at this drugstore where all the actors hung out and somebody said, 'Hey, they're filming a movie in the Bronx.' I went up there and I got a part.") Billed as Dolores Vitina, she received excellent reviews playing John Drew Barymore's mother who dies shortly after giving birth to her son who grows up to be a racketeer. The film is most famous though for introducing a young Steve McQueen

put on this lovely negligee and chose a scene. I played the character imagining her mannerisms of a child but in a grown woman's body. I played her without the conventional ideal. Apparently, I must have done a good job because Lee Strasberg gave me a very positive analysis.

"A few of us did a workshop play and invited agents to come watch. I had my pick of all the top agencies in the city. The next thing I knew I was starring in a live television show and flown to Hollywood. I went out there to test for *Rio Bravo*. Angie Dickinson got the part. She was a semi-star then but I was a young nobody. While there I did do a leading role in a *Schlitz Playhouse* TV episode."

to movie audiences. "I didn't work with Steve McQueen in the movie but I appeared with him in a regional production of *A Hatful of Rain*," says Vitina. "He terrified me while he was driving several of us around. He drove down this steep hill at full speed. I thought we were going to die! He loved frightening us. A few years later when he was married and living in Hollywood, I was invited to one of his parties at his home."

With her career going strong, the dark-haired ingenue was off to Hollywood. A friend, who unknown to Vitina was independently wealthy playing agent, began representing her and took the young actress to 20th Century–Fox. The studio bigwigs wanted to test her to become a contract player but she said no. "This might have been a *big* mistake," admits Vitina. "I don't know if that I had issues in my childhood. I just wanted to be free and independent, which might have made life more difficult for me. I had an aversion to being under contract to a studio because I did not want to be owned and manipulated."

Though headstrong Vitina did not sign with Fox, unbeknownst to her producer Irwin Allen had spotted the back of her head as she stepped into an elevator on the lot and was frantically trying to track her down. Allen contacted Vitina's agent and the perplexed actress was back to the studio for another interview. "I didn't know I was going to meet Irwin Allen," says Vitina. "When I walked in he said, 'Do you know why you are here?' I really

In *The Lost World* (20th Century–Fox, 1960) Vitina Marcus and David Hedison are trapped in a giant spider's web.

didn't know who he was. The next thing I know I'm testing for and then cast in *The Lost World*. At that time my daughter was only about seven months old. I hired a private nurse to stay at my house to take care of my baby while I was working."

A hit with the teenage drive-in crowd, *The Lost World* (1960) was based on a story by Sir Arthur Conan Doyle and was a remake of the 1925 movie. In this version, Claude Rains played a zoology professor and discoverer of the "lost world." He rounds up a group including Michael Rennie as a big game hunter, Jill St. John as an adventuress, Ray Stricklyn as her brother, David Hedison as a newsman, and Fernando Lamas as a pilot to accompany him on his next exploration. The group becomes stranded in the "lost world" when a brontosaurus destroys their helicopter. Vitina played a native girl who is spotted by the explorers and flees from them. She is nearly caught in the web of a giant spider but is saved by Hedison. The agitated girl keeps trying to escape but when Stricklyn saves her from Lamas' travel partner who attempts to rape her, she becomes appreciative. The native girl eventually escapes and returns to her tribe but she becomes the group's savior when they are captured and are to be sacrificed to the natives' God. She frees the group as the rampaging natives pursue them. Marcus leads the explorers through a passageway complete with the huge remains of a monster in the Graveyard of the Damned, a narrow ledge above a pit of seething lava, and the hideous Fire Monster. When they reach safety, Stricklyn, who has fallen for the jungle beauty, decides to bring her back to civilization.

Vitina only has the fondest memories of making *The Lost World*. It was a fun experience for her. Though she had no lines, as her character doesn't speak English, she needed to express emotions with her face and body, which she did excellently. Her character also does a lot of running and climbing. ("I had some training as a dancer so I was used to being very physical.") Vitina too enjoyed working with the entire cast but what sticks out in her mind is the friendliness of Michael Rennie ("He was a very sweet, kind person") and the generosity of Jill St. John, of all people. "I had just learned to drive and I owned this big old Chrysler convertible," recalls Vitina with a laugh. "One night it was pouring rain when we left the studio and the top of my car would not go up. I couldn't drive the car home. Jill very graciously invited me to stay in the guestroom at her house. She was married at that time to Lance Reventlow. Jill was very friendly and we drove back to the studio the next day. I was relieved to be able to be on time."

Overall, the press praised the special effects in *The Lost World* and highly recommended the adventure film to adolescents but felt the story was too plodding and the characters uninteresting for adults. The reviewer in *Variety* was the exception and exclaimed, "Watching 'The Lost World' is tantamount to taking a trip through a Coney Island fun house." As for Vitina, her most notable notice came from the *New York Times*, whose critic remarked that she was "a comely lass in a revealing suede outfit."

The Lost World got Vitina noticed by casting directors at all the studios, but more importantly it boosted her career, as producer Irwin Allen would go on to cast her in three of his television series though never in a regular role. "Irwin Allen was a Gemini and he had two sides to him," remarks Vitina. "He was very touched by my baby and me. He always wanted to make sure my little girl was all right. Professionally, he was all over the place, talking very fast and shaking people up. He was here—he was there. No matter what department it was, he was there supervising. I was kind of surprised about our friendship because even though he made most other people very nervous he usually spoke in a calm, considerate matter to me. In other ways I found him frustrating, especially if I got a part in another show he'd grill me and ask, 'Who did you work for?' That upset me because I was fearful that he might influence other people not to hire me. There were many things I liked and admired about Irwin Allen; however, he was known to be very possessive of the people he employed."

With her long jet-black hair, olive complexion, high cheekbones, and dark penetrating eyes, the aspiring actress began getting typecast as Native Americans on TV westerns. She played a woman accused of killing her tribe's chief on *Gunslinger*, an Indian maiden who takes up with a widower on *Gunsmoke*, and a squaw named Wankshum on *Rawhide*. Back on the big screen, Vitina won a medium-size role as a hot-blooded gypsy opposite Tony Curtis and Yul Brynner in the epic film *Taras Bulba* (1962), about the powerful Cossack leader and his tribe in 16th century Ukraine. But unfortunately most of her scenes were excised from the movie. ("It was very disappointing for me.") However, that didn't stop the producers from using Vitina's lovely visage on a few of the film's poster ads. Recalling the shoot, Vitina says, "All my scenes were with Tony Curtis but he was busy with his new love Christine Kaufmann [who was also in the movie] so he wasn't always available. Yul Brynner stood in for him all the time. I had admired him since seeing him in *The King and I* and here he was now playing stand-in for me! He was very nice. Soon the rumors started about us. All a man has to do is talk to a woman on a set and the tongues start to wag. Some guys started to say a few derogatory things to me and Yul made them apologize. I always respected him for that."

Vitina's last film appearance was playing a tiny role in *Bedtime Story* (1964) starring David Niven and Marlon Brando. ("I don't remember anything about this film. It was a very small part, but work is work. At the time I needed the money to support my daughter and me.") It wasn't a lack of talent that kept Vitina off the big screen but a lack of guidance. "I didn't vigorously try for film roles," she reveals. "I didn't do more in the movie business because I wasn't 'out there' socializing and I didn't have a manager."

Irwin Allen though kept Vitina busy on television. In "Turn Back the Clock" on *Voyage to the Bottom of the Sea*, she reprised her role from *The Lost World* as the ever cost conscious Allen used footage and outtakes from that film, which he incorporated into this episode. Captain Crane (David Hedison) and Admiral Nelson (Richard Basehart) of the Seaview accompany a recently rescued scientist (Nick Adams), who is suffering from temporary amnesia, and his photographer girlfriend (Yvonne Craig) to the spot where he, Craig's father (Les Tremayne) and two others were lost. Their diving bell is swept up into a lost world full of dinosaurs and jungle people. From this point the plot follows almost exactly the story in the movie. Hedison sees Vitina's jungle girl and chases her through a cave complete with a giant spider. This entire sequence was lifted from *The Lost World*. After being captured by the girl's tribe, the group is held prisoner in a cave waiting to be sacrificed to the tribe's gods. They then discover that Craig's father is still alive. As in the movie, Vitina's native girl helps them escape and leads them to safety.

Understandably almost forty years later, Vitina does not recall much about making "Turn Back the Clock." But she does remember fondly her second appearance on *Voyage to the Bottom of the Sea* in "The Return of the Phantom," where she played a dead Island girl who returns in a ghost-like form and a woman whose body is picked as a vessel for the deceased's spirit. "I enjoyed playing two roles in this episode," says Vitina with a smile. "One character was a wild dancer in a nightclub and the other a very spiritual woman who was very ethical and moral and attempts to have her ex-love do the right thing. However he wants her back so badly that he wants to find a different body (the nightclub dancer) to put her soul into. I found these roles interesting."

Television roles continued coming Vitina's way, including playing a gypsy fortune teller on *The Travels of Jaime McPheeters* and the lead guest role as a female Tarzan on an episode of *The Man from U.N.C.L.E.* Unfortunately, this is considered the silliest of the popular spy show's output and a big disappointment for the series' fans. David McCallum's Illya Kuryakin disappears while on assignment in an African country, and Robert Vaughn as agent Napoleon Solo is sent to find him. He encounters Vitina as Girl, a beauty raised by apes and who has a pet gorilla named Baby. She teams up with Solo to find the missing U.N.C.L.E. agent. "I exaggerated to get this role," reveals Vitina. "They asked me if I would be able to carry Robert Vaughn over my shoulder. I said sure and that I was lifting weights since I was a teenager, which was true. I military pressed seventy pounds at age fourteen. However, Robert Vaughn was very heavy for me."

Though Vitina enjoyed playing the roles she was offered and needed the money to support her daughter, she was frustrated that none of the parts offered her required much of an acting stretch. Her looks seemed to have typecast her in these exotic roles. "People were always wondering what my nationality was," says Vitina. "In fact, one of my agents told me I belonged in Europe and that I would probably get a lot of work there. At that time in Hollywood there was a certain typecasting and of course now it's changed. I felt very sad because I didn't want to leave America to go work in Europe."

Vitina remained in Hollywood and soon she played her most remembered role that of Athena, the Green Lady on two episodes of Irwin Allen's hit science fiction TV series, *Lost in Space*. She is perhaps one of the sexiest space babes to appear on any '60s TV fantasy program. With a number of roles under her belt, the dark-haired beauty did not have to test for the role of Athena (the character was named by Allen after Vitina's daughter Athena), as the wise producer knew enough of her ability to handle the part extremely well. She walked into his office with the *Lost in Space* sponsors and as he introduced her he said, "Gentlemen, this is the Green

An intense looking Vitina Marcus as a gypsy fortune teller on an episode of the TV western series *The Travels of Jaime McPheeters* (MGM-TV, 1964).

Lady." Vitina told writer Will Viharo, "Before anything was filmed, I worked with the stuntman. It was an experience for me being in a harness, hanging way up there, and even going upside down. There was a technique to having your head face the floor, your legs straight up, then getting yourself back!"

In her first appearance on *Lost in Space*, the cat suit clad Athena floats in space as she hypnotizes Jonathan Harris' Dr. Smith (summoning him Lorelei style) to join her and to bring her the Jupiter 2's fuel that her race needs for sustenance. Vitina was such a hit as the green alien that the show's advertisers asked for her to be brought back in another episode. Allen had one specially written for Vitina, as Athena turns up on the planet where the Robinson family has landed. She is still infatuated with wily Dr. Smith ("handsome, pretty, handsome" she coos) and draws him in to fight off her ex-boyfriend, the green ogre Urso from her home planet who wants Athena back. Vitina only has the fondest of memories of playing the Green Lady. "Athena was the most fun role to play. Paul Zastupnevich created the costume specifically for me and the head of the studio makeup department, Ben Nye, did the makeup every morning. It was a very intricate process because he did a lot of shading with gold, blue and green. I would come to work extra early for him to do it.

"I so enjoyed working with Jonathan Harris," continues Vitina. "I was fascinated with his wit. All these clever remarks would just pop out of his head. He was so very witty. He had a way of doing and saying things that is strictly *Jonathan Harris*."

Vitina ended the decade appearing in two episodes of Irwin Allen's *Time Tunnel*, one of which she worked with Robert Duvall. "He saved my daughter's life when some of us went horseback riding up in North Hollywood," whispers Vitina. "The horse my little girl was on sped away and Robert galloped right after them. He stopped the horse just in time before it was about to either run into a block wall or jump over it. When I think about this it terrifies me about what could have happened if not for him." Vitina also appeared in three episodes of the John Forsythe sitcom *To Rome with Love*, playing an Italian professor and love interest to Forsythe's American living in Italy with his daughters. "I was so surprised to be finally cast as a regular woman after all the other roles I played. These were not always the parts I wanted to do but eventually I resigned myself to this.

Vitina Marcus makes an enticing Green Lady on Irwin Allen's cult science fiction series *Lost in Space* (20th Century–Fox Television, 1966).

So you can imagine how shocked I was to get *To Rome with Love*."

Unfortunately, *To Rome with Love* was Vitina's swan song in Hollywood. Though she seemed a perfect choice to play biker chicks or flower children on the drive-in movie screen ("I was sort of a free spirit back then and went to some love-ins at a park"), none of these roles came her way. The actress has admitted to being constantly distracted from her career by the drama with the men in her life. In 1970, she decided to leave show business after spending time in an Ashram. Vitina recalls, "When I finally decided to leave Hollywood, Irwin Allen said to me, 'You can't leave!' After I left acting I'd occasionally call him. I was traveling a lot, living a different lifestyle. I was teaching what I learned in the Ashram in different parts of the country and in Canada. I felt that it was important for people to understand these teachings to add on to what was happening at that time—early seventies. It was an expansion of awareness and culture. To have a spiritual way of life—to alleviate selfishness and other problems people run into. I also learned in the Ashram about nutrition and holistic health care because I feel that healing and holistic health (mind, body and spirit) is extremely important."

Today Vitina resides in Las Vegas. Her daughter Athena (who was voted "The Most Beautiful Showgirl in the World") and her son Giuliano are both successful in their careers. Vitina is now in the real estate business and is actively working on a spiritual path. Her hair is still long but now blonde and she is honored that people still remember her from the '60s. During the hoopla surrounding the release of the movie version of *Lost in Space*, some promoters contacted Vitina and invited her to attend their celebrity autograph convention. Touched by the graciousness of her colleagues and her fans' response, the former '60s pin-up has done a few more conventions and established a web site. She is a strict vegetarian and is involved "inspiring compassion, understanding and kindness between the human, animal and plant kingdoms." She states, "How else can this planet evolve?"

Film Appearances

1958   **Never Love a Stranger** (Allied Artists) d. Robert Stevens

1960   **The Lost World** (20th Century–Fox) d. Irwin Allen

1962   **Taras Bulba** (United Artists) d. J. Lee Thompson

1964   **Bedtime Story** (Universal) d. Ralph Levy

Television Appearances

Kraft Television Theatre "The Other Wise Man" 12/25/1957 NBC
Schlitz Playhouse of Stars "Curfew at Midnight" 6/27/1958 CBS.
Have Gun, Will Travel "Lady on the Stagecoach" 1/17/1959 CBS
Mickey Spillane's Mike Hammer "Doll Trouble" 7/31/1959 SYN
Wagon Train "The Vittorio Bottecelli Story" 12/16/1959 NBC
Sea Hunt "Mercy Ship" 4/29/1961 SYN
Gunslinger "The Death of Yellow Singer" 5/11/1961 CBS
Gunsmoke "The Squaw" 11/11/1961 CBS
Rawhide "The Peddler" 1/19/1962 CBS
I'm Dickens, He's Fenster "A Small Matter of Being Fired" 9/28/1962 ABC
Gunsmoke "Old Comrade" 12/29/1962 CBS
The Travels of Jaime McPheeters "The Day of the Wizard" 1/12/1964 ABC
Voyage to the Bottom of the Sea "Turn Back the Clock" 10/26/1964 ABC
Voyage to the Bottom of the Sea "The Return of the Phantom" 3/20/1966 ABC
Lost in Space "Wild Adventure" 9/21/1966 CBS

The Man from U.N.C.L.E. "The My Friend the Gorilla Affair" 12/16/1966 NBC
Lost in Space "The Girl from the Green Dimension" 1/4/1967 CBS
Time Tunnel "Chase Through Time" 2/24/1967 ABC
Time Tunnel "Attack of the Barbarians" 3/10/1967 ABC
To Rome with Love "The Telephone" 11/2/1969 CBS
The F.B.I. "Conspiracy of Corruption" 1/11/1970 ABC
To Rome with Love "Birds, Bees and Bushes" 3/8/1970 CBS
To Rome with Love "Pretty Little Girl" 3/15/1970 CBS

Also

The Jackie Gleason Show, The Colgate Comedy Hour, Checkmate, Adventures in Paradise, The Virginian, Death Valley Days, and *Rawhide*

☆ ARLENE MARTEL ☆

Arlene Martel is one of the many talented Hollywood actors whose face fans recognize but whose name may elude them. In her case it's even more so since she started out in Hollywood using her real name of Arline Sax. On the big screen Martel had the female lead in the cult film noir *The Glass Cage* (1964) and played a biker chick in the popular film *Angels From Hell* (1968), the follow-up to *Hell's Angels on Wheels* (1968). But it was on TV where Martel excelled, essaying a variety of roles usually hidden under different hair colors and gobs of make-up or speaking in a foreign dialect in such series as *The Outer Limits, Star Trek, The Monkees* and *Bewitched*. The exotic, shapely beauty played so many varied roles that she was dubbed "the Chameleon" by honchos at Universal Studios. "I think this was a hindrance because no one knew it was the same actress from week to week," comments Arlene. "In fact, in one week I was on three different shows. And nobody knew it was the same person. I think it is very good to have that versatility when you are established as a star. They say, 'Look she can do this and do this.' But if the audience doesn't know it's you, it is not to your advantage."

Arlene was born Arline Sax on April 14, 1936 in New York City. Growing up in the slums of the Bronx, her mother's millionaire boss plucked her from the city's dirty streets and enrolled her in the Cherry Lawn School, a private boarding school in Darien, Connecticut. At the age of eleven she learned of her desire to act after appearing in a production of *Six Who Passed While the Lentils Boiled*. She then auditioned and was accepted into The High School for the Performing Arts in New York City, where her classmates included Suzanne Pleshette, Susan Harrison and Tony Mordente. During the summers, Arlene lied about her age to work as an actress at the Berkshire Playhouse, where you had to be eighteen or older. While a student, Arlene met and became romantically involved with film icon James Dean. She saw him on a live television program before he was famous. "My mother called me over to the television set to look at this actor who she thought was quite good," recalls Martel. "I agreed with her. So the next day I called information—I was sixteen and totally innocent—and James Dean was listed. Jimmy answered the phone and I told him, 'I was just calling to tell you how wonderful I thought

The alluring Arlene Martel.

your work was.' He was sleeping and told me he'd call me back. He did and we met at the Museum of Modern Art. It then ensued into a relationship that lasted until he died. Jimmy's presence in my life profoundly affected my future choices in *all* areas, including the men I chose after." Arlene can be seen discussing Dean in Robert Altman's documentary *The James Dean Story*, which was released in 1957. In the film she reveals that they listened to classical music together and that Dean would read his favorite book, *The Little Prince*, to her. She comments in the movie, "Once I told him I loved him, but he pretended he didn't hear. Then he said, 'You can't love me. I don't think anyone can yet.'"

After graduating high school, Arlene worked odd jobs while landing roles Off-Broadway. With much television work shifting to the West Coast, she decided to give Hollywood a try. Arlene (using her real name Arline Sax) was cast as a Flamenco dancer in an episode of *Matinee Theatre*. Trouble was that Arlene did not dance the Flamenco, so she rushed out and hired a choreographer to teach her a whole routine. Arlene proved limber on-camera but a mishap occurred as the camera dollied in for a close up, hitting her. She remarked jokingly in the *Angels from Hell* pressbook, "You might say that was my first real contact with a television camera." After her inauspicious television bow, Martel returned East to make her Broadway debut in the comedy *Uncle Willie* followed by appearances in a series of one act plays at the Circle in the Square Theatre.

In 1958, Arlene once again headed to Hollywood. She began landing many TV roles, including two on *The Twilight Zone* written by Rod Serling. ("He was just as people would imagine him—brilliant, warm and real.") Martel then won the lead role of Nanoa in the 20th Century–Fox film *The Little Savage* (1959) directed by Byron Haskin. She reported to the Mexican location only to find out that the producer's girlfriend was replacing her. "This was such a terrible experience for me," remembers Arlene. "When I was cast in the lead role I managed to persuade the producer to cast my husband, actor Robert Palmer, as my love interest. I thought he'd be wonderful in the part and we could really make it happen on screen. When I arrived on location, they said, 'Thank you so much but Christiane Martel will play your part.' She was Miss Universe of 1953. Here I managed to get my husband the role opposite *me*, only to find that he was going to play opposite *her*." A few years later, Arlene moved to a street in Hollywood called Martel Avenue. "The coincidence was too much and I decided that there was going to be some justice in all this so I took the name Arlene Martel. Everybody mispronounced Arline and there were many puns on the name Sax like 'sex' and 'Saks Fifth Avenue.' Martel was easy to say and it went nicely with Arlene."

Due to her talent, professionalism and expertise with foreign dialects, Martel began getting steady work on television. The first of Martel's three classic guest stints came about due to Byron Haskin, the director of *The Little Savage*. When he was assigned to direct the Hugo award-winning "Demon with a Glass Hand" by Harlan Ellison on *The Outer Limits*, he remembered Martel. He brought her in to read for the role of Consuela and she got the part. "When I first read Harlan's script I felt inspired by it," exclaims Martel. "I felt I could do a lot in the role of Consuela. This part had a lovely substance that I connected with. Byron Haskin was our director and he was wonderful! He was the reason I got this role. When they replaced me with Christiane Martel, Byron told me, 'One day I will make it up to you and find something else for you.' And sure enough he did."

"Demon with a Glass Hand" (perhaps the best of *The Outer Limits* episodes) starred Robert Culp as Trent, who is pursued by aliens from the future. Trent has a robot hand that is missing three fingers. He learns from one of the aliens that he too is from man's future. Martel played Conseula, a poor garment worker who, while working late, is discovered by Trent as he tries to find and destroy the aliens' "Time Mirror," which they use for time travel. The pair is chased relentlessly by the aliens in the deserted office building. After locating his missing extremities, Trent discovers that he is a robot and holds man's fate inside of him. Recalling the shoot, Martel says, "I believe Harlan Ellison was on the set during filming, but to tell you the truth my concentration was so much on my part that, other than Robert Culp, I don't think I was aware of anyone else. I was very focused on what was happening between our characters. I found Culp to be very attractive in many ways. I got a very beautiful feeling about him. I thought that as a person he projected a lovely sanity. I enjoyed working with him. He remains a favorite.

"I also had an operation and had just been released from the hospital the day before. If you watch the episode you'll notice that as I am being pulled by Robert Culp I am running very stiffly with my arm at my side because I was nervous that the stitches would open. I was running in so much pain—up the stairs, down the stairs—but I was afraid to tell them that I just got out of the hospital, because I thought that they would replace me. I kept that to myself and just prayed, 'Oh dear God please don't let me start bleeding all over the place.'"

This episode of *The Outer Limits* may have been what led Martel to being cast in a dual role in the Avant-garde, experimental film *The Glass Cage* (1964) directed by Antonio Santean. She played a lonely young woman who shoots a prowler in self-defense and her older domineering sister. The police detective (Robert Kelljan) on the case becomes infatuated with the girl but things get stranger when her sister disappears. She is brutally raped by a beatnik (in a very racy scene for 1964) and falls into the bear pit at the local zoo, where the policeman rescues her.

Though Martel excelled in dramatic roles, her comedic talents were put to good use on some of the decade's top sitcoms. On *My Favorite Martian*, she played the dual role of a ditzy silent movie star, who chooses Tim (Bill Bixby) to be her next leading man when Martin (Ray Walston) sends them back in time to Hollywood 1925 and her granddaughter, a cub reporter. Martel, sporting nifty strawberry blonde hair, made six appearances on *Hogan's Heroes* as Tiger, the seductive French spy working for the Allies. The character of Tiger was introduced on *Hogan's Heroes*' second episode entitled "Hold That Tiger." The agent was sent by the underground to Stalag 13 to obtain the blueprints to the German's new Tiger tank from Hogan and his men. At first Hogan, played by Bob Crane (whom Martel found to be "cynical in terms of romance and love. I find cynicism of any kind to be unappealing"), is perturbed that they sent a woman, but a playful rapport edging on romance develops between them. Describing the character, Martel comments, "Tiger was charming, ingenious, sexy, and flirtatious. It was a fun role to play."

Though Tiger and Hogan had a romantic spark, their situations—he a prisoner of war, she a spy for the Allies—kept them from taking it further.

Martel could also be found portraying a bungling foreign spy and Count Dracula's niece on two different episodes of *The Monkees*. "This was such a zany show to work on," recalls Arlene. "The guys were having a ball doing this series. I had an especially good rapport with Peter Tork and Davy Jones. There was a great deal of joviality on the set." Being one of the more outrageous TV shows from the sixties, it is no wonder that *The Monkees* spoofed the spy genre so wonderfully in the madcap "The Spy who Came in from the Cool." As foreign

Arlene Martel and Robert Culp in the classic episode "Demon with a Glass Hand" of *The Outer Limits* (United Artists Television, 1964).

enemy agent Madame Olinsky, Martel leaves a microfilm in a pair of red maracas for her sidekick Boris to pass off to one of their comrades. But the maracas end up with Davy Jones. To retrieve them, Olinsky disguises herself as a mod hipster and crashes the Monkees' discotheque, causing all sorts of mayhem. Martel worked well with this zany foursome and was invited back to do another episode. But this time she wound up in a bit of trouble. Screen Gems had a room, dubbed the Black Box, built below the studio where the Monkees could hang out, play a little music and smoke some grass. Sometimes the guest stars would be invited in. "I hung out with them one day and it was the first and only instance where I wasn't on time getting back to a set. The air was thick with smoke and I guess I innocently inhaled. I was twenty minutes late and the director berated me mercilessly in front of the cast and crew."

Returning to the science fiction genre, Martel was cast in her most popular role—that of T'Pring, the woman who jilted Spock in "Amok Time," on *Star Trek*. "This was the third role I was up for on *Star Trek*," reveals Arlene. "The first role was in 'Where No Man Has Gone Before' and I would have had to wear contact lenses. But my eyes are very sensitive and I couldn't do that. So I had to say no—it was the part Sally Kellerman played. She probably would be very upset to read that but it's true. The second episode was 'Catspaw.' On my audition I heard them whispering and they said, 'We'd like to bring you back for something else we have in mind.' They did, but I never realized that it would become one of the classic episodes."

"Amok Time" was the first *Star Trek* episode televised during the show's second season. Spock becomes so overwhelmed by his mating drive that he commandeers the *Enterprise* on a course for Vulcan. The Vulcan ruler T'Pau (Celia Lovsky) begins the wedding ceremony to T'Pring, the woman betrothed to Spock when they were children. But T'Pring rejects Spock and chooses Captain Kirk, who now must fight Spock to the death. The role of T'Pring was an acting stretch for Martel. Usually cast in highly dramatic roles, as a Vulcan she couldn't show any emotion. Her director, Joseph Pevney, felt she was too animated at first. "Pevney kept guiding me towards doing less and less and less," says Martel. "Finally he said, 'Do even less than what you're doing.' I said, 'But I wouldn't be doing *anything* at that point.' He replied, 'That's exactly what I want. It will come through.' So this very dry, icy, intellectual quality came forth and that is exactly what he was after. But it was very different from everything else I had done." She also had to spend hours in the make up chair to achieve a Vulcan look. This didn't bother her because, "I loved to work so much that what someone calls difficult to me is a pleasure. What I did find odd though was the costume they designed for me. Many actresses who played aliens on *Star Trek* wore very skimpy outfits. My dress was very boxy and hid my figure—I looked pregnant in it. I thought maybe at one point the character was supposed to be carrying Stann's child and would come back in another episode."

Though what was happening in front of the camera on "Amok Time" was very somber, it was anything but off-camera. "Every time Celia Lovsky pronounced one of the Vulcan words Shatner would whisper something funny about it and get me to laugh, which was terrible to do," says Arlene with a chuckle. "*It was just terrible of him!* Of course Ms. Lovsky wasn't aware of this. But she had difficulty pronouncing the Vulcan words. Bill was like a naughty schoolboy and suddenly I became five years old too. At one point, the direc-

Teaser print ad for *Angels from Hell* (AIP, 1968).

tor threatened to throw us both off the set. I have very good concentration, but Bill just broke me up." Though she got along wonderfully with Shatner, Nimoy was another story. "Leonard was rather removed. Maybe he was maintaining his character—I don't know. Or maybe he genuinely didn't like me! I have no idea to this day. We were cast together in three different shows. Before *Star Trek* we played a mountain couple in the western *The Rebel* with Nick Adams, and I also worked with him later on *Mission: Impossible*. I thought I was very good to work with and that I gave a great deal in my work. For some reason, he remained very aloof.

"When I played T'Pring it was another job. I certainly didn't think it would become legendary," continues Martel. "Who would have ever thought *Star Trek* would turn into this phenomenon? I was just so happy to be working and playing a part that was so challenging in terms of what I had done before. I had no idea it would continue even to this day. Fans purchase my *Star Trek* photos at conventions where I sign autographs. I had no idea that T'Pring would be so memorable to people."

Detail from Australian daybill for *Angels from Hell* (AIP, 1968) starring Tom Stern and Arlene Martel.

Despite giving skilled performances and proving she was not just another Sixties' starlet–a-go-go, Martel could not get much film work. She muses, "When I worked with Peter Falk—I did *three* episodes of *Columbo*—he said, 'How come you are not a movie star?' I looked good, I could act and I didn't have any personal problems. But I didn't have the agent or the connections to catapult me forward into films. My agent dropped out of the business. I also didn't have a PR person, who would say, 'Hey, wait a minute. We'll publicize the fact that you are on three different shows this week.' I never knew how to make more of what was happening."

Despite her lack of big screen output, sixties drive-in fans remember Martel for playing a biker chick named Ginger in *Angels from Hell* (1968), directed by Bruce Kessler. The film was released on a double-bill with another biker film, *The Mini-Skirt Mob* starring Diane McBain. "I have no idea how I got the role of Ginger," says Arlene with a laugh. "I auditioned for this and there were a lot of other actresses that were right for it too. I know Bruce Kessler liked my acting. So they offered me the part of the *biker chick*."

Shot on location in Bakersfield, California, *Angels from Hell* was the first film produced by Fanfare Productions, which was formed by producer Joe Solomon from the money he made on three previous biker films. This one starred Tom Stern as Mike, a disillusioned GI just returning from Vietnam, out to combat the establishment for sending him off to war. He heads for a new town where his buddy Smiley (Ted Markland) and his other former gang members are part of a new biker club, the Madcaps. Backed by his military experience, Mike takes out the club's leader and beds the mini-skirted Ginger (Martel), who lets the bikers hang out at her farm because "they amuse her." Unlike the other biker chicks, Ginger "hangs loose" and doesn't want to be any man's old lady. She rides with Mike and the gang to Hollywood to see a former member, Dude Marshall (Steve Rogers), who is now a movie star. Ginger gets jealous of Mike's attention towards Dude's bimbo girlfriend (Susan Holloway), and when Mike makes time with a go-go dancer she calls the girl's lesbian lover who catches them in bed. During the course of the film the Madcaps drink beer, smoke pot, make love and tangle with "the squares." ("We don't want them to love us—just leave us alone.'") Mike's power as leader of the gang goes to his head as he dreams of uniting all the biker gangs, after biker Speed (Stephen Oliver) is "accidentally" killed by the police. When an innocent flower child is raped and murdered by one of the drugged-out bikers (Paul Bertoya as Nutty), the police close in as Mike tries to cover it up, to the consternation of Ginger. Now out of control, an enraged Mike calls for an all-out war against the cops, only to die defiantly opposing the oppression of the establishment.

Also appearing in the exciting film (complete with a rockin' theme song by Stu Phillips, Guy Hemric and Byron Coleand, sung by the Peanut Butter Conspiracy) were Jack Starrett, Jimmy Murphy, Saundra Gayle, and real-life members of the Hell's Angels. "They [Hell's Angels] were the most courteous and polite people we encountered. Some of the townspeople on the other hand, were so rude. One day Paul Bertoya and I were eating at this restaurant. This guy comes up to Paul and says, 'I didn't think we let any hippie fags into this town.' He then assaults Paul and they started fighting. *Nobody did anything*! I was so scared. After my frantic prodding somebody *finally* called the police. It was a frightening moment—let me tell you. I had not been exposed to anything quite like that before."

In *Angels from Hell* (AIP, 1968) bikers Ted Markland (left) and Tom Stern (right) hit the open highway looking for trouble with their girls, Saundra Gayle (left) and Arlene Martel (right).

Sporting a long auburn colored wig, Martel plays the role with amused detachment as she gets more and more involved in the gang's activities. The *New York Post* reviewer commented, "Keeping up with the times, the script includes more pot than usual and a bit of the hippy scene." The film also pokes fun at itself and biker films in general as Dude's producer wants to interview the bikers for his own motorcycle picture. The film also showed that even by 1967 Elvis Presley had become uncool in the eyes of the young: "Don't you go to drive-ins any more," asks Mike. "Dude Marshall is the biggest thing to hit Hollywood since Elvis." "Elvis who," responds one gang member.

Martel ended the sixties still playing varied roles on TV, including a tempestuous Indian squaw hired by series star Dale Robertson to guide him to the land of the Sioux on *Iron Horse* and a beautiful Greek woman being fought over by two suitors on *Here Come the Brides*. The seventies found Martel in supporting roles in a few made-for-TV movies including *Adventures of Nick Carter* (1972) with Robert Conrad, *Indict and Convict* (1974) with William Shatner and, again cast as an Indian squaw, this time aiding an outlaw played by John Saxon, on an episode of *Gunsmoke*. But it is Martel's tour-de-force performance as the loathsome witch Malvina in the two-part "How Not to Lose Your Head to Henry VIII" on *Bewitched* that is her most memorable seventies role. In this famous episode, while the Stephens' are on vacation in London, Samantha reverses another witch's spell put on a nobleman centuries ago. Furious with Sam for tampering with her incantation, the wicked Malvina sends her back in time. An amnesiac Sam lands in the court of King Henry VIII. Darrin and Endora then follow to rescue her before she becomes his next wife. Martel is simply marvelous as Malvina. Writing on *The Bewitched Critic* web site Scott Viets remarks, "Looking like something out of a Tim Burton movie, Ms. Martel is perhaps one of *Bewitched*'s scariest guest witches and her incantation is wickedly executed and worthy of rewind." Arlene comments, "I just threw myself into the role of Malvina like I threw myself into every role. I had no inhibitions playing this part. I just went for it and it was a fun role to play. The whole cast was a joy to work with. Elizabeth Montgomery was especially delightful. She was a talented and generous actress."

Later in the decade Martel surprisingly turned up along with Candice Rialson, Rip Taylor and Prof. Irwin Corey in the cult classic *Chatterbox* (1977), a musical about a talking vagina. "I was cast as a lesbian—talk about over-the-top," says Martel with a laugh. "I thought the part was really funny. But it was just one of those ludicrous things that slips into one's career."

Another film falling into this category was the low-budget horror film *Dracula's Dog* (1978). Reggie Nalder played a Transylvanian manservant who journeys with Dracula's bloodthirsty pooch Zoltan to Los Angeles in search of the Count's last remaining descendant (Michael Pataki). Martel played a Communist military commander who unleashes the hound, and Jose Ferrer was cast as a Van Helsing-type. The film however is not as awful as it sounds. Writing in *Terror on Tape*, James O'Neill described it as "One of those dumb but fun movies efficiently directed and acted with gusto...."

"A neighbor of mine [Frank Ray Perilli] wrote and produced *Dracula's Dog*," says Arlene. "He said to me, 'I wrote a script, but there is nothing for you in it unless I change this role from a male into a female.' So that's what he did. I played some sort of Russian military commander. My scenes were with Jose Ferrer. What is interesting is that a

Publicity pose of Arlene Martel as spy gal Tiger and series star Bob Crane from the hit sitcom *Hogan's Heroes* (Paramount Television, ca. 1968).

few years before Ferrer had wanted to meet me after watching me eat in the studio commissary—but I declined his 'amorous' invitation. Now here we were working together. Thankfully he didn't remember me because I looked so different."

Arlene Martel took a hiatus from show business in the eighties. With her children "out of the nest," she is re-establishing herself in Hollywood. (Daughter Avra Douglas is a screenwriter whose film *Teacher's Pet* was a hit in Europe. Son Jod Kastan is a writer for the *New York Times*. And son Adam Palmer is a writer/producer.) Martel too is an accomplished writer and her screenplay entitled *Whisper into My Good Ear* will be going before the cameras soon. "I co-wrote this with my new son-in-law Joseph Brutsman," says Arlene proudly. "It is about two elderly friends who have a suicide pact, but on the day that they are supposed to fulfill this agreement one of them changes his mind. He then has to convince the other to dissolve the pact. On route to their destination each of them reveals something to the other that they have never told before. It has humor and it has pathos. William Shatner is slated to direct and Martin Landau is interested in playing one of the leads."

And Arlene is in the process of rejuvenating her acting career. She has been appearing at autograph shows ("I like the exchange of energy meeting and talking with the fans") and has her own web site where film buffs can read more about her career and purchase autographed photos.

Film Appearances

1957   **The James Dean Story** (Warner Bros.) [as herself] d. Robert Altman

1964   **The Glass Cage** (Futuramic Releasing) d. Antonio Santean

1968   **Angels from Hell** (AIP) d. Bruce Kessler

1972   **The Adventures of Nick Carter** (TV-movie) d. Paul Krasny

1973   **Indict and Convict** (TV-movie) d. Boris Sagal

1975   **Conspiracy of Terror** (TV-movie) d. John Llewellyn Moxey

1977   **Chatterbox** (AIP) d. Tom De Simone

1978   **Dracula's Dog** (Crown International) d. Albert Band

1981   **The Day the Loving Stopped** (TV-movie) d. Daniel Mann

1982   **Eleanor, First Lady of the World** (TV-movie) d. John Erman

Television Appearances

The Restless Gun "A Bell for Santo Domingo" 12/22/1958 NBC
The Twilight Zone "What You Need" 12/29/1959 CBS
Playhouse 90 "In the Presence of Mine Enemies" 5/18/1960 CBS
Death Valley Days "Human Sacrifice" 6/2/1960 SYN
The Rebel "The Hunted" 11/6/1960 ABC
The Untouchables "A Seat on the Fence" 11/24/1960 ABC
Route 66 "A Legacy for Lucia" 11/25/1960 CBS
Have Gun, Will Travel "The Princess and the Gunfighter" 1/21/1961 CBS
The Twilight Zone "Twenty-Two" 2/10/1961 CBS
Hong Kong "The Hunted" 2/15/1961 ABC
The Detectives "An Eye for an Eye" 2/24/1961 ABC
The Gunslinger "The Diehards" 4/20/1961 CBS
Route 66 "The Newborn" 5/5/1961 CBS
The Untouchables "The Genna Brothers" 11/2/1961 ABC
Ben Casey "My Good Friend Krikor" 11/27/1961 ABC
Bus Stop "Cry to Heaven" 1/14/1962 ABC
Perry Mason "The Case of the Absent Artist" 3/17/1962 CBS

The New Breed "The Man with the Other Face" 4/10/1962 ABC
Cheyenne "Indian Gold" 10/29/1962 ABC
Breaking Point "My Hands Are Clean" 4/27/1964 NBC
The Outer Limits "Demon with a Glass Hand" 10/17/1964 ABC
Valentine's Day "Bride and Gloom" 11/27/1964 ABC
The Man from U.N.C.L.E. "The King of Knaves Affair" 12/22/1964 NBC
Profiles in Courage "Edmund G. Ross" 3/21/1965 NBC
Hogan's Heroes "Hold That Tiger" 9/24/1965 CBS
My Favorite Martian "Martin of the Movies" 9/26/1965 CBS
I Dream of Jeannie "Russian Roulette" 12/11/1965 NBC
Perry Mason "The Case of the Dead Ringer" 4/17/1966 CBS
The Monkees "The Spy Who Came in from the Cool" 10/10/1966 NBC
Hogan's Heroes "A Tiger Hunt in Paris" 11/18 & 11/25/1966 CBS
The Fugitive "Blessings of Liberty" 12/20/1966 ABC
Iron Horse "Hellcat" 12/26/1966 ABC
Hogan's Heroes "Heil Klink" 2/10/1967 CBS
Star Trek "Amok Time" 9/15/1967 NBC
The Wild Wild West "The Night of the Circus of Death" 11/3/1967 CBS
The Flying Nun "Tonio's Mother" 1/4/1968 ABC
The Monkees "Monstrous Monkee Mash" 1/22/1968 NBC
Hogan's Heroes "Never Play Cards with Strangers" 11/9/1968 CBS
It Takes a Thief "Guess Who's Coming to Rio?" 1/7/1969 ABC
Hogan's Heroes "The Defector" 11/28/1969 CBS
Mission: Impossible "Terror" 2/15/1970 CBS
Here Come the Brides "To the Victor" 2/27/1970 ABC
Mannix "Murder Revisited" 3/10/1970 CBS
Hogan's Heroes "Operation Tiger" 11/29/1970 CBS
Bewitched "How Not to Lose Your Head to Henry VIII" 9/15 & 9/22/1971 ABC
McCloud "The Disposal Man" 12/29/1971 NBC
The Doris Day Show "The Sorrow of a Sangapur" 1/10/1972 CBS
McCloud "A Little Plot at Tranquil Valley" 1/12/1972 NBC
Columbo "The Greenhouse Jungle" 10/15/1972 NBC
Mannix "The Danford File" 3/11/1973 CBS
The Delphi Bureau "The Terror Broker Project" 3/17/1973 ABC
Columbo "Double Exposure" 12/16/1973 NBC
Banacek "The Three Million Dollar Piracy" 11/21/1973 NBC
The Six Million Dollar Man "The Last of the Fourth of Julys" 4/5/1974 ABC
The Rookies "Vendetta" 11/18/1974 ABC
Petrocelli "A Very Lonely Lady" 11/27/1974 NBC
Columbo "A Friend in Deed" 12/29/1974 NBC
Gunsmoke "The Squaw" 1/6/1975 CBS
The Rockford Files "Trouble in Chapter Seventeen" 9/23/1977 NBC
Richie Brockelman, Private Eye "The Framing of Perfect Sydney" 3/17/1978 NBC
Battlestar Galactica "The Long Patrol" 10/15/1978 ABC
The Love Boat "Return of the Ninny/ Split Personality/ Touchdown Twins" 2/14/1981 ABC
Knots Landing "Homecoming" 12/1/1983 CBS
Berrengers "Overture" 1/5/1985 NBC
The Young and the Restless [recurring role as Mavis MacDonald] 1986 CBS

Also

Matinee Theatre

☆ MARLYN MASON ☆

With her big blue-green eyes and button nose, Marlyn Mason was an unconventional beauty who had the talent to play comedy and drama to good effect. Film producers irrationally ignored her throughout most of the swinging '60s, but Mason became a mainstay on television. Being an extremely versatile performer, she played a variety of roles on all the top series, including *My Three Sons*, *Burke's Law*, *Ben Casey*, *Dr. Kildare*, *Bonanza*, *Gomer Pyle, USMC*, *Hogan's Heroes*, *Mannix*, *Love, American Style*, etc. Mason also proved herself to be a more than competent singer and dancer on two TV variety spectaculars and on Broadway. Her talent was finally put to good use on the big screen when she won a lead role opposite Elvis Presley in *The Trouble with Girls* (1969), one of his last drive-in movie hits. Two years later, Marlyn bared more than her talent as the older woman who seduces one of her husband's students in the youth-oriented comedy, *Making It* (1971).

Marlyn Mason was born on August 7, 1940, in the San Fernando Valley. The unusual name of Marlyn was also the name of a friend of her mother's. ("My mother loved that name and said that when she had a child she was going to name her Marlyn.") When Mason was five years old she performed the song "Santa Claus Is Coming to Town" at her local church and decided at that tender age that she wanted a life on the stage. Mason once commented to a reporter, "Oh, God, ambition is my middle name. I've wanted to perform since I crawled out of my mother." To keep her happy, Mason's family enrolled their determined daughter in singing, dancing, and piano classes. She then began performing with local groups and making appearances on talent shows such as *The Doyle O'Dell Show* on KTLA.

By the time she reached high school, she had played roles on stage with the children's wing of the Players Ring Theatre in productions of *Cinderella*, *Heidi*, and *Tom Sawyer*. She also appeared in a few episodes of the TV series *Matinee Theatre*. "I went on to do five episodes," says Mason. "That was great training. A lot of good actors and directors came out of this. My first show was with Keith Andes and Margaret O'Brien. I played her girlfriend. In another episode I played Dennis Hopper's sister. Constance Bennett, who was Joan Bennett's sister, played my mother in another show. I worked with some heavyweights and people who later became heavy weights in the business like Lamont Johnson, who is a wonderful director."

In 1958, Mason graduated high school and worked at a coffeehouse. She still continued pursuing her acting career and landed a bit in the melodramatic teenage film *Because They're Young* (1960), starring Dick Clark, Michael Callan, and Tuesday Weld. ("I had one teeny line coming down the stairs in the high school. I don't even think my name showed up in the credits.") Mason and her sister then auditioned as dancers for Harold Minsky at the Dunes in Las Vegas and were hired to entertain at a bankers' convention in Chicago. The California native remarked to *TV Guide*, "I thought *Las Vegas* was East. So it was a big thrill to go all the way to Chicago."

Mason worked at the Desert Inn in Las Vegas before landing what would be the "launching pad" for her career, when she was cast in the Los Angeles production of *The Billy Barnes Revue* in 1962. Also in the cast were Ken Berry, Steve Franken, and Joyce Jameson. But it was Mason's performing of the number "The

Marlyn Mason and Elvis Presley played flirtatious adversaries working for a Chautauqua, a religious educational traveling fair in *The Trouble with Girls* **(MGM, 1969).**

Pink Pussycat School" that was the showstopper. "This really opened up television to me," says Marlyn. "I got great reviews and then the work just kept coming—one [TV] show after another. I got a real nice career out of that for about ten to twelve years."

During the sixties, Marlyn Mason could be seen playing sexy, kooky, naive, or evil characters on sitcoms, westerns, science fiction, medical, and other types of dramatic series. Her roles ranged from an adulterous wife who plots to pin the murder of her lover's wife on Richard Kimble (David Janssen) in *The Fugitive*, to a free-spirited heiress who winds up engaged to series star Michael Callan after a wild night on the town in *Occasional Wife*. On *Gomer Pyle, USMC*, she played the sister of bellowing Sgt. Carter (Frank Sutton), who objects to her choice for a husband so she uses innocent Gomer (Jim Nabors) to make her brother change his mind. She was an innocent girl accidentally blinded by Little Joe (Michael Landon) in a hunting accident on *Bonanza*, while *The Big Valley* featured Mason as an alluring flirt who distracts Nick Barkley (Peter Breck) while her family plots to rob and murder him. On *Laredo* she played the charmingly named Belleflower Ferne who is in a hurry to marry Ben Conrad (Peter Graves) when two penniless actors pretending to be ministers (British pop stars Chad and Jeremy) come to the town to con the congregation out of money. *Mannix* featured Mason as a beautiful model who hires the virile detective (Michael Connors) to find her missing boyfriend.

Mason was such a sought after actress that in an unprecedented move, she appeared in a seven-part story arc on *Ben Casey* as Sally Weldon, and the day after her run ended she began a seven-part story arc on its chief rival *Dr. Kildare* in 1965. "I had known Richard Chamberlain [of *Dr. Kildare*] for a long time because we had the same singing teacher," remembers Mason. "But I didn't work that much with him on the show. Most of my scenes were with Robert Reed who played my husband. I had heard that Vince Edwards [of *Ben Casey*] was very volatile and I was prepared to have this guy blow up. But he never did. He was always off talking on the phone betting the horses. I never saw him raise his voice once. He was great and behaved himself when I was working with him."

Marlyn Mason also made a guest appearance on the cult sci-fi series *The Invaders* starring Roy Thinnes. In her episode, directed by Richard Benedict, she played a woman who helps David Vincent (Thinnes) prove his innocence when the aliens frame him for the apparent death of a communications plant owner. "What sticks out in my memory about *The Invaders* is that we shot some scenes near a dam off of Mulholland Drive," recalls Mason. "There are a lot of trees around it and they film a lot up there. Roy Thinnes and I were on a hillside slope. He wasn't very tall and I'm 5'7". They had to dig a little trench for me. Roy was sweet about it."

While Marlyn Mason was swinging from one TV show to another, it seems producers forgot or did not know that this talented lady could also sing and dance. Television audiences finally got their chance to see her perform when she was cast in the Emmy-Award–winning TV special *Brigadoon*, starring Robert Goulet, Sally Ann Howes, and Peter Falk in 1966. Mason played Meg and sings "My Mother's Wedding Day." She was such a hit that she appeared again with Goulet the following year in the TV special *Carousel* as Carrie. In this Rodgers and Hammerstein musical, Marlyn sings the solo "When I Marry Mr. Snow" and duets with female lead Mary Grover playing Julie Jordan, singing "You're a Queer One, Julie Jordan!"

These two appearances may have led Mason to be cast in the Broadway musical *How Now, Dow Jones* with music by Elmer Bernstein and lyrics by Carolyn Leigh. The musical spoof on Wall Street starring Tony Roberts, Brenda Vaccaro, and Mason opened on December 7, 1967, and closed on June 15, 1968, with a run of 220 performances.

"*How Now, Dow Jones* was a rough show to do and not a fun experience for me," says Marlyn, with a trace of disappointment in her voice. "It was not a good production and no hit song came out of it. I was in it because of Arthur Penn. Out of the blue, he called me and asked if I wanted to do a Broadway musical that he was directing. At that moment I did not know what to say. I had auditioned for him for a role in a film that he directed called *Mickey One* with Warren Beatty. I told him I would get back to him and then I called my friend Gene Saks who told me, 'If it is a role that you can do and it has one good song then go for it. It can't hurt you.' It had a song that I thought was pretty good and it was a David Merrick production, so my instincts told me to do it. Ultimately, Penn left the show when we were on the road and George Abbott came in. He was over eighty years old. While I respected him, I didn't care much for him because of the way he treated actors. But I learned one thing from the old man. We went out to dinner just after he came aboard and I asked him, 'What's your secret [for working so long]?' He replied, 'I have never taken it too seriously.' That really didn't sink in until after the show closed. I was twenty-seven years old then but it became my philosophy for life. You can't take show business seriously. Yes, you have to be on time, know your lines and be professional. But other than that it is all fluff and make believe."

Despite Mason's displeasure with it, *How Now, Dow Jones* received very good reviews from most of the major New York newspapers and a number of Tony Award nominations. However, the *New York Times* critic Clive Barnes, who had the power to close a show, panned the musical (he nicknamed it "How to Try in Business without Really Succeeding"), aiding in the production's demise. As for Mason, she won raves. For example, Edward Sothern Hipp of the *Newark Evening News* called her "a honey of a miss with a song-belting voice" while Whitney Bolton of *The Morning Telegraph* described Marlyn as "a handsome and melodious newcomer to our Broadway, and most welcome."

Returning to Hollywood, Mason finally landed a movie role that could fully tap her talent. She was cast opposite Elvis Presley in the period musical *The Trouble with Girls* (1969), Presley's last drive-in movie. It was based on the book entitled *Chautauqua* (the film's working title) by Day Keene and Dwight Babcock and directed by Peter Tewksbury. Purportedly, Presley's manager Colonel Tom Parker and the producers wanted actress Jean Hale for the lead. Hale came right out and told them that she could dance but not sing. Her singing voice was going to be dubbed when Tewksbury brought Marlyn Mason to their attention. Mason got the role and did not learn of the behind-the-scenes maneuverings until years later. "The only thing that was told to me was by Chuck Briles, who played one of the college boys [Amherst]," reveals Marlyn. "He called me out of the blue some years ago while I was in L.A. and asked me if I knew that Peter Tewksbury almost walked off the Elvis movie. I said, 'No, why?' He said, "Because they wanted some buxom blonde and Peter said, 'If you don't hire Marlyn Mason, I am not directing.' The Colonel always wanted busty blondes with Elvis and of course I was just the opposite. All I know is that I got a call from my agent that the film was offered to me. I don't recall reading or having to interview for it. I just had the role."

Before filming began, rehearsals were set up for the dance sequences and that is where Marlyn Mason met her leading man for the first time. "We rehearsed with choreographer Jonathan Lucas for a week," recalls Mason. "Elvis seemed to be at his peak then. He had just filmed his first TV special and had signed to play Vegas. He was in fantastic shape. Soon after, we recorded the songs [for the film]. I was told that I was one of only a handful of his leading ladies to actually record with Elvis though none of the songs we did became hits or anything. It was wonderful singing with Elvis. Mac Davis was at the recording session because he wrote one of the songs for the movie. Elvis had a good time. He said, 'You just love to sing, don't you Marlyn?' I sighed, 'Oh, yeah!' Elvis and Robert Goulet were the best guys to work with. They were so professional, fun and knew what they were doing. Their celebrity just fell by the wayside. They became just good buddies to work with."

Following the western *Charro!* (1969) that starred Elvis as an outlaw trying to go straight and the drama *Change of Habit* (1969) where he played a doctor who runs a clinic in the ghetto, *The Trouble with Girls* (1969), set in 1927, also offered Elvis a change of pace role. He played Walter Hale, the new manager of a chautauqua, a traveling show consisting of performances and lectures, which has just come into Radford Center, Iowa. Hale immediately locks horns with pretty Charlene (Mason) who is trying to unionize the troupe's performers. She infuriates the town's dignitaries when she chooses the daughter (Anissa Jones) of the town trollop Nita (Sheree North) for the lead in the children's pageant. Hale is romantically interested in Charlene, but the perky gal doesn't want to fraternize with management until the performers' grievances are addressed. Meanwhile, evil druggist Harrison Wilby (Dabney Coleman) is murdered. Chautauqua performer Clarence (Anthony Teague) is arrested when it is revealed that Wilby cheated him out of his gambling winnings. Walter investigates and uncovers the fact that Nita is the killer, as she murdered Wilby in self-defense after he forced her into an affair. Walter convinces Nita to confess and to do it during a chautauqua performance. Charlene is outraged of how Walter exploited Nita just to make a profit and quits in protest. Walter however convinces her of his integrity and she rejoins the company. During the course of the movie Mason gets to duet with Elvis on the novelty song "Signs of the Zodiac," with most of the singing surprisingly done by Marlyn.

One of the standout scenes in *The Trouble with Girls* is when Walter and Charlene finally kiss in one of the tents just as fireworks explode all around them. Though it looked dangerous for the actors, it wasn't according to Mason, but there was another scene that concerned her more. "The one stunt that worried me a bit was at the end when Elvis had to pull me onto the moving train," reveals Marlyn. "I had heard Elvis talking and I think he said that he had been smoking a little grass. I never knew that he did anything because he was always on his toes. I went to him and said, 'I don't know if this is true or not but if you have been smoking grass and I get hurt while doing this stunt I am going to sue you for every penny that you have.' Elvis just laughed. He thought that was so funny. So if he was stoned, I couldn't tell. There was no hint to me that he had any kind of drug problem. He and I were pretty close a lot of the time and I never smelled or detected anything."

Despite that misunderstanding, Mason has nothing but praise regarding working with the King. "Elvis was so polite and such a southern gentleman," comments Mason endearingly. "He always called Peter Tewksbury, 'Mr. Tewksbury.' I don't ever recall Elvis calling him Peter. Throughout the film, if Peter Tewksbury wanted a certain reaction from you during your close-up, he'd tell the other actor off-camera to do whatever he needed to do to get that reaction. So sometimes there were just crazy things going on off-camera that the audience just has no idea. Peter did that a lot with Elvis. Peter would tell me, 'I don't care what you do but this is what I need from him.' I'd do things, but Elvis was so spontaneous to work with. I was just so well trained it didn't bother me too much.

"Elvis got along with everybody and everybody just loved Elvis," continues Marlyn. "I have never heard of anybody having a hard time with Elvis. He was just fabulous to work with. If I had never done another thing in my life the fact that I was Elvis' leading lady fascinates somebody. I'm getting more fan mail now for that movie and for some of my old TV shows that are airing on cable than I ever have."

When it came time to release the movie, the producers were concerned that Elvis' fans would not pay to see a film entitled *Chautauqua*, especially since most of them probably could not even pronounce it correctly, let alone know what it meant. So they saddled it with the generic title of

In *The Trouble with Girls* (MGM, 1969) Marlyn Mason and Elvis Presley settle their union differences and get romantic.

The Trouble with Girls, relating to the batch of mid-sixties films Elvis starred in, even though the new title meant absolutely nothing to the film. To make matters worse, the film's posters added a subtitle and it was called *The Trouble with Girls (and How to Get Into It)* and was released on a double-bill with *The Green Slime* in some parts of the country. Suffice it to say this film was not one of Presley's biggest hits.

Though Marlyn Mason has fond memories of *The Trouble with Girls* ("I thought it was a cute movie, though it is kind of long"), it received only middling reviews from the critics. Though they felt it was good thing that Elvis was trying to branch out, his material was weak. Mason though received mostly positive reviews. William Tusher, writing in *The Hollywood Reporter*, described her as "a vivacious charmer who would have risen above the material if she did nothing but get in the way of the camera." David Austen of *Films and Filming* also found Marlyn to be "vivacious" and stated that she was "the real 'find'" of the movie.

Marlyn Mason did develop a following of new fans from *The Trouble with Girls*, but two years later she must have shocked them when she bared her bosom across the drive-ins of America playing a bored wife who seduces one of her husband's students in *Making It* (1971). This youth-oriented serio-comic film, directed by John Erman, followed the sexual adventures of a seventeen-year-old named Phil (Kristofer Tabori) who doesn't dig the establishment but doesn't fight it either. Instead, he concentrates on making it with chicks. When he meets his gym teacher's spouse (Mason), he is immediately attracted to her though the beautiful woman has a phobia regarding growing older and losing her looks. The older woman seduces him, but the randy teen dumps her on her thirtieth birthday. Phil then turns his attention to his high school girlfriend (Sherry Miles), who thinks she is pregnant. It turns out to be a false alarm but in the process Phil learns that his trying-to-be hip mother is expecting and has arranged for an abortion. Though theirs is a strained relationship, it draws mother and son closer and a friendship evolves.

Unlike other actresses of her generation, Mason had no qualms regarding her nude scene. "It didn't bother me and was easy to do," says Marlyn matter-of-factly. "John Erman, Kristofer Tabori and I got together before we even left for the shoot in Albuquerque. We talked it over and it felt very comfortable. When we were shooting the scene, I said before I took off my blouse, 'Okay guys get ready. Here it comes!' I told them that one breast was slightly larger than the other one so they nicknamed me 'Big Lefty.' It was probably more uncomfortable for the on-lookers than it was for me.

"Looking back on it now, I didn't even think about how young and how much of a good time Kristofer Tabori must have been having," continues Marlyn with a laugh. "But he was seventeen going on *forty-five*. That kid was so bright and so articulate. His parents were Viveca Lindfors and director Don Siegel. If I would put Kristofer in a category, I would say he was like Timothy Hutton—he had that little boyish way about him. I'm assuming he is now living in New York because he was a very sophisticated guy. If I

Pretty Marlyn Mason (right) in "Love and the Eskimo" on *Love, American Style* (Paramount Television, 1970), one of her many appearances on that show. Also pictured are Anthony Caruso, Bill Bixby, and Naomi Stevens (left to right).

were going to be intimidated in conversation with anybody it would have been Kristofer. He was so smart but also so sweet."

Critics were evenly split down the line concerning *Making It*. They either loved it or hated it. The ones who preferred the movie did so because it was atypical of the exploitative youth and generation gap movies being churned out at the time. To prove this point, Frances Herridge of the *New York Post* remarked that in *Making It*, "There are no weird exaggerations, no mind-blowing drug scenes with psychedelic camerawork, no crazy jaunts, no sex violence and the usual trappings that adult or sick adolescent writers dream up for average young America." Rex Reed on the other hand suggested that *Making It* was "For the garbage can" and that it was a "plodding, pointless waste of time." Kristofer Tabori won raves for his film debut and Mason received good reviews also, though some critics found her character not to be a shining example of womanhood. Leo Mishkin of the *Morning Telegraph N.Y.* remarked that Marlyn Mason "contributes handsomely," while Bruce Bahrenburg of *The Evening News, N.J.* commented that she gives a "fine performance."

During the remainder of the seventies and into the eighties, Mason kept busy on television. She was hired to replace Martine Beswicke as Nikki Bell in the detective drama *Longstreet* after the pilot was picked up as a series. Nikki was the assistant to blind insurance investigator Mike Longstreet (James Franciscus), who lost his eyesight in a bomb explosion. "I never had to audition for the role of Nikki Bell," reveals Mason. "I did go to lunch with Stirling Silliphant [the series creator] and James Franciscus at the Brown Derby. Jimmy wanted Diane Baker for the role of Nikki Bell. But Sterling Silliphant and the network wanted someone with a little more life. The character was light and free-spirited—types of roles that I played a lot. We all got along fine but Jimmy was slight so he was concerned that I would be taller than he was. I told him he never had to worry about that because I had a way of bending my knees to make myself shorter and in the two-shot scenes I'd take my shoes off. The height issue was never mentioned again."

Longstreet was well received by the critics due to Silliphant's above-average scripts and the talented cast, but the gimmick of a blind detective may have worn off quickly for the viewing public. Regarding Marlyn's performance, critic Cleveland Amory wrote in *TV Guide*, "At least part of the good scenery is Marlyn Mason. She plays understandingly—but not too understandingly—Longstreet's girlfriend." The show's earlier episodes gave Mason more to do, such as "A World of Perfect Complicity" where Mike Longstreet and Nikki pose as a married couple while investigating a series of robberies at an exclusive high rise. But as the series continued on she found herself with less to do. This coupled with a leading man who was not the friendliest guy in the bunch would have discouraged most actresses, but the spirited Mason took it all in stride. "I found Jimmy Franciscus to be very quiet and very aloof most of the time," remarks Marlyn. "From day to day you never knew how friendly he was going to be. It was not that he was never sociable but sometimes he was very unapproachable. He could walk right by you and not say hello. In all the shows that we did we never once had lunch together. He was extremely private. I didn't know any more about him after twenty-six shows than I knew before. But actors all have a different way of working. Some of us are quiet, and I think women tend to be more out there in front. I always had a good time on the set and I was what you'd call

High school student Kristoffer Tabori and his coach's wife Marlyn Mason find that they dig more than football in *Making It* (20th Century–Fox, 1971).

a great crew gal. I'd bake cookies and bring stuff to the crew. That was sort of my old training. Somebody compared me once to Barbara Stanwyck. She and Bette Davis always took good care of their crew. I was raised with that so I always thought it was important to treat them nicely—you get treated nicely in return."

Longstreet was cancelled in 1972 after only one season, but as in the sixties Mason kept busy for the next twenty years playing a variety of roles on television. Her most famous made-for-TV movie was the groundbreaking, Emmy-award–winning drama *That Certain Summer* (1972) starring Hal Holbrook as the divorced father who reveals his homosexuality to his teenage son (Scott Jacoby) during a summer visit. Mason played the supporting role of a woman who hires Holbrook to work on her house. "I just had two small scenes with Hal Holbrook but it was wonderful," says Mason. "I was the lady with the leaky roof. Hal was an architect I hired to redesign my roof. It was like an unspoken attraction to him because he comes back with his son. But my character had no idea that he was gay. I believe *That Certain Summer* was one of the first TV movies to deal with homosexuality and it was so well done. I never had any qualms appearing in this, especially not with that cast. Hal was great but I never did get to meet Martin Sheen [who played Holbrook's young lover]."

Mason's other TV-movie roles included the kidnapped daughter of a scientist in the sci-fi adventure *Escape* (1971), starring Christopher George, and the wife of Robert Culp ("He was very nice but he was not real approachable"), playing a vigilante in *Outrage* (1973). Avid television viewers could catch Marlyn playing a gambler in debt to the mob on *The Magician*, the head of a call girl ring on *Barnaby Jones*, and a motorbike daredevil determined to break a long distance jump record on *Vega$*. *The New Adventures of Wonder Woman* featured Mason as a wicked woman who is in cahoots to sell a stolen missile system to the highest bidder on the black market. Comedy wise, Mason was a standout in her two appearances on *The Odd Couple*. During the show's first season she played a cooking contestant who tries to entice Oscar Madison (Jack Klugman) to reveal the secret recipe of her rival, Felix Unger (Tony Randall). She then appeared during the series' third season, playing a con artist.

In the nineties, Marlyn Mason was still getting work and played her first grandmother role in the made-for-TV movie *Fifteen and Pregnant* (1998). "This was fun because I had just come off of foot surgery," recalls Mason. "I was still in a removable boot and on crutches. I drove up and read for it. Before I had even got to my car I learned I had gotten the part. When the director [Sam Pillsbury] informed me of my first shooting date, I told him I would be using a cane but I won't have the boot. He said, 'I don't care what condition you are in, I just want you for this part.' That was a nice compliment. My using a cane added to the character. I played her as a tough old, not terribly attractive, farmer lady from Kansas. It was great."

Looking back on her long and varied career, Marlyn jokes, "I never did a *Batman* nor a *Gunsmoke*. On my tombstone I'm going to have them inscribe that 'She never did a *Love Boat* and never slept with Warren Beatty.'" But Mason does get serious and opines "I had a good career in terms of making a living at it. But I didn't have a real *juicy* career. I think my being so versatile hindered me because there were a lot more serious roles that I thought I could play that I wasn't considered for. My looks—with my big blue eyes and tiny nose—sort of typed me in cute rather than more dramatic roles."

Today Marlyn Mason resides in a beautiful town in Oregon. Though she has left the rat race of Los Angeles behind her, she still has not given up on her acting career. "In 1992, a series of events happened—my car died, my agent died and thusly my career died," laughs Mason. "And it wasn't much alive at that time anyway. I was fifty-two and I always felt there would come a time when I just wouldn't want to do it anymore. It's a mean business. People say you are wonderful and behind your back they'd say, 'God, she looks like hell! She's too this, she's too that. She's not aging very well.' Hollywood could be a terrible place. When I decided to relocate to Oregon it felt like a lot of baggage was lifted off my shoulders. I never regretted the move and I've done two movies while living here. I am still getting scripts and am ready to work if they want to hire me. I live a stress free life here. When I do have to go down to L.A. to audition I feel very strong because I haven't been hanging in there with the business. I see a lot of these actresses that I used to know with these faces that I don't recognize anymore. They've all had plastic surgery. What's the point of having a forty year-old face on a sixty year-old body?"

Film Appearances

1960 **Because They're Young** (Columbia) [uncredited] d. Paul Wendkos

1969 **The Trouble with Girls** (MGM) d. Peter Tewksbury
1970 **A Storm in Summer** (TV-movie) d. Buzz Kulik
1971 **Making It** (20th Century–Fox) d. John Erman
      Harpy (TV-movie) d. Jerrold Freedman/ Gerald Seth Sindell
      Escape (TV-movie) d. John Llewellyn Moxey
1972 **That Certain Summer** (TV-movie) d. Lamont Johnson
1973 **Outrage** (TV-movie) d. Richard T. Heffron
1974 **Christina** (New World) d. Paul Krasny
1975 **Attack on Terror: The FBI vs. the Ku Klux Klan** (TV-movie) d. Marvin J. Chomsky
1978 **Last of the Good Guys** (TV-movie) d. Theodore J. Flicker
      The New Adventures of Heidi (TV-movie) d. Ralph Senensky
1985 **My Wicked, Wicked Ways … The Legend of Errol Flynn** (TV-movie) d. Don Taylor
1986 **Trapped in Silence** (TV-movie) d. Michael Tuchner
1991 **Lonely Hearts** (Gibraltar Entertainment) d. Andrew Lane
1992 **Miles from Nowhere** (TV-movie) d. Buzz Kulik
1998 **Fifteen and Pregnant** (TV-movie) d. Sam Pillsbury

Television Appearances

Ripcord "The Sky Diver" 1962 SYN
My Three Sons "The Girls Next Door" 2/1/1962 ABC
The Real McCoys "The Incorruptibles" 3/31/1963 CBS
Burke's Law "Who Killed Billy Joe?" 11/8/1963 ABC
The Lieutenant "Instant Wedding" 11/9/1963 NBC
The Bill Dana Show "Jose the Agent" 11/17/1963 NBC
Burke's Law "Who Killed Jason Shaw?" 11/22/1963 ABC
The Greatest Show on Earth "Leaves in the Wind" 11/26/1963
Channing "A Hall Full of Strangers" 12/25/1963 ABC
Bonanza "A Bullet for the Bride" 2/16/1964 NBC
The Eleventh Hour "To Love Is to Live" 4/15/1964 NBC
Destry "The Infernal Triangle" 5/1/1964 ABC
Burke's Law "Who Killed the Surf Board Broad?" 9/16/1964 ABC
Kentucky Jones (pilot) 9/19/1964 NBC
The Rogues "The Project Man" 11/1/1964 NBC
Tell Aggie (unaired pilot) 1965 NBC
The Man from U.N.C.L.E. "The Fiddlesticks Affair" 1/18/1965 NBC
Bonanza "The Ponderosa Birdman" 2/11/1965 NBC
Valentine's Day "A Muffin Is Not a Tart" 4/23/1965 ABC
Ben Casey "War of Nerves" 9/13/1965 ABC
Ben Casey "O' the Big Wheel Turns by Faith, by Faith" 9/20/1965 ABC
Ben Casey "A Nightingale Named Nathan" 9/27/1965 ABC
Ben Casey "Run for Your Lives, Dr. Galanos Practices" 10/4/1965 ABC
Ben Casey "Because of the Needle, the Haystack" 10/11/1965 ABC
Ben Casey "What to Her Is Plato?" 10/18/1965 ABC
Ben Casey "Francini? Who Is Francini?" 10/25/1965 ABC
Dr. Kildare "The Life Machine" 10/26/1965 NBC
Laredo "A Question of Discipline" 10/28/1965 NBC
Dr. Kildare "Toast the Golden Couple" 11/1/1965 NBC
Dr. Kildare "Wives and Losers" 11/2/1965 NBC
Dr. Kildare "Welcome Home, Dear Anna" 11/8/1965 NBC
Dr. Kildare "A Little Child Shall Lead Them" 11/9/1965 NBC
Dr. Kildare "Hour of Decision" 11/15/1965 NBC
Dr. Kildare "Aftermath" 11/16/1965 NBC

I Spy "Weight of the World" 12/1/1965 NBC
Gomer Pyle, USMC "A Groom for Sgt. Carter's Sister" 12/3/1965 CBS
Laredo "That's Noway, Thataway" 1/20/1966 NBC
The Big Valley "The Fallen Hawk" 3/2/1966 ABC
Perry Mason "The Case of the Final Fade-Out" 5/22/1966 CBS
The F.B.I. "The Escape" 10/2/1966 ABC
Brigadoon (special) 10/15/1966 ABC
Twelve O'Clock High "Fighter Pilot" 11/11/1966 ABC
Run for Your Life "The Shock of Recognition" 12/26/1966 NBC
Hey Landlord "Stranger in the Night Than in the Morning" 2/5/1967 NBC
Occasional Wife "The New Secretary" 2/14/1967 NBC
Occasional Wife "Engagement, Christopher Style" 2/28/1967 NBC
The Fugitive "Goodbye, My Love" 2/28/1967 ABC
Captain Nice "May I Have the Last Dance?" 4/17/1967 NBC
Carousel (special) 5/7/1967 ABC
The Invaders "The Condemned" 5/9/1967 ABC
The Big Valley "Ladykiller" 10/16/1967 ABC
Mannix "The Cost of a Vacation" 10/21/1967 CBS
The Man from U.N.C.L.E. "The Deadly Quest Affair" 10/30/1967 NBC
The Joe Franklin Show 2/15/1968 SYN
The F.B.I. "Moment of Truth" 3/30/1969 ABC
Love, American Style "Love and the Living Doll" 10/6/1969 ABC
Bracken's World "The Chase Sequence" 12/26/1969 NBC
Hogan's Heroes "Six Lessons from Madame LaGrange" 2/27/1970 CBS
Love, American Style "Love and the Eskimo" 10/30/1970 ABC
The Most Deadly Game "Photo Finish" 11/14/1970 ABC
The Odd Couple "They Use Horse Radish, Don't They?" 1/7/1971 ABC
Hogan's Heroes "Rockets or Romance" 4/4/1971 CBS
Longstreet (series regular as Nikki Bell) 9/16/71 to 8/10/1972 ABC
Love, American Style "Love and the Married Bachelor" 11/5/1971 ABC
Ironside "Class of '57" 12/16/1971 NBC
Insight "Friends" 1972 SYN
It's Your Bet 7/10 to 7/14/1972 NBC
Banacek "Let's Hear It for a Living Legend" 9/13/1972 NBC
Banyon "The Decent Thing to Do" 9/15/1972 NBC
The FBI "The Fatal Showdown" 10/1/1972 ABC
The Bold Ones: The Doctors "A Quality of Fear" 11/14/1972 NBC
Ghost Story "Elegy for a Vampire" 12/1/1972 NBC
Mission: Impossible "Crack-Up" 12/9/1972 CBS
Of Men and Women "Why Was He Late for Work?" (pilot) 12/17/1972 ABC
The Odd Couple "Don't Believe in Roomers" 12/22/1972 ABC
The Mod Squad "Don't Kill My Child" 1/18/1973 ABC
Medical Center "Night Cry" 2/7/1973 CBS
Love, American Style "Love and the Burglar Joke" 2/16/1973 ABC
Cannon "Press Pass to the Slammer" 3/14/1973 CBS
Barnaby Jones "See Some Evil … Do Some Evil" 4/8/1973 CBS
The Magician "The Manhunters" 10/2/1973 NBC
Love, American Style "Love and the Man of the Year" 11/23/1973 ABC
Lucas Tanner "Instant Replay" 9/18/1974 NBC
Caribe "The Mercenary" 3/10/1975 ABC
Joe Forrester "Powder Blue" 10/21/1975 NBC
Matt Helm "Squeeze Play" 11/1/1975 ABC
Joe Forrester "An Act of Violence" 1/3/1976 NBC
Marcus Welby, M.D. "Prisoner of the Island Cell" 1/20 & 1/27/1976 ABC
The Streets of San Francisco "Who Killed Helen French?" 2/3/1977 ABC
Tales of the Unexpected "The Mask of Adonis" 2/9/1977 NBC
Most Wanted "The Driver" 3/14/1977 ABC
Barnaby Jones "Child of Love, Child of Vengeance" 3/15 & 3/22/1977 CBS
Handle with Care (pilot) 5/9/1977 CBS
Barnaby Jones "Daughter of Evil" 11/3/1977 CBS
Great Performances "The Good Doctor" 11/8/1978 PBS

Project UFO "Sighting 4022: The Island Incident" 11/30/1978 NBC
The Amazing Spider-Man "The Kirkwood Haunting" 12/30/1978 CBS
The New Adventures of Wonder Woman "The Richest Man in the World" 2/19/1979 CBS
Cross-Wits 3/12 to 3/16/1979 SYN
Vega$ "A Way to Live" 5/2/1979 ABC
Cross-Wits 1/16/1980 SYN
Skag "In Trouble at 15" 1/17/1980 NBC
Cross-Wits 2/4/1980 SYN
House Calls "Bombing Out" 2/2/1981 CBS
Two the Hard Way (pilot) 8/11/1981 CBS
Boone "The Front Line" 8/4/1984 NBC
Scarecrow and Mrs. King "Ship of Spies" 1/7/1985 CBS
Hardcastle and McCormick "Poker Night" 3/3/1986 ABC
Newhart "Baby, I'm Your Handyman" 4/7/1986 CBS
The Bronx Zoo "Ties That Bind" 4/13/1988 NBC
Dynasty "Here Comes the Son" 4/27/1989 ABC
Charles in Charge "Walter's War" 9/9/1989 SYN
Jake and the Fatman "Sweet Leilani" 11/15/1989 CBS
Charles in Charge "Three Dates and a Walnut" 1990 SYN
Dead by Sunset (mini-series) 11/19 to 11/20/1995
Candid Camera 2/5/2000 SYN

Also

Matinee Theater (5) and *Father Knows Best*

☆ QUINN O'HARA ☆

Once described as a "red-headed gasser" and a "scorching sizzler," Quinn O'Hara was very popular with teenage audiences during the sixties. A former Miss Scotland, this titian-haired beauty began on television before appearing in minor film roles with major stars such as Jerry Lewis and Jack Lemmon. Audiences remembered her best for her role as Smitty in the second incarnation of Vic Damone's popular summer series *The Lively One*s in 1962. Two back-to-back starring roles in *A Swingin' Summer* (1965) and *The Ghost in the Invisible Bikini* (1966) propelled her to the top of the teen heap. However, disenchanted with the roles being offered her, O'Hara fled to England where she worked on stage, TV and an occasional film. When she returned to Hollywood in the mid-seventies, she undeservedly got the cold shoulder from the town. She was just another in a long line of sixties starlets who saw their careers unceremoniously end during that decade. Quinn persevered and eventually went into real estate and nursing.

Quinn O'Hara was dramatically born in a hospital's elevator going up in Edinburgh, Scotland. The date was January 3, 1941, and her Welsh father and her Scottish-Irish mother named the impatient newborn Alice Jones. Most of her childhood was spent in a convent boarding school in Wales. When she turned fourteen, she and her mother moved to Quebec, Canada, where the blossoming teenager learned to speak French. After three years, they moved to Long Beach, California, where the red haired beauty stood out from the myriad of California blondes. "While I was living in California someone wanted me to enter the Miss California contest as Miss Lakewood," recalls O'Hara. "When they found out that I was born in Edinburgh I couldn't compete as Miss Lakewood, because if I won and went on to the Miss Universe pageant it wouldn't have been too cool if Miss USA was born in Scotland. There had not been a Miss Scotland until that time. The countries franchise the title and the Royal Order called and dubbed me Miss Scotland. I didn't actually compete but they gave me the title. I always played down the Miss Scotland title even though the PR guys always tried to play it up. You don't get much credit for being a beauty queen and it was all so very odd the way the whole thing came about."

The one thing you do gain as a beauty queen is attention, and O'Hara began to get a lot of it. With the acting offers coming in, she decided the name Alice Jones did not seem right for a redheaded aspiring actress. "When you first start out you usually have only an 8 × 10 black and white photo of yourself," explains O'Hara. "Red hair doesn't come up in black and white. I wanted a name that would make people think of a redhead. I immediately thought of O'Hara, but it was a question of what first name would go with it. After about three months of great thought, I was looking down the roster of people at Goldwyn Studios and came across Quinn Martin's name. Quinn O'Hara had a nice sound to it. A couple of other people thought it sounded good so I went with that."

O'Hara's first official acting role that got her into the Screen Actors Guild was a commercial for Lifeogen, which was oxygen in a can. In case of an emergency, you were supposed to put it over somebody's mouth until the paramedics got there. Her big screen debut was in an uncredited bit part in *The Errand Boy* (1961) starring Jerry Lewis, where he plays a goofball hired by the CEO of a movie studio, Paramuteul Pictures, to spy on his employees. O'Hara would go on to work with Lewis again in *The Patsy* (1964), playing the minor role of a cigarette girl. "Jerry was fantastic to work with," exclaims Quinn. "Of course he is a crazy man but he is also a real perfectionist. There was an actor he worked a lot with—comedian Del Moore—and they would break each other up on the set. But Jerry is quite a deep person too and has a lot more depth than people think. His office had clowns all around it. He was quite different than he comes across on film." Lewis also hired O'Hara for a role in *Who's Minding the Store?* (1963), but her scenes were cut. Coincidentally, Lewis' costar in that movie is another fiery redhead, Jill St. John (whom O'Hara describes as being "an unbelievably cruel person who I am not fond of in the least!").

O'Hara's first taste of fame came when she was selected to appear with Vic Damone in his 1962 summer series *The Lively Ones*. Barry Shear produced this Emmy nominated variety series and to make *The Lively Ones* different, he featured an array of guest stars ranging from dancer Barrie Chase to the Benny Goodman Sextet, and Charlie Byrd to Bulwinkle the Moose performing in various venues around the country. "This was a wonderful experience for me," exclaims O'Hara. "Working on *The Lively Set* was great because I got to work with so many fantastic people. It was incredible. Gloria Neil and I were like two ding-a-lings or bookends. We did most of the commercials for Ford, the show's sponsor. In fact, it was my commercial agent who got me this. We would be sitting watching other performers, sometimes in a nightclub setting. We'd do a lot of fun things like ride a roller coaster. One time we were mermaids at the beach. We were really there on the show as decoration."

The Lively Ones brought O'Hara notoriety. She became very much in demand on TV but she wasn't having much luck with films. She played a hospital nurse in *The Caretakers* (1963), but all her scenes were deleted except for one where you can see her hand as she is holding down patient Polly Bergen. ("I knew it was my

All eyes are on Quinn O'Hara, the redheaded knockout of *The Ghost in the Invisible Bikini* (AIP, 1966).

hand because I had a ring on that my mother had given me on my twenty-first birthday.") Her whole body was on display in her next film, *Good Neighbor, Sam* (1964) where she played the small role of a curvy secretary to recently promoted ad man Jack Lemmon (whom O'Hara describes as being "just wonderful! He was darling and very modest."). O'Hara contributes her lack of movie roles to mistakes she made regarding agents. "I was just never good at picking one," says Quinn with a laugh. "At the time the one I had told me, 'You don't want a studio contract. You're going be hemmed in with this, that and the other thing.' That was the wrong thing to say! I should have had a contract for a little while. But by the time I actually started there weren't many contracts being offered. Warner Brothers, Paramount and MGM were the only studios with contract players."

O'Hara kept persevering. She began getting press in all the movie rags of the time and she was chosen by *Photoplay* to be photographed on a pre-arranged "date" with teen idol Fabian. But surprisingly, the duo hit it off and it developed into a relationship that lasted a year. ("Fabian had a temper so I broke it off with him," reveals Quinn.) Regarding the lull in her career at that time, her good friend actor Aron Kincaid says "I constantly told Quinn that once they put her in color everything would change. In black and white, she looked great and but *nothing* like she did in person." Kincaid was absolutely correct. In 1965 Quinn O'Hara starred in the teenage film *A Swingin' Summer,* directed by Robert Sparr and produced by Reno Carell, who was also responsible for *Winter a-Go-Go* that same year. Though it was not her first color movie, it was her first lead role. She looked terrific and more than held her own with co-star Raquel Welch. "Linda Evans was set for the lead and I went in to see about the part Lili Kardell did," reveals O'Hara. "Then Linda backed out because she got cast in the series *The Big Valley*. I had tested for that also but she won out. Linda had to give up the movie so the producers called me in and I got her part at the last minute." Not only did Quinn have to quickly learn her lines but she also had to put a wardrobe together during the course of the filming. ("Linda Evans is taller than I am so her clothes didn't fit me.") That didn't bother O'Hara as much as the altitude and the film's cameraman [Ray Fernstrom]. "I remember that this was his first color movie. He

Fabian and his date Quinn O'Hara are all smiles at a celebrity shindig, ca. 1964. *Courtesy of Quinn O'Hara.*

had done a lot of black and white television. He really blasted us with those reflectors."

To set itself apart from the myriad of beach films being released in 1965, *A Swingin' Summer* is set in Lake Arrowhead, a real life area in the mountains popular with teenagers at that time. O'Hara essayed the role of Cindy who, along with her boyfriend Rick (William Wellman, Jr.) and his friend Mickey (James Stacy), plans to work the summer booking musical acts at a dance pavilion at the resort. When the owner threatens to close it down, Cindy secretly arranges for her wealthy father to put up the security. Complications ensue when lifeguard Turk (Martin West), a rival for the spot, tries to sabotage the upcoming show and vies with Rick for the charms of Cindy. Also appearing in the film is Raquel Welch as an intellectual bookworm who loses her glasses and learns to swing and Mary Mitchel as the wisecracking, bubble gum chewing friend of Cindy.

"William Wellman Jr. and James Stacy were both delightful," remarks Quinn. "Jim was married to Connie Stevens at the time. I saw Connie—she looks fabulous—at a luncheon in the Valley about two years ago. I had heard a lot of nasty rumors about Jim Stacy so I asked her, 'Is it true what I've heard about Jim?' She said, 'Yes.' Jim was so charming and such a good-looking guy. I thought he had everything going for him and was destined for stardom." The fans thought so too and were shocked when Stacy (who survived a motorcycle accident in the early seventies but lost a leg) was arrested for child molestation in the nineties.

As the ad copy proclaimed, "Spread out the beach towels.... Grab your gals! It's gonna be *A Swingin' Summer*!" And the movie is just that. As it was described by *Variety*, "A breezy bouncing bunch of boys, babes, bosoms, buttocks and bodies bob about in this bucolic beach-bash broth." O'Hara looks fantastic and acts wonderfully, prompting *Variety* to rave, "Miss O'Hara is a knockout who can go places." Teenage boys desired her and teenage girls wanted to be her. She became so popular that readers of *Teen Screen Magazine* voted her the year's 'Most Promising Female Personality.' ("I still have the award in a box somewhere.")

Though O'Hara got good notices and the fans' attention, it is no secret that Raquel Welch (despite her untrained singing voice) is the one who became the superstar. Surprisingly, Quinn and Welch got along very well during the filming and there was no competition between them. "I had no trouble with Raquel," says O'Hara. "But everybody else did—including the cameraman and make up person. Lori Williams, who was such a nice girl, also had a terrible time with Raquel. I wasn't on the set but I heard that Lori had the same color bikini on as Raquel and she told the director to go make Lori change her bathing suit! When we went to do promotion for the film in conjunction with Suzuki, Raquel and I both showed up wearing pink. I said to somebody, 'If she thinks I'm going to change, she's crazy.' Raquel didn't say a word and went and changed her outfit.

"I remember saying one day on the set to Lori and Irene Sale, 'You know what—this girl is going to be a star. She's got enough *bitch* in her to make it,'" continues Quinn. "Raquel knew exactly what she wanted it and that's what it takes to make it big. I have great admiration and respect for her, believe me. She looks terrific, she's hung in there and she has done very well. Raquel is a businesswoman and a smart lady. I wish I had been a bit more like her." Much of Raquel's early success has to do with her manager and then husband Patrick Curtis, who guided her to stardom. He was a very noticeable presence on the set of *A Swingin' Summer*. According to O'Hara she had an opportunity to have him manage her also, but "I thought Patrick was a very delightful person but full of bull. I told him to stick with Raquel and put in a couple of years with her. So she then became a big star! *Would I like to eat my words!*"

Quinn O'Hara next auditioned at AIP for the role of the sexy though bumbling Sinistra in what was then titled *Bikini Party in a Haunted House*. It was not her first encounter with the studio. The producers and director Don Weis originally wanted her for a role in *Pajama Party* (1964), but she declined because "I didn't want to be just one of the beach girls so I turned it down. I also didn't want to do it because I was appearing in a lot of other things that were better at that time."

"They originally wanted a tall buxom blonde for the part of Sinistra," continues Quinn laughing. *"They ended up with a short redhead instead.* When I read for Don Weis, he said, 'I forgot what a good actress you are. You got it.' Even though they wanted a blonde he went with me. While I was working on the film, I asked him, 'If I had taken that part last year, would I have been able to get this part this year?' He said, 'No, probably not.'"

AIP decided they needed to pump new life into their beach genre, so they came up with an idea of combining it with a horror angle, which had worked so well for them with the series of Edgar Allan Poe films. Previously, *Pajama Party*, which starred Tommy Kirk as an alien who invades the beach party, did very well at the box office, so it was felt this would too. Domenic Priore, writing in *Hollywood Rock*, commented that the film "presents the sci-fi goofiness of *Pajama Party* kicked into a chamber of horrors." The premise of *The Ghost in the Invisible Bikini*, originally titled *Bikini Party in a Haunted House*, was that three heirs, Chuck Philips (Tommy Kirk), Lili Morton (Deborah Walley) and Myrtle Forbush (Patsy Kelly), gather at the creepy mansion of dead millionaire, Hiram Stokely, to hear the reading of his will. His crooked attorney, Reggie Ripper (Basil Rathbone), informs them that the money is hidden somewhere in the house. Myrtle invites her nephew Bobby (Aron Kincaid) to come along, and he brings with him a gaggle of surfer boys and bikini girls (including Nancy Sinatra, Claudia Martin, Piccola Pupa, Ed Garner, Luree Holmes, etc.). Erik Von Zipper (Harvey Lembeck) and his Rat Pack also invade the haunted house to get their hands on the hidden loot. Ripper plans to eliminate each heir with the help of his inept gang led by fumbling Jesse White and sexpot Bobbi Shaw. To get rid of Bobby, he sets his shapely, brainy, though blind-as-a-bat daughter Sinistra (O'Hara) on him. But her nearsightedness keeps getting in her way. The Bobby Fuller Four appears poolside to get the kids dancing, lip-synching to "Make the Music Pretty" and "Swing-A-Ma-Thang." They also back up Nancy Sinatra on arguably the film's best song, "Geronimo."

O'Hara also gets to sing. Her rendition of "Don't Try to Fight It" is one of the film's highlights. "When I heard Nancy Sinatra was singing I thought, '*I guess I can too,*'" cracks Quinn with a laugh. "That is actually me singing. I took two years of voice lessons with a very good teacher. I do not consider myself a singer. But I did enjoy singing in the movie because I got to dance with it, which distracts from the singing. When I hear it now, there are a couple of notes I hit that make me want to hide under the bed. I feel lucky that I had the opportunity to do that and it was a lot of fun to do."

O'Hara also had some wonderfully comedic scenes as she fumbles in her attempts to knock off the young blonde surfer (Kincaid). After Sinistra entices

Bobby away from his girlfriend Vicky (Sinatra), Ripper says, "Men do seem to like her for some reason." Myrtle responds sarcastically, "I can think of three reasons—38-24-36. Yiish!" Quinn's Sinistra misplaces her glasses and tries to seduce a suit of armor (thinking it is Bobby) into drinking her deadly concoction. When that fails, she sings "Don't Try to Fight It" while dancing around it. Later the inept girl mistakes a statue for Bobby and rubs its neck ("Ooh, aren't you built!") before pushing it over a cliff. "I had more fun playing this role than any other. It is my favorite, as a matter of fact. I got to be really campy with the English accent. My walk was accidental because I couldn't see a damn thing with those glasses on. The lenses were as thick as Coke bottles. They didn't even have any holes to see through, so the only way I could see was to look over them. When I had to walk wearing them I couldn't see a thing."

Another highlight of doing this film for Quinn O'Hara was the opportunity to play the esteemed Basil Rathbone's daughter. Though she had worked with some big stars before, Rathbone left an indelible impression on her. "He was delightful," gushes O'Hara. "When I first met him I was so afraid I'd say, 'Rasil Bathbone' that I actually did! He was a charming man. I heard that during his heyday in Hollywood he and his wife would throw the most magnificent parties. I was just so happy to play his daughter." Regarding her other co-stars, Quinn continues, "Aron Kincaid is one of the nicest people you ever want to meet. He is cheerful, upbeat, considerate and very talented. He is a lot of fun to work with. He is also a very skilled artist. I didn't have much of an occasion to work with Tommy Kirk or

Michael Blodgett and Quinn O'Hara do the Frug in *A Swingin' Summer* **(United Screen Arts, 1965).** *Courtesy of Quinn O'Hara.*

Deborah Walley. I thought Deborah was a very fine person. Tommy Kirk was a bit strange but he was nice."

The head honchos at AIP decreed that *Bikini Party in a Haunted House* was unreleasable. Purportedly, the script was being rewritten daily on the set and the film went over budget. According to O'Hara one reason may have been due to cameraman Stanley Cortez. "When I began working with Stanley, he'd always call me 'Miss' and say things like 'Miss, could you move over here.' After two days of this I went up to him and said, 'Mr. Cortez my name is Quinn O'Hara. Would you mind calling me Quinn?' After that we got along wonderfully. He told me that he liked my cheekbones. He really took a lot of time with the shots and the producers got mad at him because we were going over budget. I thought he was a fantastic cameraman." The extra time Cortez took with his shots really did help the film and O'Hara never looked more gorgeous on screen, despite the thick glasses she wears. *Variety* noted, "All other technical credits are excellent, particularly Stanley Cortez' Panavision camera...."

To salvage the film, scenes with Boris Karloff as the recently departed Hiram Stokely and Susan Hart as his long-dead wife, Cecily, were added and the film was re-titled *The Ghost in the Invisible Bikini*. Hiram must do a good deed to get into heaven, so Cecily (the girl in the title) is sent down to Earth to make sure the rightful heirs get his money. With the name change came the excising of the film's big opening song, "Bikini Party in a Haunted House" with lead vocals sung by Aron Kincaid and Piccola Pupa. The entire cast was carted out to the Disney Ranch for this big production number which never saw the light of day, though Kincaid does have the song on CD.

As directed by Don Weis, *The Ghost in the Invisible Bikini* is the weakest of the *Beach Party* films. It is not too surprising since one of the film's stars was Italian "singing sensation" Piccola Pupa, whom AIP was pushing onto the public as perhaps their new Donna Loren. "Piccola Pupa was discovered by Danny Thomas," remarks Quinn. "Her name translates into 'Little Doll' in English." Whatever her name means, the public wisely rejected her and sent her packing. Quinn though received good reviews for her performance. *Variety* took notice and commented, "Almost all the girls are still good—Nancy Sinatra, Quinn O'Hara and Deborah Walley coming over best." But the film on the whole did not—"standard AIP mindlessness" is just one of many dismissive reviews.

O'Hara deserved better than her next AIP film *In the Year 2889* (1967), co-starring Paul Petersen of *The Donna Reed Show*. The film was directed by self-described "schlockmeister" Larry Buchanan, who had a four-picture deal with the studio to remake some of their cult fifties movies on minuscule budgets. ("I think the budget for *In the Year 2889* was $28.89," jokes O'Hara.) This film was an uncredited remake of Roger Corman's *The Day the World Ended* (1956). O'Hara played a stripper who is one of a handful of people (including Petersen as the good-looking hero, Neil Fletcher as a retired Navy officer and Charla Doherty as his daughter) who survive an atomic blast. Hiding in a big house in the mountains, they argue amongst themselves as they are menaced by a group of ravaging cannibalistic human mutants with telepathic powers. O'Hara is lucky, as her character meets her demise mid-way through the film.

Buchanan, writing in his autobiography *It Came from Hunger!*, described Quinn as "a stunning sexpot with a comic temperament." He went on to relay how the beautiful redhead was such a cut-up on the set and how the crew loved her so much that he decided to kill her character off just to send her packing early. O'Hara loved the idea because she got to do a death scene and he got the attention of his crew back. "I adored what Larry wrote but some of it was not true," refutes Quinn. "My character was always supposed to die. She originally was to be pushed off a cliff by the mutants, but they changed it so they'd drown her in the pool."

Quinn next appeared in the Oscar nominated short film *Prelude* (1968), directed by John Astin. Only in swinging 1960s Hollywood could a starlet go from low budget teenage schlock to a prestigious award-winning movie within a year. Astin originally asked O'Hara to play Startling Girl, the fantasy woman Astin's put-upon character meets in the supermarket. However, actress Karen Jensen was brought to Astin's attention and he asked O'Hara to play his wife instead. "I had no problem switching roles because the wife was a real bitch," remarks O'Hara. "I didn't get the opportunity to play many roles like that."

It was shortly thereafter that Quinn O'Hara departed Hollywood after appearing on *The Dating Game*. This was her second appearance as one of three celebrity bachlorettes. The first time was in 1967, where on a special St. Patrick's Day program, the eligible bachelor chose the Irish lass, actress Eileen O'Neill. But in a special program in honor of the Academy Awards in 1969, O'Hara got picked and went on a chaperoned trip to Nepal. She decided to return home via Europe but never made it back to the U.S. "I got hung up in London and decided to move there because I could do theatre," says Quinn. "I had a problem with doing theatre in the U.S. because I wasn't a citizen. Actor's Equity is very hard on British actors. It was very bad timing on my part because I still had a lot of things going on in Hollywood."

A number of reasons contributed to her decision to leave California, but one of the major ones was her frustration with the film roles being offered her. These parts required her to go topless and she turned them all down—even a role as a stewardess in *Bob & Carol & Ted & Alice* (1969). "The only roles I was being offered had gratuitous nudity," comments Quinn. "*I was brought up in a convent!* I didn't even undress in front of women! I had done some sexy posing for various magazines but that was as far as I would go. I was offered to appear in *Playboy* many times but I wouldn't do it."

One of the films Quinn O'Hara did while in Europe was a small role in the AIP horror film *Cry of the Banshee* (1970). Vincent Price ("He was delightful—absolutely wonderful," raves Quinn) starred as Lord Whitman, a wicked sixteenth century Irish magistrate who takes pleasure in torturing people suspected of witchcraft. When his followers murder the members of a Druid cult, their leader, Oona (Elisabeth Bergner), summons a demon banshee who takes the form of a studly stable boy (Patrick Mower) to procure revenge against Whitman and his family. O'Hara played Maggie, a wench working at a tavern, who is discovered to be a witch when she drops her ingredients for a potion. She is the catalyst for the nightmare that follows. As Whitman's men rip off her top and threaten to rape and kill her, she reveals the whereabouts of Oona and her cult. Despite cooperating, Maggie is disposed of anyway. "I wasn't really sure when I did this if I was a witch or a wench. I know I got killed in it. I had to wait until the end credits where I was listed as a witch. I guess I was a witch wench."

O'Hara's last movie was *Rubia's Jungle* (1971), which was shot in the Netherlands. "This was a good movie," remarks Quinn. "It was sort of a film noir, shot in black and white. It was very solemn and heavy. My character is obsessed with this guy who is married. I end up killing him and then myself. *I die very well*. The lead in it was a black actor named Milton Irons who was modeling and doing the Amsterdam version of *Hair*. He was very nice and he had half the male and female population after him. The director interviewed me in England and we met at a hotel. He told me when I walked into the lobby he knew I was right for Rubia. It was the Dutch entry in the Edinburg Film Festival."

During her time in England, O'Hara made periodical trips back to Hollywood to maintain her working status. She could be seen on *To Rome with Love*, *The Smith Family* and *Ironside* ("This was one of my favorite acting experiences because I found

Quinn O'Hara played an obsessed woman in love with a married man in *Rubia's Jungle* (Scorpio Films, 1971) Courtesy of Quinn O'Hara.

Raymond Burr to be such a pro."). Then Quinn disappeared from show business. "I went to Africa to visit my father, who was working for an English company. I stayed for about five months and met an Italian guy there. We were going to be wed so I went with him to Italy but we didn't marry. I had a lot of fun in Italy and when I came back to Hollywood [in the late seventies] it was like everybody had forgotten me. It was very hard to get any work. Don Weis gave me a part in an episode of *CHiPs*. Other than that and two small roles on *One Day at a Time*, I couldn't get arrested."

Like a number of her contemporaries, O'Hara took up real estate to make ends meet. After a short-lived marriage ("He was an idiot"), Quinn met Bill Kirk, who is twenty years her junior, in 1981. "I met him when he was about twenty-one and just legal," laughs O'Hara. "We got married about five years after we had met, after living together for a short while. But I was going through a very dark period during that time." O'Hara had a problem with alcohol, which she successfully overcame. Getting her life in order meant becoming a U. S. citizen. "I became a citizen in 1992 and had the opportunity to change my name legally. I wasn't doing much acting, so instead of Quinn O'Hara I kept my real first name Alice and used Kirk even though Bill and I were divorced by then. I liked the name Kirk because it's Scottish for church. I am now legally Alice Kirk. Bill and I are living together again and we may re-marry."

Today, Quinn O'Hara works as a nurse ("I like to help elderly people out so they will not have to go to a nursing home. As people get older they deserve to have a decent quality of life.") She would also love another chance to act again. "Two years ago I went to a lot of showcases and met a number of casting directors. The people I knew are all retired and these new people just don't know who I am. I would love to be able to act again, especially in comedy. I used to say, *'I might be seventy-six but one of these days I'm going to get an Oscar!'* Margaret Rutherford and Jessica Tandy did. These ladies are my idols. Who knows? They brought Gloria Stuart back for *Titanic*, so you never know. I'm hoping that one of these days something like that could happen to me."

Film Appearances

1961   The Errand Boy (Paramount) d. Jerry Lewis

1963   The Caretakers (United Artists) d. Hall Bartlett *

Who's Minding the Store? (Paramount) d. Frank Tashlin *

1964   Good Neighbor Sam (Columbia) d. David Swift

The Patsy (Paramount) d. Jerry Lewis

1965   A Swingin' Summer (United Screen Arts) d. Robert Sparr

1966   The Ghost in the Invisible Bikini (AIP) d. Don Weis

1967   In the Year 2889 (AIP) d. Larry Buchanan

1968   Way Out West (Universal) [edited episodes of Pistols n Petticoats] d. various

Prelude (Excelsior) [short] d. John Astin

1970   Cry of the Banshee (Great Britain, AIP) d. Gordon Hessler

1971   Rubia's Jungle (Netherlands, Scorpio Films) d. Pim de la Parra

*Scenes deleted.

Television Appearances

G. E. Theatre "A Very Special Girl" 3/11/1962 CBS
Surfside 6 "Love Song for a Dead Redhead" 4/30/1962 ABC
The Red Skelton Show "Freddie and the Daily Freeloader" 6/12/1962 CBS
The Real McCoys "Meeting Hassie's Friends" 6/28/1962 CBS
The Red Skelton Show 10/30/1962 CBS
I'm Dickens … He's Fenster "The Yellow Badge of Courage" 11/30/1962 ABC
The Red Skelton Show 12/18/1962 CBS
The Real McCoys "The Incorruptibles" 3/31/1963 CBS
The Lively Ones (series regular as Smitty) 7/25 to 9/12/1963 NBC
Arrest and Trial "The Witnesses" 11/3/1963 ABC
Burke's Law "Who Killed Jason Shaw?" 11/22/1963 ABC
My Three Sons "The Chaperone" 1/30/1964 ABC
Channing "The Face in the Sun" 2/19/1964 ABC
The Beverly Hillbillies "Granny vs. the Weather Bureau" 3/25/1964 CBS
Bob Hope Chrysler Theatre "A Case of Armed Robbery" 4/3/1964 NBC
Kraft Suspense Theatre "Rumble on the Docks" 10/22/1964 NBC
The Rogues "Death of a Fleming" 10/25/1964 NBC
Burke's Law "Who Killed Lenore Wingfield?" 11/4/1964 ABC
Burke's Law "Who Killed the Strangler?" 1/6/1965 ABC
The Tycoon "Johnny on the Spot" 3/2/1965 ABC
Burke's Law "Who Killed the Card?" 5/5/1965 ABC
The Smothers Brothers Show "Pay the Man the $27.95" 10/15/1965 CBS
The Man from U.N.C.L.E. "The Arabian Affair" 10/29/1965 NBC
Run for Your Life "The Savage Season" 11/8/1965 NBC
The Man from U.N.C.L.E. "The Adriatic Express Affair" 12/17/1965 NBC
My Three Sons "Charley the Pigeon" 12/30/1965 CBS
The John Forsythe Show "On an Island with You and You and You" 3/14/1966 NBC
Bob Hope Chrysler Theatre "Brilliant Benjamin Boggs" 3/30/1966 NBC
The Saint "Interlude in Venice" 10/7/1966 NBC
Pistols 'n' Petticoats "Quit Shootin' Folks, Grandma" 11/26/1966 CBS
Dragnet "The Suicide Attempt" 2/29/1968 NBC
To Rome with Love "Making the Scene" 1/5/1971 CBS
The Smith Family "All the Good Neighbors" 2/17/1971 ABC
Ironside "Grandmother's House" 4/1/1971 NBC
UFO "Ordeal" 4/21/1971 SYN

One Day at a Time "The Singles Bar" 3/8/1977 CBS
CHiPs "Drive, Lady, Drive Part 2" 11/10/1977 NBC
One Day at a Time "The Race Driver Part 1" 1/3/1978 CBS

Also

Day in Court and *The Dating Game* (3)

☆ MELODY PATTERSON ☆

Pretty, blonde Melody Patterson will forever be remembered as shapely cowgirl Wrangler Jane on the cult TV comedy series *F Troop*. Patterson brought a fresh-faced feistiness to the role, which was a bit reminiscent to real-life western heroine Calamity Jane. Proving she could play strong-willed women convincingly, the biker film genre took advantage, as she was cast as a Hollywood starlet in *The Angry Breed* (1968) and a former motorcycle gang member trying to go straight in *The Cycle Savages* (1969). Patterson's last drive-in movie appearance was as the heroine in the cult horror opus *Blood and Lace* (1971), about an ax-wielding psycho terrorizing an orphanage for teenagers.

Melody Patterson was born in Inglewood, California on April 16, 1949. Her mother was a dancer so Melody inherited her mother's love of performing. The youngster was singing and dancing by the time she was four years old. "I think this just came naturally and I was just that kind of a child," remarks Melody Patterson. "My grandmother taught me how to sing the words to some songs before I was even in kindergarten. My mom and dad loved to eat out and, being an only child, they took me with them everywhere. I do have some vague memories of being put on this piano in some place and singing 'Glow Little Glowworm.' Of course, when you are four years old everybody thinks you're adorable. My mother then enrolled me in dance class. She was involved with getting the Downey Community Players going and then the Downey Children's Theatre. I danced in their first production, which was *Heidi*. Then before I knew it, I was in *Alice in Wonderland* and other productions. It was so much fun. I practically grew up in children's theatre."

During her formative years, Patterson attended a Catholic elementary school while still appearing on stage, which eventually led to small parts on television and in film. "I did a few episodes of *Day in Court*," recalls Patterson. "The nuns were really excited about that. Then in the eighth grade I was cast as a dancer in the movie *Bye Bye Birdie*. I worked for three weeks on this [in the "Honestly Sincere" number performed by Jesse Pearson when he first arrives in Ann-Margret's hometown]. When I did this there were hundreds of kids, so they had to hire at least eight teachers for us." With her budding acting career starting to blossom, Patterson transferred to the Hollywood Professional School in the ninth grade, which she loved because "everybody there was in show business of some sort. They were extremely proud of you and didn't react negatively if you had an interview. They'd work around you, plus school went from nine in the morning to one in the afternoon. They expected you to go on auditions after that. There was never any homework because all the kids were professional kids. It was a great school and I loved it!"

Patterson eventually left the Hollywood Professional School to go to Downey High School. ("I thought I was missing out on something. I found out that I wasn't missing out on a *thing*.") It was here that she learned of the role of Wrangler Jane in a proposed new comedy series called *F Troop*. Though she was only fifteen at the time, Patterson immediately felt a connection to the part because her favorite movie was *Calamity Jane*, starring Doris Day. Melody knew every scene and line from the film and felt that Wrangler Jane was a close cousin to her big screen counterpart. Because of this, she knew she had a good shot for the part but her age would be a hindrance. "It seemed that during that time when I was thirteen, fourteen and fifteen years old, if a studio could get a girl who was over eighteen to play a fifteen-year-old they did," says Patterson. "There were quite a few actresses around then that could pull it off. The studios didn't want to be hassled with a minor going to school or paying for a teacher. I was going on a lot of auditions and working hard at my craft, so I was dying to get a role. There were quite a few roles that I felt I might have gotten if I had been eighteen. One part that I did get was a student on *Mr. Novak*. It was a big deal because they had to hire a teacher for me. But all in all the studios would rather not do it.

"I did well on the *F Troop* audition

Curvy, bikini-clad Melody Patterson poses with what every '60s drive-in movie starlet needed—a stuffed leopard.

and I knew it," continues Patterson. "So when the producers asked me, 'You're eighteen, right?' I didn't argue with them. I said, 'Right.' Then they said, 'Well, you can ride a horse, right?' I didn't argue about that either. I thought to myself, 'If I can just get tested, then I will have some film.' Then when they offered me the role, I thought, 'Well if I can just do the pilot I'll still be ahead of the game.'" Melody and her mother knew she could get into trouble if she took the part without revealing her true age. But they had told Downey High School that the family was moving to Texas so Melody could do the pilot. She was lucky that it was filmed during Christmas vacation because Melody didn't miss any school.

F Troop was a broadly played, ambitious, innovative and funny lampoon on the western genre, full of slapstick and pratfalls. These elements made the show a hit as the veteran cast of vaudeville-style actors brilliantly brought the show's oddballs to life. The show's opening theme song set up the premise as the bumbling but well-meaning Captain Wilton Parmenter (Ken Berry) is given command of Fort Courage after his sneeze accidentally started a battle that the Union won over the Confederates. Though Parmenter was officially in charge of the fort located somewhere west of the Missouri River, it was actually run by the scheming and always looking for a quick buck Sergeant Morgan O'Rourke (Forrest Tucker) and his lackey Corporal Randolph Agarn (Larry Storch). The duo was in cahoots to make a profit, selling Indian souvenirs and anything else they could get their hands on, with the peaceful Hekawi tribe ("We're lovers, not fighters") led by the equally scheming Chief Wild Eagle (Frank DeKova) and his flunky Crazy Cat (Don Diamond).

The *F Troop* pilot was well received, and ABC picked it up to begin airing in the fall of 1965. This was a role of a lifetime for Melody Patterson so nobody could begrudge her for continuing with the sidestepping of her age, considering how frugal the studios were at the time. "I missed a semester of school because I had to learn to ride and rope and shoot a shotgun at the studio before filming began," says Patterson. "I thought I'd make up the missed classes later at the Hollywood Professional School. But before I knew it, we had filmed seven shows. Then they hired a little boy to play a guest role and his teacher had been my teacher on *Bye Bye Birdie*. She knew I was a minor and went to the producer and said, 'Do you know this little girl is not eighteen but only fifteen?' The cat was out of the bag. But by that time *F Troop* was airing. We were already a hit and had appeared on the cover of *TV Guide*. When it came up to a vote, I don't think ABC wanted to rock the boat and I don't think it bothered Jack Warner too much. I was off for a week and when I came back I had a teacher. I went to school for four hours a day,

The TV sitcom *F Troop* (Warner Bros. Television, 1965) featured Melody Patterson as cowgirl Wrangler Jane.

which is an extra hour than you were supposed to, but I had to make up the four months of school that I had missed."

When Paterson returned to the soundstage after her true age was revealed, she was delighted to find that it had not change her interaction with her fellow cast members, particularly Ken Berry, her romantic interest. "Ken Berry was wonderful regarding the whole situation and he is still wonderful," exclaims Melody. "Forest Tucker, Larry Storch and the rest of the guys were so much fun to work with. A lot of these guys came from vaudeville. But then again I had been in a form of vaudeville as an entertainer [since I was a child]. We were all professionals who really worked on our craft and had mutual respect for each other's talent. So when they discovered I was a minor, nothing changed except that Forest Tucker would tease me because he knew I got embarrassed."

Melody Patterson expertly played the amorous Wrangler Jane Angelica Thrift, general store owner and sharp shooter, who was intent on marrying the reluctant Wilton. One of the series' running gags was that every time Jane would flirt with the bashful Wilton he'd respond, "Please, Jane, not in front of the men." Patterson and Berry were perfect together and made a charming romantic couple. "Ken's character was a rather innocent and very naïve kind of a guy," says Patterson. "I think Wrangler Jane was savvier than Wilton anyway. She was extremely independent—she owned her own store, she ran the mail and she could out ride and out shoot anybody else in town. She was a very self-reliant teenager, which I always saw her as." Other goofballs populating the fort included the inept bugle player Trooper Hannibal Dobbs (James Hampton), the fort's oldest member Trooper Duffy (Bob Steele) and very near-sighted lookout Trooper Vanderbilt (John Mitchum).

Overall *F Troop* received quite positive reviews. John Horn of the *N.Y. Herald Tribune* wrote "what counts is that a situation comedy—good burlesque, really—has arrived that could tickle the fancy of the entire family." Kay Gardella of the *Daily News N.Y.* described *F Troop* as an "insane cavalcade of wild and wooly happenings." The *New York Post* dubbed it the "first slapstick western," while the *Christian Science Monitor* remarked that "this wild romp is ... quite funny." Cleveland Amory singled Melody out in his review for *TV Guide* and commented, "[the] beauteous Wrangler Jane is well played by Melody Patterson."

One favorite episode of Melody Patterson's is "The Girl from Philadelphia," where a jealous Jane vies for Wilton's attention with his snooty former flame (Linda Marshall), who comes to town to persuade him to return East. Another is "The Courtship of Wrangler Jane," where Sergeant O'Rourke plays Cupid for Jane and Wilton just to get the Captain out of the fort so he could expand his trading operation. In "That's Show Biz," Patterson revealed her vocal talents and sweetly sang the song, "Lemon Tree." Melody admits to liking all the show's guest stars but was in awe of one in particular—Vincent Price. "I was a big Edgar Allan Poe fan, so of course I saw Vincent Price in *The House of Usher* and *The Pit and the Pendulum*," says Melody Patterson. "So when he guest starred, I was like, 'Wow, it's Vincent Price!' I was also very impressed with Milton Berle. Actors used to just adore appearing on *F Troop* and we definitely did not have a reputation of being aloof around them like some other shows."

During the two-year run of *F Troop* Patterson cut a record called "You're the One" and sang it on *Shindig*. She received a 1965 *Photoplay* Gold Medal Award nomination for Most Promising New Star (Female) and she was voted a Hollywood Deb Star in 1967, where actor Aron Kincaid escorted her to the ceremony. "The Deb Star Ball was a tradition in Hollywood and the Deb Stars were nominated by the studios' hairdressers and make-up artists," explains Melody. "It had been going on for a long, long time. It was a great honor and an absolute thrilling evening. The wardrobe department was delighted in finding me the perfect gown and my hairdresser and make-up people were very proud. It was a marvelous wonderful thing. But now I look at photos of me from that night and I think I can't believe that hair-do and eyelashes. Gosh, my hair went up about four inches."

F Troop was cancelled after only two seasons, but according to Patterson, it wasn't done in by low ratings but because studio head Jack Warner had a stroke. "The studio was really his alone to control and he hadn't diversified at that time," reveals Melody. "When he got sick and then died, everyone got the pink slip—from his son-in-law, who was the head of the television department, to the lowliest grip. The studio basically shut down for awhile." An enterprising Forrest Tucker then made a trip scouting studio locations in Spain to continue the series in syndication. He knew it would be too costly to shoot a syndicated show in Hollywood. However, when he went to discuss purchasing the rights to *F Troop*, he learned in New York that the studio had just sold the series for re-broadcast in syndication. Continuing the series with new episodes was then out of the question.

Lobby card for *The Cycle Savages* (Trans American, 1969) with Chris Robinson and Melody Patterson.

In 1968, Patterson began branching out, doing TV guest shots, films, game shows and radio. She played a hillbilly in an amusing episode of TV's *The Monkees*. "I really remember doing this show because it was the first show I guest starred on [after the cancellation of *F Troop*]," says Melody sadly. "I recall sitting in the make-up chair and thinking it just didn't feel right. I didn't mind doing the part but it *wasn't* my studio, it *wasn't* my make-up department, and it *wasn't* my show. It was that hang of a great loss. It was hard for me. As for the Monkees, I didn't have any trouble with them but I just thought there was something strange about them. Of course, now I know why. They weren't real friendly—not that they were unfriendly." During this time Patterson also became a deejay for Armed Forces Radio, hosting a weekly show that aired in Vietnam. Like fellow deejay actress Chris Noel, who hosted a daily show, Patterson too journeyed to Vietnam to boost the morale of the GIs. She went there twice as part of Johnny Grant's entourage. Her first trip was with Diane McBain and the second was with Vicki Lawrence.

Movies finally took advantage of Patterson's beauty and talent, as she was cast as a movie starlet named April, whose boyfriend was the leader of a motorcycle gang in the exploitation film, *The Angry Breed* (1968). "During the late sixties, Hollywood seemed to be always trying to portray itself as being populated by dope-crazed, LSD-taking weirdoes," remarks Patterson. "I think that is what this movie was supposed to be about. But I am not really sure. It is the worst movie ever made." *The Angry Breed* tried to merge the world of violent bikers with the hip pill-popping Hollywood set, but it was not a success. The reviewer in *Variety* noted that the film "[had] the look of a mismatch between an out and out sexploitation item and the type of actioner that has proven such a formula for American International."

Though billed fifth, *The Angry Breed* starred Murray McLeod as Johnny Taylor, an actor and Vietnam vet who has just returned to Hollywood with a script from a writer whose life is saved in battle. ("Good God, Murray wore his pants practically up to his armpits and was supposed to be the *big* hero," jokes Melody laughing.) Johnny's attempts to sell the script are unsuccessful. Broke, he begins living on the beach in Malibu, where he comes to the rescue of Diane Patton (Lori Martin), who is being harassed by a Nazi-clad biker gang headed by Deek Stacey (James MacArthur). Patton's father Vance (William Windom), a film producer, is so grateful to Johnny that he agrees to finance the film. He hooks Johnny up with greedy homosexual agent Mori Thompson (Jan Murray), whose favorite client is none other than biker Deek, who wants to star in the film. Mori convinces Vance to throw a costume party to celebrate the film's start but he and Deek plot to do away with Johnny. At the party, which turns into a freak-out complete with LSD, Johnny's leading lady April Wilde (Melody Patterson) pursues him but he wants Diane. A crazed Deek in disguise tries to kill Johnny but he escapes, thanks to a diversion caused by Patton's mute maid. The next day on the set Johnny recognizes Deek and has him thrown off the lot. That night Johnny learns that Vance has pulled his financing since he is unhappy about the budding romance between Johnny and Diane. Furious with her husband, his neglected wife (Jan Sterling) sabotages the cable car that takes Vance down to the beach for his nightly swim. Deek shows up bent on revenge and during the struggle with Johnny ends up in the cable car along with Vance. The car crashes, killing Deek, while an injured Vance realizes the error of his ways.

Recalling the shoot for *The Angry*

Psycho biker Bruce Dern threatens his ex-girlfriend Melody Patterson in *The Cycle Savages* (Trans American, 1969).

Breed, Melody says, "This fellow's [David Commons] only credit was a ketchup commercial and he thought he could direct a feature. How he got all of us—it was a good cast—in this movie to begin with I'll never know. I haven't the foggiest idea what my character was supposed to be doing and why. I ran around for a week sporting a mustache. It was difficult wearing it trying to flirt with Jimmy MacArthur, who was dressed in a Nazi uniform." Mustache or not, Patterson was a knockout and got MacArthur's attention—so much so that they were wed two years later.

The following year Melody Patterson had a more defined role and gave a convincing performance as Lea, a troubled young woman trying to go straight while keeping her distance from her former biker gang in the violent film, *The Cycle Savages* (1969), directed by Bill Brame. Interestingly, the movie was produced by Top 40 deejay Casey Kasem and record executive Mike Curb, who later became the lieutenant governor of California. As the trade ads proclaimed, "Hot steel between their legs.... The wildest bunch on wheels!" The film also featured a great exploitation cast including Bruce Dern, Chris Robinson, Scott Brady, Gary Littlejohn and Maray Ayres. Though panning the film, *Variety*'s critic commented that "the whole cast really tries." Melody remarks, "Bruce Dern was wonderful and an absolutely exciting actor. Chris Robinson and I had the same manager so we knew each other pretty well. I loved the director because he was an editor and knew what he was doing."

An artist named Romko (Chris Robinson) gets on the bad side of crazed gang leader Keeg (an intense Bruce Dern) for sketching him and his outlaw bikers as they terrorized the patrons of a hamburger drive-in. Keeg is determined to retrieve Romko's sketches, because they could incriminate him and his renegade roughnecks in a white slavery operation they run. They slash Romko's midsection and his neighbor Lea nurses him after Keeg threatens her to keep Romko away from his apartment. To stall Romko, Lea allows the artist to draw her nude while the gang ransacks his pad looking for his drawings. Lea falls for Romko and they make love, but when the police come to investigate his attack they reveal that Lea was a decoy for the gang and was pressured to distract him. Meanwhile, Keeg and his gang have coerced a high school girl over to their lair where they give her LSD and gang rape her. After being rejected by Lea, the bikers capture Romko and torture him by squeezing his hand in a vise. A pistol-packing Lea arrives to save him but she lacks the courage to shoot anyone. As the police close in, the gun is grabbed by biker chick Sandy (Maray Ayres), who chases a fleeing Keeg and shoots him dead.

"I had a better experience working on *The Cycle Savages* than *The Angry Breed*, though I can't say it was a better movie," comments Patterson. "I was in the midst of my Method acting period and it seemed like everybody was taking long pauses before saying their lines. I didn't like doing nudity but I agreed to do a back shot and a love scene. That is when I found out that I had a curvature of the spine. My mother was on the set to make sure everything was on the up and up. It was done with the utmost care and on a closed set. What I found amusing the most was that the sketch of me drawn by Chris' character was a lot bustier than I was."

By 1970, Patterson's acting credits began to trail off, because "I was terribly in love with Jimmy [MacArthur] and spending most of my time in Hawaii." On TV, she was hyped to guest star on *Death Valley Days* but dropped out at the last minute to appear in a TV pilot for *The Flip Wilson Show*. ("The producers of *Death Valley Days* were really pissed off with me. I made the wrong choice here. The pilot was awful because the writing was bad. They threw this pilot out and it never aired.") Her last drive-in movie before relocating to the island paradise was the gory *Blood and Lace* (1971), starring former forties glamour queen and Academy Award–winning actress, Gloria Grahame. ("I was quite impressed with Gloria. She was an absolute dear and wonderful to work with.") As directed by Philip Gilbert, this horror movie was considered to be one of the sickest PG-rated films released at the time. This film's trade ad promised, "Shock after shock after shock as desire drives a bargain with murder!" Patterson says, "This movie I liked and it has turned into a cult hit. But to me it wasn't really gory because the special effects were so bad. Even Vic Tayback's mask that he wears running around was phony looking."

In *Blood and Lace*, Patterson played a teenager named Ellie who witnessed the axe murders of her prostitute mother and one of her johns. A lust-filled detective (Vic Tayback) tells her that the killer can still be around. The pretty seventeen-year-old is sent to a home for wayward youths run by Dorothy Deere (Grahame), a crazy widow who is bilking the county out of money. Her drunken handyman (Len Lesser) runs around killing runaways with a meat cleaver and stores their bodies in a freezer. When the inspector shows up the

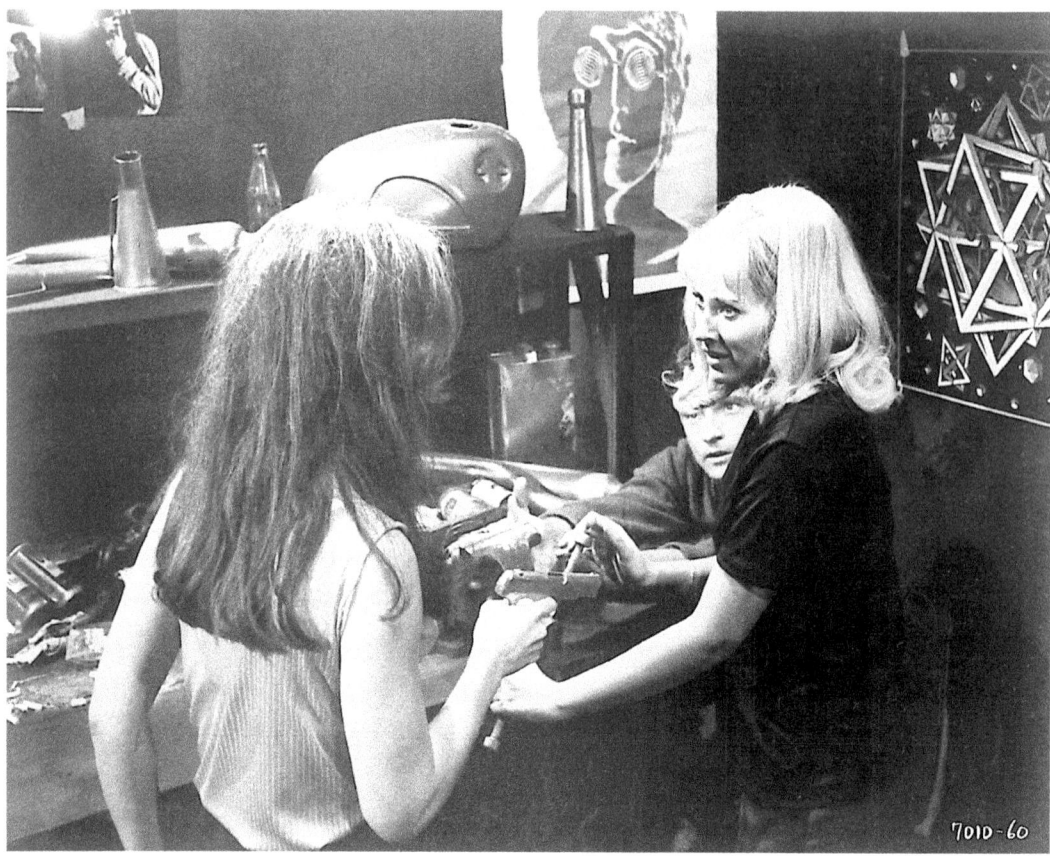

In *The Cycle Savages* (Trans American, 1969) Melody Patterson (right) tries to protect Chris Robinson from the pistol-packin' biker chick Marah Ayres (left).

corpses are put into beds and Deere pretends they are sleeping due to illness. Deere despises the lonely Ellie because her mother was sleeping with the loony woman's dead husband, whose corpse she talks to for advice. Soon Ellie discovers another runaway held captive in the attic, rotting corpses in the infirmary and the meat-locker full of dead bodies. When things can't seem to get any worse, the masked hammer killer shows up and stalks Ellie. However, the audience soon learns just before the end credits roll that the psycho and Ellie are not what they seem to be.

"I really worked hard on *Blood and Lace*," remarks Patterson. "On the first day of shooting I came down with the flu. They weren't going to let me off the hook and for some reason we were shooting very, very late in this big house. The producer got her doctor to give me some kind of antibiotic and basically they just put me into bed. When it was my scene they just dragged me out of bed and put me in the shot and then put me back to bed. I was very sick for the entire first week of shooting. I had a high fever and was feeling really awful."

After filming *Blood and Lace* Melody Patterson married James MacArthur on July 12, 1970, and moved to Hawaii, where he was living while co-starring in the hit TV detective series *Hawaii Five-0* with Jack Lord. ("Jack had a reputation for not being nice to his fellow actors including

Jimmy. But he was never rude to me and I never had any problems with him.") Patterson literally put her film and TV career on hold while being Mrs. MacArthur, although she made three guest appearances on her husband's show. Her most memorable performance was as a suspected money launderer's secretary, who was not as ditzy as she pretended to be in "The Devil and Mr. Frog."

Trying to keep busy in Hawaii, Patterson also began modeling and doing commercials. She also returned to the stage in productions of *Butterflies Are Free* with Dirk Benedict and Barbara Rush, *House of Blue Leaves*, *The Front Page* opposite her husband, and the lead role in *Miss Julie*. During the show's hiatus in 1972, the MacArthurs spent some time in Hollywood and Patterson's agents got her an interview for the film *The Harrad Experiment* (1973). "This was an odd experience for me," comments Melody. "It was a small role [of a coed] and I only worked for one day. Basically it was a really good love scene with Don Johnson that we did in the backseat of a car. Years later I rented the video and realized my scene was cut from the film."

After Patterson's marriage to MacArthur ended in the late seventies, she relocated to New York when she was accepted into the prestigious Academy of Dramatic Arts. She attended for two years but did not put her experience to use, as she married a businessman named Robert Seaton and traveled around with him and his children from a former marriage. The

In *Blood and Lace* (AIP, 1971) orphan Melody Patterson is threatened by a masked psycho—or is she?

family relocated to Los Angeles for a bit in the mid-eighties and Patterson tried to revive her acting career. "I did a musical called *Double Your Pleasure* at a theatre in Hollywood," recalls Melody. "I also was starting to do some little things when I went on this interview for a film called *The Immortalizer* [1987]. I got that part. This was a good little movie but it never got released." In this low-budget fright film, Patterson played an evil nurse who works for a derelict doctor (Ron Ray) who transplants the brains of young people into old bodies, creating a race of mutants.

In 1993 Patterson divorced Seaton and relocated to Nevada to take care of her ailing mother. The duo first lived in Carson City and then moved to Lake Tahoe so Melody could attend Sierra Nevada College. "When I was in high school I absolutely hated school," admits Patterson. "I didn't realize then though that I was a life long learner. I loved and adored college. I wasn't in a hurry to get a degree so I took every class I could get my hands on. As long as my funding was there I took a class. My degree is in Visual and Performing Arts with a concentration in Theater. My goal is to be a drama teacher for secondary education."

In 1998, Patterson met her current husband Vern Miller, a banjo/mandolin/guitar player with a band called the Comstock Cowboys. They reside near Reno, Nevada. In between classes and directing productions, Melody still finds time to attend celebrity autograph shows and reunion luncheons with her former *F Troop* cast mates. When asked why the show is so beloved, Patterson opines, "It is because of the universal humor and talented cast. There is nobody who could do what Ken Berry did with those pratfalls. Think of all the characters that Larry Storch played—a Russian, a French fur trapper and a Mexican bandito—or the array of guest stars that were fabulous. The writing was superb and the jokes were universal in the fact that it will never be a dated show and still will be funny in the year 2090. Like Lucille Ball, I think *F Troop*'s humor will transcend the decades."

Film Appearances

1963   **Bye Bye Birdie** (Columbia) [uncredited] d. George Sidney
1968   **The Angry Breed** (Commonwealth United) d. David Commons
1969   **The Cycle Savages** (Trans American) d. Bill Brame
1971   **Blood and Lace** (AIP) d. Philip Gilbert
1973   **The Harrad Experiment** (Cinerama)* d. Ted Post
1987   **The Immortalizer** (Direct-to-laser disc) d. Joel Bender

*scenes deleted

Television Appearances

Mr. Novak "The Tower" 3/10/1964 NBC
Wendy and Me "You Can't Fight City Hall" 4/5/1965 ABC
F Troop (series regular as Wrangler Jane) 9/14/1965 to 8/31/1967 ABC
Shindig [singing "You're the One"] 12/2/1965 ABC
The Hollywood Deb Stars of 1966 (special) [Hollywood Deb Star] 1/7/1966 ABC
Dateline: Hollywood 5/26/1967 ABC
The Hollywood Squares 7/3 to 7/7/1967 NBC
The Hollywood Squares 8/14 to 8/18/1967 NBC
The Monkees "Hillbilly Honeymoon" 10/23/1967 NBC
Adam-12 "Log 141" 9/28/1968 NBC
Green Acres "Eb's Romance" 10/23/1968 CBS
The Donald O'Connor Show 1/21/1969 SYN
The Flip Wilson Show [unaired pilot] 1969 NBC

Hawaii Five-0 "The Devil and Mr. Frog" 12/10/1969 CBS
It Takes Two 3/23 to 3/27/1970 NBC
It's Your Bet 6/26 to 6/30/1972 NBC
It's Your Bet 3/5 to 3/9/1973 NBC
Hawaii Five-0 "Nightmare in Blue" 2/5/1974 CBS
Hawaii Five-0 "Bomb, Bomb Who's Got the Bomb?" 10/8/1974 CBS
Vicki! 3/31/1993 SYN

Also

Day in Court

☆ CYNTHIA PEPPER ☆

Pert, perky, and pleasant were some of the adjectives used to describe talented Cynthia Pepper. The daughter of a vaudevillian and his dancer wife, this green-eyed blonde was destined for show business. She co-starred on the sitcom *My Three Sons* for a year before landing her own series, *Margie,* in 1961. After the show was cancelled after only one season, Pepper played a supporting role in *Take Her, She's Mine* (1963) starring Sandra Dee. But drive-in fans remember her for her turn as a WAVE who is romanced by a blond Elvis Presley in the hit film *Kissin' Cousins* (1964). More teenage films should have come her way, but like some of her contemporaries, caring for her child became her number one priority.

Cynthia Pepper was born in Los Angeles on September 4, 1940. Her father Jack Pepper was a veteran vaudeville, radio and nightclub entertainer. Once described as "a bouncy song-and-dance man," Jack Pepper's big number was "Melancholy Baby." Cynthia's mother Dawn was a dancer and a former showgirl for theatrical producer Billy Rose. Cynthia grew up in show business as she traveled around with her parents. "I lived in New York for awhile while my dad was doing a radio show," recalls Cynthia Pepper. "We stayed in a hotel and I literally slept in a drawer as a baby. When I was four years old I was cast in a Broadway play [*It's a Gift*] with Julie Harris. We played sisters. She was eighteen and making her debut. We worked together in rehearsals, but I never got to go on stage because the union said I was too young."

Cynthia literally lived out of a trunk as a small child, as she accompanied her parents who performed at small clubs across the country. When Jack Pepper went off to war, first as a soldier and than as part of Bob Hope's USO Troupe, Cynthia stayed back and went to school. ("As I got older I began taking classes in singing, acting and piano.") While a student at Hollywood High School, Pepper would participate in her father's act, performing at local American Legion socials and church picnics. Though determined to become an actress, Cynthia's parents also wanted her to have a grounded childhood, so they forbade her to work professionally until she graduated high school. And although she had grown up in show business, like most teenage girls, Cynthia too was star struck. "My dad was very friendly with Chill Wills and visited him on the set of *Giant*," recalls Pepper. "On my fifteenth birthday I got a phone call from him and he said, 'Someone wants to talk to you.' It was James Dean wishing me a happy birthday. I was in awe and all I could get whisper was 'thank you.' Three weeks later he was killed."

While her high school classmates

The fetching Cynthia Pepper in *Kissin' Cousins* (MGM, 1964).

were spending their free time hanging out on the beach, Pepper concentrated on her craft. According to *TV Guide*, her father once advised her, "Keep out of Schwab's. No matter what the fan magazines say, nobody ever got famous out of a drugstore. You've got to study." After graduating Hollywood High School, Pepper signed with agent Sam Armstrong. She took classes with drama and vocal coaches and began getting small roles on television. "I think I had one line on *Surfside 6*," says Cynthia. "I did a lot of TV at Warner Bros. where I had one or two lines. I was engaged at the time to a guy named Buck Edwards, who worked in the production office at Warner Bros. He knew I wanted to be an actress so he introduced me around."

In 1960, Pepper read for the recurring role of Jean Pearson on *My Three Sons*. To her delight, she was cast as the perky girlfriend of oldest son, Mike Douglas (Tim Considine). Her character was introduced during the show's Thanksgiving Day episode entitled "Chip's Harvest." Though this show was not centered on her character, she had more to do in later episodes. In "The Elopement," Steve Douglas (Fred MacMurray) mistakenly thinks his son Mike and Jean are running off to get married, and in "The Delinquent" it is Jean's turn to make mistaken assumptions as Mike keeps disappearing at night. She thinks he is hanging out with hooligans but in fact he is building a hi-fi set as a birthday present for her. "I appeared in eight shows during that season [1960 –1961]," says Cynthia. "This was really the start of me working a lot. I loved doing this show and loved everyone on it. It was like my first home in acting. Tim was fine to work with and we were peers. I had just gotten married so we'd go out on double dates. Fred MacMurray was very nice but he kept to himself. He filmed a lot of his scenes all at once and then he'd leave for a week. He always seemed to bring his lunch in a paper bag and eat in his trailer. The person I got along with best and really liked was William Frawley. We went to lunch almost every day. He knew my dad so he kind of looked out for me. Every one on the show was great. I was thrilled to death to play this part." Pepper's character was written off the show at the end of the first season, as her character relocates to Europe with her family, when Cynthia was cast in *Margie*.

My Three Sons brought the talented newcomer a lot of attention. Desilu Studios wanted Pepper for a proposed series called *Sweet Sixteen*, while producers Larry Klein and Hal Goodman asked her to test for a TV pilot entitled *Margie* at 20th Century–Fox. *Margie*, based on the movie starring Jeanne Crain, was a typical early sixties family sitcom centering on a mischievous teenager. According to *TV Guide*, Pepper thought she had a better chance of getting the show at Desilu, but it never materialized and she was cast as Margie instead. ("I was thrilled when my agent called and said, 'Hi, is this Margie?' I knew right away that I got it.") Producer Hal Goodman remarked to *TV Guide*, "We looked at a hundred kids, tested maybe 20 time after time, and there was nobody who had the talent and capabilities Cynthia had. But the main reason [that she won the part] is that she *is* Margie." He may have felt that way about Cynthia because as she reveals, "I always, until this day, loved the twenties. One of my last parties in high school had a 1920s theme so we all dressed in flapper outfits and danced to that era's music. I always had an affinity for that decade. I guess I just fit right in playing a teenager from then."

Unlike other series such as *The Roaring Twenties* and *The Untouchables* that were set in the 1920s, *Margie* was a family sitcom so there were no gangsters, bootleg gin, or speakeasies in sight. Instead it focused on the everyday problems of high school girl Margie Clayton, her bewildered parents Harvey and Nora Clayton (Dave Willock and Wesley Tackitt), her precocious brother (Johnny Bangert), and her friend Maybelle Jackson (Penney Parker). Typical episodes included "Madame President," where Margie runs for her school's office, and "Shimmy Dress," where Margie is prohibited from buying a flapper-type dress to wear to the school dance. Watching *Margie* today however you can sit through an entire episode without realizing that it is supposedly set in the 1920s. That Shimmy dress could have been a mini-skirt and no one would have noticed. It looks and plays just like the typical family sitcoms of the late fifties and early sixties, such as *The Donna Reed Show* and *Father Knows Best*. All the stereotypes are there—the well-meaning but bungling father, doting mother, wise-cracking brother and the rambunctious teenager trying to assert her independence. What made *Margie* popular with audiences, especially the teenage kind, was Cynthia Pepper. Not just perky, she enlivened her character with warmth and maturity not usually found in teenage characters of that time.

Since Pepper was playing younger than what she was, the studio instructed the newlywed not to say anything about her husband. Fox was giving Pepper and the show a big publicity build-up and the studio probably wanted their star to come across as being available for the teenage boys in the audience and as someone you'd want to identify with for the teenage girls. Cynthia saw her face plastered across everything from the covers of teenage movie fan magazines to the covers of local newspaper TV listing sections across the country. "I was under contract so I just did what they told me," says Pepper, matter-of-factly. "Nowadays, they don't care. During the show, it eventually came out that I was married but it didn't matter and it didn't create a big deal."

Though she loved doing the series, Pepper did have a minor working problem. "One of my co-stars—I will not say who—always tried to upstage me," reveals Cynthia. "I was sort of naïve and this other person had much more working experience. The cameraman took me aside and told me, 'Cynthia, if you do this—that won't happen.' The crew guys I worked with were very protective of me and I always loved working with them. One funny story happened when we celebrated my twenty first birthday on the set. I was coming down this staircase and at the bottom they had a cake for me. Well, I tripped and fell. I never swore in public but I let out a loud, 'Oh, shit!' I was *so* embarrassed. I apologized profusely and everybody was laughing."

Margie was a modest hit with the

Cynthia Pepper and Jimmy Hawkins in publicity photo for the TV series *Margie* (20th Century–Fox Television, 1961).

critics, who admired the show due to the charm of Cynthia Pepper. For example, the reviewer in *Variety* raved, "Cynthia Pepper is a real find…" and "Besides being a doll, she also appears to have talent and enthusiasm." *Show* magazine's critic remarked, "The brightest of all television's bright young things this fall is a teenage flapper named Margie. Cynthia Pepper is a piquant performer…" *Margie* was also a hit with the viewers and was the twentieth most popular program on the air, according to the Nielsen Ratings. Unbelievably, the sitcom was not renewed for a second season. "I don't know the full story but I think we were cancelled due to network politics," guesses Pepper. "There was a conflict with sponsors who had a choice of our series or another. They decided to go with the other show. Then one of the other networks was going to pick us up but the timeslot when we were normally on was filled and they didn't like the time where they would have had to put us. That was my understanding of the whole thing. We had no idea when we wrapped filming that we weren't coming back for a second season."

Though *Margie* was cancelled, Fox still had confidence in Cynthia Pepper and kept her under contract. She was their Hollywood Deb Star in 1962, but the only film role that was offered to her was a small part as one of Sandra Dee's college roommates in the comedy *Take Her, She's Mine* (1963). As the boy chasing Adele, Pepper is amusing as the coed out to land a Harvard man. "They made me a brunette for this because Sandra Dee was a blonde," comments Pepper. "I had to do what they told me so I let them dye my hair. I didn't care for being brunette. I hung out with Charla Doherty who played Sandra Dee's younger sister. Sandra was not around very much and never socialized with us. She was nice but I was shocked that she was a chain-smoker."

In 1963, Pepper, along with most of Fox's contract players, was let go due to the ornate movie *Cleopatra*, which almost bankrupted the studio. "I was kind of depressed after Fox dropped me," admits Cynthia. "I was literally praying for a job. Things just weren't happening for me and all actors think that their last job is their *last job*." In the sixties, lots of sitcom stars saw themselves typecast and couldn't get decent roles after their series ended. Though *Margie* was not a huge hit, Pepper become very popular and may have been typed as a TV performer. But her luck was about to change. "I was out one

In *Take Her, She's Mine* (20th Century–Fox, 1963) coeds Sandra Dee, Cynthia Pepper, and Jenny Maxwell (left to right) ogle the frat boys from their dorm window.

day and when I returned my housekeeper told me to call my agent. I asked what for and she said, 'If you can get over to MGM in forty-five minutes you have a part with Elvis Presley in *Kissin' Cousins*.' I ran over there—this was on a Friday—and had to report to wardrobe. Sam Katzman [the producer] must have seen a picture of me because he told my agent if I fit into the uniform the role was mine. Thankfully, I did. Monday we were off to Big Bear to shoot for a week." The role Pepper won without auditioning was that of Midge, an Air Force secretary who accompanies her boss to Smoky Mountain and falls in love with hillbilly Jody Tatum, played by Elvis.

Former dancer Gene Nelson ("I loved Gene—I always had a crush on him so I was thrilled to be working with him") directed *Kissin' Cousins* (1964), and it was produced by Sam "the King of the B-Movies" Katzman. So it is no surprise than that this film became the first of what was termed the "quickie Elvis movie." In that regard, Cynthia opines, "Though Elvis' films were very entertaining, his acting talent was bigger than that. I think he really wanted to do more serious movies. Elvis had more to him than just singing and shaking his hips. But he really never got the chance. All his movies made a lot of money, so I guess they just kept sticking to the same type of films."

In *Kissin' Cousins*, Elvis Presley played dual roles—dark-haired Lt. Josh Morgan and his blond hillbilly cousin Jody. Josh is sent to Tennessee by the Air Force when they learn that he grew up near the Tatum family, who owns the property on Big Smoky Mountain, where the U.S. government wants to build a missile base. While trying to convince Pappy and Ma Tatum (Arthur O'Connell and Glenda Farrell) to give up the land, handsome Josh attracts the romantic attention of his cousins, the Daisy Mae-ish Selena (Pamela Austin) and Azalea (Yvonne Craig), as well as the Kittyhawks, twelve man-starved beauties who prowl the mountainside. Pappy is afraid the Internal Revenue Service will close down his illegal still so he refuses to sign any agreements. When Josh finally meets Jody everyone is amazed of how identical they are. Pepper's Midge drives up alone to the mountain cabin and almost runs over Jody Tatum. He immediately becomes moonstruck over the pretty blonde and when he approaches her she flips him over her shoulder. This makes him attracted to her even more, as Jody wails while chasing her, "Ah loves yo somethin' powerful, li'l ole speckled pup. You's gotta git tired sometime, so say you'll marry up with me." Josh finally recalls that his great aunt married a Tatum and that they are all kissin' cousins! The Tatums reach an agreement with the Air Force while Josh gets Azalea and cousin Jody wins over Midge.

Cynthia Pepper found this film truly a blessing, since she met so many wonderful people through the years because of it. As for working with Elvis Presley, she is just one of many who has nothing but raves for the King. "I remember getting a rose and card from Elvis in my dressing room," recalls Pepper with a laugh. "It said, 'To Cynthia, Love, E. P.' I thought, '*Oh my Gosh! He's in love with me!*' But he did that with all his co-stars. He couldn't have been sweeter. Our first scene together was when I had to flip him. Elvis took the time out to teach me the different karate moves. He treated me like a little sister. Later I got to dance with Elvis but not sing with him. I would have loved to have a duet with Elvis. But singing was not why I was hired.

"I think Elvis preferred playing the dark-haired cousin though," continues Cynthia. "Actually that wasn't his true color either. Elvis had brown hair but they were always darkening it. He kept the set on an even keel. Usually on a set the main star's demeanor sets the tone for the working environment. With Elvis, it was always fun. He didn't hang around much but he would stand there behind the camera if you had to do a take for a close up. He wouldn't leave—unlike some other stars. He was also very gentlemanly. A number of times he offered me his chair when he saw me standing."

Recalling some of the other people she worked with, Cynthia remarks, "Sam Katzman was funny and always joking with me. He'd say, 'Why didn't you nudge me when you got up this morning?' I would get so embarrassed. Of course he just wanted to see my expression. Jack Albertson was a friend of my father's. He would look out for me and tell the crew, 'Don't you swear in front of this little lady.' I hit it off immediately with Yvonne Craig and we became friends. I didn't get to know Pamela Austin very well. When I worked I liked to hang around and talk to the crew. I loved being in that environment. If the crew liked you they'd do anything for you."

Though production was completed in less than two weeks on a lesser budget than previous Elvis movies, *Kissin' Cousins* still went on to become another box office hit, grossing $2.8 million. The soundtrack album for the movie also sold extremely well and Presley had another chart-topping record with the film's title track. What the movie lacked in budget, it made up for it with two Elvis Presley's for the price of one and three lovely leading ladies. The trio, Pamela Austin, Cynthia Pepper, and Yvonne Craig was described as being "button-cute" by Kathleen Carroll in the *Daily News, N.Y.* and "luscious" by the reviewer in *Variety*.

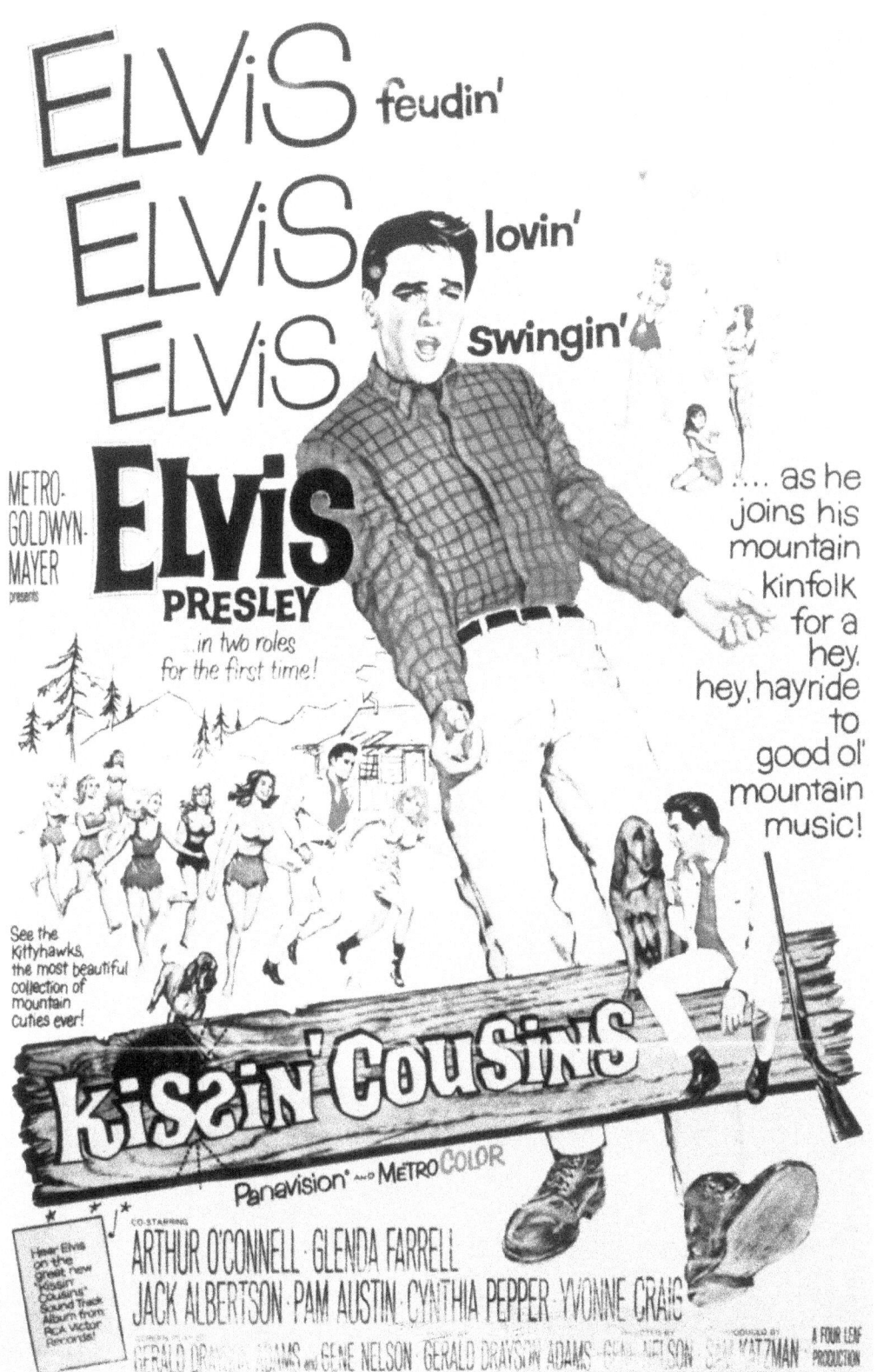

Poster art for *Kissin' Cousins* (MGM, 1964).

Though *Kissin' Cousins* was not Pepper's last acting job, it turned out to be her last movie. However, she continued landing guest roles on various TV series. She made a well-handled return appearance on *My Three Sons* as Jean Pearson, where former boyfriend Mike Douglas is afraid to tell her that he is engaged to Sally Morrison (Meredith MacRae). Another memorable moment for Pepper was playing a newlywed who moves into the house next door to that creepy *Addams Family*. "Carolyn Jones and John Astin were very sweet," remembers Cynthia. "Ted Cassidy [who played Lurch] was so tall. The actor who played my husband and I had to fall back into his arms. I didn't think Cassidy would be able to catch us but he was so big he caught us just fine."

In 1965, Cynthia made what was to be her last attempt at TV stardom. She appeared in two TV pilots but neither was picked up as a series. The first was called *Sally and Sam*, created by Hal Kanter and starring Pepper and Gary Lockwood as two singles trying to platonically share an apartment. The second was the more elaborate *Three Coins in the Fountain*, based on the movie of the same name and just remade the year before as *The Pleasure Seekers*. It was directed and written by Kanter and stuck closely to the original movie. Cynthia Pepper was the sticky sweet girl newly arrived in Rome who becomes

Cynthia Pepper as a WAF lands the blond Elvis Presley as a hillbilly in *Kissin' Cousins* (MGM, 1964).

roommates with the acerbic Joanna Moore and the levelheaded Yvonne Craig. No expense was spared, as the pilot was shot on location in Italy. "We spent six weeks filming this and it was a dream come true for me," exclaims Pepper. "Yvonne and I really became friends while shooting this. Afterwards, we took about a week and a half off and went to Venice, Paris and London on vacation. Joanna Moore was married at that time to Ryan O'Neal and her children, Tatum and Griffin, were just babies. I got along really well with Joanna, but she was having some emotional problems. She was the complete opposite of Yvonne who is like Earth mother to me. Joanna was a very Southern lady. I was somewhere in between. We all threw coins in the fountain thinking we'd be back in Rome, but it didn't happen." Though the studio put a lot of effort into this, it was not picked up by any of the networks. Surprisingly, the pilot didn't air until almost six years later.

Cynthia Pepper's last acting roles included playing a schoolteacher on the groundbreaking sitcom *Julia*, starring Diahann Carroll, and the wife of a down-on-his-luck fisherman on *Lassie*. She didn't appear on screen until seven years later, when she played a small part in the made-for-TV movie *Crisis in Mid-Air* (1979), starring George Peppard as an air traffic controller who may have been responsible for a fatal air crash. As for why she faded from the Hollywood scene, Pepper states, "I had my son in 1965. I then went through a divorce and raising a child. I quit the business for twenty-five years. I'm still paying for it now because it is very hard to get back in. But I don't have any regrets. I don't live like Baby Jane and think my acting days were the best years of my life. It was a good time and a part of my life, but I like what is happening now."

Film Appearances

1950 **Cheaper by the Dozen** (20th Century–Fox) [uncredited] d. Walter Lang

1963 **Take Her, She's Mine** (20th Century–Fox) d. Henry Koster

1964 **Kissin' Cousins** (MGM) d. Gene Nelson

1979 **Crisis in Mid-Air** (TV-movie) d. Walter Grauman

Television Appearances

77 Sunset Strip "The Attic" 9/16/1960 ABC
My Three Sons "Chip's Harvest" 11/17/1960 ABC
Thriller "Fatal Impulse" 11/29/1960 NBC
My Three Sons "The Elopement" 12/22/1960 ABC
My Three Sons "Mike in a Rush" 1/19/1961 ABC
My Three Sons "The Delinquent" 2/16/1961 ABC
My Three Sons "The Man in the Trench Coat" 2/23/1961 ABC
My Three Sons "Deadline" 3/2/1961 ABC
My Three Sons "Trial by Separation" 5/25/1961 ABC
My Three Sons "The Sunday Drive" 6/1/1961 ABC
American Bandstand 10/6/1961 ABC
Margie [series regular as Margie] 10/21/1961 to 8/31/1962 ABC
The Bob Hope Show (special) [Hollywood Deb Star] 12/13/1961 NBC
Here's Hollywood 2/2/1962 NBC
The U.S. Steel Hour "The Inner Panic" 9/12/1962 CBS
Wagon Train "The Sandra Cummings Story" 12/2/1963 ABC
Perry Mason "The Case of the Drifting Dropout" 5/7/1964 CBS
Many Happy Returns "Walter Meets the Machine" 9/21/1964 CBS
My Three Sons "Goodbye Again" 11/12/1964 ABC
The Addams Family "The New Neighbors Meet the Addams Family" 11/13/1964 ABC

90 Bristol Court: Tom, Dick and Mary "Simplify, Simplify" 11/23/1964 NBC
Sally and Sam (pilot) 7/5/1965 CBS
Julia "Who's a Freud of Ginger Wolfe?" 10/22/1968 NBC
Julia "Too Good to Be Bad" 11/19/1968 NBC
The Flying Nun "The Boyfriend" 2/13/1969 ABC
Lassie "The Road Back" Part II 2/11/1970 CBS
Three Coins in the Fountain (pilot—produced in 1966) 8/10/1970 NBC
The Jimmy Stewart Show "Price Is Right" 2/13/1972 NBC

Also

Day in Court, Surfside 6, Bourbon Street Beat, and *The Many Loves of Dobie Gillis*

☆ HILARIE THOMPSON ☆

A cute baby-faced brunette, Hilarie Thompson excelled at playing the girl-next-door gone rebel in the late sixties. Besides her natural talent, Thompson was so convincing in these roles because she was an actual teenager at the time she essayed these parts, unlike other '60s actresses who were playing college coeds well into their late twenties. Hilarie made her film debut at age eighteen playing a pot-smoking high school student in *Maryjane* (1968). She then went on to play for laughs defiant but loveable good girls clad in outrageously mod mini-skirts and go-go boots in *How Sweet It Is* (1968) and *If It's Tuesday, This Must Be Belgium* (1969). More serious roles followed in *The Model Shop* (1969), as a hippie, and in *Getting Straight* (1970), as a protesting college student. The barely released *Hex* (1973) combined two staples of drive-in movie fare, bikers and the supernatural, and featured Thompson as an Indian maiden with mystical powers who becomes entangled with a motorcycle gang on the South Dakota prairie in 1910.

Hilarie Thompson was born March 2, 1949, in Birmingham, Michigan. Her mother wanted to name her child Hilary if it was a girl, while her father was leaning towards Valerie. Since her father was out of town on the day of her birth, her mother compromised and named her newborn Hilarie, much to her husband's dismay. A short time later the Thompson family moved to Hollywood. "I think my mother and father moved there because they had some dream—not that they ever did anything about it," says Thompson. "My sister Victoria and I grew up with show business in our blood. We would go to a nearby park where a group of children would put on a show every week. We learned all the routines and would act them out on our front porch when we lived on Santa Monica Boulevard. Samuel Goldwyn would walk by on his way to his studio and we'd always hoped that he would discover us. We also wrote in to *The Mickey Mouse Club* and asked to be on the show, but they always said no. We were interested in acting from the get go."

In school, Hilarie took music classes and Victoria enrolled in drama. The Thompson sisters were in all the school productions. Outside of school, Hilarie began taking tap dance lessons. Her teacher's husband was an agent who approached the fresh-faced teenager and signed her as a client. Her first audition was for a Kodak Camera television commercial. "I bought a hamster at the Farmer's

Market and took it with me on the interview," says Hilarie. "I showed them the hamster and I guess they liked me since they offered me the part. The commercial debuted during the Academy Awards in 1966."

Hilarie next appeared in an episode of the TV series *Lassie*, playing a lonely teenage mountain girl trying to protect her pet fox named Riddle from some nearby boys and their hunting dogs. Recalling her TV series debut, Thompson says, "*Lassie* was filmed in North Carolina, so it was the first time I was ever on an airplane. I flew there with my mother. The funniest thing about this was that in one scene I had to slide down this great big rock into this river with Lassie's *understudy*! We then had to do another shot with the actual Lassie coming out of the water with me. After the director yelled cut, Lassie was immediately blown dry while I was given an old horse blanket."

During her senior year at Hollywood High School, Hilarie finally won a lead role—that of Eliza Doolittle in *My Fair Lady*. A casting director from Screen Gems, the television subsidiary of Columbia Pictures, came to see the show and was so impressed by the talented brunette that her offered her a contract. Thompson made her debut at Screen Gems in an episode of *I Dream of Jeannie*, playing a hippie. She was the studio's representative in the Hollywood Deb Star competition for 1967.

Hilarie was loaned out to AIP for her first released film *Maryjane*, where she played a hippie-ish pot smoking high school student. It was the type of role that the cherubic Hilarie would become synonymous with. Recalling an interview she did back in the '60s, Hilarie says laughing, "I asked the writer, '*Why do they always cast me as a hippie?*' In the actual article the reporter wrote something like, 'She asked, 'Why do they always cast me as a hippie?'

Precocious hippie chick Hilarie Thompson.

as she stood there wearing Indian beads and a headband.' I guess I was a hippie, so they cast me as one very often. But I felt they never portrayed the hippie scene as it really was. Maybe I just thought I was so cool but I think I was much more in the know about it than how forty-five year old men portrayed hippies in their scripts."

Maury Dexter directed the drive-in camp classic *Maryjane* (1968) from a screenplay by comedians Dick Gautier and Peter Marshall. The film tried to take a serious and sincere look at the growing number of high school students who were beginning to experiment with marijuana or Maryjane, as it was called. The movie's ad copy took full advantage of this using sensational headlines to exploit the subject. Thompson played Hilarie, one of the members of student Jordan Bates' (Kevin Coughlin) pot smoking clique, the "Maryjanes." Other members included Michael Margotta (Jerry), Patty McCormack (Susan), Teri Garr (Terry), and Jo Ann Harris (Jo Ann). Art teacher Phil Blake (Fabian) tries to help insecure Jerry, who is just trying to fit in with the gang. Jerry rebuffs Phil's help and Jordan frames the teacher for marijuana possession. Fellow teacher Ellie Holden (Diane McBain) bails Phil out of jail. He later learns that Ellie is the real drug pusher and that Jordan has set up Jerry to deliver a fake package of "Acapulco Gold" to some young toughs. Phil rescues a badly beaten Jerry and leaves Jordan to the wrath of the gang. Needless to say, the film was a hit with the indiscriminate drive-in crowd but not the critics. Of all the negative reviews, the *Variety* critic's remark about the movie, "More teenagers going to pot," was the wittiest.

Recalling *Maryjane*, Thompson says jokingly, "It was all innocent fun and not a puff of marijuana was anywhere to be found. We all thought the movie was very silly, but I had a really good time working on it. I had a very brief romance with my co-star Michael Margotta. I became friendly with Kevin Coughlin and hung out on the set with Patty McCormack, Teri Garr, and Jo Ann Harris. Fabian and Diane McBain were much older than the rest of us, so we didn't have much off-screen contact with them. The really wonderful thing about this movie though was that we filmed some scenes at this little amusement park that used to be where the Beverly Center is now in Los Angeles. For me, it is now become a historical thing."

Though made before *Maryjane*, *Where Angels Go ... Trouble Follows* (1968) was released after it and Thompson was again cast as a high school student named Hilarie, this time attending a Catholic school. ("No hippies here—we were perfect little girls in this one," quips Thompson.) This was the sequel to the very popular film *The Trouble with Angels* (1966), starring Hayley Mills. Hip nun Sister George (Stella Stevens) and her students (including Susan Saint James and Barbara Hunter), along with doting Mother Superior Simplicia (Rosalind Russell), journey by bus from Pennsylvania to California to attend an ecumenical rally with anticipated misadventures along the way, including an encounter with a biker gang. "This was also a lot of fun to do," exclaims Hilarie. "We went to Pennsylvania for three weeks and then New Mexico for three weeks. There were sixteen of us girls living together. We all got along, but there were two who hated each other. Each would come to me and talk about the other one. I wasn't familiar with that type of behavior at that point of my life. I found myself talking about one with the other and vice versa."

Regarding the esteemed cast that also included Milton Berle, Robert Taylor, and Van Johnson, Thompson admits, "Back then, I was young and callow—only thinking about myself. I had heard of all these stars but I didn't appreciate them until years later. Looking back, it was so great that I worked with them. Stella Stevens and Rosalind Russell were very pleasant but I just hung out with the girls that I was working with."

In *How Sweet It Is* (1968) Hilarie Thompson finally was able to really get noticed by the critics and the public when she was cast as a mini-skirted, go-go boot wearing free spirit named Bootsie. ("She was sort of a hippie but it was portrayed very cutesy-like.") Decked out in mod late sixties duds, Bootsie heads out to Europe on an all-girls photo tour for her father's magazine, leaving her lovelorn boyfriend David (Donald Losby) back home. His mother Jenny (Debbie Reynolds) conspires to get her photographer husband

Poster art for *Maryjane* (AIP, 1968) featuring Hilarie Thompson in her film debut as a pot-smoking, high school student.

Grif (James Garner), who works for the magazine, this photo assignment so he can bring David along as his assistant. However, the blossoming romance between David and Bootsie takes a back seat to the unfunny sitcom misadventures of Grif and Jenny, who rents a villa in France to be close to her husband.

Hilarie Thompson continued acting on television for Screen Gems but, unlike other fellow contract players such as Bridget Hanley, she was able to land roles, albeit small ones, in films at Columbia. The studio cast her in the cameo role of a hitchhiking hippie in Jacques Demy's *The Model Shop* (1969), starring Anouk Aimée and Gary Lockwood. ("All that I remember about Gary is that he took me out on a date and tried to seduce me—unsuccessfully I might add," laughs Hilarie.) In Demy's tribute to Los Angeles and its youth culture, Lockwood played George Matthews, an alienated twenty-six year old architect waiting to be drafted and facing an overdue car payment. During the course of a twenty-four hour period, he rebuffs his grasping starlet girlfriend (Alexandra Hay), who wants to get married, and walks out on his job. While trying to borrow money to keep his car, he spots a beautiful French woman named Lola (Aimée) who works as a model, posing semi-nude for amateur photographers. George blows some of the money he gets from his friend to photograph Lola, just to get to know her. Hilarie Thompson enters the picture in a small role as a hitchhiker George picks up. They talk in the car as George drives and he lets her off at a bottom of a hill. By the end of the film George gets his draft notice, loses his car and girlfriend while Lola returns to Europe to reunite with her young son.

Despite her brief appearance in *The Model Shop*, Thompson found the part to be the closest to reality regarding the hippie scene. She muses, "I hardly remember the picture itself but as I was playing this role I felt more like myself. I usually felt like a cartoon caricature of a hippie in most of the hippie roles that I played. It's hard to talk seriously about 'hippies' these days because it is conceived as a silly, youthful fad. But I *was* a hippie. Having survived a harrowing, bohemian childhood, to finally be able to be the neurotic, war protesting, free loving and thinking person I was "raised" to be was quite liberating. The late sixties liberated me from that fifties and early sixties bourgeois lifestyle of the normal and functioning, which my family *was not*. One could be open about one's life experiences and the crazier or more horrendous your life had been or was, the more interesting you were. Show business made 'hippies' and 'the revolution' a caricature, but to me on a personal level it was not a silly, youthful fad but a time that changed the world as we knew it and saved my life. It opened up the world to many, many things that before that time were unmentionable. People opened up and began to talk and I think it was a great time."

Thompson credits *How Sweet It Is* as the reason she landed her next big screen role. "I think the casting director knew me from that film," speculates Hilarie. "I just walked into the interview, they said great, and I got the part." The movie was *If It's Tuesday, This Must Be Belgium* (1969), whose title alone usually brings a smile to fans of '60s comedies. Inspired by a *New Yorker* cartoon and a television documentary, the amusing film directed by Mel Stuart starred Ian McShane as a charming womanizing tour guide who shuffles a group of wacky American tourists (Suzanne Pleshette, Mildred Natwick, Michael Constantine, Sandy Baron, Norman Fell, Reva Rose, etc.) around Europe. Hilarie was cast as the perky Shelly Ferguson (described by Thompson as being "a silly little girl trying to be hip"). Her parents, played by Murray Hamilton and Peggy Cass, bring Shelly along on their vacation to keep her from having sex with her boyfriend back home. But to their chagrin, Shelly falls for a young hippie named Bo (Luke Halpin) in Amsterdam. "This was complete magic but Mel Stuart was a tough director," remarks Hilarie. "He was very hard on poor Luke Halpin. I felt badly for Luke who was a sweet guy. I never had any trouble with tyrants, so Mel and I got along fine. To be fair to Mel, he must have been going crazy traveling across Europe with a troupe of actors. Stan Margulies was the producer and he was a wonderful man.

"Making *If It's Tuesday, This Must Be Belgium* was incredible because we filmed throughout Europe for three months," continues Hilarie. "I was nineteen at the time and had not moved out of my parents' home yet. They flew me to England all by myself. We started there and went to Amsterdam, Brussels, Luxembourg, Venice, and Rome. It was first class all the way and an unbelievable experience. Everybody was delightful to work with. I hung out mostly with the younger cast members but I did enjoy the older actors as well. I was particularly friendly with Sandy Baron. He was very serious and intense about his work. Marty Ingels was just having a good old time and Michael Constantine was a darling man—I loved him."

By 1970, Hollywood was beginning to shift its focus from the peace-love hippies to the rebellious university student as

How Sweet It Is (National General, 1968) co-starred Hilarie Thompson as Bootsie, the mini-skirt clad, go-go boot wearing hippie wannabe. *Courtesy of Hilarie Thompson.*

exploitation drive-in movie fodder. Thompson was cast as a college radical named Cynthia in *Getting Straight* (1970), Columbia Pictures' contribution to the genre, which was warmly received and is considered a very good satire. "I was friendly with the writer [Robert Kaufman] who was kind of a funny character," comments Hilarie. "He somehow got me a part. I don't remember how or why, since we were strictly just friends. Of all my movies, this was the most realistic." The exciting movie, set entirely on a college campus, starred Elliot Gould and Candice Bergen.

Pop star Donovan sings a love song to tourist Hilarie Thompson in *If It's Tuesday, This Must Be Belgium* (United Artists, 1969). *Courtesy of Hilarie Thompson.*

("He was a pain in the ass and just thought he knew *everything* about acting, while Candice was totally down-to-earth with no 'movie star' persona about her at all.") Gould gave an excellent performance as Harry Bailey, a Civil rights activist and Vietnam veteran pursuing a master's degree, who begins teaching remedial English at the university he is attending. While on campus, the graduate student rejects black militant Ellis (Max Julien) pleas to join student protests. Instead he concentrates on his studies and flippantly bedding available coeds (Jeannie Berlin, Brenda Sykes, etc.), while continuing his affair with steady girl friend Jan (Bergen), an undergraduate caught between her radical ideas and her dream of a home in the suburbs. Eventually, Harry is dragged into the college conflict by the dean to act as a student liaison when riots break out on campus. Here Thompson and the other actors' rebel-rousing student characters become "traumatized, shocked, unprepared or polarized" when faced with the reality of it. Torn between saving his job and his ideals, Harry eventually walks out on his teaching job and joins the revolution.

Getting Straight was shot on location at Lake Community College in Oregon. *Variety* accurately described the outstanding and earnest movie as being "a comprehensive, cynical, sympathetic, flip, touching, and hilarious story of the middle generation—those millions a bit too old for protest, a bit too young for repression." Director Richard Rush (whom Thompson describes as being "an intensely hip and happening guy") does a deft job, especially with the harrowing student protest and riot scenes, which employed a number of local residents. According to Hilarie, "People were going absolutely nuts. I was getting slugged and pushed. I am tough and not a wuss, but they were wild. After getting hurt I said, 'Forget it—I am not going to be in this.' I just slipped out. Nobody noticed.

"I was in a weird place at that time," continues Hilarie. "I was going through some personal situations so I was not very social during this but I did become friendly with an unknown actor named Harrison Ford, who went on to do some nice little films. I also liked Jeannie Berlin, who was madly in love with Elliot Gould."

Getting Straight was Thompson's sixth movie and sixth film role where she was cast as the rebel or hippie. While some actresses would have been frustrated regarding being typecast, Thompson, who admits to not being driven in terms of her career, just relished the chance to act. "If somebody gave me a job I was a happy person," says Hilarie matter-of-factly. "I was thrilled to be working but I was a complete innocent in terms of career goals."

Screen Gems handed Hilarie her next role, as she was the first actor cast in the new "relevant" counterculture series called *The Young Rebels*. The drama was a sort of *The Mod Squad* set during the American Revolution two years after Bunker Hill and the Continental Army's retreat after losing the battle at Brandywine Creek. Thompson was cast as Elizabeth Coates, the only female member of the Yankee Doodle Society, which was described by ABC-TV as being "a fictional company of guerillas who carry the fight to the Redcoats through sabotage, propaganda and espionage."

"This was the last thing I did for Screen Gems," recalls Hilarie. "I was sort of in on the casting because the studio thought I'd play the girl—not that the producer John Epstein was very happy about it. They forced me on him. Before the show began he made me take lessons in talking lower and slower—not being this kind of crazy person that I am." Of the actors who tested for the role of Jeremy Larkin, the leader of the group and Elizabeth's love interest, Thompson says, "I thought Rick Ely was wonderful. They asked me for my opinion and I said, 'I like Rick.' *What did I know?*" Ely was not well received in the part but the producers hit a home run in their choice for the role of Isak Poole, a freed slave and the town's blacksmith. Louis Gossett Jr. got the role and went on to win an Academy Award for *An Officer and a Gentleman*. Others in the cast included Alex Henteloff as Henry Abington and Philippe Forquet as Marquis de Lafayette.

The Young Rebels premiered with lots of fanfare. It was scheduled for Sunday nights at 7:00 pm, replacing the popular but very expensive science-fiction series *Land of the Giants*. However, after only thirteen episodes, the series was cancelled, as it was not able to attract that evasive younger audience. Critical reaction was mixed to this show about "the long-haired youths of another time." Tom Macklin, writing for the *Newark Evening News*, commented that the show "has much to recommend," while the critic in *Variety* remarked that it has "Nothing honest to say; it's strictly on the make." The public may have rejected it due to the saturation of *Mod Squad*-type socially relevant rip-offs airing then, including *The New People* and *The Young Lawyers*. Thompson opines, "This was an interesting failure. We filmed right next door to *The Partridge Family*, which started the same year. Both shows were aimed at the teenage audience. Somehow that show connected and we didn't. If I were guessing why, I'd say it was because of the actors. I believe that the television audience watches a particular show because they want to spend time with the people. They just didn't catch on to us particularly—not that I took it as a personal affront. It was the show's whole chemistry. But I could be wrong. Maybe it was the whole Revolutionary War setting. The audience went, 'huh?'"

With *The Young Rebels* cancelled and her contract with Screen Gems terminated, Thompson went freelance in 1971. Television kept her busy, but she was still cast in hippie roles on such series as *Matt Lincoln*, *Room 222*, *Love, American Style*, *The F.B.I.*, and *The Odd Couple*. Back on the big screen, Thompson, who had now matured from a cute baby-faced teenager into a sleek stunning beauty, was cast as a fair-haired Indian maiden in *Hex* (1973), which was filmed on location in South Dakota. ("We all froze to death the entire time. It was very cold and the crew was shoveling snow out of scenes.) Set in 1919, the strangely eerie *Hex* (originally titled *Grassland*) centered on two sisters, Acacia (Thompson) and Oriole (Tina Herazo a.k.a. Christina Raines), descendants of an Indian mystic, who become involved with a ragtag bunch of motorcyclists led by Keith Carradine as Whizzer. The gang (also consisting of Robert Walker, Scott Glenn, Gary Busey, Mike Combs, and Doria Cook) is lost on the South Dakota prairie when they are driven out of the nearest town after winning a race against a Model-T driven by one of the locals. They come upon the weird sisters, who hesitantly give them refuge. After smoking some "loco weed" one of the bikers tries to rape Acacia, who is saved. This sets off a chain of events where the sisters' supernatural powers are revealed. However, Acacia's are for good while Oriole's are for evil, as she kills three of the gang members in revenge. In the end, Oriole heads off with the equally malicious Whizzer to California, while Acacia remains behind with shy orphan Golly (Combs).

"This was a crazy movie but I loved the script when I read it," says Hilarie. "I thought, 'How different!' I just adored the whole idea of a motorcycle gang in the early 1900's involved with two Indian girls. It just shows my taste and how well I would have done if I had to choose what scripts to produce! But at that time we all thought this movie was very deep and meaningful. It was all about *the light and the dark* and *the night and the day*. That's what Acacia and Oriole represented in the film—opposites. I had to be a blonde in this so my light hair would indicate Acacia's side of the road, which was light, good, and day."

Hex should have been a drive-in hit, with its motorcycle gang violence and supernatural elements. But by 1972, the biker genre was waning. 20th Century-Fox entered the film in a few film festivals in 1973 to test audience reaction. The feedback was not encouraging. The critic for *Variety* remarked that the film was an "untidy mix of occultism, bike gangs and 1919 rural Americana [with a] thin out look." However, he did find the cast to be "promising." The studio unfortunately decided to shelve the movie and not release it. Due to the determination of director Leon Garen, *Hex* resurfaced on laser disc in the 1980s with the title *The Shrieking*. Its release was probably due to the fact that most of his cast of unknowns had become bona fide movie stars. "Gary Busey just astounded me with his talent and overwhelming energy," remarks Hilarie. "He would play a guitar and just hold you riveted. Keith Carradine was incredibly dedicated. But I was most surprised of Scott Glenn's fame. He was probably the best actor of the group and has lasted the longest. He was *so* serious about acting. An intense guy, he would go off to a corner for an hour before a scene and go over it and over it by himself. I considered myself a *very* serious actress but

I thought, 'This is ridiculous!' But you know what? His incredible dedication paid off."

Hilarie Thompson kept working steadily through 1974 and then stopped for close to two years. When she resumed her career in 1976 she was able to shake off being typecast as a hippie. "My brother was killed in an accident when I was twenty-three," reveals Hilarie. "That knocked the wind out of my sails completely. I worked a little bit more after that but I just kind of lost interest. When I was about twenty-eight years old I sort of recovered and returned to work. By then it was a different era and I was a different person. I was more of a grown up than a kid." Thompson was able to stretch her acting muscles playing a variety of roles. ("*I'm an actress, darling. I do different roles. I'm not just a hippie!*") She was a regular on the TV shows *Manhunter* playing the worried sister of farmer-turned-bounty hunter Ken Howard, *The New Operation Petticoat* as a navy nurse, and *Number 96* as an aspiring actress. None of the series, however, lasted more than one season.

Other TV roles that Thompson essayed during the late seventies and early eighties included the snooty comic strip character Veronica Lodge in two failed *Archie* pilots and impersonating Kate Jackson's Sabrina in "Counterfeit Angels" on *Charlie's Angels*, one of that show's better episodes. "This was a kick. I had been watching the show so I was lucky when I went on the audition, because I was able to do enough of an impression of Kate Jackson to get the part. It was funny because we didn't have any contact with the Angels at all. Our scenes were separate from theirs. But Kate came in one day wanting to see who was playing her. She marched in, looked at me and said, 'Oh.' She then turned around and walked out. That was that."

Thompson's big screen output during

The college protest movie *Getting Straight* (Columbia, 1969) starred (*left to right*) Hilarie Thompson, John Rubinstein, Jeannie Berlin, and Candice Bergen as rebellious students. *Courtesy of Hilarie Thompson.*

Hilarie Thompson in a publicity shot for Screen Gems, 1970. *Courtesy of Hilarie Thompson.*

veals Thompson. "Stallone was one of the funniest and wildest guys I've met. He was your typical crazed star type—a control-freak and a womanizer. But he was very generous too. He gave me a part, so I will always be grateful to him for that."

Like so many of her '60s contemporaries who had the talent and luck to continue working in their thirties, Thompson saw her career come to an end partly due to a bad career move and partly her own choice. "I was represented by ICM and I left them, which I feel was a mistake," comments Hilarie. "I don't think I should have done that, because they liked me a lot and I liked them. I worked as much as I did because of ICM. We had a very nice relationship, which could have gone on for years. They probably wouldn't have sent me out on interviews, but if I had proceeded to stick with them maybe something would have happened later. When I left I was still naïve and wasn't a big pusher so I really didn't try hard to get another really good agent.

"I also started mostly working on myself," continues Thompson earnestly. "In my early thirties I was trying to get my life together because I had a lot of difficult emotional times like most actors do. When I turned thirty-five my big goal was to have a relationship and land a husband. I was always dating actors and loved actors. I couldn't wait to see what next cute boy was on the next show."

Hilarie did find a husband, an actor-

this time had trickled down to only a handful of films. She did have a small role in the psychological thriller *The Fury* (1978), Brian De Palma's follow-up to his more successful *Carrie*. ("He was the only director who ever gave me an acting direction—which I didn't follow," laughs Hilarie.) In 1981, she was cast as Pam in *Nighthawks*, starring Sylvester Stallone and Billy Dee Williams as two specially trained New York police officers tracking a crazed terrorist menacingly played by Rutger Hauer. "I got this part because I was in a relationship with one of Sly's good friends so I knew him off the set," returned-writer named Alan Ormsby. Drive-in movie fans know him from the cult horror film *Children Shouldn't Play with Dead Things* (1972), which he starred in and wrote. He later went on to author the screenplays for *My Bodyguard* (1980), *Cat People* (1982), and *The Substitute* (1996), among others. "Alan is a wonderful, wonderful man. We got married in 1988 when I was thirty-nine years old and I had my son Austin three years later. We are extremely happy, and I am one of the luckiest women in the world. It's a fabulous life even without show business. There is a sense [from the public] that acting is the pinnacle of anybody's experience. Once you are no longer an actor your life is over. It is not true at all! Not being an actor for the last fifteen years has been the most joyful time of my life, though I was saddened when my career ended."

Hilarie Thompson worked as a kindergarten teacher for the past four years but has decided to give show business one more try. She excitedly explains, "I feel I can go back into acting with such a sense of myself and not having it be the end-all and be-all, which I really think it was back then. I am going to try to sell diapers and arthritis medicine. This time I don't really care about any kind of ego thing. Now it is really more—*give me some money*! I am going to be a lot pushier and really go for it!" Still youthful and as vibrant as she was in the sixties, playing her hippie roles on drive-in screens across America, Hilarie Thompson will no doubt succeed in Hollywood once again.

Film Appearances

1968   **Maryjane** (AIP) d. Maury Dexter
        Where Angels Go … Trouble Follows (Columbia) d. James Neilson
        How Sweet It Is! (National General) d. Jerry Paris

1969   **The Model Shop** (Columbia) d. Jacques Demy
        If It's Tuesday, This Must Be Belgium (United Artists) d. Mel Stuart

1970   **Getting Straight** (Columbia) d. Richard Rush

1972   **A Great American Tragedy** (TV-movie) d. J. Lee Thompson

1973   **Hex** (20th Century–Fox) d. Leo Garen

1974   **Manhunter** (TV-movie) d. Walter Grouman

1978   **Cruise into Terror** (TV-movie) d. Bruce Kessler
        The Fury (20th Century–Fox) d. Brian DePalma

1980   **The Falls** (British Film Institute) d. Peter Greenaway

1981   **Nighthawks** (Universal) d. Bruce Malmuth

1984   **The Dark Ride** d. Jeremy Hoenack

Television Appearances

Lassie "Lassie the Voyager Part 4" 11/6/1966 CBS
I Dream of Jeannie "The Mod Party" 4/24/1967 NBC
I Dream of Jeannie "Jeannie, My Guru" 12/30/1968 NBC
Lassie "Walden" 3/2/1969 CBS
The Outcasts "The Town That Wouldn't" 3/31/1969 ABC
Bewitched "And Something Makes Four" 10/16/1969 ABC
Gunsmoke "Hawk" 10/20/1969 CBS
The Flying Nun "Operation, Population" 3/27/1970 ABC
The Young Rebels (series regular as Elizabeth Coates) 9/20/1970 to 1/3/1971 ABC
Matt Lincoln "Karen" 1/7/1971 ABC
Room 222 "I Hate You, Silas Marner" 3/10/1971 ABC
Love, American Style "Love and the Oldboy" 11/12/1971 ABC

Love, American Style "Love and the Free Weekend" 11/12/1971 ABC
Insight "The Freak" 1972 SYN
The F.B.I. "The Corruptor" 2/27/1972 ABC
The Odd Couple "Natural Childbirth" 3/10/1972 ABC
Insight "Roommates on a Rainy Day" 1973 SYN
Here We Go Again "The Times They Are A-Changing" 3/24/1973 ABC
The Brady Bunch "The Cincinnati Kid" 11/23/1973 ABC
Hec Ramsey "Scar Tissue" 3/10/1974 NBC
The Manhunter (series regular as Lizabeth Barrett) 9/11/1974 to 4/9/1975 CBS
Harry O "Forty Reasons to Kill" 12/5 & 12/12/1974 CBS
Barnaby Jones "Hostage" 1/15/1976 CBS
Risko (pilot) 5/9/1976 CBS
Archie (pilot) 12/19/1976 ABC
Quincy, M.E. "Visitors in Paradise" 2/18/1977 NBC
The Streets of San Francisco "Dead Lift" 5/5/1977 ABC
McLaren's Riders (pilot) 5/17/1977 CBS
Fantasy Island "Reunion"/"Anniversary" 4/29/1978 ABC
Chico and the Man "Ed Brown's Car Wash" 6/9/1978 NBC
The Archie Situation Comedy/Musical Variety Show (pilot) 8/5/1978 ABC
The New Operation Petticoat (series regular as Lt. Betty Wheeler) 9/18 to 10/16/1978 ABC
Barnaby Jones "Nest of Scorpions" 10/26/1978 CBS
Charlie's Angels "Counterfeit Angels" 1/24/1979 ABC
Starsky and Hutch "Targets without a Badge, Part 2" 3/11/1979 ABC
Barnaby Jones "The Final Victim" 3/6/1980 CBS
Camp Grizzly (pilot) 6/30/1980 ABC
Number 96 (series regular as Sharon St. Clair) 12/10/1980 to 1/2/1981 NBC
Automan "Murder, Take One" 3/19/1984 ABC
Washingtoon (pilot) 8/15/1985 SHO
Jake and the Fat Man "The Man That Got Away" 10/13/1987 CBS
Alf "Tequila" 3/28/1988 NBC

Also

9 to 5

☆ DARLENE TOMPKINS ☆

Pretty Darlene Tompkins had a banner first two years in Hollywood. She made her debut as a mute princess in the cult science-fiction movie *Beyond the Time Barrier* (1960) and followed it up in a co-starring role opposite Elvis Presley in one of his biggest hits, *Blue Hawaii* (1961). Playing a high school student, Tompkins was one of four shapely young ladies Elvis guided around the islands in this lush romantic musical. With two popular drive-in movie hits, more roles should have come Tompkins' way, but an early marriage sidelined her acting career. By the time she returned to performing during the seventies, thirty-three year old ingenues were not in vogue.

Darlene Tompkins was born Darlene Perfect on Nov. 16, 1940. Her parents divorced when Darlene was five years old. Her mother remarried and Darlene took the last name of her stepfather. Darlene's father also wed again and Darlene gained four half-brothers, Mark (who would become the country's top archer in 1978), Scott, Bobby, and Lee Perfect. ("I didn't see much of them as a child, but we became close when we got older.") As a youngster Darlene had a desire to act, which may have been in her blood. Her mother's sister Audrey was a dancer and her younger sister was child actress Beverly Washburn. But Darlene's aspirations of making it in Hollywood were cut short when at the age of twelve a dog viciously mauled her. "I got my chest scarred up from that," recalls Tompkins. "I always wore blouses and sweatshirts to cover myself. It made me become very introverted, so when I was sixteen years old my mother entered me into a beauty pageant to try to overcome my shyness. But I just couldn't wear a bathing suit in public. My Aunt Audrey loaned me her bathing suit, but I still wasn't going to do it. I remember holding it while I was sitting on my bed crying. My younger sister Georgia saw me and took money out of her bank to give to me. She thought I was crying because I had to wear a hand-me-down bathing suit. She gave me the money to buy a new one. That made me feel so good. She and my Aunt Audrey wanted me to do the pageant so much, and since my mother had already entered me, I did it. By sheer luck, I won."

Tompkin's winning streak continued as she entered and won her second pageant, Miss Optimist. By this time she had an agent who sent her on an interview for a low-budget science fiction movie. Purportedly, among the other candidates for the role of mute Princess Trirene in *Beyond the Time Barrier* were Yvette Mimieux (whose manager wanted too high a salary for his client) and Marjorie Helen (who changed her name to Leslie Parrish and did *Li'l Abner* instead). "I think the producers saw my picture in a newspaper, because they said that they had heard of me," says Darlene. "They wanted to see my expressions and if I was photo-

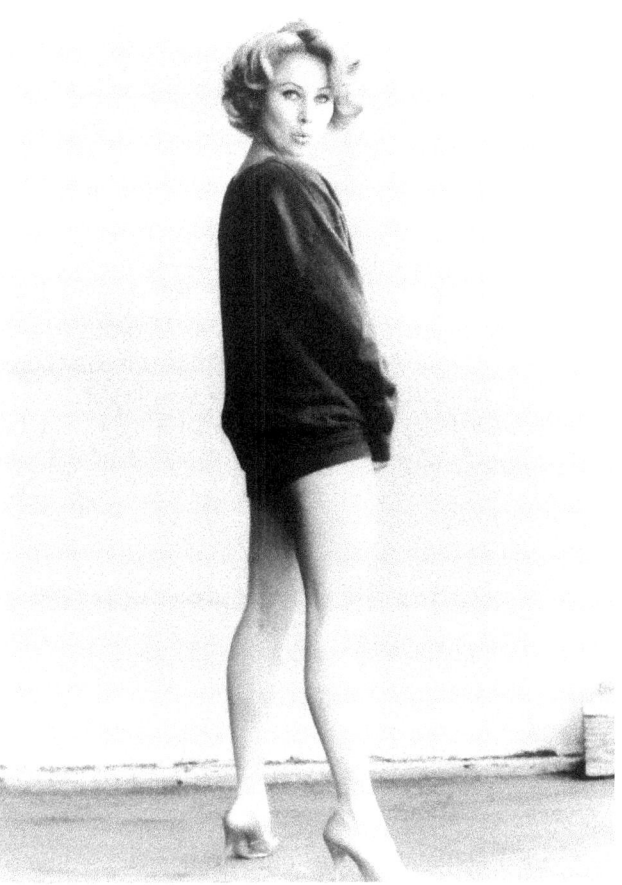

Darlene Tompkins poses provocatively. *Courtesy of Darlene Tompkins.*

genic. They also wanted to see if I could carry a scene without talking. The audition process lasted a couple of days and I tested with Robert Clarke, who told me that they wanted someone with Yvette Mimieux's quality." The veteran actor produced the film and played the lead role as well.

Beyond the Time Barrier, as directed by Edgar G. Ulmer, began production in 1959. It was filmed on the site of the 1959 Texas State Fairgrounds in Dallas, using the desolate exhibit space and an abandoned airplane hangar as futuristic sets. Tompkins traveled to Texas accompanied by her mother. The novice actress had a lot to learn, but her leading man made it very easy for her. "Robert Clarke was one of the most charming men I ever met," remarks Tompkins fondly. "He was very kind and easy to work with. It wasn't like acting opposite a *movie star*. It was like working with a gentleman, which made everything so simple. He also helped me with my acting more than Edgar J. Ulmer did." In his autobiography, Robert Clarke revealed that he and screenwriter Arthur G. Pierce had a number of disagreements with Ulmer. But the only time Tompkins saw Clarke lose his cool is when she accidentally got chocolate syrup on his rented flight suit during the scene where her character is shot and bleeding and he had to carry her in his arms. When the director yelled cut, Tompkins instinctively reached up to grab his neck and soiled the outfit. Though he didn't take it out on her, he was very upset due to the cost.

Recalling the shoot, Tompkins says, "The one thing that was sort of curious for me was that the soundman said to me one day, 'You know it really is funny working with you because when I close my eyes I always know it's you coming.' I asked, 'Why is that?' He replied, 'It is because of your shoes.' We were shooting in the hangar and it was like an echo chamber. In those days one of the most popular brands of footwear was called Springolaters. They didn't have a back to them. I was the only one who wore them so every time I took a step there was a clicking sound. The soundman was trying to keep that sound out of the film. They liked my shoes but didn't like the noise they made. I tried to walk softly, but there was no way I could."

Since *Beyond the Time Barrier* was made on an extremely low budget, Tompkins not only had to deal with a fast shooting schedule but some less than competent crew members. "I would never want to see the hairdresser on this film again in my life," exclaims Darlene. "The back of my hair was gone after she got through with me! I had to wear a ponytail and it naturally started at the nape of my neck. The producers wanted it up high. Since my hair was so long and thick, she didn't know how to wrap it to get it high. She then cut the middle and put in a false piece, which was the extension and then wrapped my hair around it. I didn't know this until a couple of days later when I was combing the back of my hair and saw this butcher's spot. It was like a two-inch circle that was just stubble. I'm assuming she wasn't union because I worked with so many hairdressers afterwards and they were so good." However, not all the creative members were this inept, and Tompkins only had praise for make-up man Jack Pierce of *Frankenstein* fame. "He was very meticulous. Remember this was so long ago and nobody was doing make-up the way he did it. He was very gentle and caring. Everything was perfect with him."

A bit reminiscent of *The Time Machine* by H. G. Wells, *Beyond the Time Barrier* told the story of jet pilot Major William Allison (Clarke), who crosses the fifth dimension when he breaks the sound barrier and gets transported into the year 2024. Due to nuclear testing during the 1960s, Earth is now ruled by mutants living above ground while a civilization of sterile mute humans ruled by The Supreme (Vladimir Sokoloff) resides below. Tompkins played The Supreme's beautiful daughter Trirene, who has ESP and who is the only fertile inhabitant. When Allison is captured by the mutants, Trirene saves him. She later is killed, and Allison must return to pre–1960 Earth to save mankind. For the most part, this low-budget film received dismal reviews, even from *Variety*, which labeled it "an uninspired sci-fi meller with a message." However, the *Variety*'s critic was much kinder to Darlene and remarked, "Any doubts that glamour won't exist in 2024 are dispelled by Darlene Tompkins." Clarke too

The cult sci-fi drive-in movie *Beyond the Time Barrier* (AIP, 1960) with Darlene Tompkins, Robert Clarke, and Vladimir Sokoloff (left to right). *Courtesy of Darlene Tompkins.*

had only praise for Darlene and described her as being "a very conscientious actress" in his autobiography.

After filming wrapped on *Beyond the Time Barrier*, Tompkins returned to Hollywood and entered and won a beauty contest sponsored by the Los Angeles Press Photographers, which led to a contract with 20th Century–Fox. Though she attended their acting school, the only film work she got was an uncredited bit as a bathing beauty in the service comedy *Wake Me When It's Over* (1960), starring Dick Shawn and Ernie Kovacs. After leaving Fox, Tompkins was signed for a small role in the Jerry Lewis comedy *CinderFella* (1960), but that part fell through. "During rehearsals Jerry Lewis was going up the stairs and he had his first heart attack," explains Tompkins. "I really liked him and he was very nice. When he recovered, I think our scene was cut because it would have been too active for him."

While on the Paramount lot, Tompkins tested for a new Elvis Presley musical to be shot on location in Hawaii, appropriately titled *Blue Hawaii* (1961). Producer Hal Wallis was looking for four actresses to play students on vacation with their attractive chaperone who hire Elvis as a tour guide to show them the islands. "I went on a number of interviews for this," recalls Darlene. "There were *so* many girls trying out. It was probably the biggest audition I ever went on. I really hadn't heard that much rock and roll because I was really into Johnny Mathis, so I didn't know much about Elvis as the other girls had. I treated this interview like any other interview. As I was auditioning everybody was telling me about what Elvis Presley was like. I started to listen to his records and found them to be very exciting. I just got lucky and was cast in a part."

Darlene Tompkins did not get to meet Elvis until shooting began in Hawaii. Recalling their relationship, Darlene says, "My first reaction was that I thought he was just so handsome. Elvis was also extraordinarily polite with me because I think I was the *only* girl there that he didn't date. I felt so sad about that actually. But we just hit it off as friends. We just liked to sit and talk—*to my forever regrets*!" One of their conversations revolved around potatoes, as Elvis confessed that though they were his favorites he didn't eat them anymore because, per Darlene, "he didn't want to gain weight."

After Elvis' dramatic turns as a halfbreed caught between warring whites and Indians in *Flaming Star* (1960) and a juvenile delinquent with writing aspirations in *Wild in the Country* (1961), *Blue Hawaii* was very lightweight fare as directed by Norman Taurog. ("He was from another era—such a gentleman and a phenomenal director.") Presley played recently returned GI Chad Gates (described in the press notes as a "free-singing, ukulele playing, lava boy"). Trying to avoid his overly protective family, Chad hides at a beach hut surfing all day. His half–French and half–Hawaiian girlfriend, Maile Duval (Joan Blackman) finally convinces him to face his parents Sarah Lee and Fred Gates (Angela Lansbury and Roland Winters). He does but he rejects their offer to work on the pineapple plantation Fred operates. Instead he takes a job as a tour guide at the agency where Maile works. The girl is thrilled until Chad's first group of clients is sophisticated high school teacher Abigail Prentace (Nancy Walters) and four of her students—pleasant Patsy (Tompkins) who loves to eat, sweet Sandy (Pamela Akert a.k.a. Austin), intellectual Beverly (Christian Kay) and spoiled Ellie (Jenny Maxwell). One of the film's most suggestive and witty exchanges occurs when Abigail first meets Chad and inquires, "Do you think you can satisfy a school teacher and four teenage girls?" Chad replies, "Well, uh, I'll sure try ma'am. I'll do all I can."

While a jealous Maile looks on, Chad packs up Abigail and the girls into the agency's convertible and heads off on a scenic island tour. The group, sans Ellie, then sings a pleasant song, but Darlene reveals that "it is not our voices singing with Elvis. They got professional singers to record it. We just lip-synched to the song." Ellie is continually rude to Chad but changes her tactics that night at a luau and kisses him. Chad rebuffs her, calling her a youngster, and Ellie becomes furious. She then flirts with a tipsy tourist and when the inebriated fellow begins to respond, Chad punches him out and lands in jail. The agency fires Chad, but Abigail hires him to take her and the girls to Kauai. Misunderstandings of the romantic kind abound between Chad with Ellie, Abigail, and Maile. By the fade out Ellie has matured, Abigail finds love with Fred's boss Jack Kelman (John Archer), and Elvis and Maile are married in a lavishly filmed boat wedding ceremony.

Recalling some of her other co-stars, Tompkins states, "Joan Blackman and Elvis were very close. She was one of his girlfriends and Pamela Austin was the other one. Joan was very quiet and the only one I really didn't talk to. But she did one thing that interested me. She didn't want to blink into the camera so she would look—she has the most beautiful pale eyes you ever saw—into the sunlight so she could practice not blinking when looking at the production lights. I tried to copy her but my eyes just watered. Joan was very dedicated and worked hard.

"I didn't realize how fascinating and wonderful Angela Lansbury was until about two years after finishing this movie," continues Darlene. "If I had known that then, I would have been sitting there watching her every move because she became my favorite actress. Nancy Walters was great fun to work with and Jenny Maxwell was very flamboyant. She was gunned down on the streets of Los Angeles years later. We all got along greatly. All the actresses were there to do our jobs and that is what we did. We'd have one day off a week and some of us would just go out and tour Hawaii."

When *Blue Hawaii* opened it received mostly positive reviews, but no one expected it to be such a huge hit. It grossed $4.5 million, becoming the fourteenth highest grossest film of 1962, and was voted a Laurel Award for Best Musical of the Year placing fourth. "The movie's success really, really surprised me because it was done so light-hearted," admits Tompkins. "We had so much fun just filming it, nobody expected it to be as big as it was. You'd think if a movie were going to be such a hit you'd put your blood, sweat and tears into it. But on *Blue Hawaii* we just had fun." The soundtrack album too was huge, selling over six million copies. It contained two standout songs "Rock-a-Hula Baby" and the poignant "Can't Help Falling in Love Again," which was touted for an Academy Award nomination. However, at that time the stuffy old guard members of the Academy's music branch wouldn't hear of bestowing a nomination on a song from an Elvis Presley movie. As for Elvis, the film's success had a negative effect on his acting career in that his manager Colonel Parker steered him away from anything different and challenging. The majority of Presley's remaining movies followed *Blue Hawaii*'s formula—pretty scenery, plenty of shapely beautiful gals and lots of songs. Not that these films were bad, but the logic was that all Elvis needed to do on screen was sing a few songs, romance pretty girls, and fight the bad guy in a lush locale and his fans would flock to the theaters, and flock they did.

As for Darlene Tompkins, her screen presence in *Blue Hawaii* impressed the folks at Paramount so much that the studio's hair and make-up people voted her a Hollywood Deb Star in 1961. Darlene's career was on the rise but she had recently gotten engaged, and her fiancé Larry McFall was not very encouraging. "At the Deb Star Ball for instance, the charming Dwayne Hickman was my escort. [It was customary to have a promising young actor squire a Deb Star.] Larry came as my date but he got upset because they were only taking pictures of Dwayne and I."

Tompkins continued pursuing her acting career. She took lessons with esteemed dramatic coach Jeff Corey and, as with most sixties starlets, had to do the proverbial cheesecake photos. "I enjoyed posing for pictures," reveals Darlene. "It was fun and you received a lot of attention. That had never happened to me before. You would pose and the photographer would yell, 'look here, now look there.' It was exciting and very flattering. I never felt exploited—I didn't even know what the word meant back then!"

Back on the big screen, Tompkins landed a small role as the bitchy Ava in the comedy *My Six Loves* (1963), the first feature directed by choreographer Gower Champion. A Paramount release, the film starred Debbie Reynolds as a harried theater actress who escapes to her country home in Connecticut to get a respite from the pressures of show business. While there she reluctantly takes in six children whose guardian has abandoned them. Tompkins played a vile ingenue and daughter of Reynold's maid (played by Alice Ghostley). "I first stood in for Debbie Reynolds because we are about the

In *Blue Hawaii* (Paramount, 1961) Elvis Presley played a tour guide surrounded by girls galore: (left to right) Christian Kay, Jenny Maxwell, Darlene Tompkins, Pamela Akert (a.k.a. Austin), Joan Blackman, and Nancy Walters.

same height," says Darlene. "This was the second time I got a part by taking my make-up off. I have white eyelashes so when I was standing in for Debbie I had make-up on, which made me look older. When it came time to interview for the role they wouldn't let me. I asked if I could take off my make-up and come back. When I returned and read a second time they gave me the part. Without make-up I looked much younger. After we filmed one of my scenes a crew guy said to me, 'you were wonderful—even I hated you.'" Critics agreed. The reviewer in *Variety* stated, "The opening momentum is sustained for awhile with the advent of an insolent servant (Alice Ghostley) and her sniveling, would-be-actress daughter (Darlene Tompkins), but when the kids arrive, the whole show goes poof."

During this whole time Tompkins also made a few appearances on television, between movie roles. She played the girlfriend of an obstinate scuba diving student who hampers the efforts of Lloyd Bridges as Mike to recover a pair of radioactive cylinders on *Sea Hunt*, and she co-starred in the well-received pilot *Five's a Family*, whose working title was *Grandpa Was a Cop*. It starred comedian Joe E. Brown as a retired police detective who moves in with his son (Dick Foran) and his family. Tompkins played Foran's daughter and Brown's granddaughter. "I loved working with Joe E. Brown," exclaims Darlene. "This is another instance

Darlene Tompkins (left) ignores the catty barbs traded by Joan Blackman and Nancy Walters over Elvis Presley in *Blue Hawaii* (Paramount, 1961).

where my wearing make-up caused confusion. After filming the pilot, I had to go in and loop some dialog with Joe E. Brown. He didn't recognize me because I was wearing make-up and looked older. He went to the producer and said, 'I am not doing this unless you get Darlene.' I had to reassure him it was me." Though the pilot had a sponsor, NBC could not find a suitable timeslot for the show and it did not become a series. It was disappointments like this and the birth of her sons, Scotland and Tyler, that made Tompkins stop acting. ("I just couldn't do both.") She auditioned intermittently and landed a small role in *A Guide for the Married Man* (1967) as a woman Walter Matthau's amorous husband flirts with. But the scene was re-shot with Sue Ane Langdon, one of the film's leading players.

Darlene Tompkins' marriage came to an end in the mid-seventies and she tried to resume her acting career but to little avail. "By then no one had heard of me," says Darlene. "I was thirty-three years old, so I started doing extra work. I became Cheryl Ladd's stand-in on *Charlie's Angels* and in the TV-movies *A Death in California* [1985] and *Crossings* [1986]. I also stood in for Dawn Wells in *Rescue from Gilligan's Island* [1978]. They put a wig on me. I liked stand-in work better than acting because there was no pressure. You didn't have to worry if you had a wrinkle or a pimple or if your hair was out of place because it was not going to be on camera where everybody was going to see it. You still needed to work hard, and doing that just worked very well for me."

Today, Darlene Tompkins is remarried and she has begun appearing at autograph shows across the country. "I enjoy it so much. If I weren't signing autographs, I'd be paying to get in. During the last convention I attended, I'd run around and get the other celebrity autographs during my break. Now that I am older I do not feel so self-conscious asking for them. When I was working with a big star, I didn't want to bother them or I thought, 'what would they think of me?' Now I think of all the big stars that I came in contact with who would have easily given me their autographs but I didn't have the nerve to ask!"

Film Appearances

1960   **Wake Me When It's Over** (20th Century–Fox) [uncredited] d. Mervyn LeRoy
       Beyond the Time Barrier (AIP) d. Edgar J. Ulmer

1961   **Blue Hawaii** (Paramount) d. Norman Taurog

1963   **My Six Loves** (Paramount) d. Gower Champion

1967   **A Guide for the Married Man** (20th Century–Fox)* d. Gene Kelly

*Scene deleted.

Television Appearances

Hennesey "The Hat" 1/2/1961 CBS
Alfred Hitchcock Presents "The Museum Piece" 4/4/1961 CBS
Sea Hunt "Hot Tracer" 5/6/1961 SYN
Five's a Family (pilot) 7/14/1961 NBC
The Bob Hope Show (special) [Hollywood Deb Star] 12/13/1961 NBC
The Bill Dana Show "The Beauty and the Baby" 12/29/1963 NBC
Wendy and Me "George Burns While Rome Fiddles" 9/28/1964 ABC

☆ BEVERLY WASHBURN ☆

Pretty and petite, Beverly Washburn began as a child actress during the fifties, working with everyone from Bing Crosby to Superman. Her ability to cry at the drop of a hat kept this talented tot busy for years. As a she matured into her teens, she co-starred in the classic Walt Disney tearjerker *Old Yeller* (1957) with Tommy Kirk and in the rock and roll musical *Summer Love* (1958) with John Saxon. During the swinging '60s, Washburn continued acting steadily on television, but film roles were scarcer. However, she will go down in drive-in cinema infamy for playing one of the cannibalistic sisters in the horror spoof *Spider Baby* (1964). Though the film received sporadic release, it has developed a fervent cult following. Washburn then played a racing groupie in *Pit Stop* (1969) and a small town girl attracted to a free-spirited drifter in *When the Line Goes Through* (1973) opposite newcomer Martin Sheen.

Beverly Washburn was born in Los Angeles on Thanksgiving Day, November 25, 1943. She is the three years younger aunt of actress Darlene Tompkins. Beverly began modeling children's clothes for a company called Little M'lady Fashions at a very young age and entered show business due to her older siblings. "My sister, Audrey, and brother, George, acted in plays and such," says Washburn. "I just tagged along and my mother got me an agent. He'd send me out for parts, but I wouldn't get anything because I didn't have any credits. It is pretty funny when you are only five to get rejected *because you don't have any credits.* At one of the benefit shows my sister Audrey was doing she was performing a dance routine. Jock Mahoney [of *Yancy Derringer* fame] was there and we met. I was six years old at that time.

"About a month or so later I was on an audition at Columbia Studios," continues Washburn. "Jock happened to be under contract at the time. My mother was with me and we were looking at the script, which said, 'there sits little Waloo Kowalski with her big brown eyes and her long brown hair.' I have blue eyes and blonde hair. My mother, who was always very supportive and very sweet, just turned to me and said, 'Honey, you're not going to get this part because you're not really right for it but just do your best.' A few minutes later Jock walked through the lobby of where we were sitting. He remembered me and asked my mother what I was doing there. She told him about the audition and how I didn't have the right look for the role. He then went in and talked to the producer, Harry Cohn, and told him that I had done this and that. Of course, I hadn't done a thing. Jock brought me in and Harry said, 'She is very cute but can she cry?' Jock turned to me and asked, 'What would you do if somebody stole your dog?' I said, 'Well, I'd cry,' and I immediately started weeping. I got the part." The film was *The Killer That Stalked New York* (1950), starring Evelyn Keyes, William Bishop and Dorothy Malone. An exciting film noir, the movie was about a female diamond smuggler who is chased by the police, unaware that she has brought a deadly disease into the city. Beverly's character actually dies in the film after contracting the Small Pox.

With a screen credit under her belt, the talented young Washburn was cast as a French war orphan in *Here Comes the Groom* (1951) with Bing Crosby and Jane Wyman. The film won an Academy Award for the song, "In the Cool, Cool, Cool of the Evening." "Bing Crosby was very nice to me," recalls Beverly. "We finished the movie in December and he gave me a beautiful doll for Christmas. Every year until he died he sent me a Christmas card. I have two autographed photos with him. One he signed, 'To Beverly, Hope to play in your next picture. Love, Bing.' It was very cute." Washburn then went on to play the "little girl" who befriends Jimmy Stewart as a clown in *The Greatest Show on Earth* (1952) and who Danny Kaye sings "Thumblelina" to outside the jail in *Hans Christian Andersen* (1952). However, genre fans remember Beverly most from *Superman and the Mole Men* (1951), where she portrayed the little girl who plays ball with the Mole Men in her bedroom. Washburn didn't work with series star George Reeves on this, but a few months later she played his daughter in the episode "Heart of Gold on Footlight Theater."

Describing her experience as a child actress, Washburn remarks, "I was very fortunate because my parents were very supportive but they never forced me into doing anything. They tried to keep me grounded and normal so I went to public school. They would always ask me if this was something I wanted to do. For some reason I really enjoyed acting and it was always fun for me. When I was a child I had a photographic memory and I could instantly memorize the script. *Now I can't even remember my own name!* That was a plus because I was able to retain lots of dialog quickly."

Washburn was also cast as a regular on the short-lived series *Professional Father* in 1955, which starred Steve Dunne as a crackerjack child psychologist who is a klutz at home, Barbara Billingsley as his put-upon wife, and Ted Marc and Washburn as their children. The series lasted only one season. Washburn then returned to the big screen, playing a child abducted

Beverly Washburn (left) and Jill Banner (right) as deranged sisters in the cult horror movie *Spider Baby* (American General Pictures, 1964).

by a savage tribe of Indians in the film version of *The Lone Ranger* (1956). But it was her next movie that catapulted Washburn into teen screen stardom.

Old Yeller (1957) was the first movie about a boy and his dog produced by Walt Disney. Based on the novel by Fred Gibson, it was a heartwarming tale (excellently directed by Robert Stevenson) about a young lad named Travis Coates (Tommy Kirk), living with his family in 1869 frontier Texas, who is put in charge when his father (Fess Parker) goes off on a cattle drive. At first Travis has only contempt for the stray yellow mongrel found by his younger brother Arliss (Kevin Corcoran). However, his love and respect for the dog grows as Old Yeller proves to be an excellent watchdog. Later Old Yeller saves an injured Travis from attacking wild pigs. The film then turns from a light-hearted adventure into a tearjerker when it is revealed that Old Yeller contracted rabies from a rabid wolf. As the dog grows more and more vicious, Travis realizes it has to be shot and killed. That sad and tender scene leaves audiences to this day in tears. Beverly Washburn played Kirk's love interest Lisbeth Searcy, the daughter of their prickly neighbor (Jeff York). Recalling how she landed the role, Washburn says, "I had to audition and audition for this. I read a number of times for Walt Disney. When we began shooting he only came on the set once or twice. He was very low-key and not particularly hands-on when it came to the making of the movie.

"I felt very blessed and fortunate to get this role," continues Washburn. "At the time Disney was doing *The Mickey Mouse Club*. There were several Mouseketeers who could have easily played the part, but they gave it to me, so I felt very honored. I became friendly with some of the kids who were Mouseketeers. We all went to the same school on the lot in a big red trailer."

Beverly Washburn has fond memories of the entire cast, including the dog that she says was found in a shelter. But she has the highest praise for her leading man. "Tommy Kirk is a doll," exclaims Beverly. "We went steady for about ten minutes. He gave me a really romantic ring of a skull and cross bone! He was fun to work with. We've done a number of autograph conventions together. At one a woman came up to us and looked at our pictures from *Old Yeller*. She said, '*Old Yeller* is one of my favorite movies. I must have seen it twenty times. It is so amazing to me that you both are still alive!' I laughed and laughed, but Tommy didn't find the humor in it."

To everyone's surprise the little film about a boy and his dog was a critical and box office hit. It brought in $5.9 million dollars and was the tenth highest grossing film of 1958. ("I was totally amazed that the film became so popular.") The movie definitely lived up to its tagline—"All the heart, all the excitement of a great frontier adventure!" It won the Laurel Award from the *Motion Picture Exhibitor* for 'Top General Entertainment Film' and the Box Office Blue Ribbon for 'Best Picture of the Month.' Surprisingly, it took six years for Disney to produce a sequel titled *Savage Sam* (1963). Though Tommy Kirk and Kevin Corcoran reprised their original roles, Washburn was not available due to her commitment to the TV series *The New Loretta Young Show*. ("They wouldn't wait for me because I was not a big enough star.") Marta Kristen wound up replacing her as Lisbeth.

Washburn's next movie was the teenage rock and roll entry *Summer Love* (1958), a sequel to *Rock, Pretty Baby* (1956). As the tagline proclaimed, "Their kind of love keeps time to the beat of their very own music. The all-new story of teenage romance as told by those *Rock, Pretty Baby* kids—with their souped-up rhythm and their mixed-up notions about romance." Most of the cast from the first movie reprised their roles, as Jim Daley (John Saxon) is hired to perform at a summer resort with his band, the Ding-a-Lings, for a two week stint. Of course, romantic complications ensue as he is torn between nice girl Joan (Judi Meredith) and not-so-nice Erica (Jill St. John). Things get even more confusing for the young hero when his family shows up and his younger brother Thomas (George Winslow) finds puppy love with Jackie (Washburn), the younger sister of the band's lead singer. Other young actors in the cast included Shelley Fabares as Twinkie Daley, Molly Bee, John Wilder, Rod McKuen, and a newcomer named Troy Donahue.

Recalling the movie, Washburn says, "Molly Bee played my sister, so most of my scenes were with her and George 'Foghorn' Winslow. But the older actors were always on the set. Molly was just a nice as can be. I knew Shelley Fabares and she is just a doll. John Wilder became a producer, and years later he cast me as an unwed mother in an episode of *The Streets of San Francisco*. Troy Donahue was just terrific. I saw him at an autograph convention and I was surprised that he remembered me. I was so saddened when I heard that he passed away. He was truly one of the nicest people that I ever met."

Though Beverly Washburn remained

Meet the creepy Merrye family of *Spider Baby* (American General Pictures, 1964): siblings Beverly Washburn, Sid Haig, and Jill Banner with family caretaker Lon Chaney, Jr (left to right).

off the big screen until 1964, she kept extremely busy on television. She got a lot of work due to her ability to turn on the waterworks. It seemed like every part that she ever got cast in she had to cry. "That always came very easy for me because I've always been extremely sensitive," says Beverly. "My brother used to tease me and say, 'You cry at supermarket openings.' *TV Guide* did an article on me one year and titled it 'Beverly Washburn Earns Her Salt by Crying on Cue.'" Among her dramatic roles during this period were that of a young orphan who befriends a homeless drifter (Lou Costello) on *Wagon Train* and an unwed teenage mother on *Playhouse 90*. On *One Step Beyond* she portrayed a young girl haunted by a vision of being crushed by the huge chandelier hanging in the ballroom of her family's mansion. Washburn could also play comedy equally as well and she appeared on *The Jack Benny Show*, *Leave It to Beaver*, and *Father Knows Best*, among others.

In 1962, Washburn was cast as one of Loretta Young's seven children in her new series appropriately titled *The New Loretta Young Show*. But unlike her critically acclaimed series *Letter to Loretta*, this show was a critical and ratings failure. Young played a widow raising seven precocious children while trying to earn a living as a magazine writer. She would eventually fall in love and marry her publisher. According to Beverly, Loretta Young did her best to deliver a quality program. "Loretta was very hands on. She was involved in everything from directing to make-up, hair and wardrobe. Once in awhile a director would get a bit annoyed with her because they were hired to direct and she was so involved that she would take over. She was just so interested in putting out a good show. On TV, very seldom did they let you see the dailies unless you were the star. But Loretta insisted that all of us go and watch the dailies every day. She felt we could learn from them. You can see things that you do that maybe you shouldn't do on screen or things that you did that you should do again."

Airing opposite the extremely popular *Ben Casey*, *The New Loretta Young Show* didn't stand a chance. "The show stunk," laughs Washburn. "Actually I'm teasing but it was just fluff. We only did a few episodes. *Ben Casey* was all the rage back then, while our audience consisted of eleven people."

Washburn had previous worked with Loretta Young on her other series and has the highest regards for the classy actress. "Of all the people that I worked with—and I worked with some wonderful stars—Loretta Young along with Jack Benny were my favorites," says Washburn. "Loretta was truly the most loving, giving, and kind woman that I have ever known. I was in touch with her up to her death. She had moved to Palm Springs. To demonstrate just what a special lady she was, she, for no apparent reason, sent me this beautiful scarf about two years before she died. She told me she was out shopping and she thought it was pretty and wanted me to have it. It was just so sweet of her."

When *The New Loretta Young Show* was cancelled in 1963, Washburn found herself unemployed. Now twenty years old, the competition for roles had become fiercer, as there were thousands of nubile ingenues looking for work as compared to when she was a kid. Roles being offered to Washburn were fewer and coming farther between. She had not been able to make the leap from child actress to star, despite her talent and body of work. Though her next project didn't make her a star in the least, it brought her infamy for drive-in movie fans throughout the world. Interestingly, it all began in a supermarket. "I was living in Hollywood at the time and I went grocery shopping," recounts Beverly. "There was a guy in the supermarket named Bart Patton. Every time I turned a corner there he was looking at me. It was very weird. Finally, he came up to me and said, 'I'm sorry to keep staring at you. Aren't you an actress? I know I have seen you before.' I said, 'Yes, I'm Beverly Washburn.' He then told me about this movie that he wanted me to come in and read for. At that time the movie was going to be called *Cannibal Orgy*. Bart told me that Lon Chaney was already lined up to star. I thought it would be cool to work with him. I thought maybe that Bart was legitimate because he didn't ask me for my phone number, instead he wanted my agent's. [Patton was the production supervisor and assistant director on the film.]

"A couple of days later my agent called me to read for the role," continues Washburn. "When I got to the audition there were tons of people in the waiting room. They'd call you in to read and then call you back in to read with somebody else. Then they say, 'Okay you can go but you stay.' They kept narrowing it down and they came out and told me I could go. I took it as that I didn't get the role. It really depressed me because I wanted that part so badly. I always tried to not get too involved on an audition so if I didn't get a role I'd think it wasn't meant to be. I really wanted to do this movie because I wanted to work with Lon Chaney Jr. and because the part was so far removed from anything that I had ever done. I had never

In *Spider Baby* (American General Pictures, 1964) Beverly Washburn (left) and Jill Banner (right) as the Merrye sisters go on a murderous rampage. *Courtesy of Beverly Washburn.*

played such a deranged character before. I usually played some pathetic person who was always crying. So to get a chance to play a killer I thought would be fun. On the way home I stopped at my mom's and told her that I didn't get the part. She saw that I was hurt so she suggested we go away for the weekend. We flew to San Francisco for a few days. The next day my sister called and told me that my agent phoned and said I got the role. I was thrilled! Later I learned that they had already chosen me at the audition but were still deciding on the role that Jill Banner wound up playing."

Spider Baby, which was originally titled *Cannibal Orgy, or the Maddest Story Ever Told*, was the directorial debut by Jack Hill, who went on to direct such '70s exploitation fare as *The Big Bird Cage* (1971), *Coffy* (1973), *Foxy Brown* (1974), and *Switchblade Sisters* (1975). In this very low-budget black-and-white horror spoof, Lon Chaney Jr. played Bruno, the chauffeur and caretaker to a family of a freakazoids and half-wits. The film opens with narration from Peter Howe, a distant cousin, who explains that the Merrye family suffers from "the Merrye Syndrome ... a progressive age regression" that may eventually "progress beyond the prenatal level—reverting to a pre-human condition of savagery and cannibalism." The Merrye family included recently deceased patriarch Titus whose deathbed request has left Bruno in charge and oldest son Ralph (Sid Haig) a bald imbecile who thinks he is a dog. Daughter Virginia (Jill Banner) is transforming into a deadly spider and youngest daughter Elizabeth (Washburn), the least affected of the bunch, goes around chastising her siblings ("Virginia, look what you've done. You're bad—*bad*!"). Down in the cellar, locked under the floorboards, are deranged cannibals Uncle Ned, Aunt Clara, and Aunt Martha.

Trouble comes to the Merrye's gothic rundown southern abode when a letter arrives via messenger (Mantan Moreland), who is dispensed by Virginia, playing her favorite game of spider with a pair of butcher knives in each hand. The telegram reveals that cousins Peter (Quinn Redecker) and Emily Howe (Carol Ohmart) will be visiting that day with their lawyer Schlocker (Karl Schanzer) and his secretary Ann (Mary Mitchel) to assess the children's living conditions. Bruno does his best to keep the wacko Merrye children in line but to no avail. As he keeps trying to run off the quartet, their insistence on staying the night increases, but Peter and Ann wisely decide to stay at a motel. During the night, the sisters discover Schlocker in the basement and in a crazed reign of madness stab and pitchfork him to death. Meanwhile, Ralph terrorizes the greedy Emily and after she runs off into the woods, the knife-wielding sisters chase after her but they can't find her. Peter and Ann return only to be terrorized by the demented children as well. Peter frees himself from Virginia's spider web and rescues Ann from Ralph, but a dazed Emily who wanders back into the mansion, becomes a midnight snack for the cannibal uncle and aunts. Realizing that the fleeing duo will bring more outsiders, Bruno does the humane thing—he blows up the mansion and the entire Merrye clan.

Two real estate developers who wanted to go into the movie business financed *Spider Baby*. They came across Jack Hill's story and commissioned him to write, direct, and edit the film. The movie's entire budget was $65,000. ("It was more like $65.00," says Washburn jokingly.) Hill assembled an eclectic cast to draw a mixed audience. Lon Chaney was at the end of his career and an alcoholic. He wanted to do the movie so badly that he stayed more or less sober during the entire shoot. He even warbles the movie's opening theme song whose lyrics include, "This cannibal orgy is strange to behold and the maddest story ever told!" Carol Ohmart was a fifties actress who had not hit the big time but was well known to horror movie fans for the classic *The House on Haunted Hill* (1959). Purportedly, director Dorothy Arzner recommended Sid Haig for the role of Ralph, as she was familiar with him through his association with the Pasadena Playhouse. Mary Mitchel was a former classmate and wife of Bart Patton. The rest of the roles were cast through auditions.

Describing how the cast approached playing such odd characters, Washburn remarks, "We played our roles kind of tongue-in-cheek. That is why they left in this one out-take where I make this face as we stalk the lawyer. It was just supposed to be a campy horror spoof. Jack Hill was fine to work with. He would tell us what he wanted but gave us free reign to do what we thought best." As for her cast mates, she says, "Lon Chaney was just wonderful too. He was as nice as could be—very soft-spoken and just a sweet gentle soul. It was a well-known fact that he had a drinking problem but he kept it under control. They'd let him go to his trailer and have a couple of drinks. It never interfered with the making of the movie. He gave Jill Banner and myself nicknames. For whatever reason he called me 'Bubble Butt' and her 'Cracker Ass.' Lon used to make Jill and I laugh all the time. This was one of the first things Jill ever did and she was terrific. We got along marvelously but we didn't become real close because we shot this very fast [in thirteen days]." Sadly, Banner was killed in a car accident in 1982.

Due to bankruptcy troubles, *Spider Baby* did not get released until 1967. By that time color films were dominating the drive-in screens across the U.S., and the film was relegated to the bottom half of double features mostly in the Deep South. A truly bizarre and fascinating film, it wasn't until years later when the movie was released on video that *Spider Baby* became a cult classic, due to the wonderfully over-the-top performances by most of the talented cast and its combination of traditional horror with tongue-in-cheek comedy. "I get fan mail to this day about this movie," gasps Beverly. "It is so cute because people, mainly teenagers, will write and say it is their favorite movie. I'm amazed and think '*Have these people never seen Gone with the Wind?*' *Spider Baby* has become quite popular in Europe and all over. There was a special showing of it a few years ago in Los Angeles. They invited me to attend the midnight showing. I thought, '*Midnight?* That's past my bedtime.' I told them I'd be there but I didn't think anybody else would. I was shocked to see people lined up around the block. It was very flattering."

After filming *Spider Baby*, Washburn continued working on TV. She made a few appearances on Sally Field's *Gidget* (one particularly funny episode has Washburn and Paul Lynde as a feisty daughter and her high-strung father driving around with a pajama-clad Gidget) and played a girlfriend of Patty Duke in *The Patty Duke Show*. "Patty was very down-to-earth," comments Washburn. "We are the same height. I remember that I hadn't even met her yet and I was in wardrobe. Patty walked in and said, 'What's going on?' The wardrobe person said, 'We're trying to find something for Beverly to wear.' Patty's exact reply was, 'Hell, give her something of mine.' I thought that was unbelievable because the stars never would want you to wear their clothes. I never forgot that." During this time, Washburn, sponsored by her dear friend Jack Benny, was chosen a 1965 Hollywood Deb Star.

In 1967, Jack Hill began filming *Pit Stop* (1969) and as he was so impressed with Beverly's performance in *Spider Baby* he offered her a role. Working again with a tight budget ($60,000), Hill presents a decent effort about the dangerous sport of Figure 8 racing, whose two-loop track has an intersection in the middle to ensure as many crashes as possible. Actual Figure 8 night races were filmed and inserted into the movie. The available budget and lighting dictated shooting these sequences in black and white so the entire movie had to be as well. Hence the flick was relegated

Poster art for *Pit Stop* (Distributors International, 1969).

to the bottom half of double bills with the biker movie *Naked Angels*. Dick Davalos ("He was a really good actor and very nice to work with") played Rick Bowman, a street hot rodder and aging delinquent itching to break into the big time. After beating local track hero Hawk Sidney (Sid Haig) in a race and stealing his slutty teenage girlfriend Jolene (Washburn) in the process, the head of a stock-car racing organization, Grant Willard (Brian Donlevy), decides to sponsor Rick. Enraged, Hawk tracks Rick and Jolene and demolishes Rick's car while terrorizing his former flame. Rick enters the Phoenix Internationals intent on beating both Hawk and Willard's protégé Ed McLeod, played by the late George Washburn, Beverly's brother. ("George was wonderful in this," remarks Washburn fondly. "I miss him so much.") Rick becomes more and more ruthless as he beds McLeod's wife Ellen (Ellen McRae, later Ellen Burstyn) and drives McLeod out of the race in a spectacular car crash. Though Rick achieves stock car fame he loses his self-respect and Jolene who turns out to be the most moral person in the film.

"When I did *Pit Stop* I had blonde hair and as did Dick Davalos," says Washburn. "They asked me if I minded dyeing my hair brunette because they thought it would look better on screen. I didn't care, but back in those days they didn't have the chemicals like they do now. They put this dye on my hair and it made all my hair fall out. The only thing that they could do was to cut it really short because it was all broken off. Nevertheless, Jolene was a fun part for me to play because again it was a stretch."

Reviews for *Pit Stop* were more on the positive side than expected. Jack Hill once again showed a flair for directing as he did with *Spider Baby*. For instance, John Mahoney, writing for *The Hollywood Reporter*, remarked, "For its time and type, the film has been given sound scripting and characterization by director-writer Jack Hill, who packs plenty of solid daredevil action into its 91 minutes of playing time." As for Beverly, Mahoney commented, "Beverly Washburn has one striking scene in which she vaguely discusses the evening's assignation while devoting her fullest energy to subduing a jawbreaker."

In 1970, Washburn, Iris Adrian, and Peggy Mondo performed with Beverly's long time friend Jack Benny on TV's *The Hollywood Palace*. They then began traveling with Benny, playing nightclubs in Vegas, Lake Tahoe and the East Coast. Washburn remembers, "We did a skit where Iris, who is very loud and nasal, Peg, who weighed about 400 pounds, and

Pit Stop **(Distributors International, 1969) starred Richard Davalos as a heartless racecar driver and Beverly Washburn as his infatuated groupie.** *Courtesy of Beverly Washburn.*

very petite me played the Smothers Sisters. He'd pretend we were three local girls from whatever city we were playing and were auditioning to become part of his act. We'd come out all dressed alike and for about ten minutes Jack just stared at us with his hand on his chin and the audience laughing hysterically. We'd do a horrible song and dance number. At the end I'd ask if we got the job and tell him that we are not very choosy about money. Peggy, the heavy-set one, then would say that we'd work for just three meals a day. Jack would quip, 'I didn't intend to go that high.' It was all very slapstick and silly. Jack always played the stingy tightwad but he was probably the most generous, giving man I have ever known. He was just a kind person. One year for Christmas he gave me a string of real pearls and another time a St. Christopher's medal that was inscribed 'To Beverly, with love, Jack Benny.' He was the best and we remained close to the day he died."

In 1971, Washburn was charming as a dizzy chatterbox who sticks teen idol Bobby Sherman as an aspiring songwriter with the tab for a $845 set of encyclopedias on his sitcom *Getting Together*, before appearing in her last movie, the obscure *When the Line Goes Through* (1973). Directed and written by Clyde Ware, the film starred newcomer Martin Sheen, playing a footloose drifter named Bluff Jackson who wanders into a small Appalachian town. He becomes romantically torn between two twin sisters—Rayme (Washburn), the shy, flustered, responsible homebody who cares for her grandfather, and Mayme (Ware's real life wife Davey Davison), the bored sexpot just itching to leave town. "This was filmed very quickly," recalls Washburn. "It was one of Martin Sheen's first movies. I was so enamored of him because he was such an intense actor. I was not at all surprised that he became so famous. He was also such a nice guy. This wasn't a very good movie but it was fun to do. We filmed it in a little town called West Union in West Virginia. It is where Clyde Ware had grown up. The town was so small that it didn't even have a motel, let alone a hotel. They had to pay the townspeople to put up the cast and crew in their homes. We actually lived with these families. It was very bizarre." Washburn

Video box art for *When the Line Goes Through* (Jud-Lee Productions, 1973).

gave another excellent performance (Lee Reynolds of *The Hollywood Reporter* found Beverly to be "especially endearing"), but as with her two previous movies, not too many people saw her in it.

Beverly Washburn's career, like most of her '60s contemporaries, slowed down considerably during the seventies. Among her TV roles were three episodes of *The Streets of San Francisco* where she played an unwed mother, a tour guide at Alcatraz and the mother of a murdered girl. "I then got married and slowly got out of acting," reveals Beverly. "I didn't want to, but the parts were not being offered. I then got divorced and wound up in an unhealthy relationship. I moved to Spain for seven months and came back to Los Angeles. I got a job working as a receptionist. One day I bumped into Marvin Paige, who was working as the casting director on *General Hospital*. He used to cast me a lot when I was a child. He didn't have a part for me, but I was hired to do the voice of the person who paged the doctors. I worked on that for four years. I got remarried and my husband, Michael Radell, was then transferred to Dallas. I lived there for awhile. Now I live in Las Vegas."

Presently, Beverly has been doing some print work and local TV commercials. "I would love to act again," sighs Beverly. "I miss it so much. It's just like that old cliché that once it's in your blood you can never get rid of it. I don't have any aspirations of becoming a big star but I would love another chance at it. I didn't realize how much I wanted to act again until I started doing some of these [celebrity autograph] conventions. The fans are so appreciative and supportive. I still get fan mail—only about one or two pieces a week but I am so amazed that people would take the time to sit down to write to me. It is very flattering and I feel honored. It's just really nice." Beverly also travels the country on the lecture circuit with her program titled "Beverly Washburn: Hollywood, Television and Me," where she speaks candidly about her life as a child actress and what it was like maturing into young womanhood in a place like Hollywood. In 2001, she was asked to appear in the documentary about the making of *Old Yeller* for the DVD version and in 2002 Beverly returned to TV playing a doctor in three episodes of *General Hospital*.

Film Appearances

1950 **The Killer That Stalked New York** (Columbia) d. Earl McAvoy

1951 **Here Comes the Groom** (Paramount) d. Frank Capra
      Superman and the Mole Men (Lippert Pictures) d. Lee Sholem

1952 **The Greatest Show on Earth** (Paramount) d. Cecil B. DeMille
      Hans Christian Andersen (RKO Radio Pictures) d. Charles Vidor

1953 **Shane** (Paramount) d. George Stevens
      The Juggler (Columbia) d. Edward Dmytryk

1956 **The Lone Ranger** (Warner Bros.) d. Stuart Heisler

1957 **Old Yeller** (Buena Vista) d. Robert Stevenson

1958 **Summer Love** (Universal) d. Charles F. Haas

1964 **Spider Baby, Or the Maddest Story Ever Told** (American General Pictures) d. Jack Hill

1969 **Pit Stop** (Distributors International) [completed in 1967] d. Jack Hill

1973 **When the Line Goes Through** (Jud-Lee Productions) d. Clyde Ware

Television Appearances

Fireside Theatre "Hired Girl" 5/16/1950 NBC
The Jack Benny Show 11/30/1952 CBS
The Adventures of Superman "The Unknown People" 7/20 & 7/27/1953 SYN
Footlight Theater "Heart of Gold" 7/31/1953 CBS
Fireside Theatre "His Name Is Jason" 9/22/1953 NBC
Lux Video Theatre "Moment of the Rose" 11/19/1953 CBS
Schlitz Playhouse of Stars "The Closed Door" 11/27/1953 CBS
A Letter to Loretta "Big Little Lie" 2/24/1954 or 2/21/1954 NBC
Cavalcade of America "Crazy Judah" 4/13/1954 ABC
Dragnet "The Big Pair" 9/16/1954 NBC
Four Star Playhouse "The Man in the Cellar" 9/30/1954 CBS
The Ray Milland Show "Christmas Story" 12/23/1954 CBS
Professional Father (series regular as Kathryn "Kit" Wilson) 1/8 to 7/2/1955 CBS
Studio '57 "Miss Jeremy and the Bran Sergin" 1/25/1955 SYN
Fireside Theater "Marked for Death" 2/22/1955 NBC
Treasury Men in Action "The Case of the Swindler's Gold" 2/24/1955 ABC
Science Fiction Theater "The Strange People of Pecos" 10/14/1955 SYN
The Loretta Young Show "Katy" 10/23/1955 NBC
Fury "Joey Sees Through It" 1/21/1956 NBC
The Millionaire "The Rita Hanley Story" 3/14/1956 CBS
Studio '57 "The Magic Glass" 3/18/1956 SYN
Four Star Playhouse "Autumn Carousel" 4/12/1956 CBS
Telephone Time "The Man with the Beard" 4/15/1956 CBS
Star Stage "The Guradian" 5/11/1956 NBC
Telephone Time "The Key" 7/15/1956 CBS
Spotlight Playhouse "The Magic Glass" 7/31/1956
The Loretta Young Show "Take Care of My Child" 11/4/1956 NBC
G. E. Theater "The Road That Led Afar" 11/25/1956 CBS
Dick Powell's Zane Grey Theater "Stars Over Texas" 12/28/1956 CBS
Schlitz Playhouse of Stars "One Left Over" 2/1/1957 CBS
Jane Wyman Theater "Farmer's Wife" 2/19/1957 NBC
20th Century–Fox Hour "The Men in Her Life" 4/17/1957 CBS
Wagon Train "The Willy Moran Story" 9/18/1957 NBC
Code Three "The Search" 11/23/1957 SYN
Shirley Temple's Storybook "Rip Van Winkle" 5/8/1958 NBC
G. E. Theater "Stopover" 4/27/1958 CBS
Wagon Train "The Tobias Jones Story" 10/22/1958 NBC
The Texan "No Tears for the Dead" 12/8/1958 CBS
Alcoa Presents: One Step Beyond "Premonition" 3/10/1959 ABC
Playhouse 90 "In Lonely Expectations" 4/2/1959 CBS
Leave It to Beaver "The Blind Date Committee" 10/3/1959 ABC
The Texan "Trouble on the Trail" 11/23/1959 CBS
The Texan "Badman" 6/20/1960 CBS
The Law and Mr. Jones "A Question of Guilt" 12/16/1960 ABC
The Best of the Post "Martha" 2/18/1961 SYN
Father Knows Best "The Spelling Bee" 4/4/1961 CBS
Thriller "Parasite Mansion" 4/25/1961 NBC
Target: The Corruptors "Nobody Gets Hurt" 6/1/1962 ABC
Ichabod and Me "Dear Debbie" 6/19/1962 CBS
The New Loretta Young Show (series regular as Vickie Massey) 9/24/1962 to 3/18/1963 CBS
Hawaiian Eye "Passport" 4/2/1963 ABC
77 Sunset Strip "Lover's Lane" 1/3/1964 ABC
Mr. Novak "Visions of Sugar Plums" 10/6/64 NBC
90 Bristol Court: Karen (episode—title unknown) 11/30/1964 NBC
The Hollywood Deb Stars of 1965 (special) [Hollywood Deb Star] 1/2/1965 ABC
Mr. Novak "From the Bow of Zeus" 1/5/1965 NBC
Gidget "Chivalry Isn't Dead, It's Just Hiding" 11/10/1965 ABC
The Patty Duke Show "Cathy Leaves Home—But Not Really" 12/15/1965 ABC

Gidget "Take a Lesson" 3/10/1966 ABC
Star Trek "The Deadly Years" 12/8/1967 NBC
The Hollywood Palace 1/20/1968 ABC
Divorce Court (episode—title unknown) 1/25/1968 SYN
Getting Together "The Great Pretender" 12/25/1971 ABC
The Streets of San Francisco "Most Feared in the Jungle" 12/20/1973 ABC
The Manhunter "The Ma Gentry Gang" 9/11/1974 CBS
The Streets of San Francisco "Let's Pretend We're Strangers" 5/19/1977 ABC
Scarecrow and Mrs. King "Remembrance of Things Past" 1/9/1984 CBS
Hotel "Hearts and Minds" 8/21/1985 ABC
General Hospital 11/20, 25 & 26/2002 ABC

Also

Matinee Theater, Day in Court, Arrest and Trial, The Jack Benny Show, McMillian and Wife, Most Wanted, Tales of the Unexpected. The Streets of San Francisco, and *Murder, She Wrote*

☆ CAROLE WELLS ☆

Carole Wells is a gorgeous gal with big green eyes and long silky flaxen hair. She once rightly told a magazine reporter, "When you're a blonde, people always notice you." Talented and charming with just the right movie star look, she should have become a superstar, but contractual TV obligations, her interest in opera singing, and her commitment to her family seemed to get in the way of big screen stardom. Instead, Wells co-starred on television in the family drama series *National Velvet* and the wild and wooly sitcom *Pistols 'n' Petticoats*. Drive-in fans remember Wells for playing the blonde tease who vamps college student Doug McClure in the hot rod film, *The Lively Set* (1964). She was off the big screen for close to ten years when she surprised her old fans by accepting a part in the cult horror film *The House of Seven Corpses* (1974). But in her next feature Wells faced an even more terrifying monster in Barbra Streisand, when she accepted a supporting role in *Funny Lady* (1975).

Carole Maureen Wells was born August 31, 1942, in Shreveport, Louisiana. She is the fourth child in a family of two boys and four girls. Wells' first taste of celebrity came at the tender age of three when she made an appearance on Art Linkletter's radio show. "I told him I was going to *be* an actress," recalls Carole. "He said, 'Well, most children say I *want* to be an actress. What do you mean that you're *going* to be an actress?' I said, '*That's* what I'm going to be.' I always knew it. I took singing and dancing lessons—all those things little girls do."

Wells' father was a doctor, and when Carole was six years old the family moved to California, where the very athletic child began riding horses. Her family was very close and Sundays were restricted to church going and big family dinners. Though an intelligent child, by the fifth grade she was in real danger of being left back. "I couldn't read because I had such bad eyes," remembers Wells. "My parents would take me to get my eyes checked with my sisters and brothers, but by the time the doctor got to me they would just pat me on the head and send me on my way. I couldn't read well so I'd memorize all the two and three letter words like 'or' 'the' and 'but' and put them in the sentence where I thought they should be. I just struggled through math because I

Carole Wells

Winsome starlet Carole Wells.

couldn't make out the numbers. When they put me in private school I was immediately given an eye test and they found out what the problem was. After that I would go over to our neighbor Lurene Tuttle's house and she'd have me read to her all the other parts in the script that she had to learn that week for the TV show *Life with Father*. That got me up to speed with my reading and cold reading."

Carole Wells' first professional acting job was at the Burbank Little Theater where Debbie Reynolds got her start. Lurene Tuttle's agent came to see the young girl and signed her as a client. As a child she was cast in every role that she auditioned for. Appearances on *Eddie Fisher Coke Time*, *The Red Skelton Show*, and Dial Soap commercials led to her film debut in *Lizzie* (1957), directed by Hugo Haas.

Known for his fifties B-movies starring Marilyn Monroe wannabe Cleo Moore, *Lizzie* (based on Shirley Jackson's novel *The Bird's Nest*) was Haas' first big studio production. The film starred Eleanor Parker as a mousy museum employee named Beth who develops three distinctive personalities after being raped by her mother's boyfriend when she was a child. One of Beth's personalities is Lizzie, a wild party girl. Wells played a young Beth in flashback sequences. "Hugo Haas was a big brawny man and he tried to get me to do some things that weren't in the script,' says Wells. "Instead of having the actor who played my boyfriend come into my bedroom and put his hand over my face as the scene was written, Haas wanted him to throw himself on top of me. That scared me. My mother stood up to him and said, 'No! She won't do that. I won't have it!' I was so relieved and proud when she did that. No one on a movie set ever yelled 'stop' to the director. I'm sure Hugo Haas was a very nice man but at that age I was frightened of him."

In 1960, MGM signed the now blossoming teenager to a contract. She played a small role of a gossipy young woman living on a cavalry outpost in the rugged western *A Thunder of Drums* (1960), starring George Hamilton, Luana Patten, and a newcomer named Richard Chamberlain. She began getting the big studio publicity build-up. She posed for a myriad of photographs, had her faced splashed across every major movie magazine including *Photoplay* and *Modern Screen*, and was romantically linked to most of MGM's male roster. "George Hamilton and I became friends," says Carole. "We were friendly for a long time. I have lots of magazine clippings where they had us as an item.

Most of what they wrote about me was not true. I was going to college [two years at UCLA and a year at USC] while I was at MGM and I had a boyfriend. The only time I went out was when the studio wanted us to do publicity. I remember once they set up a 'date' between Richard Chamberlain and me to go play miniature golf. We did this on our lunch hour as he was filming *Dr. Kildare* on the soundstage next door. They also had me paired with Clint Eastwood, who was doing *Rawhide* at the time. But nothing was going on with any of them. My boyfriend was away in college and I was looking forward to a weekend when I could drive up to see him or he could come home to see me. They paired us with different actors for different occasions. I never had a romance with any movie star. But I did have a crush on Van Williams [of TV's *Surfside Six* and later *The Green Hornet*]—was he gorgeous!"

In the spring of 1960, Wells beat out over 500 other young hopefuls to play a supporting role in the highly awaited TV series *National Velvet*, based on the hit movie starring Elizabeth Taylor. As with the film, the series focused on the adventures of Velvet Brown (Lori Martin) and her horse. However, the locale was shifted from England to a dairy farm in the midwest. Wells played Martin's mean older sister Edwina. Though Carole's experience was for the most part a pleasant one, her unhappiness with her character and Martin's emotional problems made this a rough go at times. "My main problem with my character is that they didn't make her very human," remarks Wells. "It's one thing to be a teenager and to be involved in your own issues—like most teenagers are—but it was a bit excessive [for my character]. Now I know because I'm a writer that you have to show contrast. They always made Lori Martin's character the good girl, so that was kind of maddening. My biggest peeve was that they wanted me to not use correct English. Though my character lived on a farm she was supposed to be one of the best students in her class. She wouldn't say 'ain't' and wouldn't speak incorrectly. I complained to MGM and then NBC. I said to them, 'This isn't right. Why should we be showing children all over America how to speak incorrectly. As a writer and as an actress we need to lift them up and make this a better world—not to downplay to the lowest denominator.' I fought with the producers over this and then went to the heads of NBC, who backed me up. Afterwards, the producers and writers treated me very respectfully. It wasn't so pleasant in the middle of the battle though. They thought I was just being uncooperative and difficult.

"As for Lori Martin, I don't think she knew how to handle it [fame]," continues Carole. "Looking back now, she was just a very young girl who really didn't know what to do. She had a twin sister she was jealous of because her sister had a more mature body. She just wasn't a very happy person and she really didn't know how to deal well with what was going on, because all of a sudden she was made bigger than life. Everyone was trying to please her and do whatever she wanted. But she wasn't very comfortable within her own self, and I don't think she was ever a happy girl all through her life. Her behavior affected everybody, but we all just coped and didn't pay much attention. Lori cried a lot. There were times where she would be off weeping and we couldn't help her. I felt more frustrated that there wasn't anything I could do to make her feel better. I tried."

MGM was so impressed with Carole Wells that they chose her as their Hollywood Deb Star for 1961. After *National Velvet* was cancelled in 1962, MGM kept her under contract for about another nine months before dropping her option. "It was a very weird experience for me," admits Wells. "I had an overture made to me that if I cooperated I would stay under contract longer. I thought 'cooperated' meant getting to the studio on time and doing your job. I soon learned that that was not what this man was talking about. It made me feel very badly. I basically told him he could take his contract and stuff it. It turned out fine because I went under contract twice with Universal."

Back on the big screen, Wells was cast in a blink-and-you'll-miss-her role as Tony Bill's girlfriend in the hit comedy *Come Blow Your Horn* (1963), starring Frank Sinatra as a swinging bachelor who teaches his younger brother (Bill) the ropes. Due to the film's overlong running time, most of Wells' scenes were excised from the movie. "The producer, Howard Koch, was very apologetic and felt badly about it," says Carole. "He said, 'We really wanted to leave in those scenes but we couldn't.' They were nice about it though—not like when Barbra Streisand cut me out of *Funny Lady*. People warned me that that would happen, but I didn't believe it."

Though she didn't have much screen time in *Come Blow Your Horn*, Wells did become friendly with Ol' Blue Eyes. "I loved Frank Sinatra and thought he was an amazing man," exclaims Carole. "We actually remained friends for a long time. I'll never forget the time when I walked into a party he was throwing at his suite in the Waldorf Towers about three or four years

In the teenage hot rod flick *The Lively Set* (Universal, 1964) Martin Blaine, Doug McClure, Pamela Tiffin, Peter Mann, and Carole Wells react to racecar driver James Darren's dangerous antics.

after my husband, Larry Doheny, had died. Frank was on the other side of the room. He dropped everybody and walked over to me, took my hand and said, 'Hello, Mrs. D. I've been wondering how you are.' He always called me Mrs. D. The guys in the Rat Pack never said your last name. He wouldn't let go of my hand and wanted me to meet a good friend of his. He was always just charming to me."

In June of 1963, Wells married Edward Lawrence Doheny IV. The Doheny name in Los Angeles is comparable to what the Rockefeller name is to New York. There is Doheny Drive, Doheny Estates, and at one time most of Beverly Hills was Doheny property. The family fortune is black gold and real estate, as a Doheny was one of the first men to discover oil in Southern California. Wells soon learned however that being married to a very rich man had its drawbacks in Hollywood. Wells bemoaned to *TV Guide*, "Being Mrs. Doheny is not the big help people think for an acting career. There's the other side—the resentments, the actresses with their snide remarks, the whole idea that I am taking a job from someone who really needs it." Looking back, Wells says adamantly, "I still think how I felt was all true. I even had producers say to me on interviews, 'Why are you working? Why are you here?' I never had to work even when I was a child. But I *wanted* to work. I loved doing it. I worked during the first six years of my marriage and when I decided it was time to have children, I just altered my life."

In 1964, Wells finally struck drive-in movie gold playing a sexpot named Mona in the hit film *The Lively Set* (1964). ("I was working a lot for Universal Television and they called me to meet with the producer.") As the tagline proclaimed, "Romance and racing are in their blood ... and the faster the action ... the more the fun!!!" James Darren starred as Casey Owens, a builder and racing car driver who enters college after serving two years in the army. He meets Chuck Manning (Doug McClure) and his beautiful sister Edie (Pamela Tiffin) when he challenges Chuck to a drag race in their souped up hot rods. Casey has an idea regarding a gas turbine engine and, when his professor encourages him to expand on it, he quits school and goes to work in his father's garage. Casey's invention comes to the attention of millionaire racing enthusiast Stanford Rogers (Peter Mann) and his beautiful but neglected girlfriend Mona (Wells). Rogers hires Casey, but when Casey cracks up one of his cars while trying to attain high speeds, Rogers lets him go. Casey's family, with the help of friends, buys the turbine engine back from Rogers. Now heeding the advice of his professor, Casey builds a car around the engine. He and Chuck enter the Tri-State Endurance Race where Rogers is their chief competitor. Though engaged to a singer named Doreen Grey (Joanie Sommers), Chuck can't help being attracted to Mona, who vamps him in his hotel room after Rogers ignores her one too many times. However, Mona is a good girl at heart and when Chuck confesses how much he loves Doreen, Mona and he become friends. When Mona returns to his room in her pajamas just for a friendly dinner, Doreen makes a surprise appearance. Thinking the worst, she breaks off the engagement. In the end, Casey wins the race and Edie's heart and Chuck marries Doreen.

The Lively Set was a sort of *Grand Prix* for the teenage set. However, the film's seriousness may have turned off a number of younger viewers looking for something goofier, like what was found in the *Beach Party* movies. Compared to other movies of its ilk though, *The Lively Set*, as directed by Jack Arnold, was definitely above average. It was well acted and contained some nifty songs composed

In *The Lively Set* (Universal, 1964) Carole Wells played a lovelorn lass who acts like a pit stop tramp, but underneath is just the girl-next door. *Billy Rose Theatre Collection, The New York Public Library for the Performing Arts, Astor, Lenox and Tilden Foundations.*

by Bobby Darin, including the jazzy theme song sung by James Darren. The film was meticulously produced and the racing sequences so realistic (the reviewer in *Variety* remarked that these scenes were "some of the most exciting shots seen in a long time") that the movie received an Academy Award nomination for 'Best Sound Effects Editing.' (It lost to *Goldfinger*.) The film also proved it was not just teenage fluff with its realistic incorporation of a gas turbine engine into the plot. According to Carole Wells, "That turbine engine really worked. They let us drive these cars for about six months to test them out. I was supposed to go testify for the engine makers in Sacramento. The day before I was supposed to go my father-in-law [Mr. Doheny] called me and asked, 'Carole, are you aware that the shirt on your back is brought to you by our oil companies that comprise Union Oil?' I replied, 'Yes.' He then said, 'Do you think that it is a smart move to go try to ruin the oil business with your testimony tomorrow when that's what's feeding you?' I got the message and didn't go. But I should have stuck to my guns and done it anyway, but since I was married [to his son] I'd thought I'd be loyal to my husband."

As for the film's two leads, Wells found Darren "fun" to work with. Regarding Tiffin, she opines, "Pamela definitely was not a happy camper during the making of *The Lively Set*. I loved her and we stayed friendly for a long time. Pamela was darling, but I think she wanted to be home with her husband, Clay Felker. When she wasn't with Clay she was unhappy. Also everybody was hitting on her—actually the world was hitting on Pamela! She was very esoteric and had this kind of mysterious veil around her. Pamela didn't talk to people and didn't let everybody know who she was. I think that kind of worked for her in many ways, because people stayed interested in her. She didn't seem like an actress and I always thought to myself, 'I don't think she is going to have a long career because she just isn't interested in it.' I don't know why, but I always felt like that when I was with her. Pamela really wasn't happy in Hollywood."

Doug McClure on the other hand was a prankster, according to Wells. "He was sweet and funny. I liked him a lot, but

Doug was drinking all of the time—just *always* drinking. It was terrible because being under contract at Universal everybody sort of knew what everyone else was doing. People worried about him then. I can't believe he lived as long as he did—bless his heart. Joanie Sommers was very pleasant and very normal considering all the commotion around her. She was a big singing star at that time but she was very down-to-earth."

Carole Wells was not very active on television or in films during 1965 and 1966. Needing a break from acting in front of the movie and TV cameras, she decided to concentrate on performing on stage, where the feedback from a live audience is instantaneous. She took opera lessons in New York—she is an accomplished Light Soprano—and did musical theater, beginning with a starring role in *The Wizard of Oz* in Hawaii. But it is still a mystery why no producer of a beach or Elvis movie offered her a role. "I was always working in some medium," says Carole. "I did have to turn down roles because of conflicts but I don't recall being offered any beach or Elvis movies. I even knew Elvis Presley. I liked him a lot and thought he was a wonderful, cool guy. While I was working at Universal, I was still getting my hair done at MGM studios. Elvis was getting his hair done there also and we would sit in the dye room together. He was getting his hair darkened and I was getting my hair lightened. We got to be friends. He was always fascinated about the socialite part of my life because he wanted to be more a part of society but felt he never could fit in. He also told me a story about how he bought his parents a black Cadillac when he first got money because they always dreamed of owning one. After he gave it to them, they complained that they didn't have money to buy gas for it."

In 1967, Wells was cast at the last minute to play Lucy Hanks, just back from finishing school, in the western sitcom *Pistols 'n' Petticoats*. Ann Sheridan (the

In *The Lively Set* (Universal, 1964) Carole Wells entices goodguy Doug McClure to make her boyfriend jealous. *Billy Rose Theatre Collection, The New York Public Library for the Performing Arts, Astor, Lenox and Tilden Foundations*

"Oomph Girl" of the movies) starred as Henrietta Hanks, the head of a pistol-packin' family who combats varmints, desperadoes, and warring Injuns to the dismay of the town's sheriff (Gary Vinson) in Wretched Colorado, ca. 1880. The series pilot had actress Chris Noel in the role, but when CBS tested it, she along with co-star Jody McCrea (as the sheriff) received a less than enthusiastic response from the audience as compared to the others. Though Universal still wanted Noel in the series, CBS demanded the part be recast. "I really felt badly for Chris Noel," remarks Wells sincerely. "It's a shocking thing to have happen. You make the pilot and you feel excited when it is picked up as a series only to be pulled out of it. I didn't think it was fair the way they treated Chris. I worked with the show's producer Joe Connolly on *Leave It to Beaver*. He called me one day and asked me if I'd be interested in doing another television series. I said, 'I'm not really sure.' TV series are a lot of work. You get up in the morning at 5:30 a.m. and you are on the set all day. You don't have another life. I thought about it and talked it over with my husband, and he felt it would be fine to do. So I called him on a Thursday to say yes. He told me to report to the set on that Monday. I met with Ann Sheridan and the rest of the cast and crew and then began costume fittings. This was one of the easiest ways I ever got an acting job. I got *Funny Lady* that way too."

The critics were not kind to *Pistols 'n' Petticoats*, but even still, Wells loved playing Lucy and working with Ann Sheridan. "I thought Lucy was a great character and not snooty at all. They made her very feminine, just coming back from Finishing School, but as you saw through the show she would get out there and fight with the rest of the family—hitting people over the head or tangling with the Indians. She was fun to play. I thought Lucy was a rare gem that people didn't know what to do with until they saw that she was human.

"Ann Sheridan was a fabulous woman and she died before my eyes," continues Wells sadly. "I never saw somebody expire with such grace and elegance. She was in pain and I would say, 'Hi Annie. How are you today?' She'd reply, 'Well, sweetie I wish I felt as good as you do.' That's all she would say."

Though the hippie movement was in full swing in late-sixties Hollywood, Wells' lifestyle was very far from it. She hung out with the older Hollywood stars and shied away from the Peter Fonda and Dennis Hopper crowd. "They were the ones having the most fun," admits Wells with a laugh. "They all stuck together and I never knew why I didn't fit in. I'd walk into a party somewhere and I always felt like that I was just not the same as everyone around me. I realized later that it was because I definitely was still stuck in the morality of the fifties, having such strict parents. That was just my mentality." Instead of hanging with Hollywood's newest in-crowd, Carole concentrated on her singing. She performed on stage in such musical productions of *The Sound of Music*, *Call Me Madam* with Ethel Merman ("She was a big diva and she let everyone know it"), *Wildcat* with Martha Raye, and *State Fair* with Roger Smith.

In 1969, Carole Wells quit performing to raise a family, but that didn't stop the offers coming in. As fate would have it, she was offered a part in a James Bond movie [most likely *The Man with the Golden Gun*] but had to turn it down due to her pregnancy. After her two sons were born, Wells was determined to be a stay-at-home mom. But circumstances changed when her husband suddenly died. Maybe needing to mingle with the adult world again, Wells decided to revive her acting career in 1973.

One of her first roles was playing a

film actress in the cult horror movie, *The House of Seven Corpses* (1973), produced, directed, and written by Paul Harrison, the writer of the children's series *H.R. Pufnstuf*. ("I only did this film because I hadn't worked in a long time and needed a job.") In this creepy movie, a movie crew inhabits a haunted house as they film a low-budget horror movie. The cast included John Ireland as the film's director, Faith Domergue as its leading lady who revives the murderous corpse with her readings from the Tibetan Book of the Dead, and John Carradine as the house's caretaker. Carole Wells essayed the role of the film's beautiful ingenue and, as with the rest of the cast, meets a grizzly end. In real life, she almost died doing this movie. Wells explains, "At the end when I'm going down the river I was so cold that the hairdresser on the film knew of a spa nearby that had warm Jacuzzis and things. We did that scene at night in the freezing rain. After we finished I wrapped myself up, put my hair in a towel and went to the spa. They had these old fashioned barrels that were made of aluminum that were like a Jacuzzi for one. My hair was real long and it got caught on the suction and started pulling me under. My sister-in-law, Lucy Doheny, was with me and she heard me gurgling for help. I could have drowned so easily. She saved my life."

According to Wells, the movie was made on a shoestring budget and the cast and crew stayed in some cheap motel outside of Salt Lake City. Even so, the cast for the most part had a good time making this

The House of Seven Corpses (International Amusement Corp., 1974) featured Carole Wells and Jerry Strickler playing ill-fated actors who wake the undead while filming a horror movie.

film. "We all got along fine on the set," says Carole. "I liked the director and it was all very professional. John Carradine was fascinating. We'd go out afterwards in a group and have dinner together. John would just regal us with his tales of his early working days [in Hollywood]. He was a great storyteller. Faith Domergue kept to herself. I never got to be friends with her and never felt that she wanted to be friends with me. After we completed the movie they showed us a rough-cut. Everybody was patting each other on the back, telling one another how wonderful they were. *I just wanted to get out of there!* The funniest story about this movie is that when I was doing *Funny Lady*, Barbra Streisand and Roddy McDowall had to go downtown to do a scene outside of a theater. Wouldn't you know it but on the marquee was *The House of the Seven Corpses* with my name above the title. Roddy teased me so badly. He said, 'Well, I see you've done some of those horror movies too.'"

Funny Lady (1975) was a huge step up from *The House of the Seven Corpses*, but Carole had a better chance of surviving that hideous walking corpse than the power wielding Barbra Streisand. According to Wells, Streisand only agreed to reprise her role of Fannie Brice in this sequel to the Academy Award–winning *Funny Girl*, co-starring James Caan as Billy Rose and Omar Sharif as Nicky Arnstein, if she had some authority over the production, which extended to the cutting room. Hence, Wells saw some of her best scenes excised from the final print.

Carole got the role of Norma Butler due to her friend, Fannie Brice's daughter Fran, who was married to the film's producer Ray Stark. They thought Wells was just perfect for the role of the sexy but klutzy showgirl. However, the film's director may have disagreed. "I don't think Herb Ross liked me because of that," guesses Carole. "He never gave me the time of day during that movie until I finally lost my temper with him. He basically was just getting through my scenes so he could get on to Barbra. That was his main interest. Finally I was on this gigantic stage at MGM for the scene before a Broadway opening where this moose comes in and knocks down the scenery. It was a huge undertaking to do. I was supposed to walk from the back of the stage. Roddy McDowall and Jimmy Caan were walking up the aisle and we were supposed to meet directly at a certain place on the stage. The scenery is going back and forth and the moose is knocking things over while showgirls with big headdresses are running by. Well I can't see—I'm nearsighted. I asked the assistant director to give me a cue light but nobody paid attention. So of course I missed the spot. Herb is just like Cecil B. DeMille, sitting on top of this huge crane. He yelled through a megaphone, '*Miss Wells, do you realize I have 175 extras on the set today? This is one of the biggest production numbers in this movie. It is costing me thousands of dollars. We don't have time for you to miss your cue!*' I pulled up all this energy and said loudly, '*Well get me a god damn cue light! I cannot see!*' It was so funny because I don't like confrontation. It is not my style. I was ornery back to him and sure enough he was nice to me after that. He yelled, 'Miss Wells needs a cue light! Get Miss Wells a cue light!'"

For the most part Wells got along pleasantly with Barbra Streisand during the making of *Funny Lady*. ("Barbra was always very nice to me, but I kept my distance. We had a nice rapport but—she may have evolved since then—she was totally just interested in her own work.") It wasn't until after *Funny Lady* was released that Wells' opinion of La Streisand dropped dramatically.. "Barbra had the power in the editing room and had me cut out three times," exclaims Wells. "I had a dance scene with Ben Vereen, but it was dropped. I think this was a shame because here you had a Tony winner and a great entertainer in Vereen and she cut him out so much. There are a lot of things I did in that movie that people won't see because Barbra omitted my scenes. Jimmy Caan jokes how the movie was about the back of his head. It was Barbra's face on everything. The film needed more of a balance because you had a lot of good actors, funny scenes and a lot of people beautifully costumed by Bob Mackie and Ray Aghayan for it to have so much cut out. Everybody was sick about it. We saw how long it took to film some of these scenes and they never got shown." With most of her scenes on the cutting room floor, it is no wonder that most critics never mentioned Wells in their reviews. However, the reviewer in *Variety* took notice and commented, "Carole Wells has some flashy moments...."

Wells made a few more TV appearances and played a small role in *The Cheap Detective* (1978) before abandoning her career again. Five years after her first husband passed away she remarried. Her around the world honeymoon turned into a nightmare in India when the plane they were on was hijacked. ("That is a story for another book.") After her safe return to Los Angeles, Wells gave birth to another son and then a daughter. Her marriage broke up shortly after that. Her acting career became a distant memory, though Wells got involved in other aspects of show business. "I was busy being a mother and started writing," says Carole. "I produced some TV shows too. Interesting enough, none of my children went into show business." Wells developed the game show pilot *Caesar's Comedy Bingo* and the motion picture *Loophole* (1980), starring Albert Finney. She also created the TV pilot *Far Beyond Nearby* and directed and wrote for the reality series, *How to Learn to Fly Fish*. In between projects, Carole wrote a book called *Love Letters to My Daughter*, detailing her child's harrowing experiences with a life threatening back disease. In 1991, she produced and played a supporting role in the independent movie *Molly and the Ghost*.

Carole Wells models one of the exquisite Oscar-nominated costumes from *Funny Lady* (Columbia, 1975).

Looking back on her career, Wells says, "My timing was always off. I was asked to be in the Burt Reynolds film where he starred with Sally Field for the first time [*Smokey and the Bandit*]. Burt hadn't met Sally yet and asked me to play her part. I couldn't do it because I had another obligation at the time. I had met Burt and thought, 'God this would be fun to work with him!' I would have loved to do more movies but most of the films I was offered conflicted with my TV roles, which I had to do since I was under contract. The studios would not release me."

As for the future, Carole Wells remarks, "I probably will do some acting now. After eighteen years of being single and raising my children alone, I am enjoying married life again. I also just finished my book called *Once Rich, Always Rich* about the jet set life in the '60s and '70s. But I feel my greatest achievements are my four children and the charity work [Golden Light Institute, Young Musicians Foundation, S.H.A.R.E., etc.] I have participated in all my adult life. I loved acting, but the fulfillment of rearing great kids basically by myself and educating them through college is the most satisfying of all."

Film Appearances

1957   **Lizzie** (MGM) d. Hugo Haas

1961   **The Absent Minded Professor** (Buena Vista) [uncredited] d. Robert Stevenson

        A Thunder of Drums (MGM) d. Joseph M. Newman

1963   **Come Blow Your Horn** (Paramount) d. Bud Yorkin

1964   **The Lively Set** (Universal) d. Jack Arnold

1968   **Way Out West** (Universal) [edited episodes of *Pistols 'n' Petticoats*] d. various

1974   **The House of Seven Corpses** (International Amusement Corp.) d. Paul Harrison

1975   **Funny Lady** (Columbia) d. Herbert Ross

1978   **The Cheap Detective** (Columbia) d. Robert Moore

1991   **Molly and the Ghost** (Direct-to-video) d. Don Jones

Television Appearances

Medic "She Walks in Beauty" 8/6/1956 NBC
Climax "The Blessed Midnight" 12/18/1956 ABC
Father Knows Best "Revenge Is Sweet" 2/26/1958 NBC
Bachelor Father "Bentley's Clubhouse" 5/25/1958 CBS
Maverick "The Lass with the Poisonous Air" 11/1/1959 ABC
Maverick "Maverick and Juliet" 1/17/1960 ABC
Fury "Packy's Dream" 3/19/1960 NBC
The Donna Reed Show "Mary's Crusade" 5/12/1960 ABC
The Donna Reed Show "Love's Sweet Awakening" 6/2/1960 ABC
National Velvet (series regular as Edwina Brown) 9/18/1960 to 9/10/1962 NBC
Here's Hollywood 9/18/1961 NBC
Wagon Train "The Mary Beckett Story" 5/9/1962 NBC
The Wide Country "Tears on a Painted Face" 11/29/1962 NBC
Laramie "Gun Duel" 12/25/1962 NBC
Leave It to Beaver "The All Night Party" 5/30/1963 CBS
Ben Casey "The Echo of a Silent Cheer" 10/16 & 10/23/1963 ABC
Bob Hope Presents the Chrysler Theatre "Time for Elizabeth" 4/24/1964 NBC
Arrest and Trial "We May Be Better Strangers" 5/3/1964 ABC
Perry Mason "The Case of the Golden Venom" 1/21/1965 CBS
Password 9/16/1966 CBS
Pistols 'n' Petticoats (series regular as Lucy Hanks) 9/17/1966 to 8/19/1967 CBS

Something Special: An Hour with Tony Martin (special) 1/10/1967 SYN
The Virginian "The Welcoming Town" 3/22/1967 NBC
The Sixth Sense "Whisper of Evil" 4/8/1972 ABC
The Brian Keith Show "Sean the Swinger" 11/2/1973 NBC
The Tonight Show Starring Johnny Carson 8/1/1975 NBC
Switch "Mistresses, Murder and Millions" 12/23/1975 CBS
Police Woman "The Trick Book" 9/28/1976 NBC

Also

Playhouse 90, Lux Video Theatre, Gunsmoke, Eddie Fisher Coke Time, The Groucho Marx Show, The Adventures of Ozzie and Harriet, The Many Loves of Dobie Gillis, The Red Skelton Show, Dr. Kildare, The Joey Bishop Show, He Said, She Said, The Dean Martin Show, The Doris Day Show, and The AM Show

☆ LORI WILLIAMS ☆

Lori Williams is a shapely blonde who began working as part of choreographer David Winters' dance troupe. She made a number of uncredited appearances shaking her wild mane of hair and curvaceous body in a gaggle of beach and Elvis films, including *Pajama Party* (1964), *Roustabout* (1964), *Viva Las Vegas* (1964) and *Girl Happy* (1965). Her first credited role was a beach girl in *A Swingin' Summer* (1965). But the part that propelled her to drive-in cinema fame was that of go-go dancer Billie, who joins Tura Satana's Varla and Haji's Rosie on a wild, for-kicks back road journey in the Russ Meyer classic, *Faster, Pussycat! Kill! Kill!* (1966). When the film first opened, it was a hit with the drive-in crowd but ignored by everyone else. It wasn't until years later that the film developed a massive cult following. Williams followed this with a small role in *It's a Bikini World* (1967), before abandoning Hollywood to get married.

Lori Williams was born in Pittsburgh on March 23, 1946. When she was in her teens she began taking classes at the Town Modeling Agency. Modeling led to acting and dancing at the Pittsburgh Playhouse where she landed a small part in *Daddy Long Legs*. After graduating high school, Lori bought a one-way ticket to Los Angeles to visit a friend for the summer. "I saved the money I had made from an income tax check I received for modeling to finance my trip," recalls Williams. "My friend Chris was about eight years older than I was. She was also an actress and she came out to L.A. with a boyfriend. Just after I arrived, Chris broke up with her boyfriend and went back East. I decided to stick with my plan and stayed the summer. I got a job working and modeling at the Wilhelmina Agency."

With the money she was earning from modeling by day and swinging on a red velvet swing over the bar at a club called the Roaring 20's, Williams was able to take dance classes again. Her instructor was renowned choreographer David Winters, best known for playing A-rab, one of the Jets gang members, in the stage and film versions of *West Side Story*. By 1964 he had focused his attentions behind the screen and choreographed many of the beach party and Elvis Presley movies. Winters was impressed with Lori and plucked her and Teri Garr out of his class to dance in some of the films he was working on. "David and I became really good buddies," remarks Lori. "We hung out together when we weren't working. I'd spend time at his house eating Chinese food and watching movies. He was like a brother to me. Professionally, he was very proficient and very tough. He didn't want the dance sequences in the movies he was working on to look choreographed. All the dancing and gyrating was choreographed loosely to give it a natural style. I had to go on auditions for each of the dance jobs even if David was the choreographer."

In 1963, Williams worked as a dancer in the Paul Newman film *The Prize*. During filming, the writers expanded the scene and there was a speaking role created for a young woman. Paul Newman and director Mark Robson had all the dancers line up and asked the ones who had a SAG card to raise their hands. Lori's hand quickly went up but she reveals, "I didn't have my SAG card. You needed a speaking job to get one—I never had one before." Newman went down the row of beautiful young dancers and selected Lori to be in the scene with him. Since the new scene was going to be shot after lunch, Williams raced down to the Screen Actors Guild to get her SAG card now that she landed a speaking role.

Now that she was a bona-fide Screen Actors Guild member, choreographer David Winters kept Lori very busy in 1964, using her as a dancer in five drive-in films aimed at the teenage set. In *Get Yourself a College Girl* (1964), starring Mary Ann Mobley and Chad Everett, Lori is in all the dance sequences but stands out at the ski lodge costume ball where, wearing a gold lamé teddy, she does "The Swim," sung by the Standells. Williams is more noticeable in *Kissin' Cousins* as one of the man-hungry Kitty Hawks who have their sights set on the brunette and blonde Elvis, playing look-alike cousins. Williams also danced in one of the King's biggest hits, *Viva Las Vegas*, where Elvis played a down-on-his-luck racecar driver determined to enter the Las Vegas Grand Prix. He gets a job as a waiter in a hotel to earn the entrance fee and pursues the gorgeous Ann-Margret as a swimming instructor. Before long the red-hot duo are singin', dancin' and romancin'. Complications begin when Cesare Danova, as Presley's suave friendly rival on the track, also competes for the affections of Ann-Margret. Performing in the numbers "The Lady Loves Me" and "What I'd Say," set in a club where the dance floor is patterned after a roulette wheel, Lori recalls, that "In *Viva Las Vegas* there was major dance rehearsals. David Winters was very much a perfectionist and a very good choreographer. He wanted every dance sequence just right."

As for Elvis, Williams remarks, "He

The voluptuous Lori Williams in publicity shot from *Faster, Pussycat! Kill! Kill!* (Eve Productions, 1966). *Courtesy of Lori Williams.*

was the sweetest, nicest, most insecure guy I ever met. He liked the same people around him all the time. That's why he had those guys—the Memphis Mafia—always with him. They were all cousins and close friends of Elvis. I knew them all—Joe Esposito, Sonny West. Elvis tried to get people that he worked with jobs on the movies he was making. I also dated Elvis for awhile but it was a very sweet thing. We went together between the making of *Roustabout* and *Kissin' Cousins*. Then he met Ann-Margret, who really was the love of his life. Our courtship was not some bizarre story. It was very sweet and Elvis was the perfect gentleman."

Williams last movie in 1964 was *Pajama Party* from American International Pictures, starring Tommy Kirk as a Martian who crashes the beach party and falls in love with Annette Funicello as Connie despite the presence of her moronic boyfriend Big Lunk (Jody McCrea). *Pajama Party* was the only AIP beach film choreographed by Winters and it shows. The regular AIP cast of beach boys and girls are shoved to the background as Winters' dancers (most notably Toni Basil and Teri Garr) come front and center during the film's production numbers. Williams could be seen dancing in a bikini during the film's rousing extended opening song "It's That Kind of Day" and gyrating in her PJs at the pajama party in the film's finale. She is also seen modeling a purple negligee during Dorothy

In *Girl Happy* (MGM, 1965), Elvis Presley is surrounded by fetching beach bunnies Lori Williams, Lyn Edgington, Chris Noel, and unidentified actress (left to right).

Lamour's number "Where Did I Go Wrong" sung at a dress shop. Purportedly, the songwriters composed the tune especially for Lamour.

Lori Williams continued working as a dancer for David Winters in 1965. She played a vacationing coed who can be seen doing "The Clam" with Elvis Presley in *Girl Happy* and one of the shapely denizens of a spa for women who flip over handyman Elvis Presley in *Tickle Me*. Williams has a nice dance bit with Elvis in this as he warbles the song "Dirty Feelin'" at the ranch's horse stable. Recalling her drive-in films, Williams opines, "The kind of movies I worked in weren't like *A Tale of Two Cities*. They were all fun, beach party-type of films oriented toward a young audience. That was the atmosphere on the sets too. Everything was so light and fluffy. On most of these pictures, the actors and dancers were more like a company. The dancing was very important in these movies, as was the singing. The story line took a back seat to that. I cannot tell you the plot to a single one of these movies. So when you were working, you were in a united group and you stayed that way. For the most part, there wasn't this star system working on these films. If you worked and were on the film, you were a part of it. Unless somebody like a Raquel Welch with his or her nose out of joint came on board, everybody was together.

"I didn't have any bad or horrible experiences working with other actors," continues Lori. "But there were a couple of prima donnas. Mary Ann Mobley comes to mind when I worked on *Girl Happy*. What happened with her is so miniscule it is not worth repeating. Pamela Austin and I became friends while working together on *Kissin' Cousins*. We both lived at the Hollywood Studio Club at one time. She was a sweetie and I really liked her a lot. I ran into her at Neiman-Marcus during the 1980s and she looked fabulous. She told me she was going to try to resurrect her acting career, but I don't think she did. Yvonne Craig was also a great gal to work with, as was Teri Garr. She was neat."

While continuing to get film work, Williams began branching out into other areas as she danced on TV's *Hullabaloo* and *Shindig*. "I only danced on *Hullabaloo* twice," says Lori. "I did a few more episodes of *Shindig*. I was the girl in the cage when Bobby Vinton was the host. I was asked to dance more on *Shindig* but I was working in films a lot of the time. They needed you every week for those shows and I wasn't available." Williams also started to accept stunt and stand-in work to earn extra money. She replaced Wende Wagner as the stunt girl on the popular TV series *Run for Your Life*, starring Ben Gazzara.

Despite being a sexy aspiring actress trying to make it in Hollywood while working in the lower echelons of the business, Williams surprisingly did not run into the casting couch very often. "I don't know why but I didn't" says Lori. "The one guy that gave me problems was producer Martin Ransohoff. He was talking about putting me under contract. I had met him while I was doubling for Sharon Tate during her test for *The Cincinnati Kid*, which she didn't get. Another guy that liked me and said that he could get me work in Europe was Roger Vadim. But I suspected there was a hitch to his offer."

While standing in for Sharon Tate, Lori Williams became the next starlet on Steve McQueen's hit list. Seeing how stunning Williams looked, who could blame this Hollywood Romeo for making his move. "I was reading *Gone with the Wind* on the set and Steve asked to borrow the book for a second to see what I was reading," recalls Lori with a smile. "He put his phone number in the book. Nothing ever came of it. Sometime later I went one night to the Whiskey a-Go-Go and Steve was there. We danced together the whole night and that was it. He was funny and very childish—not the brightest guy in the world."

Though she had few lines, the film where Williams finally received notable billing was *A Swingin' Summer* (1965). Cast once again as a beach girl, Lori and the other gals (Diane Bond, Irene Sale, Diane Swanson and Kathy Francis) were described as "A Bevy of Bountiful Beauties in a Blazing Bikini Bonanza at the Beach." The film starred James Stacy, William Wellman Jr. and Quinn O'Hara as college students who persuade the manager of the Lake Arrowhead Village to let them run the dance pavilion for the summer. The film also introduced "TV's Hollywood Palace Billboard Girl" Raquel Welch to movie audiences, playing a book worm who learns to groove, as her manager Patrick Curtis was one of the film's backers. Recalling her first look at Raquel, Lori remembers, "James Stacy knocked on the door of the room I shared with another actress. He said to me, 'Come down to the set Lori. I think you met your Waterloo.' I asked, 'What do you mean?' He said, 'There is somebody down there and she is with a guy named Patrick Curtis.' At that point, for whatever reasons, a lot of people thought I had the look and body to do very well. All I needed was the right part. They were shooting one of the scenes from the beginning of the movie down on the beach where Raquel's character is rather plain and wearing glasses. I was on a bluff looking down on her with her drop-dead

Lori Williams as the curvaceous, hot rod-racing, go go-dancing Billie in *Faster, Pussycat! Kill! Kill!* **(Eve Productions, 1966).**

body and you just knew she was going to make it. She had a tremendous force behind her pushing her to the top."

Lori, clad in a black-and-white zebra-striped bikini, is first seen in *A Swingin' Summer* on the beach, throwing a beach ball around with the other girls and James Stacy as ladies man Mickey. She then is partnered with Mike Blodgett, energetically dancing to Gary Lewis and the Playboys. Later dressed in a green midriff and matching Toreador slacks, she is seen doing the Swim as "Mr. Personality" Donnie Brooks sings "Penny the Poo." But she finally gets the spotlight all to herself when she and Blodget do a wild dance solo while the other kids cheer them on. Though she is a knockout dancing or frolicking in her wild bikini, Williams was not happy with it due to Raquel Welch. "Raquel Welch was a problem on this movie and she was a major, major bitch," says Williams emphatically. "She wanted to have her signature bikini in the film. I had bought my bikinis before we got to Lake Arrowhead and she wouldn't let me wear any of them. I had to go out and buy new swimsuits. She then accused the makeup lady—who was a nice older woman who I had worked with many times—of putting the makeup too high up her thigh. I was right behind her and she remarked, 'You really don't need to be putting the body makeup there, do you!' Working with her was not a lot of fun. She kept trying to get people fired. We lost two cameramen who quit because she was just wretched. For me, she was just the worst person I ever met during the time I worked.

"Despite Raquel, I still enjoyed myself working on *A Swingin' Summer*," continues Lori Williams. "Everyone else was nice and we really didn't deal with Raquel a lot. Mike Blodgett was fun to dance with. Quinn O'Hara was great and we became very good friends. I also became very friendly with Diane Bond. She later became a feminist artist. She even changed her appearance. She was very pretty with a great body and totally changed her appearance to look more like a feminist. I stayed in touch with her up until about fifteen years ago."

Though Lori danced in a number of popular films, the one that will go down in infamy is the Russ Meyer cult classic *Faster, Pussycat! Kill! Kill!* This low budget movie filmed in glorious black and white for an estimated budget of $45,000, was done entirely on location outside of Los Angeles. Williams was cast as the go-go dancing Billie, a hot blonde thrill seeker out for kicks who goes on a wild melee with her fellow dancers Tura Satana, as the tough, menacing Varla, and Haji, as the exotic Rosie. "I was with the Paul Konar Agency and had a pretty good agent," recalls Williams. "For whatever reason, Russ Meyer cast Tura Satana and Haji after seeing them dancing in clubs. Tura had some minor acting credits, but I believe Haji did not. [Haji actually co-starred in Meyer's *Motorpsycho!* released in 1965.] Meyer wanted the blonde to be a completely different type. For my role and the Sue Bernard role of the kidnapped teenager, he wanted to get 'an actress.' He put a call out to the agents and Pat Konar sent me to the interview. It was like a big cattle call. After I got the third callback there were just a few of us left. Russ wasn't going to hire me because I wasn't busty enough. I wasn't really a 'Meyer girl.' But he liked my look and form and said we'd work it out somehow.

"I, in the meantime, had no clue who Russ Meyer was," continues Lori. "I just thought this was an interview for a regular movie. I didn't know he made films like *Lorna* and *Mudhoney* before this. Even though this film had no swearing, no nudity—I have a backless scene but my front is completely covered—it was still considered really exploitative. I thought, 'Oh God, what type of picture is this?' I was also taken aback regarding the violence in the film. But little did I know it was going to be the best thing for me."

Faster, Pussycat! Kill! Kill! opens with narration describing "a new breed of superwomen emerging out of the ruthlessness of our times" and then quickly dissolves to dancers Varla, Rosie, and Billie shaking their scantily clad bodies to the Bostweeds' title song at a seedy go-go club, as the intense male customers grotesquely yell encouragement, "Go baby, go! Faster! Harder!" The girls then hit the highway in their revved up hot rods and drive to the desert. They stop by a lake and Billie jumps into the water—clothes and all—for a swim. When Varla, the leader of the pack dressed appropriately in a black jumpsuit and showing ample cleavage, tells her smitten lover Rosie to fetch Billie out of the water, Billie yells back, "Here Rosie baby, I got it all nice and wet for ya." This is just one of many fabulous quotable one-liners Williams delivers with gusto in this over-the-top film, which leads to the first of the film's many catfights. The girls then find an open stretch of desert sand to race each other in a game of chicken. When teens Tommie (Ray Barlow) and Linda (Sue Bernard, *Playboy's* Miss December 1966) approach by car, Billie remarks, "Can't be my agent—he couldn't afford the gas! My desert fan club! They went thataway partner...." Varla challenges the "All-American he-man man" to a drag race after watching him race against the clock as Linda times him. With his male pride on the line, Tommie hesitantly agrees. After Varla wins by cheating, she goads him into a fight and breaks his spine, killing him.

Recalling the racing scenes, Williams says, "I had never driven until I moved to L.A. after high school. I was about twenty years old when I did this film and had no idea how to drive a stick shift. During the interview Russ asked me if I knew how to drive one and I lied and said sure. But I had never even been in a sports car. This caused a lot of problems because I didn't know how to drive. I had to learn very quickly. What grief there was for me on *Pussycat* was over this."

After dumping Tommie's body in her trunk, Varla drugs Linda and takes her hostage. Stopping at a gas station, the man-hungry Billie spots a dim-witted muscular blonde named Vegetable (Dennis Busch). "What a hunk of stuff! Woof," she yells lewdly. The girls then learn from the creepy gas station attendant that Vegetable's father (Stuart Lancaster), a dirty old man in a wheelchair, has hidden on his dilapidated ranch a stash of insurance money. Varla plots to steal it, but when Rosie and Billie balk, Varla threatens that the law would consider them accomplices—not witnesses—to Tommie's death. Billie retorts to Varla, "Oh, you're cute—like a velvet glove cast in iron. And like the gas chamber—a real fun gal!"

The character of Varla intimidates her cohorts just like off-screen Tura Satana intentionally or not intimidated her co-stars. Being of Japanese and Cherokee heritage, Satana is incredible in appearance and makes an imposing figure clad all in black—never smiling. According to Lori, "I was scared to death of Tura, who is a phenomenal woman and had an amazing life. But she really was a tough chick. She argued with Meyer constantly. When I saw Russ—who is hard to take on—back down a few times from her I thought, 'Whoa, this lady is not to be tangled with.' At one point, she didn't want to do a scene a certain way. She slammed her hand against some railroad equipment and broke her hand. This was enough to frighten anybody. Off camera, I kind of hid a lot with Sue Bernard. I felt I was out of my realm around Tura and if I made her mad she'd whip me. But she was very nice to me and I never had any problem with her I think because I kept my distance."

The girls follow Vegetable and his father to their isolated shack and pretend that they need water for a long trip home. The lascivious old man invites the gals to lunch. They accept and while Varla calculates their next move, Billie showers under the water tank. In a typical Meyer touch, the audience is treated to seeing the naked back of Williams as Billie squeals in delight from the refreshing water. "Oh, this is such a gas!" Varla's plot to fleece the old man hits a snag with the panicky Linda begging to be let free and the appearance of Kirk, the normal son (Paul Trinka). While Varla and

Rosie case the ranch, Billie comments to Linda, "Those two make the Mafia look like Brownies." When Linda questions Billie of why she is involved with them, she replies, "It's kicks. But I'm not under contract to them and I have a strong feeling option time is around the corner."

But before Billie decides to go freelance, she tries to seduce Vegetable under the pretense that she wants to see him lift weights. As the shirtless muscleman begins to pump iron, Billie makes her move. After lightly caressing his handsome physique and getting no reaction from him as he concentrates on his barbell, the frustrated bombshell raves, "Look, me, Jane—you, Tarzan. Now why don't you drop that tree you're holding and let's grab a vine and swing a little?" Their idyll is interrupted with a crash when Linda pushes the old man's wheelchair over and flees only to be captured again by Varla. While everybody is out searching for the girl, Billie gets Vegetable alone again, but his freaking out when a train thunders by puts a halt to the romancing.

After having lunch with the men, where Billie gets drunk, Varla announces that they have to kill them all. This is the last straw for Billie, who wants no more part of this caper and takes off with a parting shot, "See you girls in church!" But as she triumphantly walks towards her car, Varla grabs Rosie's knife and throws it into Billie's back, killing her. The body count quickly mounts as Vegetable pulls the knife out of Billie and stabs Rosie while Varla runs down the old man. Seeing her girlfriend lying in a pool of blood, an enraged Varla crushes Vegetable with her car. She then catches up with the fleeing Kirk and Linda. After a violent fight with Kirk, Varla is about to finish him off when Linda jumps into a truck and runs down Varla, who is thrown into the air and lands near a battered Kirk. Defiant to the end, Varla lifts her hand to give him a karate chop but her hand drops as the life is snuffed out of her. Hysterically crying, Linda sobs, "I killed her like she was an animal! Like she was nothing!" Kirk responds, "She was nothing—nothing human!" As the closing credits roll, the title song sung by the Bostweeds once again is played.

Though Lori Williams was at first skeptical about working with Meyer on *Faster, Pussycat! Kill! Kill!*, he quickly put her fears to rest once filming began. "After Russ hired me, we quickly began rehearsals," remembers Lori. "He turned out to be very professional—the reason being that he had only so much money. He wanted to get this film released because it was going to be his entry to direct at 20th Century–Fox to make himself 'legitimate.' He ran the set like a boot camp. It was very stringent. Everybody had to go to bed early. There was no drinking allowed because Russ didn't want the actors looking bad. The shooting was run on a very tight schedule because we had only four weeks to do it in. To make us look Amazonian, Russ used low angle camera shots throughout the film. He also had me padded way more than the other girls to make me bigger on top. The only thing that made me uncomfortable is that Russ directed me to swing my hips as I walked. No real person walks that way, but everything in this film was over-the-top. It all contributed to the camp element of the film. Meyer put a lot into this film and, even though it didn't do that well when it first came out something in his psyche told him that this film would be a cult hit. It turned out that he was right."

As for the rest of the cast, Williams comments, "Haji was sweet and very quiet. She just wanted to be exotic all the time and would always say she was from another galaxy. She was almost esoteric. Sue Bernard was nice but she had a stage mother from hell with her. Stuart Lancaster was a doll and he would work with

Russ Meyer's hot rod racing wildcats from *Faster, Pussycat! Kill! Kill!* (Eve Productions, 1966) Haji as Rosie, Lori Williams as Billie, and Tura Satana as Varla (left to right). *Courtesy of Lori Williams.*

me to try to teach me things about acting. He was a phenomenal man. I heard that Dennis Busch died in car accident a long time ago. He was sweet and kind but you couldn't have more than a two-sentence conversation with him."

When *Faster, Pussycat! Kill! Kill!* was first released, it pretty much went unnoticed or critics ignored it due to its excessive violence. One of the few publications to review the film was *Variety*, whose critic commented that the film "is a somewhat sordid, quite sexy, and very violent murder-kidnap-theft meller, which includes elements of rape, lesbianism, and sadism clothed in faddish leather and boots and equipped with sports cars." Meyer purposely kept his trademark nudity out of this film to gear it to the teenage audiences that flocked to the drive-in. According to Lori, "*Faster Pussycat* opened the same weekend as *Harper* and it out grossed it on the East Coast. I still have the trade ads. When the film was first released it didn't do as badly as people say now." As for Williams' performance, the *Variety* reviewer remarked, "Miss Williams has a fresh, but sensual air that is promising in both heavy and sympathetic characterizations."

Williams next movie was filmed before *Faster, Pussycat! Kill! Kill!* was released. It was back to the sand-and-surf for Lori, playing, what else, a beach girl in *It's a Bikini World* (1967), starring Tommy Kirk and Deborah Walley. This late-in-the-cycle beach movie, the first feature directed by Stephanie Rothman, had a feminist angle to it, as Walley's bikini-clad redhead challenges Kirk's pompous surfer boy to a series of athletic contests to see who is the better person. By the time *Faster, Pussycat!* was released, Williams was contracted to another project and couldn't take advantage of the notoriety she received from it. "Andy Williams was mounting this big revue that was going to feature two showgirls—one blonde and one brunette—and they were not going to be topless," explains Lori. "My agent called me about this and said it could be a nice experience. I went to Las Vegas about six weeks after *Faster, Pussycat!* opened. My agent then began getting a lot of calls for me. I was even offered *Playboy* several times and looking back I should have done it but I didn't. I was locked into this revue and couldn't accept any acting offers. The reason I did it was because the pay was excellent and that they chose a very good friend of mine as the brunette. We'd thought we'd have so much fun together in Vegas and we did. We rented a house from a friend and stayed there for six months until the show closed.

"The lull in my career continued because I met my then husband in Vegas. He was a musician from Pennsylvania. After the show closed just before the holidays, I was supposed to go to Europe with a good friend of mine, actress Diane Bond. Our agents planned to get us a lot of the sexpot Barbarella-type roles that were being offered there. I went back to Pennsylvania with Tony and told Diane that I would meet up with her in Rome sometime in January. I never went. I married Tony and took a two year break." During her time back East, Williams continued modeling until she became pregnant with her daughter Julie.

When her marriage collapsed, Williams returned to Hollywood in 1969. She began making recurring appearances as one of the blackout players on the hit TV series *Love, American Style*. ("I worked a lot with Stuart Margolin and Phyllis Davis. Charlie Rondeau directed most of these segments. Working on this show was like a big party.") Williams then returned to stunt work when she was hired to play one of the ill-fated ocean liner passengers in the granddaddy of all disaster movies, *The Poseidon Adventure* (1972) and acted for director John Frankenheimer in his gangster film *99 and 44/100 Percent Dead* (1974) starring Richard Harris.

Lori Williams studied acting at the Actor's Studio with Lee Strasberg for a short period but she abandoned acting after an embarrassing experience while on an audition in the mid-seventies. "Even though I was in my early thirties my agents started to send me out to test for T&A beach party types of films,' says Lori. "I hadn't changed that much from the sixties and my body hadn't changed either. I'd going out on these auditions and everybody else was from about eighteen to twenty-three. I remember thinking, 'Been there—done that. I don't want to do these films being the oldest person on the set.' Finally, on one audition as this twenty-one year old came out of the room I was walking in and I remember hearing the casting director say to the producer, 'The next girl is Lori Williams. I want you to seriously take a good look at her. She is an oldie but goodie.' I was only about thirty-one! My face was just boiling hot in embarrassment. That is when I gave up acting.

"I think my type either became very big stars [like Raquel Welch] or you had to transcend like Shelley Fabares did into more mother-type roles," opines Williams. "I could make myself look like a mom but I really wasn't that type, though I did play Danielle Brisbois' mother on an episode of *Baretta*. For the most part, I was in that nowhere zone, so since I hadn't become a star I needed to wait until I got older to get acting work."

Williams teamed up with casting director Gene O'Havens and formed a casting company. They worked together for a few years and were very successful casting some episodes of *Tenspeed and Brownshoe*, *Family Ties*, *Cheers* and the Emmy winning "Who Am I," an installment of *ABC After-School Specials*. When that came to an end, Lori went into real estate. Her quiet life outside of show business was jolted in the mid-nineties when director John Waters commented on a few TV talk shows that *Faster, Pussycat! Kill! Kill!* was "Beyond a doubt the best movie ever made. And it is possibly better than any film that will be made in the future." Renewed interest led to the film being re-released, where the critics had a field day with their glowing tributes: "Pop Art fantasy image of powerful women" (Roger Ebert); "one of those rare legends that glides easily from its own time into our own, its charms intact and its powers as combustible as ever" (B. Ruby Rich, *The Village Voice*); "this rabid Z movie stretches double-entendres into warped figure-eights and offers some truly delicious bizarro strokes" (*The New Yorker*); and "a monument to raunch, it's Meyer's finest hour" (*Premiere Magazine*).

Today, Lori Williams, Tura Satana and Haji are much sought after to appear at film festivals and celebrity autograph conventions around the country. The film's popularity has also rejuvenated their acting careers, as Lori will be seen in the upcoming film *Beneath the Flesh*.

Film Appearances

1963   **The Prize** (MGM) d. Mark Robson

1964   **Kissin' Cousins** (MGM) [uncredited] d. Gene Nelson
Viva Las Vegas (MGM) [uncredited] d. George Sidney
Roustabout (Paramount) [uncredited] d. John Rich
Pajama Party (AIP) d. Don Weis
Get Yourself a College Girl (MGM) [uncredited] d. Sidney Miller
The Disorderly Orderly (Paramount) [uncredited] d. Frank Tashlin

1965   **Baby the Rain Must Fall** [uncredited] d. Robert Mulligan
Girl Happy (MGM) [uncredited] d. Norman Taurog
A Swingin' Summer (United Screen Arts) d. Robert Sparr
Tickle Me (Allied Artists) [uncredited] d. Norman Taurog

1966   **Our Man Flint** (20th Century–Fox) [uncredited] d. Gordon Douglas
Faster, Pussycat! Kill! Kill! (Eve Productions) d. Russ Meyer
The Swinger (20th Century–Fox) [uncredited] d. George Sidney

1967   **It's a Bikini World** (Trans American) d. Stephanie Rothman

1972   **The Poseidon Adventure** (20th Century–Fox) [stunts] d. Ronald Neame

1974   **99 and 44/100 percent Dead** (20th Century–Fox) d. John Frankenheimer

Television Appearances

Shindig [dancer] 12/2/1964 ABC
The Long, Hot Summer "A Day of Thunder" 1/19/1966 ABC
Love, American Style [recurring blackout player] 9/29/1969 to 9/18/1970 ABC
Baretta "The Dream" 5/4/1978 ABC

Also

Shindig, Hullabaloo, The Man from U.N.C.L.E., The Girl from U..N.C.L.E. and *Honey West*

MORE DRIVE-IN DREAM GIRLS

☆ BRENDA BENET ☆

A fetching brunette who some said reminded them of a younger Natalie Wood, Brenda Benet was a more than marginal actress during the '60s and '70s who had the drive to keep working. The fragile-looking beauty frolicked on the Malibu shore in *Beach Ball* (1965), danced with Elvis Presley in *Harum Scarum* (1965), and was romantically pursued by two racecar drivers in *Track of Thunder* (1967) on drive-in screens across the nation. She also did lots of television. However, movie fans knew her more for being famously wed (and divorced) to actors Paul Petersen and Bill Bixby than for any particular acting role.

Brenda Benet was born Brenda Nelson on August 14, 1945, in Hollywood. Her family moved to South Gate, just outside of Los Angeles when Brenda was a small child. Her father deserted the family soon after, and her mother Leona purportedly had to take in laundry to help support her children. Encouraged by her mother, Brenda began taking piano, ballet, and drama lessons. While attending South Gate High School, Benet acted at Hollywood's Shakespeare Festival, appearing in *A Winter's Tale*, *A Midsummer Night's Dream*, and *Twelfth Night*. She also expanded her talents to the musical stage, co-starring in the Long Beach Civic Light Opera productions of *Kismet* and *Oklahoma*. After graduating high school in 1963, Benet deferred her enrollment to Los Angeles City College for a year while she worked with the San Francisco Ballet Company and toured with the International Dance Company.

When Brenda returned to Los Angeles she decided to give acting a try while still taking college courses at LACC majoring in languages. She changed her name from Nelson to Benet, after a French cabaret singer, Vicki Benet. Things started happening quickly for the newcomer. She landed a small role in the comedy *A Global Affair* (1964), starring Bob Hope as a bachelor put in charge of a baby found at the United Nations. Co-star Susan Hart remarks, "Brenda was a very moral girl. When the director told us we had to strip down to our bras we both called our agents and screamed, '*You didn't tell us we had to take off our blouses!*' We both got dismissed from the film." Even still, Benet made enough of an impression for United Artists to choose her as its Hollywood Deb Star for 1964.

Benet began honing her acting craft with roles on a few sitcoms before making her film debut in one of the better *Beach Party* knockoffs, *Beach Ball* (1965). In the film Chris Noel, Benet, Gail Gilmore, and Mikki Jamison played four straight-laced college coeds who shed their bookworm ways, tease up their hair, and don bikinis to try to convince a quartet of college dropouts played by Edd Byrnes, Aron Kincaid, Robert Logan, and Don Edmonds to return to school. But the guys dig playing their musical instruments more than cramming for the next test. Benet made a fetching beach girl and was charming as Samantha, who is paired with Edmonds as Bob. Co-star Aron Kincaid described Benet as being "very warm and honey-voiced. She had that sort of June Allyson gravelly sound to her speech."

The Elvis Presley feature *Harum Scarum* (1965) reunited Brenda with *Beach Ball* co-star Gail Gilmore. Benet played Amethyst, a dancing gypsy and member of a band of thieves in a mythical Middle Eastern country who help a kidnapped singing star (Presley) thwart a plot to assassinate the King. Benet and her fellow dancers, Gilmore (as Sapphire) and Wilda Taylor (as Emerald), perform an exotic dance in the town square while Elvis croons "Shake That Tambourine." Recalling Benet, Gail Gerber (a.k.a. Gilmore) says fondly, "I used to drive Brenda home every day after shooting. She was a nice, sweet Catholic girl from the Valley."

Late in 1965 Benet took over the role of fashion model Jill McComb on the daytime drama *The Young Marrieds*. When the soap was cancelled in 1966, Benet worked steadily on television due to her talent and versatility. The sultry brunette was able to go from portraying an Arabian princess on *The Girl from U.N.C.L.E.* to astronaut Tony Nelson's would-be girlfriend on *I Dream of Jeannie*, to a rebellious Indian maiden on *Daniel Boone* to a Parisian model on the run from the Gestapo on *Hogan's Heroes*. In 1967, Benet married actor Paul Petersen of *The Donna Reed Show*. The marriage lasted only four years, as Petersen blamed it on Hollywood and Benet's ambition. He remarked in *TV Guide*, "When I rapidly turned into what passes for failure in this town, all Brenda kept saying was, 'This can't be happening to me.' She traded me in for Bill [Bixby], a guy whose career was going up."

Benet returned to the drive-in movie screen as the female lead in the racecar actioner *Track of Thunder* (1967). Filmed around the Nashville area, the film co-starred Tommy Kirk as Bobby Goodwin and Ray Stricklyn as Gary Regal—longtime friends and rivals both on and off the track. When the guys aren't trying to out drive each other, they are competing for the charms of Shelley Newman (energetically played by Benet). She is torn between the two, as Gary is ambitious and wants to keep racing for a long time while Bobby wants to quit and settle down on a farm. Meanwhile, the manager of the track (H. M. Wynant) is desperate to get gamblers interested in the stock car races and cultivates reporter Georgia Clark (Majel Barrett) to write embellished stories on the intense rivalry between Bobby and Gary. The bitterness grows between the two as they enter the stock car championship race, the International 500. *Track of Thunder* received dismal reviews for its implausible characterizations and predictable plot. Even among drive-in film aficionados, this less-than-exciting movie is not well regarded.

For the next couple of years, Benet

Lobby card for *Track of Thunder* (United Artists, 1967), starring Brenda Benet as a pit stop cutie.

once again remained a television actress. She had the gumption and talent to keep landing lead guest star roles on all the top sitcoms, westerns, and drama series. Her name was back in the movie fan magazines in 1971 when she married Bill Bixby, whom she had previously dated in the '60s. Then she appeared in one of the seventies' biggest drive-in hits, *Walking Tall* (1973), an exciting but exploitative, violent look at real-life baseball bat-wielding Tennessee sheriff Buford Pusser, played by Joe Don Baker. Benet played Luan, Pusser's informant working as a "hostess" in a gin mill roadhouse run by slatternly Callie Hacker (Rosemary Murphy).

In 1975, Benet and Bixby's son Christopher was born, and Brenda took time off to devote to being a fulltime mother. She returned to making guest spots in 1978, including playing a psychic on her husband's series, *The Incredible Hulk*. She then landed what would become her most popular role—seductress Lee Dumonde on the hit soap opera, *Days of Our Lives*. Benet was an instant hit and became one of the most popular villains on daytime television as the vile woman who comes to town to break up the show's super couple Doug and Julie. Benet revealed in *Soap Opera Digest*, "I was mildly interested in the idea of working a two-day work week, but when I heard the character was going to be a lady of questionable scruples, well that intrigued me; it was something I had never had the chance to play before."

Benet finally found that "brass ring" former husband Paul Petersen said she was always searching for, due to her success on *Days of Our Lives,* and she should have been happy but her life slowly began to unravel. Bixby left her in 1979 (they divorced in 1980), and then in March of 1981 her son tragically died during an emergency tracheotomy while accompanying Benet and friend Don Edmonds on a weekend outing to Mammoth Lake. The guilt surrounding her son's death seemed to be too much for her to take, despite her sunny outward appearance. Sadly, on April 7, 1982, a despondent Benet killed herself from a self-inflicted gunshot wound to the head. She was only thirty-six years old.

Film Appearances

1964 **A Global Affair** (MGM) d. Jack Arnold
1965 **Beach Ball** (Paramount) d. Lennie Weinrib
 Harum Scarum (MGM) d. Gene Nelson
1967 **Track of Thunder** (United Artists) d. Joe Kane
1972 **Horror at 37,000 Feet** (TV-movie) d. David Lowell Rich
1973 **Walking Tall** (AIP) d. Phil Karlson

Television Appearances

Hollywood Deb Star Ball (special) [Deb Star] 12/28/1963 ABC
Wendy and Me "East Is East and West Is Wendy" 12/7/1964 ABC
Wendy and Me "How Not to Succeed in Stealing" 3/1/1965 ABC
McHale's Navy "Will the Real Admiral Please Stand Up?" 4/2/1965 ABC
The Young Marrieds (series regular as Jill McComb) 7/1965 to 3/25/1966 ABC
This Is the Life "Crisis in Hearts" 4/2/1966 SYN
Mona McCluskey "Mike's Birthday Present" 4/14/1966 NBC
The Girl from U.N.C.L.E. "The Prisoner of Zalamar Affair" 9/20/1966 NBC.
Daniel Boone "The Matchmaker" 10/27/1966 NBC
My Three Sons "Happy Birthday World" 11/17/1966 CBS
Three's a Crowd (a.k.a. *Two for JJ*, un-aired pilot) 1967 ABC
Iron Horse "Banner with a Strange Device" 2/6/1967 ABC
The Green Hornet "Alias the Scarf" 2/24/1967 ABC
I Dream of Jeannie "Jeannie Goes to Honolulu" 12/26/1967 NBC
Hogan's Heroes "Is There a Doctor in the House?" 1/6/1968 CBS
It Takes a Thief "A Matter of Royal Larceny" 4/23/1968 ABC
The High Chaparral "The Lion Sleeps" 3/28/1969 NBC
To Rome with Love (pilot) 9/28/1969 CBS
The F.B.I. "Flight" 10/26/1969 ABC
My Three Sons "Came the Day" 11/22/1969 CBS
Hogan's Heroes "The Antique" 12/12/1969 CBS
Love, American Style "Love and the Bachelor" 12/22/1969 ABC
It Takes a Thief "The Scorpio Drop" 12/25/1969 ABC
Mannix "Medal for a Hero" 1/3/1970 CBS
My Three Sons "Double Jealousy" 1/17/1970 CBS
Paris 7000 "Call Me Ellen" 2/5/1970 ABC
Death Valley Days "The King of Uralde Road" 4/25/1970 SYN
It's Your Bet 6/22 to 6/26/1970 NBC
Love, American Style "Love and the Young Executive" 11/20/1970 ABC
The Most Deadly Game "The Lady from Praha" 1/9/1971 ABC
Mannix "The Judas Touch" 1/16/1971 CBS
It's Your Bet 1/25 to 1/29/1971 NBC
The Men from Shiloh "The Town Killer" 3/10/1971 NBC
The Courtship of Eddie's Father "The Lonely Weekend" 3/31/1971 ABC
Dinah's Place! 10/5/1971 NBC
The Virginia Graham Show 2/9/1972 SYN

Love, American Style "Love and the Test of Manhood" 2/11/1972 ABC
Wednesday Night Out (pilot) 4/24/1972 NBC
The Mike Douglas Show 6/22/1972 SYN
I've Got a Secret 9/19/1972 SYN
I've Got a Secret 10/31/1972 SYN
Search "The Adonis File" 11/15/1972 NBC
Friday Night Group (unaired pilot) 1973 NBC
Joanne Carson's VIPs 1/16/1973 SYN
The Magician "Illusion in Terror" 10/23/1973 NBC
Celebrity Sweepstakes 6/24 to 6/28/1974 NBC
Mannix "A World Called Courage" 1/5/1975 CBS
Tattletales 6/16 to 6/18, 6/21 & 6/22/1976 CBS
Dinah! 10/26/1976 SYN
Tattletales 4/19 to 4/22, & 4/25/1977 CBS
The Love Boat "Message for Maureen/ Gotcha/ Acapulco Connection" 10/15/1977 ABC
Wonder Woman "Diana's Disappearing Act" 2/3/1978 CBS
Fantasy Island "Charlie's Cherubs" 12/9/1978 ABC
Days of Our Lives (series regular as Lee Dumonde) 7/1979 to 4/1982 NBC
The Incredible Hulk "The Psychic" 2/22/1980 CBS
Father Murphy "The Heir Apparent" 2/23/1982 NBC

Also

Mr. Novak and The Fugitive

☆ DIANE BOND ☆

Diane Bond was a real looker with long straight red-auburn hair, a bit of a pug nose, and a distinctive look that set her apart from the blonde drive-in movie starlets of the day. A shapely beauty (the press book for *A Swingin' Summer* extolled her measurements as being "36-23-36"), Bond was bikini-clad in every one of her drive-in film appearances. The fact that she never achieved a modicum of stardom may have been for a lack of determination on her part to obtain bigger roles. She certainly was beautiful enough.

Diane Bond was born in Los Angeles but spent her childhood on her father's ranch in the mountains of Colorado. The athletic Bond quickly became an expert skier, skater, and horse rider. In her mid-teens an executive of the Rose Marie Reid Bathing Suit firm spotted her on the beach at Malibu and offered her a job as a model. Between modeling assignments, the shapely redhead began working with a troupe of trapeze artists. The group was hired to perform on the TV series *The Greatest Show on Earth* in 1963. She made her film debut a year later as one of the beach girls in *Pajama Party* (1964). It is here where she met actress Lori Williams. The two became friends and would work together numerous times. As with Williams, Bond also began doing stunt work between acting assignments, where, according to the *A Swingin' Summer* press book, she was tagged "Hollywood's prettiest stunt girl."

In Diane Bond's next movie, she was again cast as a beach girl but she received featured billing as "The Girl in the Polka Dot Bikini" in *A Swingin' Summer* (1965). The colorful beach movie starred James Stacy, William Wellman, Jr., and Quinn O'Hara as college students who take summer jobs operating a dance pavilion at Lake Arrowhead. As the film's opening credits roll, Diane, in her signature pink and white polka-dot bikini, is dancing on water skis to the surf-rock instrumental composed by Harry Betts. She and the "Swingin' Summer girls," which included Lori Williams and Irene Sale, were bikini-clad vacationers who are romanced by Lothario James Stacy. Though Bond filled out her swimsuit nicely, a buxom newcomer named Raquel Welch, playing a bookworm who learns to groove, outshone her and the other beach girls.

Like most young actresses of the mid-sixties, Bond too got to work with Elvis Presley. She joined Lori Williams and a myriad of other starlets playing essentially themselves—young actresses and models at a spa for women who flip over handyman Presley in *Tickle Me* (1965). Bikini-clad Bond has much less to do than in her previous movie and is seen only in the scenes around the pool. On television, Bond turned up twice on *The Beverly Hillbillies,* playing a beach movie extra and then a harem girl. After doubling for Claudia Cardinale in *Blindfold* (1966), Diane was back on the big screen the following year in two drive-in movies.

First up was the role of Jan, one of debonair secret agent Derek Flint's three consorts, in her best known film *In Like Flint* (1967), the successful sequel to the extremely popular *Our Man Flint* (1966). None of the actresses who played Flint's attendants returned in the new film and the number dropped from four to three. Diane Bond, blonde Jacki Ray as Denise, and dark-haired Mary Michael as Terry were costumed in mod fashions just as their predecessors, were but they did not fawn over Flint as overtly as the girls did in the original. The witty spoof was released with the tag line: "Flint's back. In action ... In danger ... In the Virgin Islands.... Where the bad guys ... *Are girls!*" Flint (James Coburn), who is still reporting to ZOWIE, must thwart a secret society of women who are plotting to take over the world. Led by Lisa Norton (Jean Hale) and the world's three top female fashion leaders, they operate from a lavish spa in the Virgin Islands called Fabulous Faces. Their plan is to take over a space station that controls nuclear weapons. To reach

Bikini-clad Diane Bond (second from left) in *In Like Flint* (20th Century–Fox, 1967) with Mary Michael, James Coburn, and Jacki Ray (left to right). *Billy Rose Theatre Collection, The New York Public Library for the Performing Arts, Astor, Lenox and Tilden Foundations.*

their goal, they disguise two of their women as golf caddies and kidnap the President of the U.S. and replace him with imposter Trent (Andrew Duggan). Knowing Flint is away, Lisa lures Jan and the others to the island where they and the paying clientele get "brain and hair washing at the same time" as a way to get the rest of the female population to support their nefarious plot. However, the brainwashing doesn't take on the three bikini-clad charmers and they are frozen in the cryonics lab. When Trent turns on the women with the help of General Carter (Steve Ihnat), they join forces with Flint to stop them.

In 1968, Diane Bond relocated to Europe to find film work. She was to be accompanied by her good friend Lori Williams, but Williams' marriage plans prevented her from going. Bond departed alone and landed a small part in AIP's *House of 1,000 Dolls* (1968), starring Vincent Price as a mad magician and Martha Hyer as his willing assistant, who sell nubile women who volunteer to be in their act into white slavery. Bond played Liza, one of the bikini-clad captives, who is shackled and whipped. George Nader was the hero. *House of 1,000 Dolls* was filmed in Tangiers and Spain and was released on a double-bill with the teen exploitation film, *Maryjane* (1968).

Bond next played a bit part in the pop art science fiction cult classic *Barberella* (1968), starring Jane Fonda. But you'll have to strain your eyes to pick her out as one of the outrageously costumed inhabitants of the planet Lythion. It is her last known credit. According to Lori Williams, "Diane became a writer of feminist issues." How ironic—the years of being exploited, exposing her luscious flesh in bikini-roles across the drive-ins of America, finally must have gotten to this intelligent starlet.

Film Appearances

1964 **Pajama Party** (AIP) d. Don Weis
1965 **A Swingin' Summer** (United Screen Arts) d. Robert Sparr
       Tickle Me (Allied Artists) [uncredited] d. Norman Taurog
1967 **In Like Flint** (20th Century–Fox) d. Gordon Douglas
1968 **House of 1,000 Dolls** (W. Germany/Spain, AIP) d. Jeremy Summers
       Barbarella (Paramount) [uncredited] d. Roger Vadim

Television Appearances

Petticoat Junction "Mother of the Bride" 12/15/1964 CBS
The Beverly Hillbillies "Elly in the Movies" 1/20/1965 CBS
The Beverly Hillbillies "The Sheik" 9/29/1965 CBS

Also

Ben Casey and The Greatest Show on Earth

☆ CINDY CAROL ☆

Cindy Carol was a cute dark-haired blonde with velvety brown eyes who had the right amount of perkiness to assume the role of Gidget from predecessors Sandra Dee and Deborah Walley in *Gidget Goes to Rome* (1963). Carol also had the acting expertise as she had been performing since she was a child under her real name of Carol Sydes. After her success as Gidget she should have reached drive-in nirvana in other teenage B-movies but she only graced the big screen in one more film, playing James Stewart's daughter in *Dear Brigitte* (1965).

Cindy Carol was born Annette Carol Sydes on October 11, 1944, in Los Angeles. Her father Thomas was an English teacher and her mother, the former Ruth Meadows, a housewife. Carol was the second of four children. Her older brother Anthony was a child actor, and Carol's career in acting began accidentally while accompanying him on an audition for the TV series *Medic*. The producer, Jim Moser, was charmed by the sweet ten-year-old and asked her to play a retarded girl who sings the song "Never Come Sunday." Carol followed this up playing one of teacher Jennifer Jones' students in the film *Good Morning, Miss Dove* (1955). Unfortunately, Carol's time in Hollywood was cut short since her parents disapproved of an acting career for her.

Sydes then concentrated on her schoolwork and was one of Riverside Elementary School and North Hollywood Junior High School's top students. But Carol, now sixteen, still had the acting bug and when she broached the subject with her father he absolutely forbid her. However, the coy teenager had the ingenuity to get her parents' permission to give it another try. She recounted to *Family Weekly* in 1963, "I knew that, on a teacher's salary, he [her father] couldn't afford to send us all to college. So when he poured cold water on my wanting to be an actress, I reversed tactics and told him I wanted to be a teacher—but that I would need money to go to school. If I could just do a TV show once in a while, I could make enough money to pay my tuition. What could he say but yes?"

A talent agency quickly signed Sydes and before she knew it she was appearing in TV commercials for Crest, Noxema, Fritos, and Frisky Cat Food, among others. Her work on these ads caught the attention of TV show producers and Carol began making appearances as high school classmates to Noreen Corcoran on *Bachelor Father* and Tony Dow on *Leave It to Beaver*. In one particularly funny episode entitled "Wally and Alma," Carol played the brash Alma, whose name is picked by Wally (Dow) to take to an upcoming school picnic. Though Wally has no interest in the chatterbox, her mother keeps setting them up on after school dates. Desperate, Wally keeps bringing different friends with him to Alma's house, hoping that she will like any of them better than him.

In 1962, Carol was cast as Binkie, "a typical teenager" and one of Loretta Young's seven children in her new series appropriately titled *The New Loretta Young Show*. Young

As Gidget #3, Cindy Carol proves that the third time is not necessarily the charm in *Gidget Goes to Rome* (Columbia, 1963).

played a widow raising seven precocious children while trying to earn a living as a magazine writer who was being wooed by her publisher. Dack and Dirk Rambo, Beverly Washburn, Celia Kaye, Sandy Descher, and Tracy Stafford played the other children. Beverly Washburn remarks, "Carol and I got along wonderfully. We stayed friendly and are still in touch. It was a very close knit cast."

While Carol Sydes was working on the TV show, producer Jerry Bresler at Columbia Pictures was conducting a mammoth quest to find a new Gidget. The second sequel to the popular *Gidget* (1959) starring Sandra Dee was going into production. Deborah Walley, the star of *Gidget Goes Hawaiian* (1961) was originally going to essay the role again but she was newly married and about to have a baby. Bresler tested over 500 actresses for the part. Laurel Goodwin, Elvis Presley's co-star in *Girls! Girls! Girls!* (1962), came close to nabbing the role but at 5'7" was deemed too statuesque to play the petite surfer. After a nationwide search, Bresler found his Gidget right in his own backyard as *The New Lorettta Young Show* was produced by Screen Gems, a subsidiary of Columbia. Recalling her screen test with co-star James Darren, Carol told *Movie Stars Magazine*, "When I was called in to test with him I almost died. He was so darling I couldn't believe it. He gave me pointers on the two scenes we did."

Before Carol could accept the role, Loretta Young had to release her from the show, which she did. Young sprung the news on the ingenue at a New Year's Eve party at her house. Sydes told *Photoplay*, "She [Young] couldn't have been more pleased. When I walked in, she came running up to me. And she said to me, 'The studio just phoned and asked for your full release. You got it! You got it! And then she hugged me. And gosh, we were both excited."

Sydes was signed to a seven-year contract with Columbia starting at $300 per week to increase to $1,250 if all options are renewed. But with this came major adjustments for Sydes. The studio changed her name to Cindy Carol ("I didn't mind too much, although I wasn't crazy about the new name") and her hair was lightened to a golden blonde, which photographed better than her natural color. The private teenager was also given the big studio publicity build up. Her face was splashed across such major movie fan magazines as *Photoplay*, *Screen Stories*, *Movie Teen*, *Screen Album*, and *TV Star Parade*, among others. When asked about following in the footsteps of Sandra Dee and Deborah Walley, Carol remarked to *Seventeen*, "I'm not worried about being the same as or different from the other two girls.... I'm just going to be myself. I think they hired me because of the way I am."

Cindy Carol made a very charming Gidget and more than held her own when compared to Dee and Walley. Regarding his casting choice, producer Jerry Bresler remarked in *Photoplay*, "Cindy isn't the typical kind of beauty, is she? But she *is* exactly what *Gidget* is supposed to be—a girl every girl loves to have as a friend, a girl every boy loves to be with." In *Gidget Goes to Rome* (1963), the surfing sweetie leaves the sunny shores of Southern California for a vacation in Italy's Eternal City with her boyfriend Jeff (James Darren) and four friends. Of course romantic complications quickly ensue as Gidget falls for older suave journalist Paolo Cellini (Cesare Danova) unaware that he is secretly chaperoning her as a favor to her father while Jeff becomes infatuated with tour guide Daniela Serrini (Danielle de Metz). By the end of the film, after the viewer is treated to some spectacular shots of Rome, Gidget and Moondoggie are reunited and head home.

Regarding her leading man, Cindy Carol told the teenage readers of *Seventeen* what they were expecting to hear about their handsome idol, "It's been wonderful working with James Darren. He's such a professional. He complains of course—he didn't want to do another Gidget picture—but finally when it was ready to go, he was just marvelous…. He always knows his lines, and he has a great sense of humor."

Reviews for *Gidget Goes to Rome* were mixed, but Cindy Carol received mostly positive notices. Louis Calta of the *New York Times* said she played the role "with the proper pout and correct ingenuousness," while the critic of the *N.Y. Post* described her as "cute and clever." She received a 1964 Laurel Award for Best New Face—Female, placing eleventh in the poll, and a 1963 *Photoplay* Gold Medal nomination for Most Promising New Star (Female) [She lost out to Tippi Hedren]. Box office-wise, the film was a hit with the teenage drive-in movie crowd, and Carol became hugely popular among them especially with adolescent girls.

After a whirlwind tour to promote *Gidget Goes to Rome*, Cindy tested at 20th Century–Fox for the role of Pandora, James Stewart's teenage daughter in *Dear Brigitte* (1965). According to Jerry Asher, writing in *Screen Stories*, Cindy was so sure that she didn't get the part that she flew off to the Indianapolis car races. The studio tracked her down and told her to return

Lobby card of *Dear Brigitte* (20th Century–Fox, 1965) featuring Cindy Carol as an entrepreneurial coed and Fabian as her beau.

quickly. *Dear Brigitte* was originally titled *Erasmus with Freckles* and centered on Billy Mumy as a boy genius who has the hots for Brigitte Bardot. When Pandora learns her brother is a mathematical whiz, the shrewd coed begins to have him do her homework and later handicap horse races for her and her boyfriend Kenneth (Fabian). As the money piles up, Erasmus saves his share to pay for a trip to France to meet his gorgeous idol. Things get complicated when the kids' parents discover their scheme and a con artist plans to exploit Erasmus' talents. Reportedly, Fabian and Cindy filmed their kissing scene on the first day of shooting and director Henry Koster let the scene go on and on. "Just thought I'd give you a chance to get acquainted," the director teased them.

Dear Brigitte was Cindy Carol's last movie. Her big screen stardom petered out very quickly, most likely due to the fact that she lost the interest of the teenage audience—a very fickle bunch. She wasn't sexy enough to keep teenage boys enticed, while her female admirers had gotten older and shifted their attention to the male heartthrobs of the day. To keep acting, Carol accepted a starring role in *Never Too Young*, a soap opera geared for the teenage audience set in Mailbu. Other young players on it included Tony Dow, Michael Blodgett, Dack Rambo, and Joy Harmon. Carol also may have lost interest in performing as well, as around this time she wed a doctor named Ken L. Coombs. The marriage was short-lived.

When the soap came to an end in June of 1966, so did Cindy Carol's once up-and-coming career. Three years previously Carol had remarked to UPI, "I hope that 'Gidget' is as lucky for me as it was for Sandra and Deborah. It's much more exciting to look forward to acting than teaching for a living." Alas it was back to the classroom for this drive-in movie starlet.

In 1968, Cindy Carol purportedly met actor Christopher Connelly (of *Peyton Place* fame) at the Daisy Club and they began dating. The couple wed in April of 1969 and they had two sons, Joseph and Daniel. Carol divorced Connelly in 1988 and he passed away from cancer shortly after. Nestled somewhere in Southern California, the former Gidget is now a schoolteacher and shuns all interviews regarding her Hollywood past.

Film Appearances

1955 **Good Morning, Miss Dove** (20th Century–Fox) d. Henry Koster

1962 **Cape Fear** (Universal) d. J. Lee Thompson

1963 **Gidget Goes to Rome** (Columbia) d. Paul Wendkos

1965 **Dear Brigitte** (20th Century–Fox) d. Henry Koster

Television Appearances

Medic "Never Come Sunday" 5/23/1955 NBC
Medic "General Practitioner" 6/13/1955 NBC
Leave It to Beaver "Wally's Girl Trouble" 12/6/1957 CBS
Bachelor Father "Woman of the House" 4/13/1958 CBS
The Red Skelton Show 6/2/1958 CBS
Mickey Spillane's Mike Hammer "Doll Trouble" 7/31/1959 SYN
Leave It to Beaver "Wally's Test" 1/23/1960 CBS
Leave It to Beaver "School Sweater" 3/5/1960 CBS
Leave It to Beaver "Wally and Alma" 3/19/1960 CBS
Leave It to Beaver "Wally, the Lifeguard" 10/22/1960 CBS
Leave It to Beaver "Eddie's Double Cross" 11/19/1960 CBS

My Three Sons "Man in a Trench Coat" 2/23/1961 ABC
The Bob Newhart Show 12/6/1961 NBC
Wagon Train "The Dick Pederson Story" 1/10/1962 NBC
The New Loretta Young Show (series regular as Binkie Massey) 9/24/1962 to 3/18/1963 CBS
The Donna Reed Show "To Be a Boy" 10/4/1962 ABC
The Eve Arden Show (pilot) 7/20/1964 CBS
Never Too Young (series regular as Susan) 9/27/1965 to 6/24/1966 ABC
Tattletales 10/22, 24, 28, 30 & 11/5/1974 CBS

☆ REGINA CARROL ☆

Buxom blonde Regina Carrol was the late '60s equivalent of '50s sexpot Mamie Van Doren. And just like Mamie, Regina received no respect from the mainstream as she too hooked up with a B-movie director who made her a "star" with a fervent cult following. In Carrol's case it was schlockmeister Al Adamson who featured her in a number of his low-budget exploitation movies—from violent biker films such as *Satan's Sadists* (1969) and *Angels' Wild Women* (1972) to grade-Z horror trash like *Dracula vs. Frankenstein* (1971).

Regina Carrol was born Regina Gelfan on May 23, 1943, in Boston. When she was a child, the Gelfan family relocated to Los Angeles. Regina's mother encouraged her to dance and reportedly would lie to get her daughter out of school to attend auditions. The girl had talent and under her real name landed roles in stage productions of *The Children's Hour*, *Daddy Long Legs*, and a touring company of *West Side Story*. When Regina was fifteen, her mother passed away from cancer. Regina then relocated to Las Vegas to work as a dancer. Hollywood beckoned when family friend Steve Cochran helped Regina land a small role as a beatnik in his new movie *The Beat Generation* (1959), co-starring platinum blonde bombshell, Mamie Van Doren.

After playing very minor roles in a few mainstream movies and on TV, Regina was cast as a dancer and had one line in *Viva Las Vegas* (1964), starring Elvis Presley and Ann-Margret. She told writer Al Ryan, "Elvis was very kind. You see, at the time, his mother had just died and my mother had just died, so we spent a lot of quiet time together. I was one of the only girls in Vegas that didn't jump in bed with him." Years later, writing in her column for the *Las Vegas Panorama*, Carrol mused about her relationship with Elvis and revealed that he gave her a ring that she never took off her index finger.

Regina's acting career seemed not to have taken off during the early to mid-sixties because she was continually bouncing back and forth between performing her nightclub act in Las Vegas and Europe and auditioning for roles in Hollywood. Then in 1968, Carrol met at a coffee shop director Al Adamson, whom she would eventually wed in 1972. He asked Regina to read for the lead female role in his new biker movie called *Satan's Sadists* (1969). Adamson cast the curvy, hard-looking blonde as Gina or, as she was referred to in the film's poster, "The Freak-Out Girl," the girlfriend of a psychotic gang leader nicknamed Anchor (Russ Tamblyn). Gina is the catalyst for the gangs' violent rampage. After a café owner insults her while she does a sexy dance on top one of the restaurant's tables, Anchor and his gang kill him and all his customers except a

Voluptuous Regina Carrol in *Angels' Wild Women* **(Independent-International, 1972).**

hitchhiking Vietnam veteran named Johnny Martin (Gary Kent). During the course of the rest of this sadistic, far out biker flick, Johnny kills one biker by smashing his face in a mirror and another one by drowning him in a toilet bowl. The cyclists meanwhile encounter three college coeds on a geology outing and after spiking their coffee with LSD, rape and murder them. After Anchor decides to cut loose from Gina, the devastated biker chick drives her chopper over a cliff. Busting out all over in her skimpy tops, Carrol couldn't help but get noticed in this role. The critic in *Variety* remarked, "Big blonde Regina Carrol plays her hard cookie role for what it's worth."

Carrol had the intelligence, drive, and cleavage to make a name for herself in B-movies. She got to demonstrate her vocal capabilities in her next role as a Vegas showgirl in *The Female Bunch* (1969), starring Russ Tamblyn and Lon Chaney, Jr. as a ranch hand. Carrol portrayed the role of Libby the friend of a despondent woman named Sandy who contemplates suicide over a failed romance to a lounge lizard. Libby, then introduces her to Grace (Jennifer Bishop), the vicious leader of a group of women who hate men and who make a living through a thriving heroin trade. Sandy becomes a full-fledged member but trouble comes to the gang when one of the girls falls for a stud (Tamblyn) first seen taking a leak. After having sex with one of the Female Bunch, he is branded like a cow and later killed. Besides the film's excessive violence and kinky lesbian sex, *The Female Bunch* received notoriety because it was filmed on the Spahn Ranch in Chatsworth,

California, where the Manson Family was settled. Soon after filming completed, Charlie Manson and some of his followers were arrested for the murders of Sharon Tate and the others. The producers made sure to exploit this fact in their trade ads.

In *Brain of Blood* (1971) the hapless, top-heavy starlet, playing a double D agent, is terrorized by a creature that is a result of a medical experiment gone awry in a plot to take over a dictator's oil-rich country. As the ad proclaimed, "A Blood-dripping Brain Transplant turns a Maniac into a Monster...." Career-wise things got even worse for Regina Carrol when Adamson included her in new footage that was added to his horror film *Psycho-a-Go-Go* (1965). Retitled *Blood of Ghastly Horror* (1971), Carrol played the daughter of a mad doctor (John Carradine) who transforms a Vietnam vet into a zombie. Her last fright flick of 1971 was *Dracula vs. Frankenstein*, which has developed a cult following over the years due to its profound ineptness in every department from bad scripting to horrendous acting to amateurish directing, which surprisingly added up to a weirdly entertaining film. Regina is cast as a lounge singer who goes to a creepy amusement park looking for her missing sister. Instead she encounters Dr. Frankenstein (J. Carrol Naish), his mute assistant Groton (Lon Chaney, Jr.) who decapitates mini-skirted girls, and Count Dracula (the inept Zandor Vorkov) who wants to use Frankenstein's creation (John Bloom) to take over the world. Believe-it-or-not, Carrol's character still finds time to sing, dance, and trip on LSD.

The pinnacle of Regina Carrol's career is her first-rate turn as a whip-slashing motorcycle mama in *Angels' Wild Women* (1972). As with most Al Adamson productions, this film, originally titled *Screaming Angels*, sat on the shelf for a year or two due to the number of biker films that saturated the drive-in screens across the U.S. By the early '70s, the appeal of these movies had waned, but the ever-shrewd director picked up on the popularity of the tough females in prison movies of the time. He then re-edited the movie, added extra footage of Regina kicking some male butt, and released it as *Angels' Wild Women* with the tag line, "Hot, Hard and Mean.... Too Tough for Any Man! They'll Beat'em, Treat'em and Eat'em Alive."

Carrol convincingly played Margo, one of the biker chicks left behind when their leader Speed (Ross Hagen) and his gang go off on an extended run. Just as rowdy and tough as their boyfriends, the girls extract revenge on a rapist and sexually assault a naïve farm boy. As the press book proclaimed, "The slashing sound of a whip cuts through the air.... In the hand of tough, blonde and sexy Margo, the rawhide behaves just as it's told. And the girls love every minute of it." When they raid the Spahn Movie Ranch they run into trouble with evil leader King (William Bonner) and his hippie cult. (This was an obvious way to link the film to Charles Manson and his family.) After one of the biker girls is killed after sleeping with King and Speed's girl Donna is selected to be a human sacrifice in a weird ritual, Margo flees the ranch to find Speed. He and the Angels race to Donna's rescue, but it is too late. The bikers, though, quickly put an end to the hippie's happening and King is killed in a wild chase with Speed. Regarding the film, Carrol commented, "That was quite a switch for me, having a chance to play a wild, aggressive female. But what I do on screen has no relation to the woman that I am in real life."

Angels' Wild Women was not Carrol's last box office hit. She went on to star in such '70s drive-in genre films as the ribald comedies *Naughty Stewardesses* (1974) and its sequel *Blazing Stewardesses* (1974), playing a sexy flight attendant, and the blaxpoitation quickie *Black Heat* (1975) as

In *Angels' Wild Women* (Independent-International, 1972) Regina Carrol, as a tough biker chick, bullwhips her man as Diana Ross look-alike Maggie Bembry playing Cool Chick peers on.

a nightclub singer. In between film appearances, Carrol found time to host her own local Las Vegas television program called *The Regina Carrol Show* during the early '70s. Her guests included such stalwarts as Dinah Shore and Zsa Zsa Gabor.

A heavy smoker like her mother, Regina gave up acting in the late '70s when she was diagnosed with cancer. With the disease in remission during the '80s, she wrote a column for the *Las Vegas Panorama* and returned to the stage performing her one-woman show tribute to Isadora Duncan. Looking back on her acting career, she commented, "I always wanted to be a great dramatic actress and win an Academy Award. But after doing *Satan's Sadists* and some others, I said, 'Hey, I'm not going to get an award for these pictures!' But I still tried to bring truth and beauty to the screen, no matter what the film was."

Regina Carrol's cancer returned in 1989 and she passed away on November 4, 1992. She was only forty-nine years old. Though her screen persona was that of an outrageously tough chick, in real life she was anything but. Co-stars remembered her for being very straight-laced and passive. She enjoyed knitting and was truly in love with her husband Al Adamson until the day she died.

Film Appearances

1959   The Beat Generation (MGM) d. Charles Haas

1960   From the Terrace (20th Century-Fox) d. Mark Robson

1961 **Two Rode Together** (Columbia) d. John Ford

1964 **Viva Las Vegas** (MGM) [uncredited] d. George Sidney

1965 **The Slender Thread** (Paramount) [uncredited] d. Sydney Pollack

1966 **The Glass Bottom Boat** (MGM) d. Frank Tashlin

1969 **Satan's Sadists** (Independent-International) d. Al Adamson

The Female Bunch (Independent-International) d. Al Adamson & John 'Bud' Cardos

1971 **Dracula vs. Frankenstein** (Independent-International) d. Al Adamson

Brain of Blood (Hemisphere Pictures) d. Al Adamson

Blood of Ghastly Horror (Hemisphere Pictures) [originally released as *Psycho-a-Go-Go* (1965) and as *Fiend with the Electronic Brain* (1969)] d. Al Adamson

1972 **Angels' Wild Women** (Independent-International) d. Al Adamson

1974 **Naughty Stewardesses** (Independent-International) d. Al Adamson

Blazing Stewardesses (Independent-International) d. Al Adamson

I Spit on Your Corpse [uncredited] d. Al Adamson

1975 **Jessi's Girls** (Manson Distributing) d. Al Adamson

Black Heat/ The Murder Gang (Zenon Entertainment Group) d. Al Adamson

1981 **Carnival Magic/ Doctor Dracula/ Svengali** (Independent-International) d. Al Adamson & Paul Aratow

Television Appearances

The Adventures of Ozzie and Harriet, Route 66, The Dinah Shore Show, and *The Regina Carrol Show*

☆ PATTI CHANDLER ☆

Among the AIP beach girls sexy Patti Chandler seemed the one most destined for film stardom. She was relegated to the background in her first two beach films, *Bikini Beach* (1964) and *Pajama Party* (1965), but audiences could not help but be drawn to the curvy beach bunny with the honey-brown hair when she was on screen. The folks at AIP took notice too, and soon Patti was given lines and more to do in *Beach Blanket Bingo* (1965), *Ski Party* (1965), and *How to Stuff a Wild Bikini* (1965). Inexplicably, it was back to the background for Patti for her next couple of films at AIP, until she went to Hong Kong to play an assassin in *The Million Eyes of Su-Muru* (1967), her last drive-in movie appearance.

Patti Chandler was a true beach girl in every sense of the word. She was born Patricia Ann Lauderback in 1945 in Southern California and never owned a winter coat in her life. She literally grew up on the beach and was working as a Water Sports Counselor at a hotel in Waikiki where a photographer asked her to model bikinis. Soon after the founders of American International Pictures discovered her. According to *Look* magazine, "She saw an advertisement in the paper for a Bikini-girl contest at American International. An hour later, she had been selected from over 100 contestants for *Bikini Beach*, which was starting production that day in Pomona, Calif. In another hour, she was on location, and an hour later, she was in front of the cameras." Her rise at AIP was meteoric. Her second film was *Pajama Party* (1964) and Patti was again just one of the background beach girls. But in this film not only was she competing for screen time with AIP regulars Mary Hughes, Linda Opie, and Luree Holmes, but choreographer David Winters brought in his gaggle of female dancers (including Teri Garr and Lori Williams) to play bikini-clad beauties as well. When *Look* magazine produced a color spread on *Pajama Party* and its young stars, Patti was featured prominently throughout, even getting more attention than the film's female lead, Annette Funicello!

In 1965, Chandler was signed to a seven-year contract with AIP and with much fanfare by the studio entered their "Starburst of Youth Program" which was really just a promotional gimmick created by AIP founder Jim Nicholson for the exhibitors. In Chandler's first film in 1965, she is seen dancing with Jody McCrea as Bonehead in the beginning of *Beach Blanket Bingo*. A supposed love interest for the dumb surfer, Patti is quickly replaced in his fickle heart by Lorelei (Marta Kristen), a mermaid who saves his life after a surfing accident. *Ski Party*, starring Frankie Avalon, Dwayne Hickman, and Deborah Walley, gave Patti lots more to do as Janet, one of the many girls lusting after suave ski champion Freddy (Aron Kincaid). He has to fight Janet off on his first date with her, as she practically mauls him with kisses in his sporty convertible.

Patti Chandler and Aron Kincaid in a publicity pose from *Ski Party* **(AIP, 1965).** *Courtesy of Aron Kincaid.*

Freddy promises her a second date before graduation and time alone together on their ski vacation, but the determined coed will not take no for an answer. She and the other girls lose Freddy to Nora who is actually one of the guys in drag (Hickman) trying to see what women want in a man.

It was at this point in Chandler's career that she broke out from the rest of the beach girls, as *Look* magazine did a cover story on her entitled "Success Overtakes Patti Chandler." A special photo shoot was set up in the desert where Chandler, her *Ski Party* co-stars Aron Kincaid and Salli Sachse (along with her husband Peter) were photographed frolicking on skis in the sand dunes of Palm Springs. The joys of being Patti Chandler, a starlet on the way up, were exalted. "For 20-

year-old Patti Chandler, the glittery world of Hollywood has become wonderfully real. Patti is about to succeed in movies, and the rewards are already at hand. She has a contract calling for five pictures this year. She has a gloriously rich boyfriend [businessman Burt Sugarman] and time as well for the less serious young actors who work with her. Instead of making her own clothes and bikinis, she buys them in expensive shops." Chandler's success carried over into the world of fashion, as she appeared in print ads for Sheer Magic make-up.

Back on the big screen in *How to Stuff a Wild Bikini* (1965), Chandler stood out again as Patti, one of the girls featured prominently in the song "What About Us?" When adman Mickey Rooney is turned down by mysterious Beverly Adams to be the center of his new campaign, beach girls Marianne Gaba, Mary Hughes, and Chandler ask, "What about me?" before breaking into song extolling their brains, charms, and looks. As the curvy, bikini-clad girls dance on the sand and sing "We're the chicks who know all the tricks, hey what about us," who could disagree? The spy spoof *Dr. Goldfoot and the Bikini Machine* (1965) starring Vincent Price, Frankie Avalon, and Susan Hart, featured Chandler as one of Dr. Goldfoot's bikini-clad robots created to marry and then kill some of the world's wealthiest men.

Regarding Chandler during this period of time, former co-star Aron Kincaid remarks, "Patti was like a kid sister—half brat and half angel. She was this slaphappy kid racing about the set and she was always coming up with these new plans for everybody. I enjoyed Patti and always had a good relationship with her but at the same time I was smart enough to keep my distance."

Chandler's last beach party-type film was *The Ghost in the Invisible Bikini* (1966), starring Tommy Kirk and Deborah Walley, but she is not featured very prominently. After playing one of racecar driver Fabian's groupies in *Fireball 500* (1966), Patti journeyed to Hong Kong along with Frankie Avalon and Salli Sachse to star in *The Million Eyes of Su-Muru* (1966). She and Sachse played two of the evil Su-Muru's (Shirley Eaton) deadly assassins, who are plotting to take over the world. Chandler commented in *Photoplay* magazine that she was delighted to play this role because "I usually run around in bikinis or play good girls. In *Su-Muru* for the first time in my life I play—a killer!"

Chandler went on to play varied roles but not at American International Pictures. She was dropped from the studio after returning from Hong Kong, as AIP's film output now consisted of biker and alienated youth movies because the beach party genre was dead. In 1967, Patti hung up her bikini to play an Indian maiden opposite her current beau at that time, Lee Majors, on the TV western *The Big Valley*. She had met Majors in May of 1965 (he inscribed a photo of him astride a horse, twirling a lasso: "To Patti: Now that I've roped you, I'll never untie the knot. Love, Lee") and soon after Chandler moved into his nine-acre ranch located north of Malibu. Majors admitted in *Modern Screen*, "Patti's the most marvelous, unselfish girl—different from other girls in that she isn't possessive. I am absolutely free in every way." Which was true, as the fan magazines reported that Majors squired such lovelies as Natalie Wood, Juliet Prowse, Jill St. John, and Barbara Parkins

Opposite: **Poster art for** *The Ghost in the Invisible Bikini* **(AIP, 1966)**.

around Hollywood while involved with Patti. Still gossip columnists had a field day trying to predict when and if the sexy pixie would get the notorious playboy to propose. Alas she did not. When the romance cooled, so did Hollywood's interest in *Look*'s one-time cover girl. Chandler's chance for stardom quickly waned as she went on to play small roles in the TV-movie *The Feminist and the Fuzz* (1971) as a women's libber and on *Love, American Style* as a hippie chick, before her career sunk back into the Pacific. As the song says, "*Wipe out!*"

During the '70s, Chandler dried herself off and retired from show business after marrying a very successful businessman, which is not too surprising since she confessed to *Photoplay* in 1967 that her goal was to be "a homemaker and have lots of children." Purportedly, Patti and her husband now spend time commuting between their homes in Southern California and Arizona.

Film Appearances

1964 Bikini Beach (AIP) d. William Asher
Pajama Party (AIP) d. Don Weis
1965 Beach Blanket Bingo (AIP) d. William Asher
Ski Party (AIP) d. Alan Rafkin
How to Stuff a Wild Bikini (AIP) d. William Asher
Sergeant Deadhead (AIP) d. Norman Taurog
Dr. Goldfoot and the Bikini Machine (AIP) d. Norman Taurog
1966 The Ghost in the Invisible Bikini (AIP) d. Don Weis
Fireball 500 (AIP) d. William Asher
1967 The Million Eyes of Su-Muru (AIP) d. Lindsay Shonteff
1971 The Feminist and the Fuzz (TV-movie) d. Jerry Paris

Television Appearances

The Wild Weird World of Dr. Goldfoot (special) 11/18/1965 ABC
The Big Valley "Plunder!" 3/13/1967 ABC
Mannix "To Kill a Writer" 3/9/1968 CBS
Alias Smith and Jones "Night of the Red Dog" 11/4/1971 ABC
Love, American Style "Love and the Fountain of Youth" 12/17/1971 ABC

☆ NANCY CZAR ☆

Nancy Czar was a platinum blonde beauty (and dead ringer for actress Carroll Baker) who graced a few drive-in movies during the '60s. She played a dancer in *Wild Guitar* (1962), a bikini-clad bathing beauty in *Girl Happy* (1965), and most memorably a bubble headed sexpot in *Winter a-Go-Go* (1965).

Not much information is available about Nancy Czar's early life. She is a graduate from Hollywood High School and a championship figure skater, who was sidelined from competing due to an injury. She was also friendly with Elvis.

Czar made her film debut in *Wild Guitar* (1962), directed by B-movie maven Ray Dennis Steckler a.k.a. Cash Flagg and produced and written by Nicholas Merriwether a.k.a. Arch Hall, Sr. Czar played Vicki, a dancer working at a café while trying to make it big in Hollywood. She meets Bud (Arch Hall, Jr.), described as "a guitar-playing, motorcycle-riding hipster," who comes to town to become a rock 'n' roll star. Before he knows it, Bud has replaced an ailing singer on a TV talent show and is discovered by a record company promoter (William Watters). However, Bud's good luck is short-lived, as the promoter organizes a payola scam to get Bud's records played, pays off high school students to start up Bud's fan club, and then begins to cheat the newcomer out of royalties. When Bud quits and goes to work with Vicki at the café, the promoter has him kidnapped and tries to force the starry eyed youngster to return to performing. Vicki and her brother rescue Bud and help him obtain a new contract.

In the no-budget comedy *What's Up Front?* produced by Arch Hall, Sr. Czar played a customer of door-to-door bra salesman Bob Wehling. In the Elvis Presley musical *Girl Happy* (1965), she was "the blonde on the beach." Clad in a leopard skin-spotted bikini, Czar is a knockout as she lies on her blanket in the sand distracting Gary Crosby from keeping an eye out on Shelley Fabares, who he and Elvis have been paid to secretly chaperone on her Fort Lauderdale vacation.

In *Winter a-Go-Go* (1965) Czar was finally offered a part that highlighted her comedic talents and landed her a place in drive-in movie history. She played Gloria Jones, nicknamed Jonesy, an amorous but addlebrained blonde ("I like people very much, *especially* men," she coos) who is one of a bevy of college coeds hired by Danny

Poster art for *Wild Guitar* (Fairway International, 1962).

(James Stacy) and Jeff (William Wellman, Jr.) to work at their ski resort, which Jeff has just inherited. Promotion man Danny immediately uses Jonesy's interest in him to get the curvaceous ski bunny to attract guests. One of his stunts is to have Jonesy wear a fur coat and slip it off as cars come by, revealing herself in a bikini with a sign on her back plugging the resort's vacancies. Soon she has a caravan of cars following her back to the lodge. Czar gives an amusing performance and demonstrated a flair for

Winter a-Go-Go (Columbia, 1965) was a beach party in the snow featuring Linda Rogers, Nancy Czar, Duke Hobbie, Julie Parrish, Tom Nardini, and Jill Donohue (left to right) as college students who swap their surf boards for skis. *Billy Rose Theatre Collection, The New York Public Library for the Performing Arts, Astor, Lenox and Tilden Foundations.*

light comedy. She even received a special mention in the *Variety* review that stated, "Nancy Czar, a blonde looker, has some very good comedy moments in a substantial part not indicated by her credit position." Despite being one of the leads, Czar is billed eleventh after Stacy, Wellman, Beverly Adams, Anthony Hayes, Jill Donohue, Tom Nardini, Duke Hobbie, Julie Parrish, Buck Holland, and Linda Rogers.

Good reviews aside, the best this sexy blonde drive-in movie starlet could follow *Winter a-Go-Go* up with was another bit role (she's more-than-just-a-fan who kisses Elvis Presley goodbye backstage after he finishes his act) in the beginning of *Spinout* (1966). Czar was then off the big screen for four years until she essayed her last movie role in *The Wild Scene* (1970), about a psychiatrist (Alberta Nelson) who discusses case histories and how they relate to her domestic situation with a hippie college daughter named Diane (Anita Eubank). Czar played Clarette, one of Diane's friends.

By 1971, Czar became just another '60s starlet who had faded into obscurity after flickering on drive-in movie screens across America. She did, though, make a comeback in the early nineties, but it was short-lived. No matter, as Nancy Czar became hugely successful in the garment industry and currently resides in Bangladesh and Los Angeles.

Film Appearances

1962 **Wild Guitar** (Fairway International) d. Ray Dennis Steckler
1963 **What's Up Front?** (Fairway International) d. Bob Wehling
1965 **Girl Happy** (MGM) [uncredited] d. Boris Sagal
Winter a-Go-Go (Columbia) d. Richard Benedict
1966 **Spinout** (MGM) [uncredited] d. Norman Taurog
1970 **The Wild Scene** (Four Star Excelsior) d. William Rowland

Television Appearances

Perry Mason "The Case of the Golden Girls" 12/19/1965 CBS
Gypsy 4/25/1966 SYN
Counterstrike "Dead in the Air" 7/8/1990 USA
Hidden Room "Dream Child" 7/23/1991 Lifetime

☆ JACKIE DeSHANNON ☆

Millions of music lovers remember prolific singer and songwriter Jackie DeShannon for her beloved Top 10 singles "What the World Needs Now Is Love" and "Put a Little Love in Your Heart" during the '60s. But what they might not know is that the pretty, slender blonde embarked on an acting career for a short period of time during that swinging decade. Her drive-in movie hits include the beach romp *Surf Party* (1964) and the teenage college musical *C'mon, Let's Live a Little* (1967).

Jackie DeShannon was born Sharon Lee Myers on August 21, 1944 in Hazel, Kentucky but was raised in Chicago. She made her radio debut at age eleven and as a child used the name Sherry Lee. Moving to the West Coast in 1960, Jackie became the lead singer with groups like the Nighthawks. Also a talented songwriter, Jackie (now DeShannon) penned with writing partner Sharon Sheeley hit records for such artists as Brenda Lee ("Dum Dum") and the Fleetwoods ("The Great Imposter"). At this time, Jackie began making some early singing TV appearances. "I got a fan letter from Johnny Mercer who saw me on *The Jackie Gleason Show*," recalls Jackie. "When he tells you that you can sing—*you can sing*."

Jackie was signed as a solo artist to Imperial Records and her first album entitled *Jackie DeShannon* was released in 1963. She charted with "Needles and Pins" but the British pop group The Searchers re-recorded the song and it became a smash Top 40 hit in Great Britain and the U.S. Jackie's songwriting style was a crossbreed between rock and folk and she is considered "the mid-wife to the birth of folk-rock." Though DeShannon was not a household name insiders in the music business knew of her accomplishments as a songwriter and talent as a live performer so it was no surprise to them when The Beatles chose her to be one of their opening acts on their first big U.S. tour.

Despite having a very hectic year in 1964, Jackie was able to squeeze in her first acting role. Her friend Kenny Miller was cast in the beach film *Surf Party* and he introduced her to director Maury Dexter who hired her for one of the female leads. *Surf Party* was 20th Century-Fox's answer to the hit movie *Beach Party* (1963). As the tagline proclaimed, "When Beach Boys meet Surf Sweeties it's a real swingin' splash of Fun, Fun, Fun!" Filmed in glorious black-and-white, the movie offers some catchy songs and exciting surfing sequences. DeShannon played the doe-eyed, tomboy Junior who accompanies her friends Terry (Pat Morrow) and Sylvia (Lory Patrick) to Malibu from Arizona to visit Terry's brother Skeet (Jerry Summers) who is the leader of an elite surfing group called The Lodge. Sylvia falls for Skeet who is secretly being kept by an older woman, while Terry is romanced by Len (Bobby Vinton) the operator of a local surf shop. Junior pairs up with Milo (Miller) a surfer who breaks his arm trying to gain entrance into Skeet's group.

DeShannon made a fetching beach girl despite her lack of surfing experience. "*Surf Party* was my first time on a surfboard and it was hysterical," says Jackie laughing. "I went to get up on the board during the shoot and my top fell down!"

DeShannon's acting career was put on hold in 1965 when she scored her first Top 10 hit with the Burt Bacharach-Hal David song, "What the World Needs Now Is Love." The record reached #7 on the national charts and DeShannon became very in demand to perform on all the teenage music television series of that period such as *Shindig* and *Hullabaloo*. ("We were making history appearing on these programs. Those shows were the MTV of the time.") Imperial released her next album *This Is Jackie DeShannon*, which included her hit record along with other less rock and more orchestrated pop ballads like "A Lifetime of Loneliness."

DeShannon wanted to act more but being a young woman who wanted to do it all—compose, sing, produce, and act—in a time when most women were home having babies was arduous. "Today it would be called versatility. A lot of people sing, act, write songs, and do everything that's included in the current view of what I call the woman power mogul. In the sixties, it was very hard because I was way ahead of my time as far as being an artist. One of the things I always believed in was that you could be multi-faceted. But I ran up against a lot of brick walls. I wasn't the only one. Elvis Presley had the same problem.

"I had to sneak around and try to learn as much as I could. I was going to art school and taking acting classes while I was writing songs and singing. You tell people that now and they say, 'So what. What's new.' Well it was *very* new back then because I was the only woman out in LA producing, writing, and recording coming from a pop base. Now when I look back I sort of give myself a pat on the back because I did follow my goal and my dreams. But it was one step up and four hundred backwards. It was extremely difficult."

In 1966, Jackie returned to the big screen in the low-budget drama *Intimacy* where she was cast against type as a prostitute being paid to entice a businessman (Jack Ging) into a compromising position. "People weren't enlightened and didn't have a clue about the real me," says Jackie. "Every time I was cast playing 'a real person' I jumped at the opportunity. But these parts were just few and far between. I turned down a lot of things because I wanted acting credits where I didn't have to break into song. Today casting popular female vocalists in non-singing roles is commonplace but not back then."

DeShannon's final theatrical movie was the college musical *C'mon, Let's Live a Little* (1967) co-staring Bobby Vee, Suzie Kaye ("she was so talented"), and John Ireland, Jr. To distinguish it from similar films such as *Get Yourself a College Girl* (1964) and *When the Boys Meet the Girls* (1965), the plot included a student protest movement for "free speech on campus" to

During the time of hippies and love-ins, Jackie DeShannon and Bobby Vee played square college students in *C'mon, Let's Live a Little* **(Paramount, 1967).**

make it a bit more relevant for 1967 audiences. Vee played Jesse, a country boy who is accepted into Waymount College after rescuing Judy, the dean's daughter (DeShannon), from a fiery car wreck. On campus his singing talent is noticed and he becomes the innocent pawn of the campus radical (Ireland, Jr.) to draw students to a free speech rally to rile them up against the university. But the dean makes a surprise appearance and appeases the students while Jesse is convinced by Judy to stay in school.

C'mon, Let's Live a Little is DeShannon's ultimate movie. She looks great, acts convincingly, and sings two good tunes "Baker Man" and "For Granted." Critical reaction was for the most part favorable. Howard Thompson of the *New York Times* wrote, "some of the youngsters are appealing especially Bobby Vee and Jackie DeShannon, who is very nice indeed as the dean's comely daughter" while William Pepper of the *N.Y. World Journal Tribune* found them to be "attractive leading players [who] sing pleasantly."

For Jackie, the movie was "eye candy. I was grateful to work because you can only do so much in the classroom. I don't know how Bobby Vee felt about acting but for me it was an opportunity to have a lead role and be in front of the camera knocking down another barrier."

In 1969, Jackie had her second Top 10 hit single with "Put a Little Love in Your Heart" that reached #4. Her album released that year was named for the hit single and also contained the minor hit called

"Love Will Find a Way." DeShannon was a mainstay on TV appearing on the myriad of variety programs that dominated the networks' schedules during the late '60s and early '70s. She continued acting too joining Jordan Christopher and Tisha Sterling as students protesting nuclear testing on *The Name of the Game*. ("I had to fight like hell to get that part.") Her last acting role was in the TV-movie *The Catcher* where she also wrote and sang the title tune. This was a pilot for a proposed series starring Michael Witney and Jan-Michael Vincent ("he was a very cool guy") as private detectives hired to find people who have "vanished."

In 1971, Capitol Records released DeShannon's LP *Songs* and later she collaborated with Van Morrison on his album *Hard Nose The Highway* where she sang background. She kept busy touring, writing songs, and recording during the '70s. In 1981, Kim Carnes covered a song called "Bette Davis Eyes" that DeShannon co-wrote with Donna Weiss for Jackie's 1975 album titled *New Arrangement*. Carnes' rendition took the song to No. 1 on the charts and Jackie received a Grammy Award as it was named "Song of the Year."

Today, Jackie DeShannon keeps writing, as such artists as Cher, Bruce Springsteen, Marianne Faithful, the Carpenters, and Dolly Parton have covered her songs over the years. She released a well-received CD in late 2000 called *You Know Me* after a twenty-year hiatus and performed live at such venues as The Knitting Factory and The Bottom Line to promote it. Jackie currently lives in Los Angeles with her husband of twenty-five years, Randy Edleman, a film composer whose credits include *Kindergarten Cop*. Their son Noah has entered the management end of the music business. "I wish he could represent me but I can't afford him," Jackie joked in *Biography Magazine*.

Though she has been dubbed everything from "Princess of Pop" to "Goddess of the Love Generation" to "Torchy Tunesmith," to drive-in movie fans Jackie will best be remembered as the beach bunny from *Surf Party* and the mini-skirted college coed of *C'mon, Let's Live a Little*.

Film Appearances

1964   **Surf Party** (20th Century-Fox) d. Maury Dexter

1966   **Intimacy** (Goldstone Film Enterprises) d. Victor Stoloff

1967   **C'mon, Let's Live a Little** (Paramount) d. David Butler

1972   **The Catcher** (TV-movie) d. Allen H. Miner

Television Appearances

American Bandstand 8/18/1961 ABC
American Bandstand 2/8/1964 ABC
American Bandstand [singing "When You Walk in the Room"] 5/15/1965 ABC
Hollywood a Go-Go [singing "I Remember the Boy"] 5/17/1965 SYN.
Shindig [singing "Something's Got a Hold of Me (It Must Be Love)"] 5/26/1965 ABC
Shivaree [singing "I Remember the Boy"] 5/29/1965 SYN
Hollywood a Go-Go [singing "What the World Needs Now Is Love"] 6/21/1965 SYN
Where the Action Is [singing "What the World Needs Now Is Love"] 6/30/1965 ABC
Where the Action Is [singing "What the World Needs Now Is Love" & "Needles and Pins"] 8/6/1965 ABC
Shindig [singing "What the World Needs Now Is Love" & "Feels So Good"] 8/18/1965 ABC
Hollywood a Go-Go [singing "Over You"] 9/6/1965 SYN
Where the Action Is 9/7/1965 ABC
Shindig [singing "Shop Around"] 9/18/1965 ABC
Where the Action Is 9/24/1965 ABC

Shivaree [singing "What the World Needs Now Is Love"] 10/2/1965 SYN

Let's Go-Go 10/7/1965 SYN

Hollywood a Go-Go [singing "A Lifetime of Loneliness"] 10/8/1965 SYN

Shindig [singing "It's Love Baby," "I Go Crazy" & "A Lifetime of Loneliness"] 10/9/1965 ABC

Where the Action Is [singing "A Lifetime of Loneliness"] 11/9/1965 ABC

Hullabaloo [singing "A Lifetime of Loneliness"] 11/29/1965 NBC

Shindig [singing "We Can Work It Out" & "As Tears Go By"] 1/8/1966 ABC

American Bandstand [singing "What the World Needs Now Is Love"] 4/30/1966 ABC

Where the Action Is 10/4/1966 ABC

American Bandstand 10/15/1966 ABC

Where the Action Is 10/26/1966 ABC

Where the Action Is 12/5/1966 ABC

My Three Sons "Both Your Houses" 1/12/1967 CBS

The Mike Douglas Show 5/18/1967 SYN

The Clay Cole Show [singing "That's the Name of the Game"] 5/20/1967 SYN

The Pat Boone Show 10/16/1967 NBC

Music City U.S.A. [singing "Trouble" & "Mame"] 11/18/1967 SYN

The Woody Woodbury Show 1/22/1968 SYN

Happening '68 3/2/1968 ABC

Happening '68 3/16/1968 ABC

The Steve Allen Show 4/16/1968 SYN

The Woody Woodbury Show 6/4/1968 SYN

Upbeat 9/7/1968 SYN

It's Happening 9/13/1968 ABC

The Joey Bishop Show 10/9/1968 ABC

Upbeat! 10/26/1968 SYN

Upbeat! [singing "What the World Needs Now Is Love"] 11/30/1968 SYN

The Name of the Game "Love-In at Ground Zero" 1/31/1969 NBC

The Buddy Greco Show (special) 2/9/1969 SYN

The Wild Wild West "The Night of the Janus" 2/15/1969 CBS

Jack Cassidy's St. Patrick's Day Special (special) [singing "Greensleaves"] 3/16/1969 SYN

Playboy After Dark 4/26/1969 SYN

The Glen Campbell Good Time Hour [singing "Put a Little Love in Your Heart"] 10/8/1969 CBS

The Andy Williams Show [singing "Love Will Find a Way"] 11/15/1969 NBC

The Buddy Greco Special [singing "Hollywood"] 2/8/1970 SYN

The Virginian "A King's Ransom" 2/25/1970 NBC

The Red Skelton Show [singing "Love Is Blue"] 3/3/1970 CBS

The Johnny Cash Show 3/25/1970 NBC

Kraft Music Hall [singing "Hurt So Bad" & "You Keep Me Hanging On"] 4/8/1970 NBC

The Everly Brothers Show [singing "You Keep Me Hangin' On"] 7/15/1970 ABC

The Glen Campbell Good Time Hour [singing "Let It Be"] 11/1/1970 CBS

The Tim Conway Comedy Hour [singing "You Keep Me Hangin' On" & "Hurt So Bad"] 11/6/1970 CBS

Johnny Cash and Friends [singing "Dark As a Dungeon"] 12/16/1970 NBC

The Jim Nabors Hour [singing "Have I Stayed Too Long at the Fair?"] 3/4/1971 CBS

Midnight Special [singing "All Night Desire"] 7/9/1976 NBC

Midnight Special [co-host] [singing "Put a Little Love in Your Heart"] 10/15/1976 NBC

The Jim Nabors Show 1/27/1978 SYN

The Jim Nabors Show 1/31/1978 SYN

The Jim Nabors Show [singing "Don't Let the Flame Burn Out" & "To Love Somebody"] 7/7/1978 SYN

Dinah! & Friends 2/14/1980 SYN

Dinah! & Friends 5/2/1980 SYN

Hollywood Rocks the Movies: The Early Years (1955-1970) (special) 7/2/2000 AMC

The Late Show with David Letterman 2001 CBS

Also

Ready, Steady, Go!, The Jackie Gleason Show, The Ed Sullivan Show (2), and *Speaking Freely.*

☆ JILL DONOHUE ☆

Attractive Jill Donohue was similar to older actresses Dina Merrill and Barbara Rush in that she brought a touch of sophistication to her two teenage drive-in movies, *Winter a-Go-Go* (1965) and *Nobody's Perfect* (1968). However, classy actresses were not a sought after commodity in B-movies, which may explain Donohue's short-lived movie career.

Jill Donohue was born in Stockholm, Sweden shortly after the outbreak of WWII. Her father was stage and television director Jack Donohue and her mother was former Scandinavian actress Tutta Rolf. Jill attended Marymount schools in New York and Los Angeles. When her parents divorced, she returned to Sweden to live with her mother and her new husband Hasse Ekman, an actor and director. Now tall and slender, the lithesome teenager began studying ballet and other forms of dance at the Calleflyger School in Stockholm. She then switched to dramatic arts and entered the Royal Academy. Donohue's first professional acting role was a minor bit in the American-financed film *Face of Fire* (1959), starring Cameron Mitchell and James Whitmore, which was shot in Europe. Jill remarked, "The company was making a big thing about hiring local people for small parts, and they picked me because I spoke good English." She used the name Jill Ekman for the movie but switched back to Donohue for an appearance on the Swedish TV series *13 Demon Street*, which was created by Curt Siodmak. Unfortunately, the horror anthology never aired, but years later a few episodes, including Donohue's, were released on video.

In 1963, Donohue almost accepted an offer to travel to Paris to become a model ("I would have loved living there but not on the diet I would have had to follow") but instead she returned to Los Angeles to pursue an acting career. American audiences' first glimpse of the Swedish beauty was in an episode of *Burke's Law* in 1964, where she played just one of the many glamorous women brought on to the show as potential love interests for Gene Barry's detective. She was one of twenty actresses who auditioned for Columbia Pictures. The field was narrowed down to eight promising newcomers who were all screen tested. Jill was the only one signed to a contract with the studio. She remarked to a press agent, "My contract came just before Christmas and it's the nicest present I've ever had."

Jill Donohue's first and only film for the studio was the teenage drive-in movie *Winter a-Go-Go* (1965) whose tag line proclaimed, "Ski buffs and ski babes.... The go-go crowd goes ga-ga on skis!" In the film, William Wellman, Jr. inherits a deserted ski lodge, and with help from his buddy James Stacy and girlfriend Beverly Adams, tries to turn it into a popular resort. Donohue brought a touch of class to the movie, as it was populated by a bunch of top-heavy starlets billed as the "ski honeys." Jill played the confident and spoiled Janine, a French vacationer who is the ex-girlfriend of chief troublemaker Anthony Hayes as Burt. She arrives at the resort accompanied by tomboyish Dori (Judy Parker) and doting, bespectacled Roger (Bob Kanter, who also penned the screenplay). Janine makes a play for both Stacy and Wellman's characters but is rebuffed. Not used to being rejected, she decides to cause trouble, which results in a dangerous ski race between the guys. After Burt is saved from dangling over a cliff, he decides to inform on the resort's mortgage holder who paid him to ruin the lodge. Impressed by his honesty, Janine and Burt reconcile. Jill does well in her role, and the critic in *Variety* remarked, "Jill Donohue plays a snooty chick and shows promise in sophisticated parts, either sympathetic or heavy," while Ann Guarino, writing in the *N.Y. Daily News,* commented that Donohue "gives able support."

Donohue was off the big screen for the next two years as she worked steadily on TV, making three appearances on *The Virginian* and two on *Tarzan,* among others. She returned to the drive-in screen in the youth-oriented service comedy *Nobody's Perfect,* (1968) starring Doug McClure and Nancy Kwan. McClure played the Chief Petty Officer of the U.S.S. Bustard, who spends most of his time try to finagle shore leave to return a stolen Buddha to its rightful owners while chasing pretty women, including Kwan as a Japanese nurse and Donohue as a civilian named Marci Adler.

Due to her ability to assume various dialects, Donohue continued working on television, playing a variety of roles including a beautiful model on *The Name of the Game,* a Bulgarian agent and then an Italian actress on *It Takes a Thief,* and a French girl on *Hogan's Heroes.* In the made-for-TV movie *San Francisco International Airport* (1970), she played the kidnapped wife of pilot David Hartman. This was a pilot for a proposed television series starring Pernell Roberts as the airport's head of security who must deal with three crises in one day. When it was picked up as a series, Lloyd Bridges replaced Roberts.

San Francisco International Airport was Donohue's last credit. She faded from

Pressbook art for *Winter a-Go-Go* (Columbia, 1965) with Jill Donohue and James Stacy pictured. *Billy Rose Theatre Collection, The New York Public Library for the Performing Arts, Astor, Lenox and Tilden Foundations.*

the Hollywood scene but fifteen years later resurfaced in a supporting role in a *Hart to Hart* made-for-TV movie starring Robert Wagner and Stefanie Powers. Her current whereabouts are unknown.

Film Appearances

1959   Face of Fire (Allied Artists) d. Albert Band

1965   Winter a-Go-Go (Columbia) d. Richard Benedict

1968   Nobody's Perfect (Universal) d. Alan Rafkin

1970   San Francisco International Airport (TV-movie) d. John Llewellyn Moxey

1985   Hart to Hart: Secrets of the Hart (TV-movie) d. Kevin Connor

Television Appearances

13 Demon Street "Fever" [unaired] 1960 Swedish TV

Burke's Law "Who Killed Half of Glory Lee?" 5/8/1964 ABC
Mona McCluskey "Snow Valley Snow Job" 3/24/1966 NBC
Tarzan "The End of the River" 12/16/1966 NBC
I Spy "Father Abraham" 12/21/1966 NBC
Tarzan "Pride of Assassins" 1/27/1967 NBC
The Virginian "Doctor Pat" 3/1/1967 NBC
The Virginian "Ah Sing vs. Wyoming" 10/25/1967 NBC
Ironside "The Past Is Prologue" 12/7/1967 NBC
The Virginian "With Help from Ulysses" 1/17/1968 NBC
Dragnet "The Big Goodbye" 2/29/1968 NBC
It Takes a Thief "The Radomir Miniature" 4/9/1968 ABC
The Name of the Game "The Fear of High Places" 9/20/1968 NBC
Hogan's Heroes "Man in a Box" 12/28/1968 CBS
It Takes a Thief "A Matter of Grey Matter" 2/11 & 2/18/1969 ABC
Dragnet "Burglary—Baseball" 4/9/1970 NBC

Also

Kentucky Jones

☆ JOAN FREEMAN ☆

Winsome Joan Freeman was one of four Joans—the others being Joan O'Brien, Joan Blackman, and Joan Staley—who graced movie drive-in screens during the '60s. Producers deemed these gals interchangeable, as all four Joans worked with Elvis Presley, two of them with Jerry Lewis, and two with Don Knotts. How to tell Joan Freeman apart from her counterparts? She is the blue-eyed, honey blonde who was usually cast as the sweet girl-next-door rather than the bikini-clad swinger in such films as *Panic in Year Zero* (1962), *Roustabout* (1964) with Elvis, *The Reluctant Astronaut* (1967) with Knotts, and *The Fastest Guitar Alive* (1967) with Roy Orbison.

Joan Leslie Freeman, a purported descendant of Daniel Freeman, the state of Nebraska's first homesteader, was born on January 8, 1942, in Council Bluffs, Iowa, though she spent most of her childhood in California when her family moved to Burbank when she was two years old. Her father was a railway postal clerk and her mother a housewife. When Joan was three she began taking dancing lessons and by nine she was a regular on a local Saturday morning children's program called *Fantastic Studios Ink* in 1951, along with youngsters Jill St. John and Richard Beymer. That same year Freeman made her film debut playing Joan Leslie as a young girl in *Pistol Harvest*.

During the remainder of the fifties, Freeman continued appearing on live TV, along with the occasional film appearance, while attending public school. After graduating from John Burrough High School in 1959, she enrolled at San Fernando Valley College to study accounting, but her parents encouraged her not to give up on an acting career. Freeman commented in *TV Guide*, "I loved to dance and Mother had no objection to my being in these [TV] shows. But she certainly didn't push me. I wasn't really what you'd call a dedicated actress. I'm still not for that matter. There were long, long periods of time between each show I did. It was more just for fun than anything else. I would have hated working all the time and going to those studio schools."

Things began picking up for Freeman in 1959. She played one of Clifton Webb's many children in *The Remarkable Mr. Pennypacker* (1959) and one of the college students along with Sandra Dee and Bobby Darin who crash at an Italian villa owned by Rock Hudson in *Come September* (1961). Joan confessed in *Show Business International* to having a crush on Hudson. "Once I saw him in a white dinner jacket and black pants and I just stood there with my mouth hanging down to my shoe tops. He probably felt very self-conscious."

After transferring to UCLA, Freeman became a member of its famous Javanese Gamelin Orchestra where she sang and played the xylophone-like stenten. She still continued pursuing acting parts, and after losing out to Carole Wells for a continuing role on the TV series *National Velvet*, Joan was cast as waitress Elma Gahringer in the anthology series *Bus Stop*, loosely based on the 1956 movie. The TV show debuted in September of 1961 and focused on big name guest stars playing characters that stop by the Sherwood Bus Depot and Diner while passing through sleepy Sunrise, Colorado. *Bus Stop* only lasted a season but is remembered for a violent episode starring Fabian as a wild-eyed youth on a murder spree, which caused one of the earliest public outcries against violence on television.

After *Bus Stop* was cancelled, Joan guest starred on all the top dramatic series, particularly westerns, and also began landing leading roles in movies. She was out of her depth, though, playing Lady Margaret to Vincent Price's ruthless Richard of Glouchester in the Roger Corman directed film *Tower of London* (1962). The deranged Richard holds Margaret, one of the Queen's ladies-in-waiting, hostage in the tower as he begins a rampage, killing everybody standing between him and the throne. *Panic in Year Zero* (1962), directed by and starring Ray Milland, is "a skillfully made exploitation picture" featuring Joan Freeman as Marilyn Hayes, one of the survivors of a nuclear blast that has destroyed Los Angeles. She is discovered hiding in a farmhouse on the outskirts of the city where a trio of toughs has murdered her parents. Harry Baldwin and his son Rick, played, respectively, by Milland and Frankie Avalon, rescue her from the hoodlums and take her back to the cave where they've been hiding with the rest of the Baldwin family. Several days later the lone surviving gang member (Richard Bakalyan) returns to extract his revenge. Rick disarms the youth but a furious Marilyn picks up the rifle and shoots him dead. The film concludes "with the feeling that, as the Baldwins and other good people have survived the atomic attack, civilization will be renewed again soon, perhaps for the better this time." After making this film, Freeman bemoaned in

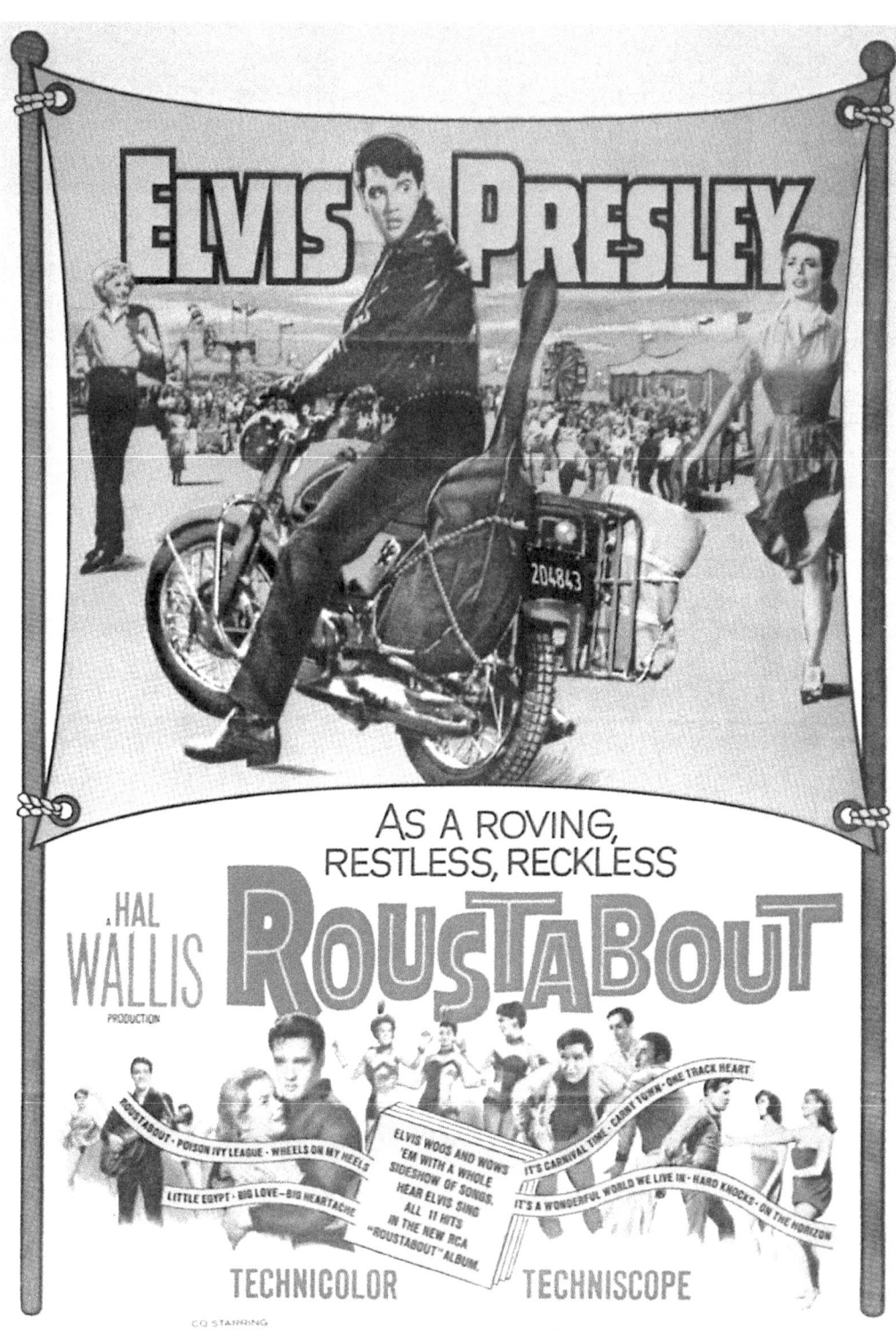

Poster art for *Roustabout* (Paramount, 1964).

Life magazine, "For sexy parts it's blondes. If you're a blonde you don't get the stable part."

In 1962 Freeman received a *Photoplay* Gold Medal Award nomination for Most Promising New Star (Female) and in 1963 she was voted a Hollywood Deb Star. The pretty blonde landed her first "stable part" in *The Three Stooges Go Around the World in a Daze* (1963). She played Amelia Carter, an American tourist who is rescued from a pair of thugs in Calcutta by Phileas Fogg III (Jay Sheffield) and his servants (The Three Stooges). Fogg has made the same bet his grandfather did with the Reform Club members when one of them makes an accusation that the elder Fogg cheated in his global journey. The next year Freeman followed in the footsteps of Joan Blackman and Joan O'Brien by being romanced by Elvis Presley on drive-in screens across the country. In *Roustabout* (1964) Joan was the good girl vying for the King's affections with vixen Sue Ane Langdon as Madame Mijanou, amidst a traveling carnival setting. Freeman frets throughout the movie, as she is either catching Presley's Danny in a clinch with Mijanou or arguing with her bitter father (Leif Erickson), a drunken carnie. The reviewer in *Variety* remarked, "Miss Freeman hasn't much to do except wring her hands ... but does it prettily." Freeman was nominated that year for the *Photoplay* Gold Medal Award for Best Female Star [Ann-Margret won].

In her next film, *The Rounders* (1965), starring James Stewart, Glenn Ford, and Sue Ane Langdon, Freeman was reduced to a supporting role as a farm girl who pursues a reluctant Ford throughout the movie. Could the fall from lead to support be because early in her career Joan had let it be known that she was not going to play by the rules? "The last thing in the world I want to be is a glamour girl. I just had a fit when they wanted to take pictures in a bathing suit. That's so Hollywood. I hate to think of myself as a starlet," remarked the "starlet" in *Show Business Illustrated*.

Freeman did progress back to leading roles in two more films that were hits on the drive-in movie circuit. Who better to pack the cars in than Don Knotts in the comedy *The Reluctant Astronaut* (1966),

Carnival workers Joan Freeman and Elvis Presley get romantically involved in *Roustabout* (Paramount, 1964).

where he played a timid fellow with a fear of heights who gets accepted into the space program? Freeman was cast as his childhood sweetheart. According to the film's press book, Joan tested for the female lead in Knotts' previous movie *The Ghost and Mr. Chicken* (1966) and lost out on the role to Joan Staley. Director Edward Montagne remembered her from it and offered her this role without even an audition. In the western *The Fastest Guitar Alive* (1967), Freeman was finally able to let loose on the big screen, playing Sue Chestnut, a dancing barmaid with a fondness towards "scanty undies and silk tights" who travels across the US with her sister Flo (Maggie Pierce) and their beaus as part of a medicine wagon. What Sue doesn't know is that her guitar-playing boyfriend (Roy Orbison) is really a Confederate spy planning to rob the government mint. The *Variety* critic panned the movie but praised Freeman and wrote that of all the cast members she was "most at ease and competent, showing ability far beyond this script." Roy Orbison was smitten with his lovely co-star too and remarked in the film's press book, "I ought to be paying the studio for the chance to do love scenes with Joan."

The Fastest Guitar Alive was Freeman's last '60s movie. As with most of Elvis Presley's early sixties co-stars, such as Juliet Prowse, Anne Helm, and Laurel Goodwin, Joan Freeman too fell out of favor with teenage drive-in movie fans during the late sixties. But Joan had the talent and perseverance to continue working well after other drive-in movie starlets had long retired from the big screen. She finally began to out grow the sweet ingenue roles, playing the wife of drug addict on *Insight* and a grasping cold-hearted spouse who browbeats her husband to commit a crime on *Land of the Giants*.

In the eighties Joan Freeman must have surprised her old fans when she turned up playing the mother of terrified teens Kimberly Beck and Corey Feldman in *Friday the 13th: The Final Chapter* (1984). Freeman continued working, playing matrons and snooty rich ladies roles well into the nineties. Joan Freeman is alive and well in 2003 and reportedly she and her husband are avid sailors.

Film Appearances

1951 **Pistol Harvest** (RKO Radio) d. Lesley Selander

1956 **Teenage Rebel** (20th Century–Fox) d. Edmund Goulding

1959 **The Remarkable Mr. Pennypacker** (20th Century–Fox) d. Henry Levin

1961 **Come September** (Universal) d. Robert Mulligan

1962 **Tower of London** (United Artists) d. Roger Corman
Panic in Year Zero (AIP) d. Ray Milland

1963 **The Three Stooges Go Around the World in a Daze** (Columbia) d. Norman Maurer

1964 **Roustabout** (Paramount) d. John Rich

1965 **The Rounders** (MGM) d. Burt Kennedy

1966 **The Reluctant Astronaut** (Universal) d. Edward Montagne

1967 **The Fastest Guitar Alive** (MGM) d. Michael Moore

1974 **Warhead/ Prisoner in the Middle** (Worldvision Enterprises) d. John O'Connor

1978 **Death Moon** (TV-movie) d. Bruce Kessler

1982 **Jinxed!** (MGM) d. Don Siegel

1984 Friday the 13th: The Final Chapter (Paramount) d. Joseph Zito

Television Appearances

Fantastic Studios Ink (series regular) 1951 to 1953 KTLA
Lux Video Theatre "Meet Jo Cathart" 9/30/1954 CBS
The Life and Legend of Wyatt Earp "The Frontier Theatre" 2/7/1956 ABC
Father Knows Best "The Art of Romance" 5/15/1957 NBC
National Velvet "The Beauty Contest" 3/12/1961 NBC
The Real McCoys "The Sorority Girl" 5/3/1961 CBS
Bus Stop (series regular as Elma Gahringer) 10/1/1961 to 3/25/1962 ABC
Empire "A Place to Put a Life" 10/9/1962 NBC
Gunsmoke "Phoebe Strunk" 11/10/1962 CBS
The Virginian "The Devil's Children" 12/5/1962 NBC
Dr. Kildare "An Ancient Office" 12/6/1962 NBC
Walt Disney's Wonderful World of Color "The Mooncussers" 12/2 & 12/9/1962 NBC
Perry Mason "The Case of the Fickle Filly" 12/13/1962 CBS
The Dakotas "Trouble at French Creek" 1/28/1963 ABC
The Bob Hope Special [Deb Star] 3/13/1963 NBC
Hawaiian Eye "Blow Low, Blow Blue" 3/5/1963 ABC
Laramie "Trapped" 5/14/1963 NBC
Wagon Train "Alias Bill Hawks" 5/15/1963 ABC
The Greatest Show on Earth "Lion on Fire" 9/17/1963 ABC
Arrest and Trial "Whose Little Girl Are You?" 10/27/1963 ABC
The Virginian "Stopover in a Western Town" 11/27/1963 NBC
The Travels of Jaime McPheeters "The Days of the 12 Candles" 2/23/1964 ABC
The Outer Limits "Behold, Eck!" 10/3/1964 ABC
The Littlest Hobo "Anniversary Guest" 12/23/1964 SYN
The Littlest Hobo "The Near-Sighted Moose" 2/17/1965 SYN
The Virginian "Timberland" 3/10/1965 NBC
Bonanza "The Trap" 3/28/1965 NBC
The Loner "The Vespers" 9/25/1965 CBS
Lassie "Crisis" 12/5/1965 CBS
The Virginian "Blaze of Glory" 12/29/1965 NBC
Mister Roberts "Black and Blue Market" 1/14/1966 NBC
The Man from U.N.C.L.E. "The Bat Cave Affair" 4/1/1966 NBC
Insight "Snow in Summer" 6/18/1967 SYN
Bonanza "Night of Reckoning" 10/15/1967 NBC
The Red Skelton Show 12/19/1967 CBS
To Rome with Love "To Rome from Iowa" 10/12/1969 CBS
Land of the Giants "Chamber of Fear" 11/16/1969 ABC
Family Affair "Nobody Here But Us Uncles" 1/7/1971 CBS
Lassie (series regular as Sue Lambert) 10/7/1971 to 3/10/1972 SYN
Adam-12 "Excessive Force" 12/3/1974 NBC
Marcus Welby, M. D. "Loser in a Dead Heat" 3/11/1975 ABC
Code R [recurring as Barbara Robinson] 1/21 to 6/10/1977 CBS
Project UFO "Sighting 4005: The Medicine Bow Incident" 3/26/1978 NBC
Quincy "No Way to Treat a Flower" 9/20/1979 NBC
CHiPs "Dynamite Alley" 3/30/1980 NBC
CHiPs "Things That Go Creep in the Night" 4/10/1983 NBC
The Facts of Life "Just My Bill" 10/12/1983 NBC
Riptide "Four Eyes" 3/6/1984 NBC
Hardcastle and McCormick "There Goes the Neighborhood" 1/7/1985 ABC
The Commish "Dead Drunk" 4/2/1994 ABC
Renegade "Teen Angel" 11/21/1994 SYN

Also

Four Star Theatre, Medic, Bachelor Father, The Many Loves of Dobie Gillis, The June Allyson Show, and *McKeever and the Colonel*

☆ SUSAN HART ☆

Dark haired and sultry, Susan Hart's film career consisted of mostly "bikinis and monsters." It's no wonder considering her measurements were usually touted as 37-23-36, as she was being groomed to become Hollywood's newest sex symbol. But Hart had talent and a charm that merited more important roles. After fleeing from *The Slime People* (1963) in her film debut, Hart hit the beach as a half-Hawaiian in *Ride the Wild Surf* (1964) and as a shapely bikini-clad girl in *Pajama Party* (1964). Signed to a contract by American International Pictures, she was given her first starring role in *War-Gods of the Deep* (1965), where she was back to being chased by monsters again—this time by lizard creatures. The spy spoof *Dr. Goldfoot and the Bikini Machine* (1965) was Hart's first chance to shine and she did, playing a robot programmed to seduce, marry and kill a bungling playboy. After stepping in to save the last official *Beach Party* film, *The Ghost in the Invisible Bikini* (1966), as the title character, Hart faded from the scene.

Susan Hart was born on June 2, 1941, in Wenatchee, Washington—the apple capital of the world. When she was in the second grade her family began spending the winters in Palm Springs, California and the summers in Washington because her mother had contracted tuberculosis. Entering Palm Springs High School, Hart continued acting in the school's theatrical productions and was recruited with other

The enticing Susan Hart.

high school students to do a few walk-ons and very minor parts in plays produced at Herb Rogers' Theatre-in-the-Round, which was nearby. This was the second theatre-in-the-round Rogers built—the first being located in Highland Park, Illinois. Hart also landed a small role in a local production of *Will Success Spoil Rock Hunter?* in what was then called the El Paseo Theatre.

After graduating high school, Hart took a job as a telephone operator and saved enough money to go to Hawaii with a girlfriend for three months. She went back again a year later and was working at the International Market Place when a fellow named Morton Smith came in one day and handed her his card. He was an agent and also a photographer on assignment for *Playboy* Magazine. He took some snap shots of her on a surfboard and told her if she was ever interested in becoming an actress to look him up in Hollywood.

Susan Hart returned to Palm Springs and got a job managing a dress shop. With Smith's words of encouragement and praise still in her head, she decided to take him up on his offer. She went to his office, and within a month he sent her out on an interview for *The Joey Bishop Show*. She got the part, which consisted of about four or five lines.

Hart later landed an agent named Bill Schuyler, who kept her busy playing small parts on TV while honing her craft to make the leap to features. She screen tested at MGM but did not land a contract. However, photos of her turned up in the film *Boys Night Out* (1962), as she was the centerfold wrapped in a towel while answering the phone in a magazine that Tony Randall and James Garner open up.

In Hart's next feature, she is not only seen but heard as well, as she was cast as Robert Hutton's leading lady in the horror film, *The Slime People* (1963). This low-budget horror film was shot at KTLA Studios. After about nine days of filming, the cast stopped getting paid and the make-up man left. However, Hart proved to be a trouper and continued with the production.

In *The Slime People*, nuclear testing decimates Los Angeles, leaving the city enshrouded in a blanket of fog. A small group of survivors try to make it out of the deserted metropolis while battling subterranean creatures roused from hibernation. Robert Hutton, stars playing a hot shot pilot with Robert Burton as a professor and Susan Hart and Judee Morton as his daughters. One of the films many unintentional laughs is that despite the fact that she is being terrorized and chased by the Slime People, Hart's character Gwen keeps on her four-inch high heel shoes and never lets go of her oversize black pocketbook.

The ad copy for *The Slime People* proclaimed, "Up from the Bowels of the Earth Come…. The Slime People." Needless to say, the film did not receive rave reviews. It is no wonder then Hart tried to distance herself from the movie as much as she could. To keep journalists from asking about the film, when she landed one of the lead roles in her fourth movie, *Ride the Wild Surf* (1964), it was touted as a first starring role.

Before appearing in *Ride the Wild Surf*, if you blinked you missed Hart's bit in the Bob Hope comedy *A Global Affair* (1964). The audience would have seen more of her in a locker room scene, but she balked at doing it because she had to strip down to her bra. That same year, Hart turned up along with Nancy Sinatra and Claudia Martin as one of Pamela Tiffin's sorority sisters in the beach film *For Those Who Think Young* (1964).

The movie that put Susan Hart in the spotlight was the film *Ride the Wild Surf* (1964), which aficionados consider the best of the beach movie genre because of the awesome surfing footage. Three California surfers travel to Hawaii during Christmas vacation for the yearly surfing event at Waimea Bay. Recent college dropout Jody Wallis (Fabian) debates the life of a surf bum versus returning to school and falls for Brie, a vacationing coed (Shelley Fabares sporting bitchin' blonde hair) not impressed with his quitter's attitude. Reliable, down-to-earth Steamer (Tab Hunter) falls in love with sultry Hula-swaying, island girl Lily, played by Susan Hart, to the consternation of her stern and disapproving mother (Catherine McLeod). Staid law student Chase Colton (Peter Brown) is attracted to the playful, athletic Augie Pool (Barbara Eden), who teaches him to loosen up.

Ride the Wild Surf garnered good reviews from the critics. It set itself apart from the other beach films by taking itself more seriously and by highlighting the surfing footage. *Variety* described the film as being "exciting" and "lushly and sometimes sensationally filmed." As for the cast, *Variety* raved, "the principals without exception are excellent." Kathleen Carroll, writing in the *New York Daily News*, singled Hart out and called her "a brunette enchanter." Though *Ride the Wild Surf* did not prove as popular at the box office as *Beach Party*, it was still a hit. And with the good notices received by the cast, Columbia took action, purportedly putting the entire cast on a six-month option. But unbeknownst to Hart, AIP founder James

Bountiful beach babes Susan Hart, Shelley Fabares, and Barbara Eden (left to right) in *Ride the Wild Surf* (Columbia, 1964).

H. Nicholson had access to the dailies of *Ride the Wild Surf* and that is the first time he saw Susan Hart. When they met, the duo hit it off both professionally and personally.

After signing with American International Pictures, Susan Hart was cast in the small role of Gilda in *Pajama Party* (1964). This was a bit of a comedown from her much bigger role in *Ride the Wild Surf*. Hart doesn't have many lines in the film but is a major presence throughout. Though all she did was wiggle her shapely body, she did so with panache. That year Hart received a *Photoplay* Gold Medal nomination for Most Promising New Star (Female), but she lost out to Barbara Parkins of TV's *Peyton Place*.

AIP then began really pushing Susan Hart to become a star. She was voted a Hollywood Deb Star for 1964 and was touted as one of AIP's chosen few to enter their Starburst of Youth program. Louella Parsons touted Hart as being on the verge of stardom in one of her columns and remarked, "She's beautiful and so very talented." Back on the big screen, Hart starred in her next two features for AIP. The fantasy film *War-Gods of the Deep* (1965) reunited her with her *Ride the Wild Surf* co-star, Tab Hunter. The film was inspired by the poems "City Under the Sea" and "A Descent into the Maelstrom" by Edgar Allan Poe. Set in the turn-of-the-century, Hart played Jill Tregellis, a young American lass who owns a converted manor house hotel on the Cornish coast of England. In the middle of the night, she is dragged off by ancient gill-men to an underwater city called Lyonesse. complete with a tyrannical ruler called The Captain (Vincent Price), his cadre of thieves and a threatening volcano. Life in Lyonesse is eternal except for people who commit a crime and then are thrown to the gill-men. The Captain thinks Jill is his reincarnated wife as her daffy artist friend (David Tomlinson) and a hunky American guest at the hotel (Tab Hunter) go to her rescue.

Hart next gave an amusing, well-received performance as a bikini-clad robot in *Dr. Goldfoot and the Bikini Machine* (1965), a goofy take-off on the James Bond film *Goldfinger*, co-starring Frankie Avalon and Dwayne Hickman. Surprisingly, this spy spoof was quite entertaining and grossed $2.5 million, a smash hit by AIP standards. *Dr. Goldfoot and the Bikini Machine* (1965) was filmed on location in San Francisco by director Norman Taurog. The script was by Elwood Ullman and Robert Kaufman, based on a story by James Hartford. The film stars Vincent Price as mad scientist Dr. Goldfoot (named for his wearing of gold slippers), who plans on capturing the fortunes of the world's richest men with the aid of his invention. As lights blink, dials wiggle, horns blow, and the machine vibrates, manufactured bikini-clad robots (Patti Chandler, Salli Sachse, Deanna Lund, Luree Holmes and Marianne Gaba, among them) are produced one by one. Hart played Goldfoot's most prized robot, No. 11 named Diane, who is sent out to entrap playboy millionaire Todd Armstrong (Hickman) but is hampered by the bumbling of inept Secret Agent 00.5 Craig Gamble (Avalon).

Hart showed a lot of promise in her role as Diane and handled the physical comedy aspects of the role excellently. As Diane is programmed to speak many different languages, Hart used an array of accents (including Southern, French, British, etc.). Susan Hart received very good notices for her hard working performance. *Variety*, in particular, raved, "Susan Hart is very good in a role which demands several dialects, human warmth, and robot inanimity, often in rapid sequence." Hart credits her well-received performance to director Norman Taurog, because of the confidence he instilled in her.

Poster art for *Dr. Goldfoot and the Bikini Machine* (AIP, 1966).

Aron Kincaid only has a cameo in *Dr. Goldfoot and the Bikini Machine,* but he and Hart immediately hit it off. "Susan is a doll,' exclaims the actor. "I went to Paris in April of 2001 and this big box arrived at my house just before I left. It was the 'Susan Hart Don't Get Bored' package for me to take away. There were playing cards and audiotapes. She told me that she used to do that for her son when he went off to school. It was about the sweetest gift that I ever got."

Hart's last feature was not even supposed to include her in the cast. *The Ghost in the Invisible Bikini* was originally titled *Bikini Party in a Haunted House.* Tommy Kirk and Deborah Walley played heirs to a fortune who must spend the night in a haunted house in order to collect their inheritance hidden somewhere in the creepy mansion, complete with a chamber of horrors, an escaped gorilla, surfer boys, and bikini girls. The weak film was deemed unreleaseable by AIP and a quick fix was needed. It was Jim Nicholson's idea to add a sexy ghost in the invisible bikini, and who better to play the role than his shapely wife?

Boris Karloff and Hart were added to the cast to play, respectively, millionaire Hiram Stokely and his young blonde wife Cecily. The recently deceased Hiram must perform a good deed to get into heaven and as a bonus is promised eternal youth. Cecily, who died as a young woman, is sent down to Earth to make sure Hiram's rightful heirs inherit his money. Their scenes together were tacked on to the beginning and the end of the film. During the interim, shots of Hart in her invisible bikini are superimposed on the film, as she seems to be dictating the action.

Hart was wasted in *The Ghost in the Invisible Bikini,* and unfortunately this was her big screen swan song. A number of things contributed to that, including the caring of her son and the problems that arose between Jim Nicholson and Sam Arkoff, who gained controlling interest in AIP after Nicholson's divorce from his first wife. Purportedly, Arkoff was not interested in having Susan Hart star in any more AIP movies.

Though Susan left AIP, Jim Nicholson continued with the company until 1972 when he signed a deal with 20th Century–Fox. He was the executive producer for *The Legend of Hell House* (1973) and was readying *Dirty Mary, Crazy Larry* (1974) for production when he was diagnosed with a brain tumor. He passed away on December 10, 1972, before *The Legend of Hell House* was released. After his death, Susan Hart got involved in a lawsuit that dragged on for years with the two men who were left in charge of his production company. Other lawsuits followed, including one with the late Sam Arkoff regarding the rights to some of AIP's earlier films from the fifties and two pending lawsuits regarding the rights of privacy. Today, Susan Hart is happily remarried and is a champion precision figure skater. And in 2003 she was awarded a "star" on the Palm Springs Walk of Stars.

Film Appearances

1962   **The Slime People** (Hansen Enterprises) d. Robert Hutton

1964   **A Global Affair** (MGM) d. Jack Arnold
For Those Who Think Young (United Artists) d. Leslie H. Martinson
Ride the Wild Surf (Columbia) d. Don Taylor
Pajama Party (AIP) d. Don Weis

1965   **War-Gods of the Deep** (AIP) d. Jacques Tourneur
Dr. Goldfoot and the Bikini Machine (AIP) d. Norman Taurog

1966   **The Ghost in the Invisible Bikini** (AIP) d. Don Weis

Television Appearances:

The New Bob Cummings Show "Roamin' Holiday" 11/2/1961 CBS
Cain's Hundred "The Debasers" 1/16/1962 NBC
The Alfred Hitchcock Hour "The Door without a Key" 1/16/1962 CBS
77 Sunset Strip "Brass Ring Caper" 2/9/1962 ABC
Laramie "The Runt" 2/20/1962 NBC
77 Sunset Strip "Reunion at Balboa" 4/12/1963 ABC
Channing "A Doll's House with Pom Poms and Trophies" 12/4/1963 ABC
The Beverly Hillbillies "The Race for Queen" 2/5/1964 CBS
The Bob Hope Show (special) [Hollywood Deb Star] 3/13/1964 NBC
The Beverly Hillbillies "Another Neighbor" 4/1/1964 CBS
The Clay Cole Show 11/13/1965 SYN
The Wild Weird World of Dr. Goldfoot (special) 11/18/1965 ABC
Gypsy 2/24/1966 SYN
Death Valley Days "Major Horace Bell" 4/26/1967 SYN
The Wild Wild West "The Night of the Fugitives" 11/8/1968 CBS
It Conquered Hollywood! The Story of American International Pictures (special) [as herself] 5/1/2001 AMC

Also

The Joey Bishop Show and *The Many Loves of Dobie Gillis*

☆ ANNE HELM ☆

A petite dark haired blonde, Anne Helm was one of the '60s busiest actresses. She worked non-stop on television while also lighting up the drive-in screens across the country in a variety of roles, most notably as a princess in *The Magic Sword* (1962) and Elvis Presley's love interest in *Follow That Dream* (1962). Super stardom eluded the perky talented Helm, but that is not surprising since her later films included such drivel as *The Swingin' Maiden* (1963), *Mother Goose a-Go-Go* (1966), and *Nightmare in Wax* (1969).

Anne Helm was born on September 12, 1938, in Toronto, Canada. Her father was a real estate broker and her mother, Isabel, ran a dairy farm and country inn. Her early childhood was spent in the tiny hamlet of Ste. Marguerite, which she described to *The Courier-Journal* as being "a village of four houses, a railway stop, 23 horses, seven cows, five dogs and 11 cats." At age twelve Helm began taking ballet lessons at the National Ballet Guild of Canada and two years later she was studying at the Metropolitan Opera Ballet School in New York. To pay expenses, she began modeling, which led to TV commercials. By the time she was seventeen years old she was earning $25,000 a year. She commented in *TV Guide*, "I realized that I wanted money more than the strict life of the dancer. So I let the dancing drift."

Helm made her TV debut on *The Phil Silvers Show*, playing a beauty pageant contestant and followed this with an appearance on the *U.S. Steel Hour*. She also began honing her acting craft on stage, first in an Off-Broadway production of *Clerambard* and then in two Broadway shows, *Cloud Seven* with Ralph Meeker and *Edwin Booth* with Jose Ferrer, who also directed. Unfortunately, both productions flopped, though Helm received good notices. Soon Hollywood beckoned and Helm received national press when she was selected to play Sleeping Beauty on TV's *Shirley Temple's Storybook* in 1958. Her acting career took off like a rocket. Her film debut was in the turgid Southern soap opera *Desire in the Dust* (1960), as the sister of a sharecropper (Ken Scott) wrongly accused of running down a little boy who returns to town to reclaim his rich girlfriend (Martha Hyer), the real culprit.

During the remainder of the swinging '60s, Helm worked constantly on television, appearing on all the top drama, western, and comedy series as well as action-syndicated shows such as *Sea Hunt* and *The Beachcomber*. On TV, her varied roles included playing a hardworking pioneer on *Wagon Train*, a fortune hunter on *Bonanza*, an Indian maiden on *Daniel Boone*, and a hip undercover cop on *Hawaii Five-O*. Helm had the talent to play sweet and virginal one week and nasty and slutty the next. Film-wise, Helm had a busy year in 1962, appearing in four movies. Though she never received raves for any of her big screen performances, critics usually found her to be "attractive" and "decorative." She played a kittenish woman who tries to entice psychopath Grant Williams up to her room in *The Couch* and the self-absorbed socialite fiancée of a two-timing cad of a doctor played by Michael Callan in *The Interns*. Helm's first film to become a drive-in hit was the exciting fantasy film *The Magic Sword*, produced and directed by Bert I. Gordon. The film starred Basil Rathbone as an evil magician who abducts Helm's enchanting Princess Helene and

Anne Helm tries to hide her romantic feelings for her stepbrother Elvis Presley in the comedy *Follow That Dream* (United Artists, 1962).

gives her would-be rescuer Saint George, played by Gary Lockwood, seven deadly challenges to complete to win her back.

But Helm's biggest hit of 1962 and the film she is most remembered was the sweet comedy *Follow That Dream*, starring Elvis Presley (about whom Helm remarked in *TV Guide*, "I thought—well, that he was just a rock 'n' roll singer. I changed my mind. He's very warm and—well, sincere. And a beautiful actor."). A bit atypical from the usual Presley fare, *Follow That Dream* did not have many songs or a gaggle of bikini-clad girls going gaga over Elvis. Instead the film focused on Pop Kwimper, played by Arthur O'Connell, who with his son Toby (Elvis), a army vet, and four unofficially adopted children including nineteen year old Holly (Helm), homestead on an unopened stretch of highway in Florida. (The film was shot on location in Crystal River, Florida ninety miles northeast of St. Petersburg.) The state tries to legally remove them, but the Kwimpers win the right to stay in court. They build a shack to live in and open a fish-and-tackle store. Soon business is booming and more homesteaders join them. Toby is elected sheriff when local gangsters set up an illegal gambling den. Toby also has to deal with the advances of a brazen social worker played by Joanna Moore who, when spurned, decides to have the state take away the minor children. In the end, the Kwimpers plead, in a heartwarming scene, their case to the judge, who renders a verdict in their favor calling them "hardy pioneers" while Toby finally recognizes that he has feelings for Holly, who has tried to hide her crush on him. Trading her blue jeans for a "purty" dress, Holly comes to him as he sings on the porch and they embrace during the film's fade out. Helm had a sweet angelic quality that really shines through in this movie. She was awarded a *Photoplay* Gold Medal Award nomination for Most Promising New Star (Female) [she lost out to Suzanne Pleshette] and received a Laurel Award for New Female Personality, placing eighth in the poll.

Anne Helm was also one of Presley's few co-stars to speak openly about her sexual relationship with the King. He showed up at her hotel room with flowers on the first day of shooting (Elvis however did this for all his leading ladies), and Helm immediately developed a crush on Presley, just as her character did in the movie. The feeling was mutual. Helm remarked in the book *Down at the End of Lonely Street*, "I actually wrote some poetry about him when we were making the movie. It was that kind of romance. He really liked sex. A lot of nights I didn't go back to my own bungalow. I felt a little ashamed about it the next morning, because I knew that people on the set realized what was going on." Helm's romance with Elvis lasted throughout the entire shoot of *Follow That Dream* (despite co-star Joanne Moore's designs on the King too) and continued back in Hollywood. The relationship ended as abruptly as it started. One night they were "goofing around" and Anne closed the piano top down on Elvis' finger after he made a comment that upset her. Though she apologized and he forgave her, he never called Helm again.

In 1963, Anne Helm was hired to co-star as Joan Blondell's axe wielding daughter in the fright flick *Strait-Jacket*. However, when the producers learned that Joan Crawford was interested in the role, Blondell was sacked. Reportedly the diva movie star was unhappy with the choice of Helm to play her daughter and she made life hell during rehearsals for the promising newcomer who she thought was going to upstage her. Crawford pressured producer William Castle to have Helm removed from the movie and replaced her with the bland Diane Baker. Describing the situation, Helm commented in *Fangoria*, "She was a very hypocritical woman. She really wanted me off the picture, and I knew that. But by that point, there was no way I even wanted to be on the picture. She was a very sick woman."

Helm's remaining '60s big screen output was ho-hum. Playing the daughter of rich American tycoon Alan Hale, she accompanies one of his British business associates, engineer Michael Craig, in a steam locomotive rally in *The Swingin' Maiden* (1963). In *Honeymoon Hotel* (1964) Helm again has fiancé trouble as groom Robert Morse rightly jilts her snooty character at the altar and spends the honeymoon with the best man, Robert Goulet.

Is she in danger or did she just read the script? Anne Helm screams in fright in *The Swingin' Maiden* **(Columbia, 1963) with Michael Craig.**

The wildly titled *Mother Goose a Go-Go*, from producer/director/screenwriter Jack H. Harris, featured Helm as a virginal newlywed whose young husband Tommy Kirk can't perform his conjugal duty so he is treated with a LSD-spray that makes his fairy tale fantasies become reality.

Helm married novelist John Sherlock in 1968. The marriage was short-lived, though they produced a son named Peter. After giving birth, Helm returned to work and her last theatrical release of the decade was the Grade-Z horror film *Nightmare in Wax* (1969). Cameron Mitchell played a vengeful, scarred owner of a wax museum seeking revenge against the head of Paragon Pictures who disfigured him when he worked there as a make-up man in a dispute over the studio's biggest star, Anne Helm. Mitchell's character begins injecting a secret formula into some of the studios brightest contract players, turning them into living statues for his museum.

During the seventies, Helm spent two years playing Nurse Mary Briggs on the TV soap *General Hospital* and made the expected guest appearances on most of producer Quinn Martin's detective series. She married actor Robert Viharo in 1972 (they divorced in 1977) and she had a daughter named Serena. Helm tried to give acting another shot in the mid-eighties but after appearing opposite John Lithgow in his Emmy winning performance on an episode of *Amazing Stories*, Helm packed it in. Today, she is an accomplished artist and appears frequently at Elvis Presley conventions across the country.

Film Appearances

1960 Desire in the Dust (20th Century–Fox) d. William F. Claxton
1962 The Couch (Warner Bros.) d. Owen Crump
      The Interns (Columbia) d. David Swift
      The Magic Sword (United Artists) d. Bert I. Gordon
      Follow That Dream (United Artists) d. Gordon Douglas
1963 The Swingin' Maiden/ The Iron Maiden (Great Britain, Columbia) d. Gerald Thomas
1964 Honeymoon Hotel (MGM) d. Henry Levin
      Ready for the People (Warner Bros.) d. Buzz Kulik
1966 Mother Goose a-Go-Go/ The Unkissed Bride (U.S. Films) d. Jack H. Harris
1969 Nightmare in Wax (Commonwealth United) d. Bud Townsend
1971 A Tattered Web (TV-movie) d. Paul Wendkos
1980 Hide in Plain Sight (MGM) d. James Caan

Television Appearances

The Phil Silvers Show "Miss America" 2/28/1956 CBS
Studio One "The McTaggart Succession" 5/5/1958 CBS
Father Knows Best "A Matter of Pride" 6/4/1958 NBC
Shirley Temple's Storybook "The Sleeping Beauty" 6/8/1958 NBC
Du Pont Show of the Month "The Human Comedy" 3/28/1959 CBS
Alcoa Theatre "You Should Meet My Sister" 5/6/1960 NBC
Mr. Lucky "Operation Fortuna" 5/21/1960 CBS
Tales of Wells Fargo "The Killing of Johnny Lash" 11/21/1960 NBC
Sea Hunt "Storm Drain" 11/26/1960 SYN
The Du Pont Show Starring June Allyson "A Thief or Two" 12/1/1960 CBS
Alfred Hitchcock Presents "The Changing Heart" 1/3/1961 CBS
Wagon Train "The Dick Pederson Story" 1/10/1961 NBC
Shirley Temple Theatre "King Midas" 1/15/1961 NBC
Route 66 "The Clover Throne" 1/27/1961 CBS
Gunsmoke "Bad Seed" 2/4/1961 CBS
Rawhide "Incident Near Gloomy River" 3/17/1961 CBS
Hawaiian Eye "The Humuhumunukunukuapuaa Kid" 3/22/1961 ABC
The Americans "The Bounty Jumpers" 4/17/1961 NBC
Malibu Run "The Frankie Adventure" 4/26/1961 CBS
The Brothers Brannagan "Equinox" 5/13/1961 SYN
Gunslinger "The New Savannah Story" 5/18/1961 CBS
Perry Mason "The Case of the Duplicate Daughter" 5/20/1961 CBS
Bus Stop "Afternoon of a Cowboy" 10/1/1961 ABC
Bronco "Cousin from Atlanta" 10/16/1961 ABC
Rawhide "The Inside Man" 11/3/1961 CBS
Adventures in Paradise "The Pretender" 11/12/1961 ABC
The Untouchables "Man Killer" 12/7/1961 ABC
Window on Main Street "The Mechanic" 12/11/1961 CBS
Frontier Circus "Mr. Brady Regrets" 1/25/1962 CBS
Follow the Sun "A Choice of Weapons" 2/4/1962 ABC
Cain's Hundred "The New Order" 3/6/1962 ABC
Death Valley Days "Girl with a Gun" 3/8/1962 SYN
Route 66 "From an Enchantress Fleeing" 6/1/1962 CBS
Alfred Hitchcock Presents "The Big Kick" 6/19/1962 CBS
The Beachcomber "Man with a Guitar" 10/2/1962 SYN

The Beachcomber "Paradise Lost" 11/13/1962 SYN
The Wide Country "The Girl in the Sunshine Smile" 11/15/1962 NBC
Laramie "Protective Custody" 1/15/1963 NBC
Route 66 "Narcissus on an Old Red Fire Engine" 3/29/1963 CBS
Wagon Train "Heather and Hamish" 4/10/1963 ABC
Empire "The Convention" 5/14/1963 NBC
Temple Houston "The Third Bullet" 10/24/1963 NBC
Dr. Kildare "The Backslider" 12/5/1963 NBC
Wagon Train "The Story of Cain" 12/16/1963 ABC
The Lieutenant "The Art of Discipline" 12/21/1963 NBC
The Eleventh Hour "The Only Remaining Copy Is in the British Museum" 2/12/1964 NBC
The Farmer's Daughter "Bless Our Happy Home" 2/19/1964 CBS
Burke's Law "Who Killed Half of Glory Lee?" 5/8/1964 ABC
Kraft Suspense Theater "A Cruel and Unusual Night" 6/4/1964 NBC
The Virginian "Ryker" 9/16/1964 NBC
Burke's Law "Who Killed Lenore Wingfield?" 11/4/1964 ABC
The Fugitive "Ballad for a Ghost" 12/29/1964 ABC
Gunsmoke "One Killer on Ice" 1/23/1965 CBS
Daniel Boone "The Courtship of Jericho Jones" 4/29/1965 NBC
The Long Hot Summer "A Time for Living" 9/23/1965 ABC
The Big Valley "Heritage" 10/20/1965 ABC
Bonanza "The Meredith Smith" 10/31/1965 NBC
Run for Your Life "The Carnival Ends at Midnight" 1/10/1966 NBC
A Man Called Shenandoah "Muted Fifes, Muffled Drums" 2/28/1966 ABC
The Jean Arthur Show (pilot) 9/12/1966 CBS
Run for Your Life "The Day Time Stopped" 9/12/1966 NBC
Run for Your Life "The Treasure Seekers" 11/14/1966 NBC
12 O'Clock High "Long Time Dead" 1/6/1967 ABC
The F.B.I. "Force of Nature" 4/9/1967 ABC
Run for Your Life "At the End of the Rainbow, There's Another Rainbow" 10/25/1967 NBC
Run for Your Life "One Bad Turn" 1/10/1968 NBC
The Big Valley "Devil's Masquerade" 3/4/1968 ABC
The F.B.I. "The Ninth Man" 3/24/1968 ABC
Bonanza "A Pride of a Man" 6/2/1968 NBC
The Good Guys (episode—title unknown) 10/16/1968 CBS
The F.B.I. "The Butcher" 12/8/1968 ABC
Hawaii Five-0 "By the Numbers" 12/11/1968 CBS
Adam-12 "Log 73: I'm Still a Cop" 2/22/1969 NBC
Hawaii Five-0 "Just Lucky, I Guess" 10/15/1969 CBS
The F.B.I. "Gamble with Death" 10/19/1969 ABC
Mission: Impossible "The Double Circle" 11/9/1969 CBS
The Virginian "Journey to Scathelock" 12/10/1969 NBC
The Mike Douglas Show 1/6/1970 SYN
General Hospital (series regular as Mary Briggs, R.N.) 1971 to 1973 ABC
Medical Center "The Albatross" 11/3/1971 CBS
The Bold Ones: The Lawyers "The Long Morning After" 1/9 & 1/16/1972 CBS
The Streets of San Francisco "Mask of Death" 3/14/1974 ABC
Barnaby Jones "Conspiracy of Terror" 10/1/1974 CBS
The Manhunter "The Carnival Story" 11/20/1974 CBS
Bert D'Angelo/Superstar "A Concerned Citizen" 4/3/1976 ABC
Hart to Hart "Too Many Cooks Are Murder" 5/6/1980 ABC
Airwolf "The Hunted" 10/20/1984 CBS
Amazing Stories "The Doll" 5/4/1986 NBC

Also

Kraft Playhouse, The U.S. Steel Hour, and *The Steve Allen Show*

☆ Mary Hughes ☆

Not much is known about statuesque blonde sexpot Mary Hughes, except that this Brigitte Bardot look-a-like appeared in every *Beach Party* movie except the original. Prancing around the Malibu shore in the skimpiest of bikinis, Hughes must have interrupted many a drive-in movie necking session as young males couldn't take their eyes off this statuesque beauty.

According to American International press releases, Mary Hughes was born and raised in Southern California and was discovered on the beaches of Malibu. Along with another *Beach Party* regular, Salli Sachse, Mary made her film debut in *Muscle Beach Party* (1964). Tall and curvaceous with measurements of 36-22-36, audiences could not help but wonder who was AIP's newest sun-bleached blonde beach girl. The studio took notice of Hughes too and cast her in *Bikini Beach* (1964) and *Pajama Party* (1964). In the latter film, Hughes steals the attention from the rest of the beach girls. *Pajama Party* also received a lot of press including a photo spread in *Look* magazine, but most of the attention was given to rival beach girl, Patti Chandler.

Mary Hughes quickly became a fan favorite, and AIP signed her to a contract. She was sent on many public relation tours around the country to promote the beach films. Though fans may not have known her name, they could not help but recognize the flaxen-haired knockout who was used a number of times, dancing bikini-clad during her film's closing credits. In Hughes' first movie of 1965, *Beach Blanket Bingo,* she has an amusing bit during the film's opening song as she smashes an a ice cream cone into the face of cute surfer boy Mike Nader ("Right blanket, wrong miss," sing Frankie and Annette) before she fades into the background. In *Ski Party* (1965) Hughes received billing on the film's poster ads but she is hardly seen in the movie, as the beach gang heads for Sun Valley for a ski vacation. Totally under utilizing Hughes, director Alan Rafkin gave lots of screen time instead to ski bunnies Patti Chandler, Salli Sachse, and Luree Holmes. *How to Stuff a Wild Bikini* (1965) gave Hughes her first lines as she, Chandler, and Marianne Gaba try to persuade adman Mickey Rooney that they had what it takes to be "the girl next door" in his motorcycle ad campaign. In *Dr. Goldfoot and the Bikini Machine* (1965), Hughes played Robot No. 6, programmed by Vincent Price as the evil Dr. Goldfoot to marry then kill a wealthy surgeon in Denmark.

Commenting on Mary Hughes, frequent co-star Aron Kincaid remarks, "Mary Hughes was wonderful in that she had this detached Brigitte Bardot attitude. She was very naïve in a lot of ways—not in life but with PR and things like that. She'd make these little comments in the most inappropriate times."

Hughes, wearing a red headband throughout the movie, was pushed back into the background for *The Ghost in the Invisible Bikini* (1966) though she got more screen time than Chandler and Sachse. Her last film for AIP was *Fireball 500* (1966), as one of the many female fans of racecar driver Fabian. As with most of the beach party gang, Hughes was not able to crossover into AIP's biker and alienated youth movies and was dropped from the studio. She did land a few more bit roles, including playing one of the Slaygirls in the Dean Martin Matt Helm spy spoof, *Murderers' Row* (1966), and a Watusi dancer in the Elvis Presley musical *Double Trouble* (1967) before washing away with the tide.

The '70s found Mary Hughes working as a fitness instructor and she materialized for a *Beach Party* reunion in 1985.

Frankie Avalon, Annette Funicello, Mike Nader, and Mary Hughes singing the title tune from *Beach Blanket Bingo* (AIP, 1965).

According to attendee Aron Kincaid, "Mary came in and everybody just went, 'Whoa!' She looked amazing wearing this skintight black see-through gown. She had an even better body than she had in the beach movies. She came with her husband and she was quite the picture of sophistication and success."

Film Appearances

1964 **Muscle Beach Party** (AIP) d. William Asher
Bikini Beach (AIP) d. William Asher
Pajama Party (AIP) d. Don Weis
1965 **Beach Blanket Bingo** (AIP) d. William Asher
Ski Party (AIP) d. Alan Rafkin
How to Stuff a Wild Bikini (AIP) d. William Asher
Sergeant Deadhead (AIP) d. Norman Taurog
Dr. Goldfoot and the Bikini Machine (AIP) d. Norman Taurog
1966 **The Ghost in the Invisible Bikini** (AIP) d. Don Weis
Fireball 500 (AIP) d. William Asher
Murderers' Row (Columbia) d. Henry Levin
1967 **Double Trouble** (MGM) d. Norman Taurog

Television Appearances

The Wild Weird World of Dr. Goldfoot (special) 11/18/1965 ABC

☆ MIKKI JAMISON ☆

Bright-eyed Mikki Jamison was a pretty brunette who graced only two drive-in movies popular with the teenage set. Jamison was very active on TV before she made her film debut in the *Beach Party* knock-off *Beach Ball* (1965), co-starring Edd Byrnes and Chris Noel. She then joined the AIP beach crowd that same year as they traded in their surf boards for snow gear in *Ski Party* with Frankie Avalon and Deborah Walley.

Mikke Jamison was born Mikki McGoldrick on December 13, 1944, in Spokane, Washington. Described as a tomboy as a child, the athletic adolescent blossomed into a dark-haired beauty who loved the outdoors and natural foods.

After graduating from Lewis and Clark High School, she passed on college to enroll at the Pasadena Playhouse where she was discovered by Warner Bros. talent scout Sollie Biano. The studio put her under option for a year in 1962 and used her in a number of their TV shows, most notably *77 Sunset Strip* where she made four guest appearances. She was also the studio's choice to represent them as their Hollywood Deb Star for 1962. Despite this accolade, Warner Bros. dropped her option soon after without using her in a single movie.

Jamison continued appearing on the small screen and became one of a myriad of young shapely freelance TV actresses who specialized in playing the girl next door on a number of sitcoms. Among her leading young men were Dwayne Hickman on *The Many Loves of Dobie Gillis*, Rick Nelson on *The Adventures of Ozzie and Harriet* and Bill Bixby on *My Favorite Martian*. Frustrated with the parts she was being offered and the publicity she was required to do, Jamison commented in *TV Guide*, "Careerwise I would like to be like Lee Remick. You won't find *her* cutting any ribbons in any supermarkets. It proves a girl *can* get along in Hollywood and not behave like an idiot at all." When asked by *Photoplay* that same year if she'd ever consider doing a nude scene for the role of a lifetime, Jamison responded, "No, thanks ... nothing's left to the imagination."

Though she never came close to being a Lee Remick or had to decide to do a nude scene for the ultimate role, Mikki Jamison finally got her chance to shine on the big

Winsome ingenue Mikki Jamison. *Courtesy of Aron Kincaid.*

screen in *Beach Ball* (1965), Paramount's answer to AIP's *Beach Party* movies. Jamison co-starred with Chris Noel, Gail Gilmore and Brenda Benet as four staid coeds who, as members of their college's finance committee, decide to give a loan to poor music student Edd Byrnes, who needs the cash to pay for his band's instruments. When the gals discover that they have been duped and that Byrnes and his buddies (Robert Logan, Aron Kincaid and Don Edmonds) are dropouts and beach bums, they rip up the check and flee the boys' swinging Malibu bachelor pad. Back in their dorm, though Jamison's Augusta wants to put them in jail, Noel's character Susan comes up with a plan to get the guys to go back to school. To reach that end, the girls take off their glasses, tease up their hair and trek to the beach. One especially amusing scene is when the girls are pressured to don bikinis and slink out of the beach cabana. Augusta is then paired with Kincaid as Jack, the lead singer of the Wigglers. As Augusta, Jamison's character is the most cynical and apprehensive of the girls and Mikki gives the character a comedic bite.

Also in 1965, Jamison turned up as one of the ski bunnies in AIP's *Ski Party* (1965), starring Frankie Avalon, Dwayne Hickman, Deborah Walley and Yvonne Craig. Aron Kincaid is also in the film as Freddie Carter, a pompous ski champion who has all the girls on campus crazy for him. As the *Beach Party* gang hits the slopes of Sun Valley, Avalon and Hickman pose as females to discover why the girls find Freddie so irresistible. Needless to say, complications ensue, especially when the arrogant Freddie falls for Hickman's 'Nora.'

"Mikki Jamison is a great gal," professes co-star Aron Kincaid. "I am still friendly with her and Salli Sachse. I first met her when she was sixteen years old and under contract to Warner Bros.. We have gone through a lot together and have had some fun times and some bad times. In *Beach Ball*, she was my leading lady and then in *Ski Party* as my billing was reduced she was reduced even further. But she wanted to go to Sun Valley. The producer knew her work and thought she'd be great. What little they gave her to do, she made the very most of it. She even stands out in scenes where she has no lines."

Jamison was off both the big and small screens for a short period of time before she was cast as Jean Reed, wife of Officer Jim Reed (Kent McCord) on the hit series *Adam-12* in 1969. She was scheduled to play a recurring role, as her character was to represent the frustrating life being married to a police officer but she appeared in only two episodes. In "A Rare Occasion," Jamison gives a particularly convincing performance. Her character becomes more and more perturbed with her husband Jim, who can't keep his mind on her dinner party due to the hospitalization of two of his fellow policemen and his need to deal with a stoned teenage neighbor (David Cassidy). Jamison left the series after marrying a stockbroker and relocated to Paris where her son Jaime was born.

After divorcing her husband, Mikki Jamison returned to the U.S. in the mid-seventies and married attorney Gary Olsen who encouraged his new wife to give acting a try again. Now billed as Mikki Jamison-Olsen, she starred opposite *Beach Ball* co-star, Robert Logan, in *The Sea Gypsies* (1978). Playing a photojournalist, Jamison's character inveigles her way onto Logan's boat to document his around the world sailboat trip with his two young daughters and a young stowaway. Off the Alaskan coast, the boat is shipwrecked and the small party is marooned on an uninhabited island where the castaways are threatened by a bear and a whale. Jamison remarked in a press release for the movie, "Frankly, although I was still in my teens, I was better equipped to deal with Kookie [of *77 Sunset Strip*]. My scenes with the bear were terrifying. He was totally unpredictable as far as I was concerned."

Today, Mikki Jamison nee Mikki McGoldrick, is living in Spokane, working as a Tour Director for Brennan Tours. Now a blonde, she is still as beautiful as ever. Besides journeying around the world, Mikki is also currently preparing a publication about her life and travel adventures.

Film Appearances

1965 **Beach Ball** (Paramount) d. Lennie Weinrib
      Ski Party (AIP) d. Don Weis
1978 **The Sea Gypsies/Shipwreck** (Warner Bros.) d. Stewart Raffill

Television Appearances

77 Sunset Strip "Big Boy Blue" 11/3/1961 ABC
77 Sunset Strip "The Cold Cash Caper" 11/10/1961 ABC
Hawaiian Eye "Big Fever" 1/17/1962 ABC
Maverick "Mr. Muldoon's Partner" 4/15/1962 ABC
77 Sunset Strip "Terror in a Small Town" 10/26/1962 ABC
The Many Loves of Dobie Gillis "What Makes the Varsity Drag?" 10/31/1962 CBS
Ripcord "Hostage Below" 1/15/1963 SYN
The Adventures of Ozzie and Harriet "Any Date in a Storm" 3/7/1963 ABC
The Donna Reed Show "Where the Stones Are" 3/7/1963 ABC
77 Sunset Strip "Reunion at Balboa" 4/12/1963 ABC
Dennis the Menace "Hawaiian Love Song" 9/22/1963 CBS
Hazel "The Baby Came C.O.D." 11/14/1963 NBC
My Three Sons "My Fair Chinese Lady" 2/6/1964 ABC
My Favorite Martian "Won't You Come Home, Uncle Martin, Won't You Come Home" 12/27/1964 CBS
My Three Sons "He Wanted Wings" 1/28/1965 ABC
Adam-12 "A Sound Like Thunder" 11/1/1969 NBC
Adam-12 "A Rare Occasion" 2/14/1970 NBC
Wonder Woman "The Pluto File" 12/25/1977 ABC

☆ CANDY JOHNSON ☆

Dubbed "Miss Perpetual Motion" by a Las Vegas columnist, Candy Johnson was the most famous go-go dancer of the early '60s. The energetic blonde twisted her way into nightclub fame and then into drive-in movie history with appearances in four beach movies—*Beach Party* (1963), *Muscle Beach Party* (1964), *Bikini Beach* (1964), and *Pajama Party* (1964)—where she did little more than shake her fanny, enthralling audiences worldwide.

Purportedly, Johnson was born on May 1, 1942, in Illinois. According to AIP press releases, she was raised in Southern California and began taking tap dance lessons when she was five years old from Mary Lou Kaiser of Arcadia. Reportedly, at six she made her television debut "and created no sensation until she and the twist found each other." Johnson graduated from San Gabriel High School and began performing the twist in local clubs when manager Red Gilson discovered her and helped her put together an act. "The Candy Johnson Show" premiered in October 1962 in the Safari Lounge at the El

Mirador Hotel in Palm Springs, California. It quickly became the hottest ticket in town with standing room only most nights for two straight years as Johnson danced her butt off to the musical accompaniment of her combo, The Exciters. After catching Candy's act, columnist Mike Jackson remarked in the *Los Angeles Herald-Examiner*, "What she does is wiggle. There's nothing new about that. But Candy's exuberant energy has an electric effect on the crowd." A reviewer in *Citizen News* described Johnson as "a vortex of vim, vigor, vitality, and verve."

All the press that Candy Johnson garnered brought her to the attention of producers Jim Nicholson and Sam Arkoff at American International Pictures, who were in pre-production on a new film called *Beach Party* (1963) starring Frankie Avalon and Annette Funicello. Not the prettiest wahine on the beach with her big bouffant hairdo, Johnson nevertheless was the perfect choice to bring the twist alive on the shores of sunny Malibu. She has a great dance sequence with Frankie Avalon who sings "Don't Stop Now" while trying to make girlfriend Annette Funicello as Dolores jealous, and she could be seen gyrating with abandon during the end credits to Avalon's solo version of the title song. 1963 was also the year that Candy released her debut album called *Ray Ryan Presents the Candy Johnson Show* on her own record label, Canjo. The LP was recorded live on her 1,500th show, featuring original songs co-written by her manager and such standards as "Baby Face," "Swing Low" and "Abba Dabba Honeymoon." Not surprisingly, most reviewers found it did not capture

The perpetual motion machine Candy Johnson (right) lets loose dancing on the backs of two surfer boys (Mike Nader is on right) while Donna Loren sings in *Bikini Beach* **(AIP, 1964).**

the exuberance of Johnson's act as she was a much better dancer than vocalist.

Muscle Beach Party (1964) featured Candy Johnson as Candy doing a wild shimmy on the beach, knocking off surfers from their boards with every bump and grind. Jody McCrea as Deadhead remarks, "Boy, I am glad I'm not out there riding the curl. Once Candy gets started it's all over." Later she is seen dancing on the tabletops to the tunes of Dick Dale and His Del-Tones at the local teen hangout. When the cameras stopped rolling during production, Johnson reportedly would race from the set and travel 250 miles to perform three 45-minute shows a night in Palm Springs. According to an AIP press release for *Muscle Beach Party*, Candy "loses five to fifteen pounds nightly when performing in supper clubs; eats six meals a day; and sleeps a minimum of twelve hours on doctor's orders." Candy told columnists that to make up for the weight loss she eats steak and potatoes for dinner every night. Her simplistic advice to readers of the *Citizen News*, "If your trouble is too much weight just twist it off!"

Back on the big screen *Bikini Beach* (1964) gave Johnson more to do than her previous two films and lines to say. Candy, along with Frankie, Annette, and the rest of the beach gang, mixes with Erich Von Zipper's motorcycle gang, a developer (Keenan Wynn) who wants to drive them off the beach, and a drag-racing English pop star called the Potato Bug (also played by Avalon). Candy's dancing prowess is especially highlighted during Donna Loren's number "Secret Weapon." She even released her second and last album on Canjo called *The Candy Johnson Show at Bikini Beach* where she sang all the songs from the movie including "Bikini Beach" and "Secret Weapon" plus other originals. Because not many LPs sold, this is now considered a rarity among record collectors.

Pajama Party (1964) was Johnson's last film appearance. An offshoot from the typical beach party movies it starred Tommy Kirk as a Martian and Annette Funicello as the beach girl he becomes infatuated with. For this film, the producers hired popular choreographer David Winters. Candy, like most of the AIP stable of beach girls, is severely pushed to the background as Winters favored his troupe of dancers in the movie. However, Candy gets to shine one last time on the big screen during Donna Loren's rockin' number "Among the Young."

Though Candy Johnson did not make any films for AIP during 1965, she was still touring for the studio promoting the beach films. New York City audiences finally got a chance to see her exciting stage act as she headlined the Gay New Orleans Nightclub on Bourbon Street at the New York World's Fair in 1964 and 1965. Reportedly, she twisted her way down Broadway for an International Variety Club charity event and performed during the intermission of a doubleheader Mets—Braves baseball game at Shea Stadium.

Post-1965, there is not much found on Candy Johnson, as she and the Twist fell from favor. There are only rumors regarding where she is now, but the most plausible one is that she is a choreographer working in Branson, Missouri.

Film Appearances

1963   **Beach Party** (AIP) d. William Asher
1964   **Muscle Beach Party** (AIP) d. William Asher
       Bikini Beach (AIP) d. William Asher.
       Pajama Party (AIP) d. Don Weis.

☆ MARTA KRISTEN ☆

Nordic blonde knockout Marta Kristen is best remembered for playing galactic castaway Judy Robinson on TV's *Lost in Space* during the '60s. However, drive-in movie fans fondly recall her performance as the sweet mermaid who falls for a dumb surfer in *Beach Blanket Bingo* (1965). Her popular television series kept her off the big screen for the remainder of the decade, but in the early '70s Kristen surprised her fans by spewing foul language as a tough convict in *Terminal Island* (1973) and by shedding her clothes as an aspiring actress in *Gemini Affair* (1973).

Marta Kristen was born Birgit Annalisa Rusanen on February 26, 1945, in Norway. Her father was a German soldier who quickly disappeared after the Nazis were driven out of the country. Her mother was ill and couldn't care for the little Birgit any longer and she put her in an orphanage. Recalling her time there, Kristen remarked in *Starlog* magazine, "I always sang to the adults, to get approval. I was a *cute* little girl. A little chubby. And they loved my songs. From then on, there was never any doubt what I wanted to do … performing." When she was four years old Birgit was adopted by an older American couple, Prof. and Mrs. Harold Soderquist of Detroit, Michigan. Her adopted parents changed her name to Marta, after the woman who had arranged the adoption. The newly arrived young girl quickly blossomed in America. She loved entertaining her family's guests by singing and dancing. A colleague of her father's was impressed enough by Marta and recommended her to the Will-O-Way Theatre in Birmingham, Michigan. By age fourteen she was doing summer stock, appearing in such productions as *The Taming of the Shrew* and *Little Women*.

Kristen's life changed when her father relocated the family to the West Coast on a sabbatical leave to do research on a new book. The striking fair-haired teenager fit right in among the other blonde denizens

Sexy Norwegian movie starlet Marta Kristen in a publicity pose promoting *Beach Blanket Bingo* (AIP, 1965).

of sunny California. When her family returned to Michigan, Marta stayed behind with a guardian and finished up high school at the Hollywood Professional School. In 1960, while having lunch with a friend one day in Santa Monica, Kristen was approached by producer Jimmy Harris, who was looking for an actress to play Lolita and asked her if she would in interested in testing for it. She stated in *TV Guide*, "I thought he was kidding, until I checked up. It is a good thing I didn't get the part. After testing I went out and read the book. There was a lot in it I didn't understand." Though she lost out on it, Kristen impressed the film's producers, Harris and Julian Ludwig, who helped her secure an agent.

Marta changed her last name to Kristen and almost immediately made her television debut in a lead guest role on *Loretta Young Theater* in 1960. She quickly followed playing roles such as the girlfriend of Don Grady's Robbie on *My Three Sons* and that of an unwed teenage mother on a two-part episode that began on *Dr. Kildare* and concluded on *The Eleventh Hour*. In "Bang, You're Dead" on *Alfred Hitchcock Presents*, she portrayed a supermarket clerk almost gunned down by a little boy, played by her future *Lost in Space* co-star, Billy Mumy.

In 1963, Kristen married college student Terence Teadwell whom she met at the beach. That same year she appeared in her first movie, as Walt Disney chose the blonde beauty to replace Beverly Washburn as Lisbeth Searcy in *Savage Sam* (1963), the long awaited sequel to *Old Yeller* (1957). Tommy Kirk and Kevin Corcoran reprised their roles as Travis and Arliss Coates who, with their trusted dog Sam, go after Lisbeth who has been abducted by Apaches. This was an inauspicious film debut that either went unnoticed or was criticized, as Eugene Archer wrote in the *New York Times*, "Tommy Kirk and Marta Kristen do little more than make puppy eyes around the wigwam." Receiving poor notices, *Savage Sam* paled in comparison to the original.

Marta made a bigger splash, figuratively and literally, as a sexy mermaid named Lorelei in her next film, *Beach Blanket Bingo* (1965), starring Frankie Avalon and Annette Funicello. While the beach gang is taking skydiving lessons, Lorelei saves a lone surfer named Deadhead played by Jody McCrea when he has an accident riding the curl. Lorelei helps Deadhead to get to shore where he is helped by singing star Sugar Kane (Linda Evans). Sugar's ambitious manager Paul Lynde plays up the incident hailing Sugar as the rescuer for the press, but Deadhead feels something is not right. Following his intuition, he surfs out to the same spot and meets the beautiful sea-maiden. Mermaids can don legs only for one twelve hour period, so Lorelei agrees to meet Deadhead for a date as he escorts her to the local teen hangout before she has to return to the ocean. Their scenes, which were sweetly enacted by Kristen and McCrea, made a nice contrast to the typical frenetic beach party shenanigans in one of the series' most beloved movies. Regarding the shoot, Kristen remarked in *Starlog*, "I remember shooting day-for-night in Paradise Cove in November, having to be out in the freezing surf to make my entrance. I'm trying to look pleasant and pop up out of the water, while trying also to keep from being dashed against some nearby rocks."

In 1965, Kristen came to the attention of producer Irwin Allen due to the fact that they were clients of the same agent. Allen was looking for someone to play Judy, the eldest daughter of John and Maureen Robinson (Guy Williams and June Lockhart) on his newest science-fiction series *Lost in Space* (which was originally titled *Space Family Robinson*), about the adventures of a family of intergalactic travelers lost in outer space. Kristen at first turned down the role because she felt that her character wouldn't have much to do and fade into the background. Allen convinced her otherwise and Kristen signed on. Her intuition proved correct, as Judy Robinson was the center of attention in only a handful of plots during the show's three-year run as the focus was on villainous Dr. Smith (Jonathan Harris), the Robot, and young Will Robinson (Billy Mumy). Two of Kristen's standout episodes were during the show's final season as the now modly coiffured Judy Robinson entered an intergalactic beauty pageant in "Space Beauty" and tangled with a talking carrot man in "The Giant Vegetable Rebellion."

When *Lost in Space* was cancelled in

1968, Marta put her acting career on hold to spend more time with her husband and daughter. When her marriage dissolved in the early seventies, she returned to work, landing a part in the action-packed film *Terminal Island* (1973) directed by Stephanie Rothman. The film featured a great exploitation cast, including Tom Selleck, Phyllis Davis, Barbara Leigh, Geoffrey Duell, Don Marshall, and Kristen, playing convicted murderers sentenced to life in prison on an island.

Gemini Affair: A Diary (1973) gave Kristen more of an acting stretch playing Julie, a hopeful wide-eyed actress newly arrived in Los Angeles. In town for a screen test she stays at the home of her friend Jessica, a Scotch swilling high-class call girl, played by a restrained Kathy Kersh, a former '60s TV starlet. When Julie's dreams of becoming a movie star are crushed and she turns a trick to make some money, she finds solace in the arms of Jessica, leading to the film's infamous nude lesbian love scenes. According to co-star Kathy Kersh, "That scene was shot in the dark and was very shadowy—not graphic at all. But it was very tough for Marta and me to do it—even with only a skeleton crew present. They showed more of her than they did of me. During the shoot Marta had an affair with the cinematographer. I knew they were seeing each other. I only saw a rough-cut of *Gemini Affair* at that time. I was surprised that the light was always on Marta and I was in the dark—what a crummy thing to do! I couldn't believe it!" Despite the appeal of seeing *Lost in Space*'s Judy Robinson (and Kersh, for that matter) in the buff, the film was barely released. It is a bit talky, but Kristen is good throughout most of the film though she becomes much too over-wrought as her character freaks out over what she and Jessica have done.

As with another Irwin Allen cast-off Deanna Lund (of *Land of the Giants*), Kristen too was another beauty who had the looks and talent to make it to the big time but was overlooked by producers. During the remainder of the '70s, Kristen mostly appeared in TV commercials and began playing roles in area theater productions. She eventually formed her own theater group and married an attorney named Kevin.

In 1980 Marta played one of the leaders of a peaceful planet overtaken by villainous John Saxon in the Roger Corman produced film, *Battle Beyond the Stars*. With her career rejuvenated, Kristen stayed semi-active on television and in low-budget

In *Beach Blanket Bingo* (AIP, 1965) surfer Jody McCrea professes his love to mermaid Marta Kristen before she must return to the sea.

movies. In 1998, she made a cameo appearance as a reporter in the long awaited film version of *Lost in Space*. Today, Kristen devotes all her energy to raising her granddaughter Lena, though she still finds time to make a commercial or attend autograph conventions across the nation.

Film Appearances

1963 **Savage Sam** (Buena Vista) d. Norman Tokar

1965 **Beach Blanket Bingo** (AIP) d. William Asher

1973 **Terminal Island** (Dimension) d. Stephanie Rothman
       Gemini Affair: A Diary (Moonstone Entertainment) d. Matt Cimber

1974 **Once** (Communication Designs) d. Morton Heilig

1980 **Battle Beyond the Stars** (New World) d. Jimmy T. Murakami

1987 **Strange Voices** (TV-movie) d. Arthur Allan Seidelman

1996 **Harvest of Fire** (TV-movie) d. Arthur Allan Seidelman
       The Living Reed (unreleased)

1997 **Below Utopia/ Body Count** (Cinetel Films) d. Kurt Voss

1998 **Lost in Space** (New Line Cinema) [cameo] d. Stephen Hopkins

Television Appearances

Loretta Young Theater "The Glass Cage" 10/30/1960 NBC
My Three Sons "Spring Will Be a Little Late This Year" 12/8/1960 ABC
Leave it to Beaver "Wally and Dudley" 3/18/1961 CBS
Alfred Hitchcock Presents "The Gloating Place" 5/16/1961 CBS
Alfred Hitchcock Presents "Bang, You're Dead!" 10/17/1961 CBS
My Three Sons "Going Steady" 12/20/1962 ABC
The Dick Powell Show "The Third Side of a Coin" 3/26/1963 NBC
Dr. Kildare "Four Feet in the Morning Part I" 11/21/1963 NBC
The Eleventh Hour "Four Feet in the Morning Part II" 11/27/1963 NBC
The Greatest Show on Earth "Clancy" 2/25/1964 ABC
Mr. Novak "Senior Prom" 4/14/1964 NBC
My Three Sons "A Serious Girl" 9/24/1964 CBS
The Man from U.N.C.L.E. "The Neptune Affair" 12/8/1964 NBC
Wagon Train "The Wanda Snow Story" 1/17/1965
Lost in Space (series regular as Judy Robinson) 9/15/1965 to 9/11/1968 CBS
Insight "Is the 11:59 Late this Year?" 1969 SYN
Mannix "A Game of Shadows" 12/24/1972 CBS
Project UFO "Sighting 4011: The Dollhouse Incident" 5/20/1978 NBC
Just Friends (episode—title unknown) 3/25/1979 CBS
Remington Steele "Signed, Steeled and Delivered" 10/29/1982 NBC
Family Feud "TV's All-Time Favorites" [celebrity contestant] 5/2 to 5/6 & 5/9 to 5/13/1983 ABC
Fame "Danny De Bergerac" 2/16/1985 SYN
Trapper John, M.D. "In the Eyes of the Beholder" 3/24/1985 CBS
Wildside "The Crime of the Century" 4/3/1985 ABC
Our Time 8/24/1985
Magnum, P.I. "L.A." 10/1/1986 CBS
Scarecrow and Mrs. King "Rumors of My Death" 1/23/1987 NBC
Murphy Brown "Fjord Your Eyes Only" 1/31/1994 CBS
The Fantasy Worlds of Irwin Allen (special) 9/30/1995 SCI
The CBS Morning Show 2/8/2002 CBS
A&E Biography "Jonathan Harris: Never Fear, Smith Is Here" 11/27/2002 A&E

Also

Shirley Temple's Storybook and *America*

☆ MEREDITH MACRAE ☆

Television fans fondly recall sleek, brown-eyed, honey-blonde Meredith MacRae as Billie Jo Bradley on *Petticoat Junction* and for her numerous appearances on practically all the celebrity game shows of the late sixties and seventies. But drive-in movie fans know MacRae from playing one of the original beach girls in the movie that started it all, *Beach Party* (1963), and as man-hungry Animal in *Bikini Beach* (1964). Her TV series kept her off the drive-in movie screens until she portrayed Broadway Joe Namath's girlfriend in his first movie, *Norwood* (1970).

Meredith MacRae was born on May 30, 1944, in Houston and was the offspring of Hollywood royalty. Her father was movie actor Gordon MacRae, who was serving time in the Army Air Corp and stationed in Texas at that time, while her mother was vocalist Sheila MacRae. After his tour of duty was complete, MacRae moved his family back to Los Angeles where Meredith was raised. The family grew to include younger sister Heather and two younger brothers, Gar and Bruce. When Meredith was four she announced that she wanted to be a singer. But her parents limited her lessons to piano only because they "did not believe in training an immature voice." In 1955 Meredith got to show the nation that she could sing when she performed a duet with her father on *The Colgate Comedy Hour*. It was her

Beach girls Meredith MacRae and Annette Funicello in publicity still for *Bikini Beach* (AIP, 1964).

television debut. Her film debut was two years earlier as she ice-skated with her father during a scene in the musical *By the Light of the Silvery Moon* (1953).

After graduating high school, MacRae enrolled in UCLA, majoring in English with theater as a minor. She also decided to concentrate on acting rather than singing because "I decided it would be more interesting to be an actress who could sing rather than a singer who couldn't act." She appeared in stage productions of *Bye Bye Birdie*, *Picnic*, *Annie Get Your Gun* with her family, and *Wildcat* with Martha Raye. In 1963, Meredith made her film debut playing one of the beach girls in *Beach Party* (1963), starring Frankie Avalon and Annette Funicello. MacRae didn't have much to do in her first beach movie other than smile, dance, and look good in a bikini, which was no trouble for the curvy lass. 1963 proved to be a very busy year for Meredith. She wed accountant Richard Berger (they divorced almost three years later) and dropped out of UCLA when she was cast as Sally Ann Morrison, a secretary at Fred MacMurray's factory who becomes the steady girlfriend of his son Mike, played by Tim Considine, on the hit sitcom *My Three Sons*. Meredith revealed in *Seventeen* that she couldn't type and kept jamming the typewriter in one episode, as she had to take a typed letter and file it. "When I finally did the scene and made it over to the filing cabinet with the piece of paper, I forgot my lines! Was my face red!" During her second year with the show, Mike and Sally get engaged culminating with their marriage on the first episode of the 1965–66 season. It was also Meredith's last appearance, as Considine wanted off the series, so his character along with MacRae's was written out.

Meredith's time on the show brought her reams of publicity. She was voted a Hollywood Deb Star in 1963, and AIP invited her back to the beach. This time she would be taking over for Valora Noland as Animal in *Bikini Beach* (1964). MacRae's character is paired with John Ashley's Johnny but goes gaga along with Annette Funicello and the other girls over the drag racing British pop star The Potato Bug (played by Frankie Avalon in a dual role), to the consternation of Avalon's Frankie and his surfing buddies. As the aggressive beach girl, MacRae is a knockout in a bikini, though she felt otherwise and modestly admitted in *Modern Screen*, "I don't think I'm sexy." In the subsequent beach movies Animal is played by two former *Playboy* Playmates, Donna Michelle in *Beach Blanket Bingo* (1965) and Marianne Gaba in *How to Stuff a Wild Bikini* (1965).

In 1966, MacRae appeared in an obscure Canadian film entitled *Footsteps in the Snow*, starring Veronica Lake, before taking over the role of Billie Jo Bradley on *Petticoat Junction*. The third actress to play the part (after Jeannine Riley and Gunilla Hutton), MacRae immediately made Billie Jo her own and fit in nicely with Lori Saunders as Bobbi Jo and Linda Kaye Henning as Betty Jo. Meredith revealed in *Screen Stories*, "I'm especially close to Lori because we're both married and have a lot in common. I came into the show this past year as a replacement for another girl, and Lori who had been a replacement herself and knew how it felt, befriended me. Like the Bobbsy twins, we're inseparable." The sitcom didn't demand any special acting prowess from MacRae, but she always looked fetching as the more cosmopolitan of the Bradley girls and was able to sing occasionally on the show, garnering her a legion of fans and two *Photoplay* Gold Medal nominations for Best Comedy Star. She and the other two girls also parlayed their popularity into the recording industry. Billed as the Girls from Petticoat Junction, they released two singles, "I'm So Glad That You Found Me" and "Wheeling, West Virginia."

In 1969, frustrated with the limited acting requirements of playing Billie Jo, Meredith MacRae enrolled in a drama workshop to enact more serious roles in hopes of improving her acting technique. She certainly had the looks and talent to warrant better parts but whatever she learned was not put to use in her myriad appearances on practically all the celebrity game shows during that period. According to a *TV Guide* article by Richard Warren Lewis in 1970, "Meredith's *What's My Line?* segment was just one of 31 game show appearances she made in little more than a month on programs like *The Match Game, Snap Judgment, Lucky Pair, PDQ, Funny You Should Ask*." MacRae quickly became known for being a "personality" and any aspirations she had to continue being a serious actress were dashed by this over exposure on the small screen. However, Meredith defended her TV forays in *TV Guide* as a way to overcome typecasting. She noted, "My image before doing game shows and talk shows was only as Billie Jo on *Petticoat Junction*. I certainly would like people to see me more as I really am—someone who certainly has more depth than Billie Jo...."

After *Petticoat Junction* was cancelled in 1970, MacRae returned to the big screen, playing the small role of Kay in *Norwood* (1970). She was the fast-driving girlfriend of returning Vietnam vet Joe William, played by Joe Namath, whose buddy Norwood, Glen Campbell, has hit the road to become a singer. (MacRae revealed in the *N. Y. Daily News*, "Joe was a bit nervous about my driving ability.") While passing through Arkansas, Norwood looks up Joe to collect an outstanding debt and is invited to a family picnic where he meets the bikini-clad, blonde Kay. Campbell meets a number of other pretty gals along the way, including Carol Lynley as a surly Southern model, Tisha Sterling as an intellectual Greenwich Village hippie, and Kim Darby as an unwed pregnant woman named Rita Lee with whom he falls in love. As for being novice actor Namath's first leading lady, Meredith, told columnist Earl Wilson, "He kept saying 'Oh, I'm really terrible, aren't I?' But I thought he just did beautifully in that scene where he had a live chick in a car and had to put it in the trunk and close the trunk and hand me the key. I expected him to be real conceited which he isn't."

In 1971, Meredith and her sister Heather got to sing and dance as regulars on their mother's short-lived syndicated variety program *The Sheila MacRae Show*. She then went the TV guest star route (including giving a standout performance as a distraught housewife whose husband is critically ill on *The Interns*) while continuing to make her daytime game show appearances. In the mid-seventies, MacRae and her husband Greg Mullavey

The beautiful Meredith MacRae in *Norwood* **(Paramount, 1970).**

(they met in a drama workshop, wed on April 19, 1969, and had a daughter named Alison Lee in 1974) became friendly with director Paul Leder who used them in a number of his bizarre, obscure low budget movies. Though hardly anyone ever saw these films due to limited release, it at least gave Meredith a chance to really emote in a variety of roles after years of only playing Miss Celebrity Game Show Panelist. She played the wife of a psycho Vietnam vet in *My Friends Need Killing* (1976), a woman who goes undercover as a hooker to trap her sister's killer in *Sketches of a Strangler* (1978), and the ambitious actress-wife of a theatrical director in *I'm Going to Be Famous* (1983). In one of Leder's films that did get distributed, MacRae received positive reviews (the critic in *Variety* found her to be "excellent") as one half of a bickering couple who kill a Federal agent and hide his body in the black comedy *The Census Taker* (1984).

By the eighties, the still gorgeous and vivacious Meredith MacRae seemed to be resigned to the fact that she was best being herself on the small screen. She co-hosted with Geoff Edwards a local talk show in Los Angeles called *Mid-Morning L.A.*, which ran for eight years, earning her a local Emmy Award in 1986, and later produced and hosted the cable series *Born Famous*, interviewing children of celebrities. But MacRae was most proud of *A Second Chance: Surviving Alcoholism*, which she co-produced, wrote, and hosted since her father was a recovering alcoholic. The acclaimed special aired locally in Los Angeles. MacRae also found the time to put her energy and talent to use recording twenty-four best-selling books on tape for Dove Audio.

In 1995, Meredith (who divorced Mullavey in 1987) married Phil Neal, a CEO of a Fortune 500 company. Sadly, MacRae passed away much too young from her battle with brain cancer on July 14, 2000. Though *Petticoat Junction* and her numerous game show appearances made her well known to the public, it also stifled what could have been an exciting movie career for the sexy blonde. But the privileged Meredith MacRae would probably want to be remembered for what she gave back to the community. She served on the boards of the National Council on Alcoholism, Women in Film Foundation, YWCA Board of Councilors, and the Celebrity Action Council of the Los Angeles Mission, among others. MacRae also worked diligently for the American Heart Association and United Cerebral Palsy, where she served as the local L.A. host of their telethons for twenty years. With all her associations, it is no wonder then she was chosen one of Los Angeles' Outstanding Women "for her contributions to the community and charitable endeavors." It was a well-deserved honor for this dedicated and generous woman.

Film Appearances

1953   **By the Light of the Silvery Moon** (Warner Bros.) [uncredited] d. David Butler
1963   **Beach Party** (AIP) d. William Asher
       Bikini Beach (AIP) d. William Asher
1966   **Footsteps in the Snow** (Peerless Films) d. Martin Green
1970   **Norwood** (Paramount) d. Jack Haley Jr.
1976   **My Friends Needs Killing** (Cinema Producers Center) d. Paul Leder
       Grand Jury (unreleased) d. Christopher Cain
1978   **Three on a Date** (TV-movie) d. Bill Bixby

Sketches of a Strangler (unreleased) d. Paul Leder
The Chinese Caper (unreleased) d. Paul Leder
1983 I'm Going to Be Famous (International Film Sales) d. Paul Leder
Vultures (Prism Entertainment) d. Paul Leder
1984 The Calendar Girl Murders (TV-movie) [as herself] d. William A. Graham
The Census Taker (Seymour Borde) d. Bruce R. Cook
1992 China Heat (Shanghai Film Studios d. William Cheung)

Television Appearances— Drama, Comedy & Variety Series:

The Colgate Comedy Hour "Roberta" 4/10/1955 NBC
The Gordon MacRae Show [singing "Little Child"] 3/12/1956 NBC
The Dinah Shore Show 11/1961 NBC
Highways of Melody (special) 4/22/1962 NBC
The Tennessee Ernie Ford Show 10/4/1963 ABC
My Three Sons (series regular as Sally Ann Morrison) 10/24/1963 to 9/9/1965 ABC
The Hollywood Deb Stars Ball (special) [Deb Star] 12/28/1963 ABC
My Three Sons "The First Marriage" 9/16/1965 ABC
Petticoat Junction (series regular as Billie Jo Bradley) 9/13/1966 to 9/12/1970 CBS
The 1967 Emmy Awards (special) [presenter] 6/4/1967 ABC
The Beverly Hillbillies "The Thanksgiving Story" 11/18/1968 CBS
The Beverly Hillbillies "The Week Before Christmas" 12/18/1968 CBS
The Beverly Hillbillies "Christmas in Hooterville" 12/25/1968 CBS
Spring Thing (special) [singing "High Heel Sneakers"] 4/28/1969 NBC
The Barbara McNair Show [singing "All of Me"] 2/22/1970 SYN
Love, American Style "Love and Grandma" 3/6/1970 ABC
Insight "Incident on Danker Street" 5/1970 SYN
The Sheila MacRae Show (co-host) 1971 SYN
Alias Smith and Jones "Something to Get Hung About" 10/21/1971 ABC
Love, American Style "Love and the Bashful Groom" 10/22/1971 ABC
Banyon "A Date with Death" 11/24/1972 NBC
The F.B.I. "The Detonator" 2/25/1973 ABC
The F.B.I. "Night of the Long Knives" 3/25/1973 ABC
ABC Wide World of Entertainment: Miss-World [co-host] 12/11/1973 ABC
ABC Wide World of Mystery: The Werewolf of Woodstock 9/21/1977 ABC
The Rockford Files "Requiem for a Funny Box" 11/4/1977 NBC
Thanksgiving Reunion with the Partridge Family and My Three Sons (special) 11/25/1977 ABC
The Phenomenon of Benji (special) 5/4/1978 ABC
Wilder and Wilder (pilot) 8/26/1978 CBS
The Next Step Beyond "Ondine's Curse" 10/4/1978 SYN
Fantasy Island "I Want to Get Married/ Jewel Thief" 10/21/1978 ABC
CHiPs "Off-Road" 2/2/1980 NBC
Steve Martin's Comedy Is Not Pretty (special) 2/14/1980 NBC
The International Guinness Book of World Records (special) [co-host] 9/21/1980 ABC
Fantasy Island "With Affection, Jack the Ripper/ Gigolo" 11/29/1980 ABC
Earthbound (pilot) 1/31 & 2/7/1982 NBC
Fantasy (series regular as roving reporter) 9/13/1982 to 10/28/1983 NBC
CHiPs "Firepower" 3/6/1983 NBC
The Fall Guy "To the Finish" [as herself] 12/7/1983 ABC
The Fall Guy "Baja 1000" [as herself] 11/28/1984 ABC
Webster "The Uh-Oh Feeling" 1/25/1985 ABC
Scene of the Crime "The Medium Is Murder" 5/26/1985 NBC
Hollywood Reporter (pilot) 12/1985 SYN
Magnum, PI "Summer School" 1/9/1986 CBS
The New Love, American Style "Love and the Beagles" 3/13/1986 ABC

Dalton's Code of Vengeance II (pilot) 5/11/1986 NBC
It's Howdy Doody Time—A 40 Year Celebration (special) 11/1987 SYN
Batman: The Animated Series "On Leather Wings" [voice only] 9/6/1992 FOX
Batman: The Animated Series "Terror in the Sky" [voice only] 11/12/1992 FOX

Television Appearances— Talk & Game Shows:

Person to Person 6/17/1960 CBS
Art Linkletter's Talent Scouts 7/4/1966 CBS
Dateline: Hollywood 8/1/1967 ABC
Art Linkletter's House Party 10/12/1967 CBS
Pat Boone in Hollywood 10/20/1967 SYN
The Mike Douglas Show 11/17/1967 SYN
Personality 2/5 to 2/9/1968 NBC
The Joey Bishop Show 3/27/1968 ABC
The Woody Woodbury Show 4/8/1968 SYN
Personality 5/20 to 5/24/1968 NBC
The Woody Woodbury Show 7/5/1968 SYN
Snap Judgement 7/8 to 7/12/1968 NBC
The Match Game 7/15 to 7/19/1968 NBC
The Match Game 8/19 to 8/23/1968 NBC
Snap Judgement 8/26 to 8/30/1968 NBC
What's My Line? 9/9 to 9/13/1968 SYN
What's My Line? 9/16 to 9/20/1968 SYN
What's My Line? 9/23 to 9/27/1968 SYN
The Match Game 9/30 to 10/4/1968 NBC
The Dating Game 10/5/1968 ABC
What's My Line? 12/23 to 12/27/1968 SYN
The Donald O'Connor Show 1/8/1969 SYN
The Match Game 2/3 to 2/7/1969 NBC
The Steve Allen Show 2/20/1969 SYN
Funny You Should Ask 2/24 to 2/28/1969 ABC
The Hollywood Squares 3/24 to 3/28/1969 NBC
The Hollywood Squares 4/7 to 4/11/1969 NBC
Funny You Should Ask 4/14 to 4/18/1969 ABC
The Joey Bishop Show 4/18/1969 ABC
The Match Game 4/21 to 4/25/1969 NBC
Kup's Show 4/22/1969 NET
The Art Linkletter Show 5/19/1969 CBS
Funny You Should Ask 5/19 to 5/23/1969 ABC
What's My Line? 5/19 to 5/23/1969 SYN
Name Droppers 9/29/1969 NBC
He Said! She Said! 1/19 to 1/23/1970 SYN

It's Your Bet 1/26 to 1/30/1970 NBC
All-American College Show [celebrity judge] 1/31/1970 SYN
PDQ 2/23 to 2/27/1970 NBC
It Takes Two 6/8 to 6/12/1970 NBC
The Movie Game 7/20 to 7/24/1970 SYN
He Said! She Said! 7/30, 8/2, 8/9, & 8/15/1970 SYN
What's My Line? 8/17 to 8/21/1970 SYN
The Real Tom Kennedy Show 9/3/1970 SYN
It's Your Bet 9/20 to 9/24/1970 NBC
The Virginia Graham Show 10/2/1970 SYN
The Choice Is Yours (unaired pilot) 11/1970
Password 6/14 to 6/18/1971 ABC
Mantrap 6/28 to 7/2/1971 SYN
Mantrap 7/5 to 7/9/1971 SYN
The Movie Game 8/16 to 8/19, 8/21/1971 SYN
Mantrap 11/22 to 7/26/1971 SYN
What's My Line 3/20 to 3/24/1972 SYN
Kid Talk 5/29/1972 SYN
What's My Line? 8/11/1972 SYN
I've Got a Secret 10/3/1972 SYN
The Mike Douglas Show 10/20/1972 SYN
This Is Your Life "Harold Krents" 10/29/1972 SYN
I've Got a Secret 12/26/1972 SYN
What's My Line? 4/2 to 4/6/1973 CBS
What's My Line? 5/14 to 5/18/1973 CBS
I've Got a Secret 6/12/1973 SYN
What's My Line? 10/8 to 10/12/1973 CBS
What's My Line? 2/12 to 2/16/1973 CBS
The $10,000 Pyramid 10/29 to 11/2/1973 ABC
What's My Line? 12/10 to 12/14/1973 CBS
The Merv Griffin Show 1974 SYN
Match Game '74 1/31–2/1, 2/4–2/6/1974 CBS
The $10,000 Pyramid 3/13 to 3/15, 3/18 & 3/19/1974 ABC
Tattletales 3/18 to 3/22/1974 CBS
The Mike Douglas Show 3/22/1974 SYN
What's My Line? 6/17 to 6/21/1974 CBS
The $10,000 Pyramid 7/22 to 7/26/1974 ABC
3 for the Money 10/27 to 10/31/1974 NBC
Tattletales 1/7 to 1/10, 1/13/1975 CBS
Match Game '75 3/17 to 3/21/1975 CBS
Rhyme and Reason 8/4 to 8/8/1975 ABC
Cross-Wits 12/17/1975 SYN
Rhyme and Reason 2/2 to 2/6/1976 ABC
Rhyme and Reason 3/22 to 3/26/1976 ABC
Tattletales 3/22 to 3/26/1976 CBS
Cross-Wits 3/29 to 4/2/1976 SYN
Break the Bank 5/3 to 5/7/1976 ABC
Rhyme and Reason 5/10 to 5/14/1976 ABC
Dinah! 6/9/1976 SYN

Rhyme and Reason 6/21 to 6/25/1976 ABC
Rhyme and Reason 6/28 to 7/2/1976 ABC
Cross-Wits 10/11 to 10/15/1976 SYN
Liar's Club 10/18 to 10/22/1976 SYN
Cross-Wits 12/13 to 12/17/1976 SYN
The Jim Nabors Show 1978 SYN
Cross-Wits 1978 SYN
Hollywood Connection 3/13 to 3/17/1978 SYN
Tattletales 3/23, 3/24, 3/27 to 3/29/1978 CBS
Hollywood Connection 3/26 to 3/30/1978 SYN
The Merv Griffin Show 6/13/1978 SYN
Celebrity Cooks 8/22/1978 SYN
Family Feud "TV's All-Time Favorites" 5/2 to 5/6 & 5/9 to 5/13/1983 ABC
All-Star Beat the Clock 1/21 to 1/25/1980 CBS
Celebrity Whew! 2/12 to 2/15, 2/18/1980 CBS
Celebrity Whew! 4/24, 4/25, 4/28-4/30/1980 CBS
Card Sharks 11/24 to 11/28/1980
Your New Day 12/8/1980 SYN
Body Language 9/17 to 9/21/1984 CBS
Couch Potatoes 4/18/1989 SYN
Vicki! 1/7/1993 SYN

Also

Insight, To Tell the Truth, The Dean Martin Show, Mid-Morning L.A., Born Famous, and *A Second Chance: Surviving Alcoholism* (special)

☆ DODIE MARSHALL ☆

Dark-haired beauty Dodie Marshall made only two film appearances and both of them were with Elvis Presley. After playing a small role in *Spinout* (1966), Marshall went on to co-star opposite the King in one of his most mod films, *Easy Come, Easy Go* (1967).

Dodie Marshall was born in Great Britain but raised in Philadelphia. As a child she professed a desire to be a star of the silver screen. She's quoted in the *Easy Come, Easy Go* press book as saying, "All the little girls I knew wanted to be movie stars. But they quit and I didn't." Dodie took drama and singing lessons in New York and her English background undoubtedly helped her in landing a spot in the chorus in the Broadway musical *Oliver*. Marshall also began singing in very small clubs in downtown New York before graduating to bigger venues.

In 1964, Marshall came to Hollywood and quickly landed a guest spot on the TV sitcom *My Favorite Martian*, playing the girlfriend of Bill Bixby's Tim who dumps him after he is exposed to a Martian bulb that gives him a "hate-me" glow. She also made singing appearances on the teenage dance programs, *Shindig* and *Hullabaloo*. After playing a receptionist on *The Man from U.N.C.L.E.* in one of the series best episodes, "The Foxes and Hounds Affair," Marshall made her film debut in the small role of Susan in *Spinout* (1966) starring Elvis Presley. Described as "the sexiest girl in the world" the role was very sought after, with Marshall purportedly beating out over 200 other aspiring actresses. Presley played a racecar driver and singer who is pursued by three marriage-minded females—a sophisticated author (Diane McBain), a spoiled rich girl (Shelley Fabares), and his perky tom-boyish drummer (Deborah Walley). After dodging the ladies intentions and pairing them up with others, Presley settles on Marshall's go-go dancing Susan who when she meets Elvis at a poolside party, says she has no intentions of marrying until she is "fifty, fifty-five—*maybe*." The film wraps up with Susan becoming Presley's combo's new drummer and possibly new love interest.

Elvis Presley and Dodie Marshall sing and dance in *Easy Come, Easy Go* (Paramount, 1967).

Marshall looks great with shoulder-length hair worn in a flip. Wanting to make an impression and keep things real, she learned to play the drums by practicing eight hours a day. She convincingly faked playing along during Elvis' number, "I'll Be Back," during the film's finale.

Marshall was upped to leading lady in her second Elvis Presley film, *Easy Come, Easy Go* (1967). This lighthearted, tuneful romp is considered by his fans to be the lowest point in Elvis' movie career even though the film made money (grossing close to $2 million) and received fairly good reviews. The movie features Elvis as Ted Jackson, a navy frogman who encounters a treasure chest in a sunken ship, a yacht full of blonde beauties, beatniks, the counterculture and yoga. Marshall played Jo, a free-spirited go-go dancing yoga enthusiast, beatnik and descendant of the ship's skipper. She aids Ted and discotheque owner Judd (Pat Harrington) in retrieving the treasure before scheming playboy Gil Corey (Skip Ward) and his viper girlfriend Dina Bishop (Pat Priest) can get to it first. Marshall was one of Elvis' more energetic leading ladies and they made a charming screen duo. She was also one of his most outrageously costumed and coiffured co-stars, as she graced the screen in outlandish hairstyles and mod sixties outfits ranging from a white striped midriff to a rust tasseled minidress.

After the release of *Easy Come, Easy Go*, Marshall exclaimed, "I want to be a star and I see no reason to conceal it. I want to get to the top of my profession and it's more than just an expression of ego. I have the desire and some of the qualifications and I hope I can acquire the others." The talented brunette also had the notices to back up her goal. Regarding her performance in *Easy Come, Easy Go,* the *Variety* reviewer described her as "an excellent young actress with appealing warmth and looks for meatier sympathetic roles." Alas, after guest starring on the long-forgotten TV western series *The Rounders,* playing a guest at a health resort for women, and *Cowboy in Africa* as a woman trying to help save a wounded rare white Rhino, the ambitious starlet vanished from the Hollywood scene. As they say, "easy come, easy go."

Film Appearances

1966 **Spinout** (MGM) d. Norman Taurog

1967 **Easy Come, Easy Go** (Paramount) d. John Rich

Television Appearances

My Favorite Martian "Won't You Come Home, Uncle Martin, Won't You Come Home" 12/27/1964 CBS
Shivaree 9/25/1965 SYN
The Man from U.N.C.L.E. "The Foxes and Hounds Affair" 10/8/1965 NBC
Shindig [singing "Round Every Corner"] 11/25/1965 ABC
The Smothers Brothers Show "Hawaiian Caper" 1/14/1966 CBS
The Rounders "The Scavenger Hunt" 10/11/1966 ABC
Cowboy in Africa "Kifaru! Kifaru!" 9/18/1967 ABC

Also

Hullabaloo

☆ CLAUDIA MARTIN ☆

While Frank Sinatra over shadowed Dean Martin in life, the same could be said of their daughters, Nancy Sinatra and Claudia Martin. Dark-haired Claudia played second fiddle to Nancy in the beach movie *For Those Who Think Young* (1964) and the last of the *Beach Party* films, *The Ghost in the Invisible Bikini* (1966). Sans Sinatra, Martin copped a lead role as an American skier on vacation in Austria in the Euro-teenage romp *Ski Fever* (1969), but Claudia never had the appeal or the determination of Nancy to become a true '60s icon.

Claudia Martin was born March 16, 1944, in Ridley Park, Pennsylvania. She was the second of four children (the others being Craig, Gail, and Deana) born to singer Dean Martin and his wife, the former Betty McDonald. As his singing career began to take off Martin moved his family from Pennsylvania to New York, then to Long Beach and finally to swanky Bel Air where they settled down. Young Claudia was attending the Bel Air Town & Country Grammar School when her parents split up and she went to live with her mother in Holmby Hills. In 1957, Claudia moved in with her father and his new wife Jeanne plus their three children, Dino, Ricci, and Gina.

Martin graduated from Beverly Hills High School in 1961 and had a secret desire to act but felt intimidated by her talented younger siblings. She remarked in *New York World-Telegraph and Sun*, "They could sing and dance and mimic people. I couldn't do a thing. I felt very out of it, to tell you the truth." What spurred Martin on was gossipmonger Hedda Hopper's taking her to task in one of her columns, suggesting that Claudia was a spoiled child who expected everything to be handed to her and that if she tried she could become a star. Infuriated, Claudia enrolled in a drama workshop conducted by Charles Conrad where she boasted that she was going to be "not just 'another' actress but a fine actress—maybe some day as fine an actress as Bette Davis."

However, classmate Gavin Murell quickly distracted the teenager and the young couple secretly eloped to Las Vegas in July of 1963. Martin quickly realized that she made a mistake and confessed in *Screen Stories*, "I should have been happy, being married. But I wasn't. Every day I missed my family terribly and longed for my old way of life." With her father's help, the hasty marriage was annulled a few months later.

Claudia Martin's acting debut was in an episode of *The Donna Reed Show*. Being Dean Martin's daughter was most likely the only reason that she was voted a Hollywood Deb Star two months later in

Publicity shot of Nancy Sinatra, James Darren, and Claudia Martin (left to right) as college students in *For Those Who Think Young* (United Artists, 1964). *Billy Rose Theatre Collection, The New York Public Library for the Performing Arts, Astor, Lenox and Tilden Foundations*

December 1963. Her film debut was in the *Beach Party* knockoff *For Those Who Think Young* (1964), starring James Darren and Pamela Tiffin. Reportedly, her father brought her to the attention of the film's producers who had already cast Nancy Sinatra and thought it would be a novel idea to have Dean's daughter play her rival. In the film, Darren played Ding Pruitt, a rich college playboy who falls for Tiffin's poor college coed Sandy. She rejects Ding, but her sorority sisters Sue and Karen, played by Martin and Nancy Sinatra, go gaga over Ding and want him for themselves. They try competing for him but he only has eyes for Sandy. Despite her smaller part than Sinatra's, Martin got noticed playing the chatty Sue, as *Variety* called her one of the "cast members who come on strong if briefly ... as a sorority type who spends more time on the phone than did the late A. G. Bell." To promote the movie, Martin modeled swimsuits along with Linda Evans in a spread for *Photoplay* magazine in June of 1964.

Martin donned sexy swimwear again for her next picture, *The Ghost in the Invisible Bikini* (1966). Though she looks terrific with her long hair and fills out her bikini very nicely, this film gave Claudia less to do than in her first movie. In one scene all she does is stand there and comfort co-star Nancy Sinatra who thinks she has lost beau Aron Kincaid to vixen Quinn O'Hara, while "Italian sensation" Piccola Pupa sings to brighten their spirits.

The following year Martin was off to Austria to star opposite Martin Milner in *Ski Fever*. This was a late in the cycle look at wholesome teenagers similar to the previous films *Ski Party* (1965), *Winter a-Go-Go* (1965), and *Wild Wild Winter* (1966). Surrounded by European actors, Martin played Susan Halsey, a beautiful but brittle California tourist on a ski vacation in Austria. Co-star Martin Milner played Brian Davis, an American student working at the lodge as a ski instructor to earn money for his tuition. The boy falls instantly in love with Susan, as does his rival Franz played by real-life ski champion Toni Sailor. They wager their season's pay to see who will win her affections. Susan is at first turned off by Brian's attitude but when she learns that Franz is only interested in her due to the bet and that Brian has thrown the ski jumping contest for her, she is convinced of his intentions and the two are united. *Ski Fever* sat on the shelf in the U.S. until 1969. It was finally released due to Milner's success in his hit TV series *Adam-12*. As expected, the reviews were dismal. *Variety* deemed it "uneventful" and "a slow programmer even in lesser markets," though they found Claudia to be "earnest."

By 1968, Claudia Martin had dropped out of show business, never coming close to her goal of becoming a Bette Davis. She married actor Kiel Martin (later of *Hill Street Blues* fame) in 1969, gave birth to a daughter named Jesse soon after, and filed for divorce in 1971. In 1978, Claudia married businessman Jim Roberts and lived an unassuming life helping her husband run his printing company in Reno, Nevada until her death from breast cancer on February 16, 2001.

Film Appearances

1964   **For Those Who Think Young** (United Artists) d. Leslie H. Martinson

1966   **The Ghost in the Invisible Bikini** (AIP) d. Don Weis

1969   **Ski Fever** (US/ Austria/Czechoslovakia; Allied Artists) [completed in 1967] d. Curt Siodmak

Television Appearances

The Donna Reed Show "Whatever You Wish" 10/3/1963 ABC
The Hollywood Deb Star Ball (special) [Deb Star] 12/28/1963 ABC
My Three Sons "Marriage by Proxy" 1/23/1964 ABC
Gypsy 7/19/1966 SYN
The Dean Martin Show 12/21/1967 NBC
The Dating Game 9/7/1968 ABC

☆ JENNY MAXWELL ☆

Blonde sex kitten Jenny Maxwell, a distant relative of Marilyn Monroe, made a career of playing teenage sirens well into her twenties, though *the* nymphet role of Lolita escaped her. On the big screen she played Carol Lynley's friend in *Blue Denim* (1959) before being cast as a high schooler who vamps Elvis Presley in *Blue Hawaii* (1961). She did another friend-of-the-star role, this time that of Sandra Dee in *Take Her, She's Mine* (1963), before appearing in the backwoods drive-in movie *Shotgun Wedding* (1963) playing a moon shiner's nubile daughter.

Of Norwegian descent, Jenny Maxwell was born on September 3, 1942, in New York City. When she was ten years old the adorable blonde was spotted by a CBS-TV talent scout on Fifth Avenue. Maxwell's mother, a former model, allowed her daughter to appear in a few live dramatic programs. She also enrolled Jenny in acting and singing classes. It was in her drama class where the teenager met an older man who introduced her to an agent, Lillian Small. Impressed with Maxwell, the agent sent her pictures to MGM. Maxwell flew out to Hollywood with her classmate, now acting as her manager, to test for the role of an unwed pregnant girl opposite George Hamilton and George Peppard in *Home from the Hill*. But Maxwell failed to get cast (Luana Patten got the role.) She admitted to columnist Dick Williams, "I didn't understand the part and I guess I didn't do very well."

But Maxwell must have done something right because she would go on to play unwed mothers in four different TV shows, most notably a *Playhouse 90* episode entitled "In Lonely Expectations" with Diane Baker and Beverly Washburn (whom described Maxwell as being "a nice girl to work with. She was fun but kind of wild.")

In 1959, Maxwell made her film debut in the controversial teenage melodrama *Blue Denim* (1959), based on the stage play about teenagers faced with an unwanted pregnancy. However, this time Maxwell was not playing another expectant teen. Brandon DeWilde and Carol Lynley essayed the roles of the parents-to-be. Jenny was cast in the small part of Lynley's friend with a reputation of being easy. That same year, the sixteen year old married twenty-four year old Paul W. Rapp, an assistant director. Their divorce made headlines three years later with nasty accusations (both parties charging "cruelty") and a bitter custody fight for their nineteen-month-old son Brian, with Maxwell winning in court.

Professionally, Maxwell dumped her manager with the help of her mother and agent after he began demanding more and more money from her. She worked steadily on TV though she was typecast as teenage vixens, which is probably why she was brought to the attention of producer James Harris in 1960 as he was searching for the right actress to bring *Lolita* to life on the big screen. For a period of time, Maxwell was the front-runner for the part of the pubescent tease. Though she was almost nineteen years old, Maxwell had the right quality and could pass for being fourteen. She commented, "I look very young but different, people see me in different ways. Some days I look like an angel. Others say I look like Brigitte Bardot." Perhaps because of her appearance, Maxwell eventually lost the role to Sue Lyon who had a softer look.

A highly sought after role that Maxwell did land was playing Ellie in *Blue Hawaii* (1961) starring Elvis Presley as Chad Gates, a returning GI from a rich family "slumming" as a tour guide in Hawaii. (Regarding the King, Jenny remarked in *Show Business Illustrated*, "Elvis is tender and understanding.") Maxwell's character was described in the press notes as being "a fresh kid with grown up ideas." Ellie is part of a small band of high school friends played by Darlene Tompkins, Pamela Austin, and Christian Kay who are chaperoned around the islands by their teacher Abigail Prentace (Nancy Walters) and Chad. Spoiled Ellie refuses to get into the spirit of the vacation and is consistently rude to Chad as she sulks in the car, refuses to eat, and flirts with a drunk resulting in a bar fight that costs Chad his job. Abigail hires Chad back to continue as tour guide. Ellie then changes her tactics and tries to seduce Chad. When he rejects her, she storms off. Chad rescues the problem teen as she tries to drown herself in the surf. As she wails on and on about how nobody cares about her, Chad takes Ellie over his knee and gives her an old fashioned spanking. (A scene that is a fetishist's delight.) This we are led to believe finally knocks some sense into the girl. Maxwell described her character as being a "psychotic adolescent sexpot on the make for Elvis Presley." She also loved the ending, calling it "great. I tried to drown myself in a pink peignoir." Maxwell handled herself well in the role and received favorable reviews such as the one in *Variety* whose critic noted that "Jenny Maxwell emotes with youthful relish and spirit."

After playing a small part as one of Sandra Dee's college roommates (the other one was Cynthia Pepper) in the comedy *Take Her, She's Mine* (1963), Max-

Blue Hawaii (Paramount, 1961) featured Jenny Maxwell as a spoiled high school student with designs on her Hawaiian tour guide, Elvis Presley.

well sort of got a consolation prize after losing out on *Lolita*. She was cast as another Lolita-ish character in the low-budget drive-in movie *Shotgun Wedding* (1963), directed by Boris L. Petroff with a screenplay by the "world's worst movie director" the incomparable Ed Wood, Jr. The film's tag line proclaimed, "Gorgeous Gals Set the Ozarks on Fire!" In this sort of hillbilly *Romeo and Juliet* tale, Maxwell played the aptly named Honey Bee Heller, the sexy daughter of a family of moon shiners in love with Rafe Ankers (Peter Holt), whose family is the Heller's arch enemy. Despite their families' feud, Honey Bee and Rafe are desperate to be together. A subplot in the movie involved the shanty-boat Anker family hiding an ex-carnival worker played by Valerie Allen (Mrs. Troy Donahue) on the run from the police. She agrees to marry the cantankerous family patriarch Buford played by J. Pat O'Malley despite being in love with a fake preacher. By fadeout true love wins out and both couples get married.

Shotgun Wedding was Maxwell's swan song on the big screen. She continued appearing on television and in 1967 she was still being cast in teenage roles when she played a college coed and friend of Don Grady's Robbie Douglas on *My Three Sons*. Maxwell left show business soon after when she married respected attorney Ervin (Tip) Roeder, who was twenty-one years her senior. They had just separated in May of 1981, when they were both shot and killed in a possible bungled robbery attempt outside Maxwell's condominium near Cedars-Sinai Medical Center in Los Angeles. Jenny Maxwell was only thirty-nine when she died.

Film Appearances

1959 **Blue Denim** (20th Century–Fox) d. Phillip Dunne

1961 **Blue Hawaii** (Paramount) d. Norman Taurog

1963 **Take Her, She's Mine** (20th Century–Fox) d. Henry Koster
Shotgun Wedding (Pat Paterson Prod.) d. Boris Petroff

Television Appearances

Father Knows Best "Two Loves Has Bud" 3/30/1959 CBS
Playhouse 90 "In Lonely Expectations" 4/2/1959 CBS
G. E. Theater "The Flying Wife" 4/5/1959 CBS
Peck's Bad Girl "Lips That Touch Lipstick" 5/19/1959 CBS
The D.A.'s Man "Flight 729" 7/4/1959 NBC
Bachelor Father "Bentley and the Teenage Siren" 7/9/1959 CBS
Bonanza "The Gunmen" 1/23/1960 NBC
Route 66 "Fly Away Home" 2/10 & 2/17/1961 CBS
The Twilight Zone "Long Distance Call" 3/31/1961 CBS
The Lawless Years "The Jonathan Wills Story" 9/8/1961 NBC
Dr. Kildare "The Patient" 11/23/1961 NBC
Bus Stop "A Lion Walks Among Us" 12/3/1961 ABC
Pete and Gladys "Hero in the House" 12/28/1961 CBS
Ichabod and Me "Bob's Teenage Guest" 2/13/1962 CBS
Wagon Train "The Lieutenant Burton Story" 2/28/1962 NBC
The Joey Bishop Show "The Big Date" 2/28/1962 NBC
Room for One More "Ribbin's and Beaus" 7/14/1962 ABC
Route 66 "Journey to Nineveh" 9/28/1962 CBS
Empire "When the Gods Laugh" 12/18/1962 NBC
Hawaiian Eye "Go for Baroque" 2/12/1963 ABC
77 Sunset Strip "Target Island" 4/5/1963 ABC
The Eleventh Hour "86 Different Kinds of Love" 2/19/1964 NBC

Death Valley Days "Peter the Hunter" 12/31/1964 SYN
The F.B.I. "Pound of Flesh" 12/19/1965 ABC
This Is the Life "The Night of the Junior Prom" 7/30/1966 SYN
My Three Sons "TV or Not TV" 1/26/1967 CBS
Judd for the Defense "To Love and Stand Mute" 12/8/1967 ABC
The Wild Wild West "The Night of the Avaricious Actuary" 12/6/1968 CBS

☆ MARY MITCHEL ☆

Pretty Mary Mitchel resembled and sounded a lot like Connie Stevens. But Mitchel was more appealing and less annoying than her famous counterpart, as she played the ingenue in various low-budget drive-in movies during the early to middle '60s. She danced in the rock-and-roll musical *Twist Around the Clock* (1961) and screamed her way through *Panic in Year Zero* (1962), *Dementia 13* (1963), and *Spider Baby* (1964). In 1965, she hit the beach for typical teenage shenanigans in *A Swingin' Summer* and *The Girls on the Beach*.

According to the *Panic in Year Zero* pressbook, Mary Mitchel was born and raised in Los Angeles. Her father was a contractor and her mother an interior decorator. As a youngster, Mary had a talent for drawing and had the unique skill of being able to write backwards. Her first ambition was to become an artist but she also had a very good singing voice, which was the impetus for her show business career. While singing with the Robert Wagner Chorale during a concert for the foreign press, she was spotted by a Columbia talent scout. She was offered a screen test to become the new Gidget. Though Mitchel lost the role to Deborah Walley, she did garner an agent.

Her first TV appearance was playing the marriage minded girlfriend of Tony Dow's Wally on *Leave It to Beaver* in 1961. That same year Mary made her film debut in *Twist Around the Clock*, which showcased her dancing prowess. This quickie was produced by the King of the B's, Sam Katzman, to cash in on the dance fad and featured guest performers Chubby Checker, Dion, Vicki Spencer, and the Marcels. Manager Mitch Mason (John Cronin), just fired by a rock-and-roll band, spots Tina and her brother Jeff doing a new dance called the Twist. Impressed, he offers to manage them along with Clay Cole and his band for a 60/40 split. A shrewd businesswoman, Tina negotiates him down to 75/25. Mitch is blocked from getting the group gigs in New York due to a jilted girlfriend named Debbie (Maura McGiveney) whose father Joe Marshall (Tol Avery) is the city's top booking agent. But Marshall allows Mitch's group to perform at a high society affair in Boston as a ploy to reunite Mitch and Debbie, but his plan backfires when the group is a hit. Mitch is able to sign the act into the Seven Club where Chubby Checker and Dion are performing. The group is a smash hit. Debbie becomes extremely jealous of the close bond between Mitch and Tina and is more determined than ever to win Mitch back. Prodded by his scheming daughter, Marshall signs the group to a contract but adds the stipulation that Tina can not marry for three years. She surprisingly agrees. However father and daughter are duped as Tina and Mitch secretly elope before signing the contracts.

For a low-budget film rushed into theatres to capitalize on a dance craze,

Twist Around the Clock is an entertaining, well-produced film. Populated with a number of peppy dance numbers, audiences could not help but want to jump out of their seats and Twist along with the cast. Notices for the film and the actors were for the most part positive. The reviewer in *Variety* remarked, "John Cronin and Mary Mitchel are an attractive pair as the romantic couple, and the latter does some competent twisting."

While pursuing acting roles, Mitchel began taking art and drama courses at UCLA. Her classmates included actors Aron Kincaid and Bart Patton, whom she began dating and would eventually marry. In her next drive-in movie, Mitchel played Ray Milland and Jean Hagen's teenage daughter who gets raped by some local toughs after a nuclear attack destroys Los Angeles in *Panic in Year Zero* (1962).

Mitchel, under the tutelage of acting coach Agnes Moorehead, then went on to receive good notices playing the female lead in a Hollywood Players Ring production of *Under the Yum Yum Tree*.

Back on the drive-in screen, Mary Mitchel made back-to-back horror movies. A very young Francis Coppola, employing some of the actors from Roger Corman's just completed film, *The Young Racers*, directed Mitchel's next film *Dementia 13* (1963), which was completed in only three days on location in England. Coppola knew Mitchel and Bart Patton from UCLA and cast them in roles. Mary played Kane, the newly arrived American fiancée of Richard Haloran (William Campbell), a bitter sculptor living in his family's castle in Ireland. As their wedding day approaches one of Richard's brothers disappears, his sister-in-law (Luana Anders) is secretly trying to drive his mother insane by making her believe she can communicate with her dead daughter, his younger brother (Patton) is acting neurotically, and there is an axe-wielding maniac on the loose. Mitchel is out of her depth in this creepy and atmospheric film but looks great, especially in the scene where Kane, wearing only a sheer nightgown with bikini panties, secretly follows Richard through one of the castle's tunnels.

Mitchel fared better in *Spider Baby* (1964), director Jack Hill's cult poverty-row horror movie about the weird in-bred Merrye family starring Lon Chaney, Jr. and Carol Ohmart. Her husband Bart Patton, who worked as production supervisor and assistant director on the film, no doubt must have helped her land the role of Ann, a legal secretary who accompanies her boss to the Mer-

Twist Around the Clock (Columbia, 1961) featured Mary Mitchel and Jeff Parker as a sister and brother twisting dance team.

ryes' home. Mitchel however makes an unnervingly vulnerable heroine as she discovers the family patriarch's skeleton in his bed, is tied and bound by the two knife-wielding sisters (Beverly Washburn and Jill Banner), and is almost pulled under the floor boards by crazed cannibals Uncle Ned and Aunt Martha.

In her next movie, Mitchel was able to show her comedic side when she was cast as Shirlee, the wise-cracking, always eating ("food inspires me") best friend of Cindy (Quinn O'Hara) in *A Swingin' Summer* (1965). Shirlee accompanies her pal, along with James Stacy as Mickey and William Wellman, Jr. as Rick, to Lake Arrowhead, where they are going operate a dance pavilion for the summer. As the college kids attempt to get the place in shape and book rock-and-roll acts, they still find time to hang out on the beach, water ski, and fight off interlopers who want the pavilion to fail. Wearing her hair up to make her look less the ingenue, Mitchel gives an amusing performance. *Variety* noted that "Mary Mitchell [sic] registers solidly in comic support." Whatever good Mitchel found in this review, the misspelling of her name (a frequent occurrence in credits and in the press) totally irked the movie starlet, according to her friend Aron Kincaid.

Despite her solid work in *A Swingin' Summer*, Mitchel was given less to do and was wasted in her next beach movie, *The Girls on the Beach* (1965). Lead roles went to Noreen Corcoran, Linda Marshall, Gail Gerber (a.k.a. Gilmore), and Lana Wood as sorority sisters who get duped by three surfers (Martin West, Aron Kincaid, and Steve Rogers) into believing that the Beatles will be playing a benefit to help raise money to pay the house mortgage. Mitchel, Anna Capri, Lori Saunders, and Nancy

Mary Mitchel (left) and Quinn O'Hara (right) in *A Swingin' Summer* **(United Screen Arts, 1965).** *Courtesy of Quinn O'Hara.*

Spry (Miss Teen USA for 1964) had lesser roles as sorority members who try to earn money for the house by exploiting their skills before the girls fall for the Beatles con.

The Girls on the Beach was Mitchel's last drive-in movie appearance. She continued acting on TV for a few more years. One of her jobs was thanks to her *Swingin' Summer* co-star, Quinn O'Hara. According to Quinn, "I got along so well with Mary Mitchel. She was a blast. Afterwards, I was cast in an episode entitled "Charley the Pigeon" on *My Three Sons*. I was one of two girls who were pool sharks. The producer, Ed Hartman, asked me, 'Is there anybody you particularly work well with?' I told him I just finished working with Mary Mitchel. When I showed up on the set she was there and I was so happy! It was just so great to work with her again." On television, Mitchel also played one of Lily Munster's hair salon clients who winds up bald on *The Munsters* and a barmaid and a German girl working for the Allied Underground on two different segments of *Hogan's Heroes*.

Mary Mitchel stopped acting in 1968 and worked behind-the-scenes on a number of films. Her son Tyler Patton is also in the film business.

Film Appearances

1961 **Twist Around the Clock** (Columbia) d. Oscar Rudolph

1962 **Panic in Year Zero** (AIP) d. Ray Milland

1963 **Dementia 13** (AIP) d. Francis Coppola

1964 **Spider Baby, Or the Maddest Story Ever Told** (American General Pictures) d. Jack Hill

1965 **A Swingin' Summer** (United Screen Arts) d. Robert Sparr
 The Girls on the Beach (Paramount) d. William Witney

2003 **Looney Tunes:** Back in Action (Warner Bros.) d. Joe Dante

Television Appearances

Leave It to Beaver "Wally Goes Steady" 9/30/1961 CBS
The Many Loves of Dobie Gillis "The Gigolo" 11/7/1961 CBS
The Many Loves of Dobie Gillis "This Town Ain't Big Enough for Me and Robert Browning" 12/12/1961 CBS
Leave It to Beaver "Wally's Chauffeur" 12/23/1961 CBS
Bachelor Father "How to Throw Your Voice" 1/2/1962 ABC
The Many Loves of Dobie Gillis "Girls Will Be Boys" 2/13/1962 CBS
Walt Disney's Wonderful World of Color "Sunny the Way Out Seal" 10/28/1962 NBC
Howie (unaired pilot) 1963
90 Bristol Court: Tom, Dick and Mary "The Joke's on You" 10/19/1964 NBC
The Man from U.N.C.L.E. "The Mad, Mad Tea Party Affair" 2/1/1965 NBC
Perry Mason "The Case of the Mischievous Doll" 5/13/1965 CBS
My Three Sons "Charley the Pigeon" 12/30/1965 CBS
Perry Mason "The Case of the Bogus Buccaneers" 1/9/1966 CBS
The Munsters "The Most Beautiful Ghoul in the World" 1/28/1966 CBS
Hogan's Heroes "Request Permission to Escape" 4/29/1966 CBS
Gomer Pyle, USMC "To Re-enlist or Not to Re-enlist" 2/15/1967 CBS
Hogan's Heroes "Everyone Has a Brother-in-Law" 2/17/1967 CBS

☆ LAURIE MOCK ☆

This dark-haired beauty, similar in looks to Hilarie Thompson, co-starred with cult B-movie actress Mimsy Farmer in two hit alienated youth movies. *Hot Rods to Hell* (1967) featured Laurie Mock as the good girl on a road trip with her family terrorized by Farmer and her speed demon friends. In *Riot on Sunset Strip* (1967) their roles were reversed as Farmer played a naïve teenager coerced by Mock and other Sunset Strip dwellers into the world of LSD.

There isn't much early biographical information available about Laurie Mock. According to press releases, she was born in Los Angeles and studied acting as a teenager. One of her drama coaches was the protégé of esteemed Russian actor

Michael Chekhov. Mock made her TV debut on the John Houseman-produced anthology series *The Great Adventure* in 1964. Each episode reenacted famous stories from American history. Laurie played a young settler kidnapped by Indians in a two-part episode about Daniel Boone and the formation of Fort Boonesborough in Kentucky.

Continuing in the western milieu, Mock made her film debut in the low-budget adventure film *War Party* (1965), co-starring newcomers Michael T. Mikler and Davey Davison. Laurie played an Indian girl named Nicoma who leads a Cavalry patrol to a mission besieged by marauding Comanche Indians. On the trek through an open pass, Nicoma helps in setting dynamite to kill the Indians but she perishes in the explosion.

After playing small TV roles as a surgical nurse on *Twelve O'Clock High* and an alien on *The Invaders*, Mock was cast in the made-for-TV movie, *52 Miles to Terror*. MGM decided that the film was too violent for television and would play better on drive-in screens across the country. Hence, it was re-titled *Hot Rods to Hell* and given a theatrical release in 1967 with the tagline "Call them punks…. Call them animals…. But you better get out of their way! They're souped up for thrills and there's no limit to what they'll do!" Mock played Tina Philips who accompanies her parents Tom and Peg, played by Dana Andrews and Jeanne Crain, and her younger brother on a road trip to the California desert where Tom has purchased a motel-restaurant. During their drive Mimsy Farmer, Paul Bertoya, and Gene Kirkwood, as three youths out for kicks, harass them. When the family meets up with them at a filling station, Tom threatens the hellions with police action, which only antagonizes them further as they call in more of their friends to give the Philips family a hard time. Once the family reaches their destination, they are appalled that the teen hoodlums have taken over the deserted motel and use it for drinking binges. The inexperienced Tina becomes interested in Bertoya's Duke who tries to unsuccessfully seduce her. The family then flees the motel to try to reach Paul's brother's house fifty-two miles away while being pursued by Duke and his buddy. Tired of fleeing, Tom turns his car around and parks it with the headlights on, blinding speeding Duke who crashes his souped-up sports car. In exchange for not calling the police, the teens vow to mend their ways.

Mock received positive reviews for her performance in *Hot Rods to Hell*, with particular praise from Howard Thompson of the *New York Times* who commented, "Laurie Mock does well as the sensitive daughter." According to the *Hot Rods to Hell* press book, MGM too was impressed with the young actress and signed to a five-year contract. However, she never appeared in another film from that studio.

After playing a naïve goody-goody in *Hot Rods to Hell*, Mock got a chance to show her wild side in *Riot on Sunset Strip* (1967). Laurie and Mimsy Farmer were teamed again in this Sam Katzman produced quickie, but Mock was cast as bad girl Liz-Ann (*Variety*'s reviewer remarked that she "registers effectively") as the out-for-kicks friend of Farmer's more conservative Andy. Katzman also recruited from *Hot Rods to Hell* cast member Paul Bertoya for a lead role in this movie. All the ingredients were present—hippies, drugs, protestors, free love, police brutality—to make *Riot on Sunset Strip* a camp classic of the alienated youth movie genre. The film opens with young people milling about on the street with deadly serious voiceover narration that begins, "These are not dangerous revolutionaries in a beleaguered city under martial law. These are teenagers on the Sunset Strip in Los Angeles, Cal-

Poster art for *Hot Rods to Hell* (MGM, 1967) featuring Laurie Mock (center).

ifornia—on a peaceful night. Irresponsible, wild, beat, protest youths with nowhere to go, nothing to do, no goal in life. Just searching for something that they have demanded throughout the ages—the right of self-expression and recognition. What you see here is happening all over the world and in every country the question is the same—what to do about the youth problem?"

Hanging out on the Sunset Strip at a club called Pandora's Box, underage high school kids Andy, Liz-Ann, and their beaus get involved in a brawl and are hauled off to jail for breaking curfew. Andy's estranged police detective father, played by Aldo Ray, who hasn't seen his daughter in four years has been informed of her arrest. When Liz-Ann and the gang decide to return to the strip the following night, Andy declines, but when she finds her mother in another alcoholic daze she changes her mind. There she hooks up again with the wild Liz-Ann and Schuyler Hayden as Herby, the bored son of a movie star. He gets a bunch of kids to break into an abandoned house on the Strip where drinking leads to marijuana then to LSD and finally a gang rape of a drugged Andy. As she is upstairs with five guys, Liz-Ann clad in a green and white striped mini-dress is freaking out downstairs dancing around and laughing. When the police raid the house, all the kids get out except Andy and Liz-Ann who fingers the guys who raped her friend. Andy's father beats Herby to a pulp with cries of "police brutality" in his ears, but he is able to stave off the impending riot.

Despite her promise to be a drive-in movie star, Mock never copped a lead role in a B-movie again. Television kept her tied to western series, playing Mexicans or homesteaders. On the big screen she turned up playing a very minor role as a waitress at a discotheque in John Cassavetes' award-winning experimental film *Faces*, about marital infidelity, starring John Marley and Gena Rowlands, which was shot in 1965 but not completed and released until 1968. Mock's last known film role was another small part in the violent urban thriller *Dirty Harry* (1971) with Clint Eastwood.

Laurie went on to study Spanish classical dance before quitting show business. She eventually married former journalist and screenwriter Frederick Samitaur-Smith and they became partners in real estate development. Samitaur-Smith remarked in *Grid*, "We were both successful, but discontent. Acting and writing movie screenplays just didn't meet our objectives. We were not in control of what we wanted to do in life. We decided to take a different pathway." Today Frederick and Laurie Samitaur-Smith are two of the most successful and admired developers in Los Angeles after transforming a depressed industrial area of Culver City into "a hot commercial address and architectural tourist destination."

Film Appearances

1965   **War Party** (20th Century–Fox) d. Leslie Selander

1967   **Hot Rods to Hell** (MGM) d. John Brahm

Riot on Sunset Strip (AIP) d. Arthur Dreifuss

1968   **Faces** (Continental) d. John Cassavetes

1971   **Dirty Harry** (Warner Bros.) d. Don Siegel

Television Appearances

The Great Adventure "Kentucky's Bloody Ground" 4/3/1964 CBS

The Great Adventure "The Siege of Boonesborough" 4/10/1964 CBS
Twelve O'Clock High "The Hollow Man" 3/14/1966 ABC
The Invaders "The Ivy Curtain" 3/21/1967 ABC
Cimarron Strip "The Last Wolf" 12/14/1967 CBS
The High Chaparral "A Joyful Noise" 3/24/1968 NBC
Gunsmoke "The Judas Gun" 1/19/1970 CBS

☆ VALORA NOLAND ☆

Sultry blonde Valora Noland was born Valor Baum in Seattle, Washington. Purportedly, her mother, Mrs. Franz Baum, was so moved by Winston Churchill's famous speech in 1939 where he uttered the immortal words, "Death and sorrow will be the companions of our journey; hardship our garment; constancy and valor our only shield" that she named her newborn daughter Valor. When she decided to become an actress the nineteen-year-old beauty added an 'a' to her first name and changed her last name. Hence, Valora Noland was born.

Noland studied at the esteemed Pasadena Playhouse where she partook in their basic curriculum, which included many theatre arts courses. She left after only a year and a half when discovered by an agent. She immediately began playing roles on *The Rifleman* and *Laramie*. She made her film debut a year later as "the girl" in Daniel Mann's *Five Finger Exercise*, but her scene was excised from the final print. Back on TV, Noland was a top contender for Billie Jo Bradley on the series *Petticoat Junction*. Noland did not get the role but she did get praise from the show's creator, Paul Henning, who gushed in *TV Guide*, "She's remarkably beautiful like a little wild deer." Noland told the magazine that when she found out that she lost out on the series she was happy because she had just won a part in a new AIP film.

That movie was *Beach Party* (1963) starring Frankie Avalon and Annette Funicello. The two stars played Frankie and Dolores, two teenage lovebirds, who come to the Malibu beach area for a private two-week vacation. But unbeknownst to Frankie, Dolores has invited their friends to join them. Noland played Dolores' best friend Rhonda who is first seen clad in a revealing yellow polka-dot bikini doing stretching exercises on the beach, which causes the "unhinged" surfers to wipeout. During the course of the film, Dolores develops a friendship, which she misinterprets as a romance, with Prof. Jason Sutwell (Robert Cummings), who is secretly studying the mating habits of Dolores and her friends. Rhonda can not understand her friend who turned her romantic love nest with Frankie into "a teenage flophouse" and offers her some advice. Later the aggressive Rhonda sits frustrated while boyfriend Deadhead (Jody McCrea) prefers eating his sandwich to making out with her. With her untamed blonde hair, Noland looked like the quintessential beach girl and played the part well, especially in her scenes with Annette.

Beach Party was such a huge hit for AIP that it immediately commissioned a sequel. Most of the young cast returned for *Muscle Beach Party* (1964). Still set on the beaches of California, the surfers and their girls tangled with a bunch of bodybuilders rather than Eric Von Zipper and his motorcycle gang. This time, though Valora played a character named Animal,

On the beach with John Ashley, Frankie Avalon, Annette Funicello, Jody McCrea, and Valora Noland in *Muscle Beach Party* (AIP, 1964). *Billy Rose Theatre Collection, The New York Public Library for the Performing Arts, Astor, Lenox and Tilden Foundations.*

the man-hungry friend to Annette's Didi, but she was really just reprising the role of Rhonda from the previous film with less to do. When the audience first encounters Animal, she and the guys are voicing their disapproval with the sleeping arrangements by Didi, who created a make shift wall to separate the boys from the girls at the beach house. Demurely clad in a leopard skin one-piece bathing suit, the boy crazy Animal has a crush on Frankie, the beach's top surfer. But her clumsiness keeps getting in her way as she goes to get him a hot dog and soft drink from the refreshment stand and winds up spilling the drink all over him.

Muscle Beach Party was Noland's swan song for AIP and but not from the beach genre. Although the character of Animal turned up in the rest of the beach movies (played by different actresses), Noland may have moved on to get more substantial roles. In 1964 she told *Show Business Beauty* magazine, "What I want is a chance at a complicated part, something that will show the scope of feeling I have to give." She was part of the teenage set in the barely released film *The Fun Lovers* (1964) that featured newcomers Charles Grodin, John Gabriel and Julie Sommars. The movie was re-released in 1969 as *Sex and the College Girl*. Valora co-starred with Stuart Anderson in the unreleased *Summer Children* (1965). Just rediscovered and restored, it is an early example of the American New Wave of filmmaking beautifully shot in b/w by cinematographer Vilmos Zsigmond on Catalina Island. Valora is wonderful in it. She next journeyed to the Philippines to play a cheating wife whose jealous husband (Michael Parsons) accidentally kills the uncle of her Filipino lover in *The Passionate Strangers* (1966) directed by Eddie Romero. Since the murdered man was a labor leader, this starts a workers riot. Though this film too went unnoticed, it was a step above the cheap horror films Romero began producing and directing in the Philippines a few years later.

Television offered Noland a variety of high profile guest star roles from a Grand Duchess trying to save her country from being overrun by enemy agents on *The Man from U.N.C.L.E.* to a mysterious beauty with a secret on *The Virginian* to a heroic freedom fighter battling a race of conquering Nazis on *Star Trek*. Noland's versatility may have led her to being cast in the second female lead in *The War Wagon* (1967). This entertaining western starred John Wayne as a vengeful rancher and Kirk Douglas as a cocky gunfighter who plot with three others to hijack an evil cattle baron's war wagon carrying a half million dollars in gold. Playing Kate, the young wife of an old supply wagon driver (Keenan Wynn) who falls for Billy, a young drunken demolitions expert (Robert Walker), Noland more than holds her own opposite some of Hollywood's biggest names. Her scene where she reveals to Walker's Billy that her husband bartered her ("My parents traded me for twenty dollars and a horse. They's poor") is very touchingly performed.

Despite her good performance in *The War Wagon*, Noland decided to leave Hollywood. She "simply wanted to act" and was unhappy with some of the promotion she had to do for the movie. That part of the business was confusing to her and one of the reasons why she abandoned her career. However, Valora left on a high note. Her last role was playing a futuristic Nazi on *Star Trek* in one of the series' best episodes, "Pattern of Force." That was her swan song, though she is credited as playing a small role in the obscure comedy *Up Your Teddy Bear* (1970) starring Julie Newmar and Wally Cox. It is not her. Per Valora, producer and friend Don Joslyn used a lookalike actress because he did not know where she disappeared to.

Film Appearances

1962   **Five Finger Exercise** (Columbia) d. Daniel Mann

1963   **Beach Party** (AIP) d. William Asher

1964   **Muscle Beach Party** (AIP) d. William Asher
The Fun Lovers [re-released in 1969 as **Sex and the College Girl**] (Entertainment Enterprises) d. Joseph Adler

1965   **Summer Children** (Unreleased) d. James Bruner

1966   **The Passionate Strangers** (U.S./Philippines, RAF Industries) d. Eddie Romero

1967   **The War Wagon** (Universal) d. Burt Kennedy

Television Appearances

The Rifleman "The High Country" 12/18/1961 ABC
Laramie "Double Eagles" 11/20/1962 NBC
DuPont Show of the Week "Two Faces of Treason" 2/10/1962 NBC
The Donna Reed Show "Everywhere That Mary Goes" 3/21/1963 ABC
Dr. Kildare "A Hand Held Out in Darkness" 5/30/1963 NBC
Burke's Law "Who Killed Billy Joe?" 11/8/1963 ABC
Wagon Train "The Last Circle Up" 4/27/1964 NBC

The Donna Reed Show "The Unheroic Hero" 3/18/1965 ABC
Burke's Law "Who Killed Hamlet?" 4/7/1965 ABC
The Man from U.N.C.L.E. "The Round Table Affair" 3/25/1966 NBC
The Virginian "The Girl on the Pinto" 3/19/1967 NBC
Mannix "Warning: Live Blueberries" 10/28/1967 CBS
Star Trek "Patterns of Force" 2/16/1968 NBC

☆ ANGELIQUE PETTYJOHN ☆

Angelique Pettyjohn was a pretty, uninhibited blonde who played trashy and tough girl roles during the late '60s. After appearing in a few risqué mid-sixties sex films, Pettyjohn copped a small role in the Elvis Presley musical *Clambake* (1967). Bigger roles followed in a variety of drive-in movie genres, including the biker film *Hell's Belles* (1969), the horror opus *The Mad Doctor of Blood Island* (1969), and the science-fiction tale *The Curious Female* (1969). But Pettyjohn is most remembered by *Star Trek* fans for her appearance in one of the series' most infamous episodes, "The Gamesters of Triskelion."

Angelique Pettyjohn was born on March 10, 1943, in California and raised in Salt Lake City, Utah. Not much is known about Pettyjohn's early life. Using only her first name of Angelique she made her acting debut playing a small role in the John Derek directed drama *Childish Things* (1966), starring Don Murray as an alcoholic ex–G.I. working for the mob and Derek's soon-to-be wife Linda Evans as the young girl who may change him. The film remained on the shelf until 1969, when Derek tried to find an interested distributor, now that Evans was well known due to her success on the TV western series *The Big Valley*. He did not get any takers until a few years later when the film was released theatrically as *Confessions of Tom Harris*. Despite Angelique's relatively tiny role, the reviewer in *Variety* who saw the film at a film festival in 1969 noticed the newcomer and remarked that she was "effective in a bit."

In 1967, Pettyjohn had just the right look to begin making TV guest appearances on a number of fantasy, spy, and science fiction series. One of her more popular roles was playing spy Charlie Watkins on *Get Smart*. The male spy goes undercover in the form of the shapely Pettyjohn as a Las Vegas cigarette girl who aids Don Adams' Maxwell Smart. So successful was her performance that she reprised the role in a second episode as Charlie disguised himself as a showgirl in the Pussycats Club.

On the big screen, Angelique played small roles in *The Touch of Her Flesh* (1967), about a husband who, after he discovers his wife in bed with another man, goes on a murderous rampage against all women, and in *The Love Rebellion* (1967), a kinky sex drama about group love-ins. Angelique began being billed as "Angelique Pettyjohn" starting with *Clambake* (1967) starring Elvis Presley. In this tuneful romp set in Miami, Pettyjohn played Gloria, one of the denizens at a swanky hotel who, along with other female guests Shelley Fabares and Suzie Kaye, flips for rich playboy Bill Bixby. Presley as a water ski instructor goes unnoticed and is befriended by the rich husband hunting Fabares, unaware that he is actually a millionaire's son incognito.

Publicity shot of hog riding Angelique Pettyjohn in *Hell's Belles* **(AIP, 1969).** *Billy Rose Theatre Collection, The New York Public Library for the Performing Arts, Astor, Lenox and Tilden Foundations*

Back on the small screen in 1968, Pettyjohn appeared in her most remembered acting role, that of Shahna in the *Star Trek* episode "The Gamesters of Triskelion." In this episode, Kirk and members of his crew are imprisoned on the planet Triskelion where the enslaved Thralls compete in combat games. The green-haired Shahna, scantily clad in a very revealing silver lamé two-piece outfit, is selected by the Providers to train Kirk as a warrior. When the Captain wagers his crew's and the Thralls' freedom versus the entire enslavement of the *Enterprise*, the captors choose Shahna to be one of the three fighters to challenge him.

The year 1969 was very busy for Pettyjohn. She looked authentic playing a saloon girl in the western *Heaven with a Gun*, starring Glenn Ford, and then was cast as a biker chick in the popular *Hell's Belles*. In the film, Adam Roarke as nasty biker leader Tampa steals a motorcycle from Dan (Jeremy Slate), a motorcycle endurance racer, and leaves his cast-off girlfriend Cathy (Jocelyn Lane) as a trade-off. Pettyjohn's Cherry becomes Tampa's new motorcycle mama as Dan with Cathy in tow pursues the gang to the Mexican border. After killing off three bikers, the rest including Cherry desert Tampa, leaving him to face Dan one-on-one. Dan breaks Tampa's shoulder and regains his bike, leaving Cathy with the beaten leader. As biker films go, *Hell's Belles* was one of the best and received semi-positive reviews even from staid publications that would never recommend a motorcycle drama. *Variety* in particular praised the movie and found that Pettyjohn "shows promise" in her role.

In the Eddie Romero-produced *Mad Doctor of Blood Island* (1969), shot on location in the Philippines, Pettyjohn played Sheila Willard, a woman who travels to Blood Island looking for her father. She meets John Ashley's pathologist who is investigating the discovery of a human corpse with green blood. On the tropical paradise, they encounter Dr. Lorca, a madman who experiments with a fountain of youth drug that turns a human into the hideous chlorophyll creature. While searching for her missing father and fleeing from the monster, Pettyjohn finds time to disrobe for the camera for a love scene with Ashley. Filmed on a shoestring budget, the movie (a companion film to *Brides of Blood*) was popular enough with the drive-in crowd to spawn a sequel, *Beast of Blood* (1971) starring Ashley and Celeste Yarnall.

Actress Jenny Maxwell's former husband Paul Rapp was responsible for Pettyjohn's last film of 1969, *The Curious Female*. In the year 2177, a totalitarian government has outlawed love, romance, and sex. A young couple defies the law and views an old film from 1969 about three coeds with sexual hang-ups. As one of the college students, Angelique's character was reared not to have sex without love.

During the '70s Pettyjohn made sporadic film appearances. She did a semi-

Biker chick Angelique Pettyjohn tries to make time with gang leader Adam Roarke in *Hell's Belles* (AIP, 1969).

nude turn as a prostitute in the bizarre comedy *Up Your Teddy Bear* (1970), starring Julie Newmar and Wally Cox, and played a high priced call girl living in Singapore who gets involved with espionage agents, Chinese defectors, and homosexual gangsters in *Dragon Lady* (1971). The latter went unreleased until Troma Pictures bought the rights and released it in 1985 as *G. I. Executioner*. During the remainder of the '70s, Pettyjohn concentrated on her burlesque act, which she performed in Los Angeles and Las Vegas. It is probably through this that she was lured to appear in a few hardcore adult films in the early eighties using the name Heaven St. John and Angelique. Though she was pushing forty, Pettyjohn was in fabulous shape and looked terrific. She returned to mainstream films, playing a stripper in *Weekend Pass* (1984), a repo wife in the cult *Repo Man* (1984), an owner of a striptease club in *Takin' It Off* (1985), an Amazon warrior named Whiplash in *The Lost Empire* (1985), and an ESP-sensitive woman in *Biohazard* (1985). Reportedly, the latter contains scenes of bloopers at the end, including Pettyjohn's platinum blonde wig slipping off during a vigorous sexual encounter.

Angelique Pettyjohn appeared in a few more films before her death from cancer on February 14, 1992. She was only forty-nine years old. Despite her '60s drive-in movie appearances, her '70s stint as a burlesque queen, and her '80s wallow in porn films, Angelique will be most remembered as the girl with green hair from *Star Trek*.

Film Appearances

1967   **Hotel** (Warner Bros.) d. Richard Quine
        The Cool Ones (Warner Bros.) d. Gene Nelson
        The Love Rebellion (Cannon) d. Joseph W. Sarno
        Clambake (United Artists) d. Arthur Nadel

1968   **Where Were You When the Lights Went Out?** (MGM) d. Hy Averback

1969   **Heaven with a Gun** (MGM) d. Lee H. Katzin
        Hell's Belles (AIP) d. Maury Dexter
        The Mad Doctor of Blood Island (U.S./ Philippines; Hemisphere) d. Eddie Romero
        The Curious Female (Fanfare) d. Paul Rapp

1970   **Tell Me That You Love Me Junie Moon** (Paramount) d. Otto Preminger
        Up Your Teddy Bear (Geneni) d. Don Joslyn

1972   **Confessions of Tom Harris** (Filmworld) [filmed in 1966 as **Childish Things**] d. John Derek/ David Nelson

1974   **Bordello** (Cambist) d. Ole Ege

1979   **Going in Style** (Warner Bros.) d. Martin Brest

1982   **Titillation** (Adult) d. Damon Christian
        Stalag 69 (Adult)
        Body Talk (Adult) d. Pedie Sweet

1984   **Weekend Pass** (Crown International) d. Lawrence Bassoff
        Repo Man (Universal) d. Alex Cox

1985   **The Lost Empire** (JGM Enterprises) d. Jim Wynorski
        G. I. Executioner (Troma) [filmed in 1971 as **Dragon Lady**] d. Joel M. Reed
        Takin' It Off (Direct-to-video) d. Ed Hansen
        Biohazard (21st Century) d. Fred Olen Rey

1986   **Famous Ta-Tas** (Adult)

1988   **The Wizard of Speed and Time**

1990 **Sorority Girls and the Creature from Hell** (Direct-to-video) d. John McBrearty

(Shapiro-Glickenhaus Entertainment) d. Mike Jittlov

Television Appearances

The Green Hornet "Corpse of the Year" 1/13 & 1/27/1967 ABC
Mr. Terrific "I Can't Fly" 1/23/1967 CBS
The Girl from U.N.C.L.E. "The Uncle—Samurai Affair" 3/28/1967 NBC
Get Smart "Smart Fit the Battle of Jericho" 2/18/1967 NBC
Felony Squad "Target!" 2/20/1967 ABC
Batman "A Piece of the Action" 3/1/1967 ABC
Get Smart "Pussycats Galore" 4/1/1967 NBC
Star Trek "The Gamesters of Triskelion" 1/5/1968 NBC
Love, American Style "Love and the Modern Wife" 10/27/1969 ABC
Hill Street Blues "Bangladesh Slowly" 11/1/1984 NBC

☆ PAT PRIEST ☆

An All-American blonde beauty, Pat Priest is best known for playing Marilyn Munster, the normal niece, on the cult TV sitcom *The Munsters*. Unlike most '60s drive-in movie starlets, who knew their acting limitations, Priest boasted at one point in her career that her greatest ambition was to give an Oscar-winning performance. Alas, all she got to do on drive-in screens across America was to shake her bikini-clad fanny at Elvis Presley in *Easy Come, Easy Go* (1966) and scream in fright in *The Incredible Two-Headed Transplant* (1971).

Pat Priest was born in Bountiful, Utah, on August 15, 1936. Her mother was Ivy Baker Priest who became the Treasurer of the United States during the Eisenhower administration. The acting bug bit Pat at age fifteen when she lip-synched to a Beatrice Kay novelty record in a show her mother was mounting for the Bountiful First Ward Church. She proved to be such a hit that she accompanied the show to other local venues and appeared on Salt Lake City television. In 1952, Priest relocated with her mother to Washington and took the town by storm. While a senior in high school she did record pantomimes on a local television program called *The Art Lamb Show* and began appearing in commercials. She attended Marjorie Webster Junior College on a drama scholarship and went on to win the Grand National Speech Contest in the dramatic interpretation division. She told a magazine reporter years later, "Once you've heard the applause of a theatre audience, you can't get it out of your system."

While in Washington, Priest had her 'coming out' party and her picture appeared in *Life* magazine. She was elected Queen of the Azalea Festival and went on to be crowned the Queen of the Virginia Apple Blossom Festival and Queen of the President's Cup Regatta. With all this publicity, it is no wonder the nineteen-year-old beauty very quickly landed a husband, Naval officer Pierce A. Jensen, Jr. When he was transferred to Point Mugu in 1962, fifty miles north of Los Angeles, Priest decided to give acting a try. She took drama classes with Jeff Corey, did commercials, tested unsuccessfully for a number of series including *Gilligan's Island* and landed bit roles in two movies.

In 1964, things began to pick up for Priest as she played Bill Bixby's girlfriend on an episode of *My Favorite Martian* and

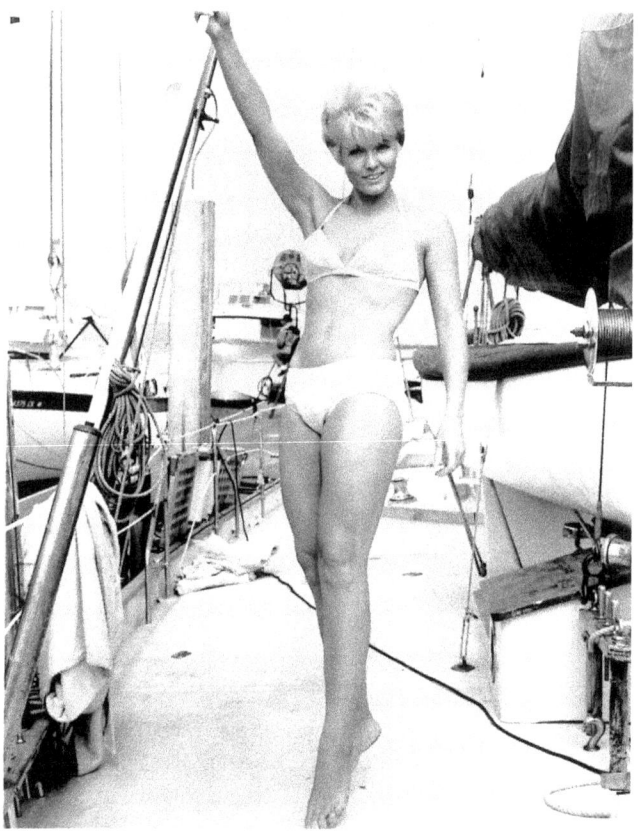

Pat Priest leaves her Marilyn Munster persona far behind in this publicity shot from *Easy Come, Easy Go* (Paramount, 1967).

a scientist's wife who becomes the first victim of a South Pole plankton experiment gone awry on *Voyage to the Bottom of the Sea*. Then as luck would have it, the twenty-eight year old wife and mother of two sons took over for Beverly Owen as Marilyn Munster in episode fourteen of the TV comedy series, *The Munsters*, in 1964 when Owen quit the series to get married. One of the sitcom's running jokes is that the Munsters, who resembled Universal Studios' series of monsters, considered themselves a typical ordinary family and looked down on their niece Marilyn for being "abnormal." But in fact she was a gorgeous blonde and it was Herman, his wife Lily, their son Eddie and Grandpa who were the strange ones. As the ingenue in the series, Priest took backseat to the broad playing of Fred Gwynne, Yvonne DeCarlo and Al Lewis. For the most part, all she had to do was look hurtful as each of her many suitors was scared away by her family, who blamed Marilyn's looks for her not being able to keep a man.

When *The Munsters* ended its second and final season, the studio signed the entire cast except for Pat Priest to appear in a feature film. The producers felt that Priest (who was pushing thirty) was too old to play a teenager and cast contract player Debbie Watson in the part instead. Priest revealed in *Written Out of Television* that when she found out, "I started to cry, I was so upset and Al [Lewis], who was like a sweet father to me, was the one that talked to me and calmed me down. They [the cast] all felt that it wasn't right, but they couldn't do anything about it."

Though she lost out on *The Munsters* film, Priest nabbed an Elvis Presley movie as a consolation. In *Easy Come, Easy Go* (1967) Presley played a navy frogman on his last assignment who, while deactivating a mine, stumbles upon a treasure chest in the hull of a ship called Port of Call. Once a civilian, he devises a way to retrieve the Spanish coins and his helped by the granddaughter (Dodie Marshall) of the sunken ship's captain while being hindered by a devious socialite (Priest). *Easy Come, Easy Go* should have co-starred British lass Suzanna Leigh, a Paramount contract player, as the society girl, but problems with SAG prevented her from taking the role. Priest stepped in and does a more than adequate job. The reviewer in *Variety* raved, "[Priest] is also excellent." This role will surprise some of Priest's *Munsters* fans as the demure blonde (though wearing an unflattering headband) looks terrific clad in a series of skimpy bikinis playing a very deceitful character. During the course of the film, the out-for-kicks playgirl distracts some navy crew members as her boyfriend (Skip Ward) secretly photographs a naval operation, tries to pick up Elvis to get her beau jealous and tries to steal the treasure.

Priest has given a number of interviews over the years where her memories of working with Elvis are fond ones, though she has one major regret—having purchased a 1967 El Dorado from Presley, she traded it in for a Pontiac two years later!

Unlike co-star Dodie Marshall, whose film career ended with *Easy Come, Easy Go*, Priest continued acting a bit longer. She guest starred on a number of TV shows, most notably playing a stewardess having to contend with the fumbling Lucille Ball as Lucy Carmichael on her way to swinging mod London in an episode of *The Lucy Show*. On the big screen, Priest appeared in what should have been an instant career killer, the distasteful horror film, *The Incredible Two-Headed Transplant* (1971) not to be confused with *The Thing with Two Heads* released the following year. In the film (whose tag line proclaimed, "One brain wants to love…. One brain wants to kill!), Priest plays the put-upon wife of a mad doctor (wild-eyed Bruce Dern) who surgically attaches the head of a psychopathic maniac loose from an asylum onto the shoulders of his retarded burly handyman. The creature

Could it be the intense look on the faces of Pat Priest, Bruce Dern, and Casey Kasem are because they are out to strangle their agents for getting them involved in *The Incredible Two-Headed Transplant* (AIP, 1971)?

then goes on a wild murder spree. During the course of the film Priest is ogled by the simpleton, kidnapped and assaulted by the psychopath, held prisoner in the laboratory by her demented husband when she discovers what he has created and then carried off by the two-headed creature to a cave.

Despite *The Incredible Two-Headed Transplant*, Priest's career limped along. She played a nurse in the film *Some Call It Loving* (1973) and then played Sue Ann Niven's (Betty White) competitive sister Lila who gets a job on a competing station as its "Happy Homemaker" on a hilarious episode of *The Mary Tyler Moore Show* in 1976. Soon after, Priest left show business. In 1988, she was lured out of retirement to join ex-cast members Al Lewis and Butch Patrick in a TBS retrospective on *The Munsters*, which preceded the start of a new syndicated series entitled *The Munsters Today*. Pat Priest is now a grandmother who resides with her second husband in Idaho, where for the past twenty years she has been restoring and selling houses. But she does find time to make occasional guest appearances at autograph shows across the country.

Film Appearances

1964 **Looking for Love** (MGM) [uncredited] d. Don Weis

1965 **Quick, Before It Melts** (MGM) [uncredited] d. Delbert Mann

1967 **Easy Come, Easy Go** (Paramount) d. John Rich

1971 **The Incredible Two-Headed Transplant** (AIP) d. Anthony M. Lanza

1973 **Some Call It Loving** (Cine-Globe) d. James B. Harris

1995 **Here Come the Munsters** (TV-movie) [cameo] d. Robert Ginty

2000 **Al Lewis: Forever Grandpa** (short) d. Lawrence Williams

Television Appearances

Big Town 9/16/1954 CBS
The Many Loves of Dobie Gillis "The Gigolo" 11/7/1961 CBS
The Jack Benny Show "Jack and Dennis Do Impersonations" 2/25/1964 CBS
Perry Mason "The Case of the Tandem Target" 5/14/1964 CBS
Valentine's Day "The Life You Save Is Yours" 9/18/1964 ABC
Voyage to the Bottom of the Sea "The Price of Doom" 10/12/1964 ABC
My Favorite Martian "My Uncle the Folk Singer" 11/8/1964 CBS
The Munsters (series regular as Marilyn Munster) 12/10/1964 to 9/1/1966 CBS
Death Valley Days "The Wild West's Biggest Train Hold Up" 3/28/1965 SYN
Marineland Carnival (special) 4/18/1965 CBS
Perry Mason "The Case of the Crafty Kidnapper" 5/15/1966 CBS
The Lucy Show "Lucy Flies to London" 10/17/1966 CBS
Dateline: Hollywood 6/29/1967 ABC
Hollywood Backstage 7/6/1967 SYN
Mannix "Beyond the Shadow of a Dream" 11/4/1967 CBS
Run for Your Life "Beware My Love" 2/28/1968 NBC
The Red Skelton Show 3/19/1968 CBS
Ironside "Alias Mr. Braithwaite" 9/18/1969 NBC
Bewitched "And Something Makes Four" 10/16/1969 ABC
Bewitched "Samantha's Lost Weekend" 1/8/1970 ABC
Bewitched "Just a Kid Again" 2/26/1970 ABC
Mission: Impossible "The Field" 1/23/1971 CBS
The Mary Tyler Moore Show "Sue Ann's Sister" 10/9/1976 CBS
The Best of the Munsters (special) 1988 TBS

Also

Dr. Kildare, *Wendy and Me*, and *The Bob Hope Show*

☆ JULIET PROWSE ☆

Leggy Juliet Prowse is best know for her singing and dancing talent, so many fans may be surprised to learn that during the swinging '60s, she was a staple of low-budget drive-in movie fare. In her second feature she co-starred opposite Elvis Presley in *G. I. Blues* (1960) and received an equal amount of publicity when she turned down a second chance to star opposite the King in *Blue Hawaii* (1961). Despite her dancing prowess and vivacious personality, Juliet was relegated to black-and-white melodramatic programmers such as *The Right Approach* (1961) with singer Frankie Vaughan and *Who Killed Teddy Bear?* (1965) with Sal Mineo.

Juliet Prowse was born Sept. 25, 1936, in Bombay, India. Her father was a British manager for Westinghouse and died when Juliet was three. Her mother Phyllis Donne then relocated to South Africa where Juliet and her brother Clive were reared. Prowse began taking ballet lessons as a young child and when she was fourteen, she was named "Baby Ballerina" of the Festival Ballet in Johannesburg. At seventeen she was pursuing a ballet career in London but she had to switch to modern dance when she grew too tall to be a ballerina. Undaunted, the 5'7" beauty landed the lead dance role of Princess Samaris in the 1955 London production of *Kismet*, which won her raves from the theater critics. She remained with the show for two years and then accepted engagements in a renowned topless club in Paris (she remained fully clothed) and as part of a traveling dance review, which she founded.

Celebrated choreographer Hermes Pan saw her dancing in Rome and was so impressed that he convinced her to go to Hollywood. He brought Juliet to the attention of the studio heads at 20th Century-Fox, who signed the vivacious dancer to a contract and gave her a small role in the big budget Cole Porter musical *Can-Can* (1960), starring Frank Sinatra, Shirley MacLaine, Maurice Chavalier, and Louis Jourdan. Dancer Barrie Chase was also in the film but when she dropped out her part was combined with Prowse's to give the newcomer more screen time. During the filming of a Can-Can number, Soviet Premier Nikita Khrushchev visited the set

Juliet Prowse kicks in the New Year.

and denounced the dance as being immoral. The story ran worldwide with a picture of Prowse in her Parisian costume. When *Can-Can* opened it received mixed reviews though Juliet won raves, especially for her dancing as the Snake in the Adam and Eve number. Years later when asked by writer Kim Garfield of *Drama-Logue* what she thought of her first film, Prowse remarked, "I didn't think it was a good movie ... it was just so—uh—un-French. Except for Chevalier and Louis Jourdan, the casting was all wrong. It was just too slick. But for me it was wonderful. I mean talk about a steppingstone!"

Not only did the Khrushchev incident bring her notoriety, but Prowse began dating her leading man, Frank Sinatra. She immediately became the toast of Hollywood gossip columnists. For her next movie, Fox loaned her out to Paramount to co-star opposite Elvis Presley in his first musical after being discharged from the army. Regarding her first reaction when learning that she was being paired with Presley, Prowse commented in *Drama-Logue*, "My first thought was, 'Oh my God. I'm going to work with a juvenile delinquent.' That was my first impression of him. Well, he couldn't have been more the opposite. A terrific guy!" *G. I. Blues* (1960) featured Presley as Tulsa McLean, a tail gunner on duty in Germany who reluctantly accepts a wager that he can "spend the night" with a frosty nightclub performer named Lili, played by Prowse. Tulsa only agrees to the bet because he is trying to save money to open a nightclub with some buddies back in the states. Complications arise when Tulsa begins to fall in love with Lili. The icy cabaret singer loosens up with Tulsa who tries to back out of the bet. An innocent babysitting gig at Lili's apartment wins Tulsa the money but the bet is revealed to Lili who storms off. However, true love conquers all as Lili accepts Tulsa's marriage proposal during an Armed Forces show. Despite playing a cabaret singer, Prowse really does not vocalize much since this was Elvis' return to the big screen after a two-year absence, but she and the King do perform a duet, "Gotta Pocket Full of Rainbows."

Juliet Prowse received stacks of fan mail from the teenage audience and kudos from the critics for her work in *G. I. Blues*. Her reviews were all favorable. *Variety* stated that "Juliet Prowse is a first rate dancer and has a pixie charm," while Bosley Crowther in the *New York Times* wrote that Prowse "makes a pleasant companion." *Time* magazine panned the movie and Elvis but found that Juliet "is absolutely out of place in this picture. She looks human." The exhibitors in *The Motion Picture Herald* voted her a "Star of Tomorrow" for 1961, and Juliet received a *Photoplay* Gold Medal Award nomination for Most Promising New Star (Female). She lost out to Paula Prentiss and Deborah Walley, who tied for the accolade.

The chemistry between Presley and Prowse continued off-screen as the duo became an item despite Prowse's on-going affair with Frank Sinatra. To keep the momentum going on screen, producer Hal B. Wallis asked Fox to borrow Prowse again for Elvis' next movie *Blue Hawaii* (1961) since they worked so well together previously. Fox agreed but fame may have come too quickly to the starlet who wanted "movie star" treatment, requesting that her own make-up man be hired for the film and the airfare paid for her secretary. Prowse explained to the Associated Press, "I have a face that is difficult to make up; I wanted someone who knew me." As for her secretary, "I wanted a companion. I didn't know anyone else in the company except Elvis, and he's always surrounded by a dozen buddies." Wallis vetoed both of Prowse's requests, and she asked to do a screen test with the Paramount makeup man. While waiting for the results, she reread the script and decided not to do the film. She commented, "[My] part had no character. I was only one of three girls in Elvis's life, and one 16-year-old had a more interesting part than mine." She also hated the dance number "Rock-A-Hula-Baby." She exclaimed to columnist Joe Hyams, "Are you ready for that title? Doesn't it get you—me doing the hula while Elvis sings?" Though Prowse had a point that the role would not take advantage of her singing and dancing abilities, the way she handled the matter by bowing out just before filming was to begin made her come across as more of a pampered prima donna than a career-conscious actress. Needless to say Hal Wallis and 20th Century–Fox were not happy with Prowse. She killed her chances of ever working with Presley again and the studio put her on suspension.

As if to punish her, Fox wasted Prowse in a string of forgettable movies all much worse than *Blue Hawaii*. *The Fiercest Heart* (1961) was set in 1837 South Africa, and Juliet's shapely gams were no where in sight as she played the granddaughter of a Boer leader who gets romantically involved with a private in the British army played by Stuart Whitman amid a marauding Zulu tribe. Prowse was top billed and starred opposite British pop singer Frankie Vaughan in her second movie released in 1961. *The Right Approach* was a sleazy look at the underbelly of Hollywood. As the tag line proclaimed, "The Pleasure Joints.... The Joy-Rides.... The Hideaway Shacks.... The Lowdown on Bachelor Boys—And Their Search for Girls!" Prowse played a golddigging carhop out to snag a rich husband while Vaughan was a vile aspiring actor who uses anybody he can to get to the top. In the comedy western *The Second Time Around* (1961) Juliet is wasted in support of the film's star Debbie Reynolds, who gets elected sheriff of a wild and wooly frontier town in Arizona.

In 1962, despite her very public romance with Elvis Presley, Prowse accepted Frank Sinatra's marriage proposal. She was once again in the headlines but even more so when six weeks later she broke it off due to the fact that the singer wanted her to give up performing. Prowse didn't give up on her career but she did give up on 20th Century–Fox and was able to get released from her contract. She immediately began to remind fans of her musical talent with numerous appearances on all the top variety shows. She remained off the big screen until she accepted a role as an aspiring actress working as a DJ at a Manhattan discotheque in *Who Killed Teddy Bear?* (1965). Her hapless heroine is harassed by an obscene phone caller who begins stalking her, propositioned by her lesbian boss, and lusted after by the investigating vice detective. Not really a drive-in movie hit, the gritty drama became a staple of grimy 42nd Street movie houses. It has now developed a cult following especially among gay men, due to Prowse's co-star Sal Mineo as a shy busboy and obvious psychopath who is clad throughout the movie in the tightest of jeans, a Speedo bathing suit, and, most daringly, white bikini briefs. One of the '60s best dance sequences occurs near the end of this film as Prowse's Norah gives Mineo's Lawrence a lesson in doing the Watusi before he reveals that he is the stalker. This is arguably Juliet Prowse's most striking image on the big screen as she demonstrates what '60s go-go dancing is really all about.

After returning to South Africa to play an attorney's sympathetic wife who believes in the innocence of a Bantu tribesman wrongly accused of murder in *Dingaka* (1965), Prowse settled on television in her own sitcom entitled *Mona McCluskey*. Premiering during the 1965–66

Juliet Prowse's final acting role on the big screen was a small role in the Italian comedy *Run for Your Wife* (1966) as a Miami beach denizen romanced by Ugo Tognazzi, out to land himself a wealthy wife. According to co-star Deanna Lund, "At the time Juliet was still having a thing I think with Frank Sinatra. She was in great physical condition and she was always exercising! That's a weird thing to remember but I was pretty young and impressionable."

Prowse's swan song in films was the documentary *Spree* (1967), which featured clips of various Las Vegas acts. Though big screen super stardom eluded her, Juliet worked constantly on stage and in television. In 1966, she wowed Vegas audiences in a production of *Sweet Charity*, which she took to London. Her performance earned her the London Evening Standard's award for "Actress of the Year." Throughout the remainder of the '60s and all of the '70s Prowse was a staple of the TV variety, talk, and game show circuit while touring the nation in productions of *Mame*, *Irma La Douce*, *The Pajama Game*, and *Follies*. Surprisingly, doing a Broadway musical is probably the only thing that eluded Prowse in her long and successful career.

In 1980, Juliet Prowse was able to take time off from her busy schedule to marry actor John McCook, nine years her junior. The marriage was short-lived, but they did have a son together named Seth. Beginning in 1987, Prowse became the hostess for the annual *Championship Ballroom Dance Competition* on PBS. In 1995, Prowse was diagnosed with pancreatic cancer. A trooper until the end, her illness did not deter her from performing with Mickey Rooney in *Sugar Babies* at the Desert Inn in Las Vegas. The following year, Prowse was awarded, along with Mitzi Gaynor, the Professional Dancers Society Gypsy Award. A few weeks later, on September 14, 1996, Juliet Prowse passed away.

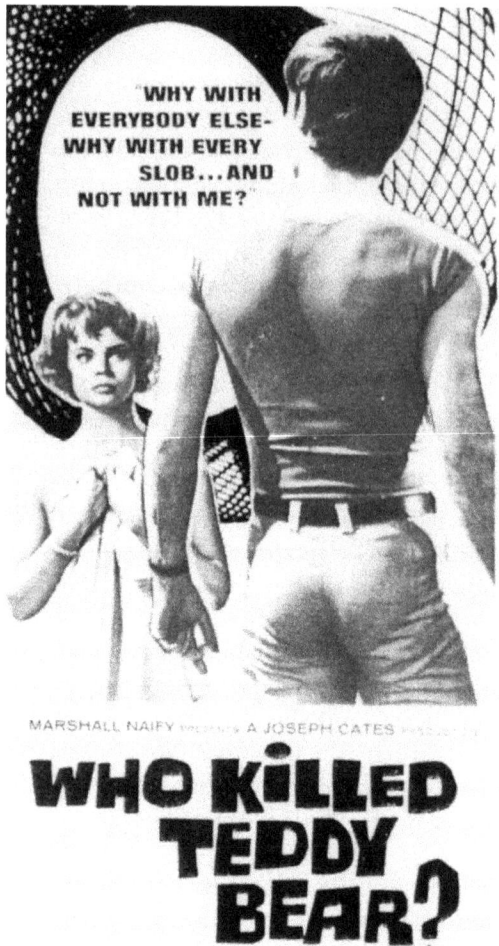

Poster art for the 42nd Street grind house classic *Who Killed Teddy Bear?* (Magna, 1965) starring Juliet Prowse as a discotheque disc jockey and Sal Mineo as a psycho-stalker with a penchant for wearing tight jeans.

season, the comedy series was an unfunny misfire lasting only one season, as Prowse energetically played a glamorous movie star who marries an air force sergeant played by Denny Miller and is forced to live on the male chauvinist's meager salary. For her performances, Prowse received *Photoplay* Gold Medal Award nominations in 1965 and 1966 for Best Female Star.

Film Appearances

1960 **Can-Can** (20th Century–Fox) d. Walter Lang
      G. I. Blues (Paramount) d. Norman Taurog
1961 **The Fiercest Heart** (20th Century–Fox) d. George Sherman
      The Right Approach (20th Century–Fox) d. David Butler
      The Second Time Around (20th Century–Fox) d. Vincent Sherman
1965 **Dingaka** (South Africa; Embassy) d. Jaime Uys
      Who Killed Teddy Bear? (Magna) d. Joseph Cates
1966 **Run for Your Wife/ Una Moglie Americana** (Italy/France; Allied Artists) d. Gian Luigi Polidoro
1967 **Spree** (Trans American) d. Walon Green & Mitchell Leisen
1971 **Second Chance** (TV-movie) d. Peter Tewksbury

Television Appearances— Drama, Comedy & Variety Series

The Frank Sinatra Timex Show (special) 12/13/1959 ABC
The Frank Sinatra Timex Show II (special) [singing w/ Frank Sinatra "Come Dance with Me" & "My Funny Valentine"] 2/15/1960 ABC
The Steve Allen Plymouth Show 3/14/1960 NBC
Adventures in Paradise "A Whale of a Tale" 11/7/1960 ABC
The Perry Como Show 12/11/1960 NBC
Remember How Great? (special) [singing "The Saga of Sadie Thompson"] 2/9/1961 NBC
The 34th Annual Academy Awards (special) 4/17/1961 ABC
The Bob Hope Buick Show (special) 5/13/1961 NBC
The Kraft Music Hall 1/10/1962 NBC
Hollywood Melody (special) 3/19/1962 NBC
Highways of Melody (special) 4/22/1962 NBC
The Red Skelton Show 10/2/1962 CBS
The Bob Hope Show (special) 10/24/1962 NBC
Story of a Songwriter (special) 1963 SYN
March of Dimes 25th Anniversary Show: Once Upon a Dime (special) 1/4/1963 SYN
Burke's Law "Who Killed Harris Crown?" 10/11/1963 ABC
The Danny Kaye Show 10/30/1963 CBS
The Ed Sullivan Show 1/19/1964 CBS
The Ed Sullivan Show 3/8/1964 CBS
The Hollywood Palace 6/6/1964 ABC
International Cabaret 7/8/1964
On Parade (special) [host] 8/14/1964 NBC
The Ed Sullivan Show 10/11/1964 CBS
The Danny Thomas Special (special) 11/13/1964 NBC
Burke's Law "Who Killed the Tall One in the Middle?" 11/25/1964 ABC
Favorite Songs (special) 11/26/1964 NBC
NBC Follies of 1965 (special) 11/27/1964 NBC
The Hollywood Palace [singing "Stop, Stop"] 12/1964 ABC
The Ed Sullivan Show 2/28/1965 CBS
The Ed Sullivan Show 5/9/1965 CBS
The Ed Sullivan Show 6/20/1965 CBS
Guest Shot 7/29/1965 SYN
Mona McCluskey (series regular as Mona McCluskey) 9/16/1965 to 4/14/1966 NBC
The Hollywood Palace [singing Dixie medley] 1/8/1966 ABC
The Dean Martin Show 2/3/1966 NBC
The Sammy Davis, Jr. Show 2/25/1966 NBC
The Andy Williams Show [singing "Call Me"] 9/18/1966 NBC
The Dean Martin Show [singing "The Very Soft Shoes"] 9/14/1967 NBC
The Danny Thomas Hour: It's Greek to Me 10/2/1967 NBC
The Don Knotts Special (special) [singing "Baubles, Bangles and Beads"] 10/26/1967 CBS
The Carol Burnett Show [singing "The Fleets In"] 11/20/1967 CBS
Showtime (co-host) 8/13/1968 CBS
The Dean Martin Show [singing "Come Back to Me" & "I Still Get Jealous"] 10/3/1968 NBC
The Name of the Game "Shine On, Shine On Jessie Gill" 11/1/1968 NBC
The Bob Hope Show (special) 11/27/1968 NBC

The Tom Jones Special [singing "Independent"] 1/9/1969 ABC
The Jonathan Winters Show [singing "We'll Get By"/ "Let's Be Buddies"/ "Friendship"] 4/10/1969 CBS
Showtime [guest host] 5/12/1969 SYN
Bing Crosby and Carol Burnett—Together Again for the First Time (special) 12/17/1969 NBC
Danny Thomas Looks At Yesterday, Today and Tomorrow (special) 1/28/1970 CBS
The Don Knotts Nice Clean, Decent, Wholesome Hour (special) [singing "Love Can Do Anything"] 4/3/1970 CBS
The Engelbert Humperdinck Show [singing "Tomorrow Never Knows"] 4/29/1970 ABC
Kraft Music Hall [singing "Do You Know the Way to San Jose?"] 7/29/1970 NBC
The Carol Burnett Show [singing "Pick Yourself Up" & "Put on a Happy Face"] 11/9/1970 CBS
The Klowns (special) [singing "Be a Clown"] 11/15/1970 ABC
The Don Knotts Show [singing "Something"] 3/16/1971 NBC
The Dean Martin Show [singing "Don't Rain on My Parade"] 12/9/1971 NBC
The Bob Hope Special [singing George M. Cohan medley] 2/27/1972 NBC
ABC Comedy Hour: A Funny Thing Happened on a Way to a Special 3/15/1972 ABC
Don Rickles—Alive and Kicking (special) 12/12/1972 CBS
Burns and Schreiver Comedy Hour 6/30/1973 ABC
United Cerebral Palsy Telethon 2/2/1974 SYN
The Fashion Awards (special) 3/19/1975 ABC
The Stars and Stripes Show (special) 7/3/75 NBC
Happy Birthday, Las Vegas (special) 10/23/1977 ABC
The Dean Martin Celebrity Roast: Angie Dickinson (special) 2/8/1977 NBC
The Muppet Show 4/25/1977 SYN
The Paul Lynde Comedy Hour (special) 5/20/1978 ABC
Bonkers 10/27/1978 SYN
The Juliet Prowse Show (special) 7/7/1979 SHO
The Love Boat "Doc's 'Ex' Change/ Making the Grade/ The Gift" 12/15/1979 ABC
The Big Show 4/22/1980 NBC
Musical Comedy Tonight (special) 2/11/1981 PBS
National Collegiate Cheerleading Championships (special) 4/1981 ABC
Women of Russia (series host) 9/1981 SYN
The Shape of Things "Episode 2" 4/13/1982 NBC
The Devlin Connection "Claudine" 12/11/1982 NBC
Fantasy Island "The Other Man—Mr. Roarke/Forbidden Love" 10/8/1983 ABC
The Love Boat "The Dream Boat/ The Parents/ Gopher and Isaac and the Starlet/ Julie and the Producer" 5/5/84 ABC
Glitter (pilot) 9/13/1984 ABC
Night of 100 Stars II (special) 3/11/1985 ABC
Placido Domingo ... Stepping Out with the Ladies (special) 5/14/1985 ABC
The 39th Annual Tony Awards (special) [presenter] 6/2/1985 CBS
The Love Boat "Who Killed Maxwell Thorn?" 2/27/1987 ABC
Murder, She Wrote "A Fashionable Way to Die" 9/20/1987 CBS
Las Vegas, An All-Star 75th Anniversary (special) 11/29/1987 ABC
Circus of the Stars (special) 12/15/1987 CBS
The Big Band Ballroom Bash (special) 1993 PBS
Championship Ballroom Dancing (annual) [co-host] 1987 to 1996 PBS

Television Appearances—Game & Talk Shows

Here's Hollywood 9/29/1960 NBC
Talent Scouts 8/21/1962 CBS
Stump the Stars 7/22/1963 CBS
Password 1/16/1964 CBS
Password 2/6/1964 CBS
Password 3/16 to 3/20/1964 CBS
Password 1/21/1965 CBS
Password 5/3 to 5/7/1965 CBS
You Don't Say 8/30 to 9/3/1965 NBC
The Tonight Show Starring Johnny Carson 10/4/1965 NBC
The Mike Douglas Show 11/18/1965 SYN
You Don't Say 4/4 to 4/8/1966 NBC
The Tonight Show Starring Johnny Carson 5/24/1968 NBC

The Joey Bishop Show 1/14/1969 ABC
The Joey Bishop Show 1/20/1969 ABC
The Donald O'Connor Show 2/28/1969 SYN
Dinah's Place 4/5/1971 NBC
The Merv Griffin Show 4/26/1971 CBS
The Movie Game 5/10 to 5/14/1971 SYN
The Merv Griffin Show 5/19/1971 CBS
The Tonight Show Starring Johnny Carson 8/20/1971 NBC
Password 12/20–12/24/1971 ABC
The Hollywood Squares [primetime] 12/24/1971 SYN
Jerry Visits 7/22/1972 SYN
The Hollywood Squares 3/5 to 3/9/1973 NBC
The Tonight Show Starring Johnny Carson 4/6/1973 NBC
The Hollywood Squares 6/17 to 6/21/1974 NBC
The Tonight Show Starring Johnny Carson 6/18/1974 NBC
Tattletales 12/30 to 12/31/1974, 1/2 to 1/3/1975 CBS
The Mike Douglas Show [co-host] 12/22 to 12/26/1975 SYN
The Tonight Show Starring Johnny Carson 12/26/1975 NBC
Tattletales 5/19 to 5/21, 5/24, 5/25/1976 CBS
Dinah! 6/9/1976 SYN
Match Game '76 6/18, 6/21 to 6/24/1976 CBS
Dinah! 9/21/1976 SYN
Match Game '77 12/7–9, 12/12 to 12/13/1977 CBS
Match Game PM 2/7/1978 SYN
All-Star Anything Goes 2/9/1978 SYN
Dinah! 5/8/1978 SYN
The Merv Griffin Show 7/12/1978 SYN
The Hollywood Squares [primetime] 1/23/1980 SYN
The Hollywood Squares 3/17 to 3/21/1980 NBC
The Mike Douglas show [co-host] 5/9/1980 SYN
Password Plus 7/7 to 7/11/1980 NBC
The Hollywood Squares [primetime] 9/29/1980 SYN
The Tonight Show Starring Johnny Carson 10/22/1982 NBC
Vicki! 9/17/1993 SYN

Also

The Merv Griffin Show, Personality, The Jim Nabors Hour and *Command Performance at the White House*

☆ BOBBI SHAW ☆

Blonde bombshell Bobbi Shaw was known for her trademark saying, "Yah, Yah," in the series of AIP beach movies beginning with *Pajama Party* (1964), where she was the sexy foil to comedian Buster Keaton. The duo was such a hit that AIP paired them again in *Beach Blanket Bingo* (1965) and *How to Stuff a Wild Bikini* (1965).

According to an AIP press release, Shaw, who was not Swedish but Jewish, was raised in Florida where she took singing and dancing lessons. She made her film debut in a bit role as Miss Miami Rendezvous in *Passion Holiday* (1963),

Yah, Yah it's Bobbi Shaw

about four young women fleeing broken relationships who run into each other in Miami and decide to vacation together. Bobbi then headed for Las Vegas where she appeared in productions of *High Button Shoes* and *Anything Goes*. Standing 5'5" with measurements of 38-23-35, the blue-eyed blonde easily stood out from the rest of her cast mates and was brought to the attention of American International Pictures. Shaw was signed to a contract and was the studio's second actress, after Susan Hart, to be groomed as a "star of the future."

Bobbi Shaw made her first beach movie appearance in *Pajama Party* (1964), starring Tommy Kirk as a Martian who comes to Earth and gets mixed up with wealthy shop owner Elsa Lanchester, her not-too-bright nephew Jody McCrea, and his frustrated girlfriend Annette Funicello. Clad in a fur bikini, Shaw played Helga, the Swedish knockout who, along with Buster Keaton as Chief Rotten Eagle, is hired by con man Jesse White to help fleece the old woman. The Chief's job is to make sure that Helga is able to entice information from McCrea's Big Lunk regarding the location of his aunt's safe. The problem is that Helga doesn't speak English and actually falls for the big lunk. According to one of the film's press releases Shaw had "to be provocative while being funny and had to perfect the Keaton deadpan style in order to blend in with his brand of comedy." She succeeded admirably, as the busty newcomer was an immediate hit with the fans and the critics. *Variety* raved, "Bobbi Shaw as a non-English-speaking Swede but who knows all the holds is a standout as the sexy lure...."

Impressed with the laughs that they brought to *Pajama Party*, AIP paired the master comedian and the blonde bombshell together again in *Beach Blanket Bingo* (1965), starring Frankie Avalon and Annette Funicello. But this time the duo were only used as a running gag and received billing as "cameo stars." Keaton's dirty old man could be seen chasing the nubile bikini-clad Shaw around the beach and the airport as the beach gang took up skydiving in the fifth movie of the series. Of course, the only lines Shaw delivers are her famous "Yah, Yah." She and Keaton could also be seen dancing during the film's end credits. *Ski Party* (1965) gave Shaw more to do as ski instructor Nita. Frankie Avalon's Todd Armstrong uses her to get his girlfriend Linda, played by Deborah Walley, jealous and he is delighted when Nita reveals in her thick Swedish accent that "in Stockholm when a boy and girl meet and they like each other—no games and very little talk." After Todd breaks a leg in a ski jump contest to impress Nita, their big date finally arrives but he is extremely disappointed when Nita decides that she wants to be treated like her chaste American counterparts with lots of talk and maybe a kiss on the cheek.

In *How to Stuff a Wild Bikini* (1965), Shaw's blonde tresses are hidden under a long dark wig as she played Khola Koku, an amorous native girl and assistant to Buster Keaton's Bwana "a witch doctor and member of the AMA." Stationed on Goona Goona Island as part of his navy reserve duty, Frankie Avalon asks Bwana to find out if his girl Dee Dee (Annette Funicello, who else?) is remaining true to him. The witch doctor sends a pelican to spy on her and conjures up Beverly Adams as the most beautiful girl on the beach to distract any of Dee Dee's potential suitors.

In Shaw's last beach party movie, *The Ghost in the Invisible Bikini* (1966), she finally gets to drop the Swedish accent and gives an amusing performance as greedy wisecracking bad girl Princess Yolanda. Bobbi was supposed to be teamed again with Buster Keaton as Chief Chicken Feathers, but due to illness he dropped out of the film and was replaced by Benny Rubin. The conniving carnival duo, along with Jesse White's J. Sinister Hulk, are hired by crooked attorney Reginald Ripper played by Basil Rathbone to knock off his client's heirs and find the dead man's fortune hidden somewhere in his huge mansion. As the inept trio keep bungling their job due to interfering Susan Hart as the ghost in the invisible bikini, Ripper tries to stall the reading of the will to the consternation of the heirs—Tommy Kirk, Deborah Walley, Patsy Kelly and Aron Kincaid as Patsy's nephew who turns up with a truckload of his surfer buddies and their girls.

When the beach party came to an end, Bobbi Shaw did not fall off the face of the map as most fans presumed. She became a member of Rob Reiner's comedy improvisational troupe called The Session. Other members included Marj Dusay, Richard Dreyfuss, Richard Mishkin, and Larry Bishop. They performed for two years in Los Angeles and on a number of TV talk shows. Shaw resurfaced on the big screen in the '70s, co-starring with David Carradine in *You and Me* (1975). She then played a prostitute named Slimey Sue working in Alaska, who befriends Gladys Knight as a woman who comes looking for her boyfriend in *Pipe Dreams* (1976).

Today, Bobbi Shaw—now Bobbie Shaw Chance—is one of Southern California's most respected drama teachers, leaving the beach party well behind her. The Bobbie Shaw Chance Actors Workshop in Studio City offers classes in all types of acting and one of her most famous students was Brad Pitt. In 1997, she also opened up her studio to kids from Free Arts for Abused Children. Her students perform skits, sing, dance, and try to get the children involved. She told the *Los Angeles Times*, "My goal is to bring in the Hollywood community. How do you think they [the children] would respond if the people they see in the movies or TV were in here? Those are the guys they look up to."

Film Appearances

1963　**Passion Holiday** (Davis Film Dist.) d. Wynn Miles
1964　**Pajama Party** (AIP) d. Don Weis
1965　**Beach Blanket Bingo** (AIP) d. William Asher
　　　Ski Party (AIP) d. Alan Rafkin
　　　How to Stuff a Wild Bikini (AIP) d. William Asher
　　　Sergeant Deadhead (AIP) d. Norman Taurog
1966　**The Ghost in the Invisible Bikini** (AIP) d. Don Weis
1975　**You and Me** (Filmmakers International, completed in 1972) d. David Carradine
1976　**Pipe Dreams** (Avco-Embassy) d. Stephen Verona

Television Appearances

The Steve Allen Show, The Joey Bishop Show, and *The Tonight Show Starring Johnny Carson*

☆ ULLA STROMSTEDT ☆

On drive-in screens across the nation, pretty, fair-haired Ulla Stromstedt's leading men were an intelligent dolphin in *Flipper's Odyssey* (1966), a former teen heartthrob in *Catalina Caper* (1967), and a guy in a loincloth in *Tarzan's Jungle Rebellion* (1970). Pure heaven for fans of B-movies, but probably the reason why when the '60s turned into the '70s, this Swedish dish was nowhere to be found.

Growing up in Sweden, the green-eyed blonde, whose mother was a sociologist, began modeling at age thirteen. A natural athlete, the young beauty excelled in swimming, skiing, and skating, which came in handy once she decided to become an actress. When she was sixteen, Stromstedt won the title of "Swedish Junior Ice Skater" and began touring with the Ice Capades. She arrived in Hollywood in 1961 with the skating show and she was hired to double as a stunt skier for Luciana Paluzzi in *Return to Peyton Place*. Her acting debut was that same year on the sitcom *The Tab Hunter Show*. But Ulla's Hollywood career was put on hold when she returned to Europe. She studied law at the University of Stockholm and art at the Sorbonne in Paris while landing the female lead in the Swedish mystery/thriller *Den Gula Bilen* (1963).

In 1965, Ulla Stromstedt was back in Hollywood as Mrs. Gilbert Cole. She met her business consultant husband in the catacombs of Italy. The newlywed turned her attention back to acting and was "saddened" when she lost out to Mary Ann Mobley for the role of April Dancer on *The Man from U.N.C.L.E.* Her spirits quickly lifted when she was added to the cast of the TV series *Flipper* in the fall of 1965 to attract more female and older male viewers. The character of Ulla Norstrand was a Swedish oceanographer who comes to Coral Key Park, Florida, to study and becomes involved with the problems of the park ranger Porter Ricks (Brian Kelly), his two sons (Luke Halpin and Tommy Nordern), and Flipper. However only a few episodes into the season and Ulla was already unhappy with her role because it was not much of an acting stretch. She bemoaned in *TV Guide*, "Flipper is the star of the show, anyway. And we say, 'Flipper! You understan' us? Go! Go for help!'" At the end of the season, Ulla was dropped from the series. It was an amicable parting. When Luke Halpin was asked by *TV Guide* to describe Stromstedt, the flippant teenager quipped, "Her subconscious is unconscious."

In 1966, Ulla's very conscious blonde figure splashed across the movie screens of Europe and a few U.S. drive-ins in *Flipper's Odyssey,* an edited theatrical release of a three-part episode of *Flipper*. In the movie, our favorite dolphin is captured by a fishing boat and disappears, leading his adoptive family and Stromstedt's fetching oceanographer to search for him. When one of the boys gets trapped in an underwater cave, Flipper is his only hope of rescue.

Stromstedt's official U.S. film debut was in the beach movie, *Catalina Caper* (1967). Needing someone who was an expert swimmer and could learn to scuba dive plus look awesome in a bikini, film producers Bond Blackman and Jack Bartlett knew Stromstedt would be perfect for the role of Katrina. But there was one problem—another blonde named Venita Wolf was already signed for the role of her rival. Ulla quickly agreed to don a dark wig to play the part. Regarding her new appearance, she thought it made her look "more mature and fascinating."

In *Catalina Caper* Stromstedt was just fine playing a mysterious and alluring

Lobby card for *Catalina Caper* (Crown-International, 1967) with Ulla Stromstedt and Tommy Kirk.

foreigner who meets college boy Don (Tommy Kirk) on his way to Catalina Island to spend his summer vacation with his college friend (Brian Cutler) and his sister Tina (Wolf). During the journey to the island they are treated to Little Richard performing the song "Scuba Party." Don makes a date with Katrina, but as they disembark her fiancé Angelo (Lyle Waggoner) greets her. Katrina is not seen until more than thirty minutes later when the bikini-clad beauty turns more than a few heads sunbathing on the beach. She catches Don's attention when she loses the top of her swimsuit in the surf. He does the gentlemanly thing and offers his windbreaker to the half-clad beauty and the two grow close. After Angelo threatens Don for being with his woman, Katrina reveals that he is being paid "to do nothing" by a Greek tycoon. Don realizes that Angleo may be involved with the men after a priceless Chou Dynasty scroll that is now lost on the ocean floor. Katrina then helps Don and his friends retrieve it and get the goods on Angelo.

Television kept Stromstedt busy for the next few years due to her linguistic abilities (she could speak Danish, French, English, and German) playing spies, informants, and double-agents on *Hogan's Heroes*, *I Spy*, *Twelve O'Clock High*, and *The Rat Patrol*. Regarding her roles up to this point, Ulla remarked, "I may not need Aristotle to play the parts I do but it makes me a better woman—no?"

In 1967, she was cast in the female lead of a two-part episode of the TV series *Tarzan*, starring Ron Ely, that was later re-edited into the theatrical feature *Tarzan's Jungle Rebellion* (1970). Stromstedt played Mary, who was part of archeologist Sam Jaffe's party searching for an ancient relic called "the Blue Stone" hidden beneath the pyramids and worshipped by tribal people. As the damsel in distress, Mary is rescued a few times by the hunky vine-swinger.

Tarzan's Jungle Rebellion was the last time Ulla would be seen by American audiences. She never progressed to being anything more than a drive-in movie starlet so it is no surprise that Stromstedt's comment in the *Catalina Caper* press book that her ambition was to direct movies was never achieved. The striking blonde disappeared from the Hollywood scene quicker than a Swedish meatball at a smorgasboard.

Film Appearances

1963   **Den Gula Bilen** (Sweden) d. Arne Mattsson
1966   **Flipper's Odyssey** (MGM; edited episodes from TV series) d. Paul Landres
1967   **Catalina Caper** (Crown International) d. Lee Sholem
1970   **Tarzan's Jungle Rebellion** (National General; edited two-part episode from the TV series) d. William Witney

Television Appearances

The Tab Hunter Show "Dream Boy" 4/9/1961 NBC
Flipper (series regular as Ulla Norstrand) 9/18/1965 to 9/10/1966 NBC
Gypsy 7/12/1966 SYN
Hogan's Heroes "Diamonds in the Rough" 9/30/1966 CBS
Twelve O'Clock High "To Seek and Destroy" 11/18/1966 ABC
I Spy "Rome.... Take Away Three" 12/28/1966 NBC
Mr. Terrific "Try This on for Spies" a.k.a. "The Sultan Has Five Wives" 4/24/1967 CBS
The Rat Patrol "Mask-a-Raid" 4/10/1967 ABC
Tarzan "The Blue Stone of Heaven" 10/6 & 10/13/1967 NBC
Hogan's Heroes "Sticky Wicket Newkirk" 1/20/1968 CBS
Achtung 2011! (series regular) 1979 (German TV)

☆ WENDE WAGNER ☆

Exotic, dark-haired Wende Wagner began her career literally underwater as a stuntwoman on such splashy television series as *Sea Hunt* and *Aquanauts*. The athletic brunette was discovered by 20th Century–Fox, who gave her the big "new star" buildup with her film debut as an Apache in the western *Rio Conchos* (1964). She played the part so well that she was typecast playing Indians or Mexicans in major studio productions. Drive-in movies however took advantage of Wagner's aquatic skills, displaying her shapely body quite nicely in less exotic roles. She played a bungling assassin in the beach/spy spoof *Out of Sight* (1966) and an underwater photographer in the cheesy sci-fi adventure *Destination Inner Space* (1966).

Wende Wagner, of French, American Indian, Hawaiian, and German descent, was born on December 6, 1941, in New London, Connecticut. Her father was Commander John H. Wagner and her mother the former Ruth Arnold, a former champion skier. Being a navy brat, Wende and her sister Candy, lived in every state of the union but two. Wagner began modeling at three and was able to find jobs no matter where she lived. When she was sixteen, the family was living in Southern California and director Billy Wilder spotted the athletic beauty surfing off the beach in Coronado, California, where he was lensing *Some Like It Hot*. He offered her a screen test, but her parents forbade it, wanting their daughter to first get her high school diploma. After graduating in 1957, Wagner took a Hawaiian vacation and when she returned to California she contacted Wilder. Her test did not lead to any film work (she turned down a small role in *The Apartment*), but she did agree to play a traveling soprano on an episode of the TV western *Wagon Train*.

Sultry Wende Wagner.

Not yet enthusiastic about an acting career, the curvaceous Wagner took off to Europe, earning money by modeling as she lived for short periods of time in England, France, Germany, and Ireland. On her way back to the states in 1960, Wagner stopped in the Bahamas to surf and stayed for three years, becoming an official Bahamian resident. It was there that the lithesome beauty's swimming and skin-diving talents were put to excellent use. She worked as a stunt double for the guest actresses on such aquatic TV series as *Sea Hunt*, *Aquanauts*, and *Malibu Run* and for Joanne Dru in the waterlogged big screen adventure *September Storm* (1960), a 3-D movie shot in CinemaScope. Her undersea adventures led Wende to remark, "I was in the water so much that I thought I might develop gills." Wagner received probably the most press coverage ever afforded a stunt double, but with her looks it was no wonder she was much sought after. *Life* magazine dubbed her "A Substitute Sea Nymph." She even landed a husband, Courtney Brown, a stunt man and aspiring actor. They soon welcomed daughter Tiffany into their household.

Returning to Hollywood in 1964 sans Brown, the newly divorced Wende Wagner beat out hundreds of actresses to land the role of "a tough, unkempt little Apache girl—a complete savage" speaking only in native tongue in *Rio Conchos* (1964), produced by 20th Century–Fox. This exciting, rugged western (it received a 1965 Laurel Award for Best Action Drama) was the story of the attempts to stop a renegade Confederate officer from selling 2000 army rifles to the Apaches. It starred Richard Boone, Stuart Whitman, Tony Franciosa, and football great Jim Brown in his film debut. Wagner first appeared in the movie in a highly dramatic scene as the snarling, dirty disheveled girl shoots at the officers from a cliff only to be wrestled to the ground by Richard Boone. Fox promoted the hell out of the film and Wagner. As studio head Richard Zanuck's newest discovery, she became the darling of the Hollywood press, who were amazed at how much she really looked like an American Indian in the movie. She stated in the *Los Angeles Herald Examiner*, "One of my ancestors was an American Indian from the Great Lakes area. I don't know how my forebears all got together. I guess they must have been real swinging travelers." Wagner's looks weren't her only winning features; her gorgeous gams so aptly displayed in the movie won her the 28th Annual Golden Calf Award. But Wagner's moment of glory was brief, as the studio unceremoniously dropped her after only one picture.

In 1966, Wagner made a brief cameo appearance as a sexy F.L.U.S.H. assassin (the reviewer for *Variety* called her "a lovely diversion") in the beach/spy spoof *Out of Sight* (1966). She is assigned by the evil Big D (John Lawrence) to terminate secret agent John Stamp (Jonathan Daly), who has learned of his plot to sabotage an upcoming rock and roll fair. As Scuba, Wagner, clad in a bikini top and scuba wear, confronts Stamp on the docks. After revealing her name he asks, "What do your friends call you?" She replies with a seductive look, "Easy." The wily agent jumps into the water as Scuba aims her spear gun at him but he escapes. After being reprimanded by Big D for missing her target, she is told to "go practice."

Wagner could also be seen along with Scott Brady, Sheree North and Gary Merrill as undersea lab inhabitants who come across an alien spaceship with a pod that grows into a monster in the low-budget sci-fi adventure *Destination Inner Space*. Wagner's swimming talents were put to use again as she played an underwater photographer clad in a very mod black-and-white checkered scuba outfit (*Variety* described her as "wonderful to look at"). Wende received lots of publicity, but another actress wearing a tight-skinned diving outfit—Raquel Welch in *Fantastic Voyage* (1966)—quickly overshadowed her.

Television once again brought Wende Wagner notoriety when she was cast as Lenore "Casey" Case in *The Green Hornet*, which premiered during the 1966–67 season. Producer William Dozier, trying to cash in on his successful *Batman* series, also was responsible for this less campy crime adventure starring Van Williams as the Green Hornet and Bruce Lee as his sidekick Kato. Wagner's Casey is the secretary to the Green Hornet's altar ego Britt Reid and, though she is underutilized throughout the course of the series, she is remembered fondly for this role.

Sometime in 1967 or 1968 Wagner wed actor James Mitchum, the son of Robert Mitchum. She returned to work playing a nice Mexican-American girl in the melodramatic *A Covenant of Death* (1967), starring George Maharis as a man wrongly convicted of murder who kills his hangman, and Mia Farrow's friend Tiger in the classic thriller *Rosemary's Baby* (1968). The action-packed *Guns of the Magnificent Seven* (1969), starring George Kennedy and James Whitmore, featured Wagner as a Mexican peasant girl who gets involved with a gentlemanly gunslinger played by Scott Thomas.

In 1969 Wagner had another baby. The birth of her child and the horrific murder of her good friend Sharon Tate

Wende Wagner poses as the seductive assassin Scuba in the beach/spy spoof *Out of Sight* **(Universal, 1966).** *Billy Rose Theatre Collection, The New York Public Library for the Performing Arts, Astor, Lenox and Tilden Foundations.*

must have taken its toll, as she again took time off from her career. She never really returned to acting except for a small role in the made-for-TV movie *The Bait* (1973), starring Donna Mills as a policewoman who goes undercover to trap a rapist. Giving up her acting career was probably not the end of the world for Wende. Back in 1964, when asked by columnist Dorothy Manners what would she do if her career didn't go as planned, Wagner replied that, "I'll get along. Don't forget I can do a lot of things. I've sailed in racing competitions. I can pilot a plane. I sky-dive, skin-dive, snow ski, water ski— and I've modeled professionally."

Sadly, the energetic Wende Wagner who was so full of life passed away of cancer on February 22, 1997, in San Francisco. To this day, she is missed terribly by friends and fans alike.

Film Appearances

1960 **September Storm** [stunts only] d. Byron Haskin

1964 **Rio Conchos** (20th Century–Fox) d. Gordon Douglas

1966 **Out of Sight** (Universal) d. Lennie Weinrib
Destination Inner Space (Magna) d. Francis D. Lyon

1967 **A Covenant with Death** (Warner Bros.) d. Lamont Johnson

1968 Rosemary's Baby (Paramount) d. Roman Polanski
1969 Guns of the Magnificent Seven (United Artists) d. Paul Wendkos
1973 The Bait (TV-movie) d. Leonard Horn

Television Appearances

Wagon Train "The Luke Grant Story" 6/1/1960 NBC
Perry Mason "The Case of the Feather Cloak" 2/11/1965 CBS
Flipper "Flipper's Monster" 4/10/1965 ABC
The Green Hornet (series regular as Lenore "Casey" Case) 9/9/1966 to 7/14/1967 ABC
Mannix "Skid Marks on a Dry Run" 9/23/1967 CBS
It Takes a Thief "Get Me to the Revolution on Time" 10/22/1968 ABC
Lassie "New Horizon" 12/8/1968 CBS
The Rookies "Prayers Unanswered, Prayers Unheard" 11/12/1973 ABC
Welcome to Hal-Land 1992 Cable Access

☆ DEBBIE WATSON ☆

A cross between Sandra Dee and Deborah Walley, curvy honey-blonde Debbie Watson inherited their sticky sweet teenage roles in films and on TV during the mid-sixties. She was *Karen* and *Tammy* on television, Marilyn Munster in the feature *Munster, Go Home!* (1966), and a go-go dancer in *The Cool Ones* (1967).

Watson was born on January 17, 1949, and grew up in La Mirada, California, a suburb outside of Los Angeles. She began singing and dancing when she was eleven and a year later the determined adolescent decided to become an actress. To make some money she began modeling dresses for a local clothes store and working as an usher at Knott's Berry Farm until she was accepted at the Long Beach Community Playhouse after fibbing about her age. She explained in *TV Guide*, "I was tall for my age but they only wanted high school girls. So I said I was. I don't really think that was lying exactly. I mean, I wouldn't have *gotten* the part otherwise." That part was in *Gangway* and the youngster went on to appear in productions of *Bye Bye Birdie* at the Melodyland Theatre and *Brigadoon*.

In 1963, Watson auditioned and surprisingly, since she had no TV or film credits, won the lead role in the sitcom *Karen* that was originally one-third of a ninety-minute block of comedies entitled *90 Bristol Court*. Produced by Joe Connelly and Joe Mosher, who hit it big with *Leave It to Beaver* and *The Munsters*, *Karen*, which premiered on October 5, 1964, was a forgettable series about a perky Southern California teenager and her tomboy younger sister. However, NBC and Universal had faith in the show due to the popularity of Watson, so after scraping *90 Bristol Court* in January of 1965, *Karen* was the only one of the trio of shows to be picked up for the entire season. Debbie had a charming quality that appealed to the audience, especially adolescent females. She was in such demand for interviews by the fan magazines that Universal had to declare a two-week moratorium on publicity so she could concentrate on learning her lines for the series. Despite the trappings that come with being a TV star, the sincere newcomer told *TV Guide*, "I really don't think being an actress should change *anything*. I *won't* go Hollywood." Watson's perkiness and popularity with teenage girls was not enough to keep *Karen* afloat and it was cancelled after one season.

Since *Karen* was sort of a combination Gidget and Tammy, Universal decided Watson would be the perfect choice to follow Debbie Reynolds and Sandra Dee, her screen counterparts, as Tammy the good ole backwoods Southern gal in their new series. *Tammy* premiered on September 9, 1965, as Watson's chipper and smart Louisiana Bayou orphan gets a job as a secretary to Donald Woods as wealthy businessman John Brent who has a very attractive son played by Jay Sheffield. Complications ensue for Tammy throughout the series as her backwards upbringing clashes with the extravagant lifestyle of her boss, snooty socialite Lavinia Tate (Dorothy Green) and her equally stuck up daughter Gloria (Linda Marshall). Unfortunately for Watson, *Tammy* was another sub-par series that appealed only to pubescent girls. Though Debbie made a winsome and good-natured Tammy, the series was not renewed for a second season.

In 1966, after starring in two failed series, the exhausted sixteen-year-old starlet opined to the popular teenage girl magazine, *Seventeen*, "Life as an actress has made me grow up faster than I think I would have done otherwise. When you're a regular high school student—I'm a senior—you go to school day in and day out…. You're not faced with any other responsibility other than getting good grades; you don't think about the fact that a show is riding on your back and a lot of people are counting on you. When you have a career, so many things depend on you that you learn to handle yourself and mature much earlier than you would ever imagine."

Poster art for *Tammy and the Millionaire* (Universal, 1967), starring Debbie Watson as the backwoods cutie.

Universal tried to change gears with Debbie Watson and began grooming her for film stardom. However, teenage audiences in 1966 were not receptive to goody-goody Pollyanna types as biker chicks, flower children and hippies began dominating drive-in screens across the country. Nevertheless, Universal foisted their new Sandra Dee onto a not very interested young audience. First up for Watson was *Munster, Go Home!* (1966), the full-color film version of the popular but recently cancelled series featuring all the series cast members except one.

Originally produced for television, the film was given a theatrical release at the last minute. The studio's decision to cast Watson as Marilyn Munster disappointed fans of the series loyal to the popular Pat Priest. Purportedly, Universal executives felt Priest was too old to play the teenager and they wanted to use this film to launch Watson. In the middling film, the Munsters inherit a British castle that is being used by a bunch of counterfeiters who try to scare the family back to America.

Universal then, in a surprise move, edited the first four episodes of *Tammy* into a feature entitled *Tammy and the Millionaire* (1967) that played drive-ins across the South. As the film ad declared, "Snooty debutante! Wild mountaineers! Uppity millionaire! Tammy hilariously teaches 'em the facts of life ... and love!" The backwoods girl also has to deal with the debutante's mother who reports her and her hillbilly family to the IRS for evasion of back taxes. In the end, her millionaire boss pays off the debt while Tammy wins the heart of his son, and her uncle and grand pappy come up with the deed proving they not only own their land but the socialite's as well.

After her option was not renewed at Universal, Watson copped her best role in the wild teenage musical *The Cool Ones* (1967). Not only were her acting talents on display, but her singing and dancing prowess were put to excellent use. *The Cool Ones* was a pleasant parody of teenage dance shows and Svengali-like record producers à la Phil Spector. As the tagline proclaimed, "It's the story of a teenage singing idol who had it all ... lost it ... and had to find it all over again. Oh, those Go-Go girls, and those get-get guys!"

The Cool Ones featured Debbie Watson as Hallie Rodgers, a frustrated young singer who cannot get a break. She auditions as a vocalist for the popular TV teenage dance show, *Whizbam*, but gets hired as a dancer instead. During one of the live telecasts, the go-go girl gets so excited during a number performed by Glen Campbell that she darts out of her cage, grabs his microphone and begins singing while dancing frenetically. The audience goes wild, but Hallie gets fired despite the fact that the show receives over 60,000 letters from teenagers demanding to know who that go-go dancer was. Visiting a nightclub called Stan's Cellar, Hallie becomes attracted to former teenage idol Cliff Donner (Gil Peterson), who is trying to make a comeback after being considered washed up at age twenty-three. They christen Hallie's dance The Tantrum and are able to persuade the "youngest self-made rock 'n' roll millionaire tycoon" Tony Krum (Roddy McDowall) to manage them as a team. Krum then reveals only to Hallie his plan to have the duo to start out dancing together, then singing and finally falling in love culminating with an engagement and marriage. This complicates matters for the aspiring singer who truly has fallen in love with Cliff. When the teen heartthrob stumbles upon the plan, he doesn't believe that Hallie loves him and distances himself from her. To prove her true feelings to Cliff, Hallie is a no-show when they are booked as headliners on *Whizbam*, letting Cliff sing solo. He then realizes Hallie really loves him and they are reunited.

When *The Cool Ones* was released it didn't generate any great notices. The movie was very tame and square compared to the likes of *Angels from Hell* and *Riot on Sunset Strip* being released at the time. Good teens were not in vogue during the heyday of bikers, hippies, and rebellious college students, so the film did not find an audience. However, today's rock film aficionados praise the teenage musical. Writing in *The Psychotronic Video Guide*, author Michael J. Weldon remarked that the film "is a fun piece of the 60s." Dominic Priore was more empathetic, re-

Robert Coote, Jim Begg, Debbie Watson, Nita Talbot, and Roddy McDowall in a scene from *The Cool Ones* (Warner Bros., 1967).

viewing the film for *Hollywood Rock* by Marshall Crenshaw, and described the movie as a "wonderfully rockin' bombshell-in-wimpster clothing."

The Cool Ones was Watson's final big screen appearance. She continued appearing sporadically on television until 1971. Her guest stints included playing a hillbilly named Jennie May whose family operates an illegal still on the flop series, *Mr. Terrific* starring Stephen Strimpell and Dick Gautier. After appearing in two episodes of *Love, American Style* in the early '70s, Debbie Watson left show business.

Film Appearances

1966 **Munster, Go Home!** (Universal) d. Earl Bellamy
1967 **The Cool Ones** (Warner Bros.) d. Gene Nelson
 Tammy and the Millionaire (Universal) d. Leslie Goodwins/ Sidney Miller/ Ezra Stone

Television Appearances

Karen (series regular as Karen Scott) 10/5/1964 to 4/19/1965 NBC
Tammy (series regular as Tammy Tarleton) 9/17/1965 to 7/15/1966 ABC
The Virginian "Requiem for a Country Doctor" 1/25/1967 NBC
Stars of Tomorrow (special) [Hollywood Deb Star] 1/28/1967 ABC
Mr. Terrific "Stanley and the Moutaineers" 3/27/1967 CBS
The Virginian "Eileen" 3/5/1969 NBC
Love, American Style "Love and the First Nighters" 2/6/1970 ABC
Love, American Style "Love and the New Roommate" 2/12/1971 ABC

☆ VENITA WOLF ☆

Blond and sexy, with the bluest of eyes, Venita Wolf was one of the prettiest actresses to grace the drive-in screens of America. The fact that Wolf, who resembled a cross between Carol Lynley and Diane McBain, appeared on screen in only one beach film, *Catalina Caper* (1967), was a real loss for girl watchers.

During the mid-sixties, Venita Wolf, like Andrea Dromm, first achieved fame in a series of TV commercials. She was the sparkling hair model for Lady Clairol. Casting directors quickly took notice and the acting offers came rolling in. Film producers Bond Blackman and Jack Bartlett were savvy enough to sign the fetching blonde to co-star in the feature *Catalina Caper*. According to the movie's press book, "So great a 'find' did the producers consider her, that Venita got the role without a screen test and without reading a line. They'd already seen for themselves how she looked and sounded on the commercial that told how much it was fun to be blonde!" The film, originally to be titled *Scuba Party* and then *Never Steal Anything Wet*, commenced filming in 1965 but was not released until 1967, making it a late in the cycle beach film.

Catalina Caper costarred Venita Wolf

Lobby card for *Catalina Caper* (Crown-International, 1967), featuring blonde Venita Wolf (left) as a pouting beach bunny.

as Tina, a denizen of Catalina Island who finds herself attracted to her brother's college classmate Don (Tommy Kirk). The audience is introduced to Tina as she steers a schooner almost into another boat that is docked. Tina catches the eye of rich boy Tad (Peter Duryea), whose parents, Arthur and Anne Duval (played by Del Moore and Sue Casey), are swindlers who have "borrowed" a priceless Chou Dynasty scroll that accidentally winds up on the ocean floor. Tina tries a number of different ways to attract Don's attention, including teaching him to scuba dive, inviting him to a yacht party where the Cascades and Carol Connors perform, and pretending to be drowning, but he is more interested in the mysterious dark-haired vixen Katrina (Ulla Stromstedt). She then tries to work her feminine wiles on Tad to make Don jealous. Duval uses his son's connection to Tina to get Don and her brother Charlie (Brian Cutler) to participate in a deep-sea treasure hunt to reclaim the lost scroll before Katrina's boyfriend Angelo (Lyle Waggoner) finds it for a Greek tycoon. Wolf (who received billing as "and introducing" in the film's credits) was a visual delight as the pouting flaxen-haired beach girl but at times she is costumed in a very unflattering white mesh bathing suit, which the end credits revealed was designed by Bronson of California.

The rest of Wolf's short acting career comprised roles on commercials and TV shows. She made her TV debut replacing Sharon Tate as Miss Murray, Mr. Drysdale's enticing receptionist, in a few episodes of *The Beverly Hillbillies*. The episode entitled "Granny Tonics a Birdwatcher" gave her the most screen time as a confidante to co-worker Jane Hathaway (Nancy Kulp) who mistakenly thinks birdwatcher Prof. P. Caspar Biddle (Wally Cox) has proposed to her but in reality he only wants her to hatch a condor's egg.

Wolf made enough of an impression on *The Beverly Hillbillies* to be presented by Bob Hope as one of the "Stars of Tomorrow" along with Susan Saint James, Chris Noel, and Eileen O'Neill, among others on his comedy special in 1966.

Star Trek fans will remember Wolf as Yeoman Teresa Ross in the episode "The Squire of Gothos." She, along with Captain Kirk (William Shatner) and the others, is held prisoner on a planetoid by a childish super being named Trelane, played by William Campbell, who is fascinated with the violent history of human beings. Wolf's outstanding features were hidden under a habit as Sister Margaret on *Gunsmoke*. She and her fellow nuns shield the criminal past of an outlaw (Claude Akins) who saved their lives. Her other TV roles included a bubble-headed beach bunny enamored of Mickey Dolenz on *The Monkees* and one of the many beautiful women playboy Carlos Ramirez (Alejandro Rey) tries to deflower but whose seduction plans are constantly interrupted by Sister Bertrille (Sally Field) on *The Flying Nun*. In Wolf's case, it is the nun's wisecracking parrot that sends the blonde running from Carlos' abode.

Wolf graced the cover of *Playboy* magazine in 1967 and continued making television commercials and guest appearances. She returned to *The Beverly Hillbillies*, this time in the role of Suzy, banker Drysdale's receptionist. Venita then faded from the Hollywood scene by 1970. The *Catalina Caper* press book prediction that "this 'Girl on the Go' will soon have all the picture work she can handle" turned out to be typical publicity hyperbole.

Film Appearances

1967 **Catalina Caper** (Crown International) d. Lee Sholem

Television Appearances

The Beverly Hillbillies "Flatt and Scruggs Return" 3/23/1966 CBS
The Beverly Hillbillies "The Folk Singer" 3/30/1966 CBS
The Beverly Hillbillies "The Birdwatchers" 4/13/1966 CBS
The Beverly Hillbillies "Granny Tonics a Birdwatcher" 4/27/1966 CBS
The Bob Hope Comedy Special 11/16/1966 NBC
Star Trek "The Squire of Gothos" 1/12/1967 NBC
Gunsmoke "Ladies from St. Louis" 3/25/1967 CBS
The Monkees "I Was a 99-Pound Weakling" 10/16/1967 NBC
The Flying Nun "Polly Wants a Crack in the Head" 10/19/1967 ABC
The Second Hundred Years "Luke-a-Likes" 12/6/1967 ABC
The Wild Wild West "The Night of the Arrow" 12/29/1967 CBS
The Beverly Hillbillies "The Diner" 1/10/1968 CBS
Felony Squad "The Flip Side of Fear" 1/15 & 1/22/1968 ABC
The Beverly Hillbillies "Jed Clampett Enterprises" 2/5/1969 CBS

Web Sites

Individuals

Jackie DeShannon: www.jackiedeshannon.com
Candy Johnson: www.candyjohnson.com
Marta Kristen: www.martakristen.com
Donna Loren: www.adasa.com
Vitina Marcus: www.geocities.com/Vitina_2002/
Arlene Martel: www.arlenemartel.com
Melody Patterson: www.wranglerjane.com
Cynthia Pepper: www.cynthiapepper.TV/
Pat Priest: www.pscelebrities.com/pp.html
Wende Wagner: www.wende-wagner.org
Beverly Washburn: www.beverlywashburn.com
Lori Williams: www.faster-pussycat.com

General

Brian's Drive-in Theater: www.briansdriveintheater.com
Elvis' Women In the Movies, That Is: greggers.granitecity.com/elvis/women/
McFarland and Company, Inc., Publishers: www.mcfarlandpub.com
Sixties Cinema.com (Tom Lisanti's website:) www.sixtiescinema.com
Swingin' Chicks of the Sixties: www.swinginchicks.com

BIBLIOGRAPHY

Betrock, Alan. *The I Was a Teenage Juvenile Delinquent Rock 'n' Roll Horror Beach Party Movie Book.* New York: St. Martin's Press, 1986.

Brooks, Tim, and Marsh, Earle. *The Complete Directory to Prime Time Network and Cable TV Shows, 1946–Present.* 4th ed. New York: Ballantine Books, 1995.

Brown, Peter Harry, and Pat H. Broeske. *Down at the End of Lonely Street: The Life and Death of Elvis Presley.* New York: Dutton, 1997.

Castleman, Harry, and Walter J. Podrazik. *Harry and Wally's Favorite TV Shows.* New York: Prentice-Hall, 1989.

Cox, Stephen. *The Beverly Hillbillies.* Chicago: Contemporary Books, 1988.

Crenshaw, Marshall. *Hollywood Rock.* New York: HarperPerennial, 1994.

Ehrlich, Henry. "Hollywood's Teen-age Gold Mine." *Look*, November 3, 1964: 60–64, 66.

Eisner, Joel, and Krinsky, David. *Television Comedy Series: An Episode Guide to 153 TV Sitcoms in Syndication.* Jefferson, NC: McFarland, 1984.

Gerani, Gary, and Schulman, Paul H. *Fantastic Television.* New York: Harmony Books, 1977.

Gianakos, Larry James. *Television Drama Series Programming: A Comprehensive Chronicle, 1947–1959.* Metuchen, NJ: Scarecrow Press, 1980.

_____. _____, *1959–1975.* Metuchen, NJ: Scarecrow Press, 1978.

_____. _____, *1975–1980.* Metuchen, NJ: Scarecrow Press, 1981.

_____. _____, *1980–1982.* Metuchen, NJ: Scarecrow Press, 1983.

_____. _____, *1982–1984.* Metuchen, NJ: Scarecrow Press, 1987.

_____. _____, *1984–1986.* Metuchen, NJ: Scarecrow Press, 1992.

Goldberg, Lee. *Unsold Television Pilots, 1955 through 1988.* Jefferson, NC: McFarland, 1990.

Hardy, Phil, ed. *The Overlook Film Encyclopedia: Horror.* Woodstock, NY: Overlook Press, 1993.

Heitland, Jon. *The Man from U.N.C.L.E. Book: The Behind-the-Scenes Story of a Television Classic.* New York: St. Martin's Press, 1987.

Henderson, Jennifer. "Fun in the Sun Cinema." *Big Reel*, August, 2002: 69–75.

Holston, Kim. *Starlet.* Jefferson, NC: McFarland, 1988.

Hyatt, Wesley. *The Encyclopedia of Daytime Television.* New York: Billboard Books, 1997.

Inman, David M. *Performers' Television Credits, 1948–2000.* 3 volumes. Jefferson, NC: McFarland, 2001.

Kesler, Susan E. *The Wild, Wild West: The Series.* Downey, CA: Arnett Press, 1988.

Krafsur, Richard P., ed. *The American Film Institute Catalog of Motion Pictures: Feature Films 1961–1970.* New York R.R. Bowker, 1976.

_____. _____, *1961–1970 Indexes.* New York: R.R. Bowker Company, 1976.

Lentz, Harris M. *Science Fiction, Horror, and*

Fantasy Film and Television Credits. 2 volumes. Jefferson, NC: McFarland, 1983.
_____. _____, *Supplement: through 1987.* Jefferson, NC: McFarland, 1989.
_____. _____, *Supplement 2, through 1993.* Jefferson, NC: McFarland, 1994.
_____. *Television Westerns Episode Guide: All United States Series, 1949–1996.* Jefferson, NC: McFarland, 1997.
_____. *Western and Frontier Film and Television Credits, 1903–1995.* Jefferson, NC: McFarland, 1996.
Lewis, Richard Warren. "Those Swinging Beach Movies." *Saturday Evening Post,* July 31, 1965: 83–87.
Lichter, Paul. *Elvis in Hollywood.* New York: Simon and Schuster, 1975.
Lisanti, Tom. *Fantasy Femmes of Sixties Cinema: Interviews with 20 Actresses from Biker, Beach, and Elvis Movies.* Jefferson, NC: McFarland, 2001.
Maltin, Leonard. *Leonard Maltin's Movie and Video Guide 1995.* New York: Penguin Books USA, 1994.
Marill, Alvin H. *Movies Made for Television: The Telefeature and the Mini-Series, 1964–1984.* New York: New York Zoetrope, 1984.
Martindale, David. *Television Detective Shows of the 1970s: Credits, Storylines, and Episode Guides for 109 Series.* Jefferson, NC: McFarland, 1991.
McLafferty, Gerry. *Elvis Presley in Hollywood: Celluloid Sell-Out.* London: Robert Hale, 1989.
McNeil, Alex. *Total Television: The Comprehensive Guide to Programming from 1948 to the Present.* New York: Penguin Books, 1996.
McParland, Stephen J. *It's Party Time: A Musical Appreciation of the* Beach Party *Film Genre.* PTB Productions, 1992.
Morris, Bruce. *Prime Time Network Serials: Episode Guides, Casts, and Credits for 37 Continuing Television Dramas, 1964–1993.* Jefferson, NC: McFarland, 1997.
Morton, Alan. *The Complete Directory to Science Fiction, Fantasy and Horror Television Series: A Comprehensive Guide to the First 50 Years 1946 to 1996.* Peoria, IL: Other World Books, 1997.
O'Neill, James. *Terror on Tape.* New York: Billboard Books, 1994.
Parish, James Robert, and Terrace, Vincent. *The Complete Actors' Television Credits, 1948–1988. Volume 2: Actresses.* Metuchen, NJ: Scarecrow Press, 1989.
Phillips, Mark, and Garcia, Frank. *Science Fiction Television Series: Episode Guides, Histories, and Cast and Credits for 62 Prime Time Shows, 1959 through 1989.* Jefferson, NC: McFarland, 1996.
Prouty, Howard H., ed. *Variety Television Reviews 1923–1988.* 15 volumes. New York: Garland Publishing, Inc., 1989.
Strodder, Chris. *Swingin' Chicks of the '60s.* San Rafael, CA: Cedco Publishing, 2000.
Terrace, Vincent. *Encyclopedia of Television: Series, Pilots, and Specials.* New York: New York Zoetrope, 1985–1986.
_____. *Television Specials: 3,201 Entertainment Spectaculars, 1939–1993.* Jefferson, NC: McFarland, 1995.
Thompson, Howard, ed. *The New York Times Guide to Movies on TV.* Chicago: Quadrangle Books, 1970.
TV Guide. January 1, 1958–December 31, 1978. Weekly.
Variety Film Reviews 1907–1980. 16 volumes. New York: Garland, 1983.
Variety Portable Movie Guide. New York: Berkley Boulevard Books, 1999.
Ward, Jack. *The Supporting Players of Television, 1959–1983.* Cleveland: Lakeshore West Publishers, 1996.
_____. *Television Guest Stars: An Illustrated Career Chronicle for 678 Performers of the Sixties and Seventies.* Jefferson, NC: McFarland, 1993.
Weldon, Michael. *The Psychotronic Encyclopedia of Film.* New York: Ballantine, 1983.
_____. *The Psychotronic Video Guide.* New York: St. Martin's Griffin, 1996.
Willis, John. *Screen World.* New York: Crown, annual.

Individual Bibliography

BRENDA BENET

Associated Press. "Soap Opera Star Commits Suicide." *Poughkeepsie Journal*, April 9, 1982.

"Brenda Benet, Actress, Called Suicide Victim." *New York Times*, April 9, 1982: B6.

Murphy, Mary. "Behind the Suicide of a Soap Star Whose Career Had Seemed So Promising." *TV Guide*, March 12, 1983: 3, 4, 6, 8, 10, 15.

"Obituary." *Variety*, April 14, 1982: 98.

Rizzo, Tony. "Hiking with Brenda Benet." *Soap Opera Digest*, July 15, 1980: 127, 128, 130–134.

DIANE BOND

Swingin' Summer, A [pressbook]. United Screen Arts, 1965.

CINDY CAROL

Asher, Jerry. "Behind the Scenes: 'Dear Brigitte'." *Screen Stories*, March 1965: 59.

"Cindy Carol." *Screen Album Magazine*, July, 1963.

"Cindy Carol Playing 'Gidget' for $300 Wkly." *Variety*, January 25, 1963.

Dear Brigitte [pressbook]. 20th Century Fox, 1965.

"Everything's Changed for Cindy." *TV Star Parade*, October, 1963.

"Meet Cindy Carol: The New Gidget." *Photoplay*, August 1963: 48, 49, 88.

Miller, Edwin. "Gidget Was Here: Cindy Carol Has the Time of Her Teens As Gidget." *Seventeen*, July 1962: 94, 95, 113.

Oppenheimer, Peter J. "Cindy Carol: Hollywood's Newest Teen-Age Star." *Family Weekly*, July 28, 1963: 7.

"Private Life of the Newest *Gidget*, The." *Movie Stars Magazine*, October, 1963.

Scott, Vernon. "Gidget: Cindy Carol New Series Star." *Newark Evening News*, June, 18, 1963.

Terry, Polly. "Mrs. Chris Connelly: How It Happened—Or Go Blonde, Get Bridegroom." *Photoplay*, July 1969: 68, 70, 72.

"Valley Girl Given Role of 'Gidget.'" *Citizen News*, January 25, 1963.

REGINA CARROL

Konow, David. *Schlock-O-Rama: The Films of Al Adamson*. Los Angeles: Lone Eagle, 1998.

"Obituary." *The Hollywood Reporter*, November 16, 1992.

"Obituary." *Variety*, November 10, 1992.

"Regina Carrol Is Dead; Horror Film Star, 49." *New York Times*, November 12, 1992.

Ryan, Al. "Regina Carrol: The Early Years." *Psychotronic Video*, Winter, 1994.

PATTI CHANDLER

Allen, Jane. "Why Patti Lets Him Play Around." *Photoplay*, July 1967: 73, 88, 89.

Conrad, Sylvia. "When a Girl Loves a Man, She Has to Trust Him—No Matter What." *Modern Screen*, January 1967: 22, 23, 66–68.

Edwards, Wallace. "Why Lee Majors Runs Away from Love! A Star Overnight, Lee Still Prefers Patti Chandler!" *Screen Stories*, June 1967: 33, 76, 77.

Ehrlich, Henry. "Success Overtakes Patti Chandler." *Look*, June 29, 1965: 33–37.

Harris, Leonard. "Beach Films Figure to Make Money." *New York World-Telegram and Sun*, January 25, 1965: 15.

NANCY CZAR

Wild Guitar [pressbook]. Fairway International, 1962.

JACKIE DESHANNON

All Music Guide to Rock, 2nd Edition. San Francisco: Miller Freeman Books, 1997.

Clarke, Donald. *The Penguin Encyclopedia of Popular Music.* New York: Viking, 1989.

C'mon, Let's Live a Little [pressbook]. Paramount, 1967.

Harrison, Nigel. *Songwriters: A Biographical Dictionary with Discographies.* Jefferson, NC: McFarland, 1998.

Miller, Kenny, with Donald Vaughan. *Kenny Miller: Surviving Teenage Werewolves, Puppet People and Hollywood.* Jefferson, NC: McFarland, 1999.

Surf Party [pressbook]. 20th Century-Fox, 1964.

JILL DONOHUE

Columbia Pictures. [press release]. March 26, 1965.

Winter a-Go-Go [pressbook]. Columbia Pictures, 1965.

Andrea Dromm

Hutchison, Katie. "Andrea Dromm: The Endless Summer of a Summer Blonde." *People*, July 11, 1988: 96.
"Is This Any Way to Make a Living? You Bet It Is!" *Look*, February 7, 1967.
Mishkin, Leo. "Andrea Dromm–Happy? You Bet She Is!" *Morning Telegraph, N.Y.*, June 9, 1967.

Joan Freeman

"Bouquet of Blossoming Blondes, A." *Life*, August 17, 1962.
The Fastest Guitar Alive [pressbook]. MGM, 1967.
Greenberg, Abe. "A Matter of Figures with Joan Freeman." *Citizen News*, November 18, 1964.
Panic in Year Zero [pressbook]. American International Pictures, 1962.
"She Plays the Slentem: 'Bus Stop's' Joan Freeman Is Otherwise Quite Normal." *TV Guide*, September 30, 1961: 28–29.
"Show Business Beauty: Joan Freeman." *Show Business Illustrated*, September 19, 1961: 66.

Gail Gilmore

"On the Way Up: Gail Gerber." *Top Hit Club News*, vol. 7, no.1, 1955.

Susan Hart

Carroll, Kathleen. "Hart Rides Wild Surf and Winds Up a Star." *Sunday News (N.Y.)*, November 28, 1965.
Parsons, Louella. "I Nominate for Stardom ... Susan Hart." *Modern Screen*, January 1965: 12.
Weaver, Tom. "The Bride of AIP." *Fangoria*, November 1991, Issue 108.

Anne Helm

Bolton, Whitney. "Anne Helm Clicks in Hollywood." *N.Y. Morning Telegraph*, September 7, 1962.
"From 'My Sister Eileen' to Elvis Presley: Anne Helm's Career Has Taken Some Wild Bounces." *TV Guide*, May 12, 1962: 6–7.
Mercer, Charles. "Sleeping Beauty Has Golden Touch." *The Courier-Journal, Louisville*, June 1, 1958.
Weaver, Tom. "At the Helm for Horror." *Fangoria*, August 1998: 12–17.

Sharyn Hillyer

"The World's Most Low-Pressure Actress." *TV Guide*, May 8, 1965: 27.

Mikki Jamison

Alexander, Greg. "Photoplay Asks Eighteen Actresses: Would You Do a Nude Scene If the Role of a Lifetime Called for It?" *Photoplay*, July 1963: 31, 32, 91.
"What's an Agent? Mikki Jamison Soon Learned the Answer—And a Lot of Others, Too." *TV Guide*, July 27, 1963: 27–28.

Candy Johnson

"Beauty Secrets of the Stars: Candy Johnson—Energy Plus." *Citizen News*, August 10, 1964.
Harris, Leonard. "Candy Johnson Keeps Moving." *New York World-Telegram and Sun*, June 30, 1965.
Jackson, Mike. "How Girl Proves Candy Is Loaded with Energy." *Los Angeles Herald-Examiner*, February 12, 1963: A-19.

Marta Kristen

Clark, Mike. "Marta Kristen: Viking Princess of the All-American Space Family Robinson." *Starlog*, October 1988: 63–68, 81.
"Norwegian Cinderella." *TV Guide*, November 20, 1965.

Sue Ane Langdon

Bender, Harold. *Pictorial TView*, November 24, 1957: 14.
Cohn, Al. "She's Black and Blue from Fighting for Fame." *Newsday*, July 6, 1966: 3.
Fagen, Herb. "A Deserving Star for Sue Ane." *Classic Images*, June 1997.
UPI. "Sue Ane Langdon Resigns as TV 'Wife.'" *Newark Evening News*, November 18, 1961: 6.

Wilson, Earl. "Sue Ane Langdon: Take the Stand…" *New York Post*, July 9, 1966: 4.

DONNA LOREN

Gardner, Christopher. "Up from the Beach." *New York Sunday News*, August 1, 1965.
Harrington, Nannette. "Donna Loren Brings Paris to Paniolo Country." *KonaViews*, 2000: 23.
Rath, Paula. "Cutting-Edge Retailers." *Island Business Magazine*, December, 1999: 10.
"Two on a Beach Blanket." *Modern Screen*, July 1965: 40–43.

MEREDITH MACRAE

Engels, Mary. "Meredith Keeps It Cool, Casual." *N.Y. Daily News*, September 20, 1969.
Groves, Bill, and Saryl T. Radwin. "Petticoat Junction." *Television Chronicles*, April 1996.
Lewis, Richard Warren. "Petticoat Junction Is Not Her Only Station." *TV Guide*, January 17, 1970: 14–17, 20.
"Petticoat Junction: How Four Gorgeous Dolls Get Along Together." *Screen Stories*, August 1967: 31, 86, 87.
"Summer Love Is Fun." *Modern Screen*, August 1964: 58, 59.
"Teens Are Looking at Pop TV Personalities." *Seventeen*, February 1964: 67.
Wilson, Earl. "MacRaes' Journal." *Newark Sunday News*, August 24, 1969: E2.

VITINA MARCUS

Viharo, Will. "Lost in Vegas: An Interview with Vitina Marcus." *Planet X*, Fall 2001: 32–36.

DODIE MARSHALL

Easy Come, Easy Go [pressbook]. Paramount, 1967.

ARLENE MARTEL

Angels from Hell [pressbook]. American International Pictures, 1968.

CLAUDIA MARTIN

Evans, Peter. "Claudia Started the Star Way." *New York World-Telegram and Sun*, November 14, 1963.
"Obituary." *The Hollywood Reporter*, February 21, 2001.
Shelley, Liz. "How Her Dad (Dean Martin) Helped Straighten Out Her (Claudia Martin) Life!" *Screen Stories*, June 1964: 25, 77.

MARLYN MASON

Diehl, Digby. "Well, You Have to Laugh a Lot." *TV Guide*, April 29, 1972: 18–21.
"Hollywood Swingers, The: Or, How to Be True to One's Press Agent in One's Fashion." *Show*, November, 1963.
"Will Someone Please Send This Girl Flowers." *TV Guide*, May 15, 1965: 20–21.

JENNY MAXWELL

"Former Actress Jenny Maxwell Slain with Husband." *Variety*, June 12, 1981.
"Show Business Beauty: Jenny Maxwell." *Show Business Illustrated*, March, 1963: 59.
Williams, Dick. "Will Jenny Maxwell Be Screen's Lolita?" *Los Angeles Mirror*, June 3, 1959: 6–7.

LAURIE MOCK

Hot Rods to Hell [pressbook]. MGM, 1967.
Newman, Morris. "The Developer As Artist." *Grid*, April 2001.
Ringen, Jonathan. "Culver City Renaissance." *Metropolis Magazine*, January 2002.

VALORA NOLAND

"If Valora Can Just Live Up to Her Name…" *TV Guide*, July 13, 1963: 18–19.
"Show Business Beauty: Valora Noland." *Show Business Illustrated*, November 14, 1961.

QUINN O'HARA

Buchanan, Larry. *It Came from Hunger! Tales of a Cinema Schlockmeister.* Jefferson, NC: McFarland, 1996.
"He Wants to Bury Vaudeville." *TV Guide*, July 13, 1962.
"Her First Word Was 'Cheese.'" *TV Guide*, April 9, 1966.
A Swingin' Summer, [pressbook]. United Screen Arts, 1965.

Tusher, William. "My Love for Fabian by Quinn O'Hara." *Photoplay*, March 1964: 44, 84, 85.

MELODY PATTERSON

Fessier, Michael, Jr. "With Her, Homework Was the Hangup." *TV Guide*, June 10, 1967: 14, 15, 17.
McCandlish, James. "Skinny TV Girls Are Hurting Our Kids … Says 'F Troop' Beauty." *The National Enquirer*, May 15, 2001.

CYNTHIA PEPPER

Bender, Harold. "Cynthia Pepper, Seasoned Star." *Pictorial TView*, October 15, 1961.
Graham, Sheila. "I'm Not Hot Stuff—Pepper." *New York Mirror*, October 8, 1961: 54.
Henaghan, Jim. "A Vaudevillian's Revenge." *TV Guide*, December 30, 1961: 2–5.

PAT PRIEST

Easy Come, Easy Go [pressbook]. Paramount, 1967.
"Mother Has Long Green Calling Cards." *TV Guide*, 1965.

JULIET PROWSE

Associated Press. "Principle Is Important to Juliet." *New York World-Telegram and Sun*, March 21, 1961.
Galloway, Doug. "Obituary." *Variety*, September 23, 1996: 138.
Garfield, Kim. "It's 'Kismet' for Juliet Prowse." *Hollywood Drama-Logue*, June 1994: 14.
Hyams, Joe. "Juliet Prowse Bolts Presley Songfest." *New York Herald-Tribune*, 1961.
Johnson, Hope. "No Tears for This Juliet: The Prowse Girl Is Dancing Her Way to a Successful Career. *New York World-Telegram and Sun*, March 6, 1965.
Thomas, Robert McG., Jr. "Juliet Prowse Is Dead at 59; Star of Musicals and Clubs." *New York Times*, September 16, 1996: B9.

BOBBI SHAW

Bond, Ed. "Healing Acts." *Los Angeles Times*, February 19, 1997.

ULLA STROMSTEDT

Crail, Ted. "*I Have Never Been a Field Idiot*: That's Ulla Stromstedt's Way of Saying There's More to Life Than 'Flipper.'" *TV Guide*, March 26, 1966: 22–25.
Gent, George. "Flipper Flips for a Blonde." *New York Times*, June 27, 1965.

DARLENE TOMPKINS

Weaver, Tom. "Tompkins Talks About Ulmer, Elvis and More." *bmonster.com*.

WENDE WAGNER

Manners, Dorothy. "About Wende Wagner: A Gasp a Minute." *Los Angeles Herald Examiner*, October 1, 1964.
"Mere Maid's Fate, A." *TV Guide*, November 13, 1960: 6–7.
"Strange Mixture." *Los Angeles Herald Examiner*, September 26, 1964: 4.
"A Substitute Sea Nymph," *Life*, November 28, 1960.

BEVERLY WASHBURN

Mitchell, Charles P. and Paul Parla. "Beverly Washburn: *Spider Baby* Sister and TV Veteran." *Filmfax*, Nos. 75–76: 108–111.
Weaver, Tom. "Thriller, Science Fiction, Theater, *Superman*, *Star Trek* and *Spider Baby*: The Amazing Genre Career of Beverly Washburn." *Chiller Theatre Magazine*, Issue 16, 2001: 15–20

DEBBIE WATSON

Cool Ones, The [pressbook]. Warner Bros., 1967.
Gordon, Stanley. "Debbie Watson: She'll Be Dangerous at 20." *Look*, November 25, 1966.
"That's Debbie's Problem." *TV Guide*, January 16, 1965: 22, 24.
Watson, Debbie. "I Like People to Like Me." *Seventeen*, January 1966: 37.
Wilkie, Jane. "Daughter Is a TV Star: The Plight of the Parents of Miss Debbie Watson, Who Is 16 and Is 'Tammy.'" *TV Guide*, February 12, 1966: 12–14.

Carole Wells

"Bouquet of Blossoming Blondes, A." *Life*, August 17, 1962.
"She's Mrs. Doheny…and They Won't Let Carole Wells Forget It." *TV Guide*, March 25, 1967: 11–13.

Lori Williams

Frasier, David K. *Russ Meyer—The Life and Films*. Jefferson, NC: McFarland & Company, 1990.
Swingin' Summer, A [pressbook]. United Screen Arts, 1965.

Index

Aaberg, Kemp 20
Abbott, George 119, 120
ABC After-School Special 215
Adam-12 267, 285
Adams, Beverly 234, 238, 244, 314
Adams, Don 49, 299
Adams, Nick 101, 111
Adamson, Al 228, 230, 231
The Addams Family 158
Adler, Stella 22, 30
Adrian, Iris 189
The Adventures of Nick Carter 113
The Adventures of Ozzie and Harriet 44–46, 50, 266
Agar, John 68
Aghayan, Ray 203
Aimée, Anouk 164
Akert, Pamela *see* Austin, Pamela
Akins, Claude 327
Albert, Eddie 5, 64
Albertson, Jack 86, 156
Albright, Vicky 67, 68
Alfred Hitchcock Presents 272
All in the Family 85
Allen, Irwin 99–102, 104, 272
Allen, Rex 8
Allen, Steve 82, 83
Allen, Valerie 18, 288
Allyson, June 218
Altman, Robert 106
The Amazing Colossal Man 29
Amazing Stories 261
American Bandstand 89
American Beauty 11, 12
An American in Paris 4
Amory, Cleveland 124, 143
Amsterdam, Morey 56
Anders, Luana 290
Anders, Merry 68
Anderson, Herbert 80
Anderson, Loni 43
Anderson, Michael, Jr. 42
Anderson, Stuart 297
Andes, Keith 117
Andrews, Dana 293

The Andy Griffith Show 76
Angelique *see* Pettyjohn, Angelique
Angels from Hell 2, 105, 106, 110–113, 324
Angels' Wild Women! 228–231
The Angry Breed 2, 64, 72, 140, 145, 147
Animals 71
Ankles Aweigh 75
Ann-Margret 42, 140, 206, 207, 228, 249
Annie 42
Annie Get Your Gun 4, 276
Antonio, Lou 95
Anything Goes 314
The Apartment 319
The Apple Tree 84
Aquanauts 318, 319
Archer, Eugene 272
Archer, John 176
Archie 169
Arkin, Alan 16
Arkoff, Samuel Z. 54, 56, 59, 61–63, 257, 269
Armstrong, Sam 22, 24, 152
Arnie 75, 84–86
Arnold, Jack 197
Arnold, Phil 80
The Art Lamb Show 303
Arthur, Maureen 83
Arzner, Dorothy 187
Asher, Jerry 226
Asher, William 58, 59
Ashley, John 55, 56, 276, 297, 301
Astin, John 136, 137, 158
Astor, David 50
Astronauts 68
Attack of the Puppet People 29
Austen, David 122
Austin, Pamela 45, 156, 176, 178, 208, 287
Austin, Patti 64
Avakian, Aram 32
Avalon, Frankie 54, 56–58, 60,
61, 91, 93, 233, 234, 247, 255,
264–266, 269, 270, 272, 276,
296, 297, 314
Avery, Tol 289
Axelrod, David 92
Ayres, Maray 146–148

Babcock, Dwight 120
Bach, Dr. George R. 62
Bacharach, Burt 240
Bachelor Father 76, 224
Bagetta, Vincent 73
Bahrenburg, Bruce 124
Baio, Scott 86
The Bait 321
Bakalyan, Richard 247
Baker, Carroll 236
Baker, Diane 124, 260, 286
Baker, Joe Don 219
Ball, Lucille 5, 94, 150, 305
Bangert, Johnny 153
Banner, Jill 182, 184, 186, 187, 291
Barberella 223
Bardot, Brigitte 227, 264, 287
Baretta 214
Barlow, Ray 211
Barnaby Jones 126
Barnes, Clive 84, 120
Barnum, H. B. 93
Baron, Sandy 164, 165
Barrett, Majel 41, 43, 218
Barry, Gene 46, 244
Barrymore, John Drew 98
Barth, John 32
Bartlett, Jack 316, 326
Basehart, Richard 101
Basil, Toni 207
The Bat People 52
Batman 91, 93, 126, 320
Battle Beyond the Stars 274
Beach Ball 1, 21, 28, 68, 217, 218, 266, 267
Beach Blanket Bingo 1, 59, 89, 92, 95, 232, 233, 264, 265, 270–273, 313, 314

Index

Beach Boys 23, 24, 89–91
The Beach Girls and the Monster 3, 5–8
Beach Party 1, 54, 56, 57, 91, 136, 197, 218, 239, 252, 254, 264, 266, 267, 268, 269, 275, 276, 285, 296
The Beachcomber 259
Beany and Cecil 7
Beast of Blood 301
The Beat Generation 228
Beatles 23, 92, 239
Beatty, Warren 119, 126
Beau Brummels 29, 68
Because They're Young 117
Beck, Kimberly 250
Bedtime Story 101
Bee, Molly 183
Begg, Jim 325
Bells Are Ringing 5
Bembry, Maggie 231
Ben Casey 117, 119, 185
Beneath the Flesh 215
Benedict, Dirk 149
Benedict, Richard 119
Benet, Brenda 2, 27, 28, 71, 217–221, 267
Benet, Vicki 217
Bening, Annette 12
Bennett, Constance 117
Bennett, Joan 117
Benny, Jack 185, 189, 190
Benny Goodman Sextet 130
Bergen, Candice 165, 166, 169
Bergen, Polly 130
Berger, Richard 276
Berger, Senta 42
Bergner, Elisabeth 137
Berle, Milton 93, 94, 143, 162
Berlin, Jeannie 166, 167, 169
Bernard, Sue 210–212
Bernardi, Hershel 84
Bernstein, Elmer 119
Bernstein, Leonard 66
Berry, Ken 117, 142, 143, 150
Bertoya, Paul 112, 293
Beswicke, Martine 124
The Beverly Hillbillies 222, 327
Bewitched 105, 113, 114
Beymer, Richard 66, 247
Beyond the Time Barrier 172–175
Biano, Sollie 266
The Big Bird Cage 186
The Big Valley 118, 132, 234, 299
Bikini Beach 56, 57, 89, 90, 232, 233, 264, 268–270, 275, 276
Bikini Party in a Haunted House see *The Ghost in the Invisible Bikini*
Bill, Tony 196
Billingsley, Barbara 181
The Billy Barnes Revue 117
Biohazard 302
Birney, David 73
Bishop, Jennifer 229

Bishop, Joey 47–49, 94
Bishop, Larry 315
Bishop, William 181
Bixby, Bill 50, 51, 70, 71, 107, 123, 217–219, 266, 281, 299, 303
Bixby, Christopher 219
Black Heat 230
Blackman, Bond 316, 326
Blackman, Joan 176, 178, 179, 246, 249
Blaine, Martin 196
Blazing Stewardesses 230
Blindfold 222
Blodgett, Michael 135, 209, 210, 227
Blondell, Joan 260
Blood and Lace 140, 147–149
Blood of Ghastly Horror 230
Bloom, John 230
Blossoms 90
Blue Denim 286
Blue Hawaii 39, 172, 175–179, 286, 287, 307–309
Bob & Carol & Ted & Alice 137
Bobby Fuller Four 134
Bolton, Whitney 120
Bonanza 76, 117, 118, 259
Bond, Diane 209, 210, 214, 221–223
Bonner, William 230
Boone, Richard 320
Born Famous 278
Bostweeds 210
Bowen, Jimmy 89
Bowen, Roger 85
Bowers, Hoyt 10
The Boy Friend 68
Boys Night Out 253
Brady, Scott 146, 320
Brain of Blood 230
Brame, Bill 146
Brando, Marlon 101
Breck, Peter 118
Bresler, Jerry 225
Brice, Fanny 202
Brides of Blood 301
Bridges, Beau 30
Bridges, Lloyd 178, 245
Brigadoon 119, 322
Briles, Chuck 120
Brisbois, Danielle 214
Brooks, Donnie 209
Brooks, Richard 10
Brown, Courtney 319
Brown, James 90
Brown, Jim 320
Brown, Joe E. 178, 179
Brown, Peter 254
Bruhl, Linda 39, 40
Brutsman, Joseph 115
Brynner, Yul 101
Buchanan, Larry 136
Burke's Law 46, 49, 117, 244
Burr, Raymond 138
Burton, James 89

Burton, Robert 253
Bus Stop (TV series) 247
Busch, Dennis 211, 213
Busey, Gary 168
Butterflies Are Free 149
By the Light of the Silvery Moon 276
Bye Bye Birdie 140, 142, 276, 322
Byrd, Charlie 130
Byrnes, Edd "Kookie" 28, 218, 266, 267

Caan, James 42, 202, 203
Caesar's Comedy Bingo 203
Caesar's Hour 64
Calamity Jane 141
Call Me Madam 200
Callan, Michael 117, 118, 259
Calta, Louis 226
Camelot 8–10
Campbell, Glen 277
Campbell, William 290, 327
Can-Can 307, 308
Cannibal Orgy see *Spider Baby*
Capri, Anna 23, 291
Cardinale, Claudia 222
Carell, Reno 132
The Caretakers 130
Cargman, Jered 95
Carnes, Kim 242
Carney, Art 76
Carol, Cindy 2, 39, 223–228
Carousel 119
Carpenter, John 31
Carpenters 242
The Carpetbaggers 5
Carradine, David 315
Carradine, John 201, 202, 230
Carradine, Keith 168
Carrie 86, 170
Carrol, Regina 2, 228–232
Carroll, Diahann 159
Carroll, Kathleen 48, 156, 254
Carroll, Leo G. 47
Carson, Johnny 82
Caruso, Anthony 123
Casey, Sue vii, 3–14, 327
Cass, Peggy 165
Cassavetes, John 76, 295
Cassidy, David 267
Cassidy, Ted 158
Castaways 71
Castle, William 260
Cat People 171
Catalina Caper 3, 8,9, 316–318, 326, 327
The Catcher 242
The Census Taker 278
Chabot, Amedee 57
Chad and Jeremy 118
Chakiris, George 66
Chamberlain, Richard 119, 194, 195
Champion, Gower 177

Championship Ballroom Dance Competition 310
Chandler, Patti 54, 56, 61, 62, 232–236, 255, 264
Chaney, Lon, Jr. 40, 184–187, 229, 230, 290
Change of Habit 72, 120
Channing, Carol 83
Chaplin, Saul 66
Charles, Ray 91
Charlie's Angels 169, 179
Charro! 120
Chase, Barrie 130, 307
Chatterbox 114
The Cheap Detective 203
Checker, Chubby 289
Cheers 215
Chekhov, Michael 293
Cher 242
Chevalier, Maurice 307, 308
The Cheyenne Social Club 79, 84
Childish Things 299
Children Shouldn't Play with Dead Things 171
The Children's Hour 228
China Beach 53
CHiPs 138
Christian, Roger 89
Christopher, Jordan 242
Churchill, Winston 296
The Cincinnati Kid 208
CinderFella 175
Clambake 64, 69, 70, 299
Clark, Dick 89, 117
Clark, Petula 92
Clarke, Gary 68
Clarke, Robert 173–175
Claxton, William F. 40
Cleopatra 154
Clerambard 258
Clive, Henry 4
Cloud Seven 258
C'mon, Let's Live a Little 64, 71, 239–242
Coburn, James 222
Cochran, Steve 228
Coffy 186
Cohn, Harry 181
Cole, Clay 289
Coleand, Byron 112
Coleman, Dabney 121
The Colgate Comedy Hour 275
Collins, Jo 57
Collins, Sheldon 17
Columbo 112
Combs, Mike 168
Come Blow Your Horn 196
Come September 247
Come Spy with Me 14, 18, 19
The Comedy of Terrors 56
Comer, Anjanette 26
The Comic 72
Commons, David 146
Conan Doyle, Sir Arthur 100
Conboy, Jon 73

Confessions of Tom Harris 299
Connelly, Christopher 227
Connelly, Daniel 227
Connelly, Joe 227, 322
Connery, Sean 75, 82, 83
Connolly, Joe 200
Connors, Mike 119
Conquest of the Planet of the Apes 10
Conrad, Charles 284
Conrad, Robert 113
Considine, Tim 152, 276
Constantine, Michael 95, 164, 165
Convy, Bert 64
Conway, Russ 71
Cook, Doria 168
The Cool Ones 322, 324, 325
Coombs, Ken L. 227
Coote, Robert 325
Copper and Brass 75
Coppola, Francis Ford 290
Corcoran, Kevin 182, 183, 272
Corcoran, Noreen 23–25, 224, 291
Corey, Prof. Irwin 114
Corey, Jeff 177, 303
Corey, Wendell 68
Corman, Gene 24
Corman, Roger 54, 62, 136, 247, 273, 290
Corsaro, Frank 98
Cortez, Stanley 135, 136
Costello, Lou 184
The Couch 259
Coughlin, Kevin 162
A Covenant of Death 320
Cowboy in Africa 283
Cox, Wally 298, 302, 327
Craig, Michael 260, 261
Craig, Yvonne 60, 61, 101, 156, 159, 208, 267
Crain, Jeanne 293
Crane, Bob 108, 114
Crawford, Joan 260
Crawford, Johnny 30
Crawling Arnold 64
Crenshaw, Marshall 325
Crisis in Mid-Air 159
Cronin, John 289, 290
Crosby, Bing 4, 180, 181
Crosby, Gary 26, 237
Crossings 179
Crowther, Bosley 308
Cry of the Banshee 137
Culp, Robert 107, 108, 126
Cummings, Robert 56, 296
Curb, Mike 146
The Curious Female 299, 301
Curtis, Patrick 133, 134, 209
Curtis, Tony 76, 101
Cutler, Brian 8, 317, 327
The Cycle Savages 2, 140, 146–148
Czar, Nancy 236–239

Daddy Long Legs 228
Dale, Dick 89, 91
Dale, Lenny 64

DaLie, David 8
Daly, Jonathan 320
Damone, Vic 129, 130
Daniel Boone 218, 259
Danova, Cesare 206, 225
Darby, Kim 47, 277
Darin, Bobby 64, 198, 247
Darren, James 25, 39, 196–198, 225, 226, 284, 285
The Dating Game 137
Davalos, Dick 189
Dave Clark Five 90, 92
David, Hal 240
Davis, Bette 125, 284, 285
Davis, Mac 120
Davis, Pepper 50
Davis, Phyllis 214, 273
Davison, Davey 190, 293
Day, Doris 141
Day in Court 140
The Day the World Ended 136
Days of Our Lives 219, 220
Dean, James 105, 106, 151
Dear Brigitte 224, 226, 227
A Death in California 179
Death Valley Days 147
DeCarlo, Yvonne 40, 304
Dee, Sandra 42, 50, 51, 59, 68, 151, 154, 155, 223, 225, 247, 286, 287, 322, 323
Deems, Mickey 80
Dekker, Albert 18
DeKova, Frank 142
Delaney, Dana 53
Dementia 13 289, 290
De Metz, Danielle 225
DeMille, Cecil B. 202
Demy, Jacques 164
Den Gula Bilen 316
De Palma, Brian 170
Derek, John 299
Dern, Bruce 146, 147, 305
Descher, Sandy 225
DeShannon, Jackie vii, 2, 71, 239–243
Desire in the Dust 259
Destination Inner Space 318, 320
DeWilde, Brandon 46, 286
Dexter, Maury 161, 239
Diamond, Don 142
Diary of a High School Bride 55
Dick Dale & His Del-Tones 56, 269
The Dick Van Dyke Show 76
Dickinson, Angie 98
Dingaka 309
Dion 289
Dirty Harry 295
Dirty Mary, Crazy Larry 257
Disney, Walt 8, 89, 180, 182, 272
Dmytryk, Edward 5
Dr. Goldfoot and the Bikini Machine 60, 62, 234, 252, 255, 256, 264
Dr. Kildare 93, 117, 119, 195, 272

Dr. Strangelove 26, 28
Doctor, You've Got to Be Kidding! 50, 51
Doheny, Larry 197
Doherty, Bill 46
Doherty, Charla 136, 154
Dolenz, Mickey 50, 327
Domergue, Faith 201, 202
Donahue, Troy 18, 19, 25, 183, 288
Donlevy, Brian 189
The Donna Reed Show 136, 153, 218, 284
Donne, Phyllis 307
Donohue, Jack 244
Donohue, Jill 238, 244–246
Donovan 166
Doohan, James 15
Double Trouble 264
Double Your Pleasure 150
Douglas, Avra 115
Douglas, Donna 80, 83
Douglas, Kirk 298
Douglas, Paul 5
Dow, Tony 224, 227, 289
The Doyle O'Dell Show 117
Dozier, William 320
Dracula vs. Frankenstein 228, 230
Dracula's Dog 114
Dragon Lady 302
Dreyfuss, Richard 315
Dromm, Andrea vii, 2, 14–21
Dru, Joanne 319
Duell, Geoffrey 273
Duggan, Andrew 223
Duke, Patty 39, 188
Duncan, Isadora 231
Dunne, Steve 181
DuPont, Elaine 6
Duryea, Peter 8, 327
Dusay, Marj 315
Duvall, Robert 103

Eastwood, Clint 10, 195, 295
Easy Aces 68
Easy Come, Easy Go 281–283, 303–305
Easy Rider 30–32
Eaton, Shirley 234
Ebert, Roger 215
The Ed Sullivan Show 22
Eddie Fisher Coke Time 194
Eden, Barbara 254
Edgington, Lyn 207
Edleman, Randy 242
Edmiston, Walter 6, 7
Edmonds, Don 28, 65, 68, 218, 220, 267
Edwards, Geoff 278
Edwards, Vince 119, 152
Edwin Booth 258
87th Precinct 296
Eisley, Anthony 80
Ekman, Hasse 244
Ekman, Jill *see* Donohue, Jill
Elam, Jack 86

The Eleventh Hour 272
Ellison, Harlan 107
Ely, Rick 167
Ely, Ron 73, 318
Emrek, Jack 75, 76
End of the Road 32
Epstein, John 167
Erickson, Leif 76, 249
Erman, John 122, 123
The Errand Boy 5, 130
Escape 125
Esposito, Joe 35, 207
Eubank, Anita 238
Evans, Linda 132, 272, 285, 299
Everett, Chad 206
The Evictors 86
Exciters 269

F Troop 2, 140–145, 150
Fabares, Shelley 26, 69, 70, 80, 183, 214, 237, 254, 281, 299
Fabian 132, 162, 226, 227, 234, 247, 254
Face of Fire 244
Faces 295
Fader, David 80
Faithful, Marianne 242
Falk, Peter 112, 119
Family Affair 9
Family Ties 215
Fantastic Studios Ink 247
Fantastic Voyage 320
Far Beyond Nearby 203
Farmer, Mimsy 292, 293
Farrell, Glenda 156
Farrow, Mia 320
The Fast and the Furious 54
Faster, Pussycat! Kill! Kill! 2, 52, 205, 206, 209, 210, 212–215
The Fastest Guitar Alive 246, 250
Father Knows Best 153, 184
Fathom 18, 19
Faylen, Frank 78
The F.B.I. 168
Feld, Eliot 65
Feldman, Corey 250
Felker, Clay 198
Fell, Norman 164
Felton, Norman 46
The Female Bunch 229
The Feminist and the Fuzz 236
Fernstrom, Ray 132
Ferrer, Jose 114, 115, 258
Field, Sally 188, 204, 327
The Fiercest Heart 309
Fifteen and Pregnant 126
52 Miles to Terror see Hot Rods to Hell
A Fine Madness 75, 82
Finney, Albert 203
Fireball 500 234, 264
Five Finger Exercise 296
Five's a Family 178
Flagg, Cash *see* Steckler, Ray Dennis

Flaming Star 176
Fleetwoods 239
Fletcher, Neil 136
The Flip Wilson Show (pilot) 147
Flipper 8, 316
Flipper's Odyssey 316
The Flying Nun 327
Follies 310
Follow That Dream 258–260
Fonda, Henry 78, 79, 84
Fonda, Jane 42, 223
Fonda, Peter 30–32, 86, 200
Fonda, Shirlee 79
Footlight Theater 181
Footsteps in the Snow 276
For Those Who Think Young 253, 283–285
Foran, Dick 178
Ford, Glenn 78, 79, 300
Ford, Harrison 167
Forquet, Philippe 167
Forsythe, John 76
Foxy Brown 186
Franciosa, Tony 320
Francis, Connie 64, 78
Francis, Kathy 209
Franciscus, James 46, 124
Franken, Steve 68, 117
Frankenheimer, John 214
Frankenstein 174
Frankie and Johnny 75, 80, 82, 83
Franklin, Aretha 90
Frawley, William 152
Freeman, Joan 1, 77, 246–251
Freeman, Joel 8
Freeman, Kathleen 64
Friday the 13th: The Final Chapter 250
The Front Page 149
The Fugitive 118
The Fun Lovers 297
Funicello, Annette 1, 54, 56–59, 61, 89, 91, 92, 207, 233, 264, 265, 269, 270, 272, 275, 276, 296, 297, 314
Funny Girl 202
Funny Lady 193, 196, 200, 202, 203
Funny You Should Ask 277
The Fury 170

Gaba, Marianne 234, 255, 264, 276
Gabor, Zsa Zsa 4, 47, 231
Gabriel, John 297
Gardella, Kay 143
Gardner, Christopher 89
Garen, Leon 168
Garfield, Kim 308
Garland, Judy 4
Garner, Ed 61, 134
Garner, James 164, 253
Garr, Teri 162, 205, 207, 208, 233
Gary Lewis & the Playboys 209
Gautier, Dick 161, 325

Gaye, Marvin 90
Gayle, Saundra 112, 113
Gaynor, Mitzi 310
Gazzara, Ben 208
Gemini Affair 271, 273
General Hospital 191, 261
Gentrys 71
George, Christopher 126
Gerber, Gail *see* Gilmore, Gail
Gershwin, George 78
Gershwin, Ira 78
Get Set, Go 75
Get Smart 49, 299
Get Yourself a College Girl 206, 240
Getting Straight 2, 160, 165–167, 169
Getting Together 190
The Ghost and Mr. Chicken 250
The Ghost in the Invisible Bikini 54, 62, 129, 131, 134–136, 234, 235, 252, 257, 264, 283, 285, 314
Ghostley, Alice 177, 178
G. I. Blues 307, 308
G. I. Executioner 302
Giant 151
Gibson, Fred 182
Gibson, Gail *see* Gilmore, Gail
Gidget 225
Gidget (TV series) 188
Gidget Goes Hawaiian 225
Gidget Goes to Rome 2, 39, 223–226
Gilardi, Jack 58
Gilbert, Carole 8
Gilbert, Melissa 68
Gilbert, Paul 68
Gilbert, Philip 147
Gilligan's Island 303
Gilmore, Gail vii, 2, 21–33, 64, 218, 267, 291
Gilmore, Glen 24
Gilmore, Voyle 91
Gilson, Red 268
Ging, Jack 240
Girl Crazy 78
The Girl from U.N.C.L.E. 218
Girl Happy 21, 26, 27, 205, 207, 208, 236, 237
Girls! Girls! Girls! 33–39, 225
The Girls on the Beach 1, 21, 23–25, 28, 289, 291
Glaser, Paul Michael 73
The Glass Cage 105, 107
Gleason, Jackie 39, 40, 43, 76, 98
Glenn, Scott 168
A Global Affair 217, 253
The Glory Guys 33, 41, 42
Goldfinger 255
Goldstone, James 16
Goldwyn, Sam 3, 160
Gomer Pyle, USMC 95, 117, 118
Good, Jack 90
Good Morning, Miss Dove 224
Good Neighbor, Sam 132
Goodman, Hal 152, 153

Goodwin, Laurel vii, 1, 15, 16, 33–44, 225, 250
Gordon, Bert I. 29, 259
Gore, Lesley 24, 90, 92
Gossett, Louis, Jr. 167
Gould, Elliot 64, 165, 166
Goulet, Robert 119, 120, 260
Grady, Don 272, 288
Grahame, Gloria 147
Grand Prix 197
Grandpa Goes to Washington 86
Grandpa Was a Cop see *Five's a Family*
Grant, Johnny 145
Graves, Peter 118
Gray, Veleka 73
The Great Adventure 293
The Great Imposter 76
The Greatest Show on Earth 181, 221
Green, Dorothy 323
The Green Hornet 195, 320
The Green Slime 122
Griffith, Corinne 39
Grodin, Charles 297
Grover, Mary 119
Guarino, Ann 80, 245
A Guide for the Married Man 47–49, 75, 84, 179
Guns of the Magnificent Seven 320
Gunslinger 101
Gunsmoke 76, 101, 113, 126, 327
Gunther, Kurt 34
Gwynne, Fred 304

Haas, Hugo 194
Hagen, Jean 290
Hagen, Ross 230
Haig, Sid 184, 186, 187, 189
Haji 2, 205, 210, 212, 213, 215
Hale, Alan 260
Hale, Jean 120, 222
Hall, Arch, Jr. 236
Hall, Arch, Sr. 236, 237
Hall, Jon 5–7
Halpin, Luke 165, 316
Hamilton, George 50, 194, 286
Hamilton, Murray 165
Hamilton, Sue 57
Hampton, James 143
Hanley, Bridget 164
Hans Christian Andersen 181
The Happy Ending 10
Harmon, Joy 24, 29–31, 47, 49, 50, 227
Harper 213
The Harrad Experiment 149
Harrington, Pat 282
Harris, Barbara 84
Harris, Jack H. 261
Harris, James 271, 272, 286
Harris, Jo Ann 162
Harris, Jonathan 103, 272
Harris, Julie 151
Harris, Richard 8, 214

Harrison, Paul 201
Harrison, Susan 105
Hart, Dolores 35
Hart, Susan 1, 60–63, 136, 217, 234, 252–258
Hart to Hart 246
Hartford, James 255
Hartman, David 245
Hartman, Ed 291
Harum Scarum 21, 27, 28, 217, 218
Haskin, Byron 106, 107
A Hatful of Rain 98, 99
Hauer, Rutger 170
Hawaii Five-O 148, 259
Hawken's Breed 86
Hawkins, Jimmy 154
Hawn, Goldie 68
Hay, Alexandra 164
Hayden, Schuyler 295
Hayes, Anthony 238, 244
Hayes, Ron 49
Hayward, Susan 39
Hayworth, Rita 11
Head, Edith 5
Heater, Mark 91
Heatherton, Joey 39
Hedison, David 99–101
Helen, Marjorie *see* Parrish, Leslie
Hell Is for Heroes 34
Hell's Angels 112
Hell's Angels on Wheels 105
Hell's Belles 299–301
Helm, Anne 1, 250, 258–263
Hemric, Guy 90–93, 112
Henderson, Dickie 75
Henning, Linda Kaye 276
Henning, Paul 296
Henteloff, Alex 167
Herazo, Tina *see* Raines, Christina
Here Come the Brides 113
Here Comes the Groom 181
Herman's Hermits 78–81, 90, 92
Herridge, Frances 124
Hewitt, Martin 18
Hex 160, 168
Hickman, Dwayne 50, 60, 61, 177, 233, 255, 266, 267
High Button Shoes 314
Hill, Jack 186–189, 290
Hill Street Blues 285
Hillyer, Sharyn vii, 2, 44–54
Hipp, Edward Sothern 120
Hit the Surf 19, 20
Hitchcock, Alfred 4, 5
Hobbie, Duke 238
Hogan's Heroes 108, 114, 117, 218, 245, 292, 317
Holbrook, Hal 125
Hold On! 75, 80, 81
Holiday, Hope 78, 79
Holiday, Judy 5
Holiday in Mexico 3

Holland, Buck 238
Holloway, Susan 112
The Hollywood Palace 189
Holmes, Luree vii, 1, 54–63, 134, 233, 255, 264
Holt, Peter 288
Home from the Hill 286
Hondells 93
Honeymoon Hotel 260
The Honeymooners 39, 76
The Hoodlum Priest 42
Hope, Bob 50, 151, 217, 253, 327
Hopper, Dennis 30–32, 117, 200
Hopper, Hedda 284
Horn, John 143
Hot Rods to Hell 2, 292–294
A Hot Summer Game 297
The House of Blue Leaves 149
House of 1,000 Dolls 223
The House of Seven Corpses 193, 201, 202
The House of Usher 143
The House on Haunted Hill 187
Houseman, John 293
How Now, Dow Jones 119, 120
How Sweet It Is 160, 162, 164, 165
How to Learn to Fly Fish 203
How to Stuff a Wild Bikini 59, 93, 232, 234, 264, 313, 314
Howard, Ken 169
Howard, Ronny 29
Howes, Sally Ann 119
H. R. Pufnstuf 201
Hud 8, 46
Hudson, Rock 247
Hughes, Mary 54, 56, 61, 62, 233, 234, 264, 265
Hullabaloo 208, 240, 281
Hunter, Barbara 162
Hunter, Jeffrey 33, 41, 43
Hunter, Tab 254, 255
Hutchins, Will 69
Hutton, Betty 4
Hutton, Gunilla 276
Hutton, Robert 253
Hutton, Timothy 123
Hyams, Joe 309
Hyer, Martha 223, 259

I Dream of Jeannie 161, 218
I Spy 317
I Was a Teenage Werewolf 55
If It's Tuesday, This Must Be Belgium 160, 164–166
Ihnat, Steve 223
I'm Going to Be Famous 278
The Immortalizer 150
In Like Flint 222
In the Year 2889 136
The Incredible Hulk 219
The Incredible Two-Headed Transplant 303, 305, 306
Indict and Convict 113
Ingels, Marty 165
Ingster, Boris 46, 47

Insight 250
The Interns 259
The Interns (TV series) 277
Intimacy 240
The Invaders 119, 293
Ireland, John 201
Ireland, John, Jr. 71, 240, 241
Irma La Douce 310
Iron Horse 113
Irons, Milton 137
Ironside 137
Isherwood, Christopher 26
It Conquered Hollywood! The Story of American International Pictures 62, 63
It Takes a Thief 245
It's a Bikini World 1, 64, 70–72, 205, 213
It's a Gift 151

The Jack Benny Show 184
Jackie and Gayle 68
Jackie Gleason and the American Scene Magazine 76
The Jackie Gleason Show 98, 239
Jackson, Kate 169
Jackson, Mike 269
Jackson, Shirley 194
Jacobs, Ronnie 72
Jacoby, Scott 125
Jaffe, Sam 318
The James Dean Story 106
Jameson, Joyce 117
Jamison, Mikki 2, 28, 45, 218, 266–268
Janis, Edward 5
Janis, Joan 5
Janssen, David 94, 118
Jay and the Americans 68
Jeffries, Fran 28
Jensen, Karen 136
Jensen, Pierce A., Jr. 303
Jewison, Norman 16, 17
The Joey Bishop Show 253
Johns, Glynis 39
Johnson, Candy 90, 91, 268–270
Johnson, Don 149
Johnson, Lamont 117
Johnson, Van 162
Jones, Anissa 9, 121
Jones, Carolyn 158
Jones, Davy 50, 94, 108, 109
Jones, James Earl 32
Jones, Jennifer 224
Jourdan, Louis 307, 308
Julia 159
Julien, Max 166

Kaiser, Mary Lou 268
Kallman, Dick 50
Kanter, Bob 244
Kanter, Hal 158
The Karate Killers 44, 47
Kardell, Lili 132
Karen 322, 323

Karloff, Boris 136, 257
Kasem, Casey 146, 305
Kastan, Jod 115
Katzman, Sam 80, 155, 156, 289, 293
Kaufman, Robert 165, 255
Kaufmann, Christine 101
Kay, Beatrice 303
Kay, Christian 176, 178, 287
Kaye, Celia 225
Kaye, Danny 181
Kaye, Suzie vii, 2, 64–74, 240
Keach, Stacy 32
Kean, Jane 75
Keaton, Buster 59, 313, 314
Keene, Day 120
Keith, Brian 9, 16
Kellerman, Sally 15, 16, 109
Kelljan, Robert 107
Kelly, Brian 316
Kelly, Claire 84
Kelly, Gene 4, 48, 84
Kelly, Grace 5
Kelly, Patsy 134, 315
Kelly, Tom 4
Kennedy, Burt 78, 79
Kennedy, George 320
Kent, Gary 229
Kersh, Kathy 273
Kessler, Bruce 112
Keyes, Evelyn 181
Khrushchev, Nikita 307
The Killer That Stalked New York 181
Kincaid, Aron vii, 23, 24, 28, 55, 60–62, 132, 134–136, 143, 218, 233, 234, 257, 264, 265, 267, 285, 290, 291, 315
Kindergarten Cop 242
The King and I 65, 101
King Kong (1976) 43
Kinks 90
Kinnear, Greg 17
Kirk, Bill 138
Kirk, Tommy 8, 30, 59, 62, 64, 71, 134, 135, 180, 182, 183, 207, 213, 218, 234, 257, 261, 270, 272, 314, 315, 317, 327
Kirkwood, Gene 293
Kismet 307
Kissin' Cousins 151, 152, 155–158, 206–208
Klein, Larry 152
Klugman, Jack 126
Knight, Gladys 315
Knotts, Don 246, 249, 250
Koch, Howard 196
Konar, Pat 210
Koster, Henry 227
Kovack, Nancy 80
Kovacs, Ernie 76, 175
Kristen, Marta 2, 183, 233, 270–274
Krump, Roy 20
Kubrick, Stanley 26

Kulp, Nancy 327
Kwan, Nancy 245

Ladd, Cheryl 179
Lake, Veronica 276
Lamas, Fernando 100
Lamour, Dorothy 208
Lancaster, Stuart 211, 212
Lanchester, Elsa 314
Land of the Giants 167, 250, 273
Landau, Martin 86, 115
Landon, Michael 118
Lane, Jocelyn 300
Langdon, Sue Ane vii, 1, 2, 75–88, 179, 249
Lansbury, Angela 176, 177
Laredo 118
Lassie 159, 161
Laven, Arnold 41
Law, John Philip 16–18
Law of the Lawless 40
Lawrence, John 320
Lawrence, Kiva 8
Lawrence, Vicki 145
Leave It to Beaver 184, 200, 224, 289, 322
Leder, Paul 278
Lee, Brenda 239
Lee, Bruce 320
The Legend of Hell House 257
Leigh, Barbara 273
Leigh, Carolyn 119
Leigh, Janet 47
Leigh, Suzanna 304
Lembeck, Harvey 56, 61, 134
Lemmon, Jack 129, 132
Lerner, Alan Jay 10
Leslie, Joan 247
Lesser, Len 147
Lessing, Arnold 6
A Letter to Loretta 184
Levinson, Janice 62
Lewis, Al 304, 306
Lewis, Jerry 5, 10, 129, 130, 175, 246
Lewis, Richard Warren 57, 277
Life with Father (TV series) 194
Li'l Abner 173
Lindfors, Viveca 123
Linkletter, Art 193
Linville, Larry 86
Lipton, Peggy 72
Lithgow, John 261
Little Richard 317
The Little Savage 106, 107
Littlejohn, Gary 146
The Lively Ones 129, 130
The Lively Set 193, 196–199
Lizzie 194
Lockhart, June 272
Lockwood, Gary 15, 16, 158, 164, 259
Loewe, Fredrick 10
Logan, Joshua 9, 10
Logan, Robert 28, 218, 267

Lolita 286, 288
The Lone Ranger 182
The Long, Hot Summer (TV series) 30
Longstreet 124, 125
Loophole 203
Lord, Jack 148
Loren, Donna vii, 1, 61, 89–97, 136, 269, 270
Loretta Young Theater 272
Lorna 210
Lorre, Peter 56
Losby, Donald 162
The Lost Empire 302
Lost in Space 104, 274
Lost in Space (TV series) 97, 102, 103, 270, 272, 273
The Lost World (1960) 97–101
Love, Darlene 90
Love, American Style 53, 117, 123, 168, 214, 236, 298, 325
The Love Boat 126
Love Is a Many Splendored Thing (TV series) 64, 73
The Love Rebellion 299
The Loved One 21, 26
Lovsky, Celia 109
Lucas, Jonathan 120
Lucky Pair 277
The Lucy-Desi Comedy Hour 5
The Lucy Show 5, 305
Ludwig, Julian 272
Luna, BarBara vii, 65, 66
Lund, Deanna 255, 273, 310
Lupino, Ida 24
Lupus, Peter 57
Lux Playhouse 76
Lyles, A. C. 40
Lynde, Paul 188, 272
Lynley, Carol 34, 42, 277, 286, 326
Lyon, Sue 287

MacArthur, James 64, 72, 145–148
Mackie, Bob 203
Macklin, Tom 167
MacLaine, Shirley 307
MacMurray, Fred 152, 276
MacRae, Bruce 275
MacRae, Gar 275
MacRae, Gordon 275
MacRae, Heather 275, 277
MacRae, Meredith 1, 2, 158, 275–281
MacRae, Sheila 275
The Mad Doctor of Blood Island 299, 301
The Magic Sword 258, 259
The Magician 126
Maharis, George 320
Mahoney, Jock 181
Mahoney, John 189
The Main Event 10
Majors, Lee 234
Making It 117, 122–125
Malibu Run 319

Malone, Dorothy 56, 181
Mame 310
A Man Called Dagger 82
The Man from U.N.C.L.E. 45–47, 84, 102, 281, 298, 316
The Man with the Golden Gun 200
Manhunter 169
Mann, Daniel 296
Mann, Peter 196, 197
Manners, Dorothy 321
Mannix 48, 117, 118
Mansfield, Jayne 25
Manson, Charles 230
Mantee, Paul 83
The Many Loves of Dobie Gillis 266
Marc, Ted 181
Marcels 289
Marcus, Vitina vii, 2, 97–105
The Marcuse 28
Margie 152
Margie (TV series) 1, 68, 151–154
Margolin, Stuart 68, 214
Margotta, Michael 162
Margulies, Stan 165
Markland, Ted 112, 113
Marley, John 295
Marshall, Dodie 1, 281–283, 304, 305
Marshall, Don 273
Marshall, Gary 68
Marshall, George 39
Marshall, Linda 23, 24, 143, 291, 323
Marshall, Peter 161
Martel, Arlene vii, 2, 105–116
Martel, Christiane 106, 107
Martin, Betty 283
Martin, Claudia 2, 134, 253, 283–286
Martin, Craig 283
Martin, Dean 5, 264, 283, 284
Martin, Deana 283
Martin, Dino 283
Martin, Gail 283
Martin, Gina 283
Martin, Jeanne 283
Martin, Kiel 285
Martin, Lori 145, 195
Martin, Quinn 130, 261
Martin, Ricci 283
Martin, Tony 44
Marvin, Lee 10
The Mary Tyler Moore Show 85, 306
Maryjane 2, 160–163, 223
Mason, Marlyn vii, 1, 117–129
The Match Game 277
Mathis, Johnny 175
Matinee Theatre 106,
Matt Lincoln 168
Matthau, Walter 47, 75, 84, 179
Maunder, Wayne 52
Maxwell, Jenny 1, 155, 176–178, 286–289, 301
McAndrew, Marianne 52

McBain, Diane 112, 145, 162, 281, 326
McCallum, David 45, 47, 48, 102
McClanahan, Rue 64
McCleod, Catherine 254
McClure, Doug 193, 196–199, 245
McCook, John 310
McCord, Kent 267
McCormack, Patty 162
McCrea, Ellen 189
McCrea, Jody 56, 59, 91, 92, 200, 207, 233, 269, 272, 273, 296, 297, 314
McDowall, Roddy 202, 324, 325
McFall, Larry 177
McGiveney, Maura 289
McHale's Navy 84
McKuen, Rod 183
McLeod, Murray 145
McQueen, Steve 98, 99, 208, 209
McRae, Ellen 189
McShane, Ian 164
Medic 224
Medley, Bill 90
Meeker, Ralph 258
Mendes, Sam 12
Mercer, Johnny 239
Meredith, Judi 183
Merman, Ethel 200
Merrick, David 119
Merrill, Dina 244
Merrill, Gary 320
Merriwether, Nicholas *see* Hall, Arch, Sr.
The Merv Griffin Show 72
Meyer, Russ 2, 52, 205, 210–212
Michael, Mary 222
Michelle, Donna 276
The Mickey Mouse Club 89, 160, 183
Mickey One 119
Mid-Morning LA 278
Mikler, Michael T. 293
Miles, Sherry 123
Milland, Ray 247, 290
Miller, Denny 309
Miller, Henry 25
Miller, Kenny 239, 240
Miller, Vern 150
The Million Eyes of Su-Muru 232, 234
Mills, Donna 73, 321
Mills, Hayley 42, 162
Milner, Martin 285
The Milton Berle Show 72, 93
Mimiuex, Yvette 173
Mineo, Sal 307, 309, 310
The Mini-Skirt Mob 112
Minsky, Harold 117
Mishkin, Leo 124
Mishkin, Richard 315
Miss Julie 149
Mission: Impossible (TV series) 111
Mr. Novak 46, 141
Mr. Terrific 325

Mitchel, Mary 2, 23, 133, 187, 289–292
Mitchell, Cameron 244, 261
Mitchum, James 320
Mitchum, John 10, 11, 143
Mitchum, Robert 10, 320
Mobley, Mary Ann 206, 208, 316
Mock, Laurie 2, 292–296
The Mod Squad 72, 167
The Model Shop 160, 164
Molly and the Ghost 203
Mona McCluskey 309
Mondo, Peggy 189, 190
Monkees 50, 94, 109, 145
The Monkees 49, 50, 94, 105, 108, 145, 327
Monroe, Marilyn 4, 98, 194, 286
The Monster from the Surf see *Beach Girls and the Monster*
Montagne, Edward 250
Montgomery, Elizabeth 114
Moore, Cleo 194
Moore, Del 8, 130, 327
Moore, Joanna 159, 260
Moore, Mary Tyler 85
Moore, Terry 83
Moorehead, Agnes 290
Mordente, Tony 105
Moreland, Mantan 187
Moreno, Rita 65, 66, 74
Morgan, Jane 75
Moriety, Nathan 54
Morrison, Van 242
Morrow, Pat 93, 240
Morrow, Vic 86
Morse, Robert 26, 47, 84, 260
Morton, Judee 253
Moser, Jim 224
Mosher, Joe 322
Mother Goose a-Go-Go 258, 261
Motorpsycho! 210
Mower, Patrick 137
Mudhoney 210
Mullaney, Jack 60
Mullavey, Greg 277
Mumy, Billy 227, 272
Munster, Go Home! 322, 323
The Munsters 1, 292, 303–306, 322
The Munsters Today 306
Murderers' Row 264
Murell, Gavin 284
Murphy, Jimmy 112
Murphy, Rosemary 219
Murray, Don 299
Murray, Jan 83, 145
Muscle Beach Party 1, 56, 57, 89–91, 264, 268, 269, 296, 297
The Music Man 64, 65
Music '60 Presents the Hit Parade 22
My Bodyguard 171
My Fair Lady 161
My Favorite Martian 107, 266, 281, 304
My Friends Need Killing 278

My Six Loves 177
My Three Sons 117, 151, 152, 158, 272, 276, 288, 291
Mysteries and Scandals 11

Nabors, Jim 95, 118
Nader, George 223, 269
Nader, Mike 56, 61, 264, 265
Naisch, J. Carrol 230
Naked Angels 189
Nalder, Reggie 114
Namath, Joe 275, 277
The Name of the Game 242, 245
Nardini, Tom 238
National Velvet (TV series) 193, 195, 247
Natwick, Mildred 164
Naughty Stewardesses 230
Neal, Patricia 8, 46
Neal, Phil 278
Neil, Gloria 6, 130
Nelson, Alberta 238
Nelson, David 45
Nelson, Gene 155
Nelson, Harriet 45
Nelson, Ozzie 44, 45
Nelson, Ricky 45, 266
Nero, Franco 8, 9
Never Love a Stranger 98
Never Steal Anything Wet see *Catalina Caper*
Never Too Young 227
The New Adventures of Wonder Woman 126
The New Interns 76
A New Kind of Love 5
The New Loretta Young Show 183–185, 224, 225
The New Operation Petticoat 169
The New People 167
Newman, Paul 46, 206
Newmar, Julie 298, 302
Nicholson, Jack 32
Nicholson, James H. 54, 55, 58, 61, 63, 233, 255, 257, 269
Nicholson, Laura 55, 57, 62
Nicholson, Loretta 55
Nicholson, Luree *see* Holmes, Luree
Nighthawks 170, 239
Nightmare in Wax 258, 261
Nimoy, Leonard 15, 33, 41, 111
90 Bristol Court 322
99 and 44/100% Dead 214
Nitzsche, Jack 29
Niven, David 101
No Time for Sergeants (TV series) 84
Nobody's Perfect 244, 245
Noel, Chris 28, 67, 68, 145, 200, 207, 217, 266, 267, 327
Noland, Valora 56, 57, 276, 296–299
Noone, Peter 80
Nordern, Tommy 316

North, Sheree 121, 320
Norwood 275, 277
Number 96 169
Nye, Ben 103

O'Brien, Joan 246, 249
O'Brien, Margaret 117
Occasional Wife 118
O'Connell, Arthur 156, 259
The Odd Couple (TV series) 126, 168
An Officer and a Gentleman 167
O'Hara, Quinn vii, 2, 129–140, 209, 210, 221, 285, 291
O'Havens, Gene 214
Ohmart, Carol 187, 290
Old Yeller 180, 182, 183, 191
Oliver 281
Oliver, Stephen 112
Oliver, Susan 41
Olsen, Gary 267
Olsen Twins 11
Olson, Johnny 64
O'Malley, J. Pat 288
One Day at a Time 138
One Million Years B.C. 19
One Step Beyond 184
O'Neal, Griffin 159
O'Neal, Ryan 10, 11, 159
O'Neal, Tatum 159
O'Neill, Eileen 46, 137, 327
O'Neill, James 114
O'Neill, Jimmy 90
Opie, Linda 57, 58, 233
Orbison, Roy 246, 250
Ormsby, Alan 171
O'Shea, Tessie 16
Our Man Flint 222
Out of Sight 318, 320, 321
The Outer Limits 105, 107, 108
Outrage 126
Owen, Beverly 304

Pacino, Al 69
Page, Geraldine 30
Paige, Martin 191
Paint Your Wagon 10
The Pajama Game 310
Pajama Party 1, 54, 59, 134, 205, 207, 221, 232, 233, 252, 255, 264, 268, 270, 313, 314
Palance, Jack 47, 86
Palmer, Adam 115
Palmer, Robert 106
Paluzzi, Luciana 316
Pan, Hermes 307
Panic in Year Zero 246, 247, 289, 290
Papa's Delicate Condition 33, 39, 40
Parker, Eleanor 194
Parker, Fess 182
Parker, Jeff 290
Parker, Judy 244
Parker, Penney 153
Parker, Colonel Tom 120, 177

Parkins, Barbara 234, 255
Parks, Bert 64
Parrish, Julie 35, 238
Parrish, Leslie 173
Parsons, Louella 255
Parsons, Michael 297
Parton, Dolly 242
The Partridge Family 167
Passion Holiday 314
The Passionate Strangers 297
Pataki, Michael 114
Patrick, Butch 306
Patrick, Lory 240
Patrick, Robert 8
The Patsy 130
Patten, Luana 194, 286
Patterson, Melody vii, 2, 140–151
Patton, Bart 68, 185, 187, 290
Patton, Tyler 292
The Patty Duke Show 188
PDQ 277
Peanut Butter Conspiracy 112
Pearce, Alice 47, 49
Pearson, Jesse 140
Peckinpah, Sam 33, 41
Penn, Arthur 119
Peppard, George 286
Pepper, Cynthia vii, 1, 68, 151–160, 287
Pepper, Dawn 151
Pepper, Jack 151
Pepper, William 241
Perfect, Bobby 172
Perfect, Lee 172
Perfect, Mark 172
Perfect, Scott 172
Perilli, Frank Ray 114
The Perry Como Show 75
Peters, Jon 11
Petersen, Paul 90, 136, 217, 218, 220
Peterson, Gil 324
Peterson, Monica 73
Petroff, Boris L. 288
Petticoat Junction 275–278, 296
Pettyjohn, Angelique 2, 69, 70, 299–303
Pevney, Joseph 109
Peyton Place (TV series) 93, 227, 255
The Phil Silvers Show 75, 258
Phillips, Stu 112
Pickett, Bob 71, 72
Picnic 276
Pierce, Arthur C. 174
Pierce, Jack 174
Pierce, Maggie 250
Pillsbury, Sam 126
Pipe Dreams 315
Pistol Harvest 247
Pistols 'n' Petticoats 193, 199, 200
The Pit and the Pendulum 143
Pit Stop 2, 180, 188, 189
Pitt, Brad 315
Playhouse 90 89, 184, 286

The Pleasure Seekers 158
Pleshette, Suzanne 39, 105, 164, 260
Poe, Edgar Allan 143, 255
Porter, Cole 307
The Poseidon Adventure 214
Powers, Stefanie 42, 246
Prelude 136
Prentiss, Paula 308
Presley, Elvis 1, 2, 21, 25–28, 33–39, 43, 64, 69, 70, 75–78, 80, 82, 83, 113, 117, 118, 120–122, 151, 155–158, 172, 175–179, 199, 205–208, 217, 218, 222, 225, 228, 238, 240, 246, 249, 250, 258–261, 264, 281, 282, 286, 287, 299, 303, 304, 307, 308
Presnell, Harve 41, 42
Preston, Billy 91
Preston, Robert 64
Price, Vincent 56, 60, 62, 137, 143, 223, 234, 247, 255, 264
Priest, Ivy Baker 303
Priest, Pat 1, 282, 303–306, 324
Priore, Dominic 324
The Prize 206
Professional Father 181
Prowse, Juliet 1, 2, 234, 250, 307–313
Psycho a-Go-Go 230
Puglia, Frank 38
Pupa, Piccola 134, 136, 285
Putnam, Cindy 17

Quigley, Linnea 36

Rafkin, Alan 59, 60, 264
Rainer, Louise 23
Raines, Christina 168
Rains, Claude 100
Rambo, Dack 225, 227
Rambo, Dirk 225
Randall, Tony 126, 253
Random, Bob 29
Ransohoff, Martin 26, 208
Rapp, Paul W. 286, 301
The Rat Patrol 317
Rathbone, Basil 56, 134, 135, 259, 315
Rawhide 101, 195
Ray, Aldo 295
Ray, Jacki 222
Ray, Ron 150
The Ray Bolger Show 75
Raye, Martha 200, 276
Rear Window 4
The Rebel 111
The Red Shoes 64
The Red Skelton Show 194
Redecker, Quinn 187
Redgrave, Vanessa 8, 9
Reed, Rex 124
Reed, Robert 119
Reeves, George 181

The Regina Carrol Show 231
Reilly, Charles Nelson 85
Reiner, Carl 16, 17, 68, 72
Reiner, Rob 315
The Reluctant Astronaut 246, 249
The Remarkable Mr. Pennypacker 247
Remick, Lee 266
Rennie, Michael 100
Repo Man 302
Rescue from Gilligan's Island 179
Return to Peyton Place 316
Reventlow, Lance 100
Rey, Alejandro 327
Reynolds, Burt 43, 204
Reynolds, Debbie 162, 177, 178, 309, 323
Reynolds, Lee 191
Rialson, Candice 114
Rich, B. Ruby 215
Richardson, Tony 26
Rickles, Don 57
Ride the Wild Surf 1, 252–255
The Rifleman 296
The Right Approach 307, 309
Righteous Brothers 90
Riley, Jeannine 276
Rio Bravo 98
Rio Conchos 318, 319
Riot on Sunset Strip 2, 292, 293, 324
Road to Bali 4
The Roaring Twenties 153
Roarke, Adam 300, 301
Robbins, Harold 98
Robbins, Jerome 65–67
Roberts, Jim 285
Roberts, Pernell 245
Roberts, Tony 119
Robertson, Dale 40, 113
Robinson, Chris 144, 146–148
Robson, Mark 206
Rock, Pretty Baby 183
Roddenberry, Gene 15, 16, 40, 41
Roeder, Ervin (Tip) 288
Rogers, Linda 238
Rogers, Steve 23, 68, 112, 291
Rolf, Tutta 244
Rolfe, Sam 46
Rolling Stones 90, 92
Roman, Leticia 47
Romero, Cesare 93
Romero, Eddie 297, 301
Rondeau, Charlie 214
Room 222 168
Rooney, Mickey 234, 264, 310
Rooney, Tim 29, 31
Rose, Billy 151
Rose, Reva 164
Rosemary's Baby 320
Ross, Herbert 202
Rothman, Stephanie 71, 213, 273
The Rounders 75, 78, 79
The Rounders (TV series) 47, 49, 283

Roustabout 75–78, 80, 205, 207, 246, 248, 249
Rowan & Martin's Laugh-In 68
Rowlands, Gena 295
Rubia's Jungle 137, 138
Rubin, Benny 315
Rubinstein, John 169
Run, Buddy, Run 68
Run for Your Life 208
Run for Your Wife 310
Rush, Barbara 149, 244
Rush, Richard 82, 83, 166
Rusoff, Lou 56
Russell, Rosalind 162, 296
The Russians Are Coming, the Russians Are Coming 14, 16–19
Rutherford, Margaret 138
Rydell, Bobby 93

Sachse, Peter 233
Sachse, Salli 54, 56, 58, 60–62, 90, 233, 234, 255, 264, 267
Sailor, Toni 285
Saint, Eva Marie 16, 17
Saint James, Susan 162, 327
St. John, Heaven *see* Pettyjohn, Angelique
St. John, Jill 75, 100, 130, 183, 234, 247
Saks, Gene 119
Sale, Irene 133, 209, 222
Salerno, Charlene 45
Sally and Sam 158
Salmaggi, Robert 19
Sam the Sham and the Pharoahs 78
Samitaur-Smith, Frederick 295
Samitaur-Smith, Laurie *see* Mock, Laurie
San Francisco International Airport 245
Sands, Anita 55
Santean, Antonio 107
Saphire, Rick vii
Satana, Tura 2, 205, 210, 211, 213, 215
Satan's Sadists 228, 231
Saunders, Lori 23, 276, 291
Savage Sam 183, 272
Sax, Arline *see* Martel, Arlene
Saxon, John 113, 180, 183, 273
Schanzer, Karl 187
Schell, Maximilian 296
Schlitz Playhouse 98
Schuyler, Bill 253
Scott, Ken 259
The Sea Gypsies 267
Sea Hunt 178, 259, 318, 319
Searchers 239
Seaton, Robert 149
Seberg, Jean 10, 11, 82
A Second Chance: Surviving Alcoholism 278
The Second Time Around 309
The Secret Life of Walter Mitty 3

Selleck, Tom 273
September Storm 319
Sergeant Deadhead 89, 93, 94
Serling, Rod 106
The Seven Minutes 52
77 Sunset Strip 266, 268
Sex and the College Girl 297
Sharif, Omar 202
Shatner, William 15, 16, 33, 48, 109, 111, 113, 115, 327
Shaw, Bobbi 1, 59, 93, 134, 313–315
Shawn, Dick 175
Shear, Barry 130
Sheeley, Sharon 239
Sheen, Martin 125, 190
Sheffield, Jay 249, 323
The Sheila MacRae Show 277
Sheridan, Ann 199, 200
Sherman, Bobby 90, 190
Shindig 72, 89–93, 143, 208, 240, 281
Shirley Temple's Storybook 259
Shore, Dinah 231
Shotgun Wedding 286, 288
The Shrieking see *Hex*
Siegel, Don 123
Siegel, Peggy 17
Silliphant, Stirling 124
Simmons, Jean 10
Sinatra, Frank 196, 197, 283, 307–310
Sinatra, Nancy 62, 134, 136, 253, 283–285
Siodmak, Curt 244
Six, Eva 56
Sketches of a Strangler 278
Ski Fever 283, 285
Ski Party 54, 55, 58–61, 93, 232, 233, 264, 266, 267, 285, 314
Slate, Jeremy 38, 300
The Slime People 252, 253
Small, Lillian 286
Smith, Morton 253
Smith, Roger 200
Smith and Dale 22
The Smith Family 137
Smokey and the Bandit 204
Snap Judgement 277
So Little Time 11
Sokoloff, Vladimir 174, 175
Solomon, Joe 112
Solow, Herb 16
Some Call It Loving 306
Some Like It Hot 319
Sommars, Julie 297
Sommers, Joanie 197, 199
Sondheim, Stephen 66
Sonny and Cher 90
The Sound of Music 200
South Pacific 64
Southern, Nile vii, 26, 32
Southern, Terry vii, 21, 25–28, 30–32
Sparr, Robert 132

Spector, Phil 324
Spelling, Aaron 72
Spencer, Vicki 289
Spider Baby 180, 182, 184, 186–189, 289, 290
Spinner, Anthony 47
Spinout 238, 281
Spree 310
Springsteen, Bruce 242
Spry, Nancy 291
The Spy in the Green Hat 44, 47, 48
Squeakin' Deacon 89
Stacy, James 133, 209, 221, 222, 237, 238, 244, 245, 291
Stafford, Tracy 225
Stage to Thunder Rock 40
Staley, Joan 46, 246, 250
Stallone, Sylvester 170
Standells 206
Stanwyck, Barbara 76, 77, 125
Star Time Kids 64
Star Trek 15, 16, 33, 40, 41, 43, 48, 105, 109, 111, 298–300, 302, 327
Stark, Fran 202
Stark, Ray 202
Starr, Ringo 24
Starrett, Jack 112
State Fair 200
Steckler, Ray Dennis 236
Steele, Bob 143
Steiger, Rod 26
Sterling, Jan 145
Sterling, Tisha 29, 30, 242, 277
Stern, Tom 111–113
The Steve Allen Tonight Show 75
Stevens, Connie 133, 289
Stevens, Inger 47, 84
Stevens, Naomi 123
Stevens, Stella 36–39, 75, 162
Stevenson, Robert 182
Stewart, James 84, 181, 224
Stone, Laurence 68, 72, 74
Stone, Marshall 18
Storch, Larry 142, 143, 150
Strait-Jacket 260
Strangers When We Meet 76
Strasberg, Lee 22, 97, 98, 214
The Streets of San Francisco 183, 191
Streisand, Barbra 10, 11, 193, 196, 202, 203
Strickler, Jerry 201
Stricklyn, Ray 100, 218
Strimpell, Stephen 325
Stroker Ace 43
Stromstedt, Ulla 8, 316–318, 327
Stuart, Gloria 138
Stuart, Mel 164, 165
Styner, Jerry 90–93
The Substitute 171
Sugar Babies 310
Sugarman, Burt 234
Sullivan, Barry 40
Summer Love 180, 183
Summers, Jerry 240

Superman 43
Superman and the Mole Men 181
Supremes 90
Surf Party 2 239, 240, 242
Surfside 6 151, 195
Sutton, Frank 118
Swamp Country 3, 8
Swanson, Diane 209
Sweet Charity 310
Swift, David 85
The Swingin' Maiden 258, 260, 261
A Swingin' Summer 1, 205, 209, 210, 221, 289, 291
Switchblade Sisters 186
Sydes, Anthony 224
Sydes, Carol *see* Carol, Cindy
Sykes, Brenda 166

The Tab Hunter Show 316
Tabori, Kristofer 122–125
Tackitt, Wesley 153
Take Her, She's Mine 151, 154, 155, 286, 287
Takei, George 15
Takin' It Off 302
Talbot, Nita 325
Talent Scouts 68
Tales of Wells Fargo 76
Tamblyn, Russ 66, 228, 229
Tammy (TV series) 322–324
Tammy and the Doctor 68
Tammy and the Millionaire 323, 324
Tandy, Jessica 138
Taras Bulba 101
Tarzan 73, 245, 318
Tarzan's Jungle Rebellion 316, 318
Tate, Sharon 208, 320, 327
Taurog, Norman 36, 38, 176, 255
Tayback, Vic 147
Taylor, Elizabeth 195
Taylor, Rip 114
Taylor, Robert 162
Taylor, Wilda 27, 28, 218
Teadwell, Terence 272
Teague, Anthony 121
Tenspeed and Brownshoe 215
Terminal Island 271, 273
Tewksbury, Peter 120, 121
Texaco Star Theater 94
That Certain Summer 125
The Thing with Two Heads 305
Thinnes, Roy 30, 119
13 Demon Street 244
This Is the Life 30
Thomas, Danny 72, 136
Thomas, Scott 320
Thompson, Hilarie vii, 2, 160–172, 292
Thompson, Howard 72, 77, 241, 293
Thompson, Victoria 160
Thorpe, Jerry 5
Three Coins in the Fountain (TV pilot) 158

Three Ring Circus 4
Three Stooges 249
The Three Stooges Go Around the World in a Daze 249
Thriller 76
A Thunder of Drums 194
Tickle Me 208, 222
Tiffin, Pamela 35, 196–198, 253, 285
The Time Machine 174
Time Tunnel 103
Tinker, Grant 85
Titanic 138
To Rome with Love 103, 104, 137
Tognazzi, Ugo 310
Tom Jones 26
Tomlinson, David 255
Tompkins, Darlene vii, 1, 172–180, 287
The Tonight Show Starring Johnny Carson 72
Torbet, Laura 62
Tork, Peter 108
Torn, Rip 30–32
Tosi, Mario 11
The Touch of Her Flesh 299
Tower of London 247
Track of Thunder 218, 219
The Travels of Jaime McPheeters 102
Tremayne, Les 101
Trikonis, Gus 68
Trinka, Paul 211
Tristan, Dorothy 32
The Trouble with Angels 162
The Trouble with Girls 117, 118, 120–122
Truscott, John 9, 10
Tryon, Tom 41, 42
Tucker, Forrest 142–144
Turner, Tina 90
Turtles 90
Tusher, William 122
Tuttle, Lurene 194
Twelve O'Clock High 292, 317
The Twilight Zone 106
Twist Around the Clock 289, 290
Two for Penny 94
Two Weeks in Another Town 5

UHF 86
Ullman, Elwood 255
Ulmer, Edgar G. 173, 174
Uncle Willie 106
Under the Yum Yum Tree 23, 290
The Untouchables 153
Up Your Teddy Bear 298, 302
The U.S. Steel Hour 258
Usher, Gary 89

Vaccaro, Brenda 119
Vadim, Roger 32, 208
The Vals 86
Van Doren, Mamie 228
Van Dyke, Dick 72

Vaughan, Frankie 307, 309
Vaughn, Robert 44, 47, 48, 102
Vee, Bobby 64, 71, 240, 241
Vega$ 126
Vereen, Ben 203
Verso, Eddie 65
Viets, Scott 114
Viharo, Robert 261
Viharo, Will 103
Village of the Giants 21, 29–31
Vincent, Jan-Michael 242
Vinson, Gary 200
Vinton, Bobby 208, 240
The Virginian 245, 298
Vitina, Dolores *see* Marcus, Vitina
Viva Las Vegas 25, 205, 206, 228
Vixen 52
Vorkov, Zandor 230
Voyage to the Bottom of the Sea (TV series) 101

Waggoner, Lyle 8, 317, 327
Wagner, Candy 319
Wagner, John H. 319
Wagner, Robert 246
Wagner, Ruth 319
Wagner, Wende 2, 208, 318–322
Wagon Train 184, 259, 319
Wake Me When It's Over 175
Walker, Nancy 75
Walker, Robert 168, 298
Walking Tall 219
Wallace, Irving 52
Walley, Deborah 39, 60–62, 71, 93, 94, 134–136, 213, 223, 225, 233, 234, 257, 266, 267, 281, 289, 308, 314, 315, 322
Wallis, Hal B. 35–37, 308, 309
Walsh, Raoul 4
Walston, Ray 107
Walters, Nancy 176–179, 287
War-Gods of the Deep 252, 255
War Party 293
The War Wagon 298
Ward, Skip 282, 305
Ware, Clyde 190
Warner, Jack 142, 144
Waronker, Lenny 95
Washburn, Audrey 173, 180, 181
Washburn, Beverly vii, 2, 173, 180–193, 225, 272, 286, 291
Washburn, George 180, 189
Waters, John 215
Watson, Debbie 2, 322–325
Watters, William 237
Waugh, Evelyn 26

Wayne, John 298
Wayne, Patrick 49
Webb, Clifton 247
Weekend Pass 302
Wehling, Bob 237
Weinrib, Lennie 68
Weis, Don 59, 134, 136, 138
Weiss, Donna 242
Welch, Raquel 18, 19, 132–134, 208–210, 214, 222, 320
Weld, Tuesday 42, 117
Weldon, Michael J. 324
Wellingtons 90
Wellman, William, Jr. 133, 209, 221, 237, 238, 244, 291
Wells, Carole vii, xi, xii, 2, 193–205, 247
Wells, Dawn 179
Wells, Delores 56
Wells, H. G. 29, 174
West, Adam 93, 94
West, Martin 23, 25, 133, 291
West, Sonny 207
West Side Story 64–69, 74, 205, 228
What's My Line? 277
What's Up Front? 237
When the Boys Meet the Girls 75, 78, 79, 240
When the Line Goes Through 180, 190
When the Whistle Blows 86
Where Angels Go...Trouble Follows 162
Where Love Has Gone 5, 39
White, Betty 306
White, Jesse 134, 314, 315
Whitman, Stuart 309, 320
Whitmore, James 244, 320
Whittaker, Johnny 18
Who Killed Teddy Bear? 307, 309, 310
Who's Got the Action? 4, 5
Who's Minding the Store? 130
The Wild Angels 2
The Wild Guitar 236, 237
Wild in the Country 176
The Wild Scene 238
The Wild Wild West 84
Wild Wild Winter 64, 65, 67, 68, 285
Wildcat 200, 276
Wilder, Billy 319
Wilder, John 183
Wilder, Yvonne 64
Will Success Spoil Rock Hunter? 253
Williams, Andy 214
Williams, Billy Dee 170

Williams, Dick 286
Williams, Esther 3
Williams, Grant 259
Williams, Guy 272
Williams, Lori vii, 2, 133, 205–215, 221–223, 233
Williams, Van 195, 320
Willock, Dave 153
Wills, Chill 151
Wilson, Brian 24, 89
Wilson, Earl 277
Windom, William 145
Winslow, George "Foghorn" 183
Winter a-Go-Go 132, 236–238, 244, 245, 285
Winters, David 27, 205–208, 233, 270
Winters, Jonathan 16
Winters, Roland 176
Wise, Robert 66, 67
Without Warning 86
Witney, Michael 242
Witney, William 24
Wolf, Venita 8, 316, 317, 326–328
Women of the Prehistoric Planet 68
Wood, Ed, Jr. 288
Wood, Lana 23–25, 39
Wood, Natalie 66, 67, 234
Wood, Walter 42, 43
Woods, Donald 323
Words and Music 3
Wyman, Jane 181
Wynant, H. M. 218
Wynn, Keenan 57, 270, 298

Yancy Derringer 181
Yankovic, Weird Al 86
Yarnall, Celeste 301
York, Francine 3
York, Jeff 182
You and Me 315
Young, Loretta 184, 185, 224, 225
Young, Skip 50
The Young Lawyers 167
The Young Marrieds 218
The Young Racers 290
The Young Rebels 167, 168
Yulin, Harris 32

Zanuck, Richard 320
Zapped 86
Zapped Again 86
Zaslow, Michael 73
Zastupnevich, Paul 103
Zieff, Howard 11
The Ziegfeld Follies 75

www.ingramcontent.com/pod-product-compliance
Ingram Content Group UK Ltd.
Pitfield, Milton Keynes, MK11 3LW, UK
UKHW050543150426
5217IPUK00026B/2058